Sigmund Freud, 1856–1939

MW01036671

Sigmund Freud, 1856–1939 draws on a wide range of primary sources to present all the datable events that took place in Sigmund Freud's life, shining new light on his day-to-day experiences.

Christfried Toegel's work provides details and context for the personal, social and political conditions under which Freud developed his theories during this time period. The book's timeline presents not only significant events but also the small and everyday interactions and experiences in Freud's life. Drawn from sources including Freud's calendars, notebooks, travel journals and lists of fees, letters and visits, this unique book provides unparalleled insight into his work.

Sigmund Freud, 1856–1939 will be of great interest to psychoanalysts in practice and in training, as well as academics and scholars of Freud, psychoanalytic studies, the history of science and the history of Europe.

Christfried Toegel is a historian of science based in Switzerland and a former director of the SALUS-Institut for Evaluation and Simulation of Mental Health Care and of the Sigmund-Freud-Center in Germany. He is the author of more than 200 publications on the history and philosophy of science, editor of several editions of letters by Sigmund Freud and author of ten books on dream research and Freud biography, which have been translated into eight languages.

History of Psychoanalysis

Series Editor

Peter L. Rudnytsky

This series seeks to present outstanding new books that illuminate any aspect of the history of psychoanalysis from its earliest days to the present, and to reintroduce classic texts to contemporary readers.

Other titles in the series:

Occultism and the Origins of Psychoanalysis
Freud, Ferenczi and the Challenge of Thought Transference
Maria Pierri, Translated by Adam Elgar

Sigmund Freud and the Forsyth Case
Coincidences and Thought-Transmission in Psychoanalysis
Maria Pierri, Translated by Adam Elgar

A Brief Apocalyptic History of Psychoanalysis
Erasing Trauma
Carlo Bonomi

Theories and Practices of Psychoanalysis in Central Europe
Narrative Assemblages of Self Analysis, Life Writing, and Fiction
Agnieszka Sobolewska

Sigmund Freud and his Patient Margarethe Csonka
A Case of Homosexuality in a Woman in Modern Vienna
Michal Shapira

Sigmund Freud, 1856–1939
A Biographical Compendium
Christfried Toegel

For further information about this series please visit https://www.routledge.com/The-History-of-Psychoanalysis-Series/book-series/KARNHIPSY

Sigmund Freud, 1856–1939

A Biographical Compendium

Christfried Toegel

Routledge
Taylor & Francis Group

LONDON AND NEW YORK

Designed cover image: ©Christfried Toegel

First published 2024
by Routledge
4 Park Square, Milton Park, Abingdon, Oxon OX14 4RN

and by Routledge
605 Third Avenue, New York, NY 10158

Originally published in German as *Freud-Diarium 1856–1913* (Psychosozial-Verlag, 2023)

Routledge is an imprint of the Taylor & Francis Group, an informa business

© 2024 Christfried Toegel

British Library Cataloguing-in-Publication Data
A catalogue record for this book is available from the British Library

Library of Congress Cataloging-in-Publication Data
A catalog record has been requested for this book

ISBN: 9781032696522 (hbk)
ISBN: 9781032696515 (pbk)
ISBN: 9781032696539 (ebk)

DOI: 10.4324/9781032696539

Typeset in Times New Roman
by codeMantra

Contents

About this book

Famous people have always been the subject of chronicles. The best known is probably *Goethes Leben von Tag zu Tag* in eight volumes (Steiger & Reimann, 1982–1996). Freud, however, was not as generous with information about his life as the German king of poets. Therefore, the endeavor to document events in Freud's life as closely as possible is also quite tedious.

In the mid-1980s, Gerhard Fichtner began to record all datable events from Ernest Jones's biography of Freud. From 1989 onward, I continued this endeavor and included not only all secondary sources available to me but also Freud's letters, works and documents related to his biography – both published and unpublished. The sources and the secondary literature used are listed at the end of each volume. For quotations, the reference is given in the entry itself.[1]

The entries have not been selected according to their significance for Freud's life, but datable items have been recorded. "Datable" means the following:

- We know the exact date of an event – the date information then reads, for example, "1856 May 6".
- The exact date is not known, but the period in which the event took place can be narrowed down to a maximum of three months – the date would then read, for example, "1926 spring" or "1915 June end".
- If we only know the year of events, they are listed at the beginning of each year.

The persons appearing in this book are briefly introduced at the first mention – where this makes sense for the understanding of the entry.[2] The index of persons contains – as far as can be ascertained – the dates of their lives. This usually enables the reader to identify them unambiguously. In the case of members of the Freud family, only their first names are given after the first mention. Most of them can be found in the family trees at the end of the book.

The following datable events were **not** included in the Compendium:

- Dates of letters written or received by Freud.[3] Only the beginning of extensive and important correspondence is recorded.
- Dates on which Freud received or visited patients: for example, for the period between 1910 and 1920, this is almost 140 patients with a total of 18,000 hours of analysis. Therefore, only the date of the beginning of the treatment/analysis of relatively known persons, and – if known – their duration, is noted.[4]
- Dates from prescriptions and fee invoices issued by F.

DOI: 10.4324/9781032696539-1

- Dates from routines such as ward rounds and duty in the Wiener Allgemeines Krankenhaus (Vienna General Hospital), receipt of manuscripts for journals edited by Freud, receipt of proof sheets from Freud's own publications and psychoanalytic journals, etc.
- Dates from income, expenditure and transfers; however, larger sums are mentioned.
- Dates of publication of Freud's writings. Only the appearance of important and well-known publications is recorded.
- Dates from Hans Pichler's detailed medical history (Jones, 1956–1958, vol. 3, pp. 497–521). Only the data that Pichler summarized for Georg Exner before Freud's departure for London are recorded.

Longer absences of Freud from his residence are set flush right for easy recognition.

Titles of books, papers, etc. by Freud are given in the language of the publication. The reader can find the English translations in the Appendix, as well as that of institutions, societies, job titles, etc.

For translations of quotations from Freud letters I have used the published English translation mainly from the following: the correspondences of Freud with Karl Abraham, Sándor Ferenczi, Wilhelm Fliess, Emil Fluss, Ernest Jones, Carl Gustav Jung, Oskar Pfister, Otto Rank, Eduard Silberstein and Arnold Zweig[5]; for texts from Freud's writings and for translation of psychoanalytic terms: and *The Standard Edition of the Complete Psychological Works of Sigmund Freud*, *The Minutes of the Vienna Psychoanalytic Society*, and *Glossary for the Use of Translators of Psycho-analytical Works* (Jones 1928).

Of course, the events recorded are not exhaustive: If, for example, ten visits by Freud to Josef Breuer are recorded for the year 1883, this does not mean that these are all visits, but merely that we know the date of only ten visits.

The Compendium gives an idea of the personal, social and political conditions under which Freud developed his theories: it shows not only important events but also small and everyday processes that we do not think of when we have Freud's grand designs in mind.

Notes

1 I have used the published English translation mainly from the following: *The Standard Edition of the Complete Psychological Works of Sigmund Freud;* the correspondences of Freud with Karl Abraham, Sándor Ferenczi, Wilhelm Fliess, Emil Fluss, Ernest Jones, Carl Gustav Jung, Oskar Pfister, Otto Rank, Eduard Silberstein and Arnold Zweig; and *The Minutes of the Vienna Psychoanalytic Society*. In most other cases, the translations are mine.
2 As a rule, the titles of nobility (knight, baron, count, prince, etc.) of Austrians and the aristocratic "von" are omitted in the diary. This is to avoid inconsistencies in the index of names due to their omission after the entry into force of the "Adelsaufhebungsgesetz" of 1919 April 3, which prohibited the use of titles of nobility. Only in the case of persons who appear throughout the literature with a title of nobility is this title retained.
3 As things stand at present, the number of letters sent by Freud is a good 17,000. It can be assumed that there were hundreds more, but many of them either fell victim to Freud's destruction actions or were not preserved by the addressees or were not made public.
4 From 1895 onward, the term "analysis" is always used and no distinction is made between the therapeutic analysis and teaching analysis, since many of the later analysts were also not sure how to classify their treatment with Freud. Before 1895, the term "treatment" is always used in connection with Freud's patients.
5 Translations from unpublished letters are mine.

Chronicles and calendars

As an introduction to this Compendium, the following pages give an overview of chronicles and calendars kept by Freud himself. Throughout his life, Freud recorded all the information that was important to him in writing – in the form of calendars, notebooks, travel journals, lists of fees, letters, visitors and much more. Some of this have been published, much else not. Some records have been lost, such as a diary kept in Greek by Freud as a youth (Jones, 1956–1958, vol. 2, p. 27) and two travel diaries from the 1870s and the 1890s.

The following pages provide an overview of Freud's preserved notes. They are usually illustrated by selected examples. All datable events contained in these records have also been included in this book.

"Index of the letters and signs of love which I have received from my dear Martha." (1882)

Freud had met his future wife Martha Bernays in the spring of 1882. At the end of May, it became clear that they were attracted to each other. And on June 11, Freud began recording Martha's "Letters and Signs of Love" (Freud & Bernays, 2011, S. 528).

Examples:

3) 13/6 Her table card, which I stole at the table, for which she squeezed my hand under the tablecloth. Together with mine.

[...]

6) 17/6 Our engagement day. In the afternoon she gave me a touchingly simple gold bracelet with a pearl, it fits on my little finger; it was too big for her.

"Our Secret Chronicle" (1883–1886)

On 1883 January 25, Freud and his fiancée Martha decided to keep a "secret chronicle". The introductory remarks to this chronicle were written by Martha:

> *Romanticism lies behind us. We have decided that these sheets should bear witness to our 'spiritual and material état', to everything that we experienced together in the years that lie ahead of us; perhaps we will both take pleasure in them later, when one event has replaced the other in our memory.*

> (Freud & Bernays, 2011, S. 531)

DOI: 10.4324/9781032696539-2

Example:

Today my Marthchen promised me to resist a long separation if possible and not to deprive me of the happiness of her presence and participation without the utmost hardship (Sigmund on 12.2.1883).

Notebooks (1901–1936)

These are 14 small notebooks, most of them 7×4 cm in size, covering the period from 1901 to 1936, with a larger gap between 1926 and 1929. The entries are very heterogeneous and contain not only ideas on psychoanalytical topics and patients but also addresses, travel plans, income, expenses and much more (Hirschmüller & Tögel, 2021).

Examples:

8.2.1901
Erogenous zones are based on sexual co-excitation (eyes)
[…]

5.6.03
Fear could also be due to the *omission* of the component of consciousness necessary to compromise the symptom.

[…]

Tuesday 8/30/04 to Athens 11h30

[…]

Illness and weakening of the ego in Pankejeff 8.7.14

[…]

Wednesday August 2nd [1916]
Mozart String Quartet in D minor
Schumann in A major
Brahms Quintett in B minor

Fee list (1906–1921)

Freud presumably kept continuous records of the fees he received from patients. Only the records between 1906 and 1921 have been preserved.[1] They provide information about

- The date
- Revenue per day
- Cumulative revenue per week
- Cumulative revenue per month
- Cumulative revenue per year
- Difference to expected revenue

Example:

February 07					
[...]	[...]	[...]	[...]	[...]	[...]
1.	305	1505	305	26845	155
2.	190	1695	495	27035	195
3.	–	–	495	27035	045
4.	295	295	790	27330	190
5.	315	610	1105	27645	355

Travel Journal America (1909)

Freud had been invited to America by Stanley Hall, the president of Clark University in Worcester (Massachusetts), to give some lectures on psychoanalysis on the occasion of the 20th anniversary of the university.[2]

He traveled on the steamer "George Washington" from Bremen via Southampton to New York. Since he could no longer send mail to his family from the ship, he kept a "travel journal" until his arrival in New York (Freud, 2002b, S. 283–297).

Example:

24 Tuesday morning, before the morning toilet.

Monday was filled with the two landings in Southampton and Cherbourg, very rich in content. Yesterday, finally, ocean voyage. The last bit of England in the morning, otherwise nothing all day except for a dolphin in the morning and sea lights in the evening. The weather was not too friendly, lots of clouds, strong wind, a little drizzle, but the ship's movements were again hardly felt. One studies carefully here and is happy when the ground really runs away.

We spent the whole day debating and laughing, not at all exhausting and very enjoyable. In between, we walked the deck, studied the waves and ate. We are on the most affectionate terms with our table stewards. The orchids are still holding up. The waiters in the café and in the lounges, where tea is served at 16ʰ, are perhaps less amiable. The bathroom, which I am waiting for again now, is precious, just opposite the cabin. The time difference is strange, that you have to move your watch back every morning and thus gain ¾ hour, which only annoys you.

In the cabin one is so safe and comfortable that it is with regret that one thinks of leaving this cosy home in less than a week.

Prof. Stern called in early, spoke to Jung and had him fogged while he turned his back on us. I watched for a while and then called Jung: Doctor, didn't we want to finish our conversation? whereupon the shabby Jew recommended himself.

Patient calendar (1910–1920)

A "patient calendar" with detailed information exists for the period from 1910 to 1920. The calendar contains exact information on the duration and frequencies of treatment[3].

Freud used "Grubers ärztliche Tages-Notizbuch-Einlage" for the patient calendar. In the Honorar column, Freud usually added up the hours of analysis.

Example:

[Monat] November	1	2	3	4	5	6	7	8	9	10	11	12	13	14	15	16	17	18	19	20	21	22	23	24	25	26	27	28	29	30	31	19[13] Honorar
NAME																																Honorar
Redlich	I	·	I	I	I	I	I	I	·	I	I	I	I	I	I	·	I	I	I	I	I	I	·	I	I	I	I	I	I	·		25
Pankejef	I	·	I	I	I	III	I	I	·	I	III	I	III	I	I	·	I	III	I	III	I	I	·	I	III	I	III	I	I	·		32
Dolinsky	I	·	I	I	I	I	I	I	·	I	I	I	I	I	I	·	I	I	I	I	I	I	·	I	I	I	I	I	I	·		25
Repine	I	·	I	I	I	I	I	I	·	I	I	I	I	I	II	·	I	I	I	I	I	I	·	I	I	I	I	I	I	·		26
Dirsztay	I	·	I	I	I	I	I	I	·	I	I	I	I	I	I	·	I	I	I	I	I	I	·	I	I	I	I	I	I	·		25
Hirschfeld	II	·	II	·	I'	I	I	I	·	I'	I	I'	I	II	·	·	II	·	I'	·	II	·	·	II	·	I'	·	II	·	·		23 ½
Fischer	I	·	I	I	I	I	·	·	·	·	·	I	·	·	·	·	I	·	I	·	I	·	·	I	·	I	·	·				12
Hoesch-Ernst	I	·	I	I	I	I	I	I	·	I	I	I	I	I	I	·	I	I	I	I	I	I	·	I	I	I	I	I	I	·		25
Schöller	·	·	I	I	I	I	I	·	I	I	I	I	I	I	·	I	I	I	I	I	I	·	I	I	I	I	I	I	·			22
Czilchert	____		I	____						I	·	·	·	·	·	I	·	·	·	·	I	·	·	·	·							4

War calendar (1916–1918)

Among the chronicles Freud kept are the calendar notes from the war years 1916 to 1918. The entries are mostly short, but nevertheless provide a supplementary insight into what moved Freud during this time (Giefer & Tögel, 2016).

Example: February 1917[4]

1.	U-boat war
2./3.	Ernst expected in vain
4.	Ferenczi
5.	American. rupture [of diplomatic relations]
12.	Anna to Sulz
18.	In Sulz
19.	Everyday life 5th edit.
21.	Anna back. Ditha married. Holl. Transl. War u Death

Travel calendar Rome (1923)

His last trip to Italy – a good quarter of a year after his cancer diagnosis – took Freud to Rome for the seventh time. He was accompanied by his daughter Anna. A kind of travel diary exists from this trip, in which Freud recorded their undertakings in keywords (Freud, 2002b, S. 377–384).

First page of the travel calendar:

Rom	Morning	Afternoon	Evening
1.	–	Corso	–
2.	Forum, Cap[itol]	Pincio	–
3.	Palatine	Gianicolo Vatican	–
4.	Museo naz[ionale]	Pantheon Coloss. P[iazza] Navona Maria s[opra] Min[erva] G. Bruno	
5.	Mus[eo] Vatic[ano]	Moses Bocca d[ella] Verità 2 Temples Port[icle of the] Octav[ia] Carcer	
6.	Museo Capitol	Janus Palatine	
7.	Sistina Punch	protest. Cemetery S. Saba S. Sabina AventinoCestius	
8.	S. Angelo	Caec. Metella Via Appia Columbar[ium]	
9.	Villa Giulia	S. Paolo Tre fontane	
10.	Vatican Loggias Bibliot.	Celio Via Latina (Tombe)	

"Kürzeste Chronik" ("Shortest Chronicle") (1929–1939)

On Freud's desk after his death were 20 large-format sheets on which Freud had made notes on events in the last ten years of his life. These notes have the same character as those from the war years 1916–1918.

Example: October/November 1929:[5]

1929	*Shortest chronicle*
31 Oct.	Passed over for the Nobel Prize
Sat. 2 Nov.	First Tarock party – Visit Rickman
Tu 4 " "	with finger suppuration at Schnitzler
We 5 "	Almanach Preface Eitingon
Th 6 ____	Kris and mounts – Flournoy
Fr 7 ____	Antisemit. Disturbances – Dioscori ring –
Mo 11 –	Neuralgia. Adda given away.
Thu 14 –	Heart warmth attack. Dr Altmann
Sa 16.	Rothschild hospital, Anna's Book
We 20 –	First evening Yvette
Th 21	At Yvette's hotel
Fr 22 –	Dedication Th. Mann. second evening Yvette At Gottlieb's
Sa 23	False alarm with Pichler
Mo 25 –	Adda back
Sa 30 –	Princess left, Eitingon's mother [†]

"Chronology" (1893–1935)

Freud began writing down a "chronology" of his publications (including all editions of his books) and their translations in the early 1920s. This list stops in 1935.

Example: 1926

1926		
Lay analysis	Sexual theory 6th	Dream interpretation French
		Hysteria span
		Sexual th. Czech
		Inhibition Sy. Russ

Visitors' list (1938–1939)

After his arrival in London at the beginning of 1938 June, Freud made notes of his visitors. He used Frank Smython's "Featherweight" notebook for this purpose.

Freud probably already kept a similar list in Vienna, but did not take it with him to London.

Example:

Visitors	
10/1	Ignotus
25/1	Repina
	Bardi
28/1	L. u V. Woolf
29/1	Trotter
1/2	K. Federn
17/2	Robson
24/2	Oppenheim
5/3	Fritz Paneth a[nd] wife
19/3	Hartmann
2/4	Sindler
9/4	Lampl a[nd] Jeanne
24/5	Marlé
	Ch. Singer & wife

List of letters received and sent (1938–1939)

Similar to visitors, Freud also kept records of letters received and sent. Only the records after his arrival in London have been preserved. Freud entered letters he received in the left-hand column and letters he sent in the right-hand column. Although extensive, the list is not complete.

Example: 20.6.1938

Pichler invoice	Bondi
Bondi	Tear
Roake	Roake
Hilda Davies	Cath Stuart
Ruth Oliver Eva (Couch)	
Sister	
Benj. Tear	
Mehta	
Cole Savage	
Tlg Union des Ami‚vs	
Stonbourough	
Wells s. a.	
Wilson	
Barnes	

Notes

1 Cf. also Tögel (2006).
2 For these lectures, see SFG 12, 1910-01.
3 In conjunction with the *Fee list,* the patient calendar also allows relatively reliable statements about Freud's income, cf. Tögel (2006).
4 The explanations for these entries can be found in Giefer and Tögel (2016), S. 170–174.
5 The explanations of these entries can be found in Freud (1996), S. 73–83.

Sigmund Freud: 1856–1939

A Biographical Compendium

1856

1856 May 6

F. is born at 6.30 PM in Freiberg in Moravia (now Příbor, Czech Republic), Schlossergasse 117. His parents are Jakob and Amalia Freud, née Nathansohn. The midwife is Caecilia Smolka. F.'s father came from Tysmenitz (now Tysmenica in Ukraine) and had been residing in Freiberg since around 1848, where he worked in the wool trade. F.'s mother hailed from Brody (now in Ukraine), approximately 150 km northeast of Lemberg (now Lviv). Jakob and Amalia got married in Vienna on 1855 July 25. F. has two half-brothers, Emanuel and Philipp, from his father's first marriage, who are over 20 years older than him. F. is born as an uncle.

1856 May 13

F. is circumcised by Rabbi Samson Frankel from Mährisch-Ostrau (part of present-day Ostrava).

1856 November 20

Birth of F.'s niece Pauline, daughter of his brother Emanuel.

DOI: 10.4324/9781032696539-3

1857

1857 June 5
F. goes with his mother Amalia and the maid Resi Wittek to Rožnau (now Rožnov), approximately 20 km south of Freiberg, for a spa treatment.

1857 July mid
Return to Freiberg.

1857 October
Birth of F.'s brother Julius.

1858

1858 April 15
Death of F.'s brother Julius. The funeral takes place in Weisskirchen (now Hranice).

1858 Summer
F. promises – after he had wet the bed – to buy his father in Neutitschein (now Nový Jičín) a nice new red bed.

1858 Autumn
F. falls off a stool in the pantry and injures himself behind the lower jaw. He is treated by the Freiberg doctor Josef Pur, who is also the town's mayor.

1858 December 31
Birth of F.'s sister Anna.

1859

1859 January
– F.'s father plans to move with his family to Leipzig.
– F.'s nanny Resi Wittek is caught stealing by his brother Philipp and is sentenced to ten months in prison.

1859 February 1
On the occasion of his imminent departure from Freiberg, F.'s father receives a certificate from the cloth-making guild, allowing him to pursue a career as a merchant.

1859 February 22
Birth of F.'s niece Bertha, daughter of brother Emanuel.

1859 February 26
The town council of Klocksdorf (a district of Freiberg) provides Jakob Freud with a certificate of good conduct, confirming that he and his family will always be welcome back in Klocksdorf.

1859 March 23
The town council of Freiberg issues a character reference for Jakob Freud.

1859 April end or May beginning
F. plays with his niece Pauline and his nephew Johannes (John) – both children of his brother Emanuel – on a dandelion meadow near Freiberg.

1859 May 9
F.'s father Jakob arrives in Leipzig together with his son Emanuel for the Easter Fair (May 9–28). Jakob stays at the Hotel Stadt Rom. Emanuel travels on to Vienna on May 16.

1859 June 10
The police department of the city of Leipzig asks the city council to provide information as soon as possible as to whether Freud's continued residence is of particular advantage to local trade.

1859 June 14–15
The wool market takes place in Leipzig, an important event for F.'s father Jakob.

1859 June 15
The city council forwards the police department's request to the chamber of commerce.

1859 Summer
F.'s brothers Emanuel and Philipp emigrate to England: Emanuel with his family, Philipp is still unmarried.

1859 June end /July beginning
Jakob Freud goes back to Freiberg, probably to dissolve the household.

1859 July 29
The chamber of commerce issues a negative opinion.

1859 July 30
The city council informs the police department that it does not approve of Jakob Freud's permanent residence.

1859 August 11

In Brno, a passport is issued for F.'s mother Amalia for further stay in Leipzig.

1859 August mid–1859 October 18
Stay in Leipzig and move to Vienna

1859 August mid

Jakob and Amalia leave Freiberg and move to Leipzig with F., daughter Anna and the maid Anna Hrazek. On the way, they pass the railway station in Breslau, and F. is reminded of the burning ghosts in hell by the gas flames there. Possibly they visit Jakob's brother Abbe, who lives in Breslau, and stay for a day or two.

1859 August 19

The police office informs Jakob Freud that his family must leave Leipzig by August 23.

1859 August 20

Jakob Freud applies to the Leipzig city council for permanent residence in Leipzig for himself, Amalia, Sigmund and Anna.

1859 August 22

The city council forwards Jakob Freud's renewed application to the chamber of commerce.

1859 August 30

The chamber of commerce again issues a negative opinion because Jakob Freud's past makes it advisable to save Leipzig "from such a businessman".

1859 August 31

The city council informs Jakob Freud's advocate Mr. Winter of the negative decision.

1859 September 10

The Austrian Consulate General issues a travel document for Amalia, son Sigmund, daughter Anna and maid Anna Hrazek to travel to Freiberg in Moravia. It can be found on the back of Amalia's passport.

1859 October 15

Jakob Freud deregisters himself and his family at the Leipzig police station.

1859 October 16

Amalia, Sigmund, Anna and the maid Anna Hrazek cross the Saxon-Austrian border at Bodenbach-Tetschen.

1859 October after 16

At some point during the train journey from Bodenbach to Vienna, F. sees his mother naked.

1859 after October 18

Once in Vienna, Anna and her children live for a quarter of a year with Amalia's parents – Jakob and Sara Nathansohn – at 726 Leopoldstadt (now Untere Donaustrasse 45). They stay there until 1860 February mid.

1859 November 8

F. sees the procession on the occasion of the Schiller anniversary. The procession passes the Freud family home only a few hundred meters away.

1859 December 10
F.'s father arrives in Vienna and stays at the Hotel National in Taborstrasse 18, one of the most luxurious hotels in Vienna.

1859 December 23
F.'s father moves to the Hotel Schröder, also in Taborstrasse.

1860

1860 January 24
The Vienna Commercial Court sends F.'s father a "reminder" to pay his debts to Benjamin Leisorowitz including interest.

1860 February 8
The *Wiener Zeitung* publishes the "reminder" and prints it twice more (on February 10 and 12).

1860 February 10
The *Brünner Zeitung* publishes a wanted poster of F.'s brother Philipp for the crime of fraud. He had accumulated large amounts of debts, had not paid them back and was a fugitive.

1860 February 17
F.'s father files for bankruptcy. After the opening of the bankruptcy proceedings, he moved in with his parents-in-law and now lives again with his wife Amalie and their children Sigmund and Anna.

1860 after February 17
The Freud family moves from Leopoldstadt 726 (II. district) to Dampfschiffstrasse 2 (now Hintere Zollamtsstrasse 1) in the III. district south of the Danube Canal; they stay there until February 1861.

1860 February 28
The *Wiener Zeitung* reports on the bankruptcy proceedings opened against F.'s father on February 17.

1860 March 21
Birth of F.'s sister Rosa.

1860 May 24
The Vienna Regional Court elects the creditors' committees and the asset manager in connection with the bankruptcy of F.'s father.

1860 July 2
The furniture of F.'s brother Emanuel is auctioned off in Freiberg. He had accumulated large amounts of debt and had not repaid them, and his whereabouts are unknown to the court.

1861

1861 February
Move from Dampfschiffstrasse 2 to Weissgärber 114 (now Hetzgasse 20, corner of Seidlgasse), also in the III. district. Freud stayed there until the spring of 1864.

1861 March 22
Birth of F.'s sister Mitzi (Maria).

1861 Summer
F. and his sister Anna pick apart a travel description of Persia with colored plates. They are overjoyed.

1862

1862 Spring
F. receives his first private lessons from his mother. She tells him that people are made of earth and therefore have to return to earth.

1862 July 13
Birth of F.'s sister Dolfi (Adolfine).

1864

Freud reads Adolphe Thiers' *Konsulat und Kaiserreich,* and André Masséna was his declared favorite, not least because of his birthday on May 6.

1864 Spring
– F. receives an edition of Shakespeare's works on the occasion of the 300th anniversary of his birth.
– Move from Weissgärber 114 (III. district) to Pillersdorfgasse 5 in the II. district. Freud stayed there until the beginning of 1865.

1864 May 3
Birth of F.'s sister Paula.

1864 May mid
F. observes his almost two-year-old sister Dolfi in the cradle and thinks that now she is no longer the youngest.

1864 September
After having been taught at home by his mother until then, F. now presumably moves to the private primary schools for boys at Obere Augartenstr. 68, about 500 m from the Freud's flat. Freud goes through a class to prepare for the religious examination, which is a prerequisite for attending the Gymnasium. The teaching of Israelite religious education at this boys' school is entrusted to Käthe Serebrenik, who is paid by the Israelitische Kultusgemeinde (Israelite religious community).

1865

F. has a dream of "people with bird's beaks".

1865 beginning
Move from Pillersdorfgasse 5 to Pfeffergasse 1 (now Taborstr. 61), also in the II. district. Freud stayed there until the autumn of 1868.

1865 June 21
F.'s uncle Josef, a brother of his father, is arrested. He is suspected of selling fake ruble notes. His accomplice Osias Weich is arrested the next day in Leipzig.

1865 Summer
F. completes the fourth grade of primary school; he receives a "very good" in Israelite religion.

1865 October 2
F. enters the Leopoldstädter Realgymnasium at Taborstrasse 24, opened in 1864 (from 1868 "Leopoldstädter Communal-Real- und Obergymnasium", since 1989 Sigmund-Freud-Gymnasium).

1865 shortly before October 3
F. visits Jakob Nathansohn, his maternal grandfather, in the Israelite hospital at Seegasse 9.

1865 October 3
Death of F.'s grandfather Jakob Nathansohn.

1865 October 18
The pupils of the grammar school have a day off school and take part in the ceremonial unveiling of the Prince Eugene Monument.

1866

- F. studies the history of Alexander the Great with his father.
- F. compares his family with the Bible.

1866 February 22
F.'s uncle Josef is sentenced to ten years in prison for his involvement in the counterfeit money affair, the Higher Regional Court reduces the sentence to six years, and finally, he is pardoned after four years.

1866 April 19
Birth of F.'s brother Alexander.

1866 after July 3
F. witnesses the arrival of wounded from the Prussian-Austrian War at the Nordbahnhof (now's freight station) and as a result prompts his class to pluck Charpie.

1866 July 14
Due to the events of the Prussian-Austrian War, the school year closes earlier than usual.

1866 October 15
- Due to the events of the Prussian-Austrian War, the school year starts later than usual.
- Eduard Silberstein moves into the I. class of the "Leopoldstädter Communal-Real- und Ober-gymnasium", which Freud has attended since 1865 and is now in the II. class. Both boys become friends, learn Spanish together, found an Academia Castellana and write humorous texts.

1867

1867 Spring
A close and intense friendship begins between F. and Heinrich Braun, the later German social democratic politician and publicist, which lasts for almost seven years. Under Braun's influence, F. considers studying law.

1867 July 29
Last day of school before the summer holidays.

1867 Summer
F. receives Alfred Brehm's *Illustriertes Thierleben* as a prize from his grammar school.

1867 Autumn
F.'s father commissions a painter to do a portrait of his children. F. talks to the painter about art and poetry. A leg is then missing from the finished picture, and the painter has to add it afterward.

1867 September 30
First day of school after the summer holidays.

1868

1868 May 22
F.'s mother Amalia goes with a child to a spa stay Rožnau (until the end of August).

1868 July 22
Last day of school before the summer holidays.

1868 August end
F.'s mother Amaliacomes back to Vienna from Rožnau.

1868 Autumn
The Freud family moves from Pfeffergasse 1 to Glockengasse 30 and stays there until autumn 1870.

1868 October 1
First day of school after the summer holidays.

1868 November 9
F. recites the *Ring des Polykrates* at a Schiller celebration at his grammar school and plays Margot in the prologue to The *Jungfrau von Orleans. The* celebration takes place in the gym hall of his school at Glockengasse 2.

1868 November 24
The pupils have a day off from classes on the occasion of the funeral service of the late Mayor of Vienna Andreas Zelinka. Zelinka had opened F.'s school in 1874.

1869

F. reads Henry Kingsley's *Hypatia*.

1869 May 6
F. receives Ludwig Börne's *Gesammelte Schriften as a* gift and reads them with great eagerness.

1869 May 21
F.'s mother goes with a child to a spa stay Rožnau (until the end of August). At the same time, Anna Silberstein is there with her sister Mina and a child, possibly with son Eduard.

1869 June 26
F. testifies for the first time as a witness in an investigation instigated by his class president Emanuel Hannak against his fellow pupils Otto Drobil and Richard Ott. The two had been accused of visiting "suspicious bars" and consorting with prostitutes, and Freud and most of the other classmates had at least known about it.

1869 June 30
F. testifies again in the investigation against his classmates.

1869 July 1
F. testifies against his fellow pupils for the last time as part of the investigation. In a subsequent teachers' conference chaired by the headmaster Alois Pokorny, Otto Drobil and Richard Ott are expelled from the school and the moral grades of the confidants, including F.'s, are lowered.

1869 July 31
Last day of school before the summer holidays.

1869 August end
F.'s mother Amalia comes back to Vienna from Rožnau.

1869 October 4
First day of school after the summer holidays.

1869 November 16
Schiller celebration of Freud's school.

1870

- F.'s brother Emanuel and his nephew Johannes (John) visit the Freud family in Vienna. F. plays "Brutus" and "Caesar" from Schiller's *Die Räuber*.
- F. and Silberstein found the "Academia Castellana" and decided to learn Spanish together. The basis for this was probably Charles Frédéric Franceson's *Grammatik der spanischen Sprache,* in which the original Spanish text of Cervantes' *El Coloquio de los Perros* was also printed for practice. F. and Silberstein borrowed their dog names "Cipion" and "Berganza" from this text.

1870 June 15
F.'s mother Amalia goes with two children to a spa stay at Rožnau (until the end of August). Anna Silberstein is also back in Rožnau.

1870 Summer
Beginning of the correspondence between F. and Eduard Silberstein.
F. offers Eduard Silberstein on behalf of his parents "to lodge him and his brother Karl** and to provide them with a room in the new apartment to which they will be moving in two months' time, and also to sign their sick notes for school" (F. to Silberstein, ca. 1870 July). Silberstein does not accept this offer, presumably because he wanted to stay close to a girl he was in love with, whom he and F. had nicknamed "Ichthyosaura". She presumably attends the school where Silberstein lives in a boarding house.

1870 July 30
Last day of school before the summer holidays.

1870 August end
F.'s mother Amalia arrives back in Vienna with her children.

1870 Autumn
- F. studies the course of the Franco-German war on maps.
- Moved from Glockengasse 30 to Pfeffergasse 5 (now Taborstr. 61). The Freud family stays there until 1873.

1870 October 3
First day of school after the summer holidays. Wilhelm Knöpfmacher comes from Nikolsburg to Vienna and enters the Leopoldstadt grammar school. F. and he become lifelong friends.

1871

1871 February 12–24
Due to a particularly strong flood in the districts around the Danube and the Danube Canal in Vienna, the pupils of the Leopoldstädter Gymnasium get the day off.

1871 Spring
F. explains the significance of the Paris Commune to his sisters.

1871 July 29
Last day of school before the summer holidays. The program of the public closing ceremony of the school year notes "5. speech and oratory exercises. a) Julius Caesar by Shakespeare. Act IV, Scene III, Brutus and Cassius, performed by the 6th grade pupil Freud Sigmund and the 7th grade pupil Löbel Samuel".

1871 July end–August end
First visit to Freiberg

F. goes to his mother in the Rožnau health resort, who has been there since July 12 with his other siblings. From Rožnau, F. visits his native town of Freiberg with Eduard Silberstein, who has also come to Rožnau. It is the first time since 1859 that F. is in Freiberg. F. and Silberstein stay with Ignaz Fluss's family, and F. meets the daughter Gisela for the first time, with whom he later falls in love. During this week, the two friends also meet "Ichthyosaura", for whom at least Silberstein feels sympathy.

1871 October 2
First day of school after the summer holidays. Samuel Hammerschlag becomes F.'s religion teacher.

1871 after October 2
– F. writes "Zerstreute Gedanken" for the school magazine *Musarion.*
– F. leads the main blow in a conspiracy against an ignorant teacher. He and his co-conspirator, the later composer and choir director Arthur Henriquez, are taken to task for this by the German teacher and "school bully" Viktor Kraus.

1871 December 31
Eduard Silberstein spends New Year's Eve with F.'s family.

1872

1872 January mid
F. is ill and cannot go to school.

1872 March 25
F. meets the brother of "Ichthyosaura".

1872 April 22
F. takes part in a prize draw for the *Illustrirtes Wiener Extrablatt*. The solution he sent in, "Ernst ist das Leben, heiter die Kunst" ("Serious is life, cheerful is art"), is correct, and he enters the final draw, which takes place on May 4; however, F. does not appear to have been among the winners.

1872 Summer
F. takes a trip through Styria with Eduard Silberstein.

1872 July 1
F.'s mother goes with two children to a spa stay in Rožnau (until the end of August).

1872 July mid
F. meets "Ichthyosaura".

1872 August beginning
F. takes a boat trip – probably with his class – on the Danube and the Danube Canal.

1872 August 3
Last day of school before the summer holidays.

1872 August 3–September 15
Second visit to Freiberg

F. goes to Freiberg. This time, he is accompanied by Ignaz Rosanes, a fellow pupil from Silberstein's class. Emil Fluss – son of the Fluss family from Freiberg, who are friends of the Freud family – and some other friends dress up and play a "mask joke". Emil tries to make his relationship with "Ichthyosaura" palatable to him after he himself has given up his inclination toward her. However, F. falls in love with Emil's 13-year-old sister Gisela. He describes her as follows: "Gisela's beauty, too, is wild, I might say Thracian: The aquiline nose, the long black hair, and the firm lips come from the mother, the dark complexion and the sometimes indifferent expression from the father" (F. to Silberstein, 4.9.1872). Occasionally, he visits his mother, who is back for a spa stay at Rožnau with his siblings.

1872 August 8

Freud is in Hochwald (now Hukvaldy) near Rožnau and begins to keep a "small travel diary into which all the outings I shall ever make will be crammed". It was "to keep Your Honour informed about my own life" (F. to Silberstein, 9.8.1872).

1872 August 17

Leon Salter from Czernowitz, who is for a spa stay at Rožnau, visits the Fluss family in Freiberg for lunch. Freud and Silberstein call him "Iguanodon" after a dinosaur genus, probably because he openly expresses his interest in "Ichthyosaura".[1]

1872 August 21

Gisela Fluss leaves Freiberg, and F. goes to Hochwald to the castle ruins for a few hours to calm his "turbulent thoughts" (F. to Silberstein, 4.9.1872).

1872 August end

F. has a toothache, so he gets drunk, and Gisela Fluss' mother Eleonore looks after him.

1872 September 1

F. goes to Rožnau to visit his mother, who in turn is there for a spa stay.

1872 September 15

F. travels back to Vienna with a short stopover in Prerau (now Přerov).

1872 September 28

Freud writes to Emil Fluss that with Ichthyosaura "that there was more irony, yes, mockery, than seriousness in this whole flirtation" (F. to Fluss, 28.9.1872).

1872 September 30

First day of school after the summer holidays.

1873

– F. runs up debts with his bookseller.

1873 January 13–14
F. writes a "memorial note" for Eduard Silberstein.

1873 March 13
The Jewish festival of Purim is celebrated, among other things, with a small play at the Freud family; the main actors are F.'s sisters.

1873 March mid
F. reads *König Oedipus* by Sophocles.

1873 March 22
F. attends a Darwin lecture by Carl Brühl at the zootomic institute, where he reads from the fragment "Die Natur" attributed to Goethe at the time, but originating from Georg Christoph Tobler. This experience provided the decisive impetus for F.'s decision to study medicine. Carl Brühl had held the chair of zootomy in Vienna since 1863 and was known to wide circles through his popular scientific lectures.

1873 April end
F. visits the Prater (probably with Eduard Silberstein). As he speaks Spanish, he is mistaken for a stranger.

1873 May beginning
F. reads odes by Horace.

1873 May 1
F. wants to "gain insight into the age-old dossiers of Nature, perhaps even eavesdrop on her eternal processes, and share my findings with anyone who wants to learn" (F. to Fluss, 1.5.1873).

1873 June
F. visits the World's Fair twice, which takes place in the Vienna Prater from May 1 to November 2. "Altogether, it is a show for the world of the aesthete, the sophisticated, unthinking world, which also for the most part makes up its visitors" (F. to Fluss, 16.6.1873). Nevertheless, he intends to go there daily after his Matura. He is particularly impressed by an exhibition of Abraham Lincoln's letters and the Gettysburg Address and obtains copies of them.

1873 June 9
F. takes the written examinations for the Matura: German, Latin, Greek and mathematics. His German Matura essay is on the topic "Welche Rücksichten sollen uns bei der Wahl des Berufes leiten" ("What considerations should guide us in choosing a profession"). In Latin, a passage from Virgil had to be translated, in Greek, one from *König Oedipus* by Sophocles had to be translated, and in mathematics, four problems from geometry and algebra had to be solved.

1873 June mid
Sigmund Bretholz, wool merchant from Tysmenica and father of the historian Bertold Bretholz from Freiberg, visits the Freud family daily with his daughter Anna and a nephew of his wife Henriette from Czernowitz. F. had an animated conversation with the latter.

1873 June 30
F.'s mother goes with three children to a spa stay at Rožnau (until the end of August). Anna Silberstein is also there with her children Karl, Adolf and Minna.

1873 July beginning
F. tries to construct a number system, for he has noticed "that everything in the real world has its equal, or equivalent, in the world of numbers" (F. to Silberstein, 6.8.1873).

1873 July 8
Because of the World's Fair, the pupils of the F.'s school are going on their summer holidays earlier than normal.

1873 July 9
F. takes the last oral examination and passes the Matura "with distinction": He receives seven "excellent" grades and a commendation in geography.

1873 before July 11
F.'s father forbids his son to go to Rožnau that summer.

1873 July 15
F. goes on a long hike in the surroundings of Vienna, among other things to the Kahlenberg; he has palpitations and sweats for the first time.

1873 July 16
F. buys Cajetan Carl Zeplichal's *Lehrbuch der Gabelsberger'schen Stenografie* in practice for Eduard Silberstein, as Silberstein wants to learn shorthand. F. also begins to take an interest in shorthand.

1873 July 19
F. sees William Shakespeare's *Othello* at the Theater an der Wien starring Ernesto Rossi.

1873 July 26
F. sees Adolf Wilbrandt's *Grachus der Volkstribun* at the Burgtheater with Friedrich Krastel in the leading role.

1873 July end
F. enrolled in "swimming classes", but "the low water level has turned the classes into a mud-bath. One cannot possibly drown, can barely dive anywhere, and with the danger the whole thrill has gone" (F. to Silberstein, 2.8.1873).

1873 August beginning
F. visits the Sophienalpe near Dornbach, picks strawberries and raspberries and becomes home-sick for Freiberg, respectively Rožnau.

1873 August 1
F. sees Friedrich Schiller's *Die Räuber* at the Stadttheater.

1873 August 6
F. orders branches of a cypress tree from Eduard Silberstein, who is in Rožnau, the needles of which have a spicy-tart taste.

1873 August mid
– F. learns French together with Heinrich Braun in the mornings, and in the afternoons, the friends deal with philosophy.

- The cypress branches ordered from Eduard Silberstein arrive at F.'s.
- F. renounces his inclination for Gisela Fluss, but Ignaz Rosanes begins to take an interest in her.

1873 August 18

F. visits Mrs. Lipska, a mutual acquaintance of him and Eduard Silberstein.

1873 August 20

- F. writes a "memorial on the subject of the Cretaceous which led to G[isela]'s dismissal" (F. to Silberstein, 21.2.1875). It presumably uses the analogy because the Cretaceous period follows Jurassic and Jurassic period stands for the Ichthyosaura.
- F. informs Eduard Silberstein that he has now renounced his inclination toward Gisela Fluss.

1873 August 22

F. attends a "festival" at the World's Fair.

1873 August 28

F.'s mother returns to Vienna from the spa in Rožnau with his siblings Alexander, Rosa and Dolfi.

1873 August 31

F. meets Eduard Silberstein, who returns from Rožnau, at the railway station.

1873 October

F.'s enrolls in the Medical Faculty of the University of Vienna.

1873 October approx.

- F. becomes a member of the "Leseverein deutscher Studenten" ("Reading Society of German Students"), whose meetings first take place at Alter Fleischmarkt 16, then at Schönlatern- gasse 9 and finally at Wollzeile 33.
- Move from Pfeffergasse 5 to Pazmanitengasse 19 (now Darwingasse 15), only a few meters from the old flat. The F. family stays there until 1874. F.'s cousin Deborah Kornhauser – daughter of F.'s uncle Josef – moves with her family into the same house at about the same time.

1873 October–1874 March

F. takes the following courses in the winter semester:

- Carl Langer: human anatomy, bones, muscles and viscera, including topography (six hours);
- Carl Langer: demonstrations and exercises in the dissecting room (six hours);
- Franz Schneider: General and Medical Chemistry, Part I: Mineral Chemistry (five hours);
- Franz Schneider: Analytical Chemistry, in conjunction with practical exercises (six hours).

1874

- Move from Pazmanitengasse 19 to Kaiser-Josef-Strasse 3 (now Heinestrasse/corner of Taborstrasse). The Freud family stays there until August 1882.
- Freud has an argument with Victor Adler, the later founder and leader of the Social Democratic Party of Austria, in the "Leseverein deutscher Studenten".
- F. acquires Jacob Henle's Handbuch der Gefässlehre des Menschen, his Handbuch der Nervenlehre des Menschen and Carl Gegenbauer's Grundriss der vergleichenden Anatomie.

1874 February 8
Carl Brühl gives a lecture on "Seescheide und Sittlichkeit", which is most likely attended by F.

1874 March 8
F. attends a lecture by Carl Brühl on the subject of the "Bau des Menschen und der Thiere" ("Construction of Man and Animals") and takes this opportunity to meet Emil Fluss, who is in Vienna.

1874 March 9
In the evening, F. probably attends Shakespeare's *Othello* with Ernesto Rossi at the Theater an der Wien.

1874 April 16–July
F. takes the following courses in the summer semester:

- Carl Langer: anatomy of the sense organs, the nervous and vascular system, including topography (six hours);
- Franz Schneider: General and Medical Chemistry, Part II: Chemistry of Organic Compounds (five hours);
- Franz Schneider: practical exercises in the laboratory and analytical chemistry (six hours);
- Carl Claus: General Zoology in connection with a critical presentation of Darwinism for listeners of all faculties (three hours);
- Carl Toldt: practical instruction on the use of the microscope and histological exercises for students (three hours);
- Gustav Tschermak: Mineralogy (five hours);
- Eduard Fenzl: on the systematics of phanerogamous plants with special consideration of medicinal and economic species (three hours);
- Ernst Brücke: physiology of voice and speech (one hour).

1874 April 20
F. starts working in Franz Schneider's chemistry laboratory.

1874 April 21
F. attends his first lecture: Franz Schneider's "General and Medical Chemistry".

1874 Summer
Eduard Silberstein teaches F.'s sister Anna shorthand and temporarily falls in love with her.

1874 July 16
F. passes the examination in mineralogy with distinction under Gustav Tschermak.

1874 August mid

F. reads Thomas Carlyle, Hermann von Helmholtz and Aristotle's *Nicomachean Ethics*.

1874 September 4

F. sends to Eduard Silberstein the second volume of Charles Dickens *The Posthumous Papers of the Pickwick Club* and a novel by Edward Bulwer-Lytton (possibly one of the recent novels *Kenelm Chillingly. His Adventures and Opinions* or *The Parisians*).

1874 September 12

F. stops keeping a diary.

1874 Autumn

– Beginning of the friendship between F. and Joseph Paneth. Both presumably get to know each other at Carl Claus' lectures in the Zoological Institute at Schottenring 22. Salomon Ehrmann also meets F. there for the first time.
– Together with his friends Joseph Paneth, Emanuel Loewy and Siegfried Lipiner, F. begins the publication of a "journal" with philosophical works. Lipiner's essay "Über das teleologische Argument autore me" ("On the teleological argument autore me") appears in the first issue.
– F. writes a piece for their journal on "Goethes Fresswerkzeuge" ("Goethe's guzzling tools") and an "occasional poem" entitled "Neues Ma-Nischtana".
– F. talks his mother out of agreeing to the marriage of his 16-year-old sister Anna to a maternal great uncle 40 years her senior, who had proposed to Anna during a visit from Odessa in Vienna.

1874 October–1875 March

F. takes the following courses in the winter semester:

– Christian August Voigt: exercises in the dissecting room and demonstrations (six hours);
– Ernst Brücke: physiology and higher anatomy (six hours);
– Ernst Brücke: anatomical-physiological exercises for beginners (six hours);
– Carl Claus: zoology for physicians and pharmacists, also teachers, in a clear presentation of the entire field, combined with microscopic demonstrations (five hours);
– Joseph Stefan: On Magnetism, Electricity and Heat, in experimental treatment (four hours);
– Joseph Stefan: On the Theory of Magnetic and Electric Forces (two hours);
– Franz Brentano: reading, explanation and critical discussion of selected philosophical writings (one hour).
– Franz Brentano: Selected Metaphysical Questions (two hours).

1874 October

– F.'s sister Anna passes the entrance examination for the Ursuline Sisters.
– F.'s sister Rosa begins training in a newly founded drawing and work school for the perfection of female handicrafts. F. has "taken charge of the rest of her education" (F. to Silberstein, 22./23.10.1874).

1874 October mid

F. takes part in a student demonstration against the Minister of Education, Karl Stremayr, because he had delayed the inauguration of the new rector Wilhelm Wahlberg.

1874 October 21
F. is at the inauguration of the new rector of Vienna University, the jurist Emil Wahlberg.

1874 October 26
F. meets the Norwegian Kristian Fredrik Grøn in the dissecting room, a medical student from Kristiana (now Oslo) who spends several months in Vienna with his father Andreas Fredrik Grøn. He learns from him how medical studies are structured in Norway.

1874 November
F. hears a colloquium with Franz Brentano on "Das Dasein Gottes" ("The Existence of God") and reads writings by Ludwig Feuerbach together with Joseph Paneth.

1874 November beginning
F. meets Etka Pineles, the fiancée of his friend Josef Herzig.

1874 December
F.'s contact with the philosophy student Richard Wahle intensifies.

1874 December beginning
F. reads Georg Christoph Lichtenberg's works "with great pleasure" and quotes him for pages in a letter to Eduard Silberstein (F. to Silberstein, 2.12.1874).

1874 December 6
The second issue of the Journal, edited by F. Joseph Paneth, Emanuel Loewy and Siegfried Lipiner, appears with a critique of Lipiner's essay from the first issue, an essay by Joseph Paneth on "Die Grundlagen der materialistischen Ethik" ("The Foundations of Materialist Ethics") together with remarks on "Spinozas Beweis für das Dasein Gottes" ("Spinoza's Proof of the Existence of God"), and an essay by Emanuel Loewy on definitions.

1874 December 14
F. visits a lecture by Karl Grün at the Engineering and Architecture Association for the benefit of the German Reading Association entitled "Über die drei Zeitalter des Menschengeistes" ("On the Three Ages of the Human mind"). This lecture "culminated in a glorification of modern science and of our most modern saints such as Darwin and Haeckel [...]" (F. to Silberstein, 7.3.1875).

1874 December 31
On New Year's Eve and the birthday of F.'s sister Anna, Gisela Fluss and her sister Sidonie, an uncle of F. (Abbe or Josef) and a friend of F.'s father from Neutitschein (now Novy Jičín) are visiting. F. is "merrier than normal" (F. to Silberstein, 17.1.1875).

1875

F. acquires a *Anleitung zu wissenschaftlichen Beobachtungen auf Reisen (Guide to Scientific Observations While Traveling)*, a *Handbuch der theoretischen Physik (Handbook of Theoretical Physics)* by William Thomson and Peter Tait, *The elements of Euclid,* Pierre Simon de Laplace's *Essai philosophique sur les probabilités*, Alessandro Manzoni's *book I* promessi *sposi: storia milanese del secolo XVII*, the fifth and sixth volumes of Charles Darwin's *Gesammelte Werke* and Gustav Theodor Fechner's Über die physikalische und philosophische Atomenlehre (On *Physical and Philosophical Atomic Theory).*

1875 January
F. reads works by Goethe, Lessing, and a chapter from *Don Quixote* by Cervantes.

1875 January mid
F. intends to spend the winter semester of 1875/1876 in Berlin to hear Hermann von Helmholtz, Emil Du Bois-Reymond and Rudolf Virchow. However, this plan is not realized.

1875 January 17
F. has himself photographed and sends the photo with a little verse on the back to Eduard Silberstein a week later.

1875 January 24
F. notices that the contact between his sisters and Gisela Fluss is intensifying.

1875 January 30
F. sends Eduard Silberstein his copy of a Spanish edition of *Don Quixote.*

1875 January end
The "Journal" published by F., Emanuel Loewy, Joseph Paneth and Siegfried Lipiner ceases publication on F.'s initiative.

1875 February
- F.'s mother suffers from a protracted lung infiltration.
- F. and Joseph Paneth write to Franz Brentano, and he invites them to his home.
- In his letters to Eduard Silberstein, who has fallen in love with a 16-year-old girl in Leipzig, F. tries for several weeks to prevent him from taking advantage of the girl.

1875 February 20
F. receives the papers of the "Academia Castellana" from Silberstein's brother Karl.

1875 February 21
F. looks through the papers of the "Academia Castellana" and finds some manuscripts written by him earlier, among them: "Memorial in Betreff der Kreide" ("Memorial on the subject of the Cretaceous"; "Nachtstück" ("Nocturen"), the torso of a novella "Die Reise nach Rožnau" ("The Journey to Rožnau"), a "Vademecum an Bord zu lesen mit Segen und Fluch auf den Bergen Rhadiska und Rhadost" ("Vademecum to be read on board ship with blessings and curses on Mounts Rhadiska and Rhadost".), a report of F.'s strange encounter with Ichthyosaura, a "Pleite-Roman" ("Bankruptcy novel") and a treatise "De mediis, quibus inamoribus efficiendis utuntur poetae", "which alone sufficed to immortalize me as Aristotle's fortunate successor" (F. to Silberstein, 21.2.1875).

1875 March
F. begins to take an interest in John Stuart Mill.

1875 March beginning
F. and Joseph Paneth wrote a second letter to Franz Brentano, who again invited them to his home. Under Brentano's influence, the decision matured in F. "to take my Ph.D. in philosophy and zoology" (F. to Silberstein, 7.3.1875).

1875 March 10
F. hears a lecture by Johannes Volkelt at the "Leseverein deutscher Studenten" on "Kants kategorischen Imperativ und die Gegenwart" ("Kant's Categorical Imperative and the Present") "that was clear, elegant, appropriately rude and entirely justified" (F. to Silberstein, 11.4.1875).

1875 March 14
F. and Joseph Paneth visit Franz Brentano for the third time and discuss philosophy and science. F. intends "to make a thorough study of his philosophy, and meanwhile reserve judgment and the choice between theism and materialism" (F. to Silberstein, 15.3.1875).

1875 March mid
F. obtains from the library of the "Leseverein deutscher Studenten" what he lacks in knowledge of recent literature. He reads, for example, *Die Ahnen* und *Bilder aus der Deutschen Vergangenheit* by Gustav Freytag and a number of Christian Friedrich Hebbel's tragedies such as *Marianne, Agnes Bernauer, Maria Magdalena, Genofeva, Gyges und sein Ring* and *Judith*.

1875 before March 27
F. receives a shipment of homeopathic writings from Eduard Silberstein. It seems to F. that the authors "are great metaphysicians, and Kantians in particular, which is most laudable but perhaps unhealthy" (F. to Silberstein, 27.3.1875).

1875 April beginning
F. reads Adolf Douai's *ABC des Wissens für Denkende (ABC of Knowledge for Thinking People)* and deals especially with the passages on proofs of God.

1875 April–July
F. takes the following courses in the summer semester:

- Ernst Brücke: physiology and higher anatomy (five hours);
- Ernst Brücke: anatomical-physiological exercises for beginners (six hours);
- Carl Claus: anatomical-physiological overview of vertebrates (five hours);
- Carl Claus: Natural History of Mollusks (two hours);
- Carl Claus: zoological-microscopic practical course for beginners (three hours);
- Franz Brentano: old and new logic, exposition of their laws on the basis of a new conception of judgment and criticism of the traditional rules (four hours);
- Josef Stefan: optics (three hours);
- Josef Stefan: theory of heat conduction and diffusion (two hours).

1875 April after 15
F. looks at the new bed of the Danube, into which the old Danube was diverted by the interruption of the Rollerdamm as part of the Danube regulation.

1875 April 27
Somebody throws a stone in a window in the Freud family flat. F. comments on the event as follows: "Anyone with imagination could easily picture the pleasure of being a minister or professor in bad times and possessing a few more windows" (F. to Silberstein, 28.4.1875).

1875 May 6
Eduard Silberstein gives F. the book by Philip Francis (pseudonym Junius) *Junius. Including letters by the same written under other signatures* with the dedication "To my dear friend Sigism. Freud at his birthday the 6th of May 1875".

1875 June 13
F. asks Eduard Silberstein to get him a second hand copy of Hermann von Helmholtz's *Handbuch der physiologischen Optik*.

1875 June mid
F. is preparing for the zoological exam and has a well-founded fear of it.

1875 June beginning
F.'s mother goes with three children for a spa stay at Rožnau (until the end of August).

1875 Summer
– From now on, F. no longer calls himself Sigismund, but Sigmund.
– F. sells a copper kettle that was in his way in his mother's absence. This made his mother very angry, and she did not forgive him for a long time.

1875 July beginning
F. acquires Charles Darwin's *Die Abstammung des Menschen und die geschlechtliche Zuchtwahl (The Descent of Man and Selection in Relation to Sex)*.

1875 July 16–1875 September 7
Visit of the brothers in England

1875 July 16
F. leaves Vienna at 7.30 pm.

1875 July 17
F. arrives in Leipzig at 17.30. He interrupts his journey for two days and stays with Eduard Silberstein, who is studying in Leipzig.

1875 July 19
F. leaves Leipzig in the evening.

1875 July 20
F. arrives in Hamburg, takes a harbor tour and travels by ferry to Grimsby in England at midnight.

1875 July 21
F. arrives in Manchester at the home of his brother Emanuel (Greenstreet 12).

1875 July end
F. is in Lytham St Anne in Lancashire and catches crabs and starfish.

1875 September 7
F. arrives back in Vienna after 7½ weeks.

1875 after September 19
Freud learns of the impending marriage of "Ichthyosaura" and shares the news with Silberstein.

1875 October–1876 March
F. takes the following courses in the winter semester:

- Carl Langer: demonstrations and exercises in the dissecting room (six hours);
- Ernst Brücke: anatomical-physiological exercises (six hours);
- Carl Claus: zoological-microscopic exercises for advanced students (ten hours);
- Ernst Fleischl: physiological discussions (two hours);
- Franz Brentano: in community with the students: reading, explanation and critical discussion of selected philosophical writings (one hour).

1875 October 1
F. writes an ironic "Hochzeitscarmen" (Epithalamium) for Eduard Silberstein, who had been in love with "Ichthyosaura" a few years earlier, on the occasion of her upcoming wedding.

1875 October 2
- F. receives a photograph by Eduard Silberstein.
- F. meets Ignaz Rosanes, who tells him from Richard Wahle that Silberstein can stay with him (Wahle).

1875 October 25
F. is assigned as a Einjährig-Freiwilliger (one-year volunteer[2]) at his own expense to the 13th Company of Infantry Regiment No. 1.

1876

Ernst Brücke becomes aware of F. because he stands out from the majority of students.

1876 February mid
F. begins working for Carl Claus at the Institute for Comparative Anatomy.

1876 February 22
F. submits a scholarship application via Carl Claus together with Johann Roscher and Karl Grobben to the Ministry of Education for zoological studies at the Zoological Station opened in Trieste in autumn 1874 on the initiative of Claus.

1876 March 10
The Minister of Culture and Education Karl Stremeyer approves a scholarship of 100 Gulden[3] for Freud's studies in Trieste.

1876 March end–April 27
First research stay in Trieste

–   F. conducts research on the sexual organs of the eel at the zoological marine laboratory in Trieste. The result of this and the next stay in September is his first publication under the title "Beobachtungen über Gestaltung und feineren Bau der als Hoden beschriebenen Lappenorgane des Aals".

–   F. starts smoking.

1876 April beginning
–   F. roams the streets of Trieste and is particularly impressed by the women there.

1876 April 23
–   F. travels with a colleague (Karl Grobben or Johann Roscher) by steamer to Muggia in a bay neighboring Trieste.

1876 April 27
–   F. leaves Trieste in the evening.

1876 April 28
–   F. arrives in Vienna in the morning.

1876 April end–July
F. takes the following courses in the summer semester:

–   Carl Claus: zoological-microscopic practical course for advanced students (15 hours);
–   Sigmund Exner: physiological demonstrations and experiments (two hours);
–   Franz Exner: spectral analysis (two hours);
–   Julius Wiesner: experimental plant physiology (three hours);
–   Franz Brentano: The Philosophy of Aristotle (three hours).

1876 June 6
F.'s report on the first part of his work in Trieste is forwarded to the Ministry of Education.

1876 July 4
Carl Claus submits a petition concerning F. to the Ministry of Education. Presumably, it concerns the awarding of a scholarship for another month.

1876 June mid
F.'s mother goes with three of her daughters for a spa stay at Rožnau (until the end of August).

1876 July 13
The Ministry of Culture and Education approves F. a further 80 Gulden[4] stipend and the "use of a work table at the Zoological Station in Trieste".

1876 July 25
F. acquires Dante Alighieri's *La divina commedia.*

1876 August mid
F.'s mother comes back to Vienna from Rožnau with her daughters.

1876 September 2–October 1

Second research stay in Trieste
1876 September 2

- F. arrives for a second stay at the zoological marine laboratory in Trieste; he possibly visits Miramare Castle for the first time on this occasion.

1876 after October 2
- F. becomes a famulus (assistant) at the Physiological Institute with Ernst Brücke and meets Sigmund Exner, Ernst Fleischl and Heinrich Obersteiner there; he possibly also meets Josef Breuer for the first time here.
- F. continues his research on the eels.

1876 October–1877 March
F. takes the following courses in the winter semester:

- Johann Dumreicher: Surgical Clinic with lectures on special surgical pathology and therapy (ten hours);
- Albert Duchek: special medical pathology, therapy and clinic (ten hours);
- Salomon Stricker: General and Experimental Pathology (five hours);
- Richard Heschl: general pathological anatomy, pathological histology and special pathological anatomy, Part I (five hours);
- Sigmund Exner: physiology and microscopic anatomy of the sense organs (three hours);
- Ernst Fleischl: Higher Mathematics as an Introduction to the Study of Physics and Physiology (three hours);
- Ernst Fleischl: Physiological Discussions (two hours);
- Samuel Basch: the physiological effect and therapeutic utilization of poisons (preferably narcotic ones), explained by experiments (two hours).

1876 before October 28
The wife of one of F.'s uncles from Odessa comes to visit Vienna – possibly Laura or Sara Nathansohn.

1876 October 28
Visit of the opera *Die Jüdin (La Juive) by* Jacques Fromental Halévy at the Hofoper with the aunt by marriage from Odessa. It is not clear whether F. was at the opera.

1876 October 30
F. acquires Ernst Fleischl's book *Untersuchung über die Gesetze der Nervenerregung.*

1877

- Eduard Silberstein gives a farewell party for his friends in Hernals, including F. and Ignaz Rosanes, before moving to Romania.
- A photographer takes a family photo in which, in addition to the members of the Freud family, the family of F.'s cousin Deborah Kornhauser and Simon Nathansohn can be seen.

1877 January beginning
F. writes his article "Über den Ursprung der hinteren Nervenwurzel im Rückenmark von Ammocoetes (Petromyzon Planeri)".

1877 January 4
Ernst Brücke submitted F.'s paper "Über den Ursprung der hinteren Nervenwurzel im Rückenmark von Ammocoetes (Petromyzon Planeri)" to the Kaiserliche Akademie der Wissenschaften and recommended its inclusion in the *Sitzungsberichte*. F. later gave one of the offprints to Heinrich Obersteiner with the dedication "Herrn Dr. Obersteiner in Hochachtung d. Verf.".

1877 March–July
F. takes the following courses in the summer semester:

- Theodor Billroth: Surgical Clinic with lectures on special surgical pathology and therapy (ten hours);
- Heinrich Bamberger: special medical pathology, therapy and clinic (ten hours);
- Richard Heschl: special pathological anatomy (five hours);
- Ernst Fleischl: nerve physiology (three hours);
- Eduard Hofmann: about special parts of forensic medicine (three hours).

1877 March 15
Carl Claus submits F.'s "Beobachtungen über Gestaltung und feineren Bau der als Hoden beschriebenen Lappenorgane des Aals" to the Kaiserliche Akademie der Wissenschaften (Imperial Academy of Sciences) without having read them at all, as F. later states.

1877 May
F. applies to start his military service as a one-year volunteer instead of on 1877 October 1, two years later. The application is granted on June 2.

1877 May end
F.'s first publications appear in the *Sitzungsberichte* of the Kaiserliche Akademie der Wissenschaften: his studies on eels and his paper on the origin of the posterior nerve roots in the spinal cord of ammocoetes.

1877 June 8
F. receives an offprint of Heinrich Obersteiner's paper "Zur Kenntniss einiger Hereditätsgesetze" ("For Knowledge of Some Laws of Heredity").

1877 June end
F. gives Ignaz Rosanes an offprint of his paper "Über den Ursprung der hinteren Nervenwurzeln im Rückenmark von Ammocoetes" with the dedication "Meinem lieben Freunde J. Rosanes".

1877 July 31
F. acquires James Clerk Maxwell's book *Matter and Motion*.

1877 August beginning
F.'s cousin Heinrich Nathansohn from Krakow, the son of F.'s deceased uncle Aron Nathansohn, is in Vienna for a few days.

1877 August 12
F. visits the Prater with Eduard Silberstein's sister Mina.

1877 August 14–15
F. reads a two-part article in the *Neues Wiener Tagblatt* by Bret Harte, a friend of Mark Twain, about protectionism and corruption in the USA.

1877 August mid
F. reads Thomas Macaulay's essay on Francis Bacon, "which could not be more perfect" (F. to Silberstein, 15.8.1877).

1877 September beginning
– F. has a longer conversation with Siegfried Lipiner; his attitude toward him is still ambivalent, but he wants to "cultivate" the relationship with him.
– F. follows the course of the Russo-Turkish War in the press with excitement.
– F. starts writing a diary again.

1877 October–1878 March
F. takes the following courses in the winter semester:

– Theodor Billroth: Surgical Clinic with lectures on special surgical pathology and therapy (ten hours);
– Adalbert Duchek: special medical pathology, therapy and clinic (ten hours);
– Theodor Meynert: Psychiatric Clinic, Nervous Diseases and Forensic Psychology. Structure and performance of the central nervous system (five hours);
– Richard Heschl: Pathological Dissection Exercises (three hours);
– Carl Langer: demonstrations and exercises in the dissecting room (six hours);
– Ernst Ludwig: Physiological and Pathological Chemistry (three hours).

1877 October 6
F. receives the offprints of his work "Beobachtungen über Gestaltung und feineren Bau der als Hoden beschriebenen Lappenorgane des Aals".

1877 November 14
Ernst Brücke recommends F. for a scholarship from the Bernhard Freiherr von Eskeles Foundation.

1878

1878 March 27
F. receives a scholarship of 100 Gulden from the Bernhard Freiherr von Eskeles Foundation for the year 1878.

1878 April–July
F. takes the following courses in the summer semester:

- Theodor Billroth: Surgical Clinic with lectures on special surgical pathology and therapy (ten hours);
- Joseph Späth: gynecologic and obstetric clinic with theoretical-practical teaching in obstetrics and in diseases of the female sexual organs and the newborn (ten hours);
- Ferdinand Hebra: Skin Diseases and Clinic (ten hours);
- Carl Sigmund: Syphilis Clinic (five hours);
- Carl Bettelheim: physical examination of the sick (five hours);
- Salomon Stricker: General Pathology of the Nervous System (one hour);
- Heinrich Bamberger (or Carl Bettelheim): physical examination of the sick (percussion and auscultation) (five hours).

1878 May 6
F. receives from a female admirer a love poem for his birthday.

1878 May 25
F. passes Julius Wiesner's botany examination with "satisfactory". He almost failed because he did not recognize any plants, but his good theoretical knowledge saved him.

1878 June 27
F. wants to evade the zoological exam at the last moment, but Carl Claus, who meets him in the corridor, stops him. He then asks exam questions that lead to the grade "distinction".

1878 June end
F.'s mother goes with two of her children for a spa stay at Rožnau (until the end of August).

1878 July 18
Ernst Brücke presents F.'s second work on Petromyzon to the Kaiserliche Akademie der Wissenschaften. F. later will give an offprint to his friend Josef Herzig with the dedication: "Seinem lieben Freunde, Herrn Chem. Dr. J. Herzig/d. Verf.".

1878 July 23
Together with the lecturer Carl Bettelheim and his fellow student Anton Bum, F. attends the funeral of Carl Rokitansky at the Hernals cemetery near Dornbach. Afterward, they visit the Prater.

1878 August beginning
- F. works for a few weeks together with Gustav Gärtner in Salomon Stricker's laboratory on the nerves of the salivary gland and salivary secretion in dogs.
- F. reads reports on voyages of discovery to Africa by Samuel Baker, Georg Schweinfurth and Henry Morgan Stanley.
- F. reads writings by Thomas Macaulay.

1878 August 6
F. sends Eduard Silberstein his first two publications: "Beobachtungen über Gestaltung und feineren Bau der als Hoden beschriebenen Lappenorgane des Aals" and "Über den Ursprung der hinteren Nervenwurzeln im Rückenmarke von Ammocoetes (Petromyzon Planeri)".

1878 August mid
F. reads Bertrand Barère and has the impression "that a man may as soon be executed with words alone as with the sharpest of guillotines" (F. to Silberstein, 14.8.1878).

1878 August 24
F. acquires J. Norman Lockyer's *Studies in Spectrum Analysis* and John Tyndall's book *The Forms of Water in Clouds, Rivers, Ice and Glaciers.*

1878 August end
F.'s mother comes back to Vienna from Rožnau.

1878 October– 1879 March
F. takes the following courses in the winter semester:

– Heinrich Bamberger: special medical pathology, therapy and clinic (ten hours);
– Ferdinand Arlt: theoretical-practical lessons in ophthalmology (ten hours).

1878 December 26
F. receives a scholarship of 100 Gulden from the Fanny Jeitteles Foundation for the year 1879/1880.[5]

1879

1879 April 8
F. acquires Charles Darwin's book *Insectivorous Plants.*

1879 June 17
F. passes the practical examination in anatomy with distinction under Carl Langer.

1879 Summer
F. makes observations on the construction of nerve fibers and nerve cells in the crayfish.

1879 July mid
F. receives Gustav Schwalbe's paper on "Das Ganglion oculomotorii", in which his work on spinal ganglia is cited several times. F. experiences this as "great scientific satisfaction" (F. to Silberstein, 22.7.1879).

1879 July 21
F. passes Ernst Brücke's practical examination in physiology with distinction. Brücke had previously asked Ernst Fleischl what he should ask F.

1879 July 22
F. says goodbye to Ernst Brücke's laboratory and spends an evening with Emanuel Loewy and Joseph Paneth.

1879 July 30
F. is transferred as a one-year volunteer to the Garrison Hospital No. 1 in Vienna.

1879 July end
F. takes over the translation of the twelfth and last volume of the complete edition of John Stuart Mill's works in German, edited by Theodor Gomperz with the contributions "Enfranchisement of Women", "Grote's Plato", "Thornton on Labour and its Claims" and "Chapters on Socialism".

1879 August beginning
F. reads essays and books by Thomas Macaulay, among others, *The History of England*, some works by Gustav Theodor Fechner, Adam Smith's main work *An Inquiry into the Nature and Causes of the Wealth of Nations,* and new books on physiology.

1879 August 18
The rector of Vienna University – Ernst Brücke at the time – grants F. the Absolutorium; i.e., he receives the graduation certificate in which the lectures attended are listed and F. is certified as having conducted himself in accordance with academic laws. However, F. needs almost two more years before he takes the Rigorosa.

1879 September
F. is called up for military service, but lives at home.

1879 September 24
F. acquires John Milton's *Poetical Works.*

1879 October 1
F. starts his Präsenz-Dienst (presence service) as a one-year volunteer.

1879 October 17
Salomon Stricker speaks to the Gesellschaft der Ärzte (Society of Physicians) about the performance of acinar glands and mentions F.'s experiments.

1879 November 12
F. acquires Tolver Preston's book *Physics of the Ether*.

1879 December 27
F. acquires Francis Bacon's *Moral and Historical Works* and Sydney Smith's *Essays Social and Political.*

1880

1880 February mid
F. attends a performance by the Danish hypnotist Carl Hansen – suggested by Eduard Silberstein and by the family doctor of the Freud, Samuel Kreisler. The scandals surrounding Hansen's performances in Vienna had probably stimulated F.'s interest in Hansen as well.

1880 March mid
F.'s German translation of the 12th volume of John Stuart Mill's *Gesammelten Werke* is published.

1880 April 20
Alexander Rollett informs Ernst Brücke that there is a vacancy for a physiological assistant in Graz. Brücke informs F. of the vacancy, and two days later, F. writes to Rollett asking whether the assistant position can be kept open until October, as he is unable to work as a one-year volunteer before October.

1880 May 6
On his birthday, F. is in custody because of eight missed war rounds and unauthorized absence from military service; the punishment had been imposed by Chief Surgeon Josef Podrazky.

1880 June 7
F. acquires Rudolph Hermann Lotze's book *Medizinische Psychologie oder Physiologie der Seele*.

1880 June 9
F. passes his first doctoral viva with Ernst Fleischl and Julius Wiesner with "excellent" in the Physiological Institute in the old rifle factory.

1880 June 23
F. passes the practical examination in pathological anatomy with distinction under Richard Heschl.

1880 July 7
F. passes the practical examination in internal medicine with "genügend" ("satisfaction").

1880 July 21
F. is studying pharmacology in preparation for the exam, and to relax takes a walk lasting several hours, during which he meets his colleague Otto Zuckerkandl.

1880 July 22
F. passes his second doctoral viva with Eduard Hofmann with "genügend" ("satisfaction"); individual results: pathological anatomy (practical): excellent; general pathology (with Carl Sigmund as a guest examiner): satisfaction; and pharmacology: good.

1880 July 24
F. visits Carl Bettelheim in the hospital.

1880 July 25–27
F. goes to Semmering for two days with his sister Rosa and Fanny Süssermann; they spend the night in the Erzherzog-Johann-Haus.

1880 August 5
F. acquires Johannes Müller's *Handbuch der Physiologie des Menschen*.

1880 September 30
F. is transferred to the reserve.

1880 October beginning
F. vows "not to play tarot again before I become a doctor, what with the waste of time and the amount of money I spend on it" (F. to Silberstein, 3.10.1880).

1880 before October 3
F. buys a pipe.

1880 October 5
F. meets with Joseph Paneth.

1880 November 11
F. passes the practical examination in obstetrics with Josef Späth with distinction.

1880 November 27
F. passes the practical examination in ophthalmology with Ferdinand Arlt with distinction.

1880 November 29
– F. acquires William Spottiswoode's book *Polarisation of Light*.
– F. is promoted to military medical 11 first-class reserve.

1880 December 1
F. is transferred to Garrison Hospital No. 6.

1880 December 18
F. passes the practical examination in surgery with distinction.

1880 December 21
F. is transferred to the Garrison Hospital in Olomouc.

1881

- The Freud family moves from Kaiser-Josef-Strasse 3 to Kaiser-Josef-Strasse 33 (now Heine-strasse/corner of Fugbachgasse). They stay there until 1884 August, but F. moves out on 1882 September 1.
- F. receives an offprint of Ernst Fleischl's article "Über die Theorien der Farbenwahrnehmung".

1881 February 13
F. passes the theoretical examination with distinction.

1881 February 15
F. fails the examination in forensic medicine. He is then asked to appear again for the third doctoral viva in forensic medicine in two months' time, i.e. on April 15.

1881 February 22
F. submits a request to the Ministry of Culture and Education asking to be allowed to repeat his examination in forensic medicine before the end of March.

1881 February 27
Gisela Fluss, F.'s early love, marries Emil Popper.

1881 March
F. starts working at Ernst Ludwig's Chemical Institute for almost three months. However, his attempts at gas analyses are unsuccessful.

1881 March 21
F. acquires the four-volume *Handwörterbuch der Physiologie* edited by Rudolf Wagner.

1881 March mid
F. flies through textbooks in preparation for the doctoral viva.

1881 March 30
F. passes his third doctoral viva with Eduard Hofmann with "excellent" and is awarded his doctorate in the Aula of the old university.

1881 April–July
During the summer semester, F. takes part in practical exercises in general chemistry with Ernst Ludwig.

1881 April 6
F.'s sister Anna meets her future husband Eli Bernays (the brother of F.'s later wife Martha) in the family of Simon and Elisabeth Weiss, where Anna teaches their daughter Mathilde.

1881 April 14
F. acquires the *Handbuch der Lehre von den Geweben des Menschen und der Thiere,* edited by Salomon Stricker.

1881 April 28
The Professorenkollegium (Board of Professors) awards F. a demonstrator scholarship at the Physiological Institute at Ernst Brücke's request. With this, F. receives 28 Gulden per month.[6]

1881 April 29
Ernst Brücke applies to the governor's office for the pay-out of the scholarship money for the period from 1881 May 1 to September 30.

1881 May 1
F. becomes a demonstrator at Ernst Brücke and remains there until the end of 1882 June.

1881 May 23
F. acquires the first part of Ernst Fleischl's *Physiologisch-optische Notizen.*

1881 May 24
F. receives Heinrich Obersteiner's paper "Experimental Researches on Attention" and "Die motorischen Leistungen der Grosshirnrinde" ("The Motor Functions of the Cerebral Cortex").

1881 May 30
One month after F. had taken up his position as a demonstrator at the Institute of Physiology, the governor's office informed the Dean's Office of the medical faculty about the pay-out of the scholarship.

1881 Summer
– F. makes observations on the construction of nerve fibers and nerve cells in the crayfish.
– Together with Heinrich Braun, F. visits Braun's brother-in-law Victor Adler at Berggasse 19[7] and spends the evening there. On this occasion, F. sees Victor Adler's then two-year-old son Friedrich, who shoots the Austrian Prime Minister Karl Stürgkh in 1916.
– F.'s father travels to Russia.

1881 July 9
The Professorenkollegium decides to extend the demonstrator scholarship for F. for another year.

1881 September 6
F. acquires Charles Darwin's book *The Effects of Cross and Self Fertilization in the* Vegetable *Kingdom.*

1881 October 27
F. acquires Julius Robert Mayer's *Die Mechanik der Wärme in gesammelten Schriften.*

1881 November 2
– F. acquires Friedrich Goltz's book Über die Verrichtungen des Grosshirns.
– F. acquires Charles Darwin's *Reise eines Naturforschers um die Welt* (Voyage of the Beagle) and volumes 1–4 of Darwin's *Gesammelten Werken.*

1881 December 8
A few minutes before the premiere of *The Tales of Hoffmann* by Jacques Offenbach, a fire breaks out in the Ringtheater. The theater is completely destroyed, and at least 386 people are killed. According to F.'s sister Anna, the F. family had tickets but could not go because they had been invited to a friend's house.

1881 December 15
F. presents his work on the nerve fibers of the crayfish at a meeting of the Mathematical and Natural Sciences Class of the Kaiserliche Akademie der Wissenschaften. Leopold Fitzinger chairs the meeting.

1881 December 22
F. acquires four works by Jacob Henle: *Handbuch der Muskellehre des Menschen, Handbuch der Knochenlehre des Menschen, Handbuch der Eingeweidelehre des Menschen* and *Handbuch der Bänderlehre des Menschen.*

1882

1882 January 5
Ernst Brücke recommends that F.'s work on the nerve fibers of the crayfish should be included in the *Sitzungsberichte of* the Academy. F. later gives an offprint to Josef Herzig with the dedication: "Seinem lieben Freunde, Dr. Josef Herzig/d. Verf.".

1882 January 21
F. acquires John Locke's *An Essay Concerning Human Understanding.*

1882 February 2
F. asked the Kaiserliche Akademie der Wissenschaften to postpone the printing of his paper "Über den Bau der Nervenfasern und Nervenzellen beim Flusskrebs" until he had seen the preliminary prints of the accompanying plate.

1882 March 21
Martha Bernays, F.'s future fiancée and wife, is invited to F.'s sister Rosa's birthday party. She makes a good impression on F.'s father.

1882 March 26
F. acquires Hermann von Helmholtz's *Popular Scientific Lectures.*

1882 April
– First encounter between F. and his later wife Martha Bernays, when the latter visited the Freud family with her sister Minna. At the time, Martha lived with her mother and sister in Matthäusgasse (official address: Radetzkystr. 6) on the other side of the Danube Canal, about 2km south of the Freuds' then flat at Kaiser-Josef-Str. 3.
– One of the students in Ernst Brücke's laboratory, the later ophthalmologist Alfred Topolansky, has fallen ill, and his mother Elise asks F. to visit him at home and judge whether he can go for a vacation to Trieste. F. does, so the next day, Alfred goes to Trieste and comes back healthy.

1882 April 12
F. acquires Felix Hoppe-Seyler's book *Physiologische Chemie* and the fourth part of his *Specielle Physiologische Chemie.*

1882 April 24
F. acquires Immanuel Kant's *Kritik der reinen Vernunft* and the *Kleinere Schriften zur Naturphilosophie.*

1882 May beginning
A "S. Freud" visits the Freud family in Vienna. This is presumably Samuel Freud, the father of Moritz Freud, the later husband of F.'s sister Mitzi. Moritz also comes to Vienna and lives with the Freud family until his wedding in 1887 February.

1882 May 31
F. goes for a walk with Martha Bernays on the Kahlenberg. It is their first conversation in private.

1882 June beginning
F. writes a "pressing love letter" to Martha (SE 5, p. 638).

1882 June 1
F. is appointed a senior physician in the reserve.

1882 June 2
F. goes on an excursion to the Kahlenberg with Martha Bernays, and they have "a very serious and profound conversation" (F. to Martha, 2.6.1884).

1882 June 3
– F. visits the Prater with Martha Bernays and her mother. His sisters accompany them.
– F. acquires Henry Chisholm's book *On the Science of Weighing and Measuring and Standards of Measure and Weight*.

1882 June 8–9
Martha goes to Munich for two days to visit the pianist and composer Max Mayer. She had made a wallet for him. F. concludes that he has little chance with Martha.

1882 June 10
F. meets Martha in a garden in Mödling and decides to court Martha.

1882 June 11
F. sends Martha the English edition of Charles Dickens' *David Copperfield* from 1850, and Martha sends F. a cake. It is clear from her letter that she is affectionate toward F.

1882 June 12
F. informs Ernst Brücke in a conversation that he has decided to set up a practice and leave the Brücke laboratory.

1882 June 13
F. is at the Bernays' family for dinner and steals Martha's place card. Martha squeezes his hand in return.

1882 June 14
F. and Martha go for a walk in the Prater.

1882 June 15
F. picks up Martha and her brother Eli Bernays from their flat in Matthäusgasse, and they go for a walk together. Before that, he has a brief opportunity to be alone with Martha in her flat.

1882 June 16
F. informs Fritz Wahle, an old friend of Martha, about their forthcoming engagement. Fritz, who is probably in love with Martha, threatens to shoot himself and F. if the latter cannot make Martha happy.

1882 June 17
F. and Martha get engaged secretly. Martha gives F. a gold ring with a pearl. In the evening, they are with friends at the inn "Zum Braunen Hirschen".

1882 June 18
– F. visits Martha in the afternoon.
– Eli Bernays and Ignaz Schönberg, the fiancé of Martha's sister Minna, are having dinner with the F. family. F. takes Martha home afterward.

1882 June 19
– Martha leaves for Wandsbek. She returns to Vienna on September 11. Before her departure, F. gives her Felix Dahn's book *Odhins Trost*.
– Eli Bernays and Ignaz Schönberg spend the evening at F.

1882 June 21
- Eli Bernays visits F., who tells him about a stay of Martha in Prague. F. shows Eli the Chemical Institute.
- In the evening, F., the Fluss brothers (Alfred, Emil and Richard), the Wahle brothers (Fritz and Richard), Ignaz Schönberg and Eli Bernays meet at Wahle's for "a little pub". The evening is concluded by a "noisy walk" (F. to Martha, 22.6.1882).

1882 June 22
F. visits the Wahle brothers, and Fritz makes envelopes with Martha's addresses so that Martha's mother will not suspect that F. is maintaining contact with her daughter.

1882 June 24–25
F. visits with family members the Prater meadows, but feels quite lonely.

1882 June 26
F. visits Ernst Fleischl and learns to play the Japanese board game Go with him.

1882 June 27
F. receives a letter from Martha with a photo of her.

1882 June 29
- F. has the date of their engagement (17.6.1882) engraved on a small box that Martha had given him.
- F. walks alone through the Prater garden.
- F. is visiting Martha's family; Fritz Wahle and Ignaz Schönberg are also present.

1882 June 30
- F. receives 100 Havana-Virginia cigars from Elise Topolansky, the mother of Adolf Topolansky, one of F.'s students.
- In the evening, F. meets with Eli Bernays. He gives him a facsimile of the American Declaration of Independence.

1882 June end
F. sends Martha photos of himself.

1882 July 1
- F. acquires John Lubbock's *Addresses, Political and Educational*.
- F. invites to the foundation of a "Union" ("Bund") in the evening: Alfred, Emil and Richard Fluss, Fritz and Richard Wahle, Arthur Ornstein, Ignaz Schönberg and Eli Bernays. Eli is elected the "president of the house", and Fitz Wahle the "president out of the house".

1882 July 2
F. travels to Mödling with Ignaz Schönberg, among other things, to visit his mother and his sisters Rosa and Paula. There, they also meet Josef Brust, an admirer of F.'s sister Rosa.

1882 July 5
- F. goes to Richard Wahle's graduation to the Doctor of Philosophy.
- Eli Bernays visits F.

1882 July 6
F.'s father returns from a trip.

1882 July 9
F. has a dispute with Fritz Wahle about his relationship with Martha.

1882 July 15
F. visits Ignaz Schönberg in Mödling.

1882 July 16–27
First visit to Wandsbek

1882 July 16

- F. leaves for Hamburg at 8.15 am to visit Martha. He has taken J. S. Mill with him as a travel book. He had told his family that he was going to Leipzig and then on a hike through Saxon Switzerland (Sächsische Schweiz). F. arrives in Bodenbach (now Děčín-Podmokly) at around 6 pm. He goes over the Elbe bridge to Tetschen (now Děčín) and takes a two-hour stroll through the town.

1882 July 17

- F. drives on from Tetschen at 2.00 am, arrives in Hamburg at 2.45 pm and goes straight to Wandsbek. In the afternoon, he sees Martha on the veranda of the house of Martha's uncle Elias Philipp in Claudiusstrasse.

- Then, he visits Bernhardine (Dina) Gompertz, the daughter of a sister of Martha's grandmother. She is an acquaintance of Max Mayer, a former admirer of Martha. F. spends the night in the Wandsbek post house.

1882 July 18

F. waits in vain for Martha from 5.15 to 6.45 am at Wandsbeker Gehölz, looks for her in other parts of town and from 8.30 am waits again at Wandsbeker Gehölz. But nothing comes of a meeting that day.

1882 July 19–20

F. and Martha see each other every day.

1882 July 21

- F. visits the Rolandsmühle in Altona-Ottensen.
- F. orders stationery with the initials "M" and "S" from a Jewish engraver at Adolphsplatz in Hamburg for correspondence with Martha.

1882 July 23

- F. meets Martha in the morning.
- F. picks up the ordered stationery.

1882 July 26

- Martha gives F. "the first warm kiss" (F. to Martha, 26.6.1882).
- F. meets Max Mayer, and both "had a businesslike conversation with each other" (F. to Martha, 29.7.1882).

1882 July 27

F. leaves Hamburg.

1882 July 28

F. arrives in Vienna.

1882 July end
F. advises his childhood friend Eduard Silberstein against marrying "a rich stupid girl" to whom he had been sent on a bridal search (F. to Martha, 7.2.1884).

1882 July 31
F. becomes Sekundararzt (a combination of resident house physician and registrar) at the Wiener Allgemeines Krankenhaus, presumably at the III. surgical department of Leopold Dittel. During an operation, he has to kneel for an hour.

1882 August beginning
F. performs a few minor operations, applies plaster casts and administers anesthesia for two operations.

1882 August 5
F. reads Alfred Meissner's book *Heinrich Heine: Erinnerungen.*

1882 August 9
F. receives "a smoked meerschaum pipe with a silver lid" from a Romanian (F. to Martha, 11.8.1882).

1882 August 10
− F. has a fever and a sore throat.
− F. receives five Gulden for a visit to the sick.

1882 August 11
− Fritz Wahle and Eli Bernays visit F.
− F. eats a cake and drinks two bottles of wine with colleagues, which his head physician Leopold Dittel had received from a patient as a thank you for an operation.

1882 August 12
Kathinka and Paula Kadisch, acquaintances of the family, visit F.

1882 August 13
F. is in the Prater with his family.

1882 August mid
− F. has a severe angina and has to stay at home.
− Eli Bernays visits F.
− F.'s brother Alexander begins an apprenticeship with Martha's brother Eli, who is secretary at *G. Roth's Coursbuch*, which gives an overview of railway, steamship and postal connections. Alexander gets a room at Radetzkystrasse 10.

1882 August 16
− F. receives a photo of Minna; he finds it "lovely, wonderfully taken" (F. to Martha, 16.8.1882).
− For F., philosophy "gains more appeal every day" (F. to Martha, 16.8.1882).

1882 August 18
− F. reads Goethe's poems with a friend and reflects on the relationship with his friends.
− In the afternoon, F. meets with Robert Franceschini.

1882 August 22
F. reads Cordy Jefferson's book *A Woman in Spite of Herself.*

1882 August 23
Eli Bernays and Fritz Wahle visit F.

1882 August 24
– F.'s direct superior Richard Wittelshöfer threatens F. to throw him out if he does not stay at home longer when he next falls ill.
– F. has to undergo a minor throat operation. Immediately afterward, the ring he had received from Martha breaks.
– F. begins to read George Eliot's novel *Daniel Deronda*.
– F. sends Martha five marks.

1882 August 26
– Eli Bernays and Fritz Wahle visit F.
– F. tells his sister Anna about his engagement.

1882 August 29
– F. visits Martha's mother Emmeline Bernays and her sister Minna at Radetzkystr. 6. He is convinced that Martha's mother "suspects more than we have believed so far" (F. to Martha, 29.8.1882).
– F. acquires Moritz Romberg's *Lehrbuch der Nervenkrankheiten des Menschen*. Romberg was one of the first psychiatrists to report cases of male hysteria.

1882 August 30
Minna Bernays visits the Freud family for dinner.

1882 September 11
Martha comes back to Vienna from Wandsbek. F. can only see her briefly as he is on duty at the hospital.

1882 September 12
Martha and her mother Emmeline are having dinner with at the Freud's.

1882 September 16
Martha visits the Freud family.

1882 September 17
F. goes for a walk with Martha in the afternoon; they have been engaged for exactly three months.

1882 September 21
F. goes for a walk with Martha in the afternoon.

1882 September 26
F. goes for a walk with Martha in the afternoon.

1882 September 30
F. goes for a walk with Martha in the Prater meadows in the afternoon.

1882 Autumn
– F. has a mild form of typhoid fever.
– F. begins to work in Theodor Meynert's brain-anatomical laboratory (until autumn 1885). Among his colleagues are Gabriel Anton (Vienna) Liweri Darkeschwitsch (Moscow), Allen Starr (New York) and Bernard Sachs, whose older brother Samuel had just founded the investment bank Goldman Sachs with Marcus Goldman.

1882 October 3
F. acquires the VIIth Treatise of Ernst Fleischl's *Untersuchung über die Gesetze der Nervenerregung*.

1882 October 4
Theodor Meynert writes a letter of recommendation for F. to Hermann Nothnagel.

1882 October 5
− F. applies to Hermann Nothnagel for an assistantship and brings him a letter of recommendation from Theodor Meynert.
− F. acquires the II. Mittheilung von Ernst Fleischl's *Physiologisch-optische Notizen*.

1882 October 6
F. presents himself to Moriz Kaposi, the head of the department for skin diseases at the Allgemeines Krankenhaus, to apply for an Aspirant position.

1882 October 7
F. meets Martha and can hold her in his arms.

1882 October 12
F. becomes an Aspirant (Clinical Assistant) at Hermann Nothnagel's I. Medical clinic and remains there until 1883 April 30.

1882 October 18
F. hears from Josef Breuer for the first time about the case of Bertha Pappenheim ("Anna O."):
"Yesterday evening I was at Breuer's until 12 o'clock, who told me among other things the highly interesting story of Miss Pappenheim's illness" (F. to Martha, 19.10.1882).

1882 October 19
− F. visits Ernst Fleischl.
− F. has lunch with Leopold Königstein, and in the evening, Königstein introduces him to the ophthalmoscope.

1882 October 21
F. visits Josef Breuer.

1882 November 14
− F. hears a "jarring Bohemian-German speech" by his "enemy" Rudolf Jaksch at the Physiological Club[8] (F. to Martha, 16.11.1882).
− F. lends Leopold Königstein 10 Kreuzer.

1882 November 16
F. goes to Josef Breuer and buys chocolate on the way because he is so hungry.

1882 November 18
F. buys a tie for 40 Kreuzer.

1882 November 20
− F. meets with Martha.
− F. visits Ernst Fleischl.

1882 November 22
F. borrows money from Josef Breuer.

1882 November 23
F. meets with Martha.

1882 November 24
F. visits Josef Breuer.

1882 November 28
Martha visits the Freud family.

1882 November end
F. has an "abbreviated typhus" (F. to Martha, 23.11.1882).

1882 December 11
F. and Salomon Stricker are invited to Hermann Nothnagel's house.

1882 December 22
F.'s sister Anna becomes engaged to Eli Bernays, the brother of F.'s fiancée Martha.

1882 December 26
F. and Martha inform Martha's mother Emmeline Bernays of their engagement. They plan to give her an illustrated edition of Schiller's "Lied von der Glocke" for New Year's Eve.

1882 December 27
F. meets with Ignaz Schönberg.

1882 December 28
F. goes shopping with Martha.

1883

– Moritz Biach, timber merchant and partner of the firm Baiersdorf & Biach, goes to F. for treatment. He remains a patient of F. until 1894.
– F. acquires John Locke's *An Essay Concerning Human Understanding*.

1883 New Year
Eli Bernays gets engaged to F.'s sister Anna.

1883 January 4
F. acquires Wilhelm Erb's *Handbuch der Elektrotherapie.*

1883 January 16
F. acquires Thomas Huxley's *Grundzüge der Physiologie* in generally understandable lectures.

1883 before January 24
F. and Martha walk for the first time after the announcement of their engagement "on the Sunday parade in the Ringstrasse" (F. to Martha, 24.1.1883).

1883 January 26
F. and Martha begin a jointly kept "secret chronicle", which they keep until 1886 September.

1883 February 5
F. and Martha spend a few hours together.

1883 February 12
F. and Martha are planning cultural activities for the next few months, including four opera performances (*Don Juan* and the *Magic Flute* by Mozart, the Faust opera *Margarete* by Charles Gounod and *Lohengrin* by Richard Wagner).

1883 February 15
F. and Martha attend a performance of Wagner's *Lohengrin at the* Vienna Hofoper. *The* news of Wagner's death had been reported by the Viennese newspapers on February 14.

1883 February 19
F. and Martha attend a performance of Gounod's *Margarete* at the Vienna Court Opera.

1883 February 23
F. and Martha attend a performance of Mozart's *Don Juan* at the Vienna Hofoper.

1883 March 31
F. and Martha meet at the Franzensbrücke. Minna and Ignaz Schönberg join them.

1883 April 3
F. is at the Physiological Club, and Josef Breuer takes him home afterward.

1883 April 4
– F. visits Hermann Nothnagel at home in the afternoon.
– F. gives "English lessons at Wahle's" in the evening (F. to Martha, 4.4.1883).

1883 April 5
F. goes for a walk with Martha.

1883 before April 16
- F. sends Martha wine.
- F. gives a new pupil her first lesson. She comes three to four times a week.

1883 April 18
F. meets Martha in the evening and gives her flowers to celebrate ten months of their engagement.

1883 April 26
F. is introduced to Theodor Meynert and is given the keys to the hospital ward of the Meynert's psychiatric department. Meynert says he is looking forward to working with F.

1883 April 27
F. gives Martha a brooch.

1883 April 28
F. receives the decree of appointment as Sekundararzt (a combination of resident House Physician and Registrar) and starts work at Theodor Meynert's Psychiatric Clinic. However, the official start of work is May 1.

1883 April 30
F. reads the "Commitment to fulfill the duties of a Sekundararzt in the Imperial and Royal General Hospital", and he confirms this in handwriting with the following text: "Everything that has just been held out to me and that I have understood in its entirety, I will fulfill exactly, which I hereby pledge. Dr. Sigm. Freud".

1883 May 1
- First official working day at the Theodor Meynert's Clinic; F. stays there until September 30. For the first three months, F. is in the men's ward, and from August in the women's ward.
- F. is given a room in the Allgemeines Krankenhaus (III. Hof, 23rd Stiege, No. 47) and no longer lives with his parents. Martha gives him a "noble tablet"[9] for the room and also helps him put together a small household.

1883 before May 4
F. sends Martha wine and money.

1883 May 6
On the afternoon of his birthday, F. meets Martha at the Zollamtsbrücke.

1883 May 6
Robert Steiner von Pfungen gives F. a photo of himself and asks him to do the same.

1883 May 7
F. is visited by his mother and sister Paula in the evening; a little later, sister Dolfi also arrives.

1883 May 9
F. meets Martha for a long excursion.

1883 May 11
F. asks Theodor Meynert to allow him to work in his laboratory. Meynert agrees and also provides him with neurological preparations.

1883 May 13
F. meets Martha for a long excursion.

1883 May 20
F. meets with Martha.

1883 May 22
F. visits Josef Breuer.

1883 May 23
F. meets Martha for a long walk in the evening.

1883 May 28
F. meets with Martha.

1883 June 6
F. acquires Charles Darwin's book *The variation of Animal and Plants under Domestication.*

1883 June 8
Ignaz Schönberg's friends organize a farewell party for him, as he leaves the next day for an extended stay at a health resort.

1883 June 9–10
Trip with Ignaz Schönberg to Bad Gleichenberg
F. accompanies Ignaz Schönberg on the journey to the Bad Gleichenberg sanatorium in Styria, where Schönberg will spend six weeks because of his pulmonary tuberculosis.

1883 June 9
Travel from Vienna to Steinamanger (now Szombathely in Hungary), where F. and Schönberg have lunch. In the early afternoon train ride to Bad Gleichenberg.

1883 June 10
F. travels back from Bad Gleichenberg to Vienna.

1883 June 11
F. meets with Martha and Minna.

1883 June 13
F. and Martha say goodbye before Martha's departure for Hamburg in Alserstrasse at the Wiener Allgemeines Krankenhaus. This marks the beginning of a three-year separation.

1883 June 14
– Martha moves with her mother and sister Minna to Wandsbek near Hamburg.
– F. acquires Theodor Meynert's Die acuten (hallucinatorischen) Formen des Wahnsinns und ihr Verlauf.

1883 June 15
F. visits Josef Breuer in the evening because he feels miserable. Both of them then go out for dinner.

1883 June 17
F. reads writings by Theodor Meynert, Bénédict Morel and Jean Etienne Esquirol.

1883 June 18
In the evening, F. gets a visit from a friend.

1883 June 20
F. visits Josef Breuer, who thinks that F. now looks better and fresher.

1883 June 21
- F. plays tarot with Alexander Holländer, a resident superior to F., and loses 80 Kreuzer.
- F. goes for a walk with his cousin Moritz and two of his sisters.

1883 June 22
- Richard Wahle visits F.
- F. acquires the third part of Ernst Fleischl's *Physiologisch-optische Notizen.*

1883 June 28
F. visits Josef Breuer. Afterward, they have dinner at the Hotel Meissl & Schadn on Neuer Markt; the former Minister of Justice Julius Glaser sits at the next table.

1883 June end
- F.'s father makes a loss of 200 Gulden in June.
- F. attends a Protestant wedding ceremony.

1883 July beginning
F. suggests to Alexander Holländer to conduct a joint study on the brain of newborns.

1883 July 4
F. spends the evening with Josef Paneth.

1883 July 5
F. spends the evening with Josef Breuer.

1883 July 6
F. meets Ernst Fleischl on the street. In the evening, he reads a chapter by Meynert's *Die acuten (hallucinatorischen) Formen des Wahnsinns und ihr Verlauf.*

1883 July 7
F. meets his cousin Moritz for lunch. He tells him that F.'s father has earned 100 Gulden through his mediation and is going to Odessa.

1883 July 8–9
F.'s cousin Moritz, at the suggestion of F.'s sister Rosa, invites all the Freud siblings on a trip to Baden. The company misses the last train, and Josef Brust organizes a hotel stay for them.

1883 July 13
F. visits Josef Breuer and stays until about midnight; one of the topics of conversation is Bertha Pappenheim.

1883 July mid
F. formed a "private dream book […] from experience" (F. to Martha, 19.7.1883). It is possible, however, that he did not put it down in writing.

1883 July 17
F. sends Martha ten marks.

1883 July 19
F.'s father travels to Odessa to open a shop there.

1883 July 20
F. visits Ernst Fleischl and Josef Breuer.

1883 July 21
F. receives a visit in the morning from Ignaz Schönberg, who has returned from Bad Gleichenberg.

1883 July 21–22
Short holiday with Josef Breuer in Gmunden

F. spends the weekend in Gmunden in the Salzkammergut at the invitation of Josef Breuer. They spend the night in Breuer's villa, which is next to the villa of Archduchess Elisabeth, the daughter of Archduke Anton Johann.

1883 July 21

In the afternoon departure for Gmunden, F. reads Gustave Flaubert's *Les Tentations du Saint Antoine* in the train. After dinner, F. and Breuer take a walk to the "Seeschloss".

1883 July 22

In the morning before breakfast, F. explores Gmunden. Later, he takes a rowing boat out on the lake with Breuer, his wife Mathilde and the composer Hugo Wolf.
In the afternoon, F. meets Richard Wahle in the Kursalon.
F. buys a silver brooch as a birthday present for Martha.
In the evening, F. returns to Vienna.

1883 July 23
F. sends Martha the silver brooch he bought in Gmunden with the remark "A young salmon trout from the Traunsee" (F. to Martha, 24.7.1883).

1883 July 25
F. goes to Döbling with Josef Paneth and his father-in-law Adolf Schwab.

1883 July 28
F. visits Ignaz Schönberg in Sankt Andrae, northwest of Vienna. Schönberg is there visiting his brother-in-law.

1883 July 29
F. is at the birthday party of his cousin Moritz. They have dinner in the garden of a historic inn.

1883 July 30
– F. visits Josef Breuer in his ordination.
– Josef Herzig visits F. and brings him "a few chemical things for new experiments" and an edition of Don Quixote with illustrations by Gustave Doré (F. to Martha, 30.7.1883).

1883 July 31
F. attends a performance of Bizet's *Carmen* at the Hofoper, and stalls, third row, with Josef and Mathilde Breuer.

1883 August
– F.'s contacts are limited to his friends Josef Herzig and Robert Franceschini, as his colleague Alexander Holländer is absent and he has taken his place as first Sekundararzt.
– F. is working on a study of facial paralysis in mental illness.

1883 August 3
F. travels with Josef Breuer to Pötzleinsdorf, where Breuer introduces him to Richard Kapell-mann, a lawyer and section councilor in the Ministry of Agriculture. F. is to give him electro-therapeutic treatment several times a week during Breuer's four-week absence. On the way back, they meet Emma Pappenheim, a relative of Martha.

1883 August 4
– F. reads Robert Hamerling's poem *Amor und Psyche.*
– F. visits his patient Kapellmann for the first time.

1883 August 6
F. acquires Albert Kölliker's *Handbuch der Gewebelehre des Menschen.*

1883 August 9–10
F. spends two days with Josef Paneth.

1883 August 12
F. buys two "picture books", one for Martha and one for Minna.

1883 August 13
Theodor Meynert comes to the clinic with his brother-in-law, the pathologist Gustav Scheuthauer.

1883 August 14
F. receives a visit in the evening from Josef Herzig.

1883 August 15
– F. buys for Martha "the most beautiful stationery I can afford" (F. to Martha, 14.8.1883).
– F. is at the wedding of Nathan Weiss.

1883 August mid
– F. has professional disputes with his colleague Robert Steiner von Pfungen.
– F. reads Don Quixote again, an edition with illustrations by Gustav Doré.
– F. reads Henry Fielding's novel *Tom Jones.*

1883 August 17
– F. receives a payment from Ignaz Schönberg, presumably because he has assumed medical duties with him.
– F.'s father returns from his trip to Odessa. His business has failed because the shop has burned down. He brings a relative of the husband of one of F.'s cousins with him.

1883 August 18
– F. introduces the relative from Odessa at the Allgemeines Krankenhaus and wants to per-suade her to have an operation.
– F. sends Ignaz Schönberg books from the series *Science Primers for the People,* which has been published since 1882 and is dedicated to the natural sciences.

1883 August 19
F. gets a visit from his mother.

1883 August 20
F. visits his family.

1883 August 21

F. visits with Josef Herzig the "Exhibition of Electricity", which was held on the grounds of the Prater from 1883 August 16 to October 31. But the exhibition is still under construction, the machines are still being repaired, and there is nothing interesting to see yet.

1883 August 23

- F. tells Martha about his hope that they will be able to marry sooner than expected thanks to a staining method he has developed. It is a procedure that allows brain sections to be made suitable for microscopic examination by hardening and staining with gold chloride solution.
- F. discusses wedding plans and their prerequisites with his colleague Ignaz Widder.
- F. receives a visit from Ignaz Schönberg.

1883 August 26

F. and his sister Rosa visit the internist Friedrich Pineles in Oberwaltersdorf, 40km south of Vienna.

1883 August 27

F. and Josef Herzig visit the "Exhibition of Electricity" again. In the evening, they listen to a lecture by William Siemens on the subject of "Temperature, Light and Total Radiation, Determination of Solar Heat by electrical Means".

1883 August 28

The publisher Franz Deuticke seeks F.'s advice on the translation of a textbook on pathological histology from English.

1883 August 29

- F. offers reflections on the "psychology of the common man", "which is quite different from ours" (F. to Martha, 29.8.1883).
- The friction with Robert Steiner von Pfungen intensifies.
- F. has the Königsberg doctor Louis Arthur Hennig as a guest for his hospital rounds.

1883 August 30

F.'s gold chloride method stops working for a short time.

1883 August end

F. has a severe migraine attack.

1883 September 1

F. receives a visit from Ignaz Schönberg and his sisters Rosa and Dolfi.

1883 September 2

F. travels with Schönberg to Pötzleinsdorf. Presumably F. visits Richard Kapellmann there, the patient whom he treats with electrotherapy in Breuer's absence.

1883 September beginning

F. visits the Exhibition of Electricity with Ernst Fleischl.

1883 September 4

- F. meets Josef Brust and his brother Hermann by chance in the city.
- F. accidentally meets Martha's relative Emma Pappenheim in Währing.

1883 September 5

F. receives a visit from Ignaz Schönberg.

1883 September 6

F. visits Ignaz Schönberg. Both then go to the "Exhibition of Electricity" together.

1883 September 7

F. is at the "Stammtisch" (regular's table) with Ignaz Schönberg in the Prater. Eli also comes by.

1883 September 8

- F. goes on an excursion to Pötzleinsdorf and Dornbach with his sister Dolfi. In Pötzleinsdorf, he again visits Richard Kapellmann.
- F.'s mother had a fever but recovered the next day.

1883 September 9

- F. has a visit from Ignaz Schönberg and Robert Franceschini all afternoon and evening.
- F.'s cousin Moritz returns from Paris. There, he had secretly become engaged to F.'s sister Mitzi who works as a nanny for a family in Paris-St. Germain and is perfecting her French.

1883 September 10

- F. is given the position of a reviewer at the *Wiener Medizinische Wochenschrift* and receives 80–100 Gulden annually.[10] He also receives foreign-language medical journals.
- F.'s father travels to Manchester to visit his sons from his first marriage. On the way, he visits his daughter Mitzi in Paris.

1883 September 13

- F. visits his patient Kappelmann in Pötzleinsdorf for the last time.
- F. receives a work table for the histological laboratory as a gift from Theodor Meynert.
- Death of F.'s friend and colleague Nathan Weiss. He hangs himself in a bath in Vienna.

1883 September 14

- The dermatologist Sigmund Lustgarten, a former classmate of F., informs him about the suicide of Nathan Weiss.
- F. is with Joseph Paneth and Sophie Schwab for dinner at Sophie's parents Adolf and Fanny Schwab.

1883 September 16

F. is at the funeral of Nathan Weiss (with Robert Steiner von Pfungen, among others). He is ashamed of the funeral orator's accusations against Nathan's wife's family.

1883 September 18

- F. begins reading Charles Dickens' novel *Bleak House.*
- F. visits Josef Breuer in the evening.

1883 September 19

- F. is transferred to the II. Department for Syphilis. Its head, Hermann Zeissl, had retired at his own request on September 1, and the post of head was vacant.
- F. registers for the IV. Department for Nervous Diseases (headed by Franz Scholz).

1883 September 23

- F. is invited to lunch with Joseph Paneth at his future parents-in-law.
- F. receives a visit from Ignaz Kohn, who was at the Allgemeines Krankenhaus until the end of 1882 and is now a practicing doctor in Brno.

1883 September 24–29
Visit to Josef Brust in Baden near Vienna

1883 September 24

F. travels from Vienna to Baden. He spends the evening with Josef Brust in the company of the "Badener Spiessbürger" (philistines) (F. to Martha, 25.9.1883).

1883 September 25

F. visits the Rauhenstein castle ruins. In the evening, F. and Brust are in Sooss near Baden and celebrate Brust's birthday.

1883 September 26

Josef Brust picks up F. for a walk. In the evening, they are at the Jägerhaus inn in Baden.

1883 September 27

F. and Brust travel together to Lilienfeld near St. Pölten.

1883 September 28

F. and Brust are having dinner at Café Otto, "where there are a bunch of blond ugly girls from 28 to 8 years old" (F. to Martha, 30.9.1883).

1883 September 29

F. travels back from Baden to Vienna.

1883 September 30

F. visits his former religion teacher Samuel Hammerschlag and beats him at chess.
F. is visited by Ignaz Schönberg in the afternoon. Both then go to the Prater.

1883 October

F. reads Gustav Freytag's novel *Die verlorene Handschrift.*

1883 October 1

F. becomes II. Sekundararzt at the II. Department for syphilis of Hermann Zeissl, who had resigned a month before. F. stays there until 1883 December 31. Abraham Anscherlik is the head of the department at this time. Besides F., Zeissl's son Maximilian also works in the department.
F. moves into a new room in the III. Hof of the Allgemeines Krankenhaus.
F. visits Josef Breuer.

– F. learns of the death of his tailor Jakob Mittler, who had died on September 28: "He was a good man, but his last suits were badly made" (F. to Martha, 1.10.1883).
– F. eats sour fish with sultanas and white bread with several Jewish colleagues for the evening on the occasion of the Jewish New Year.

1883 October 3
– F. has lunch with Ernst Fleischl and his brothers Otto and Richard. Then, he goes only with Fleischl to the "Exhibition of Electricity", where Fleischl explains the gas machines to him.
– F. receives Fleischl's paper "Zur Anatomie und Physiologie der Retina".
– F. borrows five Gulden from Alexander Holländer.
– F. visits Josef Breuer in the evening.

1883 October 4

F. moves to a new room in the same Hof; the room is higher but somewhat narrower.

1883 October 6
- F.'s first reviews appear in the *Wiener Medizinische Wochenschrift*, but without his name.
- F. tries "feverishly new methods" (F. to Martha, 6.10.1883).

1883 October 7
F. finds "finally a beautiful method again with which many things can be done" (F. to Martha, 8.10.1883).

1883 October 8
F. shows Theodor Meynert his preparations.

1883 October 9
F. gets children's brains on which he can try out his gold chloride method.

1883 October 9
F. receives a visit from Ignaz Schönberg in the evening.

1883 October 11
On Yom Kippur, the Jewish Day of Atonement, F. has lunch with his father.

1883 October 12
F.'s gold chloride method "yields preparations of such beauty, fullness of detail [...] that I may safely assume to accomplish beautiful things with its help" (F. to Martha, 12.10.1883).

1883 October 13
F. shows his preparations to Sigmund Exner, a colleague of Ernst Brücke at the Physiological Institute. He "praised them immensely". Theodor Meynert also "admires" them (F. to Martha, 13.10.1883).

1883 October 14
Wedding of F.'s sister Anna to Eli Bernays, the brother of F.'s fiancée Martha. The wedding takes place in the Jewish synagogue in Schiffgasse. F. does not go, but after being told about it, he calls it a "man-eating ceremony" (F. to Martha, 14.10.1883). He does not visit the bride and groom until the evening.

1883 October 15
- F. introduces himself to Viktor Urbantschitsch and considers taking a course in otology with him.
- F. buys a larynx case and decides to take part in a course of laryngology.
- F. asks Martha to embroider wall plaques for him with the admonition "Travailler sans raisonner" from Voltaire's *Candide* and the saying "En cas de doute abstiens toi".
- F. works with Sigmund Lustgarten on the gold chloride method in order to "make it a method of general application for all tissues" (F. to Martha, 15.10.1883).

1883 October mid
F. offers Alexander Holländer, Sigmund Lustgarten, Salomon Ehrmann and Moritz Horowitz to try out his gold chloride method in their fields of expertise.

1883 October 16
- F. believes that he has so far "succeeded best […] in staining the brain sections. These are technical feats, as in every craft, but science cannot do without them" (F. to Martha, 16.10.1883).
- F. shows Breuer his preparations.

1883 October 18
- Moritz Heitler encourages F. to take on nervous diseases.
- F. is having dinner with Josef Paneth and his fiancée Sophie Schwab at the home of Josef Paneth's future father-in-law Adolf Schwab.

1883 October 19
F. wants to publish a methodical work with Sigmund Lustgarten; however, nothing comes of it.

1883 October 20
F. visits Josef Breuer.

1883 October 21
- F. believes his "career" is beginning because he has "got enemies" (F. to Martha, 16.10.1883).
- F. gets a visit from sister Rosa.

1883 October 22
F. is playing chess in the coffee house, and a waiter pushes a lit cigar into his hand upside down, and F. also puts it into his mouth upside down.

1883 October 23
F. believes he has found a new gold dyeing method that is better than the previous one.

1883 October 24
F. visits Josef Breuer in the evening. While waiting for Breuer in his surgery, he leafs through Georg Brandes' book *Moderne Geister. Literarische Bildnisse aus dem 19. Jahrhundert.* Then, F. and Breuer take a walk together to the Karltheater, where they pick up Breuer's children.

1883 October 25
- F. visits Ernst Fleischl in the afternoon to show him his gold preparations; by chance, Ernst Brücke also comes along and remarks "Yes, you will become famous through your methods alone" (F. to Martha, 25.10.1883).
- F. visits Josef Breuer in the afternoon to show him the gold preparations. He reacts with the sentence: "Now you have the gun, I wish you a happy war" (F. to Martha, 25.10.1883).
- F. orders for Martha the book by Georg Brandes Moderne Geister. Literary portraits from the 19th century.

1883 October 27
- Joseph Paneth says goodbye to F. before a stay of several months in Villefranche.

F. receives a hat from sister Dolfi and a purse from brother Alexander.

- Hermann von Helmholtz, whose picture F. had hung in his room and whose *Populäre wissenschaftliche Vorträge* he had purchased a year before, visits the "Exhibition of Electricity", but F. never gets to see him.

1883 October 29
- F. starts a urology course with Robert Ultzmann.
- F. has a new tailor.

1883 October 31
- F. plays tarot with Alexander Holländer and is visited by Josef Herzig. Both then go to an inn.

1883 October end
F. learns of Josef Breuer's difficulties in treating Bertha Pappenheim ("Anna O.").

1883 November beginning
A Moritz Freud from Bucharest, according to F., "a real cousin" (F. to Martha, 4.11.1883) and not identical with Mitzi, the later husband of the same name, visits the Freud family. He stays at the Hotel Goldenes Lamm.

1883 November 1
F. and Ignaz Schönberg visit Ottilie Weiss, an acquaintance of the Bernays family.

1883 November 2
- F. sends Martha the book by Georg Brandes *Moderne Geister* with the dedication "Martha zum Geschenk bei einer freudigen Veranlassung Oktober 1883. Von ihrem Sigmund".
- F. and Ignaz Schönberg attend a performance of Mozart's *Don Juan* at the Hofoper. Afterward, they go to the Kleine Michaelerhaus for supper.

1883 November 3
F. attends the "Konservatorium", a Saturday lecture by Ernst Fleischl. Afterward, Fleischl and F. visit Josef Breuer.

1883 November 4
- F. visits Ernst Fleischl, and he encourages him to habilitate in neuropathology instead of histology. Then, they go together to F.'s room in the Allgemeines Krankenhaus.
- F. gets a frog for research.
- F. plays chess in a coffee house, makes a short visit to the Hammerschlag family and then visits his family, where he also meets Ignaz Schönberg.

1883 November 6
- F. gets a new pair of trousers from his tailor and a few books from his bookseller.
- F. goes to a coffee house to play chess with an elderly gentleman. F. beats him for the first time.
- F. goes to the plenary meeting of the Physiological Club in the evening.

1883 November 7
F. begins joint research work with Alexander Holländer on the treatment of histological sections.

1883 November 8
F. buys a new tie and goes to the hairdresser.

1883 November 10
F. visits Fleischl's "Konservatorium" again. He gives Fleischl a review of an experimental study by Rudolf Heidenhain. Afterward, they had a glass of wine and F. accompanied Fleischl to Döbling, where he visited his girlfriend Franziska Wertheimstein. Five years later, Franziska Wertheimstein became F.'s patient.

1883 November 10
- F. is invited to lunch at Joseph Paneth's future parents-in-law and plays three games of chess with Adolf Schwab, of which F. wins two.
- In the evening, F. visits his family and sings passages from *Don Juan* to his sisters.

1883 November 12
Sigmund Exner, associate professor and Ernst Brücke's assistant, asks F. if he would like to report on Viennese scientific life for a Polish journal. F. was to receive ten Gulden per month for this.

1883 November 13
F. visits Josef Breuer to borrow some money. There, he meets Kathinka Kadisch and her mother. Kathinka's problems while breastfeeding her first child in the spring of 1886 are the subject of F.'s first psychotherapeutic case history, which appears in 1892 December under the title "Ein Fall von hypnotischer Heilung nebst Bemerkungen über die Entstehung hysterischer Symptome durch den 'Gegenwillen'".

1883 November 15
F. visits the Hammerschlag family in the evening.

1883 November 20
- F. buys a carrying basket and vessels and has his waitress fetch food for him and his colleague Moritz Horowitz from a nearby inn.
- F. goes to the Physiological Club. Hermann Nothnagel shows an experiment, and Breuer gives a critical review.

1883 November 22
F. is at the meeting in the evening at the Psychiatrische Verein.[11]

1883 November 24
- F. visits Ernst Fleischl in the afternoon and meets Ludo Hartmann, the son of the writer Moritz Hartmann.
- In the evening, F. visits Adolf Schwab and then Josef Breuer.

1883 November 25
F. visits Emma and Wilhelm Pappenheim.

1883 November 26
- F. and Maximilian Zeissl are planning a joint paper on syphilis. However, F. is not sure whether anything will come of it.
- In the afternoon, F. meets Ottilie Weiss and her son Willy in the hospital garden and accompanies them home.

1883 November 30
F.'s cousin Moritz is visiting and tells F. about his visit to Mitzi in Paris.

1883 November end
F. takes opium because of digestive problems.

1883 December 1
- F. visits Ernst Fleischl's "Konservatorium" and then asks him about America, as he is thinking of emigrating.
- F. meets Josef Herzig in a coffee house and then shows him preparations.
- In the late evening, F. visits Josef Breuer.

1883 December 2
- F. receives a visit from Ignaz Schönberg.
- F. visits his family in the evening.

1883 December 8
F. is invited to Schwab's in the evening and plays tarot with Adolf Schwab and Samuel Hammerschlag.

1883 December 11
- F. acquires Gustav Freytag's book *Doktor Luther,* which he intends to give to Martha.
- F. sustains a minor injury to the middle finger of his right hand with a sharp knife in the laboratory.

1883 December 13
- F. visits his family and informs them about his upcoming trip to Saxony.
- In the evening, F. visits the Hammerschlag family and asks for the address of their relatives in Dresden.

1883 December Mid
F. acquires Hermann von Helmholtz''s *Wissenschaftliche Abhandlungen* in two volumes

1883 December 15–19
Meeting with the brothers
Emanuel and Philip in Saxony

1883 December 15
F. takes the night train to Leipzig at 20:45.

1883 December 16
During the train journey, F. reads Gustav Freytag's book *Doktor Luther*; in the course of an argument about the opening of a window, he receives anti-Semitic insults.
F. arrives in Leipzig at 5.30 pm and stays there in the Hotel Stadt Freiberg. His brothers Emanuel and Philipp also arrive late in the evening. The brothers chat over a bottle of Rüdesheimer until the next morning.

1883 December 17
F. and his brothers drive to Dresden in the late morning and arrive there around 2.30 pm. They take a stroll through the city and visit the Christmas market, among other things.
In the evening, F. and his brothers see a performance of Franz Grillparzer's *Esther* and Molière's *Der eingebildete Kranke* at the Dresden Residenztheater by the Herzoglich Meiningen'sche Hoftheater.

1883 December 18
F. tours the old town with his brothers in the snowfall and visits the picture gallery. He is particularly impressed by Hans Holbein's Madonna, which he describes in detail to Martha. In the afternoon, after the departure of his brothers to Reichenberg, F. visits the family of Elise, Sigmund and Emmy Altschul, who are related to Breuers, Hammerschlags and Paneths.

1883 December 19
F. travels back to Vienna on the night train at 1.00 am. He gives 36 Kreuzer to a Jewish unemployed journeyman tinsmith who had carried F.'s luggage for "night meal and sleeping money". Around 9 pm, F. is back in his room in the Allgemeines Krankenhaus.

1883 December 22
F. visits Josef Breuer.

1883 December 24
– In the afternoon, F. is at Theodor Meynert's "Weihnachtsbescherung" (handing out Christmas gifts), who has bought a "spruced-up Christmas tree for his poor charges", "gives each of them a plate with cake, apples and nuts and makes a consoling address to them" (F. to Martha, 25.12.1883).
– F. visits his family; Ignaz Schönberg is also there. As Christmas presents, F. receives stationery from sister Rosa and a desk calendar from Alexander's brother.

1883 December 28
F. sends Martha a parcel containing, among other things, Gottfried Keller's *Züricher Novellen*.

1883 December 29
F. visits Josef Breuer and his family.

1883 December 30
F. is visited by sister Rosa, cousin Moritz and Ignaz Schönberg. They all go to an inn together and "dragged [Freud] the last Gulden […] out of his pocket" (F. to Martha, 31.12.1883).

1883 December 31
F. spends the day at the Allgemeines Krankenhaus. As he has no money to celebrate with colleagues, he writes a poem for Martha.

1883 December end
F. feels that his colleague Alexander Holländer bothers him more than he helps him and decides to have his own keys made for the laboratory at the beginning of the next year so that he can work there in the evening.

1884

1884 January
- Ernst Fleischl organizes for F. the publication of his paper "A new method for the study of the course of nerve fibers in the central nervous system" in the English journal *Brain*.
- F. writes a manuscript "Über die Behandlung der Trigeminusneuralgie" ("On the Treatment of Trigeminal Neuralgia"), which remains unpublished.

1884 January 1
- F. takes up his post at Franz Scholz's IV. Department for Nervous Diseases and remains there until the end of 1885 February. He moves into a new room in the east wing of the IX. Hof of the Allgemeines Krankenhaus.
- F. receives a visit from Ignaz Schönberg.

1884 January 2
F. gets a photo of Martha.

1884 January 3
F. receives 12 Gulden fee from the *Wiener Medizinische Wochenschrift* for his reviews of the last quarter of 1883.

1884 January 4
F. gets a visit from his mother.

1884 January 5
F. visits Josef Breuer.

1884 January 6
F. goes to a coffee house to play chess.

1884 January 7
F. receives some copies of his reviews.

1884 January 8
F. gets a visit from sister Rosa at noon.

1884 January 9
- F. visits his former teacher Samuel Hammerschlag and receives a larger sum from him.
- F. begins the treatment of Emanuel Stern. His wife Rosalie, one of F.'s waitresses, had asked him to do so (until 1886 May).
- F. visits his family.

1884 before January 12
The medical student Albert Hammerschlag, a son of F.'s religion teacher Samuel Hammerschlag, visits F. daily in the evening, and F. shows him "all kinds of tricks" (F. to Martha, 12.1.1884).

1884 January 12
- F. visits Ernst Fleischl in the morning.
- F. moves into Nathan Weiss's room in the walk-in clinic for electrical treatment at the Allgemeines Krankenhaus. The head of the walk-in clinic is Moriz Rosenthal.

1884 January 13
- A friend of Eduard Silberstein visits F. and receives medical help and friendly advice from him.
- Ignaz Schönberg picks up F. at the Allgemeines Krankenhaus, and they both visit F.'s family.

1884 January 15
F. visits the Physiological Club; he sees "with annoyance how all the people throw themselves on the heritage of nervous diseases" (F. to Martha, 16.1.1884).

1884 January mid
- F. has seen something rare in the urine of a jaundiced patient and needs a microscope to trace it. But it costs 150 Gulden, and F. cannot afford it.
- F. orders a waistcoat.

1884 January 17
- A 16-year-old apprentice shoemaker is admitted to the IV. Department for Nervous Diseases with hemorrhages of the lower legs and dies the next evening. On the basis of this case, F. immediately begins work on his first clinical publication: "Ein Fall von Hirnblutung mit indirekten basalen Herdsymptomen bei Scorbut". It is finished on January 28.
- F. visits his family because his sister Paula is not feeling well.
- F. goes to a lecture by Theodor Meynert at the Psychiatrische Verein (Psychiatric Association).
- F. sends Martha a list of his income and expenditure for January. According to this, he took in 152 Gulden (including 50 Gulden each from Josef Breuer and Samuel Hammerschlag) and spent 146 Gulden. The largest sum (25 Gulden) went to support a family.

1884 January 19
F. attends Ernst Fleischl's "Konservatorium". He then visits Josef Breuer.

1884 January 20
F. receives a visit from Ignaz Schönberg.

1884 January 21
- F. completes the first part of his paper "A case of cerebral hemorrhage with indirect basal focal symptoms in scurvy".
- Theodor Meynert asks F. whether he does not think of publishing studies on special questions of brain anatomy.

1884 January 22
F. shows his preparations of brain slices to Ernst Fleischl and Sigmund Exner. Fleischl advises him to publish the method as soon as possible, which F. intends to do anyway "to keep the world in suspense" (F. to Martha, 22.1.1884).

1884 January 24
F. visits the Hammerschlag family with his sister Rosa.

1884 January 26
F. has almost finished writing his paper "A Case of Cerebral Hemorrhage with Indirect Basal Focal Symptoms in Scurvy" and reads it to Josef Breuer in the evening.

1884 January 27
F. visits Samuel Hammerschlag.

1884 January 28
F. finishes his paper "A Case of Cerebral Hemorrhage with Indirect Basal Focal Symptoms in Scurvy".

1884 January 29
F. visits the Physiological Club; he sits behind Theodor Billroth and Hermann Nothnagel; Theodor Meynert advises him to also lecture in the Gesellschaft der Ärzte (Society of Physicians).

1884 January 30
F. is visited by Eduard Silberstein, whom he has not seen for three years. Both go together to an inn, then across the Ringstrasse and finally to the Café Central. In the evening, the old friends (Ignaz Rosanes, Josef Herzig, Carl Bettelheim, Sigmund Lustgarten and Eduard Silberstein) meet at the Café Kurzweil. F. also brought Ignaz Schönberg with him.

1884 January 31
F. moves into two rooms (9th Hof, door 63) in the Allgemeines Krankenhaus, formerly occupied by Nathan Weiss.

1884 January end
In Theodor Meynert's laboratory, F. meets Bernhard Sachs from New York and the Russian neurologist Liweri Darkschewitsch, who wants to translate his work on the fiber course in the central nervous system into Russian.

1884 February
- F. writes on two manuscripts: "Die Differentialdiagnose zwischen Anästhesien ist spinalen und cerebralen Ursprungs" ("The Differential Diagnosis between Anesthesia is of Spinal and Cerebral Origin") and "Über das Überspringen der Reflexe" ("On The Skipping of Reflexes"); both remain unpublished.
- The American doctor Bernard Sachs, who is a student of Theodor Meynert, wants to report on F.'s gold chloride method in a New York newspaper.

1884 February beginning
F. finishes work on the German and English versions of his paper on "A new method for the study of the course of nerve fibers in the central nervous system". He gives a German offprint to Josef Herzig with the dedication: "Meinem lieben Freunde Dr. Josef Herzig/d. Verf.".

1884 February 1
- Eduard Silberstein visits F.
- F. is at a meeting of the Sekundarärzte to discuss the equipment of a working and operating room in the Institute of Pathology. F. is elected to a committee of four to look into the matter further.

1884 February 2
F. visits Josef Breuer.

1884 February 3
- In the morning, F.'s colleague Josef Pollak arrives from Malaga with a bottle of wine.
- F. visits Kathinka Kadisch in the evening.
- Afterward, F. is invited to Sigmund Exner's house. A "Miss Smith" from Chicago is also present, who wants to see F.'s preparations. F. shows her his preparations and explains the gold chloride method.

1884 February 4
Eduard Silberstein visits F. For lunch; they both go to an inn.

1884 February 6
Eduard Silberstein visits F.

1884 February 7
- F. produces an excerpt of his work "A new method for the study of the course of nerve fibers in the central nervous system" for Liweri Darkschewitsch.
- Eduard Silberstein visits F. and invites him and the "old revelers" back to Hernals, where he had given his farewell party in 1877; however, F. is on duty and does not go.

1884 February 9
- Liweri Darkschewitsch produces a translation of the abridged version of F.'s paper "A new method for the study of the course of nerve fibers in the central nervous system" for the Russian journal ВРАЧЬ.
- F. visits Ernst Fleischl and then Josef Breuer.

1884 February 10
Eduard Silberstein leaves Vienna.

1884 February 12
- F. visits Heinrich Obersteiner, who tells him that he has given the English translation of F.'s paper on the gold chloride method to Ernst Fleischl to send to the journal *Brain*. Fleischl sends the German version to the *Centralblatt für die medicinischen Wissenschaften*.
- F. gives a lecture at the Physiological Club on "A New Method for the Study of the Course of Nerve Fibers in the Central Nervous System".

1884 February 14
F. gives a lecture on "The Structure of the Elements of the Nervous System" at the Psychiatrische Verein (Psychiatric Association), chaired by Theodor Meynert. It was "a triumph like it had not been for a long time" (F. to Martha, 14.2.1884).

1884 February 15
F. plans a small clinical publication on the "overleaping" of reflexes and the examinations of the spinal cord. He postpones a larger clinical publication on the differentiation of insensibility from the spinal cord, resp. the brain. Instead, he wants to turn more to the lamprey (Petromyzon Planeri) and orders the fish again.

1884 February 17
F. visits the Schwab family at noon.

1884 February 18
F. has sciatica, which severely restricts him for almost six weeks and necessitates a temporary release from hospital duties.

1884 February 19
F. visits his family.

1884 February 21
F. visits Ernst Fleischl in the morning at his invitation. Fleischl had received a letter from Hugo Kronecker, the editor of the *Centralblatt für die medicinischen Wissenschaften*, asking him to compress his submitted communication on "A New Method for the Study of the Course of

Nerve Fibers in the Central Nervous System". Fleischl suggests that F. produces a short version for the *Centralblatt*, but sends the detailed article to the *Archiv für mikroskopische Anatomie*. Finally, however, the long version appears in the *Archiv für Anatomie, Physiologie und Wissenschaftliche Medicin*.

1884 February 23
- F. buys a book by Mark Twain.
- F. visits the Hammerschlag family.

1884 February 24
F. visits his family and meets Ignaz Schönberg there.

1884 February 28
F. shows his specimens to Adolf Zemann, assistant at the Department of Pathological Anatomy. He is enthusiastic and assures F. that he can get everything he needs.

1884 March
- F. has problems with Alexander Holländer regarding an agreed joint publication. F. would prefer to publish it alone, as Holländer has hardly participated in the work.
- F. works on glandular functions in Salomon Stricker's Laboratory for Experimental Pathology (until July), but without success.

1884 March beginning
- F. applies for the position of a Sekundararzt I. class at the III. Medical Department for chest patients of the Allgemeines Krankenhaus.
- F. begins to work on electrodiagnostics and wants to buy equipment for it. For the time being, Fleischl and Bettelheim lend him some.

1884 March 1
F.'s first clinical publication appears: "A Case of Cerebral Hemorrhage with Indirect Basal Focal Symptoms in Scurvy".

1884 March 3
F. visits Ernst Fleischl.

1884 March 4
Carl Bettelheim visits F.

1884 March 7
F. has to stay in bed because of his sciatica and is visited by Josef Breuer, Samuel Hammerschlag and Leopold Königstein. Hammerschlag wants to send F. a lectern so that he can write lying down.

1884 March 8
- Josef Breuer visits F. Albert Hammerschlag brings the lectern promised by his father and two volumes of Nestroy, which F. enjoys very much.
- F. gets a visit from his sister Rosa in the evening.

1884 March 10
Samuel and Albert Hammerschlag, Leopold Königstein and Alexander Holländer visit F. "They played tarot, massaged, electrified. Being ill is something funny" (F. to Martha, 11.3.1884).

1884 March 11
F. reads Fritz Reuter's story "Woans ik tau 'ne Fru kamm" ("Where Can I Find a Woman?").

1884 March 12
Samuel Hammerschlag visits F.

1884 March 13
F.'s sciatica improves a lot under Salicyl.

1884 March 14
- F. becomes a private patient in the Allgemeines Krankenhaus and pays five Gulden for meals in the first class. He stays in his room, but has his own nurse and gets food from the hospital kitchen, which, however, is hardly edible.
- Albert Hammerschlag visits F.
- F. receives a long-awaited photo of Martha.

1884 March mid
- F. gives Josef Breuer an offprint of his paper "A Case of Cerebral Hemorrhage with Indirect Basal Focal Symptoms in Scurvy" with the dedication "Herrn Dr Josef Breuer von seinem ergebenen Sigm Freud".
- F. receives daily visits from his family so that he hardly has time to read.
- F. writes intensively on his paper "A new method for the study of the course of nerve fibers in the central nervous system" for the *Archiv für Anatomie und Physiologie.*

1884 after March 15
F. gives Heinrich Obersteiner an offprint of the abridged version of his paper "A new method for the study of the course of nerve fibers in the central nervous system" with the dedication "Herrn Prof. H. Obersteiner in Hochachtung der Verf.".

1884 March 16
Engagement of F.'s sister Rosa to Josef Brust.

1884 March 17
- F. sends his paper "A new method for the study of the course of nerve fibers in the central nervous system" to the *Archiv für Anatomie und Physiologie.*
- Josef Breuer, Sigmund Lustgarten, Samuel Hammerschlag, Alexander Holländer, Ignaz Rosanes, Robert Franceschini and Albert Hammerschlag visit F. From his family come mother Amalia and sister Rosa with Fanny Süssermann.

1884 March 19
F. decides "to have no more sciatica" (F. to Martha, 19.3.1884) and has his beard trimmed by the barber; in the evening, he plays chess in a coffee house and afterward visits Samuel Hammerschlag.
- 1884 March 20
- F. orders electrical equipment from an instrument maker, which he then receives on April 19.
- F. visits Josef Breuer. There, he meets his colleagues Theodor Billroth, Carl Bettelheim and Rudolf Chrobak. At dinner, he sits next to Bertha Hartmann, the widow of the writer and publicist Moritz Hartmann.

1884 March 21

F. spends the evening with his family, who are celebrating his sister Rosa's birthday. Fanny Süssermann, Ignaz Schönberg and Josef Herzig are also invited. Afterward, F. goes to a café with the latter two.

1884 March 24

F. visits the Schwab family in the evening.

1884 March 25

F. visits Josef Breuer in the evening. Among the guests are many of Breuer's relatives, including Betty Hammerschlag with her sons Albert and Paul. F. sits next to Betty and her sister Anna Josephson. Afterward, F. goes to a café with Paul Hammerschlag.

1884 March 29

– F. decides to "exploit science instead of [being] exploited in its favor" (F. to Martha, 29.3.1884).
– F. visits the Hammerschlag family in the evening with sister Rosa. He plays tarot with Samuel Hammerschlag and the rabbi Moritz Güdemann.

1884 March 31

F. resumes work at the hospital after his sciatica.

1884 April beginning

F. introduces Ignaz Schönberg to Samuel Hammerschlag.

1884 April 2

F. buys Heinrich Heine's *Book of Songs.*

1884 April 3

– F. withdraws his application for the post of Sekundararzt I. class at the III. Medical Department.
– F. offers Carl Bettelheim to write a joint paper on testing electrical excitability in fever.

1884 April 5

F. visits the Schwab family in the evening.

1884 April 6

– F. goes on an excursion to the Kahlenberg with Samuel and Albert Hammerschlag and a Dresden relative of the Hammerschlags. After the excursion, F. writes about Samuel Hammerschlag: "[…] the old man [is] an object of veneration for me, as if he were my father" (F. to Martha, 7.4.1884).
– F. visits his family in the afternoon.
– F. visits the Hammerschlag family in the evening and plays tarot with Samuel and his son Paul. Anna Hammerschlag "was particularly gloomy, conscientious, hard-working and looked particularly bad" (F. to Martha, 7.4.1884).

1884 April 7

F. acquires Gabriel Andrals *Vorlesungen über die Krankheiten der Nervenherde gehalten an der Universität zu Paris im Jahre 1836.*

1884 April 8
F. is at the Physiological Club, where Josef Breuer gives a lecture. F. also meets Josef Paneth there, for the first time after his return from Villefranche and Nice, where he had regularly met Nietzsche for long conversations over several months and became friends.

1884 April 10
F. begins the treatment of Johanna Schönberg, Ignaz Schönberg's mother. She has a "heart affliction", and F. visits her daily.

1884 April 11
F. visits Josef Breuer and shows him his findings in brain anatomy. F. tells him about his habilitation plans and his intention to settle in Lower Austria, Moravia or Silesia. Breuer lends him money again.

1884 April 12
F. spends Easter Saturday with sister Rosa.

1884 April 13
– F. has a consultation with Dr. Braun about a pericarditis of Johanna Schönberg, Ignaz Schönberg's mother. Braun had also treated Martha's mother Emmeline Bernays in the past.
– F. visits the Schwab family.

1884 April 14
Joseph Paneth and his bride Sophie invest a capital of 1500 Gulden[12] for F. With the interest of 84 Gulden, he is to be able to finance an annual trip to Wandsbek to visit Martha.

1884 April mid
F. reads Alphonse Daudet's novel *Sappho. Pariser Sittenbild,* which has been published in installments in the *Neue Freie Presse* since 13 April. F. considers the novel "the best, most profound" that Daudet has written (F. to Martha, 30.4.1884).

1884 April 16
F. visits Josef Brust in Baden.

1884 April 17
Carl Bettelheim brings F. electrical apparatus.

1884 April 20
F. invites his sister Dolfi to a snack in order to have her correct his coat.

1884 April 21
– F. receives a visit from Joseph Paneth, who wants to arrange a patient for him.
– F. mentions for the first time his cocaine studies and the reading of Theodor Aschenbrandt's article on the effect of cocaine on the human organism. He hopes for a "lucky throw" with cocaine (F. to Martha, 21.4.1884).

1884 April 24
Josef Herzig orders cocaine for F. from the Merck company in Darmstadt. The cost of 1 gram is 1 Gulden 22 Kreuzer.

1884 April 25
F. gets his hair cut and goes to the Schwab family for lunch.

1884 April 27
F. found "a third little novelty [...] in brain anatomy" (F. to Martha, 27.4.1884).

1884 April 29
F. is at the Physiological Club and meets Josef Breuer there.

1884 April 30
– F. does self-experiments with cocaine. His pulse slows down from 88 to 72 beats.
– Josef Paneth visits F.
– F. visits Ignaz Schönberg in the evening and then Samuel Hammerschlag.

1884 May
Together with Leopold Königstein, F. conducts research on electrical reactions of the optic nerve.

1884 May beginning
– F. again conducts experiments with cocaine. The test subjects are himself and Josef Pollak. In addition, F. occasionally takes cocaine because it improves his mood and ability to work.
– F. also continues to work on cat brains. He puts them in ethyl alcohol and obtains literature on cat brains from Heinrich Obersteiner.

1884 May 2
F. visits Josef Breuer in the evening.

1884 May 3
– F. is at his sister Paula's birthday party.
– F. gets a visit from his sister Rosa.

1884 May 5
F. receives a visit from Ignaz Schönberg in the evening.

– 1884 May 6
– F. receives a visit from his sister Dolfi in the morning, who gives him a bouquet of lilies of the valley for his birthday.
– Other birthday presents he receives are as follows: a smoking table from his sister Rosa, a posh notepad from brother Alexander and a book from sister Dolfi.
– At noon, he gets a visit from his mother, who brings "bakeries" with her.
– F. suggests to Ernst Fleischl that he treat his morphine addiction with cocaine – Fleischl had had severe neuroma pain since an operation on his thumb. He was inspired to this idea by an article in the *Detroit Therapeutic Gazette*.
– F. receives a visit from cousin Moritz in the evening; he gives him gold cufflinks.

1884 May 8
F. visits Josef Breuer. He wants to persuade Breuer's wife Mathilde to take cocaine for her migraine. F. considers cocaine to be completely harmless and can be used everywhere without hesitation. Occasionally, he also issued prescriptions for cocaine to other people.

1884 May 9
F. has the impression that the cocaine helps Ernst Fleischl with morphine abstinence; Fleischl had not taken morphine for three days.

1884 May 13
F. gives a lecture on "The Structure of the Elements of the Nervous System" at the Physiological Club. He is calm during his lecture despite his lack of preparation, which he attributes to taking cocaine.

1884 May 14
F. buys a tailcoat, black trousers, shirt, tie and gloves for Ignaz Schönberg's graduation (PhD) and Joseph Paneth's wedding.

1884 May 15
- F. is at Ignaz Schönberg's graduation at noon.
- F. goes to the wedding of Joseph Paneth with Sophie Schwab in the early afternoon.
- F. visits his friend Emanuel Loewy between the Jewish wedding and the dinner.

1884 May mid
- F.'s debts to Josef Breuer now amount to 1000 Gulden.[13]
- F. has recommended cocaine to his colleague Steiner von Pfungen, who is sick to his stomach, and feels that it works well.
- F. and Karl Koller meet Leopold Königstein in the Allgemeines Krankenhaus. F. gives Königstein cocaine to treat intestinal complaints. Koller also takes some cocaine.

1884 May 16
- F. visits Ernst Fleischl in the morning.
- A wealthy student from Trieste, arranged by Fleischl, presents himself to F. He wants to take about 40 hours of lessons with F. and pay 120 Gulden.[14]

1884 May 17
- F. has lunch with Ernst Fleischl.
- F. informs his sister Rosa that Josef Brust wants to break off his engagement to her.

1884 May 20
- F. visits Hermann Nothnagel, who had liked his lecture on brain anatomy on May 13. Nothnagel invites F. to dinner on May 28 to discuss his professional future. However, this discussion does not take place at dinner, but during a walk on May 27.
- Carl Bettelheim visits F. and tells him about an operation Fleischl had had the day before; Fleischl had been in a very bad state after the operation.
- F. finishes his paper "The Structure of the Elements of the Nervous System".

1884 May 22
- F. visits Ernst Fleischl in the evening, where he meets Adolf von Lieben and Rudolf Auspitz.
- F. visits Josef Breuer in the evening.
- 1884 May 23.
- F. receives a visit from his brother Alexander, who brings a letter from their mother Amalia. It is about the precarious financial situation of the Freud family.
- F. visits his family and brings 20 Gulden with him, which he has just received from his paying student. In the evening, he goes out with his sisters Rosa, Dolfi and Paula.

1884 May 25
- F. visits his mother.
- F. visits the Hammerschlag family in the evening. The Schwab and Paneth families are also guests.

1884 May 26
- F. visits Ernst Fleischl in the morning, where he meets Sigmund Exner, Ewald Hering, Josef Breuer and Fleischl's father Karl.
- F. plays a game of tarot with Alexander Holländer.
- F. visits Ernst Fleischl in the afternoon, who is very unwell: he had become pale and started vomiting, and was in severe pain.

1884 May 27
- F. is at the Physiological Club. On a subsequent walk, Hermann Nothnagel advises him to settle in the province.
- F. visits Josef Breuer.

1884 May 28
F. visits his mother Amalia and meets his sister Anna and brother-in-law Eli there.

1884 May 30
F. visits the university observatory in Türkenschanzstrasse. F. enjoyed the "little insight into a strange, beautiful world" (F. to Martha, 31.5.1884).

1884 May end
F. declines several invitations because he thinks his clothes are too shabby and he cannot afford anything new at the moment.

1884 June
- F. asks his former fellow student Johann Pollak, who is a ship's doctor on an Austrian steamer, to experiment with cocaine on seasick people. Pollak does so, but without success.
- F. strongly recommends his colleague and friend, the ophthalmologist Leopold Königstein, to try cocaine on the eyes of his outpatients. Karl Koller also receives a cocaine sample from F.

1884 June beginning
- F. electrifies a lot and has the feeling of having cured a hysterical paralysis.
- F. electrifies a patient with leg paralysis and contraction for an hour a day, and she slowly gets her mobility back.

1884 June 2
F. asks Ignaz Schönberg to help him collect the fee for the treatment of his mother Johanna.

1884 June 3
- F. fetches young cats in a sack and meets Hermann Nothnagel on the way, who asks him what is in the sack.
- F. receives the fee for the treatment of Johanna Schönberg.
- F.'s mother goes for a spa stay at Rožnau (until August 17).

1884 June 4
- F. visits Fleischl and receives a recommendation from him so that he can use the library of the Society of Physicians.
- F. learns from Anna Hammerschlag, whom he had also given cocaine, that it did not help her.

1884 June 5
F. finds a detailed article on cocaine in the catalog of the American Surgeon General.

1884 June 9
F. buys a new suit, a black hat and a tie.

1884 June 11
F. visits Josef Breuer with Ernst Fleischl and Rudolf Chrobak.

1884 June 12
F. promises his brother Alexander to give him ten Gulden for three months so that he can learn shorthand.

1884 June 13
F. visits Josef and Sophie Paneth in the flat they moved into after the wedding.

1884 June 14
- Josef Pollak informs F. of two case histories after successful cocaine treatment, which F. includes in his paper "Ueber Coca" ("On Coca").
- F. visits Samuel Hammerschlag with his sister Rosa, who has returned to Vienna after spending several weeks with relatives in Dresden.

1884 June 17
- F. receives a patient from Braila through Eduard Silberstein. The case is complicated, and F. invites Hermann Nothnagel to a consultation.
- F. sends Martha an article by his friend and former colleague Robert Franceschini about the poor work of the Vienna Sanitary Authority.

1884 June 18
F. finishes his work "Ueber Coca" and proofreads his paper on the "Structure of the Elements of the Nervous System".

1884 June 19
- Josef Paneth visits F.
- F. visits Josef Breuer.

1884 June 20
F. goes to the consultation with Nothnagel about the patient from Braila.

1884 June 22
- F. recommends to Martha an article by Ludwig Speidel about Franz Grillparzer, which he had read in the *Neue Freie Presse* that morning.
- F. visits Ernst Fleischl; he recommends that he borrows as much money as he needs – and not only from Josef Breuer, but also from him, Fleischl.

1884 June 28
- F. goes to the Prater with his sister Dolfi.
- F. acquires Guillaume Duchenne's *Physiologie des mouvements*.

1884 June 29
F.'s sister Rosa goes with Josef Herzig to Oberwaltersdorf near Baden for three weeks. There, she helps Friedrich Pineles's family.

1884 June end
F. has a dark suit made for him by his tailor.

1884 Summer
F.'s gold chloride method causes a stir with the Leipzig anatomist Paul Flechsig.

1884 July

F. gives a free course on brain anatomy for colleagues at the hospital.

1884 July 1

- F.'s work "On Coca" is published. He gives a special edition to August Vogl with the dedication: "Herrn Prof. A. Vogl m. Dank u. Hochachtung/d. Verf.".
- F. has an inflammation of the jaw and makes an incision by himself.

1884 July 2

- The *Neue Freie Presse* publishes the contents of the *Centralblatt für die gesammte Therapie*, which also contains F.'s work "Ueber Coca". F. is introduced there as a "Sekundararzt in the Imperial and Royal General Hospital". Two days later, a "coca-loving northern railway inspector" (F. to Martha, 4.7.1884) contacted F. to be treated by him.
- F. has lunch with Ernst Fleischl.

1884 July 4

- F. has the prospect of two course participants who together could bring him 100 Gulden.
- F. has not taken cocaine for a fortnight for cost reasons.
- Osias Silberstein, Eduard Silberstein's father, consults F. and pays five Gulden.

1884 July 6

F. visits Friedrich Pineles and his sister Rosa in Oberwaltersdorf near Baden.

1884 July 7

F. has a consultation with Josef Breuer about Osias Silberstein and has to admit his "bad understanding of the case" (F. to Martha, 7.7.1884).

1884 July 8

- F. visits Ernst Fleischl, who suggests that Martha comes to Vienna as a companion of Gabriele von Todesco.
- F. visits Josef Paneth in the evening.

1884 July 11

F. applies to the management of the Allgemeines Krankenhaus for leave from July 13 to August 14. Primarius (head of department) Franz Scholz approves the application.

1884 July 12

- F. is called to Josef Hoffmann, the director of the Allgemeines Krankenhaus, because of his holiday plans. The government of Montenegro had requested three doctors to prevent the introduction of cholera at the borders. F. was to head the IV Medical Department during their absence of six weeks. He therefore has to postpone his planned trip to Martha in Wandsbek until a later date.
- F. visits Ernst Fleischl, Adolf Schwab and Josef Paneth.
- F. receives a visit from Josef Breuer, who brings him 50 Gulden.

1884 July mid

Martha's mother asks Eli and Anna if Martha, if she returns to Vienna, can live with them. F. is outraged.

- 1884 July 15
- F. is appointed the head of department (Primarius) of the IV Medical Department (Nervous Diseases) of the Allgemeines Krankenhaus. He intends to treat his patients, the warders and the secondary doctors well.

- F. sends Martha cocoa powder and writes: "Coca is enclosed today. If you are tired and out of sorts or have complaints after eating, take one half in a wine glass of water. If it does not work, take the other half after an hour" (F. to Martha, 15.7.1884).

1884 July 17
- F. receives a ring from Martha that is a little too big. F. has it made tighter.
- F. acquires Alexander Lustig as a Sekundararzt for his department.

1884 July 18
For F., the "racket [as head of department] is truly great […] cases come into the hospital which are thought to be cholera, but then turn out [to be] cardiac paralysis as a result of the heat" (F. to Martha, 18.7.1884).

1884 July 19
F. receives a decree from the director of the Allgemeines Krankenhaus appointing him as provisional primary physician and head of department; this also entails a salary increase to 45 Gulden for the next three months.

1884 July 20 approx.
F. hears that the director of the Allgemeines Krankenhaus has said "he has never had such a service-minded doctor [as F.] in the house" (F. to Martha, 21.7.1884).

1884 July 28
F. is called to Adolf Fleischl, an uncle of Ernst Fleischl. He receives ten Gulden for the visit.

1884 July 31
F. hopes to publish a small clinical note about a rare diagnosis of a patient who has just died.

1884 August 2
The post-mortem examination of the patient shows that F.'s diagnosis was correct.

1884 August beginning
F.'s family moves from Kaiser-Josef-Strasse 3 to Darwingasse 32 (until November 1885).

1884 August 1
- F. goes to the director of the Allgemeines Krankenhaus to make sure this time that he can take his leave planned from September 1.
- F. gets two new Sekundarärzte.

1884 August 7
F. sends Martha cocaine again: "[…] two coca powders, to be taken four times, best after meals or early" (F. to Martha, 7.8.1884).

1884 August 9
F. goes to the plaza music in front of the town hall with Ignaz Widder, with whom he spends many evenings.

1884 August 11
Heinrich Obersteiner gives a lecture at a medical Congress in Copenhagen "On the use of cocaine in neuroses and psychoses" and also mentions F.'s part in researching the effects of cocaine.

1884 August 13
F. gets a visit from his sister Rosa.

1884 August 14
F. visits his family in the new flat at Darwingasse 32. The family stays there until November 1885.

1884 August 17
- F. goes on an excursion to Dornbach with four colleagues. The company visits the same inn where F. and Martha had once spent a quiet evening.
- F. advises Leopold Königstein to experiment with cocaine on the eye and to publish something about it.

1884 August 18
F.'s mother comes back to Vienna from Rožnau.

1884 August 19
- F. gets a visit from his mother.
- F. visits Josef Breuer.

1884 August 25
F.'s leave is approved by Primarius Franz Scholz.

1884 August 28
F. receives 30 Gulden from a patient in Temesvar. He gives it to his mother.

1884 August 29
F. visits Josef Breuer. Sigmund Lustgarten is also there. F. tells Breuer about his idea to use cocaine in the treatment of eye diseases. However, Breuer warns of possible trophic disorders of the cornea.

1884 August end
Karl Koller discovers local anesthesia with cocaine on the eye.

1884 August 31–September 30
Second visit to Wandsbek

This visit had been postponed several times. F. received reduced tickets thanks to the mediation of Robert Franceschini.

1884 August 31

Departure from Vienna at 20.45.

1884 September 1

In the evening, F. sends a telegram from Uelzen to Martha announcing his arrival in Hamburg on September 2 at 5.15 am.

1884 September 2

F. arrives in Hamburg at 5.15 am. Martha is waiting for him at the station.

1884 ca. September Mid
- F. and Martha travel to Travemünde and spend "a nice hour" in a beach chair (Martha to F., undated); later Martha gives her husband a model of a beach chair.

1884 September 15

At the Ophthalmological Congress in Heidelberg, Karl Koller has the Trieste physician Josef Brettauer read out a "Preliminary Communication" on the anesthetic effect of cocaine.

1884 September 28

F. leaves Hamburg in the evening. On the way, he reads Benjamin Disraeli's novel *Henrietta Temple: A Love Story*.

1884 September 29

F. arrives at Hamburger Bahnhof on Invalidenstrasse in Berlin early in the morning. He takes a cab to Anhalter Bahnhof, and from there at 7.30 am departure to Dresden. Around noon, F. arrives in Dresden, washes up and has lunch. In Tetschen (now Děčín), F. changes from third to second class.

1884 September 30

F. arrives back in Vienna in the morning.

1884 September 30

F. visits Samuel Hammerschlag.

1884 Autumn

Eli claims to his wife – F.'s sister Anna – that he has started a travel agency.

1884 October 1

– Leopold Königstein visits F. because of the dispute with Karl Koller about the use of cocaine on the eye. F. advises him to give lectures on the subject at the same time as Koller at the Society of Physicians.
– F. visits the Hammerschlag family in the afternoon, then his own family. On the way, he meets Josef Breuer.
– F. gives Primarius Franz Scholz a pen stand.
– F. becomes the first Sekundararzt of the Department of Nervous Diseases at the Allgemeines Krankenhaus (until 1885 February 28).

1884 October 2

– F. is visited by cousin Moritz in the morning and later by Josef Paneth.
– F. receives a visit from Robert Franceschini in the evening. F. gives him a pipe as a thank you for arranging cheap railway tickets to Hamburg.

1884 October 3

– F. gets a visit from cousin Moritz and later from Josef Herzig.
– F. starts observing a patient whose case history he later publishes under the title "Akute multiple Neuritis der spinalen und Hirnnerven".
– F. buys an electric instrument for 15 Gulden.
– F.'s brother Emanuel comes to Vienna for a good two weeks; F. sees him in the evening with his family.

1884 October 4

– F. hands Ernst Brücke a paper on the gold dyeing method.
– F. visits Josef Breuer to give him a lampshade and borrow some money.

1884 October 5

– F. discusses family matters, mainly financial, with brother Emanuel in the afternoon.
– The Freud family is supported with 50 pounds per year by Emanuel Freud and ten Gulden per month by F.
– F. visits Ernst Fleischl in the evening.

1884 October 7
– F. is considering using cocaine to treat diabetes.
– F. is with his family for lunch, to which his brother Emanuel has invited.
– F. makes a sick call in Hernals.

1884 October 9
F. gets a visit from his brother Emanuel.

1884 October 11
– F. gets a visit from his brother Emanuel.
– The Merck company in Darmstadt offers F. to examine Ecgonine, a component of cocaine.

1884 October 12
F. visits his family. Emanuel teaches him to play whist – a precursor to bridge.

1884 October 13
F.'s sister Mitzi returns from Paris.

1884 October 14
F. visits his family in the evening.

1884 October 15
Josef Paneth visits F.

1884 October 17
F. visits the "Society of Physicians". Karl Koller gives a lecture "On the use of cocaine for anesthesia of the eye" and remarks that cocaine has become the focus of interest of Viennese doctors through F.'s publications and therapeutic experiments. After Koller's lecture, Leopold Königstein presents his studies on cocaine as a local anesthetic on the eye, without mentioning F. or Koller.

1884 October 18
– F. makes two sick calls on behalf of Josef Breuer.
– F. receives a visit from Carl Bettelheim.

1884 October 19
– F. visits the Indologist Georg Bühler and learns from him that in August a doctor in England had given a poor prognosis for Ignaz Schönberg's life expectancy.
– The first part of Leopold Königstein's lecture on cocaine as a local anesthetic on the eye appears in the *Wiener Medizinische Presse*, in which Karl Koller is not mentioned.

1884 October 20
Leopold Königstein and Karl Koller set up a court of arbitration to clarify the question of priority with regard to the discovery of cocaine as a local anesthetic on the eye. Königstein appoints F. as his representative, Koller – Julius Wagner-Jauregg. F. meets with Wagner-Jauregg, and they decide to ask Königstein to recognize Koller's priority.

1884 October 21
F. visits Ernst Fleischl and begins to try out Ecgonine with him on frogs, rabbits and dogs.

1884 October 22
– F. gets a visit from his brother Emanuel and his sister Rosa.
– Emanuel leaves Vienna.
– F. visits Josef Breuer in the evening.

1884 October 24
Edmund Jelinek reports on his cocaine experiments to the Society of Physicians in Vienna.

1884 October 26
- F. and Ernst Fleischl used Ecgonine to "kill the first rabbit […]" (F. to Martha, 26.10.1884).
- F. receives five grams of cocaine from the Merck company.
- F. visits the Schwab family in the evening. The Hammerschlag couple is also there.
- The second part of Leopold Königstein's lecture on cocaine as a local anesthetic on the eye appears; in the last paragraph, Königstein acknowledges Karl Koller's priority.

1884 October 27
F. begins to work with Moritz Heitler on a paper on electrotherapy, but it is not published.

1884 October 28
F. is at the Physiological Club. Ernst Fleischl gives a lecture "Über die doppelte Brechung des Lichtes in Flüssigkeiten" ("On the double refraction of light in liquids"). F. presents Hermann Nothnagel with his papers "Die Structur der Elemente des Nervensystems" and "Ueber Coca". The ophthalmologist August Reuss tells F. that his Coca work is revolutionary.

1884 October 29
F. visits Joseph Paneth, who is at home with a cold.

1884 October 30
F. visits the Hammerschlag family.

1884 November beginning
In the winter semester, F. offers lectures on "Electricity and electrodiagnostics" (fee 10 Gulden).

1884 November 2
F. is disappointed after taking a dose of Ecgonine: It neither suppresses hunger nor lifts the mood.

1884 November 3–4
F. has dream of a "Walk in Lübeck".

1884 November 4
F. takes 15 Gulden from two patients.

1884 November 6
F. comes to the conclusion that Ecgonine is "rubbish" and that he is "unfortunately poorer by an indefinite number of great discoveries" (F. to Martha, 6.11.1884).

1884 November 7
F. visits Josef Breuer. There, he also meets Ernst Fleischl.

1884 November 8
- F. begins to measure his strength, fatigue and reaction time under the influence of cocaine every hour with a dynamometer. Later, he publishes the results in his paper "Beitrag zur Kenntnis der Cocawirkung".
- F. meets Hermann Nothnagel, who asks him about the progress of his research.

1884 November 9
F. visits Ernst Fleischl.

1884 November 10
- F. admits a patient to the Allgemeines Krankenhaus, about whose medical history he publishes the paper "Ein Fall von Muskelatrophie mit ausgebreiteten Sensibilitätsstörungen (Syringomyelie)" one year later.
- F. examines the nerve preparation of the patient who died on July 31.

1884 November 11
F. visits the Physiological Club.

1884 November 13
An American, Dr Leslie, visits F. to inquire about the conditions for a course offered by F. He believes he can bring together five to eight participants.

1884 November 14
- F. is at the control meeting for reservists in the morning and therefore has to put on the uniform he hates.
- Dr Leslie visits F. again and informs him that the course participants prefer the afternoon from 3 to 4 pm and that F. should please teach in English. Each of the participants is willing to pay 20–25 Gulden for 25 hours.

1884 November 17
- F. begins his first neuropathology course, held in English, in front of six American listeners.
- Dr. Leslie, who praises the course, visits F. in the evening.
- F. receives a visit from Sigmund Lustgarten, who believes he has discovered a bacillus that is the causative agent of syphilis.

1884 November 18
F. visits Josef Breuer and tells him about his first course.

1884 November 19
- The number of participants in F.'s course increases to seven.
- F. visits his family.

1884 November 21
F. is in the Society of Physicians and hears a lecture by Sigmund Lustgarten on syphilis bacteria.

1884 November 22
F. visits Ernst Fleischl's "Physiologisches Conversatorium".

1884 November 24
The number of participants in F.'s course increases to nine.

1884 November 26
F. conducts experiments with Josef Herzig on the effect of cocaine on reaction time.

1884 November 30
- F. begins a series of free lectures on brain anatomy for colleagues in Heinrich Auspitz's lecture theater, from which he hopes to gain a good reputation in the Allgemeines Krankenhaus.
- F.'s sister Rosa travels via Hamburg to Manchester to visit her brother Emanuel.

1884 December
- F. gives Martha Heinrich Heine's *Buch der Lieder* with the dedication "Zur Erfüllung eines alten Wunsches/Dein Sigmund".

– An article by Robert Franceschini about F.'s cocaine paper appears in the *Neue Freie Presse*. He then receives letters from Italy, England and Hungary.

1884 December beginning
– F. starts lecturing his course on electricity and electrodiagnostics.
– F. sent Carl Weigert in Leipzig some of his preparations. Weigert had demonstrated a method of preparing nerve cells that F. thought was very good or even better than his own.

1884 December 5
F. makes an experiment with cocaine on a patient. Then, he goes to a coffee house to recover from it.

1884 December 6
F. visits Josef Breuer.

1884 December 7
– F.'s Sunday lecture for colleagues has 11 listeners.
– F. visits his family, because his father has foot problems.

1884 December 8
The Rector of the University of Vienna informs the Dean of the Faculty of Medicine about the University Jubilee Travel Grant for the academic year 1885/1886.

1884 December 9
F. visits the Physiological Club.

1884 December 13
F. visits Josef Breuer and Ernst Fleischl.

1884 December 14
– F. talks to Ernst Ludwig about a possible lectureship. Ludwig is well disposed toward him and tells F. that his lectureship would not encounter any difficulties.
– F. admits his brother Alexander to the Allgemeines Krankenhaus. He writes to Martha: "The poor boy will have to atone for an easily understandable carelessness with a few weeks in hospital. Keep quiet about it, it is a strict secret from me" (F. to Martha, 14.12.1884).

1884 December mid
F. reads Friedrich Theodor Vischer's novel *Auch Einer.*

1884 December 16
– Carl Weigert thanks F. for sending the preparations and announces that he will also send preparations himself.
– The pathological anatomist Johann Kundrat confirms a difficult diagnosis of F. and leaves him all the material F. wants.

1884 December 17
F. starts keeping records of his income and expenditure.

1884 December 19
F. has doubts as to whether the substance Merck sent him is really Ecgonine.

1884 December 20
– F. is with Ernst Fleischl on the "Physiological Conservatory".
– F. visits Josef Paneth in the evening.

1884 December 21
F. gives his third lecture for colleagues; this time, he talks about the spinal cord.

1884 December 22
– F. begins his next course, which again lasts five weeks. Among the enrolled participants is Elizabeth Sargent, the daughter of Aaron Sargent, a former senator and American envoy in Berlin.
– A 28-year-old patient from F.'s ward commits suicide by jumping out of the window. F. submits a report to the director and also presents himself to him. The director acknowledges the "blamelessness of the guards". A report to the governor's office also assumes no misconduct on the part of the guards.

1884 December 24
F. begins writing his second publications on cocaine: "Beitrag zur Kenntniss der Cocawirkung".

1884 December 25
F. visits his family.

1884 December 27
F. visits Josef Paneth in the evening and is then in a coffee house until late at night.

1884 December 28
F. visits the Hammerschlag family, where the graduation (PhD) of son Paul is celebrated. The Breuer and Schwab families are also guests.

1884 December 29
F. shows his preparations to Theodor Meynert in the laboratory. Meynert also mentions Franceschini's article about F.'s cocaine paper in the *Neue Freie Presse.*

1884 December 31
F. spends New Year's Eve in an inn with Moritz Horowitz and two other colleagues.

1884 December end
– F. urges the Sekundarärzte to draw up a petition for the acquisition of microscopes. He is himself a member of the committee that is to draw up this petition.
– F. begins to treat sciatica and neuralgia with special injections.

1885

F. gives lectures on the medulla oblongata to visiting doctors.

1885 January
F. tries to combat trigeminal neuralgia by injecting cocaine and uses the same method for Ernst Fleischl's neuroma pain, but without success.

1885 January beginning
- F. has a "combined nose-throat-palate-ear catarrh" (F. to Martha, 7.1.1885).
- F. is annoyed by letters about cocaine: "People ask for the drug or the brochure or send me their medical history and want to ordain me by letter" (F. to Martha, 9.1.1885).

1885 January 2
F. meets with Theodor Meynert.

1885 January 5
- F. goes to Josef Weinlechner and Joseph Standhartner and asks for permission to treat all neuralgia cases in their wards; he gets permission.
- F. visits Josef Breuer and meets Ernst Fleischl there.

1885 January 6
- F. receives six bottles of wine from Joseph Paneth. F. gives most of the bottles to his family.
- Duel between Karl Koller and his colleague Friedrich Zinner. Zinner had insulted Koller as a "Saujud" ("filthy Jew") and was then punched in the face by Koller. Before the duel, F. gives Koller one of Paneth's wine bottles to strengthen him. Koller remains unhurt, and Zinner sustains two injuries, one is serious. F. congratulates Koller in a letter the same evening and offers him to call each other by their first names.
- F. sends the recently published *Zur Judenfrage: Ein neuer Literatur-Schädling. Herr Isidor Singer* by the doctor and German nationalist poet Josef Winter.
- F. visits Josef Breuer in the evening; the topic of conversation is Koller's duel. Ernst Fleischl is also present.
- 1885 January 11
- F. discharges a patient who had suffered from sciatica and recovered by means of an injection he invented.
- F. gives the last lecture on the spinal cord to colleagues. Richard Wahle, who is also among the listeners, accompanies him to his room afterward.

1885 January 12
- Steiner von Pfungen informs F. that he has received permission to read a course on the same subject as F.
- Richard Wittelshöfer, the editor of the *Wiener Medizinische Wochenschrift*, promises F. to publish the papers "Beitrag zur Kenntniss der Cocawirkung" and "Ein Fall von Muskelatrophie mit ausgebreiteten Sensibilitätsstörungen" by the end of February to prevent F. from offering them to another journal.
- F. wants to do without coffee and pub visits in the future, buy a coffee machine and eat at home.

1885 January 14
- Steiner von Pfungen wants to read his course at the same hour as F.'s course.
- F. visits Josef Breuer, who encourages him to get a lectureship as soon as possible.

1885 January mid
F. completes his paper on muscular atrophy.

1885 January 16
F. goes to Hermann Nothnagel to ask his advice about applying for a lectureship. F. presents him with a list of his publications, and Nothnagel encourages him to submit the application and assures F. of his support.

1885 January 17
F. announces to Martha that one of his course participants, Richard Prichard from Wales, will visit her in Hamburg on his return journey home. Prichard struck F. with his energy, intelligence and friendliness and was very likable to him.

1885 January 19
F.'s Primararzt (head of department) Franz Scholz gives him permission to give lectures in the department.

1885 January 21
- F. applies for Privatdozent (private lectureship) in neuropathology and submits his habilitation treatise together with a curriculum, his "curriculum vitae" and 11 publications. He has previously secured the support of Ernst Ludwig and Theodor Meynert. Ludwig also tries to convince the anatomist Hans Kundrat in an inn.
- F. acquires Jean-Martin Charcot's Clinical Lectures on Diseases of the Nervous System and his Lectures on Localization in Diseases of the Brain.
- F. has some books bound for him.

1885 January 24
F.'s application for Privatdozent is assigned by the Professorenkollegium to a committee consisting of Ernst Brücke, Hermann Nothnagel and Theodor Meynert.

1885 January 29
- F. writes down his paper "A case of muscular atrophy with extensive disturbances of sensitivity (syringomyelia)".
- F. visits the Psychiatrische Verein. Theodor Meynert presents two children with clonic seizures, and Alexander Holländer gives a lecture on "Newer Theories of Epilepsy".

1885 January 30
- Of 17 registered participants for F.'s third course, 14 came. Only two registered for the "electrical course".
- F. visits Josef Breuer.

1885 February 1
Ernst Brücke declares his willingness to act as a principal consultant for F.'s application for Privatdozent.

1885 February 2
F. is at the Physiological Club. He was actually supposed to give a lecture on cocaine, but it is postponed until March 3. Afterward, all participants of the meeting go to the Riedhof, a restaurant in Weihburggasse 9 popular with the doctors of the Allgemeines Krankenhaus.

1885 February 5
- Hermann Nothnagel joins Ernst Brücke and declares his willingness to support F.'s application for Privatdozent.
- F. buys 100 cigars with which he wants to get by for the rest of the month.

1885 February 8
- F.'s third course has only nine participants.
- F. visits his family and then goes to the Breuer family. He tests the 16-year-old son Robert in anatomy, which he learns at school, and has 15-year-old Bertha tell him stories.

1885 February 9
- F.'s prospects of becoming an assistant to Meynert dwindle because of developments within the hospital. He asks Martha: "Surely you agree that I do not want to know anything about ungrateful psychiatry". (F. to Martha, 9.2.1885).
- F. loses three Gulden playing tarot.

1885 February 10
Theodor Meynert informs F. that his application for Privatdozent is at his home. F. concludes that Meynert will be the reviewer.

1885 February 13
- F. visits his cousin Dolcza Nathansohn (daughter of Hermann Nathansohn, the brother of F.'s mother) from Odessa, who is in Vienna for eye treatment.
- F. receives a letter from St. Joseph in Missouri asking for cocaine to be sent to him. It was presumably a representative of the "Missouri Meerschaum Company". He wanted to reimburse the costs later. F. does not even answer him – because of the small chance that he will be reimbursed for his expenses.

1885 February 14
Birth of F.'s niece Judith Bernays, daughter of his sister Anna.

1885 February mid
F. has "enough of all this cocaine" (F. to Martha, 13.2.1885).

1885 February 17
F. is with Josef Herzig at the Altdeutsche Weinstube and then at Café Kurzweil.

1885 February 20
- The hospital director informs F. that Primararzt (head of department) Franz Scholz wants F. to be "transferred" because he wants to meet other doctors.
- F. visits Josef Breuer in the evening.

1885 February 21
F. visits the Hammerschlag family in the evening for Betty's birthday.

1885 February 24
- The hospital director informs F. of his decision that on March 1, F. must transfer to the department for eye patients headed by Eduard Jaxtthal.
- F. goes to Theodor Meynert and tells him that he is interested in an assistantship with him.

1885 February 28
Ernst Brücke presents the committee for F.'s Privatdozent the report, signed by him, Hermann Nothnagel and Theodor Meynert. The report is accepted by 21 votes to 1, and F. is thus admitted to go ahead for Privatdozent.

1885 March beginning
F. practices with the ophthalmoscope and attends a course on it. He also learns to determine glasses and to check for people with color blindness and visual field impairments.

1885 March 1
– Ernst Ludwig informs F. that he has been admitted to the colloquium for Privatdozent.
– F. transfers to the department for eye patients and stays there until the end of May. He has to give up his courses, sees his hospital career interrupted and considers settling down as a neurologist.
– F. visits Josef Breuer in the evening; there is a "veritable dance party", including Schwabs and Hammerschlags. F. "fitted it like cholera would have fitted it" (F. to Martha, 2.3.1885).

1885 March 3
F. gives a lecture at the Physiological Club "On the general effect of cocaine". He is somewhat attacked by Hermann Nothnagel, but feels he is treated as an equal colleague. Afterward, he goes to the Riedhof inn with Sigmund Exner and Heinrich Obersteiner.

1885 March 4
F. is considering applying for the university's travel scholarship and going to Jean-Martin Charcot in Paris after his probation lecture.

1885 March 5
F. also gives his lecture "On the general effects of cocaine" at the Psychiatric Association. Afterward, the correspondent of the *Lancet* contacted him and asked for an auto-abstract.

1885 March 6
F. reports to the Dean's Office as an applicant for the travel scholarship.

1885 March 6–7
F. has a dream about a girl who falls into the water and almost drowns, but he does nothing to save her.

1885 March 10
– F. finishes his neuropathology course for English and American students.
– F. applies for the position of I. Sekundararzt at the III Medical Department of the Wiener Allgemeines Krankenhaus (Head: Isidor Hein).
– F. visits Josef Breuer.

1885 March 12
– F. believes he can bring about a methodological revolution in brain anatomy by staining whole sections, making them transparent and then transilluminating them.
– F. visits Ernst Fleischl, who has offered to lend him some money again.
– F. recommends Martha to read two speeches by Sigmund Conrad, Minister of Culture and Education, to see what prospects a Jew has at an Austrian university.

1885 March mid
– F.'s application for the position of I. Sekundararzt at the III Medical Department is rejected.
– Moritz Freud gives F. a Smyrna carpet – a Persian selvedge – for their future home together.

1885 March 16
F. is called to Ernst Fleischl because Carl Weigert from Leipzig is there and shows his preparations. Later, Theodor Meynert also joins them.

1885 March 20
F. visits Josef Breuer.

1885 March 23
– F. tries to electrify a patient, but he faints and falls on the floor.
– F. writes down his lecture of March 5 "Ueber die Allgemeinwirkung des Cocains" for publication.

1885 March 27
F. visits the Society of Physicians.

1885 March 28
F. visits Ernst Fleischl.

1885 March 31
F. visits Josef Breuer for lunch.

1885 April
– F. conducts experiments with rabbits and experiments with cocaine together with Leopold Königstein.
– F. gives Heinrich Obersteiner an offprint of his paper "Ein Fall von Muskelatrophie mit ausgebreiteten Sensibilitätsstörungen (Syringomyelie)" with the dedication "Herrn Prof. H. Obersteiner in besonderer Hochachtung der Verf.".

1885 April 1
F. reads a paper by Wladimir Bechterew in the *Neurologisches Centralblatt*, who discovers "a piece of my brain anatomy right under my nose" (F. to Martha, 8.4.1885).

1885 April 3
– F. withdraws his application for the post of I. Sekundararzt.
– F. visits Ernst Fleischl. There, he meets Philipp Karl von Liechtenstein, Rudolf Chrobak and Heinrich Obersteiner.

1885 April 5
F. gets a visit from his father, who complains of vision problems. Karl Koller diagnoses glaucoma. Leopold Königstein is then consulted.

1885 April 6
– Leopold Königstein operates on F.'s father for glaucoma; local anesthesia is administered by Karl Koller and F. Later, F. brings his father home.
– F. is invited to lunch with Königstein and his wife Henriette.
– In the afternoon, F. visits his sister Anna and her seven-week-old daughter Judith.

1885 April 7
F. visits Josef Breuer.

1885 April 9
- F. moves into a new room in the Allgemeines Krankenhaus. The "new flat is very friendly, a room on the first floor, which has air, light and space, and a cabinet opposite in the corridor". For the first time, F. is "a really intelligent and skillful waitress" (F. to Martha, 16.4.1885).
- F. visits Ernst Fleischl in the evening and stays until the next morning.

1885 April 11
The American company "Parke, Davis & Co." from Detroit offers F. 60 Gulden to compare their cocaine preparation with that of the Merck company. F. publishes the result under the title "Gutachten über das Parke Cocaïn".

1885 April 13
F. visits Ernst Fleischl in the evening and stays until the next morning.

1885 April 18
- F. applies for the University Jubilee Travel Scholarship advertised by the Academic Senate of the University of Vienna, which was announced on 1884 December 8; co-applicants are Friedrich Dimmer (II. Eye Clinic) and Julius Hochenegg (I. Surgical Clinic).
- F. visits Theodor Meynert.
- F. visits Josef Breuer in the evening. Breuer discovers small blisters on F.'s forehead and neck and diagnoses a mild form of smallpox; F. reports being sick for three days.

1885 after April 18
F. receives many visitors during his sickbed: Ignaz Rosanes, Albert Hammerschlag, his sister Dolfi and cousin Moritz. Josef Paneth gives him a chocolate cake and three bottles of wine. F. sends the wine to his parents, and eats the cake with Sigmund Lustgarten.

1885 April 20
F. invites Leopold Königstein in order to make together an experiment with cocaine.

1885 April 25
- Sigmund Lustgarten, who treats F. for smallpox, suggests that F. put his letters to Martha (including envelope) in a drying box at 120° C for a few hours before sending them so that they cannot transmit smallpox.
- Cocaine from the American company Parke, Davis & Co. arrives. F. tests it on two rabbits.

1885 April 26
F. notes that the cocaine from Parke, Davis & Co. has the same properties as that from Merck.

1885 April 28
- F. visits Ernst Fleischl in the morning.
- F. destroys all his notes, scientific excerpts, manuscripts of his works and letters (except those from Martha and his family).

1885 April end
F. occupies himself with Russian history.

1885 May
- F. treats rabies with cocaine and deals intensively with brain anatomy.
- F. gives Heinrich Obersteiner a offprint of his paper "Über die Allgemeinwirkung des Cocaïns" with the dedication "Herrn Prof. H. Obersteiner in bes. Hochachtung der Verf.".

1885 May beginning
Martha receives 4000 marks from her aunt Lea Löw-Beer from Brünn and a "family legacy" of 1500 marks. Their total assets now amount to 7000 marks.[15]

1885 May 1
F. visits with Ernst Fleischl and meets there Heinrich Obersteiner, and later, Elise von Klinkosch, whom Hans Makart immortalized in his painting "Einzug Karls V. in Antwerpen". As F. knew the picture, he immediately recognized Mrs. Klinkosch.

1885 May 2
F. is at the farewell party for Josef Pollak and Alfred Wiesenthal. F. gives a speech, which is very positively received.

1885 May 4–6
Short trip to the Semmering region

1885 May 4

F. departs from Südbahnhof at 12.30 pm. In his luggage is "an umbrella, a new penknife and Goethe's Faust in a lovely small edition" and cocaine (F. to Martha, 4.5.1885). Around 4.00 pm, he arrives in Payerbach. From there, he hikes via the ruins of Klamm castle, the Church of Maria Schutz and Sonnwendstein to the Erzherzog-Johann-Haus.

1885 May 5

F. sets off from the Erzherzog-Johann-Haus at 8.00 am and walks to Spital. There, he drinks a glass of wine at the "Goldener Hirschen" and determines his "cruising speed" at 100 m per minute. From Spital, he hikes on via Mürzzuschlag to Kapellen. He will be there at 3 pm. But as it is raining heavily, he decides to spend the night in Kapellen.

1885 May 6

On the morning of F.'s birthday, there is snow on the mountains and F. cannot go back to Reichenau on his originally planned route over the mountains without mountain boots. He makes a detour to Neuberg and then takes the train from Mürzzuschlag back to Vienna at 12.00 pm. He arrives there at 5.00 pm.

1885 May 7
- F. visits his family.
- F. orders two suits from his tailor Franz Tischer. He also buys new boots.

1885 May 8 approx.
F. shows his preparations to Theodor Meynert and receives his approval for publication.

1885 May 9
F. receives the ordered suits.

1885 May 12
- F. asks Emanuel Mendel to include a short communication in the *Neurologisches Zentralblatt* published by him; it is presumably the paper "Zur Kenntnis der Olivenzwischenschicht". In mid-May, he receives an acceptance.
- F. gives a lecture on brain anatomy at the Physiological Club.

1885 May 15
F. is at the Dean's Office to ask about his "business".

1885 May mid
- F. introduces himself to Leopold Dittel (head of the III Surgical Department of the Allgemeines Krankenhaus), Moritz Benedikt (head of the Department of Electrotherapy and Neuropathology at the General Polyclinic) and Adam Politzer (head of the University Ear Clinic).
- F. has several migraine attacks and treats them with cocaine.

1885 May 16
F. visits Ernst Fleischl.

1885 May 17
F. believes he has missed out on an important finding because a preparation in which he had placed great hopes was unusable.

1885 May 18
- F. is visited by his sisters Mitzi and Paula; they bring their friend Rosa Zeisler who is about to leave for her wedding in Chicago.
- A distant relative of F. comes to Vienna and asks for advice.
- F. goes to town to buy "drawing props", and visits the veterinary surgeon Franz Müller and later a patient.
- F. learns that rabies can possibly also be treated with cocaine. This, however, turns out to be a deceptive hope.
- F. visits his family in the evening.

1885 May 20
F. visits Ernst Fleischl and stays until the next morning.

1885 May 21
- F. receives a visit from his mother. She reports serious financial problems and insists that her son should leave the Allgemeines Krankenhaus quickly and get married. Then, he would quickly get better.
- F. talks to Josef Paneth about "future housing fatalities" (F. to Martha, 23.5.1885).

1885 May 23
An American introduces himself to F. on the recommendation of Sigmund Exner, as he might want to take lessons with him.

1885 May 24
F. visits Ernst Fleischl and stays until the next morning.

1885 May 27
The American starts taking lessons in physiology with F.

1885 May 28
F. visits Joseph and Sophie Paneth.

1885 May 29
- F. gets a microscope from Joseph Paneth so that he can show the American his preparations.
- F. visits Josef Breuer in the evening.

1885 May 30
- The medical faculty meets to discuss the awarding of the travel grant, but does not reach a decision.
- F.'s brother Alexander travels to Prague.
- F. visits the Hammerschlag family.

1885 May 31
F. visits Ernst Fleischl. He only has ½ gram of cocaine left and hopes to get a supply from Fleischl. Fleischl promises him it for the next day. He also tells F. that Heinrich Obersteiner wants F. to be his assistant at the Döbling sanatorium for three weeks. F. immediately goes to Obersteiner.

1885 June
- F. meets Josef Podrazky, who had sentenced him to arrest five years ago during his one-year military service.
- F. examines Ignaz Schönberg, who returned to Vienna in May due to his poor health after a year at the Indian Institute in Oxford.

1885 June 1
F. moves to Moriz Kaposi's department for skin diseases. Kaposi receives F. very kindly and introduces him to his listeners.

1885 June 2
- Death of Rebekka Freud, the wife of his uncle Josef.
- F. sends Martha ½ gram of cocaine, enough for five large doses. Martha replies "that coca is something heavenly" (Martha to F., 6.6.1885).

1885 June 4
- F. visits Josef Breuer.
- F. visits his family. His sister Anna also happens to be there. Both then go to the Prater with their little daughter Judith.
- In the evening, F. visits Ernst Fleischl, who has a cocaine addiction, and Ernst Brücke is already with him. F. stays with Fleischl until the next morning, writing to Martha that it was "the most terrible night I have ever experienced" (F. to Martha, 5.6.1885). F. becomes convinced that Fleischl took "terrible doses of cocaine, which finally did him a lot of harm" (F. to Martha, 8.6.1885).

1885 June 5
The College of Professors appoints a committee to award the University Anniversary Travel Scholarship, consisting of Ernst Brücke, Heinrich Bamberger, Carl Stellwag and Eduard Albert.

1885 June 6
F. receives the invitation to the colloquium, which he is to take in front of the professors on June 13.

1885 June 7
- F. takes up a three-week substitute post at the private sanatorium Oberdöbling in Hirschengasse 71 (now Obersteinergasse). He has many scientific and personal points of contact with Heinrich Obersteiner. The patients are "rich people, counts, countesses, barons and the like", among them, Wilhelm Albrecht Prince of Montenuovo, a grandson of Emperor Franz I (F. to Martha, 8.6.1885).

- F. is temporarily accommodated in the library, "a cool room with a view of all the hills around Vienna, in which there is a microscope and on the walls a treasure of literature of the nervous system, with which it is difficult to be bored" (F. to Martha, 8.6.1885).
- In the evening, F. goes into town.

1885 June 8

F. starts collecting literature for his paper "Acute multiple neuritis of the spinal and cranial nerves".

1885 June 10

- At the meeting of the committee of the medical faculty to award the university anniversary travel grant of 600 Gulden[16], Ernst Brücke speaks up for F.
- Anna Hammerschlag becomes engaged to Rudolf Lichtheim, and F. congratulates her mother Betty on the occasion. Lichtheim dies a good six months after the wedding.

1885 June 11

- F. visits Ernst Fleischl. For the first time, he has the feeling that he has come at an inopportune moment and that Fleischl is ashamed of him.
- F. meets the Indologist Georg Bühler and learns from him that he intends to send Ignaz Schönberg to India the next year.
- F. is given a room for the time of his substitute service in Döbling. He furnishes it, among other things with his books and brain preparations, which he has sent from the Allgemeines Krankenhaus, as he expects to be bored in the sanatorium.
- Heinrich Obersteiner gives him neurological books.
- In the evening, there is a society with a game of tarot, to which F. is invited.

1885 June 12

F. bought a top hat and gloves for the colloquium for admission to Privatdozent the next day and borrowed a tailcoat.

1885 June 13

- F. takes some cocaine and passes the colloquium held by Ernst Brücke and Theodor Meynert for admission to Privatdozent.
- F. visits Josef Breuer.
- F. visits Ernst Fleischl and stays until the next morning.

1885 June 15

F. receives two photos from Martha, one of them a "double picture" with Minna.

1885 June mid

- Max Leidesdorf, the official director of the psychiatric clinic in Oberdöbling, advises F. to look into nervous diseases in children.
- F. dreams of the travel grant almost every night.
- F.'s mother goes for a spa stay at Rožnau (until the end of August). Later, Mitzi and Anna also go with daughter Judith.

1885 June 15

The committee for the award of the travel scholarship proposes F.; Ernst Brücke in particular strongly supports F.

1885 June 20

The Professors' Committee approves F.'s habilitation lecture on the topic "On the time sequence of whitening of medullary bundles in the brain" by 19 votes to 3. It also nominates F. for the travel grant by 13 votes to 9. Ernst Brücke's support of F. in particular tipped the scales in his favor. But Theodor Meynert and Ernst Ludwig also stood up to the "anti-Semitic mood". He writes to his sister Rosa: "I consider it a very happy event for my education and position here in the city when I return" (F. to Rosa, 20.6.1885).

1885 June 22

Heinrich Obersteiner shows F. hypnotic experiments on a nurse, and F. then tries to hypnotize himself, but only brings it to drowsiness.

1885 June 23

F. continues his experiments with self-hypnosis.

1885 June 24

- F. gets a visit from sister Paula in the morning.
- F. visits Ernst Brücke and thanks him for his commitment to the travel grant.
- F. meets Josef Herzig and Leopold Königstein at the Allgemeines Krankenhaus.
- F. goes to a coffee house with Josef Paneth and Sigmund Exner.
- F. visits Josef Paneth in the evening; they have a cheerful dinner and play chess.
- F. visits Josef Breuer late in the evening.
- F. visits Ernst Fleischl.
- F. sends Martha an offprint of his paper "Zur Kenntniss der Olivenzwischenschicht" with the dedication "Seinem geliebten Prinzesschen als Abschreckung diesen 'Ersten Band' seiner Hirnanatomie".

1885 June 26

- F. believes that his "complicated existence" will leave traces (F. to Martha, 26.6.1885).
- F. puts his test lecture on paper in the evening.

1885 June 27

At 12.30 pm, F. gives his test lecture on "The time of whitening of the medullary fibers of the brain" in Ernst Brücke's lecture theater. Ernst Brücke, Theodor Meynert and Ernst Fleischl are among those present. Afterward, F. has lunch with Ernst Fleischl.

1885 June 29

F.'s cousin Moritz goes away for seven months.

1885 June 30

- F. moves back to Moriz Kaposi's department in the Allgemeines Krankenhaus after his work in Oberdöbling.
- F. visits Josef Breuer.
- F. visits Moritz Benedikt in the evening to inform himself about the conditions in Paris. Benedikt gives F. six letters of recommendation, including one to Jean-Martin Charcot.
- F. makes a first attempt with a "new gold method".

1885 June end

- Josef Breuer takes Ernst Fleischl's promise to give up cocaine.
- F. reads fairy tales by E. T. A. Hoffmann.

1885 July beginning
Anna Silberstein, the mother of Eduard Silberstein, is in Vienna for two days with her daughter Minna. F. asks Hermann Nothnagel for a consultation – whether because of her or daughter Minna is not clear.

1885 July 1
- F. goes to the festive farewell of Alexander Holländer.
- F. goes to Prater with Josef Herzig and the sisters Paula and Dolfi.
- The Centralblatt *für Nervenheilkunde und Psychiatrie* publishes a paper by Albrecht Erlenmeyer criticizing the use of cocaine for morphine withdrawal.

1885 July 4
- F. visits Ernst Fleischl.
- F. is to "pub" in honor of Julius Mauthner, who has become an associate professor.

1885 July 5
- F. visits Ernst Fleischl.
- The medical faculty decides to award the university anniversary travel grant to F. However, it is not released until October 1.

1885 July 6
F. Leopold Königstein tells F. about Julius Mauthner's anti-Semitic attitude toward colleagues.

1885 July 9
F. gets another, smaller room in the III Hof of the Allgemeines Krankenhaus.

1885 July 10
F. wants to stop smoking to wean himself off for Paris.

1885 July 11
- F. has a consultation with Hermann Nothnagel.
- Max Kassowitz, the director of the I. Öffentliche Kinderkrankeninstitut in Vienna, intends to expand the institute into a children's polyclinic in the spring of 1886 and to offer the department for nervous diseases to F.

1885 July 13
F. says goodbye to Josef Paneth, who goes to his parents-in-law in Reichenberg in Bohemia for a longer period of time, where they have a textile company.

1885 July 14
F. visits Josef Breuer in the evening.

1885 July 15
F. starts taking French lessons, which he wants to start with 12 lessons per month.

1885 July 16–17
F. has intestinal problems and migraine.

1885 July 17
F. visits Ernst Fleischl and stays until the next morning. In the evening, Guido Goldschmiedt, whom F. knew from Ernst Ludwig's chemical institute, is also there.

1885 July 18
- The College of Professors decides: "Since Dr. Freud has met the legal requirements and has also given the test lecture to our satisfaction, the College unanimously pronounces his habilitation".
- The Rector of Vienna University, Hermann Zschokke not only asks the Dean of the Faculty of Medicine to inform F. about the award of the travel grant but also addresses a letter to F. himself.
- F. receives several French books from Josef Breuer.

1885 July 21
F. is referred a brain-diseased child by Max Kassowitz.

1885 July 23
F. has his last day of work at the Allgemeines Krankenhaus.

1885 July 23–24
Short trip with sister Dolfi to the Semmering region

1885 July 23

At 1.30 pm, departure from Vienna-Meidling to Payerbach. From there, F. and Dolfi hike via the Klamm ruin and the Adlitzgräben to the Semmering. They arrive there late in the evening and spend the night at the "Erzherzog Johann" inn.

1885 July 24

In the morning, return journey to Vienna.

1885 July 26
F.'s habilitation documents are sent to the Ministry of Education.

1885 July 27
F. acquires Jacob Heiberg's *Atlas of the Skin Nerve Areas.*

1885 July 28
F. meets his cousin Simon Nathansohn by chance and spends the day with him. Among other things, they go to the Fürsttheater in the Prater and see *Der Zerrissene* by Johann Nestroy, one of F.'s favorite plays.

1885 July 30
- F. sees The *Magic Flute* at the Court Opera, but was disappointed: "The plot is very stupid, the libretto insane, a comparison with Don Juan is quite inadmissible" (F. to Martha, 31.7.1885).
- F. visits Ernst Fleischl.

1885 July 31
- The Ministry of Education requests the Governor for Lower Austria to "report on the political and moral conduct of Dr Sigmund Freud".
- F. buys an eye mirror.
- F. visits Ernst Fleischl and says goodbye to him, as Fleischl is going to St. Gilgen for a longer period of time.

1885 July end
- Giacomo Ricchetti, a well-known doctor from Venice, is in Vienna, and Theodor Meynert introduces him to F. Ricchetti invites him to Venice, and F. suggests to Martha that they

use this offer for their honeymoon: Ricchetti has "22 rooms and no children" (F. to Martha, 1.8.1885).

- F. reads *The Adventures of Tom Sawyer* by Mark Twain and *Paradoxes* by Max Nordau. F. reads the latter because he suspects he will meet Nordau in Paris, who lives there and is a German doctor of Jewish descent.

1885 August 1
F. signs out with the director of the Allgemeines Krankenhaus.

1885 August 3
F. is at the Riedhof with colleagues for a trout dinner.

1885 August 4
- F. is at a dinner at the Riedhof to which Moriz Kaposi has invited his staff and colleagues, including Giacomo Ricchetti, Sigmund Lustgarten, two clinical assistants and an American.
- Ricchetti lends F. the novella *Pretty Polly Pemberton* by Frances Burnett, which F. reads until the evening of the next day.

1885 August 6
F. visits Ignaz Schönberg in Baden.

1885 August 7
F. received the official letter awarding the travel grant and the announcement that he would shortly receive confirmation as a lecturer.

1885 August 8
F. visits Ignaz Schönberg in Baden. He is accompanied by Moritz Heitler, who does not believe that Schönberg will live for more than 1½ years.

1885 August 9
F.'s expert opinion on cocaine produced by the American company Parke, Davis & Co. of Detroit appears in the *Wiener Medizinische Presse.*

1885 August 11
F.'s tailor comes to fit him with a new black coat.

1885 August 12
F. receives the four volumes of George Eliot's *Middlemarch.*

1885 August 13
F. has to go to the police station, probably because of the character reference for Privatdozent.

1885 August 13–14
F. visits Ignaz Schönberg in Baden; both attend the *Beggar's Student* by Carl Millöcker at the theater there.

1885 August 15–16
F. visits the Hammerschlag family in Hainfeld. On the way back, F. goes to Leobersdorf at 7 am and continues on foot via Teesdorf and Tattendorf to Oberwaltersdorf.

1885 August 16–17
F. visits Josef Herzig in Oberwaltersdorf. There, a "company of four old people, half a dozen in middle age, five young girls, eight young people and three charming children" is gathered.

F. spends the day bowling and playing tarot in this company; in the "evening there was singing and piano playing" (F. to Martha, 18.8.1885).

1885 August 18
F.'s tailor comes for the second fitting of the black coat.

1885 August 20
– Giacomo Ricchetti promises to visit F. in Paris.
– F. visits Josef Breuer.

1885 August 21
F. visits Ignaz Schönberg in Baden.

1885 before August 23
F. is at the Riedhof with Ignaz Rosanes and Sigmund Lustgarten and meets his brother-in-law Eli there.

1885 August 24
– F. goes to the passport office, picks up his watch from the watchmaker and buys a wallet.
– F. visits his family in the evening, then Josef Breuer.

1885 August 25
– F. visits Ignaz Schönberg in Baden.
– F.'s mother comes back to Vienna from her spay stay in Rožnau.
– F.'s sister Rosa returns to Vienna from her longer stay in Manchester, accompanied by her brother Emanuel.
– F. visits his family in the evening and also meets Rosa and Emanuel there.

1885 August 26
– The governor's office informs the Ministry of Education "that Dr Sigmund Freud appears to be indecent in moral and civic terms".
– F. spends the whole day with his family.

1885 August 29
F.'s furniture is taken from his room in the Allgemeines Krankenhaus.

1885 August 30
F. packs his suitcases and in the meantime receives a visit from "a dear old woman" who tells him "that she has a bride for him in every respect, who is a close relative of Prof. [Adam] Politzer (F. to Martha, 28.4.1886).

1885 August 31–October 11
Third visit to Wandsbek and onward journey to Paris
F. visits Martha in Wandsbek and, thanks to the support of the doctor Karl Eisenlohr, is able to examine a larger contingent of nervous patients in the Hamburg General Hospital and the Heinespital. In addition, through Karl Eisenlohr he also gains access to the Klein-Friedrichsberg "lunatic asylum".

1885 August 31
F. leaves Vienna at 8.10 am on a Nordbahn express train. In the late afternoon, he meets Karl Koller during a stopover in Teplitz.

1885 September 1

F. arrives at the Venlo train station in Hamburg at 5.15 am.

1885 September 5

The Minister of Culture and Education confirms F.'s appointment as a private lecturer.

1885 September 11

Confirmation of F.'s admission as a private lecturer in neuropathology by the Vice-Dean Gustav Braun.

1885 October 11

F. leaves Wandsbek in the morning for Paris. Minna Bernays accompanied him to Münster.

1885 October 11

In the evening, F. arrives in Cologne and makes a first tour of the city.

1885 October 12

In the morning, F. takes an extensive tour of the city of Cologne. The towers of the cathedral seem too low to him. Around noon, he travels on to Brussels. There, he stays in a hotel in the Rue du Fossé aux Loups.

1885 October 13

In the morning, F. spends 3½ hours visiting Brussels, including the stock exchange, the Palace of Justice and the City Hall, which he likes much better than the one in Vienna.

1885 October 13

In the evening, F. arrives in Paris for the first part of his study stay with Charcot, which will last, with an interruption, until 1886 February 28. F. takes a room at the Hôtel de la Paix in Impasse Royer-Collard 5. The hotel is about two minutes from the Pantheon and the Jardin de Luxembourg. It is a 25-minute walk to Salpêtrière. The hotel owner's friend is a young archeologist for whom F. translates passages from German books from time to time. Martha's cousin John Philipp, whom F. meets that evening, also lives in the same hotel.

1885 October 14

– John Philipp guides F. through Paris in the morning.
– F. visits Max Nordau.
– F. continues the city tour and visits the Tuileries, Notre-Dame, the Vendôme Column and the Pantheon.
– F. meets briefly with John Philipp's brother Fabian, who lives in Paris.
– F. spends the evening with John Philipp.

1885 October 15

F. goes for a long city walk and has lunch with Fabian Philipp.

1885 October 16

F. visits Paris on the following route: Quai d'Orsay, Invalides Cathedral, Champs-Elysées, Place de la Concorde, Tuileries Gardens. The obelisk on the Place de la Concorde impresses him very much, and he writes to Martha: "Think of it, a real obelisk, scribbled with the most beautiful bird heads and sitting men and other hieroglyphics, its good 3000 years older than the lumpen people around it" (F. to Martha, 19.10.1885).

1885 October 17

F. goes to the theater with John Philipp and sees three plays by Molière: *Le Mariage de forcé*, *Tartuffe* and *Les Précieuses ridicules.* He takes great pleasure in the actors' performances.

1885 October 18
F. visits the antique section of the Louver, including the Assyrian and Egyptian sections. The things he sees – including Venus de Milo – have more historical than esthetic value for him. It is for him "a world as if in a dream" (F. to Martha, 19.10.1885).

1885 October 19
- F. goes to the Salpêtrière for the first time.
- F. buys a book by Jean-Martin Charcot in French.
- F. makes the same tour as on October 16, but includes Rue de Richelieu and Place de la République.

1885 October 20
F. meets Jean-Martin Charcot for the first time at 10.00 during the external consultation and presents him with Moritz Benedikt's letter of recommendation. He then has a conversation and a hospital tour with him. His first impression: "… a tall man of 58, top hat on his head, with dark, peculiarly soft eyes …, very expressive features, full, protruding lips, in short like a worldly clergyman, from whom one expects much wit and understanding for a good life" (F. to Martha, 21.10.1885).

1885 October 21
- F. shows Charcot some of his preparations, and Charcot asks a colleague for children's brains for F., as the latter wants to deal with degeneration symptoms after brain diseases during his stay in Paris.
- Charcot's assistant Pierre Marie gives F. material for his originally planned study of secondary atrophies and degenerations after infantile brain affections.
- F. buys new boots with English soles for 22 francs.

1885 October 23
- F. is at the Salpêtrière children's clinic with Georges Guinon to order children's brains. Afterward, he and Guinon are invited to lunch by two colleagues.
- In the afternoon, a brain is photographed for F., which he is currently examining.

1885 October 24
F. visits the histologist Louis-Antoine Ranvier, who receives him very kindly. F. promises to show him his preparations on occasion.

1885 October 25
- F. is in the laboratory in the morning and in the Louver in the afternoon.
- F. attends a performance of Victor Hugo's drama *Hernani ou l'honneur Castillan* at the Théatre-Français in the evening.

1885 October 26
F. is with Louis-Antoine Ranvier in the afternoon and shows him his preparations.

1885 October 27
F. is at Charcot's for an external consultation in the morning.

1885 October 29
F. receives a visit from John Philipp and a Russian violinist friend of his.

1885 October 31
F. visits the Musée de Cluny.

1885 October end
F. has a number of complaints, including slight balance problems, heat waves in the head and fatigue. He considers wine, pipe smoking or cigars as possible causes. He therefore wants to give up smoking as of November 1.

1885 November
Jakob Freud's family moves from Darwingasse 32 to Novaragasse 29.

1885 November 1
F. visits the Père Lachaise cemetery. First, he goes to the Jewish section and the grave of Pierre and Héloïse Abaillard. He looks in vain for the grave of Ludwig Börne.

1885 November 3
During the consultation, F. meets the Russian brain anatomist Liweri Darkschewitsch, whom he already knows from Vienna. They spend the evening together, and F. calls him his "friend in cerebro" (F. to Martha, 5.11.1885).

1885 November 5
F. makes the acquaintance of the neurologist G. Zohrab from Constantinople, who studied and obtained his doctorate in France, and of the Lithuanian physiologist Stanislaw Klikowitsch, who, however, works in St. Petersburg in the institute of Sergei Botkin, the tsar's personal physician.

1885 November 6
F. goes with Liweri Darkschewitsch to the dermatologist François-Marie Hallopeau.

1885 November 7
F. goes to the Porte Saint-Martin theater with Stanislaw Klikowitsch and sees *Théodora* by Victorien Sardou starring Sarah Bernhardt. He is disappointed by the play but delighted by Sarah Bernhardt: "I have never seen an actress who surprised me so little, I immediately believed everything she said" (F. to Martha, 8.11.1885).

1885 November 8
F. is invited to tea in the evening by Liweri Darkschewitsch.

1885 November 9
F. writes a "Critical Introduction to Nervous Pathology".

1885 November 10
– Pierre Marie encourages F. to "also occupy himself clinically" with a subject related to his anatomical work.
– F. meets his American student from Vienna, Richard Prichard, at the Consultation externe.
– F. interprets a dream of Martha in which she dreamed of her wedding but was not there herself. F. assumes the reason for this is that because he "always called Martha a princess, you wanted to allow yourself the freedom to marry by proxy. After all, it was at least our wedding and not just mine that you were dreaming of" (F. to Martha, 10.11.1885).

1885 November 11
F. edits his paper "Acute multiple neuritis of the spinal and cranial nerves" for the *Wiener Medizinische Wochenschrift.*

1885 November 12
F. visits with Darkschewitsch and Klikowitsch, an expensive restaurant.

1885 November 13

Giacomo Ricchetti arrives in Paris at F.'s invitation with his wife Louise. He wants to "enjoy science […]" with F.: F. comments on this with the words: "The man obviously thinks more of me than I do myself" (F. to Martha, 13.11.1885). The Ricchetti's rent a whole floor in a hotel near F. for 250 francs a month. F. has dinner with them, and afterward, they go for a walk on the boulevards of Paris until 9 pm.

1885 November 14

F. has dinner with Ricchetti's; they plan to make it a routine.

1885 November 15

F. visits Notre-Dame together with Giacomo Ricchetti. He wants to read Victor Hugo's novel *Notre-Dame de Paris in* this church because it is the place to fully understand the novel.

1885 November 16

F. finishes his paper "Acute multiple neuritis of the spinal and cranial nerves" and reads it to Giacomo Ricchetti.

1885 November 17

F. receives a pair of winter trousers from his tailor Franz Tischer from Vienna.

1885 November 21

- F. goes for a walk with Giacomo Ricchetti and the German psychiatrist Franz Müller-Lyer from Strasbourg, and they meet the spa doctor Ludwig Schuster from Aachen, whom F. knows through "his bad books" and whom he had "just imagined with his arrogance and ignorance" (F. to Martha, 21.11.1885).
- F. takes a bath and has his "hair done […] The hairdressers are so excellent here that you could wish for a new mane every day to have it cut" (F. to Martha, 21.11.1885).

1885 November 23

F. subscribes to Charcot's *Archives de Neurologie.* The journal is extremely important for F.'s work, but 80 francs is a lot of money for him.

1885 November 24

- F. visits Anna Kreisler, the mother of the violin virtuoso Fritz Kreisler and wife of Samuel Kreisler, the family doctor of the Freud family.
- F. characterizes Charcot as "one of the greatest doctors, a brilliantly sober person" who simply outlines his "views and intentions […] After some lectures I leave as if from Notre-Dame" (F. to Martha, 24.11.1885).

1885 November 25

F. receives a visit from John Philip in the evening.

1885 November 26

F. visits the Louver again.

1885 November 27

F. receives an offprint of Heinrich Obersteiner's paper "Über die Anwendung des Kokains bei Neurosen und Psychosen" (On the use of cocaine in neuroses and psychoses), in which the author emphasizes F.'s great merit for cocaine.

1885 November end

F. finds himself "liking *Notre-Dame de Paris* by the old Victor Hugo novel better than Nerven-pathologie […]" (F. to Martha, 1.12.1885).

1885 December beginning
- F. stops his experiments in the laboratory of the Salpêtrière.
- F. is considering writing a "Critical Introduction to Nervous Pathology".
- Giacomo Ricchetti gives F. Balzac's novel *Le père Goriot*.

1885 December 4

F. went to dinner with Giacomo and Louise Ricchetti in a restaurant near the Odéon theater, which they did not know. It turned out to be an "elegant night establishment", "where the stay after the theater had to entail other costs than food and drink. The ladies were both waitresses and company" (F. to Martha, 5.12.1885).

1885 December 5
- F. climbs the tower of Notre-Dame, his favorite place in Paris. He writes to Martha: "For the time being, I do not know of anything more magnificent than Notre-Dame and the fourth gallery with the stone devils and beasts and the view of Paris" (F. to Martha, 5.12.1885).
- F. receives a package from Martha, including winter gloves and a tie.

1885 December 7

F. visits Liweri Darkschewitsch and corrects a German paper for him.

1885 December 8

F. receives a winter coat ordered by him.

1885 December 9

Two pages of the "Critical Introduction to Nervous Pathology" are finished.

1885 December 10
- F. climbs the tower of Notre-Dame again.
- F. visits Otto Wolff, a friend of Martha's family, who had brought him a package from Hamburg. Then, they go to a café and meet Fabian Philipp on the way.

1885 before December 11

F. hears from Giacomo Ricchetti that Charcot is looking for a German translator for the third volume of his lectures.

1885 December 11
- F. writes to Charcot and asks to be allowed to translate the third volume of his lectures. Louise Ricchetti, who helps F. to write the letter, has interspersed some flattering phrases in the letter.
- F. buys two photographs of Notre-Dame as a souvenir of Paris.
- F. is back on the tower of Notre-Dame.

1885 December 12
- Charcot gives F. his consent to translate the third volume of his works. F. is sure that this will make him known in Germany and be conducive to private practice.
- F. meets with Fabian Philipp.

1885 December 13
F. begins with the translation of Charcot's *lectures*.

1885 December 16
The Viennese publishing house Toeplitz und Deuticke informs F. of its intention to publish Charcot's *lectures, which* he has translated.

1885 December 17
– F. presents Charcot with the translation of the first lecture. Charcot also responds to all the wishes of the Viennese publisher.
– F. meets John Philipp for dinner.

1885 December 18
Liweri Darkschewitsch visits F., and the latter reads him the manuscript of the Critical Introduction to Nervous Pathology.

1885 December 19
F. meets Otto Wolff for dinner.

1885 December 20–28
Fourth visit to Wandsbek

1885 December 20

F. leaves Paris for Hamburg at 7.30 am to spend Christmas with Martha.

1885 December 21

F. arrives in Hamburg at 6.18 am.

1885 December 26

F. signs the publishing contract with Deuticke for the translation of Charcot's *Leçons* (1000 copies, fee 20 Gulden per sheet).

1885 December 28

F. leaves Hamburg and travels via Aachen back to Paris. From Aachen, he spends the journey with two men whom he meets again by chance on New Year's Eve.

1885 December 29
F. arrives back in Paris and thus begins the second part of his study visit with Charcot. He is expected by the Ricchetti's, who take him to dinner at a restaurant.

1885 December 30
– F. changes his stay to the Hôtel du Brésil at Rue le Goff 10, very close to his first room at the Hotel Hôtel de la Paix.
– F. smokes smuggled Turkish tobacco that he brought from Hamburg to Paris.
– F. buys stationery and envelopes, as well as a golden Turkish ashtray.
– F. is having dinner with Ricchetti's.
– F. visits Liweri Darkschewitsch in the late evening, who is very happy about F.'s return; both drink tea together.

1885 December 31

– F. spends New Year's Eve in a German café, where he meets his traveling companions from Aachen. F. describes the subsequent stroll through the city; thus: "The spectacle on the boulevards [...] was quite indescribable. People had squeaking, squawking, screaming instruments and saw their life's work in making them sound. Every five steps there are stalls where you can buy all kinds of things, a long market, plus the gambling and shooting stalls with prizes and lotteries and the people crowding around them. They get special pleasure from hideous half-life-size dolls that you throw balls at. If you hit them on the neck, their heads fall backward, so it is a kind of revolutionary and guillotine game" (F. to Martha, 3.1.1886).

– F. is transferred to the non-active Landwehr.

1886

1886 January 2
John Philipp visits F.

1886 January 4
F. meets Martha's cousin Jules Bernays, who is a representative of his father Louise's company in Paris, in a café. Otto Wolff also happens to be there.

1886 January beginning
- F. works with Liweri Darkschewitsch on a joint neurological publication and visits him often in the evening
- F. is considering visiting Johann Georg Mezger – an expert in the field of medical massages – in Amsterdam.

1886 January 6
F. goes to a dejeuner given by the owner of his hotel, Madame Manton.

1886 January 8
F. meets a couple of American doctors at dinner who have just arrived from Vienna.

1886 January 9
F. is visited by Jules Bernays in the afternoon. They both go to a brasserie.

1886 January 10
F. visits Liweri Darkschewitsch.

1886 January 12
Charcot returned to the Salpêtrière after a few weeks, and F. witnessed how he had all the wonders of hypnotism paraded again for a "professor of the Chinese language [...]" (F. to Martha, 13.1.1886).

1886 January 13
F. is with Jules Bernays at the Café-Concert Scala, where events of the past year were presented in parodic images.

1886 January 14
F. has finished translating the first volume of Charcot's *lectures.*

1886 January 15
F. visits the sick Liweri Darkschewitsch. He tells him that he has communicated findings to a colleague who is going to use them in a publication. F. suggests that he should refrain from doing so and publish with him instead, as he had made similar findings in Vienna. Darkschewitsch agrees.

1886 January 16
F. goes to the Comédie Française with Jules Bernays and sees *Figaro's Wedding* by Pierre de Beaumarchais. F. experiences the content of the play as highly revolutionary and is "incomparably amused". Afterward, he goes to drink beer with Jules Bernays and his friend in a brasserie.

1886 January 17
- F. has a conversation with Charcot and receives another ten sheets of his lectures, which he translates.

- F. writes down the draft of the joint paper with Liweri Darkschewitsch. It is entitled "On the relation of the knitted body to the posterior strand and posterior strand nucleus, together with remarks on two fields of the oblongata".

1886 January 19

F. is at Charcot's for dinner. He buys a new shirt and white gloves and puts on his tailcoat; to disinhibit himself, he takes cocaine. Guests include the following: Ole Broch (Norwegian mathematician), Paul Brouardel, Léon Daudet (son of Alphonse Daudet), Raphael Lépine (one of the most important physiologists in France), Giacomo Ricchetti, Isidor Straus (assistant to Louis Pasteur), Edoardo Tofano (English painter), George Gilles de la Tourette. For F., it is a "highlight" of his stay in Paris so far and he felt "more comfortable than ever in a company" (F. to Martha, 24.1.1886).

1886 January 20

F. attends a lecture and demonstration by Paul Brouardel at the Morgue.

1886 January 22

F. receives from the publisher the correction of the first sheet of the translation of Charcot's *lectures*.

1886 January 23

F. and Liweri Darkschewitsch finish their paper on the medulla oblongata.

1886 January 24

- Charcot invites F. for the afternoon to discuss F.'s translation.
- F. receives bad news from his sister Rosa about Ignaz Schönberg's state of health. He is emaciated to a skeleton. F. asks Rosa to order a wreath in case Schönberg dies before F.'s return.

1886 January 25

F. sends the article on the medulla oblongata to Berlin.

1886 January 26

- F. Giacomo Ricchetti and his wife leave Paris. F. accompanies them to the railway station.
- He finishes the first part of his "Critical Introduction to Nervous Pathology".

1886 January 27

- F. has a conversation with Charcot about technical issues and believes he has made a good impression on him.
- Joseph Babinski invites F. to lunch with his colleagues, and afterward, they deal with a case of male hysteria.
- F. buys a dynamometer to examine his own nervousness.

1886 January 28

F. and Joseph Babinski present the result of their investigation of the case of male hysteria to Charcot.

1886 January 29

- Jules Bernays visits F.
- Death of Ignaz Schönberg. Before receiving the news of his death, F. had written to Martha that he wished him a quick death.

1886 February

F. sends Heinrich Obersteiner an offprint of his paper "Acute multiple neuritis of the spinal and cranial nerves" with the dedication "Herrn Prof. H. Obersteiner mit hochachtungsvollem Gruss der Verf.".

1886 February 2

- F. diagnoses himself with neurasthenia.
- F. procures the statutes of the Paris Society of Physicians for Heinrich Obersteiner.
- F. is invited to Charcot's again and takes cocaine beforehand. There are more than 40 guests present. Among other things, F. has a political conversation with Georges Gilles de la Tourette about Germany and France.
- In a letter to Martha, F. compares himself to Charcot and Hermann Nothnagel and believes he can achieve at least as much as these two men.

1886 February 3

F. receives the news of Ignaz Schönberg's death from sister Rosa.

1886 February 6

F. learns that he has been appointed the head of the neurological department of the I. Public Children's Hospital Institute in Vienna.

1886 February 7

- F. is approached in the Salpêtrière by Carl Pick, whom he knows from Vienna.
- F. meets with Jules Bernays.

1886 February 9

- F. is invited to Charcot's for dinner. F. sits next to Charcot's daughter Jeanne. Other guests include the following: Emmanuel Arêne (journalist), Marie Alfred Cornu (physicist), Alphonse Daudet, Moritz Mendelssohn (from the Berlin physiological school), Louis Ranvier (anatomist and histologist), Paul Marie Richer (Charcot's first assistant), Edoardo Tofano and Georges Gilles de la Tourette. "It was the most pleasant evening I spent here" (F. to Martha, 10.2.1886).
- Afterward, F. takes Gilles de la Tourette home to pick up a job from him.

1886 after February 9

F. has a fantasy of a carriage with horses running through it, probably a reproduction of a scene he had read in a story as a grammar school student.

1886 February 10

F. meets the New York ophthalmologist Hermann Knapp and is approached by him about his cocaine work.

1886 before February 15

F. visits Louis-Antoine Ranvier, who gives him two books.

1886 February 15

- F. has to go to the Austrian legation. There, he learns that he has been transferred to the Landwehr. He has to copy out an oath.
- F. sends Martha an offprint of his paper "Acute multiple neuritis of the spinal and cranial nerves".

1886 February mid
F. forces Liweri Darkschewitsch to leave the flat with him for the first time since his illness. The 2½-hour walk did him good, and F. considered Darkschewitsch cured.

1886 February 17
F. is invited to dine with Louis-Antoine Ranvier. Also, there are his brother Joseph-Victor Ranvier (a painter), Raphael Lépine and Joaquín Maria Albarrán y Dominguez (Cuban urologist).

1886 February 20
F. visits Jules Bernays, who has been bedridden for several days and has a severe sore throat, which F. treats with cocaine brushes and morphine.

1886 February 21
F. visits Jules Bernays twice and notices a decisive improvement in the symptoms.

1886 February 22
Charcot presents an explanation of F. for cases of hysterical paralysis with muscular atrophy in his lecture.

1886 February 23
– F. visits a Sophie Bing, who is an "aunt" to Martha and has a relative Louis who fancies Martha.
– F. says goodbye to Jules Bernays.

1886 February 24
F. acquires Immanuel Kant's *Smaller Writings on Natural Philosophy*.

1886 February 25
F. says goodbye to Charcot and asks him to sign a photograph he has bought of him. Charcot gives him another photograph and gives him two letters of recommendation for his stay in Berlin.

1886 February 28
F.'s study stay in Paria is over, and F. leaves the French capital for Berlin with a short stopover in Hamburg with Martha.

1886 March 1–March 3
Fifth visit to Wandsbek

1886 March 1

Arrival in Hamburg at 8.18 am.

1886 March 3

In the morning departure to Berlin.

1886 March 3–April 3
Study visit in Berlin

F. works for four weeks with Albert Eulenburg (private polyclinic for nervous patients), Emanuel Mendel (own "Privatirrenstalt" in Pankow) and Adolf Baginsky (own polyclinic for children's diseases, Johannisstr. 3; since 1890 director of the Kaiserin Auguste-Kaiser Friedrich Children's Hospital). At the latter, he studied mental abnormalities in children. He visits Hermann Munk and Nathan Zuntz several times. There, he met Jacques Loeb and

Benno Baginsky. During this time, F. continued to work on the translation of Charcot's *New Lectures on the Diseases of the Nervous System, especially on hysteria.*

1886 March 3

F. arrives in Berlin around noon and checks into the Central Hotel at Friedrichstrasse station. First, he looks for a flat, and then, he reads the *Fliegende Blätter* and goes for a walk.

1886 March 4

F. goes to the Charité in the morning to find out when Prof. Eduard Henoch has lectures and when he is at the clinic.
- F. visits the neurologists Carl Westphal and Martin Bernhardt.
- F. meets Fritz Gintl, an acquaintance from Vienna who wanted to do a doctorate in music history in Berlin. Both go out for a cheap meal in a pub in Behrenstrasse. Gintl died six months later of an acute lung disease.
- F. visits several rooms in the early afternoon and finally rents a room from Mrs. L. Boelckow at Karlstrasse 18a (now Reinhardtstrasse). The room is on the third floor of the front building, is furnished and costs 24 marks. All the important medical institutions in Berlin are in this area, including the Charité.
- F. reads newspapers in the Café Bauer.
- At 4.00 pm is at Emanuel Mendel's polyclinic, very close to his flat. Mendel invites him for a Sunday so that F. can tell him about his impressions of Paris.

1886 March 5

- F. is at Adolf Baginsky's at 12.00 pm, to whom he hands over a letter from Darkschewitsch.
- F. examines children in Mendel's polyclinic.

1886 March 6

- F. goes to the Austrian legation and the police, presumably because of the registration.
- F. receives the corrections of the paper on the medulla oblongata written jointly with Darkschewitsch.
- F. is in Albert Eulenburg's polyclinic.

1886 March 8

F. is at the meeting of the "Society for Psychiatry and Nervous Diseases". Carl Westphal and Martin Bernhardt give lectures, and afterward, everyone goes to the pub. F. talks to Hermann Oppenheim and Robert Thomsen, two opponents of Charcot.

1886 March 9

F. seeks out Eduard Henoch.

1886 March 10

F. visits the Royal Museum in Berlin and is particularly impressed by the finds Carl Humann had made during his excavations in Pergamon since 1878. The "battle of the gods against giants" from the ancient city was a sensation in Berlin, and F. was also impressed.

1886 March 12

- F. is in the Royal and University Libraries, but cannot borrow anything because he was not prepared for the Prussian formalities.
- F. seeks out Adolf Baginsky.

1886 March 13

F. visits a sick child with poor people with Adolf Baginsky, and Baginsky explains the streets and buildings to him on the way.

1886 March 18

F. visits Benno Baginsky, the younger brother of Adolf Baginsky, to show him his brain preparations. The physiologist Hermann Munk also looks at the preparations.

1886 March 19

F. has his "out-of-shape French beard" (F. to Martha, 19.3.1886) trimmed by the court hairdresser Richard Thomas (Unter den Linden 34). He pays one Reichsmark, but feels badly treated.

1886 March 20

F. visits Sanitätstrat Eduard Heymann, a relative of Samuel Hammerschlag.

1886 March 21

In the evening, F. visits Sally and Julius Lewisohn (Martha's grand cousin and her husband) at the Hotel Central. Sally has a cold, and F. brushes her throat with cocaine. After a long conversation, they go to the hotel's "Wintergarten", where singing plays are performed.

1886 March 22

- F. observes the large crowd on the boulevard Unter den Linden on the morning of Kaiser Wilhelm's birthday.
- F. receives a visit at noon from Paul Heymann, the son of Eduard Heymann; he is an ENT doctor and, like F., had experimented with cocaine.
- In the evening, F. is at the Deutsches Theater with Sally and Julius Lewisohn. They see a performance of Heinrich von Kleist's play *Prinz von Homburg* with Josef Kainz in the leading role. After the performance, the company went to a kosher inn, where F. "had the mishap of asking for cheese after the meat dish […]" (F. to Martha, 23.3.1886).

1886 after March 23

F. is several times in the laboratory of Hermann Munk and Nathan Zuntz, where blind dogs are kept for experimental purposes.

1886 after March 25

F. visits a sick child with Adolf Baginsky. F. does not agree with Baginsky's diagnosis.

1886 March 26

F. leaves Berlin for Hamburg in the evening.

1886 March 27–30
Sixth visit to Wandsbek

1886 March 27

F. arrives in Wandsbek in the morning.

1886 March 29

F. leaves Wandsbek in the evening.

1886 March 30

F. arrives back in Berlin early in the morning.

1886 March 30

F. goes straight to Café Bauer after arriving in Berlin.
- F. goes to see Paul Heymann to save himself the evening visit.
- F. visited Adolf Baginsky in the afternoon and showed or explained his brain preparations to him.
- F. is invited to an evening party at Adolf Baginsky's house. Skat was played, and music was played. F. believes that Baginsky has become rich "through his wife, but I would not take her off his hands for heavy money" (F. to Martha, 31.3.1886).

1886 April 1

F. summarizes the essentials of his lectures on brain anatomy in writing for Adolf Baginsky; for this purpose, he prepares a large sheet with drawings.

1886 April 2

F. is with Emanuel Mendel, who wants to see F.'s brain preparations. Afterward, they have lunch together. Mendel recruits F. as a speaker for the *Neurologisches Zentralblatt, which* he publishes.

1886 April 3

F. leaves Berlin at 8.00 am and travels via Dresden to Vienna.

1886 April 4
- F. arrives in Vienna early at 9.30.
- On the way from the train station to his hotel in Buchfeldgasse (right next to the town hall), he sees Sally Lewisohn at the farmers' market and Max Kassowitz on the Ringstrasse.
- F. visits Sigmund Lustgarten, Sophie Paneth (where he meets all the Schwabs), the Breuer family, the Pineles family (where Josef Herzig is also) and his family, including F.'s cousin Moritz. In the evening, he meets Josef Paneth.

1886 April 5
- F. meets some former colleagues from the Allgemeines Krankenhaus in a café.
- F. visits Josef Paneth.
- F. visits Ernst Brücke in his laboratory. There, he meets Wilhelm Kühne (Helmholtz's successor in Heidelberg), Sigmund Exner and Ernst Fleischl. The latter "looks miserable, more like a corpse" (F. to Martha, 4.5.1886).
- F. goes to Franz Deuticke, who pays him half the fee for the translation of Charcot's lectures.
- F. visits Leopold Königstein for lunch.
- F. seeks out Moritz Benedikt to find out whether he has a chance of working at the polyclinic.
- F. visits his tailor Franz Tischer and arranges fittings for new dresses.
- F. goes to the Allgemeines Krankenhaus and arranges meetings with some colleagues.
- F. visits Ernst Fleischl, where he meets Georg Bühler and sees a Sanskrit book that Fleischl has bought from Ignaz Schönberg's estate.
- F. visits the Hammerschlag family in the evening.

1886 April 6
- F. receives the list of persons of the academic authorities in the Dean's Office of the Faculty of Medicine, in which he is also listed.
- F. goes looking for a flat, but finds nothing suitable and, on Martha's advice, places an advertisement in the *Neue Freie Presse.*
- F. goes to his tailor Franz Tischer for a fitting.

- F. meets Moritz Heitler, who accepts him as a staff member of *the Centralblatt for the entire therapy.*
- F. visits his family.
- F. visits the Breuer family in the evening.

1886 April 7
- The advertisement for accommodation appears in the *Neue Freie Presse*: "Wanted by a young doctor, two nicely furnished rooms (waiting and consulting rooms) with service, first or second floor, in the IX. or I. district, possibly near the medical institutions. Offers with prices to be sent to the porter of the Allgemeines Krankenhaus, IX., Alserstrasse, under Dr. Freud". The first sentence of the advertisement corresponds almost word by word with a text proposed by Martha.
- F. visits Heinrich Obersteiner in Döbling.
- F. visits Alexander Holländer.
- At F.'s request, his mother rents a room for him with a neighbor at Novaragasse 29, and F. moves there from the hotel.

1886 April 8
- F. visits Theodor Meynert, who asks him to help a foreign doctor working in the laboratory.
- F. visits the Psychiatric Society.
- F. visits Moritz Benedikt in the evening.

1886 April 9
F. is having lunch with Josef Breuer.

1886 April 10
- At the constituent meeting at the I. Public Children's Hospital (Steindlgasse 2), F. is officially appointed the head of the neurological outpatient clinic. He has consultation hours there three times a week from mid-June: Tuesday, Thursday, and Saturday from 3 to 4 pm. After the meeting, Emilie Kassowitz invites F. and his colleagues to a souper.
- F. writes to Martha that he is very busy looking for a flat, but so far has not found anything suitable, but also nothing unsuitable.

1886 April 11
- F. receives a request to look at a flat at Rathausstrasse 7 and immediately sets off.
- F. gets a visit from sister Anna "with the silly and very trusting baby [Judith Bernays]" (F. to Martha, 11.4.1886).

1886 April 12
- F. decides to take the flat in Rathausstrasse. It is on the mezzanine floor and consists of an anteroom and two furnished larger rooms. The landlord and wife stay in two other, smaller rooms for another six months. The rent is 80 Gulden per month.[17]
- F. begins to write down his report on his stay in Paris and Berlin; it is dated: "at Easter 1886", (25 April), but arrived at the professors' college on April 22 at the latest.

1886 April 13
F. gives a lecture at the Physiological Club "Über den Ursprung des Nervus acusticus". Breuer told him afterward that his way of lecturing was enviable.

1886 April 14
- F. has his first consultation with Leopold Politzer with a Russian woman from Kiev. He feels it is a great honor to be called in as a consultant.
- F. orders advertisements for the start of the practice, business cards and two plaques with his

name: for the street one made of glass, with gold lettering on a black background, and one for the door made of porcelain.
- 1886 April 15
- F. moves into the flat at Rathausstrasse 7.
- F.'s book boxes and his other belongings are moved to the new flat.
- F. buys six shirts, one fine tailcoat shirt, 12 handkerchiefs, one dozen collars and cuffs for them, six undergarment dresses, six good towels and six wiping cloths with his mother at the linen and fashion shop Riedel & Beutel on Stephansplatz.
- F. has a consultation with the laryngologist Carl Stoerk in the Grüne Thorgasse and examines the eyes of an unconscious patient for an hour.
- F. receives the offprints of his paper "Über den Ursprung des N[ervus] acusticus".
- F. has dinner at the Riedhof.
- 1886 April mid
- F. begins to keep records of his income and expenditure.
- 1886 April 16
- An upholsterer covers F.'s desk with a new cloth and takes the fabric for an ottoman that F. ordered.
- An electrician comes to connect all the electrical devices.
- F. begins treatment of Sophie Klinenberger (until at least 1896).
- F. visits Josef Breuer in the evening.

1886 April 18
- F. finishes writing the report on his stay in Paris thanks to the university anniversary travel grant awarded to him and dates it "at Easter 1886".
- F. meets with brother Alexander.

1886 April 19
- F. visits Theodor Meynert and presents him with an offprint of his paper "Über den Ursprung des N[ervus] acusticus". Meynert puts his laboratory and material at his disposal.
- F. receives a visit from Mathilde and Bertha Breuer.
- For the new flat, the following are delivered: a large petroleum lamp, a small easel and a bookshelf.

1886 April 20
- The ottoman ordered by F. is delivered. F. covers it with the Smyrna carpet he had received from Moritz in 1885 March.
- F. is considering going to America if his practice does not do well in the first three months.

1886 April 21
The plaque with F.'s name is placed at the entrance to Rathausstrasse 7.

1886 April 22
F. has his second consultation with Leopold Politzer.

1886 April 23
- Josef Winter visits F.
- F.'s tailor Franz Tischer delivers a new suit.
- F. gets the medicines for the medicine cabinet and a box for reagents.
- F. visits Josef Breuer in the afternoon.

- Richard Wahle visits F.
- F. is at the Riedhof in the evening.

1886 April 24
- F. sends 100 letters with his new address so that it is known that he is back in Vienna. He plans to send another 100.
- F. is supplied with: the medicine cabinet, the chemical laboratory, medical instruments, a filing cabinet and a shelf.

1886 April 25
- The *Neue Freie Presse publishes* the announcement of Freud's opening of the practice with the text: "Dr. Sigmund Freud, Docent for Nervous Diseases at the University, has returned from his study trip to Paris and Berlin and ordains I., Rathhausstr. No. 7, from 1 pm to 2½ pm". In the first days of the practice, F. asks his sisters to sit in the waiting room so that new patients would get the impression that the consultation was going well.
- F. takes Sophie Klinenberger to the Rothschild Hospital to Leopold Oser.
- F. has headaches that made him apathetic and last for several days.

1886 April 26
F. is called to a patient who had benefited from cocaine and who had learned from the newspaper that F. is back in Vienna.

1886 April 27
- In the morning, F. visits Karl Koller's stepmother, Henriette Koller; she had asked F. to examine her nephew.
- Salomon Ehrmann refers a patient from Budweis (České Budějovice) to F.

1886 April 28
F. starts working in Meynert's laboratory.

1886 April 29
- F. begins treating a Russian woman sent by Josef Breuer.
- Moritz Horowitz comes to F.'s practice with a patient.

1886 April 30
- F. visits Josef Breuer in the afternoon.
- F. visits Hermann Nothnagel. He has the feeling of being received coolly and also does not give much to Nothnagel's promise to send him patients.
- F. visits Ernst Fleischl in the evening.

1886 April end
F. corrects the proofs of his translation of Charcot's *lectures.* Albert Hammerschlag helps him with this.

1886 May beginning
Usually, five patients come to F.'s consultation.

1886 May 1
F. is referred two new patients, one by Josef Breuer and one by Robert Ultzmann.

1886 May 3
F. is at sister Dolfi's birthday party. He congratulates with a small bouquet of flowers and cake.

1886 May 4
F. visits Josef Breuer in the evening.

1886 May 6
For his birthday, F. receives a brush box from his sisters Paula and Dolfi and two bouquets of dried flowers from Mitzi, which were complemented by feather decorations in the style of Hans Makart. His mother brings a cake, and sister Rosa brings a tissue paper frame for the desk.

1886 May 7
– F. is in the laboratory and meets Theodor Meynert there.
– F. is at the I. Public Children's Hospital.
– F. visits Ernst Fleischl in the evening and stays until the next morning. At Fleischl's, F. meets Samuel Schenk.

1886 May 10
A guide visits F. and shows him a letter from a rich Russian who wants to come to Vienna to be treated. The guide demands 20% of F.'s income and an advance of five Gulden, which F. gives him. F. writes to Martha: "Whether he has smeared me or not remains to be seen" (F. to Martha, 10.5.1886).

1886 May 11
– An American doctor comes to F. with his mistress, who finds the case so interesting that he accepts him as a patient, probably without asking for a fee.
– F. gives a lecture on hypnotism at the Physiological Club.

1886 May 12
– F. is with Rudolf Chrobak because of the American doctor's mistress, who wants to operate on her.
– A distant acquaintance calls F. to him without paying him. This is repeated two more times.

1886 May 13
– F.'s practice is busy, and the waiting room is full.
– Amalia Kompert asks F. on the recommendation of Josef Breuer what would do her husband – Emanuel Kompert – good.

1886 May 14
– F. consults Rudolf Chrobak about a patient's wife.
– The court actor Hugo Thimig visits F. on the recommendation of Josef Breuer. However, F. immediately loses him as a patient again because a minor operation that F. was supposed to perform – probably at Breuer's request – failed, and Thimig discontinued the treatment. F. sends back the fee that Thimig paid, as he blamed himself for the failed operation.

1886 May 15
– In the *Wiener Medizinische Wochenschrift,* the 24th lecture appears as an excerpt from Charcot's *Lectures* translated by F. under the title "Ueber einen Fall von hysterischer Coxalgie aus traumatischer Ursache bei einem Manne".
– F. visits Josef Breuer in the evening.

1886 May mid
– F. teaches two students in the morning and works in the laboratory.
– F. begins the treatment of Charlotte Müller (née Horowitz), the wife of the Orientalist David Müller. He deals with her a lot and is very interested in a successful therapy.

– Martha reckons that they will get married in the autumn, as her brother Eli and her mother are already making plans for that date. F. hardly dares to believe it.

1886 May 16
F. visits Josef Breuer at noon.

1886 May 18
– F. receives an electrical apparatus.
– F. visits Josef Breuer, who talks him into marrying.
– F. lends his landlady 31 Gulden, as otherwise the furniture belonging to her in F.'s room would be auctioned off.

1886 before May 19
F. receives from Paul Ehrlich an offprint of Ehrlich's paper "Ueber die Methylenblaureaction der lebenden Nervensubstanz". He had asked for it because he wanted to use Ehrlich's method for his investigations. However, the method proved difficult for F. to master.

1886 May 20
F. thinks it is possible to marry Martha in September.

1886 May 22
– The mistress of the American doctor is operated on by Rudolf Chrobak.
– F. is at Josef Paneth's trial lecture.

1886 May 23
F. visits Josef Breuer.

1886 May 25
F. is at a consultation with Josef Breuer.

1886 May 26
– In the morning, F. is a consultant at the Stefanie Hospital, whose director is his friend Ignaz Rosanes.
– F. visits a patient from Padua in the Loew Sanatorium.

1886 May 27
F. repeats his lecture on hypnotism, which he had given on May 11 at the Physiological Club, at the Psychiatric Association. He had "made a great impression on the young people, the old ones were too stupid for it" (F. to Martha, 29.5.1886).

1886 May 28
F. makes a difficult diagnosis at the pediatric polyclinic.

1886 May 29
F. visits Ernst Fleischl and stays until the next morning.

1886 May 30
F. goes on a trip to Dornbach with Josef Winter, Ignaz Rosanes and Sigmund Lustgarten.

1886 May end
F. treats a French and a Russian doctor free of charge.

1886 June [approx.]
F. begins the treatment of Mathilde Schleicher (until 1890 September).

1886 June 4

F. is in the Gesellschaft der Ärzte, but does not come to his planned lecture "Über männliche Hysterie" ("On Male Hysteria"), which is postponed to October 15.

1886 June 11

F. attends the Society of Physicians and hears lectures by Ernst Fuchs, Viktor Hacker, Karl Maydl, Josef Weinlechner and Carl Braun-Fernwald.

1886 before June 13

F. hires Rosalie Stern as a waitress, but quits her again after a week because his brother-in-law Eli Bernays supports her, and F. also knows why.

1886 before June 14

F. argues with Eli Bernays about Martha's dowry.

1886 June 14

- F. reads the news of the death of King Ludwig II of Bavaria in an extra. He believes that Bernhard von Gudden had no other option but to follow his responsible doctor Ludwig to his death.
- F. visits Josef Breuer to say goodbye to Mathilde Breuer, who is going to Berchtesgaden for the summer.

1886 June 17

F. is called to the Rudolfinum by Carl Bettelheim as a consultant to give his opinion on a difficult case. F. diagnoses hysteria.

1886 June 18

F.'s tailor Franz Tischer takes measurements for a new coat – without F. having ordered him. F. discovers that his old coat has disappeared. However, he has no idea who owns it now.

1886 June 19

F. starts working in the outpatient clinic of the I. Public Children's Hospital Institute. There, he met the pediatricians Oskar Rie and Ludwig Rosenberg.

1886 June 21

F. receives a call-up to a military exercise in Olmütz from August 9 to September 10. He had actually only expected it for 1887.

1886 June end

- F. and Martha have a serious correspondence about F.'s dealings with Eli Bernays in connection with Martha's dowry and the financial demands after the wedding (flat rent, furniture purchase, life insurance, etc.). F. even doubts whether the marriage will take place at all.
- F. gives Josef Hoffmann an offprint of his paper "Acute multiple neuritis of the spinal and cranial nerves" with the dedication "Dr J. Hoffmann in dankbarer Erinnerung d Verf.".

1886 July 5

On the recommendation of Hermann Nothnagel, F. begins treating the Portuguese envoy Fausto de Queirós Guedes with electrotherapy.

1886 July 7

- F. seeks out Hermann Nothnagel to invite him to a consultation about a patient from Braila.
- F. receives a housing register and goes looking for flats in the Alservorstadt and in the IX. district.

1886 July 8
F.'s mother goes for a spa stay at Rožnau.

1886 approx. July 10
F. is considering renting a flat in the imperial foundation house (so-called Sühnhaus) at Maria-Theresien-Strasse 8.

1886 July 13
Martha advises him against the flat at Maria-Theresien-Strasse 8 because the annual rent is half of F.'s expected income.

1886 July 14
Martha agrees to everything F. decides on the housing issue, and her future husband rents a new flat at Maria-Theresien-Strasse 8 from October 1. It is located in the Sühnhaus, which had been built on the site of the Ringtheater (until 1878 "Komische Oper"), which had burned down in 1881.

1886 after July 15
F. begins to obtain the necessary documents for the wedding in Wandsbek, such as a power of attorney for Martha and a certificate of residence ("Heimatschein") for himself.

1886 July 16
F. has a tooth extracted, and afterward, he feels bad.

1886 July 18
F. writes the preface to his translation of Charcot's *"Neue Vorlesungen über die Krankheiten des Nervensystems, insbesondere über Hysterie"*.

1886 approx. July 20
F. receives his Heimatschein, which Emil Fluss got for him in Freiberg.

1886 July end
- F.'s translation of Charcot's *New Lectures on the Diseases of the Nervous System is* published in an edition of 1000 copies. He gives a copy to Josef Breuer with the dedication "Seinem vor Allen hochgeehrten Freunde Dr. Josef Breuer, geheimen Meister der Hysterie und anderer complicirter Probleme in stiller Widmung/der Übersetzer". F. sends further copies to Charcot and Martha.
- F. wants to send Martha a catalog of the Viennese kitchen furnishings; however, Martha had already had this very catalog sent to her in mid-April 1885.
- The cabinetmaker Johann Gerersdorfer tries to convince F. to furnish the new flat in Maria-Theresien-Strasse elegantly, but this would be very expensive.
- The Vienna magistrate certifies to F. "that there is no impediment to marriage and that he recognizes the marriage concluded abroad as valid".

1886 August
F. gives Heinrich Obersteiner an offprint of his paper "Über den Ursprung des N. acusticus" with the dedication "In gewohnter Hochachtung der Verf.".

1886 August beginning
F. formulates "Secret Instructions" for his sister Rosa for the furnishing of the flat in Maria

Theresien-Strasse. The furniture should cost no more than 1700 Gulden.[18] Rosa and her friend Ottilie Weiss helped F. choose the furniture and fabrics.

1886 August 11–September 9
Maneuvers of the Landwehr (Infantry) in Olmütz

F. is in Olmütz (now Olomouc) as an army surgeon for maneuvers of the Landwehr. He lectures there "Über das Sanitätswesen im Felde" ("On Medical Care in the Field") and treats a case of paralysis agitans with arsenic injections.

1886 August 21

Martha is visited in Wandsbek by Mathilde and Josef Breuer, who are on their way from Berchtesgaden to Denmark.

1886 August 24

– A large "fortress maneuver" takes place in Olomouc, lasting 24 hours.
– Birth of F.'s niece Leah (called Lucie), daughter of his sister Anna.

1886 September 1

– F. sends Martha a list of persons to whom marriage announcements are to be sent.
– The Commander-in-Chief of the Cisleithanian Territorial Defense, Archduke Rainer Ferdinand of Habsburg arrives in Olmütz for a troop inspection.

1886 before September 4

F. is dead tired from the constant marches.

1886 September 9

F. arrives back in Vienna.

1886 September 9–29
Wedding and honeymoon

1886 September 9

F. travels from Vienna to Wandsbek.

1886 September 10

F. arrives in Wandsbek and lives with Martha's uncle Elias Philipp in Claudiusstrasse.

1886 September 13

Civil marriage in Wandsbek town hall.

1886 September 14

– Jewish wedding at Hamburgerstrasse 32, the flat of F.'s mother-in-law.
– A total of 12 people are present for lunch. The menu includes fish salad, fillet de boeuf, asparagus peas, roast goose and stewed fruit.
– Afterward, F. and Martha go on a harbor tour, during which Martha proves to be "a country bumpkin of the purest earth" (Secret Chronicle, 14.9.1886).
– In the afternoon, F. and Martha set off on their honeymoon and drive from Hamburg to Lübeck, which receives them in the fog. They stay "in the first hotel in Lübeck" (F. and Martha to Emmeline and Minna Bernays, 15.9.1886); presumably it is the Hotel Stadt Hamburg.

1886 September 15

Martha begins her "wifely duties early in the morning […] by immediately sewing a torn button back on Sigi" (F. and Martha to Emmeline and Minna, 15.9.1886).

1886 September 16

Drive from Lübeck to Travemünde; arrival at 15.00, overnight stay at the Kurhaus Hotel. At the hotel, Freud is mistaken for an Indian because of his dark beard.

1886 September 21

– F. and Martha go o.n a "sea voyage", during which Martha proves to be "a landlubber of the purest earth" (Geheim-Chronik, 21.9.1886).

1886 September 23

Drive from Travemünde to Wandsbek (arrival around noon). In the afternoon onward journey to Berlin; arrival shortly before midnight and overnight stay at the Central Hotel at Friedrichstrasse station.

1886 September 24

Presumably meeting with Adolf Baginsky, who had invited F.: "[…] I do not need to say how pleased my wife and I will be to welcome you and your dear wife in Berlin 'on our honeymoon'" (Baginsky to F., 2.9.1886).

1886 September 25

Travel from Berlin to Dresden; arrival in the evening.

1886 September 28

Journey from Dresden to Brno. There, F. and Martha introduce themselves to Lea Löw-Beer (née Bernays), a sister of Martha's father. They receive 2000 marks from her as a wedding present.

1886 September 29

Drive from Brno to Vienna. F. and Martha arrive at 7 pm and spend the night in a hotel, as the lease for their flat at Maria Theresien-Strasse 8 does not run until October 1.

1886 September 30

F. and Martha are pleased to see that the removal goods from Wandsbek have already arrived in Vienna.

1886 October 1

– F. and Martha move into the flat at Maria Theresien-Strasse 8 in the morning. They stay there until 1891 September 12. The flat (number 12) was on the mezzanine and faced Maria-Theresien-Strasse and comprises the following rooms: anteroom and passage, four rooms, a small storeroom, a kitchen, a servants' room and a bathroom. There is also a floor under the roof, a cellar and a wood store in the basement. For the furnishing of his waiting room, F. rented rental furniture: golden armchairs with red plush.
– October 1 is a Friday, and Martha is deeply upset that F. has not bought any Sabbath candles because he detests religious rituals.

1886 after October 1

– In the winter semester, F. offers lectures twice a week on the "Anatomy of the Spinal Cord and the Medulla Oblongata as an Introduction to the Clinic of Nervous Diseases". He complains to Ernst Ludwig that he cannot find a lecture hall for his lectures. He finally gives the lectures in Theodor Meynert's lecture theater. Among the first listeners are Albert Hammerschlag, Oskar Rie and Ludwig Rosenberg.

- F. offers a six-week course on "Nerve Pathology with Demonstrations of Sick People".
- F. gives a lecture on aphasia at the Physiological Club.
- F. gives Carl Todt a special edition of his paper "Ueber den Ursprung des N[ervus] acusticus" with the dedication "Herrn Prof Dr C Toldt hochachtungsvoll d Verf.".
- F. gives Carl Langer an offprint of his paper "Ueber den Ursprung des N[ervus] acusticus" with the dedication "Herrn Hofrath Prof. C v Langer hochachtungsvoll d Verf.".
- F. begins the treatment of Elise Gomperz, the wife of Theodor Gomperz (until about 1894).

1886 October 4

F. announces the beginning of the ordination.

1886 October 5

The wood shop Johann Gerersdorfer sends F. an invoice for 26.60 Gulden for furniture, including one credenza, one table, one shelf, one armchair and one laundry basket.

1886 October 13

F. feels that as a clinician he is mainly dependend on the study of hysteria and asks Karl Koller for a perimeter, since "no one can publish anything nowadays without studying the field of vision" (F. to Karl Koller, 13.10.1886). A short time later, F. received the requested perimeter.

1886 October 15

F. gives a lecture "On Male Hysteria" to the Society of Physicians. Heinrich Bamberger presides. Arthur Schnitzler is also present. F. experiences the reaction to his lecture as negative. Max Leidesdorf, however, had acted with restraint.

1886 October 22

F. finds a case of male hysteria outside the hospital, on the basis of which he hopes to convince the society of doctors of his view.

1886 October 24

- F. is appointed by the Emperor as second-class regimental physician in the non-active Imperial and Royal Landwehr, and thus also appointed a senior physician of the Landwehr medical officer corps.
- Leopold Königstein makes an ophthalmological examination of the hysterical patient referred by F.

1886 October 28

F., Richard Wittelshöfer and Eduard Schiff ask the College of Professors for permission to hold lectures in the rooms of the I. Public Children's Hospital Institute.

1886 November 5

F. and Martha visit Leopold and Henriette Königstein in the evening.

1886 November mid

- Jakob Freud's family moves from Novaragasse 29 to Praterstrasse 30.
- Moritz Freud rents a flat at Grosse Mohrengasse 29. After marrying F.'s sister Mitzi in 1887 February, the couple move in.

1886 November 26

Together with Leopold Königstein, F. presents to the Society of Physicians the "Observation of a High Grade Hemianesthesia in a Hysterical Man". It is a continuation of the lecture or discussion of October 15. This time, the reception was probably more friendly.

1886 December
F. presents Heinrich Obersteiner with an offprint of his paper "Beobachtung einer hochgradigen Hemianästhesie bei einem hysterischen Manne" with the dedication "Herrn Prof. H. Obersteiner in gewohnter Hochschätzung der Verf.".

1886 December beginning
F. and Martha are invited to the Paneths' and the Kassowitzens' and visit the Hammerschlag family.

1886 December 11
A letter addressed by Hermann Widerhofer, Eduard Albert and Carl Toldt to the College of Professors formulates concerns about teaching at the Children's Hospital Institute.

1886 December 13
F. receives the perimeter he had wanted from Karl Koller from Utrecht as a belated wedding present, and Martha receives a clay picture with frame in a Dutch style.

1886 December 15
F. and Martha are having dinner at Breuer's; there is pheasant.

1886 December 29
– F. and Martha are visited by Anna Bernays and her daughter Judith in the afternoon. Almost at the same time, Recha Pappenheim arrives with daughter Bertha.
– F. and Martha are visited by Ottilie Weiss and Samuel Weiss in the evening.

1886 December 30
Josef Herzig, Sigmund Lustgarten, Ignaz Rosanes and Julius Fürth are F.'s guests in the evening.

1886 December 31
F.'s family is visiting Maria-Theresien-Strasse on New Year's Eve.

1886 December end
F. is invited by Albert Villaret to write a few articles for the *Handwörterbuch der gesamten Medizin (Concise Dictionary of All Medicine),* which is to earn him just under 300 marks.

1887

- F. writes a series of articles for Albert Villaret's *Handwörterbuch der gesamten Medizin.*
- F. works on a paper on "Brain anatomy and general characters of hysterical affections", but it is not published.
- F. begins the treatment of Marianne Engel.
- F. begins the treatment of the later women's rights activist Louise Hackl.

1887 January 2
Arthur Schnitzler publishes a review of F.'s translation of Charcot's *New Lectures on the Diseases of the Nervous System. F.* had introduced the work to German literature and translated it in an excellent manner.

1887 approx. January 23
F. and Martha calculate their annual expenses at 4200 Gulden[19] with the greatest restriction.

1887 January 31
Moritz Freud comes back from England.

1887 February 16
Sigmund Exner proposes to the Society of Physicians that F. be admitted as a member; co-signers of the proposal are as follows: Markus Abeles, Samuel Basch, Ernst Ludwig, Julius Mauthner, Carl Stoerk.

1887 March 18
F. is elected as a member of the Society of Physicians.

1887 approx. February 20
F. receives a microtome as a gift from Josef Breuer for his planned home laboratory.

1887 February 21
During a congratulatory visit on the occasion of the forthcoming wedding of F.'s sister Mitzi to Moritz, F. meets Eli Bernays; however, the two politely pass each other by.

1887 February 22
Wedding of F.'s sister Mitzi to her cousin Moritz. For financial reasons, the Jewish ceremony does not take place in the synagogue, but at Praterstrasse 30, F. is the best man.

1887 February 23
The three now married children of Amalia and Jakob (F. and Martha, Eli and Anna, and Moritz and Mitzi) visit their parents and unmarried siblings at Praterstrasse 30.

1887 March beginning
- F.'s sisters Dolfi and Paula take jobs as teachers.
- Martha discovers that she is pregnant.

1887 March 9
F. has a consultation with Josef Breuer.

1887 approx. March 10
- Martha has a mild form of "diphtheritis", and Josef Breuer and Max Kassowitz look after her.
- F. orders a table and cabinet for his home laboratory.

1887 March 22–24
Visit to the sick in Teplice
F. travels to Teplitz (now Teplice) at the request of Karl Koller's father Leopold Koller for a consultation on his brother Gabriel, who is seriously ill with progressive paralysis.

1887 March 22
Departure from Vienna.

1887 March 23
F. meets Martha's relatives at the Koller house: Johanna Brecher, a sister of Martha's father and her husband Alois. F. goes for a half-day walk with him.

1887 March 24
- In the morning, he visits Johanna and Alois Brecher, who live only a few kilometers north of Teplice in Eichwald (now Dubí).
- F. travels in the evening from Teplitz to Schreckenstein near Aussig (now Střekov near Ústí) and from there on to Vienna.

1887 March 25
F. arrives in Vienna in the morning.

1887 March 26
Death of Gabriel Koller; F. had visited him two days earlier in Teplitz and written from there to his nephew Karl Koller: "If it continues at this rate [of progressive paralysis], life will last for another 14 days" (F. to Koller, 24.3.1887).

1887 March 27
- F. and Martha congratulate Bertha Pollaczeck and Leopold Böhm on their engagement. Bertha was a niece by marriage of Martha's aunt Lea Löw-Beer from Brünn.
- F. and Martha are visiting Breuer's in the evening. There is also Emmy Altschul, a relative of Breuer from Dresden, whom F. had met during his stay in Dresden in 1883 December.

1887 March 28
Martha's aunt Lea Löw-Beer visits F. and Martha.

1887 March 29
Alois Brecher visits F. and Martha that evening. F. had seen him a few days earlier in Teplitz.

1887 March 30
F. and Martha meet with Alois Brecher at Eli Bernays.

1887 March 31
Karl Koller comes to Vienna from Utrecht and has dinner with F. and Martha.
1887 April beginning
F.'s home laboratory is functional.

1887 April 2
F. and Martha give a "semester evening"; i.e., F.'s listeners get their lecture fees back in the form of food.

1887 April
F. offers lectures "Ueber Nervenkrankheiten des kindlichen Alters, mit Demonstrationen" ("On Nervous Diseases of Childhood, with Demonstrations") in the summer semester at the I. Öffentliche Kinderkrankeninstitut in Steindlgasse.

1887 April beginning
- F. begins the treatment of Eduard Sochor, General Director of the Galician Karl Ludwig Railway.
- F.'s home laboratory is functional.

1887 April 1
F. is in the Society of Physicians and writes a report of the meeting for the *Bulletin médical*.

1887 April 7
F. and Martha are at the Hammerschlags' Seder.

1887 April mid
F. receives a consignment of ties from his silent mother.

1887 April 16
F. gives a lecture on hysteria in the Hernals section of the "Verein der Aerzte in Nieder-Oesterreich" ("Association of Physicians in Lower Austria"). The invitation was probably issued on the initiative of the Viennese doctor Alois Biach, who had been secretary of the Association since 1883. At the time of F.'s lecture, he was the responsible editor of the association's *Mitteilungen*.

1887 April 18
F. gets a visit from Breuers and Hammerschlags in the evening.

1887 April 29
F. is in the Society of Physicians and writes a report of the meeting for the *Bulletin médical*.

1887 April end
F. and Martha consider bringing Minna and Emmeline Bernays to live with them in Vienna.

1887 May
Leopold Lichtwitz gives F. his book *Les Anesthésies Hystériques des Muqueuses et des Organes des Sens et les Zones Hystérogènes des Muqueuses. Recherches cliniques* with the dedication: Herrn Dr Freud,/Privatdocent an der Wiener/Universität, zu freund Erinnerung/der Verfasser./ Mai 1887. Dr Lichtwitz.

1887 May 6
F. is in the Society of Physicians and writes a report of the meeting for the *Bulletin médical*.

1887 May 13
F. is in the Society of Physicians and writes a report of the meeting for the *Bulletin médical*. He himself takes part in the discussion on Adolf Lorenz's lecture "Die Entstehung der Gelenkskontrakturen nach der spinalen Kinderlähmung".

1887 May 19–20
F. and Martha are on the Semmering.

1887 May 20
F. is in the Society of Physicians and writes a report of the meeting for the *Bulletin médical*.

1887 May 27
F. is in the Society of Physicians and writes a report of the meeting for the *Bulletin médical*.

1887 May 29
F. and Martha are visiting F.'s parents and unmarried siblings, and they all go to the Prater.

1886 May 30
F. and Martha visit Kathinka and Arnold Schmidl in Dornbach.

1887 June 10
F. is in the Society of Physicians and writes a report of the meeting for the *Bulletin médical*.

1887 June 17
F.'s mother goes with her pregnant daughter Mitzi for a spa stay at Rožnau (until the end of August).

1887 June mid
F.'s "main patient" is a "hysterical Russian [woman]" (F. to Minna, 19.7.1887).

1887 June 19
Mathilde Breuer sends the pregnant Martha a large amount of laundry, nappies, umbilical cloths and much more for the baby.

1887 August 4
Birth of F.'s niece Margarethe (daughter of his sister Mitzi) in Rožnau.

1887 August 7–9
Short stay in Rožnau
F. visits his sister Mitzi in Rožnau, who is not at all well after the birth of her first daughter.

1887 August 10–20
Trip to Salzburg and Reichenhall
F. and Martha are in Salzburg and Reichenhall for a few days; there, they meet Minna.

1887 August 16–17
F. takes Minna on a two-day trip to Königssee and Berchtesgaden.

1887 August 28
F. and Martha go to the Krieau in the Prater.

1887 August end
F.'s mother comes back to Vienna from Rožnau.

1887 October 10
- F. starts a course on brain anatomy for three foreign doctors: among them is Wilhelm Fliess from Berlin.
- F. offers lectures in the winter semester on "The anatomy of the spinal cord and the medulla oblongata as an introduction to the clinic of nervous diseases" (lecture hall of Theodor Meynert, fee five Gulden).
- F. offers a lecture on "Aphasia" once a week in the winter semester (fee five Gulden).

1887 October mid
Luise Zeissl, the wife of Maximilian Zeissl, begins a fattening cure at F.

1887 October 16
Birth of F.'s daughter Mathilde (named after Mathilde Breuer) at 19.45 in Maria-Theresien-Strasse 8 as the first child of F. and Martha. The doctor present was Gustav Lott, and the midwife was Maria Völkl. The family received a vase from the Porzellanmanufaktur from the Emperor on the occasion of the birth; this was the first child born in the Sühnhaus, the house that the Emperor had built on the site of the burned-down Ringtheater.

1887 October 17

F. begins the treatment of F. Anna von Lieben ("Cäcilie M") (until autumn 1893). She had been referred to him by Josef Breuer and Rudolf Chrobak. Jean-Martin Charcot had also already treated her. At times, F. visits her three to four times a week. During her treatment, F. discovers the phenomenon of transference.

1887 October 19

A wet nurse arrives from Rožnau for F.'s three-day-old daughter Mathilde.

1887 October 21

F. hears a lecture by Viktor Urbantschitsch "On the Influence of a Sensory Excitation on the Other Sensations" at the Society of Physicians and takes part in the discussion.

1887 October 22

F. is in the evening for a consultation with Max Kassowitz.

1887 October 23

– The wet nurse from Rožnau is replaced because "her milk […] became less and less; in the process she ate hair-raising quantities of all sorts of things, finally spoiled herself, became miserable and the child got a green stool on top of everything else" (F. to Emmeline and Minna Bernays, 23.10.1887).
– Carl Stoerk seeks out F. and asks him to come to Regine Friedländer whose daughter Helene is having a severe hysterical fit.

1887 October 24

F. is at a consultation with Chrobak about Anna von Lieben.

1887 October 27

F. acquires Julius Robert Mayer's *The Mechanics of Heat in Collected Writings*.

1887 October 29

F. offers lectures twice a week in the winter semester on the "Anatomy of the Spinal Cord and the Medulla oblongata as an Introduction to the Clinic of Nervous Diseases" (lecture hall of Theodor Meynert). Among the listeners is Wilhelm Fliess.

1887 November mid

– F. works on a book about aphasia and on articles for Albert Villaret's *Handwörterbuch der gesamten Medizin.*
– F. begins the treatment of Louise Benedikt ("Frau Dr. A."), the wife of Moritz Benedikt. He treats her with galvanization and baths.

1887 November 24

Beginning of the correspondence between F. and Wilhelm Fliess.

1887 December

– F. is considering translating Hippolyte Bernheim's book on suggestion and quickly reaches an agreement with the publisher.
– During the past weeks, F. has thrown himself into hypnosis and has "achieved all sorts of small but noteworthy successes" (F. to Fliess, 28.12.1887).
– F. sends a manuscript on brain anatomy to Wilhelm Fliess.

1887 December 9

F. signs the publishing contract with Deuticke for the translation of Bernheim's *Suggestion and its Healing Effects* (1550 copies, fee 20 Gulden per sheet).

1887 before December 31

F. applies to resign from the Landwehr. His resignation is approved on December 31, with the simultaneous passing of the officer's rank.

1888

- F. translates Hippolyte Bernheim's The Suggestion and its Healing Effects.
- F. is included in the *Allgemeiner Deutscher Hochschulen-Almanach* with an autobiographical entry.
- F. begins the treatment of Franziska Wertheimstein.

1888 January

F. is working on an article on hysteria for Villaret's *Handbook*.

1888 January 23

Jean-Martin Charcot gives F. his *Oeuvres complètes. Leçons sur les Maladies du Système nerveux* with the dedication "À Monsieur Le/Docteur Freud,/Excellent Suvenir/de la Salpêtrière./Charcot".

1888 February 3

A scandal breaks out in the Society of Physicians. The members should be obliged to subscribe to the *Wiener klinische Wochenschrift*, "which is intended to represent the purified, exact, and Christian views of a few Hofräte [high civil servants] who have long ago forgotten what work is like". F. feels "very much like resigning" (F. to Fliess, 4.2.1888).

1888 February 4

- F. goes for consultation with Theodor Meynert.
- F. completes the first draft of his Hysteria article for Villaret's *Handbook*.

1888 Spring

F. and his student friend Julius Fürth carry out hypnotic experiments on a young girl who was being treated as an inpatient in the Allgemeines Krankenhaus for an inflammatory change in the bursa in front of her kneecap. On one occasion, in Fürth's flat, they were unable to bring her back from hypnosis for hours.

1888 April

F. offers lectures in the summer semester "On Nervous Diseases of Childhood" (Public Children's Hospital, Steindlgasse 2, fee five Gulden).

1888 April 10

Ernst Brücke is awarded the "Medal of Honor for Art and Science" by the Kaiser. Fifty years later, F. wrote that it was the only award he wanted to receive "because his master Brücke received it" (F. to Arnold Zweig, 2.4.1937).

1888 April beginning

F. begins the treatment of the writer Elisabeth Glück (pseudonym: Betty Paoli). It lasts until the end of 1888.

1888 April mid

F. begins the treatment of the writer Elisabeth Glück (pseudonym: Betty Paoli). It lasts until the end of 1888. From the end of April, Freud treats her daily with electrotherapy.

1888 April 19

Death of Maximilian Leidesdorf. F. had known Leidesdorf since 1885, when the latter had campaigned for F. to be awarded the travel grant.

1888 May

F. is working on a paper in French on the comparison of hysterical and organic symptomatology.

1888 May 28

F. treats a patient with hypnosis.

1888 June 2

Theodor Meynert gives a lecture "On Hypnotic Phenomena" to the Society of Physicians.

1888 July beginning

Martha and daughter Mathilde travel to Maria Schutz am Semmering.

1888 August

F. writes the preface to his translation of Hippolyte Bernheim's *Die Suggestion und ihre Heilwirkung.*

1888 August 29

F. sends Wilhelm Fliess his photograph.

1888 August end–September beginning

F. goes for a week to Maria Schutz am Semmering, where Martha and daughter Mathilde have been staying since the beginning of July.

1888 September beginning

F.'s translation of Hippolyte Bernheim's *Die Suggestion und ihre Heilwirkung* appears (edition of 1550 copies).

1888 October

F. offers lectures on the "Anatomy of the Spinal Cord and the Medulla oblongata" in the winter semester (lecture hall Theodor Meynert, fee five Gulden).

1888 November 9

Death of Heinrich Bamberger. F. had heard lectures on special medical pathology, therapy and clinic from him as a student; Bamberger also presided over F.'s lecture "On Male Hysteria" at the Society of Physicians on 1886 October 15.

1888 November 22

Birth of F.'s niece Lilly, daughter of his sister Mitzi.

1889

- F. acquires Rudolph Hermann Lotze's "Grundzüge der Naturphilosophie".
- Adele Jeitteles is in F.'s consulting hours, but does not begin treatment until much later. In 1900, she married Henrik Koestler, and in 1905, their son Arthur Koestler was born.

1889 April

F. offers a weekly "Konservatorium" on the "Progress of Neuropathology" in the summer semester (fee five Gulden).

1889 May 1

- F. begins the treatment of Fanny Moser ("Emmy von N.), one of the richest women in Europe (until June 1890). She is the patient in F.'s first case history in the studies on hysteria.
- F. is at Joseph Paneth's for tarot in the evening.

1889 May 2

F. visits Fanny Moser in the evening at Anton Löw's sanatorium at Mariannengasse 20.

1889 May 2–7

F. treats Fanny Moser with warm baths and full body massage and begins with hypnosis and for the first time uses the cathartic method, i.e. remembering childhood traumas under hypnosis.

1889 May 8–17

F. visits Fanny Moser every day.

1889 June

Mathilde Schleicher gives F. Johannes Scherr's book *Germania. Two millennia of German life* with the dedication: "Dem ausgezeichneten Arzte Herrn Dr. Freud zur freundlichen Erinnerung. Als Zeichen vollster Dankbarkeit und Verehrung Mathilde Schleicher".

1889 June 13

F.'s mother goes with daughter Mitzi and her two children for a spa stay at Rožnau. Later, Jakob Freud and his daughters Anna and Dolfi arrive. They stay until the end of September.

1889 June 18

Fanny Moser leaves Vienna, and this concludes the first part of the treatment.

1889 June 26

F. reads the headline of an article in the Vienna *Neuigkeits-Welt-Blatt* as "Im Fass durch Europa" ("In the barrel through Europe") instead of "Zu Fuss durch Europa" ("On foot through Europe").

1889 July 18–August 14
Trip to Switzerland and France

1889 July 19

F. visits Fanny Moser at her estate in Au near Wädenswil on the southwestern shore of Lake Zurich. Auguste Forel is also in Au, and F. receives a letter of recommendation from him for Hippolyte Bernheim, whom he then plans to visit in Nancy.

1889 July 20

- F. arrives in Nancy and visits Hippolyte Bernheim and Ambroise Liébeault. With them, he wants to perfect his hypnotic technique. He is accompanied by his patient with Anna

von Lieben, whom he introduces to Bernheim and who is hypnotized by the latter almost daily.
– F. meets the Swedish doctor Axel Lindfors in Nancy.

1889 July 28

F. takes a longer hike to Liverdun and returns to Nancy by train.

1889 July 29

F. goes to Metz

1889 July end

F. reads Ambroise Liébault's Le sommeil provoqué, Antoine-François Prévost's L'histoire du chevalier des Grieux et de Manon Lescault and Xavier de Maistre's Le voyage autour de ma chambre.

1889 August 3

F. travels to Paris together with Auguste Liébeault and Hippolyte Bernheim to the International Congress of Experimental and Therapeutic Hypnotism. F. stays at the Hotel Byron at 30 rue Laffitte.

1889 approx. August 6

– F. finds the Congress boring, goes shopping and presumably buys the lithograph with Charcot and his pupils, which he then hangs in his study in Vienna.
– F. attends a performance by singer Yvette Guilbert for the first time.

1889 August 12

F. leaves Paris late in the evening.

1889 August 13

F. arrives in Salzburg shortly before midnight. He hopes to meet Minna at the station, who is at the spa in Reichenhall with her mother, but Minna is unable to attend.

1889 August 14

F. arrives in Vienna in the morning.

1889 August 14–September beginning
F. is in Reichenau with his family for the summer, but occasionally goes to Vienna.

1889 September 16–17
F. travels to Rožnau to visit his seriously ill sister Anna.

1889 September end
F.'s mother comes back to Vienna from Rožnau.

1889 October
F. offers a weekly "Konservatorium" on the "Progress of Neuropathology" in the winter semester (lecture hall of Theodor Meynert, fee five Gulden).

1889 after October 25
F. begins the treatment of Kathinka Schmidl (née Kadisch). She is the patient of F.'s published case history "A case of hypnotic healing along with remarks on the development of hysterical symptoms through the 'counter will'". The treatment lasts until 1890.

1889 October 29
F. refers his patient Mathilde Schleicher to the private sanatorium of Wilhelm Svetlin.

1889 November mid
Thanks to Josef Breuer's help, F.'s sister Anna recovers after being given up by nine doctors. After her return from Rožnau, she moves to Baden.

1889 December beginning
Marcel Dufour, a young doctor and friend of Hippolyte Bernheim, comes to F with a letter of recommendation from the latter. He wants to further his training in ophthalmology in Vienna.

1889 December 7
Birth of son Martin at 8 Maria-Theresien-Strasse, second child of F. and Martha.

1889 December 31
The play "Der Graben-Fiaker" is premiered at the Theater an der Josefstadt. The text is by Josef Wimmer, and the music is by Julius Stern. The couplet "solche Leut' die sterb'n aus" ("people like that are dying out") was, according to the printed version of the Buchjäger publishing house in Vienna, "dedicated to the well-known lecturer Dr. S. Freud".

1890

– Jakob Freud's family moves from Praterstrasse 30 to Grüne Thorgasse 14, a few hundred meters from F.'s flat in Maria-Theresien-Strasse.
– Richard von Krafft-Ebing gives F. his book *Neue Forschungen auf* dem *Gebiet der Psychopathia sexualis* with the dedication "Herrn Dr. F. in collegialer Hochachtung d. Verf.".
– F. begins the treatment of Josephine Benvenisti. It lasted until about 1896. F. received his couch from this patient in the autumn of 1891.

1890 January 4
Death of F.'s friend Josef Paneth. He had suffered from tuberculosis.

1890 January 6
F. attends the funeral of Josef Paneth.

1890 April
– F. offers a weekly "Konservatorium" on the "Progress of Neuropathology" in the summer semester (lecture hall Theodor Meynert, fee five Gulden).
– F.'s brother-in-law Eli goes to Bulgaria and Romania to look for new business, but returns empty-handed.

1890 April 28
Fanny Moser is back in Vienna for treatment with F. and stays until June 21.

1890 May 1
F. experiences its first workers' demonstration.

1890 May end
Mathilde Schleicher returns to F.'s treatment from Svetlin's sanatorium.

1890 June 15
F.'s mother goes with daughter Mitzi and her two children for a spa stay at Rožnau (until the beginning of September).

1890 June 21
Fanny Moser's second treatment is completed after eight weeks.

1890 August 1
F. is in Reichenau, visiting his family.

1890 August end
F. is in Salzburg for three days for the first "Congress" with Wilhelm Fliess. Both men spend the night in Hirschbühel and hike to Bad Reichenhall and Berchtesgaden, among other places. There, F. has an attack of travel anxiety.

1890 September beginning
F.'s mother comes back to Vienna from Rožnau.

1890 September 20
F. acquires Sante de Sanctis' book *I Sogni. Studi psicologici e clinici di un alienista.*

1890 September 24

Death of F.'s patient Mathilde Schleicher.

1890 October

F. offers a weekly "Konservatorium" on the "Progress of Neuropathology" in the winter semester. (lecture hall of Theodor Meynert, fee five Gulden).

1890 October 1

F. and Josef Breuer visit Anna von Lieben.

1891

- F.'s Clinical Study on Hemiplegic Cerebral Palsy in Children, written together with Oskar Rie, is published. He gives one copy to Obersteiner with the dedication "Herrn Prof. Obersteiner in Dank und Hochachtung wie immer Dr. Freud".
- F.'s sister-in-law Minna becomes the companion of Melanie and Alice Dub, later of their father Moritz Dub, on the recommendation of Joseph Paneth. Minna lived for four years in the Dub family home at Waaggasse 4, where F. visited her regularly.
  Books received and given away:
- Emanuel Loewy gives F. his book *Lysipp und seine Stellung in der griechischen Plastik* with the dedication "Mit herzlichsten Gruss d. Vf.".
- Krafft-Ebing gives F. the second edition of his *book Neue Forschungen auf dem Gebiet der Psychopathia sexualis* with the dedication "in collegialer Hochachtung d. Verf.".
- F. gives Heinrich Obersteiner his monograph *Klinische Studie über die halbseitige Cerebrallähmung der Kinder,* written together with Oskar Rie, with the dedication "Herrn Prof. H. Obersteiner in Dank und Hochachtung wie immer/Dr Freud".

1891 February 19
Birth of Oliver at Maria Theresia Street 8, third child of F. and Martha.

1891 Spring
- F.'s sister Anna moves from Baden back to Vienna, but to a new flat in the II. district, where she does not have to climb stairs after her serious illness.
- F. begins the treatment of Olga Schweinburg ("Nina R."). It lasts with interruptions until 1894.

1891 April
F. offers lectures twice a week in the summer semester on "Ueber Nervenkrankheiten des Kindesalters, mit Demonstrationen" ("About nervous diseases of childhood, with demonstrations"); fee five Gulden.

1891 April 17
F. and Oskar Rie give Hermann Nothnagel their jointly written book *Klinische Studie über die halbseitige Celebrallähmung der Kinder* with the dedication "Ihrem verehrten Lehrer Herrn Hofrath Prof. Nothnagel".

1891 May 6
F. receives a Bible with a Hebrew dedication from his father.

1891 before May 9
F. goes on foot to look for a new flat. At Berggasse 19, he finds a sign "For rent". He signs the tenancy agreement without having discussed it with Martha.

1891 May 9
F. terminates the tenancy agreement for the flat at Maria-Theresien-Strasse 8 as of November.

1891 May 14
Pauline Silberstein, the wife of F.'s childhood friend Eduard Silberstein, commits suicide in F.'s house at Maria-Theresien-Strasse 8. Presumably she had a consultation with him that day and threw herself into the stairwell before or after it.

1891 approx. May 15
Martha takes the children on a summer retreat to Reichenau.

1891 May mid
Renovation work begins at Berggasse 19: The hallway is wood-paneled and enlarged at the expense of the kitchen, and F.'s future study is wallpapered.

1891 May 22
F. makes two sick visits to Anna von Lieben and can only have lunch after 3.00 pm.

1891 May 23
F.'s tailor Franz Tischer delivers a loden suit and a summer suit.

1891 May 24
F. visits his family in Reichenau.

1891 May 26
F. visits Sophie Paneth, the wife of his deceased friend Joseph Paneth.

1891 May 27 to 31
Visit to Fanny Moser in Au on Lake Zurich
F. visits his patient Fanny Moser at her castle in Au on Lake Zurich. She had urged him to come by telegram because her 19-year-old daughter Fanny had entered a phase of abnormal development, and F. was to give a verdict on her condition.

1891 May 27
Departure from Vienna in the evening.

1891 May 28
Arrival in Au. In addition to assessing the daughter, F. takes his patient for walks on the estate.

1891 May 30
Departure from Au.

1891 May 31
Arrival in Vienna.

1891 June
The printing of F.'s aphasia book is delayed by a compositor's strike that has been going on for weeks.

1891 June 1
F. visits Josef Breuer in the evening and brings him pictures.

1891 June 2
On the occasion of Max Kassowitz's appointment as an associate professor of pediatrics, a group photo is taken with him and his colleagues, including F.

1891 June 3
– F. goes to Berggasse 19 to check on the renovation work. His study is already wallpapered – in grey-brown; previously, it was red.
– F. visits Oskar Ries' father Isidor in the evening and plays tarot with him until 2.30 in the night.

1891 June 5
– Josephine Benvenisti invites F. to lunch.
– F. visits Anna Hammerschlag.

1891 June 6–7
F. visits his family in Reichenau.

1891 June 10
F. is invited to lunch at Josephine Benvenisti's again.

1891 June 13–14
F. visits his family in Reichenau.

1891 June 16
F. visits Oskar Rie.

1891 June 18
F. is at his mother's for lunch and brings her gloves, playing cards and an inkwell for her annual stay at the spa.

1891 June 19
F. shows Mathilde Breuer the new flat in the Berggasse, which she likes "extraordinarily" and finds "cute" (F. to Martha, 19.6.1891).

1891 June 20–21
F. visits his family in Reichenau and goes to the Jakobskogel on the Rax on the 21st.

1891 June 23
F. has lunch with Minna and meets his father, who then drives to Reichenau.

1891 July beginning
– The flat in Maria-Theresien-Strasse is slowly being dissolved, and the move to Berggasse 19 is being prepared.
– F. begins treating Minna Basler, who runs a shop for ladies' riding clothes in Maximilian-strasse. It lasts until 1892.

1891 July 7
– F. makes a patient visit in Weidling near Klosterneuburg.
– F. says goodbye to Breuer, who is going on summer holiday.

1891 July 10 approx.
F.'s book *Zur Auffassung der Aphasien*, which he dedicated to Josef Breuer, is published (edition of 850 copies). When he hands Breuer a copy, he has the feeling that Breuer is not enthusiastic.

1891 July 10–12
F. visits his family in Reichenau and goes on a trip to the Rax on the 12th.

1891 July 13
F. and Martha go to Baden to visit F.'s mother, who is there for a spay stay with daughter Anna and her children.

1891 July mid
– F. gives Rudolf Chrobak his book *Zur Auffassung der Aphasien* with the dedication "Herrn Prof. R. Chrobak in Verehrung d. Verf.".

– F. gives Wilhelm Fliess his book *Zur Auffassung der Aphasien* with the dedication Herrn Dr. Wihl. Fliess/mit herzlichen Grusse/der Verf.".

1891 July 16–19
– F. visits his family in Reichenau and goes climbing on the Rax with Max Kassowitz. Afterward, they meet with their wives in Prein.
– Charcot is in Vienna on his way back from Moscow to Paris. He asks the doctor Alois Bloch about F., who tells him that F. is not in Vienna, which Charcot regrets very much.

1891 July 20
– F. visits his mother in Baden and drives back to Vienna with her.
– F. recommends Minna Edward Bellamy's book *Dr. Heidenhoff's Wunderkur,* saying it is "in fantastic form the same thing I actually do with the dear one" (F. to Minna, 20.7.1891).

1891 July 23 until August end
F. spends the summer with his family in Reichenau am Semmering
Twice a week, he went on 8- to 12-hour hikes, which gave him "a feeling of physical well-being he had not known for ages" (F. to Minna, 11.8.1891). From Reichenau, F. also travels regularly to Vienna.

1891 July 26
– For Martha's birthday, Emilie and Max Kassowitz are in Reichenau, as well as family members. The celebration takes place in the evening at the Kurhaus.
– Max Kassowitz vaccinates F.'s son Oliver against smallpox.

1891 July 27
F. travels via Sulz and Baden, where he visits his mother, to Vienna.

1891 before July 28
F. receives return gifts in the form of offprints and letters of thanks for his aphasia book, including one from Karl Eisenlohr from Hamburg, who calls the book very interesting and witty.

1891 July 28–29
– F. takes an express train to Reichenau in the morning.
– F. and Martha walk up the Rax via the Schlangenweg, spend the night there in the Schutzhaus and walk back the next day via the Thörlweg.

1891 July 30
F. and Martha go to Vienna to "arrange everything for the new flat" (Martha to Minna, 4.8.1891).

1891 July end
Anna von Lieben goes for a week to Hinterbrühl near Mödling, where her parents have a villa. F. still expects at least six months of treatment. However, this should turn out to be too optimistic.

1891 August 1
F. goes on an excursion to the Rax accompanied by Oskar Rie, Max Kassowitz, his brother Hermann and Hans Abels. Martha expects them in Nasswald in the evening, and they all wanted to go back to Reichenau in a carriage. On the way, the carriage overturns, but only

Hermann Kassowitz is slightly injured. The company stays overnight in an inn nearby and drives to Reichenau the next day.

1891 August 10

Moritz Schwarzkopf comes to Reichenau with his wife Paulina. She is the sister of F.'s student friend Julius Fürth.

1891 August 11

Arthur Schwarz from Budapest – a former colleague of F. at the Allgemeines Krankenhaus – comes to Reichenau.

1891 August 12–13

F. goes on a two-day hike on the Rax and Schneealpe with Max Kassowitz. They spend the night at Gasthof Wallner in Nasswald.

1891 August 15

Julius Fürth, one of F.'s student friends, comes to Reichenau.

1891 August 18–21

F. hikes with Max Kassowitz through the Gesäuse, a mountain group in the northeastern part of the Ennstal Alps. Then, they drive to Schladming and climb the Dachstein from the south. The return journey is via Hallstatt.

1891 August 27

Hippolyte Bernheim stays overnight in Vienna on his way back from Budapest to Paris, and F. visits him in the morning at the Hotel Munsch on Neuer Markt. Bernheim is surprised to hear that F. is translating his book *Hypnotisme, suggestion et psychothérapie, études nouvelles* into German.

1891 August end /September beginning

F. commutes back and forth between Vienna and Reichenau. In Vienna, he is busy moving from Maria-Theresien-Strasse to Berggasse.

1891 September 14

- F. moves into the new flat at Berggasse 19 (he is registered there from 1891 September 23). His family joins him a little later from Reichenau. Freud lives in Berggasse until 1938 June 4.
- F. buys a new desk set: black leather pad, inkwell with spring pin, paper stand with small calendar, blotting paper and matchbox.

1891 after September 14

F. receives his analytical couch as a gift from Josephine Benvenisti.

1891 September 15

- F. announces in the *Neue Freie Presse* that he now lives at Berggasse 19 and ordains there from 5 to 7 pm.
- F. is in the I. Public Children's Hospital Institute.
- Wilhelm Fliess visits F. in Vienna.

1891 approx. September

F. is asked by a colleague – presumably Albert Hammerschlag – to investigate Helene Weiss ("Elisabeth von R.").

1891 Autumn

F. begins the treatment of Helene Weiss. It lasts until the summer of 1892. The last of F.'s medical history of *studies on hysteria is* dedicated to her. F. tries to put her under hypnosis. But he did not succeed, and since the patient had already told him in earlier futile attempts that she could not be hypnotized, F. decided to do without hypnosis with her and, following Hippolyte Bernheim, proceeded to the following procedure: he pressed his hand lightly on the patient's forehead and ordered her to say anything she could think of. He later called this new technique "free association". In introducing this technique, F. assumed that "so-called free association will in reality prove to be unfree, because through the suppression of all conscious impulses, a determination of the ideas by the unconscious material comes to light".

1891 October

F. offers a weekly "Konservatorium" on the progress of neuropathology in the winter semester (fee five Gulden).

1891 October 2

F. acquires Theodor Lipps's writing *Der Streit über die Tragödie.*

1891 October 22

Death of F.'s friend Ernst Fleischl.

1891 November 22

Birth of nephew Edward, son of F.'s sister Anna Bernays.

1891 November end

- "Lucy R." is referred to F. by a colleague friend and is treated by him for nine weeks. Her case history is later included in the *studies on hysteria.*
- F. writes a manuscript on problems of neurasthenia and anxiety neurosis.

1891 December

F.'s brother-in-law Eli leaves for America without informing his wife – F.'s sister Anna – and stays there until 1892 March.

1892

- F. writes a series of articles for the *Diagnostisches Lexikon für praktische Ärzte* published by Anton Bum and Moritz Schnirer.
- F.'s German translation of Bernheim's *New Studies on Hypnotism* appears (edition of 1500 copies).
- Treatments:
- F. begins treating Emma Eckstein (until 1910, with interruptions). F. is friends with her brother Friedrich Eckstein, an Austrian polymath, throughout his life.
- F. begins the treatment of Francisca Biach, the wife of Moritz Biach.
  Books received and given away:
- Pierre Marie gives F. his *Leçons sur les Maladies de la Moelle* with the dedication "A M. le Dr F. cordial souvenir P. Marie".
- Richard von Krafft-Ebing gives F. the seventh edition of his book *Psychopathia sexualis mit besonderer Berücksichtigung der conträren Sexualempfindung* with the dedication "Herrn Dozent Dr. F. in collegialer Hochachtung d Verf.".

1892 January
Wilhelm Fliess visits F. in Vienna.

1892 January 7
Death of F.'s teacher Ernst Brücke.

1892 March
Eli Bernays returns from America.

1892 April
F. offers "Lectures on Nervous Diseases of Childhood" twice a week in the summer semester (fee five Gulden).

1892 April 6
Birth of Ernst at Berggasse 19, fourth child of F. and Martha.

1892 April 27
F. gives the first part of a lecture entitled "On Hypnosis and Suggestion" to the "Vienna Medical Club".

1892 May beginning
F.'s brother-in-law Eli Bernays's company goes bankrupt.

1892 May 4
F. gives the second part of a lecture entitled "On Hypnosis and Suggestion" to the Vienna Medical Club.

1892 May 5
F.'s brother-in-law Eli Bernays goes to America again. According to F.'s sister Anna, the American consul in Vienna had recommended it to him.

1892 May 31
Death of F.'s teacher – and ultimately also scientific opponent – Theodor Meynert.

1892 June
- F. writes the preface to his translation of Charcot's *Poliklinische Vorträge*.
- F. and Martha have the flat renovated and redecorated. F. moves his practice down one floor. Rooms had become available there.

- F. sends Josef Breuer the first draft of the article "On the psychic mechanism of hysterical phenomena".
- F. and Wilhelm Fliess move on to the Du.

1892 June 1

Martha goes to Reichenau with the children during the summer. F. usually visits them at least once a week.

1892 June 2

F. is having dinner with Leopold Königstein. He finds the asparagus bad, but the goose good.

1892 June 3

The dining room in the Berggasse is wallpapered and is now "very gloomy and very distinguished" (F. to Martha, 3.6.1892).

1892 June 4

F. visits Hammerschlags.

1892 June 4–6

F. visits his family in Reichenau over Whitsun. There, he meets "Lucy R." again. "She was in good spirits and assured me that her recovery had been maintained" (SE 2, p. 121).

- 1892 June 7
- F.'s surgery is almost completely renovated and furnished.
- F. is visited by Ida and Wilhelm Fliess. They go shopping together and have lunch at the Hotel Munsch.
- In the evening, Philipp Bondy, Wilhelm Fliess's father-in-law, picks F. up in the Berggasse and they drive to his family residence in the Brühl, where F. is invited to dinner.

1892 June 9

- F. receives a visit from his father and sister-in-law Minna.
- F. is at Biach's for tarot in the evening.

1892 June 10

F. meets with Ignaz Rosanes, Julius Fürth and Moritz Schwarzkopf.

1892 June mid

F.'s mother goes for a spa stay at Rožnau (until mid-September).

1892 June 14

F. goes out with Minna in the evening.

1892 June 20

F. visits Josef Breuer in the evening to hand him the finished article "On the Psychic Mechanism of Hysterical Phenomena". He then goes to Anna von Lieben.

1892 June 21

F. meets with one of Bernheim's assistants who is in Vienna. Both visit the "International Music and Theater Exhibition" and then a performance of *The Tragedy of Man* by Imre Madách. F. is thrilled by the stage design. Then, the two men go to the Riedhof for dinner.

1892 June 22

F. visits Oskar Rie in the evening.

1892 June 23

− F. waits 2½ hours in Wallnerstrasse to see Otto von Bismarck, who is in Vienna on the occasion of the wedding of his son Herbert to Marguerite Countess von Hoyos. However, F. then only sees Bismarck from behind.
− F. meets Emma Pappenheim and has a long conversation with her.
− F. is with Leopold Königstein in the evening.

1892 June 24

F. is with Josef Breuer in the evening.

1892 June 27

− Josef Breuer agrees to publish something with F. about hysteria.
− F.'s carpenter Eduard Tuczek delivers two small tables, a new bookcase and a "round frame" (F. to Martha, 4.7.1892).

1892 June 28

F. sends the first delivery of Charcot's *Poliklinische Vorträge, which he* has translated, to Wilhelm Fliess, but is still not finished with the whole translation.

1892 June 29

F. goes to his family in Reichenau.

1892 June 30

F. visits Josef Breuer.

1892 July

F. is invited to a souper in Grinzing, where Salomon Ehrmann and Olga Sachs, the sister of Hanns Sachs, are among the guests.

1892 July beginning

− F. selects books from Theodor Meynert's library and writes to Wilhelm Fliess: "Last week brought me a rare human pleasure: The opportunity to select from Meynert's library what suited me − somehow like a savage drinking mead from his enemy's skull" (F. to Fliess, 12.7.1892).
− F. is with Anna von Lieben three times a week until after midnight, and F. notices that he is missing sleep.
− F.'s ideas about the joint publication on hysteria "has, in Breuer's hands, become transformed, broadened, restricted, and in the process has partially evaporated". Nevertheless, they "are writing the thing jointly, each on his own working on several sections which he will sign, but still in complete agreement" (F. to Fliess, 12.7.1892).

1892 July 1

F. is at Hermann Teleky's for a game of tarot in the evening.

1892 July 2

− F. is called to Elise Gomperz who has an attack of facial neuralgia.
− F. gives the last lecture of the semester and concludes it with a small souper.

1892 July 3

− F. is visiting a patient in Weidling near Klosterneuburg.
− F. visits his sister Rosa.

1892 July 5
- F. is at the wedding of Annica Benvenisti's son Leon with Emmy Heymann. The wedding takes place in Währing, followed by lunch at the Hotel Sacher in Operngasse. He found it "no better tasting than at home" (F. to Martha, 7.7.1892). His dinner companion was Annica Benvenisti's daughter Sofie Russo, with whom F. was not bored.
- F. visits Oskar Rie in the evening; his brother Paul, who lives in America, is also there, as well as Emil and Albert Hammerschlag.

1892 July 11
- Anna von Lieben goes to Hinterbrühl near Mödling and intends to come to Reichenau in August to be further treated by F. there.
- F. goes on a mountain tour.
- F. visits the Bondy family in Hinterbrühl; he is again picked up from home by Philipp Bondy.

1892 July 12
An appreciative critique of F.'s book *Zur Auffassung der Aphasien* appears in the *Archiv für Psychiatrie und Nervenkrankheiten*. It was written by Friedrich Jolly, the director of the psychiatric clinic of the Charité in Berlin.

1892 July 13
F. is visiting Biach's in the evening.

1892 July 15
F. picks up Anna von Lieben in Hinterbrühl and accompanies her to Reichenau.

1892 July mid
F. reads "Psychology".
- 1892 July 17
- F. visits his sister Anna in Baden on the way back from Reichenau. Her husband Eli had written to her that "if a certain deal goes through" (F. to Martha, 19.7.1892), he wanted to take her to America with him in October.
- Josef Breuer visits F. to talk to him about the studies on hysteria.
- F. is still Josef Herzig for dinner.

1892 July 21
F. spends the evening with an assistant of Charcot and an assistant of Bernheim.

1892 July 23–24
F. visits his family in Reichenau.

1892 July 29
F. is at the Vienna Volkstheater with the assistants of Charcot and Bernheim. They see "s'Mailüfterl" (Couqin de Printemps), a four-act play by Georges Duval, and afterward, they have dinner. F. invites them to a trip to the Semmering.

1892 July end
F. visits Josephine Benvenisti in Sulz, a community in the Vienna Woods, southwest of Vienna. There was a "cold-water sanatorium" there, which F. considered the best Austrian sanatorium.

1892 August beginning–August end
F.'s family is in Reichenau am Semmering for the summer, and F. visits them regularly.

1892 August 2–5
F. and Martha go on a short trip to Gmunden (Traunsee), Hallstatt, Sankt Gilgen (Wolfgangsee) and Aussee. In St. Gilgen, they visit Hammerschlags and Wilhelm and Charlotte Rosenthal, the parents of Emilie Kassowitz.

1892 September 2
F. makes a patient visit in St. Veit, shortly after Schönbrunn.

1892 before September 12
Eli Bernays returns from America – with only one Gulden and no luggage.

1892 September 12–13
F. makes a patient visit in Sulz and in Kaltenleutgeben.

1892 September 13
Wilhelm and Ida Fliess give F. Conrad Ferdinand Meyer's *poems* with the "Ihren lieben Freunden Sigmund und Martha F. senden den ersten Gruss vom neuen Heim Wilhelm [und] Ida Fliess".

1892 September 15
F. visits Königstein's and surprisingly meets Anna von Lieben there.

1892 September mid
F.'s mother comes back to Vienna from Rožnau.

1892 September 21
– F. receives Eugen Bleuler's paper "Zur Auffassung der subkortikalen Aphasien".
– In the flat at Berggasse 19, a bathtub is being installed and the kitchen is being painted.
– F. visits Breuers.

1892 October
F. offers lectures on "The Doctrine of Hysteria" once a week in the winter semester (lecture hall of Moritz Kaposi, fee five Gulden).

1892 October beginning
F. is writing a monograph on cerebral diplegia in childhood.

1892 October 2
F. acquires the physicist Felix Auerbach's publication "Die Weltherrin und ihr Schatten. A Lecture on Energy and Entropy".

1892 October 12
F. is at a meeting of the Vienna Medical Club and takes part in the discussion of Hermann Schlesinger's lecture on a "case of eye muscle paralysis after herpes zoster".

1892 October 21
F. recommends Wilhelm Fliess to read Rudyard Kipling.
– 1892 October 22
– Eli Bernays is arrested in Baden for allegedly failing to deliver to the owners the proceeds of diamonds he had received from Viennese jewelers for sale in America.
– Josef Breuer attends F.'s lecture "The Doctrine of Hysteria".

1892 before October 27
Eli Bernays is released from prison at his own request – possibly with the legal support of F.'s friend Josef Brust – because "through an unfortunate chain of circumstances [the] suspicion aroused [...] has proved to be completely groundless" (*Neues Wiener Tagblatt*, 27.10.1892). Eli leaves Vienna in flight – as he is bankrupt – and travels to Frankfurt am Main.

1892 October 31
– Eli Bernays asks Emanuel Freud in Manchester if he can have Anna and son Edward stay with him in Manchester on their way to America. Emanuel refuses because of the illness of his wife Maria.
– F. asks friends, including Wilhelm Fliess, for money for the impoverished family of his sister Anna. Von Fliess receives the money four days later.

1892 October end
F. tries to dissuade his sister Anna from moving to America.

1892 November 2
F.'s sister Anna follows her husband to Frankfurt with son Edward. Daughter Judith stays with grandparents Amalia and Jakob and daughter Lucie with F. and Martha. F. and his father bring Anna and Edward to the Nordwestbahnhof. Around November 10, Eli, Anna and son Edward travel to New York via Antwerp and Liverpool.

1892 November 17
Birth of F.'s niece Martha (called Tom), daughter of F.'s sister Mitzi.

1892 November end
Together with Josef Breuer, F. wrote a paper on the theory of hysterical attacks, which was only published posthumously in 1940.

1892 December
F.'s first psychotherapeutic case history is published under the title "Ein Fall von hypnotischer Heilung nebst Bemerkungen über die Entstehung hysterischer Symptome durch den 'Gegenwillen'".

1892 December mid
F. begins the treatment of the journalist and Reichsrat deputy Gustav Eim. It lasts until 1893 February mid.

1892 December 22 approx.
Wilhelm Fliess comes to visit Vienna and stays until the beginning of January. F. and he decide on a joint research project on the subject of "Neurasthenia/Anxiety Neurosis". In this context, F. writes a manuscript with the chapter headings "Problems", "Sentences", "Series" and "Etiological Moments".

1892 Christmas
Wilhelm Fliess gives F. his book *Neue Beiträge zur Klinik und Therapie der nasalen Reflexneurose* with the dedication "Der 'befreundeten Seite' zur Weihnacht 1892 Wilh. Fliess" and Hermann von Helmholtz's *Vorträge und Reden* with the dedication "Seinem lieben Sigmund Freud, zur Weihnacht 1892, Wilh. Fliess".

1893

1893 January 1
F. and Josef Breuer publish the paper "Über den psychischen Mechanismus hysterischer Phänomene" with the addition of a "Preliminary Communication". It is later incorporated unchanged into the *Studien über Hysterie*.

1893 February beginning
F. writes a manuscript with the title: "The Aetiology of Neuroses"; he sends it to Wilhelm Fliess with the warning: "You will of course keep the manuscript away from your young wife" (F. to Fliess, 8.2.1893). He also writes marginal notes on a lecture by Fliess on "nasal reflex neurosis".

1893 January 11
F. gives a lecture "On the psychic mechanism of hysterical phenomena" at the Vienna Medical Club.

1893 April
F. offers lectures on "Nervous Diseases of Childhood, with Demonstrations" twice a week in the summer semester (fee five Gulden).

1893 March 31–April 5
Visit to Wilhelm Fliess in Berlin

F. visits Wilhelm Fliess in Berlin over Easter and expresses his enthusiasm for his home furnishings.

1893 March 31

Departure from Vienna.

1893 April 1

Arrival in Berlin.

1893 April 2

F. and Fliess drive to Grunewald, where Fliess owns a plot of land with a summer cottage.

1893 April 3

– F. goes for a walk in the city.
– Felix Rosenthal, musician and brother-in-law of Max Kassowitz, visits F. in Fliess' flat.

1893 April 4

Departure from Berlin at 5.30 pm.

1893 April 5

Arrival in Vienna in the morning.

1893 April 6
F. writes to Robert Binswanger, the director of the Bellevue Sanatorium in Kreuzlingen, and asks for Josef Theiler, Eduard Silberstein's father in silence, who had been treated at the Bellevue earlier. His daughter Pauline had thrown herself to her death in the stairwell of the F. house in Maria-Theresien-Strasse on 1891 May 14.

1893 April 12
Birth of Sophie at Berggasse 19, fifth child of F. and Martha. Godmother is Sophie Paneth.

1893 April mid
F. hypnotizes seven to eight patients per day.

1893 April 16
F. is looking for violets in the Prater with his sons Martin, Oliver and Ernst.

1893 April end
F. begins to write down his dreams at, "which in ten years will result in a nice job and a good bit of toilet money" (F. to Minna, 27.4.1893).

1893 May
F. begins treating Rudolf Gellert ("Herr I."), a brother-in-law of his friend Julius Fürth, and then sends him to Wilhelm Fliess in Berlin.

1893 May 5
F. receives the offprints of his paper "Les diplégies cérébrales infantiles".

1893 May 24
F. gives a lecture "On hysterical paralysis" at the Vienna Medical Club.

1893 after May 28
F. is on a condolence visit to the family of Paul Schiff, who had died on May 28. F. had treated Paul Schiff in the last few weeks and received 500 Gulden for 20 visits. There, he meets Josef Breuer, who had recommended him to Paul Schiff's family as a doctor.

1893 before May 30
– F.'s monograph Zur Kenntniss der cerebralen Diplegien des Kindesalters is published (edition of 850 copies).
– A biographical article on F. appears in Ludwig Eisenberg's *Künstler und Schriftsteller-Lexikon*. This work is designated by the Emperor for inclusion in the Imperial entail library.

1893 May 30
– F. sent Fliess his monograph *Zur Kenntniss der cerebralen Diplegien des* Kindesalters and the paper "Quelques considérations pour une étude comparative des paralysies motrices organiques et hystériques".
– F. gives Leopold Königstein his monograph *Zur Kenntniss der Cerebralen Diplegien des Kindesalters* with the dedication: "Herrn Dr. L. Königstein mit freundschaftl. Danke/der Verfasser".
– F. is having lunch with Ludwig Eisenberg. Eisenberg was the editor of *Das geistige Wien. Künstler- und Schriftsteller-Lexikon,* in which an autobiographical entry on "Freud Sigmund (Mediciner)" had been included.

1893 May 31
F. brings his family to Reichenau am Semmering for a summer stay. In the following weeks, he visits them regularly.

1893 June beginning
F.'s mother goes to the spa at Rožnau (until September mid).

1893 June 1
F. is with sister-in-law Minna at the wedding of Ludwig Rosenberg to Judith Rie, the sister of his friend Oskar Rie.

1893 June 2
- F. buys a coat with Minna for her birthday.
- F. visits Biach's.

1893 June 3
F. goes to Sulz to visit patients.

1893 June 8
F. goes to Sulz to visit patients.

1893 June 9
F. visits Oskar Rie in the evening.

1893 June 13
F. has lunch with Josephine Benvenisti. She leaves Vienna the next day for a longer period of time and travels first to Karlsbad and then to Galatz, where she wants to be present at the birth of her daughter Ernestine. She leaves F. a savings bank book, which he can – if necessary – also attack.

1893 June 14
- F. is on a visit to the water sanatorium Gainfarn (Bad Vöslau), about 40km south of Vienna. He is "received with great honor" by the director Theodor Friedmann and his wife Flora – a sister of the composer Robert Fischhof – and invited to lunch (F. to Martha, 14.6.1893). With another brother – Alfred – F. had gone to primary schools from 1864 to 1865.
- F. visits Biach's. F. only learns there that it is Francisca Biach's birthday.

1893 June mid
F.'s father is on a business trip in Pistyan (now Piešťany).

1893 June 20
F. is called to Johann Mayer, a chief engineer of Kaiser Ferdinand's Northern Railway. Presumably it is about a treatment.

1893 June 22
F. has the first tarot society with Oskar and Alfred Rie and Leopold Königstein.

1893 July 4
F. is visiting Josef Breuer.

1893 July 6
F. is at a game of tarot at Wilhelm Hendlé, the brother-in-law of Leopold Königstein.

1893 July 7
F. is at Ludwig Rosenberg's for a game of tarot.

1893 July 10
F. is in the Prater with the gynecologist Karl Fleischmann for a long talk.

1893 July 12
F. gets a visit from sister Rosa.

1893 July 13
- F. buys a hat, a tie and a shirt out of boredom; he also has his hair cut.
- F. and Martha get a second carpet from cousin Moritz.

1893 July 15–16
F. is in Reichenau.

1893 July 18
F. is at the Riedhof and speaks briefly with Max Kassowitz.

1893 July 19
F. is on a patient visit in Mödling.

1893 July 20
F. is at Ludwig Rosenberg's for a game of tarot.

1893 July 22
F. visits Hammerschlags.

1893 July 22–23
F. visits his family in Reichenau. He meets Philipp Bondy at the Südbahnhof.

1893 July 22–23
F. visits his family in Reichenau.

1893 July 27
F. is in the Riedhof.

1893 July 30
– F. visits Fanny Bardas in Baden. She is the third wife and widow of Moritz Bardas.
– F. is at Ludwig Rosenberg's for a game of tarot.

1893 August 1
– F. meets Josef Breuer.
– Max Dessoir comes to Vienna, and F. picks him up from the train late in the evening.

1893 August mid–September 4
F.'s family is in Reichenau am Semmering for summer holidays, and F. visits them regularly.

1893 August 18–19
F. goes climbing on the Rax with Oskar Rie. They spend the night in the Erzherzog-Otto-Haus. The tenant's daughter had learned that F. is a neurologist and asks him for advice, as she has been treated unsuccessfully. The story of the young woman named Aurelia Kronich and F.'s interpretation are included in the *studies on hysteria* as F.'s third case history under the pseudonym "Katharina".

1893 August end
F. gives Julius Zappert his paper "Ueber familiäre Formen von cerebralen Diplegien" with the dedication: "Herrn Dr. J. Zappert/dVerf.".

1893 September beginning
– Wilhelm Fliess is in Vienna (Hinterbrühl) visiting his parents-in-law.
– F.'s obituary of Jean-Martin Charcot appears.

1893 September 5
F. meets Josephine Benvenisti.

1893 September 7
F. is slightly ill and is visited by Wilhelm Fliess, Oskar Rie and Josef Laufer.

1893 September 8
Wilhelm Fliess visits F. in the evening and stays until the departure of his train.

1893 September mid
F.'s mother comes back to Vienna from Rožnau.

1893 September 21
F. visits Leopold Königstein in the evening.

1893 Autumn
- F.'s practice revives, and he comments on this with the words: "The sexual business attracts people" (F. to Fliess, 6.10.1893).
- F. has heart problems and reduces his tobacco consumption.

1893 before September 25
F. publishes an obituary of Charcot.

1893 September 25
- F. is with Schiff's in Baden.
- F. sends his obituary of Jean-Martin Charcot to Wilhelm Fliess.

1893 October
In the winter semester, F. offers weekly lectures on "Selected Chapters of Neuropathology" (location: lecture hall of Moritz Kaposi and lecture hall Krafft-Ebing, fee five Gulden), for which Josef Breuer enrolls too. Among them are lectures on the "Theory of Hysteria" and "On the Great Neuroses".

1893 October 5
Martha returns to Vienna from Reichenau with the children.

1893 October mid
- F. has written disputes with Josef Breuer about his debts to him.
- F. begins the treatment of a Frau Schüssler ("Dr. Ru."), a former patient of Wilhelm Fliess.
- F.'s sister Paula moves to New York. She takes Judith and Lucie Bernays, the children of her sister Anna, with her to America, who had been left in the care of the grandparents Amalia and Jakob F.'s family when they emigrated.

1893 November 16
In an advertisement in the *Neue Freie Presse,* F. is looking for "a female attendant with pleasant manners who is well versed in massage and nursing of all kinds [...] for a mast cure".

1893 December beginning
- Ida Fliess is in Vienna to look after her mother Pauline Bondy. However, F. only sees her briefly.
- F. goes to Brno for a day.
- Richard von Krafft-Ebing asks F. to take over the office of the first secretary of the Department of Psychiatry and Neurology of the "Verhandlungen der Gesellschaft Deutscher Naturforscher und Ärzte" (Conference of the Society of German Natural Scientists and Physicians) to be held in Vienna at the end of 1894 September.

1893 December end
F. visits Theodor Gomperz.

1894

Treatments:

- F. begins the treatment of Elise Goldberger de Buda (Mrs. "F."), a cousin of Edmund Goldberger de Buda. It lasts until 1897.
- F. begins the treatment of Therese Franckel. It lasts until her death in 1901. F. gives her a daily morphine injection in the late afternoon. In the summer of 1900, he is briefly replaced by Ludwig Teleky, the son of his friend Hermann Teleky.

1894 January
F.'s paper on "Abwehr-Neuropsychosen" is published. In it, F. distances himself from Breuer by assuming incompatible sexual ideas as the cause of hysteria.

1894 January 10
F. meets Philipp Bondy.

1894 February
The studies on hysteria jointly written by F. and Josef Breuer are half-finished.

1894 March end
- F. gives up smoking (temporarily).
- Eugenie Persicaner, the wife of the hose manufacturer Marcus Persicaner and sister of Fritz and Leopold Lichtwitz, starts treatment with F.

1894 Spring
Jakobine Brandeis begins treatment with F. She is the cousin of F.'s former patient Olga Schweinburg ("Nina R.").

1894 April
- F. offers lectures on the "Theory of Hysteria" once a week in the summer semester (lecture hall of Moritz Kaposi (fee five Gulden)....
- F. has heart problems, depressive states and death fantasies.

1894 April 13
F. complains in an entry in the desiderata book of the library of the Society of Physicians that the *Archive for Anatomy, Physiology is* not available in the reading room.

1894 April 18
F. goes to see Josef Breuer about his heart complaints because, in contrast to Fliess, he believes they are related less to nicotine poisoning than to chronic myocarditis.

1894 April 19
F. asks Wilhelm Fliess to be honest with him about the seriousness of the illness; he suspects that Josef Breuer is not telling him the truth.

1894 May
- F. essay on "The defensive neuro-psychoses" appears.
- F. writes a manuscript entitled "Zur Ätiologie und Theorie der grossen Neurosen", which gives an overview of the classification and theory of neuroses.
- F. acquires Leopold Löwenfeld's textbook *Pathology and Therapy of Neurasthenia and Hysteria,* reads it thoroughly and provides it with numerous notes.

1894 May mid
F. writes down the medical history of Helene Weiss, who goes down in *studies on hysteria* as "Elisabeth von R.".

1894 May 21
Fulgence Raymond, Charcot's successor, gives F. a book.

1894 May 22
Martha goes with the children to Reichenau am Semmering for the summer (until September 1). F. visits her regularly.

1894 May 24
- F. is visiting Leopold Königstein for lunch.
- F. visits Paula Frankl, the widow of Ludwig August Frankl, who had died on March 12.
- In the afternoon, F. and Minna take the rack railway up the Kahlenberg and hike from Wildgrube back to Heiligenstadt.

1894 May 25
F. decides to join the Postsparkasse check scheme so that he can pay bills without cash and is not forced to have money at home.

1894 May 29
- Josef Breuer is elected Corresponding Member of the Kaiserliche Akademie der Wissenschaften, and F. immediately goes to congratulate him.
- F. has a consultation with Hermann Teleky.
- F. is invited to Biach's for dinner.

1894 May 30
F. is invited to lunch at Josephine Benvenisti's house.

1894 May 31
F. visits Leopold Königstein in the evening.

1894 June
F. writes a manuscript entitled "How Fear Arises", which discusses the connection between sexuality and fear.

1894 June beginning
F. buys Ludwig Anzengrubers Letzte Dorfgänge. Kalendergeschichten und Skizzen aus dem Nachlass.

1894 June 4
F. visits Ludwig Rosenberg in the evening.

1894 June 5
F. is visited by Minna in the evening, and they both go to the Prater.

1894 June 7
- A storm devastates F.'s study, and hailstones break some window panes. F.'s comment is as follows: "Today it would be more worthwhile to be a glazier than a doctor" (F. to Martha, 7.6.1894).
- F. is at the Riedhof in the evening.

1894 June 8
– Josef Breuer visits F. in the morning to examine him.
– F. receives 130 Gulden from Nina Spiegler, the ex-wife of Siegfried Lipiner, which are intended for the Children's Hospital Institute.

1894 June 12
F. is in Hinterbrühl with Anna von Lieben, "she was particularly badly disposed".

1894 June 14
F. is visiting Biach's in the evening.

1894 June 16–17
F. visits his family in Reichenau.

1894 June 18
– F.'s father goes to the spa for the summer.
– F. is at the Riedhof in the evening and meets Alfred Rie and Josef Mittler, Moritz Biach's son-in-law.

1894 June 19
F. is at the Psychiatric Association in the evening.

1894 June 20
F. is at a "farewell consultation" with Hermann Teleky, followed by a "souper".

1894 June 21
– F.'s mother goes for a spa stay at Rožnau (until the beginning of September).
– F. is on a consultation with Wilhelm Hendlé.

1894 June 22
F. sends Helene Weiss's medical history to Wilhelm Fliess.

1894 June 28
F. travels to Sulz with sister Rosa and Rosenberg's; there, he visits the sick.

1894 Summer
– Fritz Lichtwitz ("Herr K."), the brother of Leopold Lichtwitz and Eugenie Persicaner, begins treatment with F. At the end of August, he sends the epicrisis to Wilhelm Fliess.
– Helene Stiassny begins treatment with F. She is the daughter of the glove manufacturer Franz Clemens Stiassny.

1894 July
– F. starts smoking again, but gives it up on the advice of Wilhelm Fliess.
– F. meets Philipp Bondy several times.

1894 July beginning
– Helene Weiss becomes engaged to Heinrich Gross.
– F. converses with Leopold Oser about "angina nicotiana".

1894 July 2
F. is at a consultation with Julius Krafft-Ebing and Ignaz Kohn about Albert Morgenstern from Brünn.

1894 July 3
F. has two consultations, one of them with Hermann Nothnagel because of Moritz Stransky. He dies on September 17.

1894 July 4
– F. is called to Jakobine Brandeis, who is very ill; she dies on July 23.
– Julius Zappert, F.'s successor at the I. Public Children's Hospital, visits F. Then, Moriz Biach and his son Philipp come, and everyone goes to the inn at noon, where Alfred Rie joins them.
– F. receives a visit from Julius Fürth in the evening.

1894 July 5
F. is at a tarot game on the occasion of the inauguration of the flat of Julius and Albertine Fürth in Heiligenstadt. Fürth had married on May 20.

1894 July 7–8
F.'s pulse is "delirious", and he takes digitalis.

1894 July 9
F. has a consultation with Hermann Teleky with James Klang, the general manager of the private insurance company Österreichischer Phönix. F. possibly knew him since his student days, as Klang was one of the supporting members of the "Leseverein deutscher Studenten". F. and Teleky then go to the Gasthof zur Linde.

1894 July 12
F. visits an inn with Philipp Bondy.

1894 July 26
F. is visiting the Rosenberg's in the evening.

1894 July 27
F. is in Sulz.

1894 August
F. begins the treatment of Edmund Goldberger de Buda ("Herr von F."), a relative of Wilhelm Fliess's wife Ida. It lasts until 1897.

1894 August 1
F. acquires Eduard Flatau's *Atlas des Menschlichen Gehirns und des Faserverlaufes*.

1894 August 8–17
Trip to Munich, Reichenhall and Bad Ischl

1894 August 8
F. and Martha drive to Salzburg in the morning and meet Minna there.

1894 August 8–10
F., Martha and Minna visit Emmeline Bernays in Reichenhall for a spa stay.

1894 August 10–15
F., Martha and Minna meet Wilhelm Fliess, who was seriously ill, and his wife Ida in Munich.

1894 August 15–16

F., Martha and Minna are in Bad Ischl.

1894 August 16

F. "of necessity" makes a four-hour night march from Weissenbach to Bad Ischl.

1894 August 17–September 1

F.'s family is in Reichenau am Semmering for the summer, and F. visits them regularly.

1894 August 17

F., Martha and Minna travel to Reichenau to visit the children who were under Rosa's care during her absence.

1894 August 18

F. sends Wilhelm Fliess a report on a case of male anxiety neurosis (Fritz Lichtwitz, "Herr K.").

1894 August 20

F. sends Wilhelm Fliess the report of a second case of male anxiety neurosis (Edmund Goldberger de Buda. "Herr von F.").

1894 August 23

F. sends Wilhelm Fliess the epicrisis on the case of male anxiety neurosis (Fritz Lichtwitz).

1894 August 29 ago

– F. begins the treatment of Adolf Engländer ("Herr D."), a distant relative of F.'s patients Jakobine Brandeis and Olga Schweinburg, and sends a short report to Fliess.
– F. begins the treatment of Julius Adler ("Dr. Z.") and sends a short report to Fliess.

1894 August end

– F. files a complaint through his lawyer Alfred Rie at the district court Landstrasse against Therese Müller, who has a criminal record for theft and fraud, and demands 50 Gulden.
– F.'s mother comes back to Vienna from Rožnau.

1894 September 1–17
Summer stay with Martha and Alexander in Lovrana

Accommodation in the "Panhans" guesthouse with extensive parkland by the sea (later Grand Hotel, today Orthopedic Clinic).

1894 September 1

Departure from Vienna in the evening.

1894 September 2

In the morning arrival in Lovrana.

1894 September 14

Celebration of the eighth wedding anniversary.

1894 September 15

Departure from Lovrana.

1894 September 16

Arrival in Payerbach.

1894 September 17

Departure from Payerbach in the morning and arrival in Vienna in the morning.

1894 September 18
F. visits Albert Eulenburg, who is in Vienna.

1894 September 19
Adolf Baginsky visits F. for ten minutes.

1894 September 20
– The official gazette of the *Wiener Zeitung* publishes a "reminder" to Therese Müller, who has meanwhile gone into hiding, to pay the 50 Gulden demanded by F. However, Therese Müller is not apprehended until the beginning of August 1896.
– F. meets Emil and Felix Rosenthal.

1894 September 21
F. travels to Trebitsch (now Třebíč) in Moravia, about 150km northeast of Vienna, probably a visit to a patient.

1894 September 23
On the eve of the 66th meeting of the Society of German Naturalists and Physicians in Vienna – at which F. is secretary of the Department of Psychiatry and Neurology – an informal gathering takes place in the Kursalon of the Stadtpark.

1894 September 24
In the morning, opening of the 66th Assembly of the Society of German Natural Scientists and Physicians in Vienna. Ernst Mach, among others, speaks at the plenary session in the Musikvereinssaal. In the afternoon, the departments are constituted. F.'s Department of Psychiatry and Neurology holds its meetings in Lecture Hall 48 of Vienna University. Lectures are given by Auguste Forel and Alois Alzheimer, among others. In the evening, excursion to the Kahlenberg.

1894 September 25
F. takes the minutes of the meeting of the Department of Psychiatry and Neurology. In the evening, social gathering in the Tiergarten.

1894 September 26
Meeting of the Department of Psychiatry and Neurology. Late afternoon, excursion to the Prater followed by a meeting at the Schweizerhaus.

1894 September 27
Meeting of the Department of Psychiatry and Neurology. At noon, reception at the town hall by the mayor Raimund Grübl.

1894 September 28
In the morning plenary session, the anatomist Albert von Kölliker speaks among others. In the afternoon, meeting of the Department of Psychiatry and Neurology. Late afternoon, excursion to the surroundings of Vienna.

1894 September 29
In the morning, excursion with the Southern Railway to Semmering; there, welcomed by the doctors and naturalists of Styria. In the afternoon, hike led by members of the German and Austrian Alpine Club.
The supporting program includes a visit to the Stephanie Observatory and a concert by the music band of the Imperial and Royal Infantry Regiment "Tsar Alexander I of Russia".

1894 October

F. offers lectures on "Selected Chapters of Neuropathology" once a week in the winter semester (location: Krafft-Ebing lecture hall, fee five Gulden).

1894 October 3

F. begins the treatment of Johanna Meyer, Paul Schiff's daughter.

1894 October end

– F.'s German translation of Charcot's *Polyclinic Lectures* appears (edition of 1500).
– Richard von Krafft-Ebing gives F. his *Psychopathia sexualis* with the dedication "Herrn Collegen Dr. F. freundschaftlich d. Verf.".

1894 December beginning

F. begins the treatment of the singer Regine Kun ("Mrs. P. J.").

1894 Christmas

F. meets with Wilhelm Fliess in Vienna.

1895

Treatments:
- Josef Goldschmidt, a textile entrepreneur from Hořice near Königgrätz, begins an analysis with Freud.
- Sophie Paneth, wife of F.'s deceased friend Josef Paneth, begins an analysis with F.
- Helene Scheu begins an analysis with F.
- Camilla Br. begins an analysis with F. It lasts about three years. She probably came to F. via Josef Breuer.

Received books and offprints:
- Christian von Ehrenfels gives F. his *Allegorische Dramen*, written for musical composition, with the dedication "Dr F. in herzlicher Freundschaft vom Verfasser".
- Max Kahane gives F. the second volume of Charcot's *Poliklinische Vorträge*, translated by him, with the dedication "Herrn Dozenten Dr Sigmund Freud in besonderer Hochachtung gewidmet vom Übersetzer".
- Wilhelm Preyer gives F. his paper "Ein merkwürdiger Fall von Fascination" with the dedication "Herrn Doc. Dr. Freud z f Bethaet".

1895 January beginning
F. writes a manuscript under the title "Melancholia".

1895 January 1
F.'s former patient Helene Weiss ("Elisabeth von R.") marries Heinrich Gross.

1895 January mid
F. writes a manuscript under the title "Paranoia".

1895 January 15
F. gives a lecture at the Psychiatric Association on the "Mechanism of Obsessions and Phobias". This is followed by a convivial dinner at the Riedhof.

1895 February 1
Wilhelm Fliess comes to Vienna for four weeks.

1895 February 12
A discussion on F.'s lecture on the "Mechanism of Obsessions and Phobias" of January 15 takes place in the Psychiatric Association.

1895 February 20 or 21
Wilhelm Fliess operates on Emma Eckstein in Anton Löw's sanatorium.

1895 after February 21
F. and Wilhelm Fliess have themselves photographed together. After receiving the photograph, F. writes: "Beautiful we are not (or no longer), but my pleasure in having you close by my side after the operation clearly shows" (F. to Fliess, 4.3.1895).

1895 February 26–27
F.'s nose is festering badly.

1895 March
F. is attacked by the psychiatrist Leopold Löwenfeld for his theory of anxiety neurosis.

1895 March beginning
Oskar Fellner ("Herr E."), co-founder of the Natural Science Association at the University of Vienna in 1882, introduced himself to F. F. had recognized it as a hysteria "but had been unwilling to try him with my psychotherapeutic treatment and had sent him on a sea voyage" (SE 4, p. 114), as Fellner was interested in Egyptology (Fellner had already donated an Egyptian mummy to the Natural Science Collections in Kremsmünster, where he had attended grammar school, in 1887). After his return at the beginning of April, Fellner begins an analysis with F. It lasts until 1902 March.

- 1895 March 2
- Emma Eckstein has severe post-operative bleeding.
- Josef Breuer has to break off a lecture in F.'s lecture on the "Theory of Hysteria".

1895 March 3
F. visits Josef Breuer in the evening and tells him about Emma Eckstein's treatment.

1895 March 4
- F. analyzes a first dream: the dream of Mathilde Breuer's nephew Rudolf Kaufmann.
- Emma Eckstein has severe bleeding in her nose again.

1895 March 5
F. visits the Bondy family.

1895 March 6
Emma Eckstein has another severe hemorrhage. Ignaz Rosanes discovers a gauze strip in Emma Eckstein's surgical wound, which Wilhelm Fliess had forgotten to remove after the operation on February 20 or 21. Rosanes and Robert Gersuny have to operate on Emma Eckstein. F. feels sick at the sight of the blood, has to leave the room and faints. Emma's sister Katharina gives him a glass of cognac, and when F. came back into the room, still somewhat dazed, Emma Eckstein received him with the remark "So this is the strong sex" (F. to Fliess, 8.3.1895). Emma then had to return to the Loew sanatorium.

1895 March 7
Ignaz Rosanes and Robert Gersuny operate on Emma Eckstein again.

1895 March 12
Mrs. Landauer sends for F. because of cramping chest pains; Josef Breuer arrives by chance.

1895 March 13 ago
F. writes 52 printed pages on the "Therapy of Hysteria", i.e. section IV of the "Studien über Hysterie".

1895 March 17–18
Emma Eckstein has severe pain and swelling again.

1895 March 23
Emma Eckstein is operated on for the third time, this time by Karl Gussenbauer.

1895 Spring
- F. is out walking with Breuer, and they meet a 16-year-old boy in Liechtensteinstrasse who is helping a butcher to bring a pig from the cart to the butcher's shop with psychological advice. The boy is Rudolf Urbantschitsch, whom F. and Breuer recommend to study psychology

instead of theology – his actual career aspiration. Urbantschitsch, who accompanies the men a few hundred meters, only sees from the nameplate at Berggasse 19 that one of the men's names is Freud. Breuer was a good friend of his father Viktor Urbantschitsch, with whom F. had attended lectures.

– F. treats a patient with stool complaints, which he thinks are hysterical.

1895 before March 28
F. talks to Rudolf Chrobak about Wilhelm Fliess's theory of labor ("Wehentheorie").

1895 April
– Helene Schiff begins an analysis with F. She is the daughter of Paul Schiff and sister of Johanna Meyer, who were also in treatment with F.
– F. has heart trouble, but refuses Wilhelm Fliess's suggestion to come to Berlin and helps himself with a cocaine brush.
– F. writes the preface to the *studies on hysteria* together with Josef Breuer.
– F. offers lectures on the "Theory of Hysteria" and "On the Great Neuroses" once a week in the summer semester (location: lecture hall of Moritz Kaposi, five Gulden).

1895 April 10
Emma Eckstein is examined by Ignaz Rosanes and has heavy bleeding again.

1895 April 12-15
Easter Trip to Abbazia
F. goes on an Easter excursion to Semmering with Oskar Rie; from there, they go to Abbazia for a day.

1895 April mid
F. looks through the correction sheets of the *studies on hysteria.*

1895 April end
– F. does not get any further with his "Psychology for the Neurologist" – today better known as a *draft of a psychology.*
– F. writes a small paper about a sensory disorder of the thigh described by the neurologist Martin Bernhardt, from which he also suffers himself.

1895 May
– F. practices 10–11 hours a day. The *Entwurf einer Psychologie* has been his "tyrant" since he came across the neuroses. He has the certainty of having "the certainty that I have the core of the matter in my hand" (F. to Fliess, 25.5.1895).
– F. again suffers from suppuration of the nose.
– F. reads Wilhelm Jerusalem's *Die Urteilsfunktion.*
– F. responds to Leopold Löwenfeld's criticism.

1895 May 3
The *Studien über Hysterie* is published (edition of 800). Mathilde Breuer is one of the first to receive a copy. Wilhelm Fliess also receives one with the dedication "Seinem theuern Wilhelm Fliess/der Einer".

1895 May 20
F. is at a meeting of the Association for Psychiatry and Neurology and takes part in the discussion about a case of tabic polyarthropathy presented by Josef Hirschl.

1895 May 25

F. believed that Josef Breuer "has become fully converted to my theory of sexuality" (F. to Fliess, 25.5.1895).

1895 May 26

Oskar Rie introduces F. Emma Strouse, the mother of Bella Strouse, his brother Paul's fiancée. She had unclear secretions on her mammary glands. F. suspected breast cancer, and many years later, the diagnosis was confirmed and her breast was amputated.

1895 May 27–September mid

F.'s family spends the summer as guests of the family of the engineer Karl Schlag (Ritter von Scharhelm) at the "Bellevue" on Cobenzl, northwest of Vienna. F. visits them regularly for several days.

1895 May 28

F. is at a meeting of the Association for Psychiatry and Neurology and participates in the discussion of three cases of chorea chronica presented by Friedrich Söldner.

1895 June

F. starts smoking again, after allegedly 14 months of abstinence.

1895 June beginning

F. presents Jeanne Steger ("Frau Dr. Re.") for unilateral facial spasms. Her husband is an acquaintance of Wilhelm Fliess.

1895 June 11

F.'s mother goes for a spa stay at Rožnau (until the beginning of September).

1895 June mid

F.'s "heart is wholly with the psychology" (F. to Fliess, 17.6.1895).

1895 June 22

F. informs Wilhelm Fliess that Martha is pregnant again.

1895 June 28–30

F. is with his father and sister Dolfi in Baden near Vienna.

1895 Summer

- Anna Hammerschlag, daughter of F.'s religion teacher Samuel Hammerschlag, starts an analysis with F.
- F. and Wilhelm Jerusalem get to know each other. Jerusalem is enthusiastic about F.'s ability to analyze psychologically. F. had already read Jerusalem's book *Die Urteilsfunktion* before their meeting, in which "I discovered two of my principal ideas: That judging consists in a transference into the motoric sphere, and that internal perception cannot claim to be evidence" (F. to Fliess, 25.5.1895).

1895 July 10

F.'s wife Martha feels the first movements of the child.

1895 July mid

F. receives from his patient Oskar Fellner "a despairing letter […] from Egypt, saying that he had had a fresh attack there which a doctor had declared was dysentery" (SE 4, p. 114).

- F. learns that his brother Emanuel, who lives in Manchester, has a limp due to an arthritic condition in his hip.

1895 July 23
- F. meets the son of an 82-year-old patient to whom he has to give two morphine injections a day.
- Oskar Rie visits F.
- Martha discusses with F. the idea of inviting Anna Hammerschlag (a family friend and patient of F.) to her birthday on July 26.
- F. writes the case history of Anna Hammerschlag late into the night and has a dream the following night in which this patient plays a central role.

1895 July 24
F. analyzes this dream, which later enters his main work *Die Traumdeutung* as the "Dream of Irma's Injection". F.'s conclusion: "The dream represented a particular state of affairs as I should have wished it to be. Thus its content was the fulfillment of a wish and its motive was a wish" (SFG 4, p. 118–119).

1895 July 26
To mark Martha's 34th birthday, a reception is held at Bellevue, to which Emma Eckstein is also invited.

1895 July 27
Death of F.'s colleague Carl Bettelheim.

1895 August beginning
F. believes he has recognized the essence of pathological defense.

1895 August mid
F. is in Reichenau for several days and then in the "Bellevue".

1895 August 24–September 2
Holiday with brother Alexander in Venice

F. travels to Venice with his brother Alexander. They stay at the Casa Kirsch, today's Hotel Metropole.

1895 August 24

Departure from Vienna in the evening.

1895 August 25

Arrival in Venice in the morning. F. and Alexander take a gondola ride through the Grand Canal and side canals.

1895 August 26

F. and Alexander climb the Campanile and walk through the city. They visit the Basilica Santa Maria Gloriosa dei Frari with paintings by Titian, and the Scuola San Rocco with paintings by Tintoretto, and have been to the Café Quadri on St Mark's Square four times. Finally, F. visits the art dealer Marco Testolini.

1895 August 27

- F. and Alexander take the boat to the Lido for a swim in the morning.
- F. and Alexander take a trip to Murano, where there has been an important glass industry since 1292, and F. buys a small gift for Ida Fliess there.

1895 August 28

F. and Alexander take a trip to Chioggia, 30km south of Venice and to the nearby seaside resort Sottomarina. F. buys a Venetian mirror for Martha.

1895 August 30

- F. and Alexander visit the fish market and the island of Giudecca.
- F. buys a Venetian oven screen for Martha.
- In the evening, gondola ride on the Grand Canal.

1895 September 1

At 2.10 pm departure from Venice.

1895 September 2

F. and Alexander arrive in Vienna at 7.50 am.

1895 September beginning

F.'s mother comes back to Vienna from Rožnau.

1895 September 3–13
Visit with brother Alexander to Wilhelm Fliess in Berlin

1895 September 3

Departure from Vienna in the evening.

1895 September 4

- Arrival in Berlin.
- F., Fliess and Alexander go to Grunewald and row on the lake.

1895 September 5

F. has an operation on his nose by Fliess.

1895 September 6

Celebration of the third wedding anniversary of Ida and Wilhelm Fliess with Rüdesheim wine and champagne.

1895 September 7

F. and Alexander go to the art museum.

1895 September 8

- F. has another nose operation by Fliess.
- Visit to the art exhibition.

1895 September 9

F. and Alexander visit the mausoleum in Charlottenburg. The Prussian king Friedrich Wilhelm III, had it built for his wife Luise, who died young, in the form of a small ancient temple.

1895 September 10

Visit to a gallery.

1895 September 13

- On the return journey from Berlin to Vienna, F. begins writing the first part of the draft of a psychology under the title "General Plan".
- One of the passengers on the train is Ernst Günther of Schleswig-Holstein-Sonderburg-Augustenburg – a brother of the Empress Auguste Viktoria – who is traveling to Austria to hunt. F. sees him briefly.

1895 September 15
F. goes to the "Bellevue" to visit his family.

1895 September 21
A dream confirms to F. that the motive of the dream is wish fulfillment.

1895 September 25
F. finishes writing the first part of the *draft of a psychology*.

1895 September end /October beginning
F. writes the second part of the *draft of a psychology* under the title "Psychopathology".

1895 approx. October
F. writes a manuscript under the title "Migraine, fixed points".

1895 October
In the winter semester, F. offers weekly lectures "Ueber die grossen Neurosen" ("About the major neuroses") in Richard von Krafft-Ebing's lecture hall (fee five Gulden). Listeners include Max Kahane, Isidor Fischer and Isidor Sadger.

1895 October beginning
F. exchanges some polemical letters with Leopold Löwenfeld. Presumably it is about Löwenfeld's planned work on the subject of "Phobias and Obsessions".

1895 October 5
F. begins writing the third part of the *draft of a psychology* under the title "Attempt to represent the normal ψ processes".

1895 October 8
F. sends Wilhelm Fliess the three parts of the *draft of a psychology*; however, the third part is not completed.

1895 October 14
F. gives the first of three lectures on hysteria at the Vienna Medical Doctors' College.

1895 October mid
– F. recognizes hysteria as the result of a sexual fright experienced in childhood and obsessive-compulsive neurosis as the result of a sexual lust. He is convinced that he also understands the neurophysiological causes of the neuroses.
– F. is deeply impressed by Jens Jacobsen's novel *Niels Lyhne.*
– F. has given up smoking once again.

1895 October 21
F. gives the second lecture on hysteria at the Vienna Medical Doctors' College. The focus of the lecture is repression.

1895 October 28
F. gives the third lecture on hysteria to the Vienna Medical Doctors' College.

1895 October before 31
F. has heart trouble again.

1895 November beginning
– F. puts aside the psychological work and devotes himself to a paper on poliomyelitis for a textbook planned by Hermann Nothnagel.

– Josef Breuer delivers a eulogy on F. and his sexual theory of neuroses in the Doctors' College.

1895 November 2
F. is in a euphoric mood because a patient provided him with confirmation for the sex-fright theory of hysteria.

1895 November 4
A discussion on F.'s lectures on hysteria of October 14, 21 and 28 takes place in the Vienna Medical Doctors' College.

1895 before November 29
– F. finds the "Lectures on the Construction and Activity of the Cerebrum" by the German neurologist Heinrich Sachs painful because he deals with the constancy of psychological energy, a problem that has occupied F. since about 1892.
– F.'s children all have colds.

1895 November 29
To F., the *Entwurf einer Psychologie* appears as "madness" and he no longer understands the state of mind in which he "hatched" it (F. to Fliess, 29.11.1895).

1895 November end
F.'s sister-in-law Minna Bernays moves into Berggasse 19 and becomes a member of the Freud family household.

1895 December
F. describes the case of a patient who, upon his insistent urging to find out the sexual background of his patient's anxiety symptoms, discontinues treatment.

1895 December beginning
F. posits that obsessions are based on accusations, and hysteria, on conflicts.

1895 December 3
Birth of daughter Anna at Berggasse 19, sixth child of F. and Martha.

1895 December 8
– F.'s practice is going well, "the city is gradually beginning to realize that something is to be had from me" (F. to Fliess, 8.12.1895).
– F. sends Wilhelm Fliess a detailed description of the case of his patient Regine Kun.

1895 Winter
F. has a dream about his daughter Sophie, who lies dead but with red cheeks in her cradle.

1895 December end
F. writes a manuscript with the sections: "The defensive neuroses", "The obsessive neurosis", "Paranoia", "Hysteria".

1896

1896 January 1
F. formulates a new variant of the physiological explanation of psychological processes.

1896 February beginning
- A review of Adolf Strümpell's studies on hysteria appears in the *Deutsche Zeitschrift für Nervenheilkunde*; F. finds it scurrilous.
- F. often suffers from migraines, and his daughter Mathilde has mild scarlet fever.

1896 February 2
A "very thoughtful" (F. to Fliess, 6.2.1896) review of the *Studien über Hysterie* by the philosopher Alfred Berger appears in the Wiener *Morgen-Presse*.

1896 February 4
F. reads a pathological study on Henrik Ibsen by Isidor Sadger in the *Neue Freie Presse*.

1896 February 5
F. sends his paper "Weitere Bemerkungen über die Abwehr-Neuropsychosen" to Emanuel Mendel, the editor of the *Neurologisches Zentralblatt*, and one on heredity and etiology of the neuroses to the *Revue Neurologique*.

1896 February 6
F. writes to Wilhelm Fliess that it is no longer possible to get along with Josef Breuer.

1896 before February 13
F. reads Hippolyte Taine's *L'Intelligence*.
1896 February 13
F. finds it "painful" that Josef Breuer "has so completely removed himself from my life" (F. to Fliess, 13.2.1896).

1896 February mid
F. is intensively occupied with his psychology.

1896 February end
F. reads Wilhelm Fliess's manuscript on "The Relationship between the Nose and the Female Genitals" in one go and comments on it in a letter to Fliess dated March 1 in a decidedly critical manner.

1896 Spring
Elsa Reiss – later headmistress of a primary school – takes over the private tuition of daughter Mathilde, Martin and Oliver. She will later also teach Ernst, Sophie and Anna privately.

1896 May
F. begins the analysis of a woman referred by Breuer and described by F. as an "evening patient". It lasted until 1900 May mid and was his "most difficult case, and the most certain as far as aetiology is concerned" (F. to Fliess, 16.5.1900).

1896 April
F. offers lectures on "Hysteria" once a week in the summer semester (lecture hall of the Psychiatric Clinic, fee five Gulden).

1896 April 2
F. uses the term "metapsychological" for the first time in a letter to Wilhelm Fliess.

1896 April 3
F. brings the manuscript of Wilhelm Fliess's monograph *Die Beziehungen zwischen Nase und weiblichen Geschlechtsorganen (The Relationship between the Nose and the Female Genitals)* to Deuticke, where the book is published in 1897.

1896 April 4–7
"Congress" with Wilhelm Fliess in Dresden

1896 April 4

F. leaves in the evening from the Nordwestbahnhof.

1896 April 5

– F. arrives in Dresden in the morning.
– F. and Fliess discuss the whole day, among other things, about somnambulism.
– Dinner on the Elbe in the same restaurant where F. and Martha had dined on 1886 September 26.

1896 April 7

F. leaves Dresden.

1896 after April 8
F. is in Aussee (Obertressen) for a few days and suffers from migraine, nasal complaints and attacks of fear of death. The trigger is the death of the well-known Viennese sculptor Victor Tilgner.

1896 April 16
F. sends Wilhelm Fliess two papers on neuroses and expresses assumptions about the psychological background of Emma Eckstein's complaints in the months after the failed operation.

1896 April 21
F. gives a lecture on the "Aetiology of Hysteria" at the Psychiatric Society. He experiences the reaction as "icy". Richard von Krafft-Ebing had remarked: "It sounds like a scientific fairy tale" (F. to Fliess, 26.4.1896).

1896 April 28
F.'s daughter Anna gets her first tooth.

1896 May
F.'s waiting room remains empty.

1896 May beginning
F. continues to work on his psychology "vigorously and in solitude", but feels "isolated" (F. to Fliess, 4.5.1896)

1896 May 2
F. gives a lecture on dream interpretation to the youth of the Jewish Academic Reading Hall.

1896 May 4
F. interprets Emma Eckstein's bleeding as a hysterical symptom.

1896 May 15
F. uses the term "Psychoanalyse" for the first time in a German paper entitled "Weitere Bemerkungen über die Abwehr-Neuropsychosen".

1896 May 17
Wedding of F.'s sister Rosa to Heinrich Graf. F. meets Josef Breuer there for the first time in a long time.

1896 May ca. 23–30
F.'s brother Emanuel is visiting Vienna for a week.

1896 May 30
F. develops the seduction theory further by specifying the temporal relationships.

1896 May 31
F.'s paper "On the aetiology of hysteria" is published. In it, he formulates his thesis on the role of sexual trauma in childhood for the development of hysteria: he was convinced that adults with hysterical or also obsessive-compulsive symptoms had been sexually abused by adults as children.

1896 June
F. writes the preface to the second German edition of his translation of Hippolyte Bernheim's *Die Suggestion und ihre Heilwirkung*.

1896 June beginning
F.'s father Jakob can only be moved in a wheelchair.

1896 June 4
F. continues to write his monograph on *Infantile Cerebral Palsy*.

1896 June 5
– Martha and the children go to Aussee for their summer holiday. They take up quarters with the publisher Ferdinand Mauskoth in Obertressen. Shortly before, Adele Bloch, who would become famous in 1907 through a painting by Gustav Klimt, had arrived in Aussee for a summer stay.
– F. climbs St. Stephen's Cathedral with his brother Alexander, and afterward, they have lunch.

1896 June 6
F. visits Alfred Rie in the evening.

1896 June 7
F. and Alexander go to an inn for dinner.

1896 June 8
F. is at the Riedhof for lunch.

1896 June 11–12
F. visits his family in Aussee with brother Alexander.

1896 June 16
F.'s sister Paula marries the Austrian-born Valentin Winternitz in New York.

1896 June 17
F. has a box of chocolates delivered to Martha on the occasion of her 14th engagement anniversary.

1896 June 21
F. drives to Hinterbrühl, presumably to visit a patient of Anna von Lieben.

1896 June 21–22
F. visits his seriously ill father Jakob in Baden, where he is staying with his daughter Dolfi. F.'s sister Rosa also comes with her husband Heinrich.

1896 June 27–29
F. visits his family in Aussee.

1896 June 30
F. cancels a meeting with Wilhelm Fliess because of his father's illness.

1896 July beginning
Flora Rosanes, wife of F.'s friend Ignaz Rosanes, begins an analysis with F.

1896 July 5
F. visits his father Jakob in Baden.

1896 July 11–12
F. visits his family in Aussee.

1896 July 15
F. again cancels a meeting with Wilhelm Fliess, as he realizes that his father is dying.

1896 July 26 August 30
F.'s family had gone to Aussee on June 6, and F. had visited them there twice since then. Now, he spends the rest of the summer with them. Also, in Aussee at the same time are Theodor Herzl, Hugo von Hofmannsthal, Karl Lueger, Karl Kautsky, Karl Kraus.

1896 August beginning
- F. makes excursions to the Schafberg and to Salzburg. In Hallein, he visits Karl Koller, who is visiting Europe from New York.
- F. takes the children on a trip to Hallstatt and the Eschern valley. Oliver is disappointed that he cannot make it to the Dachstein.

1896 August 12
F. goes on a hike to the Liechtensteinklamm.

1896 August 23–24
F. hikes through the Kaprun valley.

1896 August 26–29
F. meets Wilhelm Fliess in Salzburg (Hotel Nelboeck). Fliess gives F. Victor Hehn's book *Italien. Ansichten und Streiflichter* with the dedication "Zur Erinnerung an die Salzburger Tage im August 1896 und mit dem Wunsche einer Fortsetzung auf italischem sic Boden. Seinem lieben Sigmund Wilh Fliess".

1896 August 29–September 12
Holiday with brother Alexander in Venice

1896 August 29

Departure from Salzburg in the morning. At 10.11 pm, F. sends Martha a card from Steinach am Brenner via the postal inspector on the train.

1896 August 30

Arrival in Venice in the morning. F. and Alexander swim at the Lido and visit St Mark's Square. In the evening, they are at the Café Quadri.

1896 August 31

Morning departure from Venice; 3.30 pm arrival in Padua. There, among other things, visit to the Botanical Garden, the Church of San Antonio and the Prato della Valle. F. also wanted to visit the church Madonna del'Arena with Giotto's frescoes, but it was closed that day. In the evening, the brothers are at the Storione, a restaurant near the university. At 23.30, they continue to Bologna.

1896 September 1

Arrival in Bologna in the morning. In the morning, visit of the Museo Civico with prehistoric, Egyptian, Etruscan and Celtic antiquities. In the afternoon, visit of the leaning towers (Torre Asinelli and Torre Garisenda) and the university. Overnight, stay at the Grand Hotel Brun.

1896 September 2

Visit to the Pinakothek with the "Saint Caecilia" by Raffael and the cemetery, from which F. buys two photos.

1896 September 3

Departure for Ravenna at 5.30 am, and arrival there at 9.30 am. During the day, visit of the remains of the palace of Theoderic the Great, the Church of San Vitale, the Mausoleum of Galla Placidia with the sarcophagi of Emperor Constantine III and Valentinian III, and the tomb of Theoderic. In the evening, continue to Faenza. Overnight, stay at the "Corona" hostel.

1896 September 4

Departure from Faenza to Florence at noon. Overnight, at Casa Nardini, a guesthouse in Piazza S. Giovanni, right next to the Duomo.

1896 September 5

F. and Alexander take a tour of the city.

1896 September 6

In the morning, visit to the Tribuna in the Uffizi with the Medicean Venus and other ancient statues, including those by Praxiteles. Then, visit the Church of Santa Croce with the tombs of Cherubini, Galilei, Machiavelli, Michelangelo and Rossini. In the afternoon, visit the Boboli Gardens on the west bank of the Arno and the Torre del Gallo, near Villa Il Gioiello, where Galileo Galilei lived from 1631 until his death. They find out that rooms are available and rent for four days with full board from September 7.

1896 September 7

Move to the Torre del Gallo. The Custode shows F. and Alexander a self-portrait of Michelangelo, a telescope of Galileo, a letter from Cromwell to King Charles I, the famous portrait of Galileo by Justus Sustermann and a supposed door from Machiavelli's house.

1896 September 8

As it is the Assumption Day, all museums are closed.

1896 September 9

Visit to the Uffizi Gallery.

1896 September 10

Visit to Palazzo Pitti, one of the three important palaces in Florence with its famous collection of paintings.

1896 September 11

At 9.00 am, departure to Franzensfeste. There, the brothers separate and F. continues to Bischofshofen, where he arrives at around 7.00 pm.

1896 September 12

Drive from Bischofshofen back to Aussee.

1896 September 14

F. drives from Aussee via Bad Ischl back to Vienna.

1896 September 15

– Oskar Rie visits F in the morning.
– In the evening, F. visits Wilhelm Fliess in Hinterbrühl, who is visiting his parents-in-law with his wife.

1896 September 16

– F. has a consultation with Julius Fürth.
– F. visits his father Jakob in Baden, who is very unwell.

1896 September mid

F. reads Victor Hehn's book *Italy*.

1896 September 18

F. visits Julius Fürth in the evening.

1896 September 19

F. is at the premiere of Leo Ebermann's *The Athenian* at the Burgtheater.

1896 September 20

F. is in Hinterbrühl.

1896 September 24

– F. falls ill with influenza.
– F. acquires Ludwig Edinger's lectures on the structure of the nervous central organs of humans and animals for doctors and students.

1896 September 27–28

F. is on a patient visit to the daughter of a colleague in Oderberg (now Novy Bohumín).

1896 before September 29

A colleague of F. refuses a consultation with him on the grounds that F. is not to be taken seriously.

1896 September 29

F. believes that his father is dying.

1896 September end

Martha returns from Aussee with the children.

1896 October

F. offers "Lectures on the Great Neuroses" twice a week in the winter semester (Krafft-Ebing lecture hall).

1896 October beginning

F. writes his monograph *Die Infantile Cerebrallähmung.*

1896 October 11

- F.'s wife Martha travels alone to Hamburg to visit her mother, who has sprained her hand. On the outward journey, a short stay with the Fliess family in Berlin, on the return journey, a longer stay.
- F. is with sister Rosa and her husband Heinrich in the "Rossauer Aschanti", a "humor and sociability club".

1896 October 12

F. is at Alois Bloch's for a game of tarot.

1896 October mid

- During Martha's absence, F. has renovation work carried out in the flat, including ordering a stove for the living room from Meidinger Ofenfabriken.
- F.'s father Jakob is unconscious for several days.

1896 October 16

F. gives his daughter Mathilde a new school desk for her ninth birthday.

1896 October 23

Death of F.'s father. F. writes about this: "By one of those dark pathways behind the official consciousness the old man's death has affected me deeply. I valued him highly, understood him very well, and with his peculiar mixture of deep wisdom and fantastic light-heartedness [...] I now feel quite uprooted" (F. to Fliess, 2.11.1896).

1896 October 25

Funeral of F.'s father. F. is late because he had to wait at the hairdresser. Only a few friends and relatives are present, including Karl Drey, Heinrich Graf, Max Kahane, Leopold Königstein, Ludwig Rosenberg, Samuel (or Simon) Weiss and members of the Rie family. Alexander takes a photo of F., mother Amalia and sisters Rosa, Dolfi and Mitzi at the grave.

1896 October 26

The night after his father's funeral, F. has the dream of "squeezing his eyes shut".

1896 November beginning

- F. is again working on his monograph Die Infantile Cerebrallähmung.
- F. has seven "cures" but few patients in the consultation hours.
- F. buys the statuette "The New Shoes" by August Kühne.

1896 November 2

F. is referred a patient by Carl Wernicke.

1896 November 10

Wedding of Oskar Rie and Melanie Bondy.

1896 November mid

F. has an increased heart pain again.

1896 November 17
Salomon Ehrmann visits F. unexpectedly.

1896 December beginning
- F. buys some copies of Florentine statues and Michelangelo's "Dying Slave" and sets them up in his study. He works 10–12 hours a day, including treating a cousin of Wilhelm Fliess.
- F. thinks up mottos for certain topics of his psychology to be developed. Only one of them he actually uses later: "Flectere si nequeo superos, acheronta movebo" from Vergil's Aeneid was originally intended for symptom formation, but then became the motto of *dream interpretation*.
- Oskar and Melanie Rie visit F.

1896 before December 6
F. has dream of "theory of bisexuality".

1896 December 6
- F. dreams of a "Congress" with Fliess in Italy, preferably in Naples and Pompeii.
- F. develops a theory of the psychic mechanism of the seducer's hysteria and perversions as their cause.

1896 December 17
F. develops hypotheses on metapsychology.

1896 Winter
Ludwig Rosenberg has a life-threatening sepsis, and F., Albert Hammerschlag, the internist Arthur Klein and Oskar Rie take turns at his bedside.

1897

1897 January 3
F. develops some thoughts about the etiological significance of the first three years of life.

1897 January 11
F. develops a theory of the etiology of psychosis and epilepsy based on the recognition of the importance of sexual abuse at the age of about one and a quarter to one and a half years.

1897 January 14
Hermann Nothnagel and Richard von Krafft-Ebing again propose F. for appointment as an associate professor.

1897 January mid
- F. sees parallels between hysteria and medieval ideas of the devil and possession, and he orders the "Maleus maleficorum" ("The Witches' Hammer") because of this.
- F.'s condition stabilizes; he believes he has passed the "dangerous" age.

1897 January 24
- F. sees in perversions remnants of an old sex cult.
- F. suspects that he was passed over for nomination as an associate professor.

1897 February
F. now treats ten patients.

1897 February beginning
- F.'s monograph Die infantile Cerebrallähmung is published.
- Josef Breuer visits Martha and comments on F.'s monograph on infantile cerebral palsy.
- F. seeks out Hermann Nothnagel to give him a copy of his monograph on infantile cerebral palsy, and the latter assures him that he will stand up for his professorship.

1897 February 8
F. works 11–12 hours a day.

1897 February 11
F. attributes his siblings' hysterical symptoms to his father's perversity.

1897 February 13
- Emil Zuckerkandl raises concerns with the Ministry about the simultaneous appointment of four professors – including F. – for internal medicine. The College of Professors therefore assigns Hermann Nothnagel's and Richard von Krafft-Ebing's application to propose F. as an associate professor to a committee set up for this purpose for reporting; committee members are as follows: Sigmund Exner, Richard von Krafft-Ebing, Edmund Neusser, Hermann Nothnagel, Leopold Schrötter, Anton Weichselbaum.
- F.'s son Martin has angina.

1897 February 23
Hermann Nothnagel and Krafft-Ebing propose to the appointed committee that F. be appointed an associate professor.

1897 February 25
Death of Michael Bernays, an uncle of Martha. He was a literary scholar and Goethe specialist, critical of Judaism, and had been baptized.

1897 March beginning
Ida Fliess, the wife of Wilhelm Fliess, visits the Freud family.

1897 March 5
Death of F.'s uncle Josef, who had been sentenced to prison in 1866 for distributing forged ruble notes.

1897 March mid
F.'s daughter Mathilde is dangerously ill with septic diphtheria. Oskar Rie and Max Kassowitz reject the injection with a healing serum developed by Emil von Behring in 1894.

1897 Spring
– Wilhelm Fliess gives F. his book *Die Beziehung zwischen Nase und weiblichen Geschlecht-sorganen* with the dedication "Seinem teuren Sigmund innigst d Vf.".
– F. studies the streets of Pompeii.

1897 March 27
The Board of Professors adjourns the committee report on F.'s appointment as an associate professor.

1897 March 29
Wilhelm Fliess gives F. his lecture "*Dysmenorrhoe* und *Wehenschmerz*" ("On Dysmenorrhea and Labor Pain").

1897 March end
F. considers it lucky that he no longer sees Josef Breuer.

1897 April
F. offers lectures on "Hysteria" twice a week in the summer semester (lecture hall of the Psychiatric Clinic, fee five Gulden).

1897 shortly before April 6
F. has dream of "Herrn Zucker".

1897 April 6
– F. explains the hysterical fantasies to himself from things that children heard at the age of six to seven months but only understood afterward; Oskar Rie implores him to abandon this theory.
– F. writes his autobiography for Richard von Krafft-Ebing, who has to give a lecture on him in connection with the proposal for a professorship.

1897 April 6–7
F. has dream of Rome (street corner with German posters).

1897 April 10
F.'s son Martin falls ill again with angina; Oskar Rie and the specialist doctor for nose and throat diseases Vincenz Laufer are called in; initially, diphtheria was suspected.

1897 April 17–19
"Congress" with Wilhelm Fliess in Nuremberg
F. and Fliess talk about travel plans and the theory of bisexuality. Fliess does not like Nuremberg.

1897 April 27
F.'s old friend Josef Herzig visits F. and lets him tell him about Nuremberg.

1897 April 27–28
F. has dream of "Via Casa Secerno" and dream of "Friend R. is my uncle".

1897 May
Felix Gattel, doctor from Berlin, listens to lectures by F. and begins an analysis with F. (until September).

1897 May 2
– F. sends Wilhelm Fliess a manuscript with miscellanies.
– F. theorizes that hysteria, obsessive-compulsive disorder and paranoia have the same etiology.

1897 May 10
The committee for the "Promotion Application Regarding Lecturer Dr Freud" applies for his promotion to Associate Professor of Neuropathology.

1897 May mid
– F. has dream of "climbing stairs".
– F.'s son Martin has an attack of "poetitis" and writes a poem "Feiertag im Walde".
– F.'s daughter Mathilde begins to take an interest in mythology.

1897 May 15
The Board of Professors again adjourns the committee report on F.'s appointment as an associate professor.

1897 May 16
– F. compiles for the possible appointment as an associate professor "Inhaltsangaben der wissenschaftlichen Arbeiten des Privatdozenten Dr. Sigm. Freud (1877–1897)".
– F. feels "like the Celtic imp [Rumpelstilzchen]: 'Oh, how glad I am that no one, no one knows … No one even suspects that the dream is not nonsense but wish fulfilment" (F. to Fliess, 16.5.1897).

1897 May 24
F.'s sister-in-law Minna Bernays goes to Aussee with F.'s children. F. and Martha stay in Vienna. They live in Obertressen again with the publisher Ferdinand Mauskoth.

1897 May 25
F. sends Wilhelm Fliess the tables of contents of his scientific papers and a manuscript on hysteria and repression.

1897 before May 31
– F. has dream of "Mathilde = Hella".
– F. has dream of "climbing stairs nimbly".

1897 May 31
F. sends Wilhelm Fliess a manuscript about impulses, fantasies and symptom formation.

1897 June
Isidor Sadger sends F. his paper "The Miracle of the Thinking Protein". This triggers F.'s dream of "Norekdal Styl".

1897 June 4

Max Gruber informs the Ministry of Education that Emil Zuckerkandl has expressed reservations about the simultaneous appointment of four professors – including F. – for internal medicine.

1897 June 4–8

F. and Martha visit their children and Minna in Aussee.

1897 June 8

F.'s mother goes for a spa stay at Rožnau (until September mid). Daughter Mitzi follows with her children on June 22.

1897 June 11

- F. receives a new telephone that connects the flat and the practice rooms.
- F. has himself photographed by his brother Alexander in his brother's room in his mother's flat at Grüne Thorgasse 14. The photo bears the caption "Am historischen Eckfenster" ("At the historic corner window"), and F. sends it, dated 17.6.1897, to Martha on their 15th engagement day.
- F. is at Hermann Teleky's for dinner followed by tarot.

1897 June 12

The College of Professors decides by 22 votes to 10 to approve the application by Hermann Nothnagel and Richard von Krafft-Ebing to appoint F. as Professor Extraordinarius.

1897 June 13

F. goes to Schönbrunn with his sister Rosa and brother-in-law Heinrich Graf and visits the zoo, among other things. F. writes to his wife: "The animals were more beautiful than the people" (F. to Martha, 14.6.1897).

1897 June 15

F. sends Martha strawberries to Aussee, which were intended as a gift for the 15th engagement day.

1897 June mid

F. starts a collection of Jewish stories, probably with the intention of using them for a publication.

1897 June 17

- F. goes with his brother Alexander and Felix Gattel on a climbing tour to the Schneeberg in the Semmering area. They mainly want to take a look at the new 7-km-long cogwheel railway up the Schneeberg.
- F. wants to send Martha a telegram of congratulations on the 15th anniversary of their engagement, but "the rush [was] so great that the disgusting [Julius] Kronich [the owner of the Baumgartner House and father of Aurelia Kronich, the 'Katharina' from the *studies on hysteria*] refused to accept a telegram" (F. to Martha, 18.6.1897).

1897 June 19

- F. goes with sisters and brother Alexander to the central cemetery to visit the grave. The photos Alexander takes are not successful.
- F. visits Oskar and Melanie Rie in the evening.

1897 June 20
F. has dinner with Julius Fürth and Carl Pick at the Riedhof in the evening.

1897 June 21
F. visits Oskar and Melanie Rie in the evening.

1897 before June 23
Olga Hönig begins an analysis with F. After her mother Antonie refused her the money for therapy, F. treated her free of charge. She later marries Max Graf – their son together is Herbert Graf, "little Hans". While still in therapy, Max Graf asks F. if he should marry her. F. advises him without reservation.

1897 June 25
The Dean's Office of the Faculty of Medicine sends the decision of the College of Professors and the committee report on F.'s promotion to the associate professor to the Ministry of Education.

1897 June 26–29
Short visit to the family in Aussee

1897 June 26

F. takes the "Blitzzug" to Aussee at 3.30 pm.

1897 June 29

F. travels back to Vienna by night train (first class); by chance, a brother-in-law of his patient Oskar Fellner is traveling in the same compartment.

1897 June 30

F. arrives in Vienna in the morning.

1897 June end
Bella Rie, Oskar Rie's sister-in-law, begins an analysis with F.

1897 July
F. begins his self-analysis with systematic analysis of dreams.

1897 July 1
- F. has a consultation with Markus Hajek.
- F. goes to Baden.
- F. is with Oskar and Melanie Rie in the evening.

1897 July 4
- F. and Alexander drive to the central cemetery and arrange a few things for their father's grave, including ordering a memorial ash tree for the autumn. Alexander also takes photos again.
- F. is at Alois Bloch's for a game of tarot.
- F. is having dinner with Julius Fürth.

1897 July 7
F. believes he understands the origin of dreams and other "higher psychic structures" (F. to Fliess, 7.7.1897).

1897 July 9–11
Short trip to Salzburg and Bad Reichenhall

1897 July 9

F. leaves Vienna in the evening at 22.10.

1897 July 10

F. arrives in Salzburg at 7.19 am and meets his sister-in-law Minna. They both take short walks through Salzburg and have lunch on a boat. In the afternoon, they take a carriage to Fürstenbrunn and visit the Untersberg, which is the subject of many myths, including that Charlemagne waits there for his resurrection. On the way back, they stop at Anif and Hellbrunn. Overnight stay at the Mirabell Hotel in Salzburg.

1897 July 11

- F. and Minna drive to Bad Reichenhall at 9.30 am to visit F.'s mother-in-law Emmeline Bernays. In the afternoon, they go on a car trip to Mauthäusl near Schneizlreuth.
- F. leaves Bad Reichenhall at 10.57 pm and drives back to Vienna via Salzburg.

1897 July 12
F. arrives in Vienna at 6.45 in the morning.

1897 July 13
Birth of F.'s nephew Hermann, son of sister Rosa Graf.

1897 July 16–19
Short visit to the family in Aussee

1897 July 16

Departure from Vienna in the evening.

1897 July 18

Departure from Aussee in the evening.

1897 July 19

Arrival in Vienna in the morning.

1897 July 19
F. orders summer suits from his tailor Franz Tischer.

1897 July 24–August 19
Holiday in Aussee

F. is on holiday with his family in Aussee. Here his daughter Anna has the "omlet" dream (SE 4, p. 130).

1897 August 13

F. cancels a meeting with Wilhelm Fliess.

1897 August 14

F. refers to himself as his "chief patient" and thus indicates his self-analysis, which is "more difficult than any other" (F. to Fliess, 14.8.1897).

1897 August 18

F. is afraid of the upcoming trip to South Tyrol and Italy due to the frequent reports of railway accidents.

1897 August 19–September 18
Journey through South Tyrol and Upper Italy

F. goes on a journey through South Tyrol and Upper Italy, first with Martha, then with brother Alexander and Felix Gattel.

1897 August 20–25

F. and Martha are in Merano and Bolzano for just under a week.

1897 August 25

Drive from Bolzano to Venice. Overnight stay at Casa Kirsch (now's Hotel Metropole).

1897 August end

F. has dream of "warship".

1897 September 2

- Martha leaves Venice.
- F. visits the Accademia di Belle Ani with its famous painting gallery, including works by Giorgione and Veronese.
- F. buys a number of prints by famous artists – most of them from Vittore Carpaccio – and photos of Venice.
- F.'s brother Alexander and Felix Gattel arrive in Venice.

1897 September 3

Departure from Venice by night train to Pisa.

1897 September 4

- Arrival in Pisa in the morning.
- Climb the Leaning Tower and visit the Cathedral, Baptistery and Hall Courtyard of the Campo Santo.
- F. buys prints of the "Triumph of Death" and the "Last Judgment", paintings attributed to Andrea Orcagna.
- In the afternoon, continue to Livorno. Overnight stay at the Grand Hotel.

1897 September 5

- In the morning, departure to Siena.
- Arrival in Siena in the afternoon. Overnight stay at the Hotel Continental.

1897 September 6

Tour of the cathedral and purchase of photographs.

1897 September 7

- Visit the Palazzo Pubblico, the Church of Sant'Agostino with paintings by Giovanni Antonio Bazzi, called Sodoma, and the Church of San Domenico with remarkable frescoes by the painter.
- F. buys a new hat and an iron antique.
- Attend a performance of Vincenzo Bellini's The Somnambulist at the Siena Opera.

1897 September 8

- In the morning, departure to San Gimignano, and there, visit of the cathedral and the Church of Sant'Agostino with the frescoes from the life of St. Augustine by Benozzo Gozzoli.
- Wagon trip to Poggibonsi.

- In the evening, continue via Chiusi to Orvieto. Overnight stay at the Hotel Belle Arti.

1897 September 9
- Visit to Orvieto Cathedral with frescoes by Lucca Signorelli, whose name F. cannot remember a year later in Dalmatia.
- F. visits the Etruscan tombs in the area and buys Etruscan antiquities, presumably including the ash jar mentioned in the dream interpretation.
- In the afternoon, excursion to Bolsena.

1897 September 10
- In the morning, departure from Orvieto to Terni, and there, visit of the waterfalls.
- In the afternoon, continue to Spoleto.

1897 September 11
In the morning, carriage ride to Assisi. Overnight stay at the Hotel Subasio. The actress Eleonora Duse is sitting on the neighboring balcony. F. finds Assisi "not beautiful, the saint presses on everything" (F. to Martha, 12.9.1897).

1897 September 12
Car journey from Assisi to Perugia. There, F. and his traveling companions discover a small trattoria where they eat "very good meat and corrected French fries at the cheapest prices" and enjoy "fruit of […] fabulous quality […] large pears, figs, green and red grapes" (F. to Martha, 13.9.1897).

1897 September 14
- Drive from Perugia to Arezzo. There, F. buys photos and art prints.
- In the afternoon, continue to Florence. Overnight stay at the Hotel d'Italie.

1897 September 15
- In the morning, visit the Uffizi Gallery and Palazzo Pitti.
- In the afternoon, F. photographs a marble statuette for Oskar Rie.

1897 September 16
F. buys a Pallas Athene for his daughter Mathilde.

1897 September 17
Departure from Florence in the evening. F. travels back alone; his brother Alexander and Felix Gattel each take other routes.

1897 September 18
F. arrives back in Vienna.

1897 September 21
F. formulates doubts about his seduction theory in a letter to Wilhelm Fliess.

1897 September 25–27
"Congress" with Wilhelm Fliess in Berlin

1897 September 25
F. leaves Vienna in the evening.

1897 September 26
- F. arrives in Berlin in the morning. The discussions with Fliess fill him "with new ideas" (F. to Fliess, 27.9.1897).
- F. leaves Berlin in the evening.

1897 September 27

F. arrives back in Vienna in the morning.

1897 September 29

F. becomes a member of the "Vienna" Lodge of the Jewish humanitarian association "B'nai B'rith" founded in Vienna in 1895. He later became the chairman of the committee for spiritual interests and a member of the peace committee and the examination committee for the admission of new members.

1897 September 30

F. continues his self-analysis. He dreams, for example, of having seen his mother naked on the journey from Leipzig to Vienna (October 1859) and at that time his "libido toward matrem was awakened" (F. to Fliess, 4.10.1897).

1897 October
- F. offers lectures "On the Great Neuroses" twice a week in the winter semester (Krafft-Ebing lecture hall).
- F.'s heart complaints are replaced by gastrointestinal complaints; he attributes it to the influence of self-analysis.

1897 October beginning

F. has dream of "Hearsing".

1897 October 2

F. acquires Victor Hehn's book *Gedanken über Goethe.*

1897 October 3–4

F. has a dream about the "animal skull" and the "subscription for 20 Gulden".

1897 October 4
- In connection with F.'s promotion to associate professor, the governor's office informs the Ministry of Education about F.'s income and "moral and civic" behavior.
- Minna and F.'s children return to Vienna.

1897 October 6

F. acquires Theodor Lipps' book *Raumästhetik und geometrisch-optische Täuschungen.*

1897 before October 15

F. has "dream of the one-eyed doctor" (Josef Pur) and one of his grammar school teachers (Viktor Kraus).

1897 October mid
- F. concentrates entirely on his self-analysis.
- F. formulates the basic idea of the Oedipus complex and sees an analogy with William Shakespeare's *Hamlet.*

1897 October 27
F. sees an analogy between coercion and masturbation.

1897 October 30
F.'s first "Lectures on the Great Neuroses" in the winter semester is attended by 11 listeners.

1897 November beginning
F. spends an evening with Emanuel Loewy, professor of archeology in Rome, and one of his oldest and best friends.

1897 November 5
– F. receives James Mark Baldwin's Mental Development in the Child and the Race: Methods and Processes.
– F.'s self-analysis falters.

1897 November 9
The nanny of F.'s son Oliver pulls out his first tooth.

1897 November 12
– F. formulates the basic ideas of libido development in a letter to Fliess.
– F.'s son Oliver loses a second tooth.

1897 November 18
F. has the feeling that he has found something important, but does not know what; he believes it is connected to the therapy of hysteria.

1897 December
F.'s patient Emma Eckstein treats a patient psychoanalytically.

1897 December 2
Ida Fliess is visiting Freud's.

1897 December 5
F. recognizes his longing for Rome as neurotic and identifies with Hannibal.

1897 December 7
F. gives the first part of a lecture "Über Traumdeutung" ("On the Interpretation of Dreams") to B'nai B'rith.

1897 before December 12
F. reads the book by Rudolf Kleinpaul *Die Lebendigen und die Toten in Volksglauben, Religion und Sage*.

1897 December 12
F. visits the *Meistersinger* at the Court Opera and draws a parallel between Josef Breuer and Hanns Sachs.

1897 December mid
F. sees a parallel between masturbation as a primal addiction and alcohol or nicotine addiction.

1897 December 21
F. gives the second part of the lecture "On Dream Interpretation" to B'nai B'rith.

1897 December 22

F. uses the term "censorship" for the first time. He writes to Wilhelm Fliess: "Have you ever seen a foreign newspaper which passed Russian censorship at the frontier? Words, whole clauses and sentences are blacked out so that the rest becomes unintelligible. A *Russian censorship* of that kind comes about in psychoses and produces the apparently meaningless *deliria*" (F. to Fliess, 22.12.1897).

1897 December 25–28
"Congress" with Wilhelm Fliess in Wroclaw

1897 December 25

F. leaves Vienna at 8.00 am and arrives in Wroclaw at 2.30 pm.

1897 December 26

– F. has his nose etched by Fliess.
– F. and Fliess discuss Fliess' theory of bisexuality on an evening walk.

1897 c. December 27

– F. expresses doubts about Wilhelm Fliess's theses on left-handedness.
– Fliess's remarks about the decline of France touch F. unpleasantly.

1897 December 28

F. arrives back in Vienna.

1897 end

Rudolf Kaufmann ("Mr P. I.") begins an analysis with F. He is a nephew of Mathilde Breuer.

1898

Rosa Altmann, sister-in-law of Josef Breuer, begins an analysis with F.

1898 January beginning
- F. notes that 1897 was the best year financially of his medical career to date.
- F. self-analysis falters.
- F. has an aggressive daytime fantasy in connection with the delay in his appointment as a professor.

1898 after January 1
F. pays Josef Breuer back part of his debt (500 Gulden).[20]

1898 January 2
F. becomes a permanent contributor to the *Wiener Klinische Rundschau.*

1898 January 4
F. repeats his doubts about Wilhelm Fliess's theory of left-handedness.

1898 January 5
F. goes to the theater with Philipp and Pauline Bondy, Wilhelm Fliess's parents-in-law, and Oskar Rie and sees Theodor Herzl's play "Das neue Ghetto".

- 1898 after January 5
- F. has dream of "My son the Myop".
- F. has dream of "Auf Geseres".

1898 approx. January 6
Josef Breuer returns 350 Gulden to F.'s wife Martha.

1898 January 20
F. has a severe migraine attack.

1898 February
- F. is intensely occupied with his dream book, and his self-analysis is at rest.
- F. is annoyed at having to read so much literature on dreams; he can only warm to Gustav Theodor Fechner's ideas on dreams.

1898 February 1
F. attends an event with Mark Twain in the Bösendorfer Hall in Herrengasse, where he read the stories "The First Melon I ever Stole", "His Grandfather's Old Ram" and "The Negro's Mental History". The supporting program included a performance by violin virtuoso Fritz Kreisler, the son of the Freud family's former family doctor, Samuel Kreisler.

1898 February 6
F. is on a patient visit in Hungary with a 50-year-old lady.

1898 February 9
- F. has dream of "Professor – mother – wet nurse".
- F. hopes to be awarded the title of professor on December 2, the 50th anniversary of Franz Joseph I's accession to the throne.
- F. finishes writing his paper "Sexuality in the Aetiology of Neuroses".

1898 February beginning
F. follows with great interest the trial of Emile Zola, who was on trial in Paris for his defense of Alfred Dreyfus. He writes about Zola: "A fine fellow, someone with whom one could communicate" (F. to Fliess, 9.2.1898).

1898 February 23
Some chapters of *dream interpretation* are ready.

1898 March
F. reads Conrad Ferdinand Meyer.

1898 March beginning
- F. has the dream of the "non-stop speaker"; this probably refers to Otto Lecher, who gave a 12-hour speech in the Reichsrat on 1897 October 28 and 29).
- F. reads Pierre Janet's *Hysterie et idées fixes and is* pleased that Janet has no idea of his findings.
- F. receives a commemorative publication for Salomon Stricker on his 25th anniversary as a full professor. It mentions that the discovery of the anesthetic properties of cocaine by Karl Koller took place in Stricker's laboratory.

1898 March 5
The "best-composed" section of *The Interpretation of Dreams* is finished (F. to Fliess, 5.3.1898).

1898 March 10
- F. sees the monograph *Die Gattung Zyklamen* in a bookshop, the trigger for the dream of the botanical monograph the next night.
- F. has a long conversation with Leopold Königstein, among other things, about his patient Flora Rosanes, the wife of Ignaz Rosanes. On the way to Königstein's flat in Wollzeile, F. meets Gustav Gärtner with his wife Melanie.

1898 March 10–11
F. has dream of the "Botanical Monograph".

1898 March 15
- F. sends Wilhelm Fliess the second chapter of the interpretation of dreams.
- F. feared that Fliess would object to his comments on the dream "Professor – Mother – Nurse" of February 9.
- F. plans to read up on the Oedipus saga and feels completely disoriented in relation to hysteria.

1898 March mid
F.'s daughters have influenza.

1898 Spring
F.'s sister Mitzi's family moves to Berlin and leaves F. a Persian carpet.

1898 March 24
F. is glad to be rid of Josef Breuer.

1898 April

In the summer semester, F. offers twice-weekly lectures "On the Great Neuroses" – including "On Hysteria" (Krafft-Ebing lecture hall, fee five Gulden).

1898 April beginning

F. would prefer not to give his hysteria lecture, as he is still uncertain about it.

1898 April 2

Death of Salomon Stricker. F. had listened to Stricker's lectures and conducted investigations in his laboratory on the nerves of the salivary gland and the secretion of saliva in dogs. He was for F. "an important man, a hard personality, who succeeded in identifying his essentially mean and fanatical bent with scientific aspirations" (F. to Fliess, 3.4.1898).

1898 April 3

- F. plays the travel game "100 journeys through Europe" with his children.
- The second section of the *dream interpretation* is almost finished.

1898 April 8–12

Trip to Veneto with brother Alexander

1898 April 8

Departure from Vienna Südbahnhof in the evening.

1898 April 9

At 10.00 am, both brothers arrive in Gorizia, visit the town and spend the night there.

1898 April 10

- Travel by steamer through the canal to Grado and Aquileja (sightseeing, wine purchase), the same evening continue to Divača.
- A scathing critique of Wilhelm Fliess' book *Die Beziehungen zwischen Nase und weiblichen Geschlechtsorganen* (*The Relationship between the Nose and the Female Genitals*) appears in the Wiener Klinische Rundschau. On May 1, F. therefore ceases to contribute to the journal.

1898 April 11

- Visit to the Rudolf Cave (morning) and the caves of St. Canzian (afternoon). Karl Lueger, the Mayor of Vienna, is in the cave at the same time.
- Departure to Vienna in the evening.

1898 April 12

Arrival in Vienna in the morning.

1898 April 27

F.'s mother returns from Berlin, where she had visited her daughter Mitzi.

1898 after April 27

F. has dream of "Goethe's attack on Herr M.".

1898 May beginning

F. has dream of "dishonesty" and "inferno".

1898 May 1

- F. sends Wilhelm Fliess the third chapter of the Interpretation of Dreams.
- F. resigns from his job as a permanent contributor to the Wiener Klinische Rundschau.

1898 May 10
The Ministry of Education proposes a number of private lecturers to Emperor Franz Joseph for appointment as an associate professor: Anton Felsenreich, Lothar von Frankl-Hochwart, Ferdinand Frühwald, Moritz Heitler, Rudolf Limbeck, Maximilian Zeissl. On May 21, they are all appointed by the Emperor. F. has been passed over.

1898 May 10–11
F. has a dream of a "castle by the sea".

1898 May 23
Felix Gattel gives F. his book *Ueber die sexuellen Ursachen der Neurasthenie und Angstneurosen (On the Sexual Causes of Neurasthenia and Anxiety Neuroses)* with the dedication "Seinem lieben Herrn Dr Freud von seinem dankbaren Schüler".

1898 May 23
Part of F.'s family goes on holiday to Aussee (Martha and daughter Mathilde still stay in Vienna). They live again with Ferdinand Mauskoth in Obertressen.

1898 May 28–30
"Congress" with Wilhelm Fliess in Reichenau am Semmering.

1898 June 8
Martha and daughter Mathilde travel to Aussee.

1898 after June 8
F. has dream of "outdoor privy".

1898 June 9
- F. is prepared, on Wilhelm Fliess' advice, to cancel a dream in which he had "lost the feeling of shame required of an author" (F. to Fliess, 9.6.1898).
- F.'s wife Martha and daughter Mathilde leave for Aussee.

1898 June 10
- Emma Eckstein visits F.
- F. has dinner at Hermann Teleky's, then a game of tarot with Leopold Königstein and Pepi Engel. F.'s comment is as follows: "For the money I lost, I could have eaten in the Waldsteingarten [...]" (F. to Martha, 11.6.1898).

1898 June 11
- F.'s mother goes for a spa stay at Rožnau (until the beginning of September).
- F. is having dinner at the Riedhof with Albert Schwab and Sigmund Stiassny, the son of the architect Wilhelm Stiassny.

1898 June 12
- The renovation of the bathroom at Berggasse 19 was not finished in time. F. writes to Martha in Aussee: "We miss the bathroom very much, it makes the summer uncomfortable" (F. to Martha, 12.6.1898).
- F. is in Purkersdorf with brother Alexander and Josef Herzig.

1898 June 13
- F. visits the exhibition of the "Vienna Secession", which had opened in spring, with his brother Alexander. He wrote to Martha that it was "very beautiful and entirely in the new style. It is a pity that you are not to see it" (F. to Martha, 14.6.1898).

– In the evening, F. goes on an excursion with Julius Mayreder and Emma Eckstein. Afterward, F. accompanies them on the tram to Gumpendorfer Gürtel.

1898 June 14
– F. is in Dornbach for a consultation and then visits Hammerschlags.
– The bathroom has been renovated, and F. inaugurates it with a shower.

1898 June mid
– F. reads Conrad Ferdinand Meyer's *Gustav Adolf's Page* and "The Judge" with "great enjoyment".
– F. has dream of "house collapse".

1898 June 17–20
Short visit of the family in Aussee

1898 June 17

Departure from Vienna in the evening.

1898 June 18

Arrival in Aussee in the morning.

1898 June 19

In the evening, departure from Aussee.

1898 June 20

Arrival in Vienna in the morning.

1898 June 20
– F. sends Wilhelm Fliess an analysis of Conrad Ferdinand Meyer's story *The Judge*. He sees parallels to the mechanisms of neurosis.
– F. goes with Emma Eckstein to the exhibition of the "Wiener Secession" and then to dinner at the "Ancora verde" in Grünangergasse.

1898 Summer
Ida Bauer – the later patient "Dora" – comes to F.'s practice for the first time with her father, the industrialist Philipp Bauer. Philipp Bauer had already consulted F. earlier about his own complaints.

1898 June 23
F. changes restaurants and dines for the first time at the Matschakerhof; Julius Mayreder sits at the next table.

1898 June 24
F. is in the evening for tarot with Leopold Königstein and Hermann Teleky.

1898 June 26
F. is visiting Oskar and Melanie Rie in Hacking all day.

1898 June end
F. has dream of "open-air abortion".

1898 July 3–5
Patient visit Hořice near Königgrätz

F. visited Ferdinand Goldschmidt in Hořice near Königgrätz. He had treated his brother Josef in the mid-1890s.

1898 July 2

F. leaves Vienna in the evening. At the northwest railway station, he contracts meat poisoning during dinner.

1898 July 3

F. arrives in Hořice in the morning and first consults the Goldschmidt family doctor, who is supposed to help him with his vomiting.

1898 July 4

F. finds the stay in "Hořice […] very interesting […] From the terrace of the house one can see the battlefield of Königgrätz […]" (F. to Martha, 5.7.1898).

1898 July 5

F. arrives back in Vienna.

1898 July 5
– F. has his nose operated on by Markus Hajek because of a cold.
– F. goes out to dinner with brother Alexander.

1898 July 7
F. sends Wilhelm Fliess an early version of the seventh chapter of the Interpretation of Dreams.

1898 approx. July 8
F. orders Fritjof Nansen's book *In Night and Ice.*

1898 July 9–10
Short trip to the Wachau

1898 July 9

F. drives to St. Pölten in the evening and spends the night there.

1898 July 10

F. drives to Melk early in the morning and walks to the Aggstein ruin. From there, he takes a boat to Krems and returns to Vienna by train, arriving shortly before midnight.

1898 after July 10
F. sends Martha Fritjof Nansen's book *In Night and Ice and* Minna a book by Georg Brandes, presumably the volume *William Shakespeare.*

1898 July 18–20
Patient visit in Pörtschach

F. makes a patient visit to Emil Taussig in Pörtschach on Lake Wörthersee through the mediation of Albert Hammerschlag. He stayed at the "Wahllis" boarding house and received 500 Gulden as his fee. [21]

1898 July 18
F. leaves Vienna in the evening. On the train, he has the dream of "Hollthurn, 10 minutes".

1898 July 19

– F. arrives in Pörtschach and meets the patient.
– In the afternoon, F. goes for two walks in the forest and collects mushrooms.
– Departure from Pörtschach in the evening.

1898 July 20

F. arrives back in Vienna in the morning.

1898 July 20

– F. is at the Löw Sanatorium for a consultation. It is about Emil Taussig. His brother Theodor Taussig is also present.
– F. meets Philipp Bondy at the Matschakerhof.
– F. goes to Purkersdorf to visit his nephew Hermann and brings him a small hurdy-gurdy as a present for his first birthday.

1898 before July 22

F. drives a carriage to Dornbach.

"Congress" with Wilhelm Fliess in Berchtesgaden

1898 July 22–24

F. takes the night train to Salzburg. During the night, he has a dream about "Count Thun".

1898 July 23

F. arrives in Berchtesgaden in the morning. After the discussions with Fliess, F. is enchanted by the "Kepler of biology" (F. to Fliess, 30.7.1898).

1898 July 24

F. takes a 4½-hour hike from Berchtesgaden through the forests at Obersalzberg to Salzburg and takes the train to Aussee.

1898 July 24–August 3
Stay with the family in Aussee

1898 July 24

F. arrives in Aussee in the afternoon.

1898 August 3

F. and Minna leave Aussee. At the station, they meet some members of the Israeli Humanitarian Association B'nai B'rith, of which F. has been a member since autumn 1897.

1898 August 3–16
Holiday trip with sister-in-law Minna to South Tyrol, Upper Italy and Switzerland

1898 August 4

– In the afternoon, visit the English Garden and the Schack Gallery.
– Departure from Munich at 6.45 pm. Overnight stay in Kufstein.

1898 August 5

– In the morning, a short walk in Kufstein, then travel by express luxury train to Innsbruck.
– In Innsbruck, stay of 2½ hours. Lunch at the Hotel Goldene Sonne; afterward, F. buys a small Roman statuette, which his three-year-old daughter later calls "an old child" (F. to Fliess, 20.8.1898).

- Visit the most important Innsbruck sights, including the Hofer Monument by Heinrich Natter.
- 3.23 pm Continue from Innsbruck to Landeck. Overnight stay at the Hotel Post.
- Visit to Landeck Castle.

1898 August 6

At 12.50 pm, departure from Landeck by post coach to Pfunds. Lunch there, and then on foot to Finstermünz. Overnight stay there.

1898 August 7

Drive from Finstermünz to Prad am Stilfserjoch; overnight there.

1898 August 8

- At 7.30 am, departure from Prad via Trafoi and the Stilfserjoch (16.00) to Bormio. From the Stilfserjoch onward, it is cold, stormy and rainy.
- In Trafoi, F. learns of the death of his former patient, the neurologist Wilhelm Griendl. He had shot himself on August 2. Griendl's death plays an important role in the failure of forgetting Signorelli's name.

1898 August 9

- Drive from Bormio via Bolladore to Tirano; lunch there.
- On foot in a further "horrible dust storm" to Le Prese on Lago di Poschiavo. F. and Minna arrive "half-dead" (F. to Fliess, 20.8.1898); overnight stay at the Albergho Conzetti.

1898 August 10

F. makes the acquaintance of the spa doctor of Le Prese; he is Italian from Florence and had lived in Vienna in the early 1880s.

1898 August 11

Drive from Le Prese over the Bernina Pass to Pontresina; overnight stay at Hotel Enderlin.

1898 August 12

Excursion to the Roseg glacier and visit to an ice cave.

1898 August 13

Drive from Pontresina via St. Moritz to Maloja; F. and sister-in-law Minna stay overnight in a double room at the Hotel Schweizerhof. The entry in the guest book reads "Dr. Sigm. Freud and wife".

1898 August 14

Stay in Maloja.

1898 August 15–16

Drive from Maloja via Landeck to Aussee.

1898 August 16–31
Stay with family in Aussee

1898 before August 20

F. reads Fritjof Nansen's *In Nacht und Ei*s (Farthest North) and hopes to use Nansen dreams well, as they are very transparent for him.

1898 August 26

In a letter to Wilhelm Fliess, F. reports forgetting a name for the first time (Julius Mosen).

1898 before August 31

F. reads Theodor Lipps's *Die Grundtatsachen des Seelenlebens* and finds the "the substance of my insights stated quite clearly" reflected (F. to Fliess, 31.8.1898).

1898 August 31–September 13
Holiday trip with Mrs Martha to Dalmatia

At the beginning of 1898, Oesterreichischer Lloyd, the Hungarian-Croatian Sea Steamship Company and the smaller companies "Ragusea" and "S. Topic & Cie." had agreed to issue round-trip tickets (ticket booklets) for I. Class, which were valid for 30 days on any ship of these companies. The trip was marketed by "Thos. Cook & Son" and led from/to Fiume or from/to Trieste to Cattaro (now Kotor). The price of 45 Gulden[22] included two nights in the "Grand Hotel Imperial" in Ragusa (now Dubrovnik) with full board.

1898 August 31

- F. and Martha leave Aussee around 1.00 pm and travel via Selzthal to Bruck an der Mur. There, they board the express train from Vienna to Lake Garda, which carried first and second-class coaches to Fiume on the Adriatic. Class to Fiume on the Adriatic Sea.
- F. expresses irony about the "Tsar's Manifesto" of August 24 published by Nicholas II. He considers the Tsar's disarmament initiative to be a pretext to secure Russia's interests in China.

1898 September 1

- Arrival in Fiume.
- Visit to Tersatto, a hill with a fortress and sanctuary overlooking the entire bay of Fiume.

1898 September 2

- Departure from Fiume at 10.30 am on the egg steamer "Pannonia" of the Hungarian-Croatian Sea Steamship Company, launched in 1896.
- At 5.00 pm, arrival in Zara (now Zadar), the capital of Dalmatia.

1898 September 3

F. and Martha spend a day in Zara, the capital of Dalmatia. They will certainly have seen the cathedral with paintings by Titian and Tintoretto, two painters whose art F. had already admired two years earlier at the Scuola S. Rocco in Venice.

1898 September 4

- At 10.30 am, departure from Zara on a "slow" steamer of the Hungarian-Croatian Sea Steamship Company.
- In the early evening, the ship calls at Spalato (now Split) for a short stay.

1898 September 5

- Nightly stopover in Curzola (now Korčula).
- At 7.15 am, the steamer arrives in Gravosa (now Gruž), the port of Ragusa (now Dubrovnik).
- Overnight "Grand Hotel Imperial", opened on 1897 January 29 and designed by Viennese architect Ludwig Tischler. From the hotel – the most modern and elegant in Dalmatia – there is a wonderful view over the city.
- Probably visit the Dominican Church with a painting by Titian and the 15th-century Rector's Palace, reminiscent of the Doge's Palace in Venice.

1898 September 6

F. goes on an excursion without Martha to Trebinje in Bosnia with the Berlin assistant judge Paul Freyhan. During a conversation about art in Italy, the talk turned to the frescoes of the end of the world and the last judgment in Orvieto Cathedral. F. had forgotten the name of the painter Luca Signorelli, and despite his efforts, he could not remember it.

1898 September 7

– At 9.30 am, departure from Ragusa with the egg steamer "Pannonia", which had already taken them from Fiume to Zara.
– Around 11.30 am, the ship reaches the bay of Cattaro (now Kotor) and cruises there for two hours. Afterward, return journey with destination Spalato (now Split).

1898 September 8

– At 5.00 am arrival in Spalato, the economic center of Dalmatia, F. and Martha spend the night with the banker Stevo Perovič, who comes from Trebinje. They had possibly met him on the boat on the journey from Ragusa to Spalato.
– Martha goes shopping and buys Turkish fabrics from the merchant Popovič.

1898 September 9

F. and Martha visit the archeological museum in Spalato and sign the guest book. The museum houses, among other things, a 2700-piece collection of inscriptions, a collection of terracottas and a collection of glass objects. The oldest object in the museum is a headless sphinx from the time of Amenhotep II. The 4th-century Diocletian's Palace bordered directly on Stevo Perovič's house, and F. and Martha certainly visited it. One of the most interesting monuments on the palace grounds is the cathedral, which was originally intended as a mausoleum for Diocletian. In front of the cathedral is the counterpart to the sphinx in the museum, but with a head.

1898 September 10

– Departure from Spalato at 6.30 am with the egg steamer "Graf Wurmbrand" of Oesterreichischer Lloyd. Commissioned in the autumn of 1898, it was the largest, fastest and most modern passenger ship in the Adriatic. The cruising speed was 18 knots, almost twice as fast as the egg steamers of the competition. The ship could accommodate 96 first-class passengers, 30 second-class passengers and 100 third-class passengers. The latter were accommodated on a weather-protected part of the aft deck.
– Short stay in Zara. Since F. and Martha had spent the night in Zara on the outward journey, they will have stayed on the ship.
– Short stay in Pola. In Pola, there is a very well-preserved amphitheater from the 1st century, barely 200 meters from the landing stage of the Lloyd steamer. F. will not miss the opportunity to have a close look at the building.
– At 10.00 pm, the "Graf Wurmbrand" enters the port of Trieste.

1898 September 11

Drive from Trieste to Verona.

1898 September 12

Sightseeing tour of Verona, including a visit to the Museo di Castelvecchio with paintings Paolo Veronese including the Martyrdom of St. George.

1898 September 13

Drive from Verona to Merano. Martha stays in Merano.

September 13–18
Journey through Upper Italy

1898 September 13

– F. travels on to Brescia and stays there for two hours.
– F. acquires Pompeo Molmenti's book *Il Moretto da Brescia* in *Brescia*.
– F. visits an exhibition on the 400th birthday of Alessandro Moretto.

1898 September 14

– At 7.15 am, departure for Milan; overnight at Hotel Pozzo.
– F. acquires Giovanni Morelli's book *Della pittura italiana* and Luca Beltrami's *La Certosa di Pavia*.

1898 September 15

Attending Leonardo's Last Supper.

1898 September 16

Excursions to Pavia and Monza.

1898 September 17

– Trip to Bergamo. F. arrives there around 11.00 am and waits at the Ristorante del Sole on the Piazza Garibaldi for the Accademia Carrara to open. There, he sees paintings by Signorelli, Botticelli and Boltraffio side by side in an exhibition room: the three painters who play an important role in the blunder of forgetting the name Signorelli.
– Return to Milan in the afternoon.
– Departure from Milan at 11.15 pm.

1898 September 17–18

On the night train, F. has the dream of "Three Fates".

1898 September 18

Arrival in Vienna in the evening.

1898 September 19
F. visits Leopold Königstein in the evening.

1898 September 20
Alois Bloch visits F.

1898 September 21
– F. makes patient visits in Baden and in Purkersdorf to Babette Drey, the mother of Julius and Karl Drey.
– F. visits Oskar Rie in the evening.

1898 September 22
F. tells Wilhelm Fliess about forgetting the name Signorelli.

1898 September 27
F. sends his article "Zum psychischen Mechanismus der Vergesslichkeit" (The Psychological Mechanism of Forgetfulness) to Theodor Ziehen and Carl Wernicke as editors of the *Monatsschrift für Psychiatrie und Neurologie*. This paper becomes the basis for F.'s book *Zur Psychopathologie des Alltagslebens*.

1898 shortly before September 28
Beginning of the correspondence between F. and Eugen Bleuler.

1898 September end
F.'s family returns from Aussee.

1898 October
F. offers lectures "On the Great Neuroses" in the winter semester (lecture hall of Richard von Krafft-Ebing, fee five Gulden).

1898 October 9
F. has 10–11 psychotherapies a day.

1898 October 16
F. attends the unveiling of Ernst Fleischl's relief in the arcade courtyard of Vienna University.

1898 October mid
F. studies the "topography" of Rome.

1898 October 18
Cäcilie Graf, the daughter of F.'s sister Rosa, is born.

1898 October 23
F. receives the first volume of Max Kassowitz's *General Biology*.

1898 approx. October 26
F. has the "Non vixit" dream.

1898 October 30
F. meets Fliess' sister-in-law Marie Bondy.

1898 November beginning
F. has a painful boil that needs to be operated on and in this context has the dream of "riding a grey horse".

1898 December beginning
– F. delves into the literature about the dream again, but with reluctance.
– F. buys the missing volumes by Conrad Ferdinand Meyer: *Huttens letzte Tage*, *Die Versuchung des Pescara* and *Der Heilige*.

1898 December 6–7
F. has dream of "Mrs Doni".

1898 December 26
F. meets with Wilhelm Fliess in Vienna.

1898 end
F.'s paper "On the Psychological Mechanism of Forgetfulness" appears. He gives an offprint to Oskar Rie with the dedication "Seinem lieben Freunde Dr. Oskar Rie/F."

1899

- F. has "dream of friend Otto" (Oskar Rie).
- Ludwig Jekels, who had been running a private sanatorium for the treatment of nervous diseases in Bistrai in Silesia since 1897, visits F. to recommend his institution to him for the referral of patients.

1899 January 3
- F. concludes that fantasies are products of later times, going back to early childhood.
- F. receives a "consignment" from Gibraltar from Havelock Ellis, presumably the two off-prints "The Analysis of the sexual Impulse" and "Auto-Erotism: A psychological Study".

1899 before January 16
F. goes with Martha and Minna to the "Ancora Verde" and drinks a bottle of "Barolo".

1899 January 18
Death of Carl Claus. F. had listened to his lectures and worked in his institute for comparative anatomy.

1899 January end
F. reads Jacob Burckhardt's *Greek Cultural History*, which provides him with unexpected parallels.

1899 February 3
- F. earns 100 Gulden after 12 treatments.[23]
- F. gives a lecture to B'nai B'rith on "The Psychology of Forgetting".

1899 February
F. acquires Alfred von Sallet's book *Münzen und Medaillen*.

1899 February 6
F. thinks about death and plans a change of profession and a possible change of residence.

1899 February 19
F. verifies the thesis of the dream as wish fulfillment by means of case presentations.

1899 February 27
Beginning of the correspondence between F. and Alfred Adler.

1899 February
F. has dream of his father "on his deathbed", who looks like Garibaldi.

1899 March beginning
F.'s daughter Anna has "intestinal influenza".

1899 March 2
F. gives a lecture to B'nai B'rith on "On the Psychology of Forgetting".

1899 March 5
F. feels a strong desire to travel.

1899 March 12
F. sees Arthur Schnitzler's one-act play *Paracelsus* at the Burgtheater and writes to Fliess: "Recently I was amazed in Schnitzler's Paracelsus how much of things such a poet knows". (The premiere of the play was on 1899 March 1).

1899 March mid
F. meets Wilhelm Fliess in Baden.

1899 March 15
The Professorenkollegium formulates a reminder regarding the submissions of ten private lecturers of the medical faculty for extraordinaries, Besides F., it concerns Arthur Biedl, Conrad Clar, Salomon Ehrmann, Leopold Königstein, Josef Metnitz, Norbert Ortner, Jacob Pal, Heinrich Paschkis and Ernst Wertheim.

1899 March 19
F. examines the heavily pregnant Melanie Rie, "she looks radiant and – after no appointment at all". Six days later, daughter Margarethe is born.

1899 March end
F.'s brother Alexander becomes a contributor to the *Allgemeiner Tarif-Anzeiger*, of which he was already an editor.

1899 March 31–April 3
"Congress" with Wilhelm Fliess in Innsbruck

Overnight stay at the Hotel Sonne or the Tirolerhof; during the stay, F. has a migraine attack.

1899 March 31

F. leaves Vienna in the evening.

1899 April 1

– F. arrives in Innsbruck at 9.30 am.
– At 12.45 pm, Fliess arrives in Innsbruck and F. picks him up at the station.

1899 April 3

F. leaves Innsbruck.

1899 after April 3
F. offers lectures on "The Psychology of Dreams" in the summer semester (lecture hall of Richard von Krafft-Ebing, fee five Gulden).

1899 April mid
F. is looking for a country flat.

1899 May 6
F.'s nephew Herman Graf congratulates him on his birthday with a basket of cherries. Followed by "Cherry Dream" by Herman.

1899 May 14
F. and Martha visit Oskar and Melanie Rie and meet Bernhard Dernburg, the director of the Deutsche Treuhand-Gesellschaft. Mrs. Rie treats her guests to cauliflower and chicken, both of which F. "detest with all my heart" (F. to Fliess, 25.5.1899).

1899 after May 14
F. writes a paper "Über Deckerinnerungen" which, among other things, reproduces F.'s own memories from the beginning of his third year of life under the guise that they are the memories of an academically educated man.

1899 May 15
F. meets Gustav Gärtner during a medical consultation.

1899 May 18

Birth of F.'s niece Cäcilie, daughter of sister Rosa Graf.

1899 May 21–22
Short stay in Reichenau

1899 May 21

F. goes to Reichenau in the evening, where his sister Rosa and daughter Mathilde are staying.

1899 May 22

– F. climbs the Rax with his brother-in-law Heinrich Graf.
– In the evening, return journey to Vienna.

1899 May 25

F. sends the paper "Über Deckerinnerungen" to print.

1899 before May 28

F. acquires Heinrich Schliemann's *Ilios. Stadt und Land der Trojaner* and rejoices in its childhood story: "The man was happy when he found Priam's treasure, because happiness comes only with the fulfillment of a childhood wish" (F. to Fliess, 28.5.1899).

1899 May 28

– F. decides to publish the interpretation of dreams and in this context has the dream of "dissection on his own body".
– F.'s sons have mild angina.

1899 June beginning

Fanny Bardas begins an analysis with F. It lasts until the summer 1901. Her son Willy goes to the same dance school as F.'s daughter Mathilde and later becomes a famous pianist.

1899 June beginning

F. reads Heinrich Spitta's *The Sleep and Dream States of the Human Soul and* has the association "to spit" with the name Spitta.

1899 June 6

Minna and F.'s children (except daughter Mathilde) go to Berchtesgaden.

1899 June 9

F. comes to the conclusion that the dream seeks to fulfill the desire for sleep; i.e., the dream is the guardian of sleep.

1899 June 16

– F. goes to the Prater, then to the "Urania" for a lecture on iron and then to a Prater restaurant for dinner.
– F.'s mother goes for a spa stay at Rožnau (until September mid).

1899 June 18

F. is at the wedding of Leopold Königstein's daughter Lilli to Moritz Teich.

1899 shortly after June 18

F. has dream of "being in sixth grade".

1899 June 20

Martha goes to Berchtesgaden with daughter Mathilde.

1899 June 24
– F. receives a large antique gift from his patient Josefa Ehrenhöfer.
– The company B & L supplies F. with trousers and shirts.
– F. is at Leopold Königstein's for tarot in the evening.

1899 June 25
– F.'s daughter Mathilde has her first menstruation.
– F. has a severe migraine attack.
– F. is at Leopold Königstein's for tarot in the evening.

1899 June 28
F. sends the first sheet of the *dream interpretation to* the printer.

1899 June 29–July 2
F. is on a short holiday with his family in Berchtesgaden. Among other things, they go on an excursion to the Schellenberg Forest.

1899 after July 2
Marie Ferstel begins an analysis with F. She is the wife of the later Austrian Consul General in Berlin, Erwin Ferstel and daughter-in-law of Heinrich Ferstel, the architect of the Votivkirche. Marie Ferstel is also distantly related to Martha. Her treatment lasts until the summer of 1903.

1899 July 3
F. is at Leopold Königstein's for tarot in the evening.

1899 July 4
F. visits the Schiff family in Baden during a "terrible thunderstorm". His patient Helene Schiff "has become a different person", but still has headaches (F. to Martha, 5.7.1899).

1899 July 5
– The poet Jakob Julius David visits F. for lunch.
– In the evening, F. and Oskar Rie go to an inn.

1899 July 7
F. is with Hermann Teleky in the evening.

1899 July 8
F. visits Oskar and Melanie Rie in Hacking.

1899 July 9
F. visits Oskar Rie and meets Fliess's father-in-law Philipp Bondy there.

1899 July 10
F. is in the evening with colleagues at the "Silberner Brunnen" inn in Berggasse, corner of Wasagasse.

1899 July 11
F. has been noble with "Emma [Eckstein], Prater and Waldsteingarten" (F. to Martha, 12.7.1899).

1899 July 12
Josef Herzig has lunch at F.

1899 July 13
F. ends the First Chapter of the *Interpretation of Dreams.*

1899 July mid
– The poet Jakob Julius David visits F. several times.
– F. has dream of "autodidasker".

1899 July 16
F. goes on an excursion to Reichenau am Semmering. There, he sees Max Kassowitz and passes him out of "consideration".

1899 July 17
– F. thinks about Motti for the dream interpretation.
– F. says goodbye to the Rie family in Hacking.
– F. sends the second part of his reviews and summaries on cerebral palsy to the annual report on the achievements *and progress of neurology and psychiatry.*

1899 July 18
F. takes a trip with Markus Hajek.

1899 July 20
– F. goes to Baden to visit Bernhard Lichtenstein, who is staying there with his son, the journalist Jacques Lichtenstein, and their daughters Henriette and Lina.
– F. travels to Hietzing with his brother-in-law Heinrich Graf by tram.

1899 July 21
– F. visits Hammerschlags.
– F. assures Max Kassowitz in a letter of his admiration and devotion, as the latter had misinterpreted his "passing" on July 16 in Reichenau.

1899 July 22
F. plans to send the dream interpretation to Wilhelm Fliess for correction.

1899 July 22–September 21
Summer stay with family in Berchtesgaden

F. is on holiday in Berchtesgaden (house "Riemerlehen") and finishes writing the *dream interpretation there.* During these two months, he hikes up the Salzberg three times a week.

1899 July 22

Departure from Vienna in the evening.

1899 July 23

Arrival in Salzburg in the morning. Martha and daughter Mathilde are waiting for him there and go shopping together.

1899 July 26

The family goes on an excursion to St. Bartholomae at Königssee on the occasion of Martha's birthday.

1899 July 27

F. ends the literature chapter on *dream interpretation.*

1899 July end

F. has dream of "letter from the municipal council".

1899 August 1

F. sends the correction sheets of the first chapter of the Interpretation of Dreams to Wilhelm Fliess from Berchtesgaden.

1899 before August 6

F. wanders to Salzburg, where he acquires a few Egyptian antiquities.

1899 August 6

F. is on a short visit to Reichenhall and meets Martha's relatives from Munich. On the evening of that day, F. compares *dream interpretation to a* walk through a dark forest.

1899 August mid

F.'s brother Alexander is in Berchtesgaden for four days.

1899 August 19

F. again sends correction sheets of the *dream interpretation* to Fliess.

1899 August 20

F. has writer's cramp. It is the same day that he replaces a dream deleted by Wilhelm Fliess with a series of "dream fragments" (F. to Fliess, 20.8.1899).

1899 August 27

F. proposes a "Congress" to Fliess at Easter in Rome and begins the preparatory work for the seventh chapter of The *Interpretation of Dreams*. It will "contain 2467 mistakes" (F. to Fliess, 27.8.1899).

1899 September

F.'s paper "On Cover Memories" appears.

1899 September beginning

F. writes 8–10 pages a day on the *dream interpretation*. The Breuer family comes to Berchtesgaden, and F. meets Josef Breuer almost daily.

1899 September 11

F. asks Fliess in a letter whether or not he should rewrite the seventh chapter of The *Interpretation of Dreams*. At the same time, he informs him of his realization of the connection between the theory of the unconscious and the theory of the joke and of his sadness and bitterness at the renewed guilty verdict against Alfred Dreyfus. On the same day, F. has a migraine attack that he cannot explain.

1899 September 11–15

Severe storms hit Berchtesgaden. The town is cut off from the outside world for several days, and F. has not received any newspapers since the 13th.

1899 September 12

F. has heart problems and a slight headache.

1899 before September 15

F. completes the manuscript of the *interpretation of dreams*.

1899 September 15

F. takes a walk to flooded Salzburg.

1899 September 16

F. learns through an extra edition of the *Berchtesgadener Anzeiger about an* accident caused by the consequences of the storm.

1899 September 20

F. leaves Berchtesgaden and only has a slight headache, but no more heart complaints.

1899 September 21

F. arrives back in Vienna after an overnight stay in Budweis and a 32-hour train journey due to heavy rain.

1899 September 21

– F. learns from the press about the pardon of Alfred Dreyfus.
– F. sends 60 correction sheets of *dream interpretation to* Wilhelm Fliess and reflects on his fear of helpless poverty.
– F. relates the saying in the coat of arms of Paris ("Fluctuat nec mergitur") to his mood; later, he uses it as a motto for the writing "On the History of the Psycho-Analytic Movement".
– F. interprets the "Non vixit" dream as an expression of joy at having survived Wilhelm Fliess (F. to Fliess, 21.9.1899).
– F. visits Königsteins, gets tea there and then goes for a walk with Leopold Königstein. Afterward, Hermann Teleky comes to the tarot.
– 1899 September 22
– F. reads Émil Zola's "herzerfrischend[en]" in the *Neue Freie* Presse. Letter to Lucie Hadamard, the wife of Alfred Dreyfus (F. to Martha, 23.9.1899).
– F. has lunch with brother Alexander and brother-in-law Heinrich Graf.
– Oskar Rie visits F.
– F. went to the tarot with Leopold Königstein.

1899 Autumn

F. receives Carl Stumpf's book *Der Traum und seine Deutung*.

1899 September 25

The newspaper *Das Vaterland* announces Alexander Freud's lectures on tariff theory at the Export Academy. One day later, the announcement also appears in the *Neue Freie Presse.*

1899 September 27

F. is afraid that someone might pre-empt the publication of his dream theory. The concrete occasion was the announcement of a book by Christoph Ruths entitled *Analyse und Grundgesetze der Traumphänomene,* which never appeared.

1899 October beginning

Oskar Rie expresses serious reservations about the publication of The *Interpretation of Dreams*.

1899 October 6

F. has a mild migraine attack.

1899 before October 9

F. is driven by "obscure inner forces to read psychological writings" (F. to Fliess, 9.10.1899).

1899 October 9

– F. finds a piece of his "part of my hypothetical pleasure-unpleasure theory" in Henry Marshall's book *Pain, Pleasure and Aesthetics* (F. to Fliess, 9.10.1899).

- He has once again been passed over for promotion to professor.
- F. is considering cooperating with a "water company" in the summer.

1899 October 11
F. next intends to write a book about his sexual theory.

1899 October mid
Oskar Rie begins to warm to *dream interpretation.*

1899 October 24
F. gives Wilhelm Fliess a preprint of The *Interpretation of Dreams* with the dedication: "Seinem theuern Wilhelm/z. 24. Oktober 1899".

1899 October 27
F. is at Melanie and Oskar Rie's for tarot.

1899 November beginning
- Jakob Julius David promises F. to write a review of The *Interpretation of Dreams in* No. 17 of *Nation,* a Berlin "weekly journal for politics, economics and literature", which is published. F. then describes the review as "a kind and perceptive, somewhat diffuse" (F. to Fliess, 1.2.1900).
- F. hopes to take on a patient of Richard von Krafft-Ebing.

1899 November 4
- *Die Traumdeutung is* published (600 copies). A few days later, F. shows the book to his son Oliver in the shop window of the publisher Deuticke.
- F. has a strong splendid migraine.

1899 after November 4
- F. gives Helene Schiff a copy of *Traumdeutung* with dedication.
- F. gives Wilhelm Stekel a copy of The *Interpretation of Dreams* with the dedication "mit herzlichem Dank für sein grosses Verdienst um die Würdigung dieses Buches/dVerf.".
- F. gives Wilhelm Knöpfmacher a copy of The *Interpretation of Dreams* with dedication.
- F. shows son Oliver the *interpretation of dreams in* the shop window of Deuticke's bookshop.

1899 November 5
F. recognizes the confusion between Hamilkar and Hasdrubal in the *interpretation of dreams*.

1899 before November 7
Sophie Paneth, the wife of F.'s deceased friend Josef Paneth, terminates his friendship because she feels hurt by the mention of her husband in the dream "Non vixit". F. had wished Paneth dead in this dream.

1899 November 7
F. is toying with the idea of giving up his city flat and moving to the outskirts of Vienna.

1899 November 9
F.'s daughter Sophie has diarrhea and fever.

1899 November 10
F. writes the manuscript "A Fulfilled Dream Premonition".

1899 shortly before November 12
F.'s attention is drawn to another error in the *dream interpretation*: Friedrich Schiller's birthplace is Marbach, not Marburg.

1899 November 12
F. has heart problems and migraines.

1899 November 16–17
F. makes a patient visit in Budapest.

1899 November mid
F. has a slight writer's cramp.

1899 November 17
Heinrich Gomperz, son of the philosopher Theodor Gomperz and his wife Elise, who had previously been treated by F., begins a series of sessions with F. in which he wants to learn "the method of dream interpretation"….

1899 November 19
F. begins treatment of Maggie Haller through the mediation of Wilhelm Fliess (until 1901 and 1910 October–1911 July).

1899 November 26
F. is planning a book entitled "Sexual Theory and Fear".

1899 November end–December beginning
Wilhelm Fliess visits F. in Vienna.

1899 December 9
F. develops thoughts on sexual theory.

1899 December mid
Oskar Rie visits F.'s daughter Mathilde every day because of an abscess.

1899 December 16
A review of the *interpretation of dreams* by Carl Metzentin appears in the journal *Die Gegenwart*. F. describes it as "without content" and "deficient" (F. to Fliess, 21.12.1899).

1899 December 21
- He compares his discoveries with archeology: "It is as if Schliemann had once again dug up Troy, which was thought to be legendary" (F. to Fliess, 21.12.1899).
- In connection with an interpretation of his patient Oskar Fellner (Herr E.), F. describes his railway phobia as an "impoverishment fantasy, or rather a hunger phobia, dependent on my infantile gluttony and caused by the dowrylessness of my wife (of whom I am proud)". In gratitude, he gives Fellner the painting "Oedipus and the Sphinx" (F. to Fliess, 21.12.1899).

1899 Winter
F. sends Ernst Mach a copy of The *Interpretation of Dreams* at Mach's request; F. later learns that Mach "set it aside, shaking his head" (F. to Ferenczi, 26.11.1915).

1899 December 24
F. intends to send Ernst Ludwig Krause (pseudonym: Carus Sterne) a copy of The *Interpretation of Dreams*.

1900

- F. reads Christoph Ruth's book Experimental Untersuchungen über Musikphantome.
- Emanuel Loewy gives F. his work *Die Naturwiedergabe in der älteren griechischen Kunst* with the dedication "Sigmund Freud mit bestem Dank und herzlichsten Glückwünschen d. Vf.".
- F. hires a Czech cook.

Treatments:
- Jacob Julius David, an Austrian poet, begins an analysis with F.
- Alois Jeitteles begins an analysis with F. It lasts until 1907 October. He is a son of Richard Jeitteles, the general manager of the Kaiser Ferdinands-Nordbahn.

1900 January 1
In Austria, the Gulden currency is replaced by the Kronen as a means of payment, and F. cannot buy postcards with the new currency.

1900 January 6
The first part of a review of The *Interpretation of Dreams* by Max Burckhardt, former director of the Burgtheater, appears in Die *Zeit*. F. calls it "uncommonly uncomprehending" and "stupid" (F. to Fliess, 8.1.1900).

1900 January 7
F.'s son Martin has a fever.

1900 January 8
F. no longer expects to be recognized during his lifetime, as he believes he is "10–15 years ahead" of his audience (F. to Fliess, 8.1.1900).

1900 January 13
The second part of Max Burckhardt's review of The *Interpretation of Dreams* appears in Die Zeit.

1900 January 20
F. acquires Adolf Frey's book *Conrad Ferdinand Meyer* and immediately begins reading it.

1900 January end
- F. agrees with Leopold Löwenfeld to publish an extract from the *interpretation of dreams in* the series *Grenzfragen des Nerven- und Seelenlebens, which he* edits. It then appears under the title *Über den Traum.*
- F. buys something by Friedrich Nietzsche, but does not read it for the time being.

1900 February 1
F. considers himself less a "man of science" than a "conquistador temperament" and "adventurer": "Such people are only appreciated if they have had success, have really discovered something, but otherwise they are to be cast aside" (F. to Fliess, 1.2.1900).

1900 February 6
F. gives a lecture to B'nai B'rith on the topic "From the Soul Life of Children".

1900 February 10
Minna goes to Hamburg for three weeks to visit her mother, who is in bed with influenza.

1900 February 18
F. has a severe migraine.

1900 March
F. plays chess and reads English novels.

1900 March 1
F. receives Eugen Jonas's book *Symptomatologie und Therapie der nasogenen Reflexneurosen und Organerkrankungen.*

1900 March 10
- A review of the *interpretation of dreams* by the biochemist Carl Oppenheimer appears in the Stuttgarter *Umschau, a* journal that gives an "overview of progress and movements in the overall field of science, technology, literature and art"; F. calls it a "short, amiable and insightless paper" (F. to Fliess, 16.5.1900).
- A review of Traumdeutung appears in the Wiener *Fremden-Blatt*; F. describes it as a "quite amiable essay" (F. to Fliess, 11.3.1900). It is signed "H. K.", possibly Heinrich Kahane, the older brother of Max Kahane.

1900 March 17
F. goes to a "tarot Excess".

1900 March 18
F. and Martha attend a lecture by Georg Brandes at the "Concordia" and send him the *dream interpretation to* the hotel.

1900 Spring
- F. has dream of the "Trottoir roulant".
- Wilhelm Stekel begins an analysis with F. It ends successfully after eight sessions.

1900 March 23
F. cancels a meeting proposed by Wilhelm Fliess and indirectly admits that he is jealous of Fliess because of his biological discoveries.

1900 April
F. offers lectures on "The Psychology of Dreams" in the summer semester (until July) (lecture hall of Richard von Krafft-Ebing, fee ten Kronen).

1900 April beginning
F.'s daughter Mathilde has chickenpox.

1900 April 6
Margit Kremzir ("Mrs. M. W."), a cousin of Helene Weiss, begins treatment at F. She hangs herself in a hotel room on April 20.

1900 April mid
- F. completes the analysis of Oskar Fellner after five years.
- F. skims over Wolfgang Warda's case history of a patient he had treated with the "cathartic method of Breuer and Freud".
- A grandson of the painter Rudolf Alt, whom F. is supposed to treat, falls ill one day before the appointed appointment.

1900 April 16
F. has to cancel a planned Easter trip with brother Alexander to South Tyrol and Lake Garda, firstly because of bad weather in the destination area and secondly because all of F.'s children had come down with chickenpox.

1900 April 20
F.'s patient Margit Kremzir hangs herself in a Vienna hotel room.

1900 April 23–24
F. has a dream about a badly prepared lecture, triggered by a lecture he had to give the next day.

1900 April 24
F. gives a lecture to B'nai B'rith on Emile Zola's book *Fécondité*; the dream the night before is directly related to this.

1900 May 5
Death of Valentin Winternitz, the husband of F.'s youngest sister Paula. The couple lived in New York, where Paula had moved in 1893 November. She had met Valentin there and married him in 1895.

1900 May 7
F. speaks of his "splendid isolation" (F. to Fliess, 7.5.1900).

1900 May 12
F. begins his lecture "On the Psychology of Dreams", but has only three listeners (Hans König-stein, Dora Teleky and Gotthelf Marcuse).

1900 May mid
– F. is interested in art history and prehistory and plays a lot of chess.
– F.'s bookseller Franz Deuticke complains that The Interpretation of Dreams is selling poorly.
– F. visits the family of his deceased brother-in-law Valentin Winternitz in Zwittau (now Svitavy), with whom his widowed sister Paula and her four-year-old daughter Beatrice were to stay after their return from New York.
– F. wants to buy a small cassette for his patient Maggie Haller to store her cash. However, F. cannot find the shop where he has seen such cassettes. It turns out that the cassette company Rudolf Tanczos has its branch at Brandstätte 3, opposite Josef Breuer's house, with whom F. had no more contact after a period of estrangement.

1900 May 16
– F. is pleased that Josef Breuer seems to agree with his hysteria theory after all.
– F. visits Melanie and Oskar Rie.

1900 May 19
F. receives an album with pictures by Arnold Böcklin as a farewell gift from a patient.

1900 May 23
F. moves with his family to Bellevue on Cobenzl.

1900 May 24
F. has severe migraines.

1900 June

F. treats a 13-year-old girl ("the most remarkable case I had had in recent years", SE 6, p. 146) and diagnoses hysteria; in August, she dies of a sarcoma of the abdominal glands.

1900 June 2–6

F.'s brother Emanuel and his son Samuel from Manchester visit the Freud family in Vienna.

1900 June 6

In the evening edition of the *Berliner Tageblatt und Handels-Zeitung,* under the title "Ein wissenschaftlicher Traumdeuter" ("A scientific dream interpreter"), an unsigned review of *Traumdeutung* appears, which Wilhelm Fliess sends to F., who would like to know from Fliess who the author is.

1900 before June 12

F.'s son Ernst has angina for four days.

1900 June 12

F. asks Fliess whether a marble plaque will be placed at Bellevue in memory of the Irma dream of 1895 July 23/24 with the text: "Here, on 24 July 1895, Dr. Sigm. Freud the secret of the dream". And F. adds: "The prospects for this are so far slim"[24] (F. to Fliess, 12.6.1900).

1900 June 18

F.'s son Martin also has angina now.

1900 Summer

- F.'s school friend Sigmund Lustgarten is visiting Vienna from New York.
- Joseph Bergmann, the publisher of *Grenzfragen des Nerven- und Seelenlebens,* sends F. the correction sheets of his monograph Über den Traum and asks for them to be returned quickly. F. makes the corrections the same night, but forgets to send them for two days. F. later analyzes this failure in *Psychopathology of Everyday Life*.

1900 July 1

F.'s sister Paula Winternitz arrives in Vienna with her daughter Beatrice. She had left New York after her husband Valentin Winternitz died on May 5.

1900 July 31–August 4

F. meets for a "Congress" with Wilhelm Fliess at Achensee in Tyrol.
At this "Congress", there was a final break with Fliess. The reason was Fliess's theory of bisexuality, which F. considered his own, although Fliess had already presented it to him in Breslau in 1897.

1900 August 4–August mid
Journey with Martha through South Tyrol

1900 August 4

F. travels from Achensee to Innsbruck and meets his wife Martha there, and both travel on to Landeck.

1900 August 5

Drive from Landeck to Trafoi and overnight stay at the inn "Zur schönen Aussicht".

1900 August 6

Excursion to the Stilfserjoch.

1900 August 7

Continue to Sulden and ascend to the Schaubach Hut.

1900 August 9

Onward journey to Merano.

1900 August 10

They continue their journey to the Mendel Pass, where they meet Sigmund Lustgarten, who had come to Europe from New York.

1900 August 11

Excursion to Nonsthal (Cles), ancient findings.

1900 August 13

Martha travels home via Bolzano. F. continues to Venice, where he has another appointment with Sigmund Lustgarten to show him Venice. In Venice, F. meets his sister Rosa and brother-in-law Heinrich. Rosa is ill with oyster poisoning and has to leave earlier than planned for Annenheim, where a family reunion is planned. As a result of the poisoning, Rosa largely loses her hearing.

1900 August 15

Drive from Venice to Annenheim on Lake Ossiach.

1900 August 15–August 26
Family reunion in Annenheim on Lake Ossiach

F. and Martha are in Annenheim, where F.'s sister Anna from New York is spending the summer with her children. In addition, F.'s mother and all the other sisters have come to Annenheim. The company is accommodated in the "Berghof" guesthouse on the south side of the lake. It belongs to the composer Alban Berg, whose father had bought the house in 1894. Alban's mother asked F. to come and see the then 15-year-old boy, as he had been having asthma attacks since his father's death. After a few conversations with him, F. concluded that the attacks were psychological.

1900 ca. August 17

F.'s brother Alexander comes to Annenheim unexpectedly.

1900 August 26

F.'s sister-in-law Minna Bernays arrives in Annenheim.

1900 August 27–September 10
Journey with Minna through South Tyrol

1900 August 27

Drive from Lake Ossiach through the Puster Valley to Trento.

1900 August 28

From Trento, excursion to Castel Toblino.

1900 August 29

Drive from Trento to Lavarone.

1900 August 31

F. learns by telegram from Martha that he has again been passed over for appointment as an associate professor. Instead, Leopold Königstein has been appointed.

1900 September 1

F. and Minna go mushroom hunting and return with a carrying basket of 30 gentlemen's mushrooms.

1900 September 2

Drive via Torbole to Riva. F. meets there Gustav Czermak, Friedrich Dimmer, Anton Felsenreich, the Innsbruck philosopher Franz Hildebrand, Friedrich Jodl and Sigmund Mayer.

1900 September 4

In the afternoon, boat trip to Salò.

1900 September 5

Excursion to Arco and Torbole.

1900 September 6

Boat trip to Sirmione.

1900 September 8

F. takes Minna to Merano, where she stays until around October mid.

1900 September 10

F. returns to Vienna.

1900 September 11

F. has an idea about the psychological mechanism of superstition, namely its relationship to chance. The trigger was that the coachman who was supposed to drive him to a patient drove him to the wrong place, although he had already driven F. to the right address several times.

1900 September 15

F.'s family returns to Berggasse from their summer stay at Bellevue.
1900 September mid

– F. writes on the psychopathology of everyday life.
– F. parts with a number of medical books and offers them to a bookseller for 300 Kronen.
– F. sends 300 Kronen to a relative who is at the spa, possibly to Minna Bernays in Meran.

1900 September 23

F. cannot correctly recall Vergil's verse "Exoriar(e) aliquis nostris ex ossibus ultor!". Instead, he comes up with "Exoriar(e) ex nostris ossibus ultor!" (SE 6, p. 9). The seventh chapter of Virgil's Aeneid, from which the quotation comes, had been covered in F.'s Greek lessons in the 1872/73 school year.

1900 October

– F. offers lectures on "The Great Neuroses" in the winter semester (lecture hall of Richard von Krafft-Ebing, fee five Gulden).
– F. has dream of "company, table or table d'hôte".
– Hermann Swoboda begins an analysis with F. He learns from F. details of the theories of bisexuality developed by Wilhelm Fliess. However, Swoboda assumes that these theories are by F.

1900 October beginning
Philipp Bauer seeks out F. in order to make an appointment with von F. to start treatment for his daughter Ida.

1900 before October 14
- A review of the *interpretation of dreams* by Ludwig Karell appears in the supplement to the *Münchner Allgemeine Zeitung*. F. calls it a "stupid paper" (F. to Fliess, 14.10.1900).
- F. begins the analysis of 18-year-old Ida Bauer, called "Dora" in F.'s medical history. It lasts until December 31.

1900 October 14
F. collects material for the *Psychopathologie des Alltagslebens* and decides on the motto: "Nun ist die Luft von solchem Spuk so voll, dass niemand weiss, wie er ihn meiden soll".[25] ("Now the air is so full of such spooks that no one knows how to avoid them.")

1900 October 21
A longer review of F.'s *Interpretation of Dreams* by his patient Emma Eckstein appears in the *Arbeiter-Zeitung* under the headline "Das Seelenleben im Traum".

1900 November
F. meets with Oskar Rie several times.

1900 November mid
Minna Bernays falls ill with an ulcer.

1900 December mid
F.'s Treatise Über den Traum is published; the official date of publication is 1901. F. gives one copy to Wilhelm Stekel with the dedication "Herrn Dr. W. Stekel freundschaftlich d. Verf.".

1900 Christmas
F. gives Leopold Königstein his book Über den Traum with the dedication: "Herrn. Prof. König-stein zu Weihnacht des frohen Jahres 1900 von seinem Fr".

1900 December 25
F. gives Alfred Rie a copy of his book Zur Psychopathologie des Alltagslebens with the dedication „Dr. Alfred Rie / in alter Freundschaft".

1900 December 31
F. ends the treatment of Ida Bauer.

1901

- Richard von Krafft-Ebing gives F. his *Psychopathia sexualis with special consideration of the contrary sexual sensation* with the dedication "In collegialer Hochachtung d. Verfasser".
- Hugo Schwerdtner gives F. his book *Die stumme Seele* with the dedication "Dem Erforscher der Seele Professor Dr Sigmund Freud vom Verfasser".

1901 January
F. writes on the "Fragment of a Hysteria Analysis", the history of the illness and treatment of Ida Bauer ("Dora").

1901 January 1
- F. suggests to Wilhelm Fliess to interrupt their correspondence "for a time".
- F. "revises" his "medical book" in order to be able to send out fee invoices.

1901 January mid
Josef Breuer recommends F. to the "Philosophical Society" to invite F. as a lecturer.

1901 January 24
F. finishes the "Fragment of an Analysis of Hysteria", the "most subtle" thing he has written so far.

1901 January 31
F. indicates to Wilhelm Fliess that he wanted to meet with him.

1901 January end
Minna suffers from an ulcer, the location of which is unclear. She has to stay in bed for several weeks.

1901 February
- F. writes to Hermann Nothnagel and Richard von Krafft-Ebing asking them to renew the proposal of his professorship; both agree.
- F. seeks out Sigmund Exner about his professorship; Elise Gomperz is suggested as a mediator.
- In the Biographisches Lexikon hervorragender Ärzte des neunzehnten Jahrhunderts edited by Julius Pagel, an autobiographical article by F.

1901 February 11
The *Neue Freie Presse* announces a lecture by F. before the "Philosophical Society". However, F. cancels after some misgivings on the part of the society's representatives about touching on sexual topics.

1901 February 17 approx.
F. reads in the newspaper that a *clergyman* in Belgium has strangled boys.

1901 February 26
F. gives a lecture to B'nai B'rith on "Chance and Superstition".

1901 February end
- F. concludes the transcript of the psychopathology of everyday life.
- He lets Oskar Rie read the "Fragment of a Hysteria Analysis" at his request.

1901 March
Wilhelm Knöpfmacher gives F. Theodor Echtermeyer's *Selection of German poems for higher schools* with the dedication Widmung "Zur freundlichen Erinnerung an die Zeit unserer Bruderschaft, Willy".

1901 March beginning
F.'s son Oliver has measles. The other siblings also catch it.

1901 March 4
F. visits Marie Auspitz (née Heidenhain), the second wife of Rudolf Auspitz.

1901 March 7
A planned trip to a patient in Berlin is canceled, and F. has a dream that night in which he is in Berlin visiting Wilhelm Fliess.

1901 March 12
F. attends a lecture by Ludwig Braun at the B'nai B'rith Association on Max von Pettenkofer.

1901 Spring
– F. leads a discussion in the B'nai B'rith on the topic "On the purposes and goals of the B'nai B'rith associations".
– The Germanist Friedrich von der Leyen sends F. his paper "Traum und Märchen", in which he refers to F.'s interpretation of dreams.

1901 March end
Twelve-year-old Max Pollak came to F. with his mother Eveline because Markus Hajek, by whom he was to be operated on for adenoids in his nose, had recommended a visit to a neurologist before the operation, as Pollak suffered from insomnia. Pollak's mother was in-law to F.'s wife Martha; their son Max later became a philosopher and journalist and married Dora Kellner, later wife of Walter Benjamin, in 1912.

1901 April
F. visits his sister-in-law Minna several times, who is at Albert Konried's sanatorium in Edlach (Reichenau) for a spay stay.

1901 May beginning
F. corrects the first pages of the *psychopathology of everyday life*.

1901 May 4
Death of Robert Franceschini. F. had known him since his grammar school days, and he was one of his closest friends until about 1886.

1901 before May 8
F. acquires the fragment of a Roman fresco with centaur and faun.

1901 May mid
F. is with Martha and sister-in-law Minna in Edlach near Reichenau.

1901 May 24–27
Short trip with brother Alexander to Vorarlberg
F. is looking for summer accommodation in Vorarlberg with his brother Alexander.

1901 May 25

F. and Alexander leave Vienna. Via Innsbruck and Bludenz, they drive to Gargellen in the Montafon. They spend the night in the Hotel Madrisa.

1901 May 26

F. and Alexander drive via Bludenz to Bregenz. From there, they take a trip on Lake Constance.

1901 May 27

F. and Alexander arrive back in Vienna.

1901 June

F. follows the press reports on the excavations at Knossos led by Arthur Evans.

1901 June 8

Minna returns from a spay stay in Reichenau.

1901 June 9

– Minna goes to Reichenhall, where her mother is taking the for a spa stay.
– F. spends the evening with Oskar and Melanie Rie and Maggie Haller.

1901 June 10

The parents of F.'s patient Maggie Haller arrive in Vienna.

1901 June 12

Martin Haller, the father of his patient Maggie, gives F. Houston Stewart Chamberlain's *The Foundations of the Nineteenth Century* with the dedication "Herr Dr. Sigm. Freud In Friendly Remembrance of the Evening of 12 June 1901".

1901 June 29–30

F. visits Minna and his mother-in-law Emmeline Bernays in Reichenhall; from there, he takes a carriage trip to Thumsee. On the return journey to Vienna, F. shares a sleeping car compartment with Josef Breuer's son Robert.

1901 July beginning

Friedrich von der Leyen draws F.'s attention to Ludwig Laistner's book *Das Rätsel der Sphinx (The Riddle of the Sphinx); for the* time being, however, F. only reads the preface.

1901 July 1

Alfred Russo, a pioneer of rabbit breeding in Austria, starts an analysis at F. He is the husband of Annica Benvenisti's daughter Sofie.

1901 July 4

F. reads a report on the excavation of Knossos by Arthur Evans.

1901 July mid

– F. visits Leopold Königstein in Kaltenleutgeben near Vienna.
– F.'s paper "Zur Psychopathologie des Alltagslebens" appears in the *Monatsschrift für Psychiatrie und Neurologie*. F. gives Ernst Mach a special edition with the dedication "Herrn Hofrath E. Mach in Verehrung d. Verf.".

1901 July mid –August 30
Summer holiday with family in Thumsee

F. catches a big pike during this holiday, which is admired by everyone.

1901 August 2

F. goes on a hike to the Untersberg near Salzburg.

1901 August 5

F. plans to write a book about bisexuality as a confrontation with Wilhelm Fliess.

1901 August 7

F. confesses to Wilhelm Fliess that the two have grown apart. At the same time, he tells Fliess that he is planning a work on "Human Bisexuality", but acknowledges that the idea is Fliess's.

1901 August 8

F. and Martha attend a Don Juan performance as part of the Salzburg Music Festival, for which Marie Ferstel has arranged tickets for them.

1901 August end

Martin and Oliver are insulted by other holidaymakers such as Israelites and fish thieves. That same afternoon, Martin and Oliver – this time accompanied by their father – met the people again and F., wielding his walking stick, beat them into flight.

1901 August 30 until September 15
Trip to Rome with brother Alexander

1901 August 30

Journey from Thumsee to Merano. F. associates the Passer, which flows through Merano, with the leader of the Tyrolean uprising of 1809 Andreas Hofer. He came from the Passeier Valley.

1901 September 1

Drive from Merano via Vilpiano and Bolzano to Trento (Hotel Trento). Visit to the Castello del Buon Consiglio and the Museo del Risorgimento.

1901 September 2

Travel from Trento via Florence to Rome (Hotel Milano). Arrival at 2 pm.

1901 September 3

Visit St. Peter's Basilica, the Pantheon and the Vatican Museums with the Sistine Chapel and Raphael's Stanzas.

1901 September 4

City tour to Monte Pincio and the Nervaforum. F. could have worshipped the nearby Minerva temple "in its humiliation and mutilation" (F. to Fliess, 19.9.1901). Then, F. puts his hand in the Bocca della verità with the vow to come back to Rome.

1901 September 5

In the morning, visit to the Museo Nazionale, and in the afternoon, drive to the Via Appia.

1901 September 6

Visit to the Pantheon and the Church of S. Pietro in Vincoli with Michelangelo's statue of Moses.

1901 September 7

– Visit to the Palatine.
– F. goes to the hairdresser and buys a tie.

1901 September 8

Excursion to Tivoli; F. compares the little town with Baden near Vienna. Visit to the water-falls and the temples of Sibyl and Tiberius.

1901 September 10

Another visit to the Vatican Museums. F. writes to Martha: "Today I saw again the most won-derful things in the Vatican, from which I leave as if intoxicated" (F. to Martha, 10.9.1901).

1901 September 11

Ride into the Albanian mountains. F. and Alexander ride on donkeys.

1901 September 12

Visit to the National Museum and afternoon walk.

1901 September 14

Departure from Rome at 22.10. The last days, the brothers suffer from the Scirocco.

1901 September 16

Arrival in Vienna early at 7.50 am.

1901 after September 16

In connection with his fear of dying prematurely, F. notes the dates of death of persons who had recently died: Hermann Widerhofer (28.7.), Dezsö (Desider) Szilágyi (31.7.), Victoria Adelaide Mary Louisa, the Empress Friedrich (5.8.), Francesco Crispi (11.8.), Josef Kaizl (19.8.), Philipp Bondy (3.9.), Johannes Franz von Miquel (9.9.) and William McKinley (14.9.).

1901 September 19

F. asks himself for whom he is still writing after the loss of his "only audience", i.e. Wilhelm Fliess (F. to Fliess, 19.9.1901).

1901 Autumn

The Viennese philosopher and psychologist Otto Weininger visits F. to ask him for a suitable publisher for his book *Geschlecht und Charakter.* F. is the second person after Ernst Mach to read the manuscript – presumably an early version under the title "Eros und Psyche"; "There were no depreciatory words about Jews and much less criticism of women. He had also to a large extent given consideration to my views on hysteria" (F. to David Abrahamsen, 11.6.1939).

1901 October

F. offers lectures on "The Great Neuroses" in the winter semester (lecture hall of Richard von Krafft-Ebing, fee ten Kronen).

1901 October 28

F. acquires Auguste Forel's book *Die psychischen Fähigkeiten der Ameisen und einiger* anderen *Insekten.*

1901 November mid

F. visits Sigmund Exner to find out about the reasons for the delay in his appointment as an associate professor. Exner suggests that the Ministry of Education is plotting against him and advises him to seek "counter-influence".

1901 November 24

F. visits his former patient Elise Gomperz, and asks her to lobby for his appointment as an as-sociate professor with the Minister of Education Wilhelm von Hartel.

1901 November 25

F. writes three letters in connection with his possible appointment as an associate professor: to Hermann Nothnagel, Richard von Krafft-Ebing and Sigmund Exner.

1901 December

F. gives a lecture to B'nai B'rith "On the Aims and Purposes of the Order of B'nai B'rith".

1901 December beginning

Sigmund Exner speaks with Minister of Education Wilhelm von Hartel about F.'s appointment as an associate professor. The Minister also mentions that Elise Gomperz had stood up for F.

1901 December 5

Hermann Nothnagel and Richard von Krafft-Ebing renew their application for F.'s appointment as an associate professor.

1901 Christmas

Hermann Swoboda visits F. and tells him about his interest in periodicity, and F. then draws his attention to Wilhelm Fliess.

1902

- F. is at the B'nai B'rith for a lecture on Hermann Sudermann's drama by Max Grunwald, rabbi from Hamburg and acquaintance of F.'s mother-in-law Emmeline Bernays. At the subsequent dinner, F. provokes Grunwald with critical remarks about religion.
- F. acquires issue 6 of The Annual of the British School of Athens.

Books received:

- Paul Hartenberg, a French psychiatrist, gives F. his writing *La névrose d'angoisse* "Au Dr Prof. Sig. Freud hommage de l'auteur".
- Wilhelm Fliess gives F. his book *Über den ursächlichen Zusammenhang von Nase und Geschlechtsorganen* with the dedication "Seinem lieben Sigmund!"

1902 January 14
F. gives the introductory lecture to B'nai B'rith for the discussion "On the position of women to our union".

1902 January mid
Helene Schiff sends F. an article by the German pathologist Otto Lubarsch entitled "Schlaf und Traum" (Sleep and Dream), which had appeared in two parts in the Berlin magazin *Die Woche in* December and January and essentially deals with F.'s booklet *Über den Traum*. A little later, Wilhelm Fliess also sent him this review.

1902 before February 22
The Minister of Education, Wilhelm Hartel, does not seem to want to promote F.'s appointment as an associate professor. So F.'s patient Marie Ferstel becomes active on her own initiative and donates the painting "Kirche in Auscha" by Emil Orlik to the Modern Gallery supported by Hartel.

1902 February 22
- The Minister of Education, Wilhelm von Hartel, proposes to the Emperor that F. be appointed Professor Extraordinarius. He then informs Marie Ferstel that the act of appointment of F. as Professor Extraordinarius is with the Emperor.
- F. acquires Leonard King's book Assyrian language. Easy lessons in the cuneiform inscriptions.

1902 March
F. offers lectures on "Progress in the Teaching of Neuroses" in the summer semester (lecture hall of the Psychiatric Clinic, fee ten Kronen).

1902 March 4
F. gives the closing speech to B'nai B'rith on the discussion "On the position of women to our union".

1902 March 5
Emperor Franz Joseph appoints F. as an associate professor. F. writes to Wilhelm Fliess: "The participation of the population is great. It rains … congratulations and donations of flowers, as

if the role of sexuality had suddenly been officially recognised by Sr. Majesty, the importance of dreams had been confirmed by the Council of Ministers and the necessity of a psychoanalytical therapy of hysteria had been pushed through with a 2/3 majority in Parliament" (F. to Fliess, 11.3.1902).

1902 March shortly after 5
F. has revenge fantasies against the parents of a patient.

1902 March 13
The Minister for Cultus and Education signs F.'s certificate of appointment as an associate professor.

1902 April 1
Ida Bauer visits F. and tells him that she has no intentions of marrying. However, she changes her attitude and enters into the marriage a good year and a half later.

1902 April 30
F. gives a lecture on "Dream Interpretation" to the B'nai B'rith Association "Moravia" in Brno.

1902 before June
F. meets Ludwig Horch, who looks just like him. Horch is Melanie Figdor's brother-in-law and a board member of the Viennese Commercial Association.

1902 June 29–mid August
Summer stay with family in Schönau am Königssee
F. is with his family and brother Alexander in Schönau am Königssee in the Berchtes-gadener Land, where they are spending their summer holiday in the Villa Sonnenfels. It belongs to a baker whose shop was on the ground floor. F. undertakes an exploratory tour from Königssee to Mondsee as a possible summer stay in one of the next years. However, he was very disappointed by Mondsee and ruled it out as a summer stay, mainly because of the many cyclists.

1902 June 29
Journey from Vienna to Schönau. In Ramsau, F. notes down two aphorisms that refer to death: "Der Eine werbt, Der Andere erbt, Der Dritte sterbt" and "Si vis vitam para mortem" (If you want life, prepare for death).

1902 August mid
The student and later journalist and writer Richard Bermann meets F. on the street and receives a Havana from him.

1902 August mid
Journey back to Vienna. His niece Cäcilie welcomes him with Marguerites and his nephew Hermann with Mohn – both children of his sister Rosa.

1902 August 26–September 19
Journey with brother Alexander to Rome, Naples and Sorrento

1902 August 26
F. leaves Vienna. His sister Rosa accompanies him with her children up to Perron. He trav-els via Freilassing to Rosenheim. From Freilassing, he travels by passenger train, a "pure

massage of the soul" (F. to Minna, 26.8.1902). In the evening, he arrives in Rosenheim and continues by sleeping car to Bolzano.

1902 August 27

F. arrives in Bolzano in the morning. His brother, with whom he has an appointment there, is a little late. F. completes his travel equipment.

1902 August 28

– In the morning, departure to Venice.
– The brothers spend the afternoon in the lagoon city. They sit in a café on St Mark's Square and marvel at the ruins of the Campanile, which collapsed on 1902 July 14. F. writes to Minna: "The church [San Marco] is more beautiful than ever, like a young widow after the death of the Lord Consort" (F. to Minna, 28.8.1902).
– Then, a swim on the Lido followed by an evening gondola ride.
– At 11.00 pm, continue by night train to Bologna.

1902 August 29

– Around 2.00 am, the brothers have a "night meal" at the station restaurant in Bologna.
– At 5.00 am, continue with the express train from Munich to Orvieto.
– At 11.00 am, arrival in Orvieto. F. buys Etruscan and Roman pieces for his collection from the antique dealer Riccardo Mancini.
– At 9.00 pm, continue to Rome.

1902 August 30

Early morning, arrival in Rome. Lunch at the Rosetta Restaurant near the Pantheon; overnight at Hotel Milano.

1902 August 31

– Departure from Rome in the morning.
– Arrival in Naples in the afternoon. There, "First disappointment. Vesuvius does not smoke". Late lunch in the restaurant "Giardini di Torino": There is "noodle soup, fish, roast veal with sweet sauce, green beans as salad, a choice of three cheeses and fruit, with grapes […] The whole thing with white Ischia wine" (F. to Martha, 31.8.1902).

1902 September 1

In Naples, it is extremely hot, around 35 degrees Celsius: "[…] all capacity for enjoyment ceases. […] I lack the energy to turn the pages of the Baedeker" (F. to Martha, 1.9.1902). Nevertheless, the brothers visit the aquarium, walk along the waterfront and look at the monument Konradin von Hohenstaufen, the grandson Friedrichs II. in the church Santa Maria del Carmine. Also, F. goes to the barber, "an artist who took his time" (F. to Martha, 1.9.1902).

1902 September 2

– Drive from Naples to Sorrento. Overnight stay at Hotel Cocumella.
– In the evening, the brothers attend an open-air operetta performance.

1902 September 3

Because of the heat, the brothers forego excursions and content themselves with swimming in the sea and "dolce far niente ["sweet idleness"] (F. to Martha, 3.9.1902).

1902 September 4

– Excursion to Naples and visit Museo Nazionale, one of the most important collections of antiquities with wall paintings from Pompeii, Herculaneum and Stabiae.
– F. notes that Vesuvius is smoking in the meantime.

1902 September 5

Visit to Pompeii.

1902 September 6

F. and Alexander spend the day swimming and catching sea animals.

1902 September 7

Trip to Capri; the brothers enjoy the "magnificent cliffs" and the Blue Grotto. Lunch in the restaurant "Zum Kater Hiddigeigei" in which "[Joseph Viktor] Scheffel's pictures hang everywhere" (F. to Martha, 7.9.1902).

1902 September 8

Rest day in Sorrento. Theater in the evening.

1902 September 9

Departure for a two-day car excursion. On the first day, we travel via Amalfi to Salerno.

1902 September 10

Drive from Salerno to Paestum. The large Doric temples there are the highlight of the trip.

1902 September 11

Return journey to Sorrento.

1902 September 12

Drive from Sorrento to Naples.

1902 September 13

Visit the cave of the Sibyl in Cuma. The cave is described by Virgil in the *Aeneid*, and F. has a special relationship to this work: he borrowed the motto of *dream interpretation* from it.

1902 September 14

F. and Alexander climb Mount Vesuvius.

1902 September 15

Departure from Naples. F. considers whether to make another stop in Venice. Whether this was actually realized is unclear.

1902 September 17

Arrival in Bolzano.

1902 September 18

Departure from Bolzano.

1902 September 19

Arrival in Vienna.

1902 September 25

F. acquires Emil Laurent's and Paul Nagour's book *Occultism and Love: Studies in the history of sexual aberrations*.

1902 September 28
F. sends Theodor Herzl the *Interpretation of Dreams* via the Deuticke bookshop in the hope that Herzl will review it for the *Neue Freie Presse,* of which Herzl was the editor at the time. He also sends him a lecture on the same subject, possibly the one he gave on April 30 at the B'nai B'rith in Brno, "On Dreams".

1902 October
F. offers lectures on "Neuroses and Nervousness" twice a week in the winter semester (lecture hall of the Psychiatric Clinic, fee ten Kronen).

1902 October 1
Theodor Herzl thanks F. for sending him The *Interpretation of Dreams,* but gives him little hope of a review of the book.

1902 October 8
F. forgets the name of the spa Nervi near Genoa, although he remembers the name of the German spa doctor Gustav Ortenau whom he knew from Bad Reichenhall.

1902 October 13
F. is received by the Emperor after his promotion to Professor Extraordinarius in a general audience. As Freud is a reserve officer but has no uniform, he borrows Leopold Königstein's colorful uniform with helmet and feathers.

1902 October mid
Emma Eckstein asks F. to get her some specialist publications, presumably for the preparatory work for her book *Die Sexualfrage in der Erziehung des Kindes.* However, F. is only able to find one book and sends it to her on October 17. The bibliographical information for the other publications was wrong.

1902 October end
Wilhelm Stekel proposes the foundation of a psychological society. F. then invites some colleagues and acquaintances to meet once a week in the evening in his flat "to discuss the topics of psychology and neuropathology that interest us" (F. to Adler, 2.11.1902). Among those invited are Hermann Bahr, Max Graf, Max Kahane, Rudolf Reitler and Wilhelm Stekel as the founder. All agree, but Hermann Bahr is the only one who does not come to the meetings. F. calls these colleagues "Mittwochsherren" ("Wednesday gentlemen") because the meetings were usually held on Wednesdays.[26]

1902 November 2
F. invites Alfred Adler to the meetings of the Mittwoch-Gesellschaft (Wednesday Society).

1902 November 6
The first meeting of the Mittwoch-Gesellschaft is on a Thursday. The topic is "Smoking".

1902 December
F. gives a lecture on "Emile Zola" to B'nai B'rith.

1902 December 22
Death of Richard von Krafft-Ebing. F. had been lecturing in his lecture hall,, and Krafft-Ebing, together with Hermann Nothnagel, had proposed him for appointment as an associate professor.

1903

At the invitation of Wilhelm Stekel, Otto Pötzl attends the evenings of the Wednesday Society five or six times. At one of the meetings, F. speaks about Karl Immerman's *Tulifäntchen*.
Books received:

- Havelock Ellis gives F. the first section of the third volume of his *Studies in the psychology of sex* with the dedication "Dr. Freud, with the author's kind regards".
- F. acquires the third edition of the anthology *Sexualleben und Nervenleiden* edited by Leopold Löwenfeld.

Treatments:

- Ada Hirst, niece of Emma Eckstein, begins an analysis with F.
- Albert Hirst, the younger brother of Ada Hirst, begins a short analysis at F. A longer one follows from the autumn of1909 to the spring of 1910 spring.

1903 January
Shalom Dov-Ber Schneersohn, Rabbi from Lubavitch, comes to Vienna and visits F. several times over the next three months for health advice. He is accompanied by his son Josef Yitzchak Schneersohn.

1903 April
F. offers lectures in the summer semester "On Progress in the Teaching of Neuroses" (location: lecture hall of the Psychiatric Clinic, fee ten Kronen).

1903 April 8
Max Kahane speaks at the Mittwoch-Gesellschaft on the topic of "Mystery".

1903 April end
F. and Wilhelm Fliess meet. Fliess is in Vienna with his wife Ida on the occasion of the funeral of her mother Pauline Bondy. On this occasion, F. shows him the manuscript of *Der Witz und seine Beziehung zum Unbewussten*, which he has just begun.

1903 May
Anna von Vest, from a family of doctors and pharmacists in Klagenfurt, begins an analysis with F. It lasts with interruptions until 1926.

1903 May 8
F. complains about the irregular and insufficient cleaning of lecture theater 41.

1903 June beginning
Otto Weininger's book *Geschlecht und Charakter is* published. In it are remarks on the theory of bisexuality by Fliess, which had reached him via F. and Hermann Swoboda.

1903 July mid
F. visits the philosopher and Gestalt psychologist Christian von Ehrenfels at his family estate Schloss in the Waldviertel.

1903 July end–September 2
Summer stay with family in Schönau am Königssee
The family spends the summer holiday at Villa Sonnenfels again, as in the previous year.

1903 August 7
F. takes a trip to Aschau, south of Lake Chiemsee.

1903 August 8
F. takes a trip from Schönau to Traunstein and Aschau in Chiemgau.

1903 August 29
Hermann Swoboda asks F. for help in finding a publisher for his book *Die Perioden des menschlichen Organismus.* F. recommended him to his own publisher Deuticke.

1903 August end
F. goes to Reichenhall to go shopping. The list includes tobacco and an irrigator for his children. Apparently, he wanted to demonstrate to them how liquid can flow into a body cavity with a controlled pressure and a controllable flow rate by exploiting gravity.

1903 September 2
Departure from Königssee.

1903 September 2–20
Trip with Minna to Munich, Nuremberg and Merano

1903 September 2
Trip to Munich.

1903 September 3
F. has severe anxiety, heart pain and stomach problems.

1903 September 8
F. buys on Maximiliansplatz Russian lacquerware and terracottas, probably in the shop of the court supplier. Lehmann Bernheimer.

1903 September 8 or 9
Drive from Munich to Nuremberg.

1903 September 11
– Drive from Nuremberg to Kufstein.
– F. notes a house inscription in Kufstein, presumably on a bakery:

"Früh, eh der Tag noch graut
Morgens wenn die Erde thaut
Müssen Bäcker wachen
Brod u*nd* Semmel machen
Dies wär eine schöne Kunst
Hätten sie das Mehl
umsunst"[27]

1903 September 12
Departure from Kufstein to Bolzano at 11.00 am, arrival in Bolzano at around 15.00 pm

1903 September 13

F. reads a note in the *Neues Wiener Tagblatt* about "masterless jackpots" of the Budapest basilica cathedral lots. Since he had obviously acquired cathedral lots, he noted the numbers of the "masterless jackpots".

1903 September 14

Excursion from Bolzano to Merano.

1903 September 16

Transfer from Bolzano to Merano; overnight stay at the Savoy Hotel.

1903 September 19

Departure from Merano.

1903 September 20

Arrival in Vienna.

1903 October

F. offers lectures on "Introduction to Psychotherapy" twice a week in the winter semester (location: lecture hall of the Psychiatric Clinic, fee ten Kronen).

1903 October 23

On the day of his father's death, F. noted the location of the grave in the central cemetery: Group 50, number 53. Possibly he intended to visit the grave again after a long time.

1903 November beginning

F. acquires David Müller's book *Die Gesetze Hammurabis und ihr Verhältnis zur mosaischen Gesetzgebung sowie zu den XII Tafeln (The Laws of Hammurabi and their Relationship to Mosaic Legislation and to the XII Tablets)*, which has just been published. F. makes notes on the text.

1903 November mid

F. visits the exhibition of 80 works by Gustav Klimt at the Secession with Martha and daughter Mathilde.

1903 Christmas

– F. receives a silver box with the inscription "Christmas 1903" from his patient Anna von Vest.
– F. gives daughter Mathilde an Egyptian Isis from his collection.

1904

– Alfred Adler becomes family doctor to F.'s brother Alexander.

Books received:

– Adolf Friedemann gives F. his *Reisebilder aus Palästina* (*Travel pictures from Palestine*) with the dedication "Herrn Professor Dr. Freud verehrungsvoll Der Verfasser".
– F. receives from Theodor Heller his book *Studien zur Blindenpsychologie (Studies on the Psychology of the Blind)* with the dedication "Herrn Professor Dr Freud/verehrungsvoll überreicht/vom Verf.".

1904 February beginning
F. has influenza.

1904 February 3
F. presents the Mittwoch-Gesellschaft with a "letter of refusal" from Wilhelm Stekel. The members present instruct F. to ask Stekel to "appear in our midst next Wednesday [...], 'as if nothing had happened'" (F. to Stekel, 4.2.1904).

1904 before March 26
F. gives Friedrich Jodl a copy of *Zur Psychopathologie des Alltagslebens.*

1904 Spring
F. gives a lecture on "Hammurabi" to B'nai B'rith. F. was inspired by Friedrich Delitzsch's *Bible und Babel* and presumably also David Müller's *Die Gesetze Hammurabis und ihr Verhältnis zur mosaischen Gesetzgebung.* However, F. had forgotten the illustration of Hammurabi's tablets of law, and Max Grunwald interprets this blunder as an expression of F.'s bad conscience that he had rated Hammurabi higher than Moses.

1904 April
F. offers lectures in the summer semester "Über Fortschritte in der Lehre von den Neurosen" ("On Progress in the Theory of Neuroses") (location: lecture hall of the Psychiatric Clinic, fee ten Kronen).

1904 April beginning
F.'s book *Zur Psychopathologie des Alltagslebens* is published. The text had already appeared in 1901 in the *Monatsschrift für Psychiatrie und Neurologie.* F. donates a copy to the library of German students in Prague with the dedication: "Der wackeren deutsche Lesehalle in Prag/d. Verf.".

1904 April 10
A review of *Zur Psychopathologie des Alltagslebens* by Fritz Stüber-Gunther (actually Friedrich Stüber) appears in the *Neue Freie Presse* under the headline "Der Kobold in der Hirnkasten" ("The Leprechaun in the brain's box").

1904 April mid
F. has Emma Eckstein operated on by Josef Halban because of a fibroid. Emma subsequently falls in love with Halban and begins to drift away from F.

1904 April 16
F. gives a lecture to B'nai B'rith on Paul Möbius's book *Über den physiologischen Schwachsinn des Weibes*. Wilhelm Knöpfmacher has the impression that F. criticizes in his lecture less the fact of physiological imbecility than Möbius's reasoning.

1904 before April 17
F. receives a book from Emma Eckstein by Pyotr Kropotkin, possibly the *Memoirs of a Revolutionary*.

1904 April 17
F. offers Emma Eckstein to write a review for the *Neue Freie Presse of* her book *Die Sexualfrage in der Erziehung des Kindes, which is* currently in print. However, at the beginning of February 1905, the Neue Freie *Presse refused to* publish a review by F.

1904 April 19
F. attends a lecture by Christian von Ehrenfels before the plenary meeting of the "Gesellschaft österreichischer Volkswirte" (Society of Austrian Economists") on the topic "Über den Einfluss des Darwinismus auf die Soziologie" ("On the influence of Darwinism on Sociology").

1904 April 26
- F. writes Wilhelm Fliess that "some capable young doctors who [...] belong to my circle of students [...] are thinking of trying to publish a scientific journal soon". He asks Fliess "not to deny them your name and your contributions" (F. to Fliess, 26.4.1904).
- F. admits to Fliess that he is the "intellectual originator" of Hermann Swoboda's recently published book *Die Perioden des menschlichen Organismus* (F. to Fliess, 26.4.1904).

1904 May 18
F. admits the lawyer Felix Weiser, whom he has known since he was 13 years old, to a closed institution after a suicide attempt.

1904 May 15
F. intends to write a paper on the "sexual character of ancient architecture". However, he does not elaborate on this intention.

1904 May 24
F. receives from Emma Eckstein her book *Die Sexualfrage in der Erziehung des Kindes (The Sexual Question in Child Education)* with the dedication "Prof. Freud, meinem verehrten Lehrer, in inniger Dankbarkeit. Die Verf.".

1904 July 7
Martha drives to Königssee, where the children are already with Minna.

1904 July 16–August 28
First part of the summer stay with family in Schönau am Königssee

F. travels to his family. As in the last two years, they spend the holiday in Königssee in the Villa Sonnenfels. Leopold Königstein is also in Schönau for a while and joins many of the undertakings.

1904 July 16

On the evening of the day of arrival, F. drinks the famous Riesling from the "Schloss Johannisberg" winery in Geisenheim in the Rheingau.

1904 July 20

Wilhelm Fliess informs F. that he has received knowledge of Otto Weininger's book *Geschlecht und Charakter (Sex and Character)* "in the first, biological part of which, to my astonishment, I find the implementation of my ideas on bisexuality [...] described. [...] I have no doubt that Weininger came to know my ideas through you and that he has abused someone else's property" (Fliess to F., 20.7.1904).

1904 July 27

F. asks Wilhelm Fliess "to proofread the remarks on bisexuality in my recently completed treatise on sexual theory and to change them to your satisfaction" (F. to Fliess, 27.7.1904). This is the last letter of the correspondence with Fliess.

1904 July end

– F. completes the Three Treatises on Sexual Theory.
– Max Kassowitz comes to visit Königssee with his five children on bicycles.

1904 August 25 approx.

F. creates an "angry list" with the following names (in this order): Gustav Gärtner, Emil Redlich, Sigmund Exner, Erwin Ferstel, Wilhelm Fliess.

1904 August 28–September 9
Trip to Greece with brother Alexander

1904 August 28

Drive from Königssee via Salzburg to Graz; dinner at the Hotel Elephant; at 23.30 onward, journey to Trieste.

1904 August 29

8.30 am, arrival in Trieste; visit to the Austrian Llyod; excursion to Opicina, then bathing at Barcola, in the evening at Miramare; overnight at Hotel Buon Pastore.

1904 August 30

At 11.30 am, departure from Trieste with the steamer "Urano" of the Levant and Mediterranean Service of Austrian Lloyd (Express line to Constantinople).

1904 August 31

F. sees Heinrich Schliemann's former colleague Wilhelm Dörpfeld, who had led the excavations of Troy, Mycenae and Olympia, on the ship. F. does not approach him, but after his return to Vienna, he buys Heinrich Schliemann's report on the excavations.

1904 September 1

Around 1.30 am arrival in Brindisi; departure with 3½ hours delay approx. 3.30 am; around 1.00 pm arrival in Santi Quaranta (now Sarande in Albania); around 2.00 pm departure from Santi Quaranta; around 4.00 pm arrival in Corfu; visit to the old Venetian fortress (approx. two hours); around 7.00 pm onward journey to Patras.

1904 September 2

In the morning around 7.00 am arrival in Patras; around 7.00 pm onward journey to Athens (around Peloponnese).

1904 September 3

Arrival in Athens at 12.45 pm with a delay of three hours. Overnight stay in the Hotel Athena (first floor). F. has the first unforgettable impression of the Temple of Theseus (also called Hephaisteion) near the Agora.

1904 September 4

F. and Alexander spend the whole day at the Acropolis; F. has put on his nicest shirt for the visit. They buy what are supposed to be cheap old oil lamps from a dealer. During a rainstorm, they find a hole where the dealer had buried the lamps until they were dirty and looked old. Alexander is terribly annoyed by the swindler, but F. was amused by this idea of the trader.

1904 September 5

Visit to the National Museum. F. records the date of the museum visit in his Baedeker.

1904 September 6

In the morning small purchases; 12.00 pm train journey from Athens via Corinth (they pass the Corinth Canal at 3.30 pm) to Patras; arrival there at 7.10 pm and at 10.00 pm onward journey by steamer to Trieste.

1904 September 9

Arrival in Trieste in the afternoon and onward journey via Görz (Gorizia) back to the family's summer residence in Schönau.

September 10–18
Second part of Summer stay with family in Schönau am Königssee

1904 September 10

Arrival in Schönau.

1904 September 13

F. acquires Heinrich Schliemann's Mycenae. Report on my research and discoveries in Mycenae and Tiryns.

1904 September 17

Departure to Vienna.

1904 September 18

F. arrives back in Vienna together with the family after the end of the summer stay in Schönau.

1904 Autumn

F. learns from the Swiss psychiatrist Eugen Bleuler that he and his colleagues have been engaged in psychoanalysis for some years.

1904 October

– F. offers lectures on "Einführung in die Psychotherapie" ("Introduction to Psychotherapy") twice a week in the winter semester (location: lecture hall of the Psychiatric Clinic, fee ten Kronen).
– F. grants the journalist Rudolf Spitzer a short interview. It appears in the *Neue Freie Presse* on November 6 under the title "Magnetische Menschen" ("Magnetic People").

1904 October 2

F. congratulates Karl Kraus on his essay "Der Fall Hervay" ("The Hervay Case"), which had appeared in the *Fackel* on 1904 July 8. There, Kraus had vehemently castigated "sexual hypocrisy". The occasion was a trial in which Leontine Hervay, the wife of the Styrian district governor Franz Hervay, was accused of bigamy.

1904 November 7

Death of F.'s religion teacher Samuel Hammerschlag.

1904 November 11

F. publishes an obituary of Samuel Hammerschlag in the *Neue Freie Presse*.

1904 November 30

F. receives from Willy Hellpach his book *Grundlinien einer Psychologie der Hysterie*.

1904 December 12

F. gives a lecture "Über Psychotherapie" ("On Psychotherapy") at the Wiener medizinische Doktorenkollegium.

1904 December 15

Emanuel Loewy visits F.

1905

- Max Graf gives F. his book *Die Musik im Zeitalter der Renaissance* with the dedication "Herrn Prof. Dr. Freud hochachtungsvoll Max Graf".
- Christian von Ehrenfels gives F. his choral dramas *Die Stürmer* with the dedication "Herrn Prof. S. Freud in Freund-/schaft vom Verf.".

Treatments:

- Franz Dubsky begins an analysis with F. He is a nephew of Marie Ebner-Eschenbach, who had dedicated her fairy tale book *Hirzepinzchen to* him.
- Alfred Robitsek, Austrian chemist, begins an analysis with F. (until 1912 May).

1905 January end
F. gives an expert opinion on marriage law in connection with the revision of the Civil Code.

- 1905 February beginning
- F. reads Willy Hellpach's book *Grundlinien einer Psychologie der Hysterie* and calls it "a very clever book" (F. to Hellpach, 5.2.1905).
- The *Neue Freie Presse* refuses to publish a review by F. of Emma Eckstein's book *Die Sexualfrage in der Erziehung des Kindes.*

1905 February 13
F. concludes a contract with the publisher Franz Deuticke for the publication of his book *Der Witz und seine Beziehung zum Unbewussten* in the volume of 16 printed sheets. The fee is 50 kroner per printed sheet. The print run is 1050 copies.

1905 February mid
F. is interested in the Liverpool Architectural Society's involvement with the history of Egypt. Presumably it concerns a lecture by James Fulton on the subject of "How to attain original thought in architecture", which also contained a section on Egypt with an account of a visit to the Valley of the Kings in Thebes.

1905 March end
F. receives from Édouard Claparède his paper "Esquisse d'une Théorie biologique du Sommeil". F. then subscribed to the *Archives de psychologie,* where the article had appeared.

1905 April
- F. offers discussions on "Fortschritte in der Lehre von den Neurosen" ("Progress in the Teaching of the Neuroses") in the summer semester (lecture hall of the Psychiatric Clinic).
- F.'s cousin Jascha Nathansohn from Odessa is visiting Vienna for about two weeks.

1905 April 18
After the *Neue Freie Presse* refused to publish a review of F.'s work on Emma Eckstein's work *Die Sexualfrage in der Erziehung des Kindes*, F. offered it to another journal – also without success.

1905 April 20–24
Trip with brother Alexander to South Tyrol

The reason for the trip was the search for summer quarters.

1905 April 20

Hike from Bolzano via Waidbruck to St. Barbian and Dreikirchen.

1905 April 21

Hike from Dreikirchen to Ortisei and San Cristina.

1905 April 23

F. and Alexander are in Kastelruth.

1905 April 24

Arrival in Vienna.

1905 May

F.'s daughter Mathilde has severe appendicitis and is operated on by Freud's friend Ignaz Rosanes. She almost dies of post-operative internal bleeding.

1905 May 6

F. is interested in a series of papers by Konrad Theodor Preuss on the "Ursprung der Religion und Kunst"("Origin of Religion and Art").

1905 May 20

F.'s book *Der Witz und seine Beziehung zum Unbewussten* is published (edition of 1050 copies). He gives one copy to Emanuel Loewy with the dedication: "Herrn Prof. E. Loewy in alter Freundschaft/Freud".

1905 May 22

F. receives the first copies of his recently published book *Der Witz und seine Beziehung zum Unbewussten.*

1905 May 24

The Wednesday Society discusses the ancient and modern Electra. F. had asked the participants to prepare for the discussion by reading or visiting the theater.

1905 May end

F. sends Eugen Bleuler his recently published books *Der Witz und seine Beziehung zum Unbewussten* and *Drei Abhandlungen zur Sexualtheorie.*

1905 before May 20

F. gives Friedrich Jodl a copy of *Der Witz und seine Beziehung zum Unbewussten.*

1905 June

On the occasion of the tenth anniversary of the publication of the *Studien über Hysterie, a* banquet is held in F.'s honor at which a cake was presented on which was written: "Studies über Hysterie, 2. Auflage".

1905 Summer

– F.'s *Drei Abhandlungen zur Sexualtheorie* appears (edition of 1000 copies). He gives one copy to Emanuel Loewy with the dedication: "Seinem lieben Freunde Prof. Em. Loewy/ d. Verf." and one to Rudolf Chrobak with the dedication "Herrn Hofrat Chrobak in Verehrung d. Verf.".
– Otto Rank sends F. a manuscript for review. This is the beginning of the correspondence with F.

1905 July 7
Death of Hermann Nothnagel. Together with Ernst Brücke, he had supported F.'s application for Privatdozent and later, together with Richard von Krafft-Ebing, proposed him for appointment as Professor Extraordinarius.

1905 July 12
F. proposes to Alfred Adler to publish a manuscript on number incidents of patients under the title "Zur Psycho-Analyse von Zahleneinfällen und obsedierenden Zahlen" (On the Psycho-Analysis of Number Incidents and Obseding Numbers) and to contact directly the editor of the *Psychiatrisch-Neurologische Wochenschrift* Johannes Bresler.

1905 July mid–September 3
Summer stay with family in Aussee
- During their stay, they meet Margarethe Fürth, her husband Hugo and their children at the Grundlsee. Margarethe is a friend of Minna and Martha and the sister of Sophie Paneth and Betty Hammerschlag. He also meets Wilhelm Knöpfmacher and his family.
- F. is "indifferent to all science" and divides his time "between looking for berries and sponges and playing tarot" (F. to Emma Eckstein, 25.8.1905).

1905 July 26
F. gives Alfred Adler a testimonial and certifies "that he may be counted among the most capable and independent of the younger doctors".

1905 August 1
The American doctor Morton Prince asks F. to write a paper for one of the first issues of the *Journal of Abnormal Psychology, which* he has just founded. F. agrees but does not send a manuscript.

1905 August 18
F. has himself photographed standing between Martha and Minna.

1905 September 3–21
Journey with Minna to Upper Italy and Switzerland

1905 September 3
Drive from Aussee to Innsbruck, overnight stay at Hotel Europa.

1905 September 4
Drive from Innsbruck via Bolzano – with a three-hour break at the Hotel Greif – and Rovereto to Verona.

1905 September 5
At 11.00 am, departure from Verona to Milan.

1905 September 6
Drive from Milan to Bellagio on Lake Como.

1905 September 7
Steamboat trip on Lago di Como from Como to Bellagio; overnight stay at Villa Serbelloni.

1905 September 8
Travel from Bellagio by ferry to Menaggio, then by steam tram to Porlezzo and from there by boat to Lugano. After a short stop, continue by boat to Porto Ceresio and then by train to Luino. From Luino, boat trip to Pallanza on Lago di Maggiore.

1905 September 9

Excursion from Pallanza to Isola Madre, the "jewel of lake travel" (F. to Alexander Freud, 17.9.1905) to Isola Bella and to Isola dei Pescatori.

1905 September 10

At 11.00 am, boat trip from Pallanza to Stresa, overnight at Hotel Alpino. Short excursion to Baveno.

1905 September 11

Excursion to Monte Mottarone.

1905 September 12

Train journey from Stresa to Milan and departure from Milan at 15.30. Arrival in Genoa at 18.36, overnight at the Hotel Continental.

1905 September 13

Excursion to Pegli, 15km west of Genoa.

1905 September 16

Drive to Rapallo, and overnight stay at the Grand Hotel Savoia. In Rapallo, F. is stung by sea urchins and burned by medusae.

1905 September 17

Drive to Portofino. Overnight stay at the Hotel Piccolo.

1905 September 19

Drive to Genoa.

1905 September 20

Departure from Genoa.

1905 September 22

Arrival in Vienna.

1905 September end

F. issues Alfred Adler a certificate that supplements that of July 26.

1905 Autumn

– F. gives a lecture to B'nai B'rith "Über die Psychologie des Unbewussten" ("On the Psychology of the Unconscious").
– The Swiss poet and translator of Gogol and Tolstoy, Bruno Goetz, visits F. for some consultations. At the end of the first session, he hands the poor student an envelope with 200 Kronen.[28]

1905 October

– The first part of F.'s medical history of Ida Bauer appears under the title "Bruchstück einer Hysterie-Analyse".
– F. offers lectures on "Einführung in die Psychotherapie" ("Introduction to Psychotherapy") twice a week in the winter semester (location: lecture hall of the Psychiatric Clinic, fee ten Kronen).

1905 October 24

F. acquires *Die Akropolis von Athen* from Hermann Luckenbach.

1905 October 26

F. is visited by journalists from Die *Zeit* and asked for a statement on the case of the convicted homosexual Prof. Theodor Beer. The statement appears the next day in *Die Zeit.*

1905 November

The second part of F.'s medical history of Ida Bauer appears under the title "Bruchstück einer Hysterie-Analyse". F. gives Emanuel Loewy a special print with the dedication: "Herrn Prof. E. Loewy mit herzl. Gruss/Fr.".

1905 November 30

- Meeting of the Wednesday Society: Eduard Hitschmann speaks "On Friendship".
- F. refuses to resume the treatment of Emma Eckstein, which had been interrupted for some time. F. had treated her free of charge and justifies the refusal among other things by saying that for financial reasons, he could only accept paying patients.

1905 December beginning

F. sends Morton Prince a special print of his medical history "Bruchstück einer Hysterie-Analyse".

1905 December 21

A review of *Drei Abhandlungen zur Sexualtheorie,* written by Otto Soyka, appears in *Fackel,* edited by Karl Kraus, which describes F.'s book as "the first comprehensive presentation of a pure physics of love".

1905 December 27

Morton Prince sends F. his book *The Dissociation of a Personality* with the dedication "Prof. Sigm. Freud with the compliments of the Author".

1906

F. meets Fritz Wittels. The latter had asked him to come to the Cottage Sanatorium for a consultation, and they both returned to the city together in a horse-drawn carriage.

1906 January 3
At the general assembly of B'nai B'rith, it is decided, at F.'s request, "that all matters of a formal, administrative and business nature [...] are to be thoroughly discussed in special meetings of the council of officials, to which all members have access, and [are] to be brought to the general assembly only for formal, final decision-making".

1906 January 12
In the *Berliner Börsen-Courier*, Richard Pfennig, a friend of Wilhelm Fliess, raises accusations of plagiarism against Otto Weininger and Wilhelm Swoboda and writes that the two received their knowledge of Fliess' theories from F.

1906 January 23
F. attends Friedrich Hebbel's tragedy *Gyges and his Ring* at the Burgtheater with daughter Mathilde.

1906 January 26
F. plans to write a second part of the *Psychopathology of Everyday Life*, but he does not realize the plan.

1906 March 10
Meeting of the Wednesday Society: Eduard Hitschmann speaks about "Sexual Enlightenment".

1906 Spring
The conductor Bruno Walter begins an analysis with F.

1906 March end
Hermann Swoboda brings an action for libel against Richard Pfennig and Wilhelm Fliess before a Berlin court and writes a rebuttal under the title *Die gemeinnützige Forschung und der eigennützige Forscher. Antwort auf die von Wilhelm Fliesz gegen Otto Weininger und mich erhobenen Beschuldigungen.*

1906 April
F. offers lectures on "Einführung in die Psychotherapie" ("Introduction to Psychotherapy") in the summer semester (location: lecture hall of the Psychiatric Clinic, fee ten Kronen).

1906 April 6
Meeting of the Wednesday Society: Eduard Hitschmann speaks on the "Critique of Psychoanalysis".

1906 April 11
Beginning of the correspondence between F. and Carl Gustav Jung.

1906 May 6
On his 50th birthday, on the initiative of Paul Federn, F. receives from his students a medal with his portrait made by Karl Maria Schwerdtner. The reverse bears a verse from the final chorus of King Oedipus by Sophocles "Who solved the famous riddle and was a mighty man".

1906 May 12

F. receives Hermann Swoboda's paper Die gemeinnützige Forschung und der eigennützige Forscher. Antwort auf die von Wilhelm Fliesz gegen Otto Weininger und mich erhobenen Beschuldigungen.

1906 June

At the invitation of the lawyer Alexander Löffler, F. gives a lecture on "Tatbestandsdiagnostik und Psychoanalyse" ("Diagnosis of the Crime and Psychoanalysis") at the criminal law seminar of the University of Vienna. He learns there that Löffler uses Jung's association method.

1906 June 2

F. sends Alfred Adler a 12-year-old boy from Kiev, as his "ignorance of Russian […] causes him difficulties" in his examinations (F. to Adler, 2.6.1910).

1906 June 12

F. acquires Magnus Hirschfeld's book *Vom Wesen der Liebe,* and at the same time a contribution to solving the question of bisexuality.

1906 July 15–September 11
Summer stay with family in Lavarone and Riva

F. and his family stay in Lavarone at the Hotel du Lac. Martin's classmate and friend Hans Lampl is also in Lavarone. For F., the place is "a kind of paradise" (F. to Emma Eckstein, 4.8.1906).

1906 July 19

F. receives Wilhelm Fliess' pamphlet *In eigener Sache.* In it, he defends his claim to priority in relation to the theory of bisexuality against Otto Weininger and Hermann Swoboda.

1906 August 2

Hermann Swoboda asks F. to testify on his behalf in court in the plagiarism affair with Wilhelm Fliess. F. rejected Swoboda's request. Swoboda's libel suit was decided negatively in October 1906.

1906 August 14

F. went on an excursion to Molveno with his son Martin to find out whether it might be a good destination for the whole family. At 16.00, they set off on foot for Caldonazzo. After a tour of the town and a good coffee, they took the train to Trento. There, they visit the cathedral and the Dante monument; overnight stay in Trento.

1906 August 15–16

F. and Martin hike through the Val di Vela to Cadine (coffee break); then past Lago di Terlago to the foot of Monte Gazza. During the ascent, F. suffers a fainting spell – probably because of the heat; they return to Terlago and take a car via Trento, Mezzolombardo, Fai and Andalo to Molveno; father and son stay there for an ample day.

1906 August 24

F. begins writing his book Der Wahn und die Träume in W. Jensens "Gradiva".

1906 August 31

"Moving" with two large carriages from Lavarone – with a lunch break in Rovereto – to Riva, where F. and his family continue their holiday. They stay at the Hotel du Lac.

1906 September beginning
- F.'s brother Alexander and Leopold Königstein come to Riva.
- F. goes on a boat trip to Sirmione with Martin, Ernst and brother Alexander.

1906 September 11–ca. September 23
Trip to Viareggio with brother Alexander

1906 September 11
F. and his brother Alexander go to Viareggio and spend a week there catching crabs, among other things. They stay at the Hotel Bristol and meet the lawyer Horaz Krasnopolski and the painter Otto Brünauer.

1906 September 16
Karl Kraus asks F. to comment on the Fliess affair in the *Fackel*.

1906 September 19–20
F. and his brother Alexander are in Bologna.

1906 ca. September 22
On his way back to Vienna, F. travels via Spittal an der Drau; presumably he visits Michael Fasan's "Privatheilanstalt für Morphinisten und Nervenkranke" (Private Sanatorium for morphinists and mentally ill patients) in the Liesertal on the northern outskirts of the city.

1906 ca. September 23
Arrival in Vienna.

1906 September 24
- F. acquires Arthur Kronfeld's book Sexuality and Aesthetic Sensibility in their Genetic Interrelationship.
- F. acquires Heinrich Pudor's book Bisexualität. Investigations into the general dual sexuality of man. Against Wilhelm Fliess.

1906 September 25
F. asks Karl Kraus for a meeting in connection with the Fliess affair, since Hermann Swoboda had also contacted Kraus, and the latter wants to print a statement by F. in the next issue of the *Fackel*.

1906 October
- F. offers lectures on "Einführung in die Psychotherapie" ("Introduction to Psychotherapy") in the winter semester (location: lecture hall of the Psychiatric Clinic, fee ten Kronen).
- Havellock Ellis gives F. the fifth volume of his *Studies in the Psychology of sex* with the dedication "To Professor S. Freud with the compliments and best thanks of the Author. Oct. 1906".
- Valentin Rosenfeld seeks out F. to obtain permission to attend his lectures.

1906 October beginning
The first volume of the *Sammlung kleiner Schriften zur Neurosenlehre (Collection of small writings on neuroses)* is published (854 copies). One of the first to receive a copy from F. is Carl Gustav Jung. Heinrich Obersteiner also receives one with the dedication "Herrn Hofrat Obersteiner d. Verf.".

1906 October 3
– F. and Karl Kraus meet at the Café Landtmann.
– Meeting of the Mittwoch-Gesellschaft: formal matters are discussed.

1906 before October 8
Karl Kraus sends F. Issue 207 of the *Fackel*, which contains an article by Karl Hauer and is entitled "Spiegel sterbender Welten" ("Mirror of Dying Worlds"). F. finds the article "brilliant". In return, F. sends Karl Kraus a Magnus Hirschfeld's article "Die gestohlene Bisexualität" ("Stolen Bisexuality"), in which "the factual aspects of the Fliess affair are dealt with in a […] definitively conclusive manner" (F. to Karl Kraus, 7.10.1906).

1906 October 10
Meeting of the Mittwoch-Gesellschaft: Otto Rank speaks on "The Incest Drama and its Complications" (first part).

1906 October 17
Meeting of the Mittwoch-Gesellschaft: Otto Rank speaks on "The incest drama and its complications: The incestuous relationship between siblings" (second part).

1906 October 18
F. notes literature on the Egyptian pyramids and the excavations in Burgundy, where the Gallic Alesia was suspected.

1906 October 24
Meeting of the Mittwoch-Gesellschaft: Discussion on Rank's lecture "The Incest Drama".

1906 October 31
Meeting of the Mittwoch-Gesellschaft: Eduard Hitschmann speaks on "Affectivity, Suggestibility and Paranoia".

1906 November 1
F. names ten "good" books at the request of the Viennese bookseller and publisher Hugo Heller:

– "Multatuli, Briefe und Werk.
– Kipling, Jungle Book.
– Anatole France, Sur la pierre blanche.
– Zola: Fécondité.
– Mereschkowsky, Leonardo da Vinci.
– G. Keller, Leute von Seldwyla.
– C. F. Meyer, Huttens letzte Tage.
– Macaulay, Essays.
– Gomperz, Griechische Denker.
– Mark Twain, Sketches".

1906 November 7
Meeting of the Mittwoch-Gesellschaft: Alfred Adler speaks on "On the Organic Basis of Neuroses".

1906 November 12

F. gives a lecture on "Sexuelle Abstinenz" ("Sexual Abstinence") at the Social Science Education Association. He explains, among other things, "that prostitution and [...] sexual excesses" do little harm (interview with Rudolf Bienenfeld by Kurt Eissler, 1953 summer).

1906 November 14

Meeting of the Mittwoch-Gesellschaft: Edwin Hollerung speaks about Richard Semon's book *Die Mneme als erhaltendes Prinzip im Wechsel des organischen Geschehens* (*Mneme as the Preserving Principle in the Changing Processes of Organic Life*).

1906 before November 18

F. received Karl Kraus's essay "Der Prozess Riehl"; however, F. had already read it in the *Fackel*.

1906 November 20

Death of the poet Jakob Julius David. He had been receiving treatment from F. since 1900. After he had been diagnosed with bronchial cancer in 1905, F. had visited him together with daughter Mathilde.

1906 November 21

Meeting of the Mittwoch-Gesellschaft: Philipp Frey speaks on "On the Megalomania of the Normal Person".

1906 November 28

Meeting of the Mittwoch-Gesellschaft: Isidor Sadger speaks about "Lenau and Sophie Löwenthal".

1906 December 5

Meeting of the Mittwoch-Gesellschaft: Eduard Hitschmann reviews Wilhelm Stekel's pamphlet *The Causes of Neuroses*.

1906 December 10

Beginning of the correspondence between F. and Max Eitingon.

1906 December 12

– The flat of F.'s family is extended by the flat opposite of his sister Rosa, who had moved to Porzellangasse 45 on November 13. F. moves his practice rooms from the ground floor to the first floor. It is possibly this move that causes F. to destroy a considerable number of letters and documents.
– F. answers an inquiry from the Dean's Office about his non-appearance at expert meetings; he excuses himself with his heavy burden of psychotherapeutic work.

1907

Treatments:

- Alban Berg's mother Johanna visits F. with her daughter Smaragda and asks him if he could not take her for treatment. But after an initial conversation with F. in private, Smaragda refuses.
- Eduard Hitschmann begins an analysis with F.
- Kurt Rie, the brother of his friend Oskar Rie, begins an analysis with F. It lasted until his suicide in January 1908.
- The court and judicial advocate Oskar Thalberg begins an analysis with F. It lasts, with interruptions, until November 1918.

Books received:

- Alfred Adler gives F. his *Studie über die Minderwertigkeit von Organen (Study on the inferiority of organs)* with the dedication: "Seinem Lehrer in dankbare Verehrung gewidmet vom Verfasser".
- Carl Gustav Jung gives F. his book *Über die Psychologie der Dementia praecox* with the dedication "Ergebenst überreicht vom Verfasser".
- Emanuel Loewy gives F. an offprint of his paper "La statua di Anzio" with the dedication "Sigmund Freud freundschaftlich d. Vf.".

1907 ca. January 21–31
First visit by Max Eitingon to F. Max Eitingon begins an analysis with F.

1907 January 23
Meeting of the Mittwoch-Gesellschaft: Alfred Meisl speaks about "Hunger and Love".

1907 January 30
Meeting of the Mittwoch-Gesellschaft: discussion of the questions posed by Max Eitingon, concerning "The Etiology and Therapy of the Neuroses".

1907 February 6
Meeting of the Mittwoch-Gesellschaft: Wilhelm Stekel reviews two books: *Zur Psychologie des Landstreichers (On the Psychopathology of the Vagabond)* by Karl Wilmanns and *Über die Psychologie der Dementia praecox (On the Psychology of Dementia Praecox)* by Carl Gustav Jung.

1907 February 13
Meeting of the Mittwoch-Gesellschaft: Rudolf Reitler speaks about Frank Wedekind's *Frühlingserwachen (Spring's Awakening)*.

1907 February 20
Meeting of the Mittwoch-Gesellschaft: F. reviews Paul Möbius's book *The Hopelessness of All Psychology*.

1907 February 27
Meeting of the Mittwoch-Gesellschaft: F. presents the "Elucidation of a Hysterical Attack"; continuation of the discussion of February 20 on Paul Möbius's book *Die Hoffnungslosigkeit aller Psychologie (The Hopelessness of All Psychology)*.

1907 March 3

Carl Gustav Jung comes to Vienna for the first time. He is accompanied by his wife Emma and Ludwig Binswanger. F. goes to the hotel and presents Jung's wife Emma with a bouquet of flowers. Jung and his wife stay for almost two weeks, and Jung is with F. almost every evening for a longer conversation.

1907 March 4

F. devotes the whole day to his guests. In the evening, they attend *Don Giovanni at the* Court Opera together with F.'s daughter Mathilde.

1907 March 6

Meeting of the Mittwoch-Gesellschaft: Alfred Adler presents a psychoanalytical case. Carl Gustav Jung and Ludwig Binswanger are present as guests and take part in the discussion.

1907 March 10

F. and his family go for a Sunday walk with Ludwig Binswanger on the Cobenzl.

1907 March 17

F. warns Paul Federn "to get involved in [... psychotherapeutic] tasks in the ordination" (F. to Paul Federn, 17.3.1907).

1907 March 19

F. gives a lecture to B'nai B'rith on "Die Psychologie im Dienste der Rechtspflege" ("Psychology in the Service of Justice").

1907 March 20

Meeting of the Mittwoch-Gesellschaft: Adolf Häutler speaks about "Mysticism and Comprehension of Nature".

1907 March 27

Otto Rank gives F. his book *Der Künstler. Ansätze zu einer Sexual-Psychologie* with the dedication "Herrn Prof. F. in Verehrung u. Dankbarkeit gewidmet vom Verfasser".

1907 March 27

Meeting of the Mittwoch-Gesellschaft: Isidor Sadger speaks about "Somnambulism".

1907 March 31–April 1

F. visits Siegfried Kahlbaum in Görlitz

The psychiatrist is the son of Karl Kahlbaum, who coined the terms hebephrenia and catatonia and had taken over the sanatorium for the mentally ill founded by Hermann Andreas Reimer in Görlitz. Siegfried has run the institution since the death of his father in 1899. It is unclear why F. traveled to Görlitz. Possibly he wanted to visit the sanatorium because it enjoys an excellent international reputation. In any case, F. also visited the "Ärztliches Pädagogium für jugendliche Nervenkranke", which belonged to the institution, and saw there "a most instructive case" (F. to Jung, 7.4.1907), which he reported on two weeks later in the Mittwoch-Gesellschaft.

1907 April

F. offers lectures on "Einführung in die Psychotherapie" ("Introduction to Psychotherapy") in the summer semester (location: lecture hall of the Psychiatric Clinic, fee ten Kronen).

1907 April 10
Meeting of the Mittwoch-Gesellschaft: Fritz Wittels speaks about "Tatjana Leontiev".

1907 April 17
Meeting of the Mittwoch-Gesellschaft: David Bach speaks about "Jean Paul", and F. presents the case of a 17-year-old boy whom he had seen during his visit to the mental hospital in Görlitz two weeks earlier.

1907 April 20
F.'s first work critical of religion on "Zwangshandlungen und Religionsübung" is published.

1907 April 24
Meeting of the Mittwoch-Gesellschaft: Wilhelm Stekel speaks on "Psychology and Pathology of the Anxiety Neurosis".

1907 April 26
F.'s former patient Anna von Vest visits F.

1907 May beginning
Start of publication of the *Schriften zur angewandten Seelenkunde*. The first issue is F.'s paper *Der Wahn und die Träume in W. Jensen's "Gradiva"* (600 copies). F. receives the manuscript on May 8.

1907 May 1
Meeting of the Mittwoch-Gesellschaft: Discussion on "Degeneration" with introductory words by Isidor Sadger.

1907 May 8
Meeting of the Mittwoch-Gesellschaft: Adolf Deutsch speaks about the young poet Walter Calé who died by suicide in 1904.

1907 after May 8
F. sends a copy of his book *Der Wahn und die Träume in W. Jensens "Gradiva"* to his niece Bertha in Manchester.

1907 May 15
Meeting of the Mittwoch-Gesellschaft: discussion on Fritz Wittel's paper "Female Physicians".

1907 May 27
F. acquires Fritz Hommel's book *Grundriss der Geographie und Geschichte des alten Orients*.

1907 May 29
Meeting of the Mittwoch-Gesellschaft: Fritz Wittels speaks about "The Great Hetaera".

1907 June 11
F. acquires the first volume of Kurt Breysig's work *Die Völker ewiger Urzeit: Die Amerikaner des Nordwestens und Nordens*.

1907 June 14
Arthur Muthmann gives F. his book *Zur Psychologie und Therapie neurotischer Symptome* with the dedication "Mit dem Ausdruck ausgezeichneter Hochachtung überreicht vom Verfasser".

1907 June 22

F. gives Leopold Löwenfeld a copy of the second edition of *Psychopathologie des Alltagslebens* with the dedication: "Seinem verehrten Freunde Dr. L. Löwenfeld der Verfasser".

1907 June Summer

F. sends his sons Martin and Oliver – Ernst was not in Vienna – together with Martin's friend Hans Lampl for sexual education to Maximilian Steiner, specialist in skin and venereal diseases and member of the Wednesday Society. Steiner also explained to the boys how they could protect themselves from venereal diseases and infections.

1907 June 25

Beginning of the correspondence between F. and Karl Abraham.

1907 July 14–September 12
Summer holiday with family in Lavarone,
S. Cristina and Annenheim

The family stays in Lavarone again at the Hotel du Lac. During their stay, a young lieutenant of the Austrian army pays court to F.'s daughter Mathilde and F. invites him to the hotel for meals together. The Viennese ENT doctor and later Nobel Prize winner Robert Bárány is also in Lavarone. Finally, a reception of the Austrian heir to the throne Franz Ferdinand for officers of the local garrison takes place in the hotel.

1907 July 14

Departure from Vienna to the Semmering.

1907 July 15

Journey from Semmering to Runkelstein Castle near Bolzano.

1907 July 16

Drive from Bolzano to Lavarone.

1907 after July 16

F. makes the acquaintance of the industrial manufacturer Arturo Diena from Padua. They often go for walks together and talk about psychoanalysis, among other things. F.'s sons become friends with Diena's son Giorgio, who later becomes involved in the resistance against Mussolini and survives Dachau.

1907 July end

Arturo Diena takes F. and his daughter Mathilde on a day trip by car – a Fiat Brevetti Cabriolet-Royal – to Padua. It was F.'s first experience with a car.

1907 August mid
Change of accommodation from Lavarone to S. Cristina in Val Gardena
(Hotel Wolkenstein). Hans Lampl, who is also in Val Gardena, often
comes to go bowling with F. and his children.

1907 August 27

– Change of accommodation to Annenheim on Lake Ossiach (Hotel Annenheim and Seehof). F. often goes mushroom hunting and bathes in the lake. The then 13-year-old Paul Elbogen lives with his mother Adeline in the same hotel.

– There is another encounter with Alban Berg. F. had been called to see him because of a severe cold or an attack of bronchial asthma and comes to the Berghof by boat from the other side of the lake.

1907 September 12

F. leaves Annenheim for Italy.

1907 September 12–27
Journey with Minna to Tuscany and then alone to Rome

1907 September 12

F. meets Minna, who comes from Bad Reichenhall, in Franzensfeste, and both continue to Bolzano (Hotel Bristol).

1907 September 14

– At 10.00 am, departure from Bolzano, and at 5.00 pm, arrival in Florence.
– Dinner at Melini, the restaurant of a famous winery.

1907 September 15

– Car excursion to Fiesole, including a visit to the Roman theater.
– F. happens to meet Max Eitingon, who is also in Florence and wants to travel on to Rome.

1907 September 16

– F. buys a notebook made of light-colored leather and decorated with Florentine ornaments. He uses it for entries between 1907 September 16 and 1908 June 24.
– Minna leaves for Merano in the morning.
– F. continues to Orvieto at 5.00 pm and goes first to Riccardo Mancini's antique shop, but is disappointed and thinks it will soon be over with collecting.

1907 September 17

– Drive from Orvieto to Rome, and overnight at Hotel Milano in Piazza Monte Citorio with the column of the Emperor Marcus Aurelius.
– After arriving, F. goes to the shop of the antique dealer Attilio Simonetti in Via Vittoria Colonna.

1907 September 18

F. acquires F. Christian Huelsen's book *Die neuesten Ausgrabungen auf dem Forum Romanum* and visits the Forum, Michelangelo's Moses and the Protestant cemetery.

1907 September 19

– Visit to the Palatine and the Garibaldi Monument on the Gianicolo.
– F. buys antiques and some shopping for his children from the art dealer G. Rainaldi in Via del Babuino.
– In the evening, walk with Max Eitingon, who is staying in another hotel.

1907 September 20

– On the occasion of the anniversary of the entry of the Italian troops in 1870 and the breakthrough through the city wall at the Porta Pia, all Roman museums were closed on September 20. F. went to see the celebrations at the Porta Pia, but fled from the "crowd" to the Via Appia in the afternoon.
– F. does not feel well and considers leaving, but he feels better the next day.

1907 September 21

- Visit to the Catacombs and the Villa Borghese. The statues of Victor Hugo and Goethe prompt him to make ironic remarks in a letter to his family.
- Visit to the Borghese Museum, where F. sees, among other things, Titian's "Heavenly and Earthly Love".
- F. buys some marble bowls as ashtrays for the Mittwoch-Gesellschaft.
- F. buys the second edition of Christian Hülsen's book *Das Forum romanum. Its history and its monuments.*

1907 September 22

- Visit to the Baths of Diocletian and the National Museum.
- F. informs the members of the Mittwoch-Gesellschaft in a letter that he wants to dissolve it and re-found it as an association.

1907 September 23

- In the morning, visit the museums on the Capitol.
- F. visits the antique dealers Ettore Jandolo (Via del Babuino), Attilio Simonetti (Via Vittoria Colonna) and Giuseppe Sangiorgi (Via di Ripetta). At the latter, he smashed an antique glass after assuring the merchant that he was very skilled and that nothing would happen.
- F. notes as the "main result of the stay in Rome that I feel tiny and everything I have is worthless" (F.'s notebook, 23.9.1907).

1907 September 24

- Visit to the Vatican Museums; F. discovers the Gradiva relief there and is delighted to also see familiar things, such as the Laocoon group.
- Visit to a performance of "Carmen" by George Bizet at the Quirino Theater near F.'s hotel.

1907 September 25

- Visit to Castel Sant'Angelo, the Sistine Chapel and Raphael's Stanzas in the Vatican.
- In the afternoon, shopping again at the antique dealer Ettore Jandolo, this time probably in one of the dealer's other shops in Via Margutta or Via Sistina.
- As a farewell to Rome, visit to the Palatine. F. loses his Rome travel guide "in impatience to get away" (F.'s notebook, 25.9.1907).

1907 September 26

Departure from Rome at 11.10 pm.

1907 September 28

Arrival in Vienna at 7.50 am.

1907 October

F. offers lectures on "Einführung in die Psychotherapie" ("Introduction to Psychotherapy") in the winter semester (lecture hall of the Psychiatric Clinic, fee ten Kronen).

1907 October 1

Ernst Lanzer (the "rat man") begins an analysis with F. It lasts until 1908 January 20.

1907 October 3
F. notes down the sentence "Traumdeutung via regia zur Kenntniss des Ubw" ("The interpretation of dreams is the royal road to a knowledge of the unconscious activities of the mind"), which then appears for the first time two years later in the second edition of *Traumdeutung* (F.'s Notebooks, 3.10.1907).

1907 October 9
Meeting of the Mittwoch-Gesellschaft: Wilhelm Stekel speaks on "The somatic equivalents of anxiety and their differential diagnosis".

1907 October 13
Death of F.'s patient Alois Jeitteles. He commits suicide with gas, sleeping pills and a revolver.

1907 October 16
Meeting of the Mittwoch-Gesellschaft: Maximilian Steiner speaks on "On Functional Impotence".

1907 October 23
Meeting of the Mittwoch-Gesellschaft: Hugo Schwerdtner speaks on the subject of "Sleep".

1907 October 30
Meeting of the Mittwoch-Gesellschaft: F. gives the first part of a lecture on his patient Ernst Lanzer (the "Rat Man").

1907 November 2–4
Short trip to Kuttenberg and Prague

1907 November 2

After his Saturday lecture ("Introduction to Psychotherapy"), F. takes the night train to Kuttenberg (now Kutna Hora), about 70km east of Prague, to visit his daughter Mathilde, who is visiting her friend Johanna Teller.

1907 November 3

In the morning, Mathilde shows him Kutna Hora; around noon, F. continues to Prague and gives a lecture there to B'nai B'rith "Über den Witz" ("On the Joke"). Afterward, he takes the night train back to Vienna.

1907 November 4

F. arrives in Vienna in the morning.

1907 November 6
Meeting of the Mittwoch-Gesellschaft: F. gives the second part of a lecture on his patient Ernst Lanzer ("The Rat Man").

1907 November 13
– The writer Erich Mühsam, who had undergone successful therapy with Otto Gross, contacts F. because he is planning a paper on F.'s writings. For this purpose, he asks for F.'s books to be sent to him. However, no review of F.'s writings by Mühsam ever appeared.
– Meeting of the Mittwoch-Gesellschaft: Fritz Wittels speaks about "Venereal Disease".

1907 November 20
Meeting of the Mittwoch-Gesellschaft: Wilhelm Stekel speaks about the "Analysis of a Case of Anxiety Hysteria".

1907 November 27
– Meeting of the Mittwoch-Gesellschaft: Wilhelm Stekel speaks on "Two Cases of Anxiety Hysteria".
– F. applies for the "Heimat- und Bürgerrecht der Stadt Wien" ("Home- and civil rights of the City of Vienna").

1907 December 4
Meeting of the Mittwoch-Gesellschaft: Isidor Sadger speaks about Conrad Ferdinand Meyer.

1907 December 6
F. gives a lecture on "Der Dichter und das Phantasieren" at the Heller Art Salon. The *Neue Revue* asks F. to publish the lecture. F. agrees at the beginning of January.

1907 December 11
Meeting of the Mittwoch-Gesellschaft: Max Graf speaks on the "Methodology of Psychology of Poets".

1907 December 15–18
Karl Abraham visits F. for the first time and receives two small Egyptian bronze statues as a gift from him.

1907 December 18
Meeting of the Mittwoch-Gesellschaft: discussion on "Sexual Traumata and Sexual Enlightenment".

1907 December 20
Christian von Ehrenfels sends F. his writing *Sexualethik* with the dedication "In Freundschaft vom Verf.". F. provides it with numerous annotations.

1908

- F. receives a copy of a Pompeian relief (probably the "Gradiva" from the Vatican Museums).
- F. receives a reprint of Leopold Löwenfeld's lecture "Homosexualität und Strafgesetz" with the dedication "Mit freundlichen Grüssen Der Verf.".

Treatments:

- Otto Gross begins an analysis with F. It lasts until 1915.
- Sándor Ferenczi begins an analysis with F.

1908 beginning
Arthur Muthmann visits F.

1908 January
Hans Müller sends F. his play *Die Puppenschule (The Doll School)* with the dedication "Herrn Professor Dr Sigm. Freud in hoher Verehrung/Hans Müller".

1908 January 6
F.'s daughter Mathilde falls ill with severe peritonitis and appendicitis (perityphlitis). F. consults the surgeon Anton Eiselsberg.

1908 January 8
Meeting of the Mittwoch-Gesellschaft: Wilhelm Stekel speaks about "The border of psychosis".

1908 January 14
Beginning of the correspondence between F. and Ludwig Binswanger.

1908 January 15
Meeting of the Mittwoch-Gesellschaft: Rudolf Urbantschitsch speaks on the topic "My developmental years until marriage".

1908 January 16
F. receives the "Heimat- und Bürgerrecht der Stadt Wien" ("Home- and Civil rights of the City of Vienna").

1908 January 18
Beginning of the correspondence between F. and Sándor Ferenczi.

1908 January 22
Meeting of the Mittwoch-Gesellschaft: discussion of various topics (e.g. "The Normal Psychiatrist").

1908 January 29
Meeting of the Mittwoch-Gesellschaft: Alfred Adler gives a lecture entitled "A Contribution to the Problem of Paranoia".

1908 January 31
Kurt Rie commits suicide by shooting himself. In the morning, F. and Ludwig Rosenberg as attending physicians had sat down with Oskar Rie, Alfred Rie, Paul Rie, Kurt Rie's wife Therese and a lawyer to discuss further treatment. Rosenberg was in favor of committing him to a closed institution.

1908 January end
F. has influenza.

1908 February 2
Sándor Ferenczi visits F. for the first time, accompanied by the psychiatrist Philipp Stein.

1908 February 5
Meeting of the Mittwoch-Gesellschaft: Eduard Hitschmann speaks about "Sexual Anaesthesia".

1908 February 12
Meeting of the Mittwoch-Gesellschaft: discussion on sexual anesthesia; resolutions on work regulations.

1908 February 14
F. concludes a contract with the publisher Franz Deuticke for the purchase of the first two issues of the *Schriften zur angewandten Seelenkunde* and the continuation.

1908 February 17
F. considers offering Eugen Bleuler the chairmanship of the I. International Psychoanalytical Congress in Salzburg.

1908 February 19
Meeting of the Mittwoch-Gesellschaft: Albert Joachim speaks on "The Nature of the Symbol".

1908 February 26
Meeting of the Mittwoch-Gesellschaft: Rudolf Urbantschitsch speaks "On the significance of the psychogalvanic reflex".

1908 February 29
F.'s daughter Mathilde goes to Meran for a six-month cure after her serious illness in January. There, she meets her future husband Robert Hollitscher.

1908 March
F.'s paper "Die ‚kulturelle'" Sexualmoral und die moderne Nervosität" is published.

1908 March 4
– F. is granted the right of domicile and citizenship by the Magistrate's District Office for the ninth District of the City of Vienna.
– Meeting of the Mittwoch-Gesellschaft: brief reviews of literature and clinical communications.

1908 March 11
Meeting of the Mittwoch-Gesellschaft: Fritz Wittels speaks on "The Natural Position of Women".

1908 March 12
The surgeon Julius Schnitzler visits F. He is the brother of the doctor and poet Arthur Schnitzler.

1908 March 14
F. gives his last lecture of the semester, and afterward, he plays tarot with Oskar and Alfred Rie.

1908 March 15
Death of F.'s brother-in-law Heinrich Graf, the husband of his sister Rosa. Her friend Natalie Patzau, the wife of the director of the northern railway Josef Patzau and F.'s occasional tarot partner, spends the night with Rosa.

1908 March 19
- F. goes to the funeral of Heinrich Graf. His cousin and brother-in-law Moritz comes from Berlin for the funeral.
- F.'s daughter Anna has an appendectomy.

1908 Spring
Max Graf tells F. about the conspicuous behavior of his son Herbert. Under F.'s guidance, Max Graf carries out a kind of analysis on his son. F. later publishes the case history under the title "Analyse der Phobie eines fünfjährigen Knaben". Herbert Graf later becomes director of the Metropolitan Opera in New York.

1908 March 22
Magnus Hirschfeld visits F., and the latter writes about him: "[…] he looks good-natured and awkward and seems to be an honest sort" (F. to Jung, 14.4.1908).

1908 March 26
The women's rights activist Helene Stöcker visits F. At her request, he writes an article for the magazine *Mutterschutz on the* subject of "The 'Cultural' Sexual Morality and Modern Nervousness".

1908 March 28
F. gives a lecture to B'nai B'rith at a ladies' evening on "Kindertaufen" ("Child baptism").

1908 April
Albert Moll visits F.

1908 April
F. offers lectures on "Einführung in die Psychotherapie" ("Introduction to Psychotherapy") once a week in the summer semester (location: lecture hall of the Psychiatric Clinic, fee ten Kronen).

1908 April 1
Meeting of the Mittwoch-Gesellschaft: discussion on the third section of Friedrich Nietzsche's *Genealogy of Morals*: "On the Ascetic Ideal". Eduard Hitschmann introduces the discussion.

1908 April 8
Meeting of the Mittwoch-Gesellschaft: reviews and clinical communications. The motion to establish a library of the Mittwoch-Gesellschaft is accepted.

1908 April 10
F. buys Herbert Graf (the "Little Hans") a rocking horse for his fifth birthday – after he has been cured of his phobia of horses – and carries it up four floors to the Graf family's flat.

1908 April 15
Meeting of the Wiener Psychoanalytische Vereinigung (WPV), as the Mittwoch-Gesellschaft is called from now on: discussion of Magnus Hirschfeld's proposal for collaboration on a questionnaire on sexuality.

1908 April mid
Martha visits her mother in Hamburg.

1908 April 22
WPV meeting: discussion on Magnus Hirschfeld's proposal for collaboration on a questionnaire on sexuality.

1908 May 3
Beginning of the correspondence between F. and Stefan Zweig.

1908 May 13
Beginning of the correspondence between F. and Ernest Jones.

1908 April 25–28
I. International Psychoanalytical Congress in Salzburg

The venue for the Congress was the Bristol Hotel. At the Congress, F. meets Wilfred Trotter for the first time, who was to become his last surgeon in London. During the Congress days, F. visits the Dietfeldhof in Berchtesgaden (Bischofswiesen), which he then rents for the summer stay.

1908 April 25

Departure from Vienna in the evening.

1908 April 26

Arrival in Salzburg in the morning.

1908 April 27

– F. gives a lecture entitled "Casuistisches" ("Casuistic") about his patient Ernst Lanzer ("Rat Man"). After the set speaking time of 30 minutes, F. asked if he could continue. This was jubilantly granted, and he spoke for another 1¼ hours.
– F. spends part of April 27 with his brother Emanuel, who had come to Salzburg from Manchester.

1908 April 28

– WPV meeting in the morning.
– F. meets his brother Emanuel again and spends the rest of the day with him; among other things, they visit the fortress and Hellbrunn.
– F. travels to Vienna during the night.

1908 April 29

Arrival in Vienna in the morning.

1908 April 30
First visit of Ernst Jones and Abraham Brill to F.

1908 April end
Stefan Zweig gives F. his tragedy *Tersites*.

1908 May beginning
Abraham Brill begins an analysis with F.

1908 May 6
WPV meeting: Wilhelm Stekel gives a lecture on "The Genesis of Psychic Impotence". On the occasion of F.'s birthday, Ernest Jones and Abraham Brill are also present.

1908 May 10
F. sees Johann Nestroy's Tannhäuser parody at the Karltheater and finds it very amusing.

1908 May 13
WPV session: reviews and case reports.

1908 May 24
F. meets Robert Hollitscher, Mathilde's "friend". He writes to her: "I would have to forego all sorts of expectations if I were to imagine him as your husband already. It would be nice for me to know that you have kept your restraint" (F. to Mathilde, 25.5.1908). The next day, he meets Hollitscher's sister Marie.

1908 May 27
WPV meeting: reviews and case reports.

1908 June 3
WPV meeting: Alfred Adler gives a lecture on "Sadism in Life and Neurosis".

1908 June 10
– Paul Hollitscher, the brother of F.'s daughter Mathilde's future husband, invites Minna to give her the most precise information about his material position.
– Cozy get-together of the WPV at the Schutzengel inn on the Hohe Warte.

1908 June 22
Beginning of the correspondence between F. and Abraham Brill.

1908 June end
F. receives from Ragnar Vogt from Christiania (now Oslo) his textbook Psykiatriens grundtraek (Outlines of Psychiatry), "the first text-book of psychiatry to refer to psycho-analysis" (SE 14, p. 33).

1908 Summer
Wilhelm Stekel gives F. his book *Nervöse Angstzustände und ihre Behandlung,* to which F. had written a preface, with the dedication "Seinem Meister in unwandelbare Treue und Dankbarkeit Stekel".

1908 July
F. writes the preface to the second edition of *Studien über Hysterie.*

1908 July 1
F. spends the evening with Charles Campbell and his wife. Campbell is a Scottish doctor and co-founder of the *Review of Neurology and Psychiatry* (Edinburgh).

1908 July beginning
- F. receives his book *Balzac* from Stefan Zweig.
- F. deals with Flood myths.

1908 before July 2
The American psychologist Henry Goodard visits F. and tells him of his intention to also conduct research on mass psychology at his "Training school at Vinelande".

1908 July 15–September 1
Summer stay with family in Berchtesgaden (Bischofswiesen)
The family lives at the Dietfeldhof. Martin's friend Hans Lampl is also there. F. writes the medical history of "Little Hans" (Herbert Graf), corrects the second edition of the *Die Traumdeutung* and writes a preface for it. He also writes the papers "Über infantile Sexualtheorien" and "Allgemeines über den hysterischen Anfall". F. has "never worked so little in such a beautiful study" (F. to Alexander Freud, 12.8.1908). During his stay in Berchtesgaden, F. receives a visit from Fritz Wittels.

1908 August 4
Karl Abraham sends F. his book *Traum und Mythus* with the dedication: "Ein Werdender wird immer dankbar sein! DV".

1908 August 10
Sándor Ferenczi comes to Berchtesgaden for three weeks; F. has rented a room for him nearby. F. hoped that Ferenczi would become engaged to his daughter Mathilde.

1908 August end
William Parker from Columbia University in New York asks F. to write a paper for a textbook on psychotherapy. F. refuses because he does not know anything about the topic assigned to him (recovery and convalescence).

1908 September 1
Departure from Berchtesgaden at 7.00 am.

September 1–15
Visit of the brothers Emanuel and Philipp in England

1908 September 1
Journey via Munich to Cologne. There, F. misses his connecting train and arrives in Rotterdam late in the evening (overnight stay in Hotel Maas).

1908 September 2
F. travels from Rotterdam via The Hague to Amsterdam. There, he visits the Imperial Museum in the afternoon and is impressed by Rembrandt's "Night Watch". He then buys cigars, continues to Hoek van Holland and takes the ferry from there to Harwich.

1908 September 3
At 7.35 am, departure by train from Harwich to Manchester to visit brother Emanuel and his family. At the station, the 75-year-old carries Emanuel F.'s suitcase, saying that the old dog still has life in him.

1908 September 4

F. and Emanuel drive to the west coast to Lytham St. Annes and on to Blackpool.

1908 September 5

Trip to Southport, presumably by boat. F. has his beard removed after he was not satisfied with the one trimmed by the barber. Then drive to Lytham St. Annes and stay there until September 8.

1908 September 6

F. has a nasal infection and takes aspirin for it.

1908 September 7

F. spends the day at the beach.

1908 September 8

F. and Emanuel walk to Blackpool (just under 10km).

1908 September 9

F. and Emanuel take a train from Blackpool to Manchester at 10.30 am. F. also meets his brother Philipp there and continues to London in the late afternoon. There, he stays at Ford's Hotel in Manchester Street.

1908 September 10

F. walks through Oxford Street, buys a pumpkin pipe and visits the Assyrian section in the British Museum, where he goes more often in the following days.

1908 September 11

F. visits Tower Bridge and Westminster Abbey. At the sarcophagus of Elizabeth I, he gets the idea that Elizabeth "gave Shakespeare the character of his Lady Macbeth" (F. to Lytton Strachey, 25.12.1928).

1908 September 12

F. visits the Greco-Roman section in the British Museum, for which he had prepared himself thoroughly the day before. There, he is particularly impressed by the Rosetta Stone and a cuneiform tablet with the legend of the birth of Sargon of Akkad. He also compares two vessels depicting the transformation of Thetis into a bird as an "example of misunderstanding" (F.'s notebook, 21.9.1908).

1908 September 13

F. is in Hyde Park in the morning and then visits the National Portrait Gallery and writes a manuscript entitled "Bemerkungen über Gesichter und Männer" ("Notes on Faces and Men").

1908 September 14

F. buys Babylonian cylinder seals and goes to Regents Park. To Martha, he sends a telegram for their 22nd wedding anniversary.

1908 September 15

F. goes for a last walk. At 8.30 pm, he drives to Harwich and meets his brother Emanuel again. From Harwich, they both take the ferry to Hoek van Holland.

1908 September 16–17
Short visit with Brother Emanuel and his wife and daughter to Sister Mitzi in Berlin

1908 September 16

F. and Emanuel travel from Hoek van Holland to Berlin at 6.00 am, where they arrive at 18.49 pm.

1908 September 17

F. meets his sister Mitzi and her children Margarethe, Lilly, Martha ("Tom") and Theodor ("Theddi") at the Hotel Excelsior. At 21.45 pm, F. takes the sleeping car to Zurich.

1908 September 18–21
Visit to Carl Gustav Jung in Zurich

1908 September 18

F. arrives in Zurich at 3.23 am. Jung is waiting for him at the station. They drive to Burghölzli and take a walk in the forest.

1908 September 19

– F. visits Zurich.
– Jung drew F.'s attention to Daniel Paul Schreber's '*Denkwürdigkeiten eines Nervenkranken*', which he had read in the Burghölzli library, and suggested that F. write something about it.

1908 September 20

F. went to the "black café" with Bleuler and the doctors at Burghölzli, which "went very animatedly". Then, he visits the Okenshöhe, a vantage point on the Pfannenstiel near Zurich, which is dedicated to the naturalist Lorenz Oken.

1908 September 21

F. visits Sophie Erismann, the wife of the internist Friedrich Erismann, who was the head of the Hygiene Institute in Moscow until 1896. Then, he goes up the Uetliberg, Zurich's local mountain, and at 16.50, he takes the train through the Gotthard tunnel to Milan and from there to Desenzano.

1908 September 22–28
Journey through Upper Italy with sister-in-law Minna

1908 September 22

F.'s sister-in-law Minna arrives in Desenzano, and they both continue on to Salò, where they arrive at 12:00 pm.

1908 September 23

Drive to Manerbo, 20km south of Salò.

1908 September 24

Motorboat trip to San Vigilio and the Isola del Garda.

1908 September 25

Walk to Fasano, just north of Salò.

1908 September 26

It is raining heavily, and F. and Minna only visit the cemetery in Salò.

1908 September 27

Boat trip to Riva and from there to Bolzano.

1908 September 28

Departure from Bolzano in the late afternoon.

1908 September 29

Arrival in Vienna in the morning.

1908 Autumn

Willy Haas, a Munich philosopher, begins an analysis with F. It lasts until 1910 December. As Haas is interested in archeology, F. gives him three Egyptian pieces from his collection: two Osiris statues and a small statue of Isis with the Horus child.

1908 October

F. offers lectures on "Neurosenlehre und Psychotherapie" ("Theory of Neuroses and Psychotherapy") in the winter semester (location: lecture hall of the Psychiatric Clinic, fee ten Kronen).

1908 October beginning

William Parker again asks F. if he would write a contribution to the psychotherapy textbook; this time, he leaves the choice of topic up to him. In the end, Abraham Brill takes on this task.

1908 October 7

– Edoardo Weiss, a psychiatrist from Trieste, visits F. for the first time.
– WPV meeting: communications from von Adolf Häutler, Isidor Sadger and Wilhelm Stekel.

1908 October 9

Eugen Bleuler and his wife Hedwig visit F. Bleuler is in Vienna on the occasion of the III. International Congress for the Care of the Insane in Vienna, which took place from October 7 to 11.

1908 October 14

WPV meeting: Wilhelm Stekel speaks about "*A Dream Is life* and its Connection with Grillparzer's Neurosis".

1908 October 18

Engagement of F.'s daughter Mathilde to Robert Hollitscher.

1908 October mid

– F. sends a parcel with books Emma Jung.
– Friedrich Jodl gives F. his *textbook of psychology.*

1908 October 21

WPV meeting: Isidor Sadger speaks about the "Analysis of a case of hysterical pseudo-epilepsy".

1908 October 24

Paul Federn picks F. up from his home at his request, and they both go to F.'s lecture together.

1908 October 25

Elfriede Hirschfeld, daughter of an unsuccessful Frankfurt businessman, begins an analysis with F. This lasts until 1914 July.

1908 October 28

WPV meeting: Adolf Häutler speaks about "Friedrich Nietzsche's *Ecce homo*".

1908 November beginning

F. begins writing a "General Methodology of Psychoanalysis". However, the writing was never published; however, treatment-related writings emerged from the project between 1911 and 1914.

1908 November 4

Session of the WPV: reviews and case reports.

1908 November 11

WPV meeting: Oskar Rie speaks about Albert Moll's book *The Sexual Life of the Child*.

1908 November 12

– F. decides to stay away from the Congress of the "Gesellschaft deutscher Nervenärzte" (Society of German Neurologists) planned for 1909 autumn in Vienna and "and will also prevent my hotheads here from making an appearance" (F. to Abraham, 12.11.1908).
– F. finds in the social democratic newspaper *Vorwärts the* psychological interpretation of a slip of the tongue by the German Reichstag deputy Wilhelm Lattmann, who had spoken of "spineless" instead of "unreserved", and includes this slip in the third edition of *Psychopathologie des Alltagslebens*.

1908 November 18

WPV meeting: Fritz Wittels speaks about "Sexual Perversity", "as if I had never said a word about them in the Three Essays" (F. to Jung, 29.11.1908).

1908 November 25

WPV meeting: Otto Rank speaks on "The Myth of the Birth of the Hero: A Psychological Interpretation of Mythology".

1908 November 29

The relatives of Robert Hollitscher, the fiancé of F.'s daughter Mathilde, visit Freud's.

1908 December 9

Session of the WPV: reviews and case reports.

1908 December 15

Start of correspondence with Granville Stanley Hall. F. is invited by Hall to Worcester to give lectures and declines for the time being in a letter of 29.12.

1908 December 16

WPV meeting: Christian von Ehrenfels speaks about Fritz Wittel's paper "Die sexuelle Not".

1908 December 23

WPV meeting: Christian von Ehrenfels speaks on "A Program for Breeding Reform".

1908 December 25–27

Visit from Sándor Ferenczi.

1909

F. becomes a member of the Austrian branch of the German Dürer Association.

Books received:

- Alphonse Maeder gives F. a paper by Fanny Chalewsky entitled "Heilung eines hysterischen Bellens durch Psychanalyse" ("Curing hysterical barking through psychoanalysis") with the dedication "Hochachtungsvoll Maeder".
- Otto Rank gives F. his book *Der Mythus von der Geburt des Helden* with the dedication "Dem Vater dieses Buches in Dankbarkeit gewidmet von – der Mutter".
- Wilhelm Stekel gives F. his book *Dichtung und Neurose* with the dedication "Seinem Lehrer in treuer Anhänglichkeit Stekel".
- Isidor Sadger gives F. his book *Aus dem Liebesleben Nicolaus Lenaus* with the dedication "Seinem Lehrer, Helfer u. Berater in Treue gewidmet vom Verfasser".

1909 before January 10
F. has his beard removed; presumably he wanted to look younger in a portrait intended as a gift for the wedding of daughter Mathilde.

1909 January 10
Max Oppenheimer (called "Mopp") begins to portray F. – without a beard. After four sessions – each on Sunday – the picture was finished. F. gives Oppenheimer a copy of The *Interpretation of Dreams* as a token of appreciation.

1909 January 13
WPV meeting: Wilhelm Stekel speaks on "Poetry and Neurosis".

1909 January 18
F. sees the first sheets of the *Jahrbuch für psychoanalytische und psychopathologische Forschungen.*

1909 January mid
Beginning of the correspondence between F. and Oskar Pfister.

1909 January 20
WPV meeting: Eduard Hitschmann speaks on "Neurosis and Toxicosis".

1909 January 27
WPV meeting: Hugo Heller speaks "On the History of the Devil".

1909 January 31
Visit of the psychiatrist Philipp Stein from Budapest. F. later asks Ferenczi to take him into treatment.

1909 February
F.'s paper "Analyse der Phobie eines fünfjährigen Knaben" is published. It is the medical history of Herbert Graf, the son of the musicologist Max Graf, who was also a member of the WPV.

1909 February 2
Arthur Muthmann is a guest at F's.

1909 February 3
WPV meeting: Alfred Adler speaks on "A Case of Compulsive Blushing".

1909 February 7
– Marriage of F.'s brother Alexander to Sophie Schreiber.
– Marriage of F.'s daughter Mathilde to Robert Hollitscher. For the wedding, the bride and groom receive a portrait of F. by Max Oppenheimer, which shows F. without a beard. In the afternoon, after the wedding there is a reception at Berggasse 19.
– F. is considering a trip to Egypt.

1909 February 10
– WPV meeting: reviews and case reports; F. presents Oskar Pfister's paper "Psychoanalytic Pastoral Care and Experimental Moral Pedagogy" and Sándor Ferenczi Wladyslaw Biegan-skis *Medizinische Logik*.
– Arthur Muthmann is a guest at F.'s.

1909 February 16
F. is again invited by Stanley Hall to lecture in Worcester. Hall offers him an honorarium of 3000 marks. F. accepts by letter of February 28.

1909 February 17
WPV meeting: Isidor Sadger presents the "Recollections of a 'Sweet Girl'".

1909 before February 19
F. buys two carpets for his newly married daughter's flat.

1909 February 24
WPV meeting: F. gives a lecture "On the Genesis of Fetishism".

1909 February 25
The first volume of the *Jahrbuch für psychoanalytische und psychopathologische Forschungen* is published.

1909 February 28
Sándor Ferenczi visits F.

1909 March 3
WPV meeting: Alfred Bass speaks about "Word and Thought".

1909 March 10
WPV meeting: Alfred Adler gives a lecture on "On the Psychology of Marxism".

1909 March 24
Session of the WPV: reviews and case reports.

1909 March 25–30
Carl Gustav Jung and his wife Emma visit F. in Vienna. On the first evening, they are invited to Freud's for dinner.

1909 March 31
WPV meeting: Wilhelm Stekel speaks about "The psychopathology of Hauptmann's *Griselda*".

1909 April 7
WPV meeting: Otto Rank speaks "On the psychology of lying".

1909 April 9–12
F. goes on an Easter trip to Venice. His brother Alexander and his wife Sophie are waiting for him there. Alexander leaves Venice the next day with his dentist Hermann Löffler, and F. spends the Easter days with his sister-in-law in the lagoon city. Sophie later says, "That was my most beautiful time", and Alexander comments, "It seems to me you should have married Sigmund instead!" (interview of Sophie Freud by Kurt Eissler, 30.3.1953).

1909 April 21
WPV meeting: Eduard Hitschmann gives "A General Presentation of Freud's Theories".

1909 April 22
F.'s daughter Mathilde is operated on for an abscess.

1909 April 25
– Albert Moll visits F. He was not enthusiastic, "scolded him and almost threw him out" (F. to Ferenczi, 26.4.1909).
– Oskar Pfister visits F. for the first time.

1909 April 28
WPV session: reviews and clinical communications.

1909 May 5
WPV meeting: Isidor Sadger speaks about Heinrich von Kleist.

1909 May 11
F. attends a lecture by the Zurich educationalist Friedrich Wilhelm Foerster on "Hauptfragen der Charakterbildung" ("Main Questions of Character Formation") in the Sophiensälen. However, F. is not particularly impressed by the lecture.

1909 May 12
WPV meeting: discussion on "sexual enlightenment".

1909 May 19
WPV meeting: F. speaks "Über einen besonderen Typus der männlichen Objektwahl".

1909 May 26
WPV meeting: Continuation of the discussion on F.'s talk "Über einen besonderen Typus der männlichen Objektwahl".

1909 June
Martha is in Hamburg with her daughter Sophie for a few weeks to visit her mother. Sophie probably meets her future husband Max Halberstadt on this occasion.

1909 June 2
– WPV meeting: Alfred Adler speaks "On the Oneness of the Neuroses".
– F. receives Otto Gross's book Über psychopathische Minderwertigkeiten.

1909 June 6
F. received the *textbook of nervous diseases* edited by Hans Curschmann.

1909 June mid

F. sends Morton Prince the second installment of the *collection of small writings on neurosis*.

1909 Summer

The WPV hosts a "farewell souper" on Konstantinshügel in the Prater.

1909 July beginning

− F. has the prospect of a consultation trip to Saloniki to see a paralyzed child. However, he demanded such a high fee for the five days that the trip did not take place.
− F.'s son Martin "has got his face chopped up in a student duel" (F. to Jung, 7.7.1909).

1909 July 14–August 19

Summer stay with family in Ammerwald near Reutte in Tyrol

Accommodation in the Hotel Ammerwald. The actually beautiful house lies in the forest and offers no view. F. is visited there by Willy Haas, among others. Martin's friend Hans Lampl is also in Ammerwald. A student from Bremen asks F. to look at his swollen cheek; he wants to know whether the cause is a wasp sting or a wisdom tooth. F. reads Carl Spitteler's *Imago* and is quite enthusiastic about the book: "He came out [of his room] one Sunday and said, that is a wonderful book! After an hour he came back: A wonderful book! Came back: This is such a beautiful book!" (interview with Hans Lampl by Kurt Eissler, 1953).

1909 July 14

Departure from Vienna.

1909 July 15

Arrival in Munich.

1909 July 16

Drive from Munich to Reutte.

1909 July 18

F. undertakes a hike up a mountain slope "where nature produces such a magnificent effect with the simplest direction, with white rock, fields of red alpine roses, a patch of snow, a waterfall and a lot of green below, I hardly knew myself personally. You could have diagnosed dementia praecox" (Freud to Jung, 19.7.1909).

1909 July 24

F. orders two archeological books, but they could not be delivered because they are out of print.

1909 July 31

F. now asks Eugen Pachmayr from Bad Reichenhall/Munich, a friend of his daughter Mathilde, to have a catalog of archeological publications sent to him.

1909 August mid

The Prince Regent Luitpold Karl Joseph Wilhelm of Bavaria and his son Ludwig the III. organize a hunting day in Ammerwald. F. and his children observe the events from a certain distance.

1909 August 19–September 29
Journey to America

F. is lecturing at Clark University in Worcester, Massachusetts. He was invited by Stanley Hall on the occasion of the 20th anniversary of the university.

1909 August 19

F. travels from Reutte via Oberammergau, Munich and Hanover to Bremen.

1909 August 20

- F. arrives in Bremen at 6.10 am. He visits the city with Sándor Ferenczi (including the cathedral and town hall).
- During lunch with Carl Gustav Jung and Sándor Ferenczi in the "Essighaus", F. has a fainting fit, possibly triggered by a conversation about bog bodies and mummies in Bremen lead cellars.
- Afternoon, sightseeing with a car hired from Jung; afterward, walk along the Weser.

1909 August 21

- At 10.50 am, departure with special train to Bremerhaven.
- At 12.00 pm, embarkation on the steamer "George Washington". F. has an inside cabin for 600 marks.
- F. finds a "bouquet of the most beautiful orchids" by Elfriede Hirschfeld on the steamer.
- F. begins a "travel journal".
- On the ship, Jung tries to interpret a dream of F. in which Minna Bernays (dream of "Minna as a peasant") plays a role. F. refuses, however, so as not to jeopardize his authority.

1909 August 22

Passage from Dover, at 2 pm in Southampton and in the evening in Cherbourg.

1909 August 24

The psychologist William Stern, who is also invited to Worcester, approaches Jung on deck and engages him in conversation. F. interrupts somewhat rudely, and Stern recommended himself.

1909 ca. August 25

F. reads a book by Anatole France that Ferenczi had brought with him.

1909 August 26

Thick fog since noon, and the steamer's siren emits warning signals every two minutes.

1909 August 27

The steamer passes Newfoundland, and it gets very chilly.

1909 August 28

- The steamer launches a lifeboat in case it should run over one of the fishing boats fishing off Newfoundland in the fog.
- In the evening, festive dinner and farewell ball.

1909 August 29

- Arrival in New York harbor. Brill receives the European psychoanalysts.
- F. gives an interview to the German-language *New York State newspaper* on his arrival.
- F. stays at the Hotel Manhattan on the corner of Madison Avenue and 42nd Street and immediately takes a look at the surrounding area.

1909 August 30

- In the morning, walk along Broadway.
- F. tries in vain to visit his old friend Sigmund Lustgarten and his sister Anna.
- Brill takes F. and Jung to Central Park and shows them the windows of his flat. F. advised him never to move.
- Brill invites F., Jung and Ferenczi to his home for dinner.
- Abraham Brill shows F., Jung and Ferenczi Chinatown.

1909 August 31

- Morning visit to the Metropolitan Museum.
- In the evening, visit Coney Island, a kind of New York Prater.

1909 September 1

Evening visit to Hammerstein's Roof Garden, a variety theater founded by the theater magnate Oskar Hammerstein. There is a film full of wild pursuits. F. on this occasion for the first time Trigant Burrow, an American psychiatrist and psychoanalyst.

1909 September 2

- F. books his return journey with the "Kaiser Wilhelm der Grosse" with Norddeutscher Lloyd.
- Visit to Columbia University.

1909 September 3

- In the morning, F. visits the American Museum of Natural History and has lunch with Abraham Brill.
- In the afternoon, F. prepares for his lectures in Worcester.

1909 September 4

In the evening, departure by steamer from New York to Fall River (near Providence); overnight there.

1909 September 5

Train journey from Fall River via Boston to Worcester. F. stays the first night at the Standish Hotel. For dinner, John Burnham keeps him company. F. did not feel well and did not want to eat or drink water, but ordered a glass of Rhine wine – but to no avail, as the hotels in Worcester were not allowed to serve alcohol.

1909 after September 5

F. is present when Jung prepares for his lecture and draws squares on the blackboard that are supposed to represent Freudian complexes. F. stares at Jung's drawing and asks him what these skyscrapers are.

1909 September 6

F. moves into the house of Stanley Hall. The dinner conversation revolves around the phenomenon that brilliant students often marry "society girls" and ruin their careers. F. also mentions that homosexuality is on the rise in Vienna and that the authorities are therefore considering legalizing it.

1909 September 7–11

F. gives a lecture every day at Clark University.

1909 September 8

F. grants an interview to the journalist Adelbert Albrecht. It will appear in the *Boston Evening Transcript* on September 11.

1909 September 10

– F. receives an honorary doctorate of law.
– F. takes a long walk with William James.

1909 September 11

Adolf Meyer, a Swiss psychiatrist practicing in America, drives F., Jung and Ferenczi by car around the lake Quinsigamond.

1909 September 12

Drive from Worcester to Buffalo.

1909 September 13

Visit to Niagara Falls and a trip on the "Maid of the Mist" – for F., the highlight of the trip. On this occasion, F. steps onto Canadian soil.

1909 September 14

F., Jung and Ferenczi travel on the Pullman Express from Buffalo to Lake Placid.

1909 September 15

– Continue to James Putnam's campsite at Keene Valley at the foot of Giant Mountain; arrive around 14.30.
– In the afternoon, a hike in bad weather. After returning, Putnam's daughter Frances tries unsuccessfully to teach the men tetherball.
– At dinner, F. explains that he only came to America to see a porcupine. But so far, he has not succeeded in doing so.
– Evening party with musical performances by a young singer from Leipzig, accompanied by Putnam's sister Elizabeth on the piano, and German songs sung by Jung.
– F. learns a board game that he finds very funny. Presumably it is "Don'ts and Old Maids", a kind of humorous self-help guide on how a woman can best lose her virginity.

1909 September 16

Putnam's cousin Mary Lee and a friend offer to lead F. to a porcupine. After an arduous hike, they actually find one – but dead.

1909 September 17

F. has indigestion and rejects all suggestions for larger excursions. Instead, he and Putnam go for a walk in the camp and have extensive conversations.

1909 September 18

Departure from Putnam's camp to Albany. As a farewell gift, Putnam gives F. a metal porcupine.

1909 September 19
- Arrival in New York.
- F. buys gifts at Tiffany's.

1909 September 20
- F. visits his sister Anna.
- F. is with sister Anna, her family (except Eli, who is in Canada) and Rose Brill for tea in Central Park.
- F. gives his niece Hella Bernays, who had gained her admission to Radcliffe College at Harvard University, a business card from himself for William James – professor at Harvard University – with a recommendation for his niece.

1909 September 21
The steamer "Kaiser Wilhelm der Grosse" sets sail from New York.

1909 September 23
Passage of Newfoundland.

1909 September 24
The steamer gets caught in a storm with heavy seas.

1909 September 27
Arrival at Plymouth in the morning and Cherbourg in the early afternoon. Then sail through the Channel in calm seas and blue skies.

1909 September 29
Arrival in Bremen in the morning.

1909 September 30–October 2
Visits to Hamburg and Berlin
F. goes to Hamburg to visit his mother-in-law and then continues to Berlin.

1909 September 30
F. had himself photographed by Max Halberstadt, presumably without knowing that he was to become his son-in-law. Later, F. wrote about this visit: "Of course, I only gained a fleeting impression of you during a visit to your studio […]" (F. to Max Halberstadt, 7.7.1912).

1909 October 1
F. meets his brother Emanuel in Berlin, and they visit the family of F.'s sister Mitzi. F. also sees Karl Abraham and, together with Sándor Ferenczi, visits the fortune teller Elisabeth Seidler at Katzlerstr. 10 in Schöneberg. She had already predicted a war ten years earlier than Helmuth von Moltke.

1909 October 2
F. arrives back in Vienna.

1909 after October 2
- F. offers lectures on "Neurosenlehre und Psychotherapie" ("Theory of Neuroses and Psychotherapy") in the winter semester (location: lecture hall of the Psychiatric Clinic, fee ten Kronen).
- Auguste Forel invites F. to join the International Society for Medical Psychology and Psychotherapy.

- Albert Hirst again begins an analysis with F. (until the spring of 1910), having already been briefly treated by F. in 1903.
- Viktor Dirsztay, writer, begins an analysis with F. It lasts until March 1920.

1909 October 3

F. corrects his "Bemerkungen über einen Fall von Zwangsneurose" ("Rat Man").

1909 October 10

F. acquires Gabriel Séailles writing *Léonard de Vinci*.

1909 October 12

- F. learns from the newspaper that his former patient Ernst Lanzer ("Rat Man") has become engaged.
- WPV meeting: welcome evening of the winter semester at the Hotel Residenz.

1909 October 17

"The riddle of Leonardo da Vinci's character has suddenly become clear" to F. Leonardo converted "at an early age [...] his sexuality into an urge for knowledge and from then on the inability to finish anything he undertook became a pattern to which he had to conform in all his ventures: He was sexually inactive or homosexual" (F. to Jung, 17.10.1909).

1909 October 20

WPV meeting: Edwin Hollerung speaks on the topic of "Experiencing and emotional Experience".

1909 October 21

Max Eitingon arrives in Vienna and stays for three weeks to let F. analyze him. This happens twice a week on a night walk.

1909 October 27

WPV meeting: Fritz Wittels speaks on the "Analysis of a hysterical state of confusion".

1909 November beginning

F. receives the September and October issue of the journal *Evangelische Freiheit* from Oskar Pfister, including an article by Friedrich Wilhelm Foerster on "Psychoanalyse und Seelsorge" ("Psychoanalysis and Pastoral Care"). F. calls the paper a "formidable attack, half demented, half clairvoyant, and dipped in holy venom" (F. to Ferenczi, 10.11.1909).

1909 November 3

WPV meeting: Isidor Sadger presents the first part of "A case of multiform perversion".

1909 November 10

WPV meeting: Isidor Sadger presents the second part of "A case of multiform perversion".

1909 November mid

- F.'s paper "Bemerkungen über einen Fall von Zwangsneurose" (Rat Man) is published. F. gives Emanuel Loewy an offprint with the dedication "Seinem I. Friend/ Em. Loewy/ d. Verf.".
- F. has a brief encounter with the writer and music critic Ernst Décsey. He considers him intelligent and unreliable.

1909 November 17
- Beginning of the correspondence between F. and James Putnam.
- WPV meeting: Josef Friedjung speaks on "What can pediatrics expect from psychoanalytic research?"

1909 November 18
An article by Salomon Klein on the 25th anniversary of the introduction of cocaine appears in the *Neue Freie Presse*, in which mainly Karl Koller is credited with this achievement, but reference is also made to F.

1909 November 22
F. acquires Wilhelm Bölsche's book *Das Liebesleben in der Natur. Eine Entwicklungsgeschichte der Liebe* (*The love life in nature: A developmental story of love*).

1909 November 24
WPV meeting: Viktor Tausk speaks on "Theory of knowledge and psychoanalysis".

1909 November 30
F. is in Budapest for a consultation visit and also meets Sándor Ferenczi. On this occasion, Ferenczi gives him a sculpture of a porcupine – in memory of the dead porcupine they had seen two months earlier in the Adirondacks in America.

1909 December
- F. writes the preface to the second edition of the *Three Treatises on Sexual Theory.*
- Nikolai Osipov, a Russian follower of psychoanalysis, sends F. two offprints of his work.

1909 December beginning
F. receives the Dürerbund's Christmas catalog; in it, his writings are discussed in detail and recommended.

1909 December 1
WPV meeting: F. speaks about "Eine Phantasie des Leonardo da Vinci" ("A fantasy of Leonardo da Vinci").

1909 December 3
August Forel sends F. his book *Gehirn und Seele* with the dedication "Herrn Prof S. Freud/ Hochachtungsvoll/d. Verf.".

1909 after December 14
F. gives Emanuel Loewy an offprint of his writing "Bemerkungen über einen Fall von Zwangsneurose" with the dedication: "Seinem l. Freunde Em. Loewy/d. Verf.".

1909 December 15
WPV meeting: Wilhelm Stekel presents a case of "traumatic neurosis", and Carl Furtmüller speaks on "Education or Fatalism?"

1909 December 21
- Birth of F.'s nephew Harry, son of brother Alexander.
- F. receives the American translation of his first lecture from Worcester.

1909 December 22
– Session of the WPV: reviews and case reports
– F. gives Oskar Rie a copy of the third edition of Psychopathology of Everyday Life.

1909 December 25
F. gives Alfred Rie a copy of the third edition of his book *Zur Psychopathologie des Alltagslebens* with the dedication "Dr. Alfred Rie/in alter Freundschaft/25 Dec. 09 d. Verf.".

1910

F. obtains – after Cornelia van Mastrigt has drawn his attention to it – Anatole Frances's novel *Le Mannequin* and reads it in one night.

Books received:

- Abraham Brill gives F. the American translation of the Three *Treatises on Sexual Theory* with the dedication "With best wishes and regards from the Translator".
- Havelock Ellis gives F. the first volume of the third edition of his *Studies in the psychology of sex* with the dedication "To Professor Freud With the Author's best regards".
- Sándor Ferenczi gives F. his book *Lélekelemzés* (*Soul Analysis*) to which F. had written a preface with the dedication "Der dankbare Interpret dem Autor, Herrn Prof. Freud".
- Isidor Sadger gives F. his book *Heinrich von Kleist* with the dedication "Prof. Freud sein dankbarer Schüler".
- Hanns Sachs gives F. his translation of Rudyard Kipling's book *Barrack-Room Ballads (Soldaten-Lieder und andere Gedichte)* with the dedication "Herrn Professor Sigmund Freud in Verehrung und Dankbarkeit Hanns Sachs".

1910 beginning
F. writes on the study Eine Kindheitserinnerung des Leonardo da Vinci.

1910 January 5
WPV meeting: Isidor Sadger presents the third part of "A case of multiform perversion", and Otto Rank presents a dream that interprets itself.

1910 January 11
F. suffers from severe writer's cramp.

1910 January 12
WPV meeting: Fritz Wittels speaks about Karl Kraus under the title "The 'Fackel' Neurosis".

1910 before January 13
Alfred Knapp, a pharmacist from Bern and secretary of the "International Order for Ethics and Culture", visits F., who considers joining the Order, presumably also because Auguste Forel was the spiritus rector.

1910 January 15
Ludwig Binswanger arrives in Vienna and takes part in F.'s Saturday seminar. The subject is Shakespeare's "Hamlet". He stays until January 26.

1910 January mid
F. asks Alfred Adler to present thoughts on "Psychoanalysis and Worldview" at the Nuremberg Congress. The central question should be whether psychoanalysis is compatible with every worldview.

1910 January 16
Ludwig Binswanger and his wife are at Freud's for dinner. "He is a good sort, correct and even intelligent, but he lacks the bit of afflatus I need to lift me up, and his wife, or rather their relationship, is not an unmingled pleasure" (F. to Jung, 2.2.1910).

1910 January 19
WPV meeting: Wilhelm Stekel speaks about "A Contribution to the Psychology of Doubt". Ludwig Binswanger takes part as a guest.

1910 January 22
Ludwig Binswanger takes part in F.'s Saturday seminar. F. talks about Otto Rank's book *"On the Myth of the Birth of the Hero"*.

1910 January 23
Ludwig Binswanger and his wife are visiting Freud's from noon until the evening.

1910 January 26
WPV meeting: Eduard Hitschmann presents "Clinical Reports Bearing on Obsessional Neurosis".

1910 January 30
Sándor Ferenczi visits F.

1910 January end
Sergei Pankejeff (the "Wolf Man") begins an analysis with F. on the recommendation of Leonid Drosnes from Odessa, who also accompanied him to Vienna. It lasts until 1914 July and from 1919 November to 1920 March.

1910 February
F. is writing his Leonardo thesis and has writer's cramp, but it is slowly improving.

1910 February 9
– Ferenczi sends F. Roman clay vessels, an arrowhead, a string of glass beads and a bronze key, which he had bought from an illegal excavator from Duna Pentele (now Dunaújváros) for 20 Kronen.
– WPV meeting: reviews and clinical communications.

1910 February 10
Max Eitingon gives F. Dostoevsky's *Sämtliche Werke (Complete Works)* with the dedication "Herr Prof. Freud in Dankbarkeit M. Eitingon".

1910 February 12
F. receives the manuscript of a study in the psychology of religion entitled "Bekenntnisse der schönen Seele" ("Confessions of the Beautiful Soul") from Franz Riklin, but finds it colorless and boring.

1910 February 13
F. transfers 200 Kronen to Ferenczi[29] so that he can buy more antiquities for him from the treasure digger in Duna Pentele. F. is particularly interested in glass, rings and statuettes.

1910 February 16
– Ferenczi buys five clay lamps and a small bronze vessel for F. from the treasure digger from Duna Pentele.
– WPV meeting: David Oppenheim speaks on "Fire as a sexual symbol".

1910 February 23
WPV meeting: Alfred Adler speaks on the subject of "Psychic Hermaphroditism".

1910 March
Founding of the local psychoanalytical group in Berlin; Karl Abraham becomes a chairman.

1910 March beginning
- F. writes "in a fit of writing mania" on his Leonardo study (F. to Binswanger, 3.3.1910).
- F. acquires antiques of excellent quality in Vienna and lets Ferenczi know that the latter's treasure digger in Duna Pentele will have trouble reaching this standard.

1910 March 2
WPV meeting: Rudolf Reitler speaks on the topic "Developmental History of Neurosis".

1910 March 9
- WPV meeting: Paul Federn speaks on "The infantile preconditions of masochism".
- F.'s daughter Mathilde has to undergo an operation because of severe pain following an accidental appendectomy five years ago. Afterward, however, she has a high fever for almost two weeks.

1910 March 16
WPV meeting: reviews and clinical communications.

1910 March 23
WPV meeting: Eduard Hitschmann speaks on the "Casuistry of Obsessive-Compulsive Neurosis".

1910 March 27
Sándor Ferenczi comes to Vienna and spends Easter Monday with Freud's.

1910 Spring
- Fritz Wittels gives F. the manuscript of his planned book *Ezechiel der Zugereiste*, with which he wants to take revenge on Karl Kraus after his break with him. F. tries in vain to talk him out of publishing it. Karl Kraus tries to take legal action against the publication and, through a lawyer, also demands that F. intervene with Wittels against the publication. F. was "very uncomfortable with the 'scandal' [...] threatened by Kraus" (F. to Wittels, 24.12.1923).
- F.'s lectures on the occasion of the 20th anniversary of Clark University in Worcester in 1909 September appear under the title *On Psychoanalysis.*

1910 March 28–April 3
II. International Psychoanalytical Congress in Nuremberg

The venue for the Congress is the Grand Hotel. The Congress is held at the Grand Hotel.

1910 March 28

F. and Sándor Ferenczi leave for Nuremberg by sleeping car at 8.30 pm.

1910 March 29

F. visits the Nuremberg cemetery.

1910 March 30

- F. gives a lecture on "Die zukünftigen Chancen der psychoanalytischen Therapie".

- Foundation of the International Psychoanalytical Association (IPA); Carl Gustav Jung becomes President, and Franz Riklin, Secretary. The Vienna Group protests against the appointment of Swiss as President and Secretary of the IPA. First disagreements between Carl Gustav Jung and F.
- Founding of the *Zentralblatt für Psychoanalyse*; edited by Wilhelm Stekel and Alfred Adler.
- F. has the feeling: "The infancy of our movement has ended with the Nuremberg Reichstag" (F. to Ferenczi, 3.4.1910).

1910 March 31

In the afternoon, informal meeting.

1910 April 1

F. and Carl Gustav Jung take a trip to Rothenburg o. d. Tauber.

1910 April 2

F. travels from Nuremberg to Vienna together with Maximilian Steiner.

1910 April 3

Arrival in Vienna.

1910 April 6
WPV meeting: Epilogue to the Nuremberg Congress. F. announces his resignation as the chairman of the WPV and proposes Alfred Adler as the new chairman.

1910 April 12
Gustavo Modena, the translator of the *Three Treatises on Sexual Theory*, visits F.

1910 April 13
WPV meeting: reorganization of the Society; Alfred Adler is elected as chairman, Wilhelm Stekel as his deputy, Maximilian Steiner as treasurer, Eduard Hitschmann as librarian, Otto Rank as Secretary and Paul Federn as Auditor.

1910 April mid
As F.'s waiting room is now too small for the number of WPV members, the meetings are from now on held in the rooms of the Doktorenkollegium at Rothenturmstr. 19

1910 April 19
Carl Gustav Jung visits F. in Vienna.

1910 April 20
WPV meeting: David Oppenheim gives a report on Abraham Baer's book *Der Selbstmord im kindlichen Lebensalter (Suicide in Childhood)*, followed by a discussion on suicide in general.

1910 April 22
F. receives the American translation of his 1909 lectures at Clark University in Worcester.

1910 April 27
WPV meeting: discussion on issues of the WPV and continuation of discussion on suicide.

1910 April end
F.'s writing *A Childhood Memoir of Leonardo da Vinci is* published (1500 copies).

1910 May 4
WPV meeting: Josef Friedjung lectures on Wilhelm Strohmeyer's book *Vorlesungen über die Psychopathologie des* Kindesalters (Lectures on the Psychotherapy of Childhood).

1910 May 11
WPV meeting: Isidor Sadger speaks about "Bronchial asthma a Sexual Neurosis?"

1910 May 15
Magnus Hirschfeld sends F. his book "*Die Transvestiten. Eine Untersuchung über den erotischen Verkleidungstrieb mit umfangreichem casuistischen und historischen Material*" with the dedication "Herrn Prof. Dr. S. Freud, dem grossen Mehrer sexualpsychologischer Erkenntniss, verehrungsvoll vom Verfasser".

1910 May 15–16
F. visits Martha and daughter Sophie (or daughter Mathilde) in Karlsbad.

1910 May 18
WPV meeting: Wilhelm Stekel speaks "On the Feeling of Strangeness in Dream and in Life".

1910 May 20
F. orders Anatole France's book *Le livre de mon ami*.

1910 May 24
F. writes a prescription for a contraceptive ointment for Albert Hirst's girlfriend.

1910 May 25
WPV meeting: discussion on the harmfulness of masturbation.

1910 May 28
The psychiatrist Adolf Friedländer, director and owner of a private clinic for nervous patients in Hohe Mark near Frankfurt am Main, who had treated Sergei Pankejeff at the end of 1908, visits F. and stays until 1 am; F. believes that he is a "liar, a scoundrel, and an ignoramus" (F. to Abraham, 5.6.1910).

1910 May end
F.'s sister Anna is in Vienna for a short visit with her daughter Lucie.

1910 June
Foundation of the local psychoanalytical group in Zurich; Ludwig Binswanger becomes a chairman.

1910 June beginning
F. begins twice-weekly "conversations" with Kurt Redlich, son of Gustav Redlich and well-known Viennese intellectual, in order to be able to decide later whether to begin an analysis with him.

1910 June 1
WPV meeting: continuation of the discussion on the harmfulness of masturbation.

1910 June 2
F. reminds Franz Deuticke to increase his fee in view of the increasing number of copies of his books. The next day, F. receives the first amended contract for episodes 1 and 2 of the *collection of small writings on neurosis*.

1910 June 4
Because of the intense heat, F. holds his lecture in the Sensengasse city park and on the upper deck of a horse-drawn omnibus.

1910 June 3
F. updates his publishing contract with Deuticke for the publication of the *collection of small writings on neurosis* and concludes new contracts for the publication of the second edition of the *Three Treatises on Sexual Theory* and the Five Lectures on *Psychoanalysis.* The editions of the two books amount to 1000 and 1500 copies, respectively.

1910 June 4
Nikolai Osipov visits F.

1910 June 5
F.'s wife Martha and his daughter Sophie return from the spa in Karlsbad.

1910 June 8
WPV meeting: conclusion of the discussion on the harmfulness of masturbation.

1910 June 9
F. concludes a contract with the publisher Franz Deuticke for the publication of the third edition of *Traumdeutung*. The edition amounts to 1000 copies.

1910 June 15
WPV meeting: Isidor Sadger speaks "On Urethral Erotism".

1910 June mid
Abraham Brill comes to Vienna and stays until July 4.

1910 June 19
Abraham Brill and Sándor Ferenczi, who has come to Vienna for a day, spend Sunday with F.

1910 after June 19
F. suffers from "a recurrence of the intestinal trouble I picked up in America" (F. to Jung, 19.6.1910) and seeks treatment for it.

1910 Summer
– F.'s Leonardo study appears.
– F. receives from Wilhelm Betz the first part of his book *Vorstellung und Einstellung (Imagination and Attitude)* on "Wiedererkennen" ("Recognition").

1910 before June 26
Alfred Adler sends F. the draft of his preface to the volume *Über den Selbstmord, insbesondere den Schüler-Selbstmord*, which publishes WPV discussion papers on the subject. F. has virtually nothing to correct.

1910 July beginning
Abraham Brill arrives in Vienna.

1910 July 15–August 31
Summer trip and stay in Holland

F. travels to Holland with his two youngest sons Oliver and Ernst. They stay in The Hague at the Hotel Wittebrug, and F. has the *Wiener Zeitung* sent there. F. wrote about his stay in

The Hague: "We usually go to a nearby town in the morning – we have got to know Rotter-dam, Delft, Haarlem in this way […] – come back for the first or possibly second big meal, bathe after dinner and play cards in the evening" (F. to Mathilde, 24.7.1910).

1910 July 15

F. and his sons travel from Vienna to Frankfurt.

1910 July 16

- F. visits Elfriede Hirschfeld in her flat in Frankfurt in the Bockenheimer Anlagen.
- In the evening, continue to The Hague.

1910 July 17

- Arrival in The Hague at 7.00 am.
- In the morning, city walk with Antje van Mastrigt and visit to the Mauritshuis with its collection of paintings (including Rembrandt's "Anatomy of Nicolaas Tulp", paintings by van Dyck, Rubens and Holbein the Younger).
- In the afternoon, F. meets the Dutch doctor Jan Rudolf de Bruine-Groeneveldt, through whom F. gets to know his later student and follower Jan van Emden.

1910 July 22

- In the morning, visit Delft.
- In the afternoon, bathing in the North Sea, and F. lets his sons ride on the beach.

1910 July 23

In the evening, visit Haarlem.

1910 July 25

F.'s brother Alexander arrives in The Hague in the morning from Brussels.

1910 August 1

F. receives Minna and Martha in Leiden, and they drive from there to Noordwijk. The whole family stays at the Hotel Noordzee. There, F. reads John Motley's *Rise of the Dutch Republic, among other books.*

1910 August 5

F. visits an agent of Norddeutscher Lloyd in Leiden to find out about the possibilities of traveling by ship from Holland to Italy. He orders two cabins for himself and Ferenczi from Antwerp to Genoa.

1910 August 11

Ernest Jones comes to Noordwijk for just under three days. He recommends Karl Pearson's *The Grammar of Science to* F. F. later gets the third edition and adds numerous annotations.

1910 after August 11

Antje van Mastrigt visits F.

1910 August 16

F. changes the original plan to travel to Sicily by ship and suggests to Ferenczi to travel to Italy by train.

1910 August 18

F. visits the Leiden Museum

1910 August 23
- F. travels to Leiden at the invitation of Jan Rudolf de Bruine-Groeneveldt; there, he meets Jan van Emden for the first time.
- F. meets Gustav Mahler in Leiden and, during a long walk, analyzes the "love conditions" ("Mary complex", "mother bond") of the composer, who had contacted F. because of problems with his wife Alma. Later, F. said that thanks to this analysis Gustav Mahler's Tenth Symphony had been better than his Ninth. After the walk, they both go to a restaurant for dinner.

1910 August 25
F. learns of the death of Leopold Ozer, who had died on August 22 and whom he had held in high esteem as a university teacher.

1910 August 28
Sándor Ferenczi comes to Leiden and Noordwijk, respectively.

1910 August 31
Franz Deuticke writes to F. informing him about the state of publication of the second edition of the first volume of the *Sammlung kleiner Schriften zur Neurosenlehre*.

1910 August 31
Departure from Noordwijk.

1910 August 31–September 26
Journey with Sándor Ferenczi to Sicily and Rome
- During this trip, F. worked on his writing about the case Daniel Paul Schreber. Schreber had published *Denkwürdigkeiten eines Nervenkranken* in 1903, which F. had been dealing with since the summer and on which he then published his "Psychoanalytische Bemerkungen über einen autobiographisch beschriebenen Fall von Paranoia (Dementia paranoides)".
- He buys from various antique dealers, including a small Mercury and a Tanagra figure.

1910 August 31
Arrival in Paris. Overnight stay at the Hotel du Louvre.

1910 September 1
- Visit to the Louver. F. shows Sándor Ferenczi Leonardo da Vinci's "Saint Anne of the Blessed Virgin Mary".
- Lunch at the "Café de Paris".
- Departure from Paris in the evening.

1910 September 2–3
Drive via Milan and Genoa to Florence. Overnight stay at the Grand Hotel.

1910 September 4
In the afternoon, excursion to Fiesole.

1910 September 5
- F. shows Ferenczi the medallion with the face of the monk Girolamo Savonarola in the pavement of the Piazza Signoria at the place where he was burned.
- F. buys gloves and a tie.

– Departure for Rome at 1.20 pm, arrival in the early evening. F. continues to work on his paper on the case of Daniel Paul Schreber.

1910 September 6

In the morning, visit of the Roman Forum.

1910 September 7

F. visits the antique dealers Adriano d' Innocenti and Knill in Via del Babuino. F. buys nail scissors, toothpicks, ammonia, a tie with case, a fountain pen holder and soap for the rest of his journey.

1910 September 8

– 10.45 am departure for Naples, arrival 3.00 pm.
– In the evening with the "Siracusa" crossing to Palermo.

1910 September 9

– F. and Ferenczi arrive in Palermo in the morning and stay for five days (Hotel de FranceThis short week "was the most beautiful [Freud] had ever spent traveling" (F. to Brill, 17.10.1910).
– Visit the cathedral with the sarcophagus of Friedrich II and the Norman Palace, a fortress dating from the Saracen period and remodeled by the Normans.

1910 September 10

– In the morning visit of the Archaeological Museum.
– In the afternoon, visit the cathedral in Monreale, the most important monument of Norman art in Sicily.

1910 September 11

Visit to the Botanical Garden and the Villa Giulia Park.

1910 September 12

F. and Ferenczi visit some "ruins" in Palermo.

1910 September 13

Visit to the temple of Segesta, one of the best preserved in Sicily; continue via Calatafimi to Castelvetrano (overnight stay there).

1910 September 14

Visit to the Minerva Temple in Selinunte; then drive back to Palermo.

1910 September 15

F. seeks out the antique dealer Guiseppe de Ciccio in Palermo, who specialized in coins.

1910 September 16

Drive from Palermo to Girgenti (Agrigento) and visit the temple there.

1910 September 17

– Drive from Girgenti via Canicatti to Caltanissetta. F. buys sulfur for his son-in-law Robert Hollitscher at the sulfur mines there.
– Arrival in Syracuse in the evening; overnight stay at the Hotel des Etrangeres. F. visits the monument of Archimedes near the Arethusa spring.

1910 September 20

Drive from Syracuse back to Palermo.

1910 September 21

At 7.30 pm departure by boat to Naples.

1910 September 22
Arrival in Naples at 6.45 and onward journey to Rome at 7.45.

1910 September 24

Departure from Rome at 11.45 pm.

1910 September 26

F. arrives back in Vienna.

1910 after September 26
- First meeting between F. and Theodor Reik. The conversation is about Reik's dissertation on Flaubert and his *Versuchung des heiligen Antonius (Temptation of St. Anthony)*, among other things. F. supports Reik, who had virtually no financial means, with 200 marks a month for at least two years.
- Hanns Sachs visits F. for the first time.

1910 September end
- F. entrusts Alfred Adler and Wilhelm Stekel with the direction of the *Zentralblatt für Psychoanalyse* and Adler with the presidency of the association.
- F. asks his Dresden student Arnold Stegmann to find out something about Daniel Paul Schreber and receives interesting information.

1910 Autumn
Alfred Adler tells F. that he has problems with psychoanalysis and no longer wants to take part in events. F. persuades him not to withdraw his support for the recognition of psychoanalysis.

1910 October
- In the winter semester, F. offers lectures "Zur Elementare[n] Einführung in die Psychoanalyse" ("Elementary Introduction to Psychoanalysis"): lecture hall of the Psychiatric Clinic, fee ten Kronen. A little later, he learns that the clinic in whose lecture hall he gives his lectures is being moved elsewhere.
- F.'s 17-year-old daughter Sophie starts working for him as a "secretary" and sends out the mail, among other things.
- Sophie Freud, the wife of F.'s brother Alexander, approaches F. because of menstrual problems. It is decided that Guido Holzknecht will treat her with X-rays. Later, F. also sends her to Alfred Adler for treatment.

1910 October 1
- Death of Rudolf Chrobak. F. had held the Viennese gynecologist in high esteem, also because he had received a lot of support from him in his first years of practice.
- F.'s son Martin signed up for military service as a one-year volunteer. His father was firmly against joining the cavalry, Martin hated the infantry and so he joined the artillery.

1910 October 1–2
F. has dream of "Savonarola".

1910 October 2–3
F. has dream of "Prof. Oser" who had died on August 22.

1910 October 3
Moritz Rappaport begins an analysis with F. (until 1913 June and 1918 January). He had edited Otto Weininger's writing *Über die letzten Dinge* and provided it with a preface.

1910 October 4
– Richard Nepallek, lawyer, begins an analysis with F. (until 1913 May).
– Horaz Mallink, son of the banker Leon Mallink (Mandl), begins an analysis with F. (until 1919 July).

1910 October 5
WPV meeting: Isidor Sadger speaks "On the psychology of the only and the favorite child" (co-presenter: Josef Friedjung). The discussion turns to the question of whether a letter by Josef Breuer to David Oppenheim (pseudonym: Unus Multorum) should be published in the *Jahrbuch für psychoanalytische und psychopathologische Forschungen*. F. expresses skepticism about this – but only in a letter to Alfred Adler the next day.

1910 October 7
Maggie Haller begins a new analysis with F. after 1901 (until 1911 July).

1910 October 10
Mr. Holmos and his deaf-mute wife visit F., presumably on Ferenczi's recommendation; F. sends them both back to Budapest.

1910 October 10–11
F. has dream of Ernst Ludwig's chemistry laboratory.

1910 October 11
Mary Czilchert, daughter of Robert Czilchert, member of the leadership of the evangelical church community in Vienna, begins an analysis with F. (until 1916 November).

1910 October 12
– WPV meeting: reports and motions; discussion on the psychology of the only and favorite child.
– At the constituent general assembly of the WPV, Alfred Adler is elected chairman and F. is appointed scientific chairman, alternating in the chair with the chairman and vice-chairman.

1910 October 19
Session of the WPV: Alfred Adler gives "A Small Contribution to the Subject of Hysterical Lying".

1910 approx. October 22
Emanuel Loewy is on a "nightly" visit to F. and tells him about his contacts with the Italian royal couple.

1910 October 24
The first issue of the *Zentralblatt für Psychoanalyse is* published.

1910 October 26
WPV meeting: F. speaks "Über die zwei Prinzipien des psychischen Geschehens".

1910 October 27
Death of F.'s mother-in-law Emmeline Bernays; she dies of cancer. Martha and Minna travel to Hamburg for their mother's funeral.

1910 November 2
WPV meeting: Wilhelm Stekel speaks on the topic of "The Choice of a Profession and Neurosis".

1910 November 3
Alfred Adler and Otto Rank are at F.'s for dinner.

1910 November 5
Martha and Minna return from their mother's funeral in Hamburg.

1910 November 9
WPV meeting: discussion on Wilhelm Stekel's lecture on "The Choice of a Profession and Neurosis" of November 2.

1910 November 14
Petronella van der Linden begins an analysis with F. It lasts until the beginning of 1911 June. She is accompanied by Cornelia van Mastrigt and her daughter Antje van Mastrigt, later the wife of Johan van Ophuijsen. The first part of the treatment takes place at the Cottage Sanatorium. Later, the patient accompanied by Antje van Mastrigt comes daily to the Berggasse.

1910 November 16
WPV meeting: reviews and brief clinical and other communications, including Maximilian Steiner speaking "On the connection between prostate disease and neurosis" and David Oppenheim on "Folkloristic material on dream symbolism".

1910 November 22
Elsa Burchardt, wife of the Berlin-born banker Martin Burchardt, begins an analysis with F. (until 1918 December).

1910 November 23
WPV meeting: reviews, clinical reports and other communications, including Alfred Adler's "Contribution to Organ Inferiority".

1910 November 30
WPV meeting: reviews and brief clinical and other communications, including Carl Furtmüller speaking on "An example of poetically used symbolism" and Josef Friedjung on "On the prognosis of intensive masturbation".

1910 December 6
Max Eitingon arrives in Vienna, where he stops for a few days on his way back from Palestine and Syria.

1910 December 7
WPV meeting: reviews and brief clinical and other communications. Alfred von Winterstein speaks on Lichtenberg, and Hanns Sachs reviews Leo Spitzer's book on "Wortbildung als stilistisches Mittel" ("Word formation as a stylistic means") and Franz Grüner's poem "Das Riesenspielzeug" ("The Giant Toy").

1910 December 14

WPV meeting: reviews and brief clinical and other communications, including Margarete Hilferding speaking on a "Dream of Rosegger", Rudolf Reitler on "Sexual Fantasy and its Relationship to Suicide Symbolism" and Eduard Hitschmann on "On a Case of Melancholy".

1910 December 16

– F. finishes writing his "Psychoanalytischen Bemerkungen über einen autobiographisch beschriebenen Fall von Paranoia (Dementia Paranoides)".

– F. has "now overcome Fliess, which you were so curious about. Adler is a little Fliess *redivivus* […]" (F. to Ferenczi, 16.12.1910).

– Jan Rudolf de Bruine-Groeneveldt, Dutch doctor, begins an analysis with F. (until 1914 May).

1910 December 17

F. receives from Joseph Bergmann, the publisher of the *Zentralblatt für Psychoanalyse,* a paper by Wilhelm Stekel for correction, which he did not know would be included in the next issue. In his function as co-editor, F. asked Alfred Adler, who had taken over the editorship of the issue, to inform Stekel of his objection and to call an extraordinary editorial meeting.

1910 December 21

WPV meeting: Isidor Sadger speaks "On sexual-symbolic headaches".

1910 December 25

F. gives Alfred Rie a copy of the third edition of *Psychopathology of Everyday Life* with the dedication "Dr. Alfred Rie/in alter Freundschaft /d. Verf.".

1910 December 24–28
Short trip to Munich for a meeting with Bleuler and Jung
1910 December 24

F. takes the night train to Munich.

1910 December 25

– F. arrives in Munich at 6.00 and meets Eugen Bleuler at the Parkhotel in Munich, where he also spends the night.

– F. buys Japanese toad made of green nephrite.

1910 December 26

F. meets Carl Gustav Jung in the evening, who has arrived in Munich late in the afternoon after Bleuler's departure. Jung gives F. the first part of the manuscript of his book *Wandlungen und Symbole der Libido* to read. It appears in 1911 September in the *Jahrbuch für psychoanalytische und psychopathologische Forschungen.*

1910 December 27

F. takes the night train back to Vienna.

1910 December 28

F. arrives in Vienna in the morning.

1911

- F. begins to deal with the subject of "Totem and Taboo".
- F. explains to the 16-year-old visually impaired aspiring pianist Paul Emerich, in response to his questions about onanism, that it is not harmful. In return, Emerich explains Braille to him, which F. is very interested in.
- Valentin Rosenfeld asked F. if he should marry his cousin Eva Rosenfeld. F. said there was no reason not to marry her.
- F. gives Wilhelm Stekel a copy of the second edition of his book *Über den Traum* with the dedication "Herrn Dr. W. Stekel/freundschaftlich /d. Verf.".

Books received:

- Karl Abraham gives F. his book on *Giovanni Segantini* with the dedication: "Herrn Prof. S. Freud mit herzlichen Grüssen d. Verf.".
- Eugen Bleuler gives F. his book *Die Psychanalyse Freuds. Verteidigung und kritische Bemerkungen* with the dedication "From the Author".
- Eduard Hitschmann gives F. his book *Freud's Neurosenlehre* with the dedication "Herrn Prof. Freud in dankbarer Verehrung Dr Hitschmann".
- Ludwig Jekels gives F. the Polish translation of the five lectures *On Psychoanalysis, which* he has arranged, with the dedication "In tiefer Dankbarkeit und Verehrung Der Übersetzer".
- Max Sauerlandt gives F. his book *Michelangelo*.
- Emanuel Loewy gives F. his book *Typenwanderung II* with the dedication "Mit herzlichsten Grüssen d. Vf".
- Ignaz Zollschan gives F. his book *Das Rassenproblem* with the dedication "Herrn Prof. Dr S. Freud in Verehrung Dr Zollschan".

1911 January
- F. suffers gas poisoning from his desk lamp.
- F. becomes a member of the Society for Psychical Research.

1911 January beginning
The Swedish psychiatrist Poul Bjerre is in Vienna for a week to learn more about psychoanalysis.

1911 January 4
WPV meeting: Alfred Adler speaks on "Some Problems of Psychoanalysis". Poul Bjerre attends the meeting as a guest.

1911 January 8
F.'s son Martin suffers a fractured thigh while skiing on the Schneeberg. It took five hours before he could be rescued and he is only in hospital two and a half days after the accident. The surgeon Julius Schnitzler, the brother of the doctor and writer Arthur Schnitzler, takes over the further treatment. As a token of gratitude, F. has a medal made for Schnitzler by Karl Schwerdtner featuring a skier.

1911 January 11
WPV meeting: Margarete Hilferding speaks on "On the Basis of Mother Love".

1911 January 14–15
Sándor Ferenczi visits F., among other things, to introduce a patient.

1911 January 17
Poul Bjerre gives a lecture on "Freud's psychoanalytical method" to the Association of Swedish Doctors, in which he reports on his visit to Vienna.

1911 January 18
WPV meeting: Herbert Silberer speaks on "Magic and other topics".

1911 January 21
F. receives Theodor Kluge's paper "Der Mithrakult: seine Anfänge, Entwicklungsgeschichte und seine Denkmäler" ("The cult of Mithra: its beginnings, history of development and its monuments").

1911 January 25
WPV meeting: Alfred von Winterstein speaks on "On the Feeling of Guilt".

1911 January 29
Ferenczi visits F. again.

1911 January end
F. suspected he had end-stage arteriosclerosis. But a thorough diagnosis revealed chronic luminous gas poisoning, the cause of which was a defective hose to his desk lamp.

1911 January 31
Jung recommends F. to his fellow students the surgeon Achilles Müller, who is interested in psychoanalysis.

1911 February
- F. gives a lecture to B'nai B'rith on the "Hamlet problem".
- F. receives Hermann Swoboda's book *Otto Weiningers Tod* and comments positively on it to Wilhelm Stekel.
- Founding of the American Psychoanalytic Association; James Putnam becomes a chairman.

1911 February beginning
Otto Rank helps F. prepare the third edition of *Traumdeutung*.

1911 February 1
WPV meeting: Alfred Adler speaks on "The Masculine Protest as the Central Problem of Neurosis".

1911 February 5
Gisella Pálos, Ferenczi's mistress and later wife, visits F.

1911 February 8
WPV meeting: continuation of the discussion on Adler's talk "The Masculine Protest as the Central Problem of Neurosis". F. criticizes Adler's deviations for two hours and demands that everyone present take a stand. F. himself describes his speech "against Adler's heresies" as "moderate but decisive" (F. and Ferenczi, 8.2.1911).

1911 February 13
- F. has no objections to Karl Abraham visiting Wilhelm Fliess.

- Felix Dörmann, Austrian writer, begins an analysis with F. (until March).
- Kurt Redlich begins an analysis with F. (until 1919 May).

1911 February 14
F. invites Achilles Müller to his home and suggests that he attend a WPV meeting as a guest on February 22.

1911 February 15
WPV meeting: Hanns Sachs speaks on "On the applicability of psychoanalysis to poetic works".

1911 February mid
- F. receives an invitation from the Society for Psychical Research to stand as a corresponding member.
- F. is working on the third edition of the *Interpretation of Dreams*.

1911 February 22
WPV meeting: conclusion of the discussion on Adler's lecture "The Masculine Protest as the Central Problem of Neurosis". Board meeting: Alfred Adler and Wilhelm Stekel resign as chairman and deputy chairman, respectively.

1911 March 1
WPV meeting: F. speaks on "Further contributions to the Theory of Dreams". Extraordinary General Assembly: following the resignation of Alfred Adler as WPV Chairman and his deputy Wilhelm Stekel, F. is elected Chairman of the Association by acclamation.

1911 March 4
Wilhelm Stekel gives F. his book *Die Sprache des Traumes* with the dedication "Herrn Prof. Sig. Freud in Dankbarkeit der Verfasser".

1911 March 5
William Sutherland, the most exposed supporter of psychoanalysis in India at the time, visits F. He had begun to translate the *Interpretation of Dreams into* English, but Abraham Brill had already been given the contract by F. and was well advanced with his work.

1911 March 8
- WPV meeting: Bernhard Dattner speaks on "Psychoanalytical Problems in Dostoevski's *Raskolnikov*".
- F. receives from Wilhelm Betz the second part of his paper "Vorstellung und Einstellung" on the subject of "Begriffe".

1911 March 10
Andrew Davidson, the secretary of the neurological-psychiatric section of the "Australasian Medical Congress" to be held in Sydney in 1911 September, subscribes to the *Yearbook of Psychoanalytical and Psychopathological Research* and asks F. for an introductory paper on psychoanalysis to be printed in the Congress report. F. agrees, seeing the publication as a "business advertisement". F. then writes the paper on "On Psycho-Analysis" and sends it off on March 13. It appears in the *Transactions of the Congress* in 1913.

1911 March before 12
- F. gives himself antiques on the occasion of the 25th anniversary of his practice.

- F. receives Roman earrings from Ferenczi, which he had purchased from the treasure digger in Duna Pentele for 40 Kronen.

1911 March 15
WPV meeting: Friedrich Kraus speaks on "The corset in custom and usage among peoples of the world".

1911 Spring
In Vienna, F. writes the preface to the third edition of The *Interpretation of Dreams and* begins work on *Totem and Taboo*.

1911 March 22
WPV meeting: reviews and brief clinical communications. Margarete Hilferding presents a case of "hysterical vomiting", Hanns Sachs reports a dream with the symbolism of the cravat, David Oppenheim reads loud two poetic passages (a) from Lenaus *Faust* and (b) from Dostojewskys novel *The Growing one,* and Isidor Sadger on "moon-madness and somnambulism" and on "masturbation fantasies".

1911 March 25
F.'s answer to the question of the weekly *Der Sturm* "Ist dafür Sorge zu tragen, dass jede Konzeptionsverhütung verboten wird?" ("Is it to be ensured that all conception prevention is banned?") is published. He is of the opinion, among other things, that "the prohibition of 'traffic in means of preventing conception' […] is an entirely purposeless measure" (SFG 12, p. 171).

1911 March 29
WPV meeting: reviews and brief clinical and other communications.

1911 April
F. acquires John and Alice Cruickshank's book *Christian Rome*.

1911 April beginning
- F.'s work on Daniel Paul Schreber appears under the title "Psychoanalytischen Bemerkungen über einen autobiographisch beschriebenen Fall von Paranoia (Dementia Paranoides)".
- Rank goes on a three-week trip to Greece, which F. finances for him in return for his help with the third edition of Traumdeutung. In a letter from Athens, Rank expresses his "heartfelt thanks [for] your great kindness […] to which I owe this experience" (Rank to F., 30.4.1911).
- Samuel Jankélévitch asks F. to translate the following works into French: Drei Abhandlungen zur Sexualtheorie, die Psychopathologie des Alltagslebens and Über Psychoanalyse.

1911 April 1
- F.'s son Oliver travels to London from his first saved money.
- A local psychoanalytical group is founded in Munich. Leonhard Seif becomes a chairman.

1911 April 5
WPV meeting: reviews and brief clinical and other communications.

1911 April 6
F. receives Ludwig Jekels's lecture on "The Healing of Psychoneuroses with the Help of the Psychoanalytical Method, with Casuistry". However, only the introduction is in German, and the lecture itself is in Polish.

1911 April 14–17
Short trip with Ferenczi to South Tyrol

F. is searching with Sándor Ferenczi for summer quarters on the Ritten near Bolzano or in the Val Sugana.

1911 April 14

F. leaves Vienna at 8.05 pm with the Südbahn.

1911 April 15

Ferenczi boards the train in Villach early in the morning, and both men arrive in Bolzano at 12:55 pm.

1911 April 16

Trip to the Ritten; F. particularly likes the Hotel Post in Klobenstein; five months later, he will celebrate his silver wedding anniversary there with his wife and family.

1911 April 17

Departure to Vienna in the evening.

1911 April 18

F. arrives in Vienna in the morning.

1911 April 19
– WPV meeting: Richard Wagner speaks about *Lanval*.
– F.'s wife Martha travels with daughter Sophie to Karlsbad for a spay stay.

1911 April 26
– Otto Rank returns "blissfully" from Greece.
– WPV meeting: discussion on Wilhelm Stekel's book *The Language of Dreams*.

1911 May
Dutch psychoanalysts Jan van Emden and August Stärcke visit F.

1911 May 2
Leonid Drosnes from Odessa visits F. He informs him about the foundation of a psychoanalytical group in Moscow planned for the autumn.

1911 May 3
WPV meeting: Isidor Sadger speaks on "On skin, mucous membrane and muscle eroticism".

1911 May after 5
F. attends a guest performance of Hugo von Hofmannsthal's *König Oedipus* at the Deutsches Theater Berlin, directed by Max Reinhardt.

1911 May 10
WPV session: Viktor Tausk presents "A Contribution to the Psychology of Masochism".

1911 May mid
F. receives Auguste Forel's book *Hypnotismus*.

1911 May 12
Emil Lorenz visits F. in the evening at his invitation.

1911 May 15
Jan van Emden begins an analysis with F.

1911 May 17
WPV meeting: reviews and brief clinical and other communications; Hanns Sachs speaks about the Stekel symbols, Eduard Hitschmann discusses an interesting statement by Goethe about Kleist, and F. points out dream depictions in a Hungarian joke sheet.

1911 May 21
Martha and Sophie return from Karlsbad.

1911 May 23
F. registers with Emil Freund, Gustav Mahler's lawyer, "a fee claim of 300 K[ronen]" for "a consultation of several hours in Leiden (Holland) in August 1910" (F. to Emil Freund, 23.5.1911).

1911 May 24
WPV meeting: reviews and brief clinical and other communications, including Isidor Sadger on "On the explanation of exhibitionism", Carl Furtmüller on "On a psychoanalytically interesting illness of a schoolgirl" and F. on the castration complex and on the "elucidation of a dream act".

1911 May 27
F. received an article by Jenö Hárnik, which had appeared in the journal *Jung-Ungarn* and was essentially based on a publication by Ferenczi. The paper showed F. that Ferenczi's work "is making an impression on the best forces in your homeland" (F. to Ferenczi, 28.5.1911).

1911 May 31
WPV meeting: papers and brief clinical communications, including Richard Wagner speaking on the Oedipus complex, Rudolf Reitler on sexual symbolism and F. on dream symbolism.

1911 May end
– F.'s sister Anna from New York visits him in Vienna.
– F. demands that Joseph Bergmann, the publisher of *the Jahrbuch für Psychoanalyse,* remove Alfred Adler from the editorial board.
– Otto Rank and Hanns Sachs propose to F. that a new journal be founded devoted to literary, mythological and philosophical applications of psychoanalysis. Originally, the journal was to be called *Eros-Psyche,* but it was later agreed on *Imago.*

1911 June 1
Start of the correspondence between F. and Hanns Sachs. At the WPV meeting the previous day, F. had raised the question of evidence for the connection between the words head-skull and pot-ware. Sachs sends F. some sources on this.

1911 June 2
Alfred Adler demands that F. tell him whether he demands his resignation from the editorial office of the *Zentralblatt* or whether this is a decision of the publisher Joseph Bergmann. He said that he would remain on the editorial board until F. gave him an answer.

1911 June 11
– F. insists on Adler deciding whether or not he wants to remain on the editorial board of the *Zentralblatt für Psychoanalyse* – but without answering Adler's question of June 2 directly.
– Ferenczi visits F.

1911 June 12
In a letter to F., Alfred Adler declares his resignation from the WPV and informs him that he has informed Joseph Bergmann, the publisher of the *Jahrbuch für Psychoanalyse, of his* decision to leave the reaction. About his resignation, Adler writes: "I was never actually a psychoanalyst and a follower of Freud; I only regarded him as a trampline to jump over his head" (Adler to Moshe Wulff, ca. 1912).

1911 before 26 June
The painter Rudolf Kriser approaches F. for treatment; however, F. advises him to see his family doctor.

1911 July 9–30
Spa stay in Karlovy Vary (partly with daughter Sophie)

F. is taking the cure for a digestive disorder in Karlsbad (Haus Kolumbus). Sophie leaves after a week, and Jan van Emden and his wife Alexandrina Petronella arrive. Emden continues his analysis begun in Vienna in Karlsbad, mostly on walks. F. walks so fast that Emden finds it difficult to follow, but still has to tell him his dreams and associations.

1911 before July 13

F. makes purchases in the agate shop of the Carl Wilhelm Kessler company, including an opal for his son Martin. F.'s family knows the shop and knows that he always leaves a lot of money there so that his daughter Anna writes to him: "Doesn't Kessler already know you very well? You are probably what they call a regular at the hotel. Mama wanted to write to him that he should not sell you anything more, but I am very much against that" (Anna to F. 19.7.1911).

1911 before July 16

F. and Sophie visit the Hans Heiling Rock in the Eger Valley west of Karlovy Vary. According to a Bohemian folk tale, Hans Heiling had asked the devil to turn the wedding party of a girl he was in love with, but married someone else, into stone.

1911 July 18

F. repeats the trip to Hans Heiling Rock with Emdens.

1911 at July 20

F. is irritable and disgruntled because of his complaints. The "cure in Karlsbad is not an unmingled pleasure. I have decided to endow a votive tablet if only I get rid of all the ailments I have acquired here" (F. to Jung, 21.7.1911).

1911 July 30

Journey from Karlovy Vary to Munich. There, visit the Nymphenburg People's Garden.

1911 July 31–September 15
Silver Wedding in Klobenstein in South Tyrol

1911 July 31

F. arrives in Klobenstein coming from Munich. He stays at the Hotel Post (Hofer). During this stay, he reads books on the history of religion, among other things.

1911 August beginning

- F. makes a kind of site plan of the immediate surroundings of the Hotel Post in Klobenstein.
- F. begins the writing of *Totem and Taboo*.

1911 August 20

Sándor Ferenczi arrives in Klobenstein.

1911 August 29

Death of F.'s brother Philipp in Manchester.

1911 September 11

Nikolai Ossipov gives F. the Czech translation of the *Three Treatises on Sexual Theory,* for which Ossipov had written the preface, with the dedication "Dem hochgeehrten Herrn Professor genialen S. Freud von N. Ossipov".

1911 September 14

Celebration of the silver wedding anniversary. In addition to the celebrating couple, the following are present: the children Mathilde, Martin, Oliver, Ernst, Sophie and Anna, also F.'s sister-in-law Minna.

1911 September 15

Departure from Klobenstein. They all travel together to Innsbruck, then F. continues alone to Zurich, and his family travels back to Vienna.

1911 September 16–19
Visit to Jung in Zurich

F. writes to Jung's wife Emma about this visit, saying that "the few days in your house are among the highlights of my life [...] and that your house on Lake Zurich is at the top of my fantasy list" (F. and Emma Jung, 2.11.1911). During the nights, F. suffers from toothache.

1911 September 16

F. arrives in Zurich in the morning from Klobenstein. There, James Putnam begins an analysis with F., which is probably limited to six hours.

1911 September 17

F. talks to Emma Jung about his marriage: it has long since been amortized; there is nothing left but dying. You raise the children, then they worry you all the more, but that is the only joy.

1911 September 18

Thaddeus Ames, who is with Jung in Analysis, meets F. in Jung's house. Also present is Beatrice Hinkle, an American feminist and Jung supporter.

1911 September 19

F. travels with the couple Jung and James Putnam from Zurich to Weimar.

1911 September 21–23
III. International Psychoanalytical Congress in Weimar

The Congress takes place in the "Hotel Zum Erbprinzen". Jung as President and Riklin as Central Secretary of the IPA are re-elected by acclamation. F. meets Lou Andreas-Salomé for the first time, who attends the Congress through the mediation of Poul Bjerre. Ernest Jones asks F. to take over the treatment of his mistress Loe Kann. James Putnam has three analytical sessions with Freud.

1911 September 21

Lectures by James Putnam, Eugen Bleuler, Isidor Sadger, Heinrich Körber, Otto Rank and Carl Gustav Jung.

1911 September 22

F. gives a lecture entitled "Nachtrag zur Analyse Schreber" ("Addendum to Schreber's analysis").

1911 September 23

Visit to the Schiller House in Weimar.

1911 September 24–28

Trip to Hamburg with Abraham Brill.

1911 September 29

F. arrives back in Vienna.

1911 after September 29

- The Viennese living lady Claire Wiener is treated by F. for a short time. She had been mistakenly declared dead in the summer.
- F. signs an appeal for the foundation of the "International Association for Maternity Protection and Sexual Reform".

1911 October

F. offers lectures on "Einzelne Kapitel aus der Psychoanalyse" ("Individual Chapters from Psychoanalysis") in the winter semester (until 1912 March) (location: lecture hall of the Psychiatric Clinic, Saturday 7–21 pm, fee ten Kronen).

1911 October beginning

The Freud family has a new family doctor.

1911 October 10

René Spitz, Hungarian developmental psychologist, starts an analysis with F. It lasts until December on Ferenczi's recommendation.

1911 October 11

WPV meeting: extraordinary meeting of the WPV in the clubhouse of the Café Arkaden: Carl Furtmüller gives a speech on freedom in defence of Adler. Afterward, F. "forced" (F. to Jung, 12.10.1911) six supporters of Alfred Adler to leave the WPV: Carl Furtmüller, Franz Grüner, Gustav Grüner, Margarete Hilferding, Paul Klemperer and David Oppenheim lose the vote. Alfred Adler, David Bach, Stefan Maday and Franz von Hye had already left.

1911 approx. October 12

Sabina Spielrein visits F., unexpectedly for him.

1911 October 16

Nikolai Ossipov gives F. the Russian translation of the five lectures *On Psychoanalysis,* which he has arranged, with the dedication "Dem hochgehrt genialen Autor/der Uebersetzer".

1911 October 18

WPV meeting: Victor Tausk speaks on "Problems Dealt with in and as a Result of Psychoanalysis". The meetings now take place provisionally at Café Korb (Brandstätte 9).

1911 October 24

F. issues a receipt for the fee received for the treatment of Gustav Mahler.

1911 October 25

WPV meeting: Ludwig Klages speaks on "On the Psychology of Handwriting".

1911 November 5
- Beginning of the correspondence between F. and his nephew Sam Freud.
- F. receives a book from James Putnam about his grandfather, the judge Samuel Putnam. Presumably it is Cyrus Bartol's A discourse on the life and character of Samuel Putnam, LL.D., A.A.S., late judge of the Supreme Judicial Court of Massachusetts.

1911 November 4
The Austrian actress Claire Wallentin-Metternich begins an analysis with F. It lasts until the end of December, and she is F.'s "most interesting patient" during this period (F. to Ferenczi, 30.11.1911).

1911 November 8
WPV meeting: Wilhelm Stekel and Josef Reinhold speak on "On the supposed timelessness of the unconscious".

1911 November 13
F. makes slow progress with his work on *Totem and Taboo.*

1911 November 14
The Austrian psychiatrist Egon Köhler, who lives in Switzerland, visits F.

1911 November 15
WPV meeting: Theodor Reik speaks on "On Death and Sexuality".

1911 November 19
Arnold Stegmann, forensic doctor and psychiatrist, begins an analysis with F. (until December mid).

1911 November 22
WPV meeting: Isidor Sadger speaks about masturbation.

1911 November 25
F. receives from Alfred von Winterstein his poems, which have just been published by Hugo Heller.

1911 November 28
Eugen Bleuler informs F. of his resignation from the Zurich local group.

1911 November 29
WPV session: Sabina Spielrein speaks on "On Transformation".

1911 November end
F. penalized René Spitz "by being deprived of three hours" because he "plays something the grand" (F. to Ferenczi, 30.11.1911).

1911 December beginning
Stefan Zweig gives F. his collection *Erstes Erlebnis (First Experience)*, in F.'s opinion "subtle and psychologically significant children's stories" (F. to Zweig, 7.12.1911).

1911 December 5
F. begins to make notes of "Ideen und Entdeckungen" ("Ideas and discoveries"). He continues these notes until 1914 January.

1911 December 6
WPV meeting: continuation of the discussion on masturbation. From now on the meetings take place in the meeting room of the Vienna Medical Doctors' College at Franz-Josefs-Kai 65.

1911 December 11
F. rejects a request from the Dürerbund for more active participation in the activities of the society.

1911 before December 13
- Ferenczi visits F.
- WPV meeting: Hanns Sachs speaks on "Feeling for nature".

1911 December 20
- Sándor Ferenczi sends F. his book Lelki problémák a pszichoanalizis megvilágitásában (Psychological Problems in the Light of Psychoanalysis) with the dedication "Seinem lieben Professor Freud von Dr Ferenczi".
- Sándor Ferenczi sends F. his Hungarian translation of the five lectures *On Psychoanalysis* with the dedication "Herr Professor Freud der ergebene Übersetzer".
- WPV meeting: third discussion on masturbation.

1911 December 26
Tatjana Nacht begins an analysis with F. She is the wife of Eitingon's friend Albert Nacht (until 1912 June).

1911 December 30
Death of Siegfried Lipiner. As a student, F. had published a private "Zeitschrift" with philosophical works together with him, Joseph Paneth and Emanuel Loewy.

1912

- Karl Landauer, German psychiatrist, begins an analysis with F. It lasts until 1914 June.
- Oscar Philipp, a cousin of Martha, is in Vienna for a week with his mother Mary, and they visit F. for dinner every night for a week. After Oscar's departure, Mary moves from the hotel to F.'s flat.

Books received:

- The British psychiatrist Bernard Hart sends F. his book *The psychology of insanity* with the dedication "With the author's compliments".
- Ludwig Jekels gives F. his book *Szkic psychoanalizy Freuda* with the dedication "Herrn Prof. Dr. Freud in Verehrung u. Dankbarkeit Dr Jekels".
- Ludwig Jekels gives F. his Polish translation of *Psychopathology of Everyday Life with* the dedication "Herrn Prof. Freud in dankbarer Verehrung".
- Ernest Jones gives F. his book Der Alptraum in seiner Beziehung zu gewissen Formen des mittelalterlichen Aberglaubens (The Nightmare in its Relationship to Certain Forms of Medieval Superstition) with the dedication "To Prof. Freud with kindest regards from E. J. Ernest Jones".

1912 January
- F. donates a series of medical journals to the "Lese- und Redehalle jüdischer Hochschüler" ("Library and speech hall of Jewish university students").
- The British Society for Psychical Research asks F. to write a paper for the Society's Proceedings. F. agrees, and the paper appears in 1913 under the title "A Note on the Unconscious in Psycho-Analysis".

1912 January 2
F. receives a letter from Angelo Hesnard on behalf of the French psychiatrist Emmanuel Régis from Bordeaux "apologizing in the name of French psychiatry for its present neglect of Ψα" and announcing "his willingness to come out with a long paper about it in *Encéphale*", founded in 1906 (F. to Abraham, 2.1.1912).

1912 January 3
WPV meeting: Isidor Sadger speaks about "Hebbel's childhood".

1912 January 8
Elma Pálos, the daughter of Ferenczi's lover and later wife Gisella Pálos, begins an analysis with F. It lasts until April 5.

1912 January 10
WPV meeting: Johann Marcinowski talks about "Drawings of Dreams".

1912 January 17
WPV meeting: Isidor Sadger continues his talk on "Hebbel's boyhood".

1912 January 24
WPV meeting: fourth discussion on masturbation.

1912 January 31
WPV meeting: Paul Federn speaks on "On the sensation of flight in dreams".

1912 February 2
Wilhelm Stekel gives F. the second edition of his book *Nervöse Angstzustände und ihre Behandlung* with the dedication "Seinem Lehrer Freud in unwandelbarer Dankbarkeit! Dr. W. Stekel".

1912 February 7
WPV meeting: fifth discussion on masturbation.

1912 February 14
WPV meeting: Karl Schrötter speaks about "Experimental Dreams".

1912 February 20
The first issue of the journal *Imago is* published; F. is the publisher; the editors are Otto Rank and Hanns Sachs.

1912 February 21
WPV meeting: Theodor Reik speaks about "The parent complex as cultural ferment".

1912 February 25
Ferenczi visits F.

1912 February 28
WPV meeting: sixth discussion on masturbation.

1912 March 3
Ferenczi visits F.

1912 March 6
WPV meeting: Alfred von Winterstein presents "A contribution to the Psychoanalysis of Traveling".

1912 March 11
Elisabeth Mannes, wife of the Weimar architect and engineer Hermann Otto Mannes, begins an analysis with F. (until 1913 March).

1912 March 13
WPV meeting: seventh discussion on masturbation.

1912 March 20
WPV meeting: eighth discussion on masturbation.

1912 Spring
– *Disagreement* between F. and Wilhelm Stekel over the publication of the *Zentralblatt für Psychoanalyse.*
– F. signs the founding manifesto of the "Gesellschaft für positivistische Philosophie" ("Society for Positivist Philosophy").
– F. meets with Tatjana Rosenthal and Sabina Spielrein for three hours.

1912 March 27
WPV session: Viktor Tausk speaks on "Sexuality and Ego".

1912 March 28
F. publishes a paper "Über einige Übereinstimmungen im Seelenleben der Wilden *und* der Neurotiker"; it is the first of several publications that became the basis for his book *Totem und Tabu*, published in 1913.

1912 March 29

Jan van Emden sends F. his Dutch translation of F.'s five lectures *On Psychoanalysis* with the dedication "Mit vorzüglichster Hochachtung und dankbarer Erinnerung an Karlsbad. Überreicht vom Übersetzer".

1912 April 3

WPV meeting: reviews and clinical communications, including Herbert Silberer speaking on "On Spermatozoic Dreams", Hanns Sachs on "Sexual Symbolic Jokes" and F. on "Über eine besondere Wurzel des Kastrationskomplexes" ("On a Special Root of the Castration Complex").

1912 April 4

Allen Starr, who was F.'s colleague in Theodor Meynert's brain anatomy laboratory in 1882, attacks F.'s psychoanalytical theories at a meeting of the New York Academy of Medicine, claiming that F. had led a dissolute life and that this was the starting point of his sexually tinged theories. However, F. cannot remember having known him.

1912 April 6

Magnus Hirschfeld sends F. his book *Geschlechts-Umwandlungen (Irrtümer in der Geschlechts-bestimmung)* with the dedication "Mit besten Grüssen. The author".

1912 April 5–10

Short vacation with Sándor Ferenczi on the island of Arbe

1912 April 5

F. leaves for Fiume (now Rijeka) at 9.30 pm with the southern railway.

1912 April 6

– F. arrives in Fiume early in the morning and has breakfast with Ferenczi, who has already arrived in Fiume the day before.
– At 10.15 am, departure of the ferry to the island of Arbe (now Rab). Arrival there at 3.10 pm.

1912 April 7–9

F. will not have missed going to the Church of S. Justina in the island's main town to see the altarpiece then attributed to Titian.[30] The two also visited overgrown monastery ruins, which Ferenczi remembers as "enchanted castles" (Ferenczi to F., 22.3.1931).

1912 April 9

Departure from Arbe at 8.00 am. Arrival in Fiume around 1.00 pm. F. continues to Vienna in the evening, Ferenczi to Budapest.

1912 April 10

Early morning arrival in Vienna.

1912 April mid

Jan van Emden comes to Vienna to continue his analysis and stays until May 24.

1912 April 17

WPV meeting: reviews and clinical communications, including Eduard Hitschmann speaking on "On Symbolic Representations in Painting", Jan van Emden on a "Case of Unconscious

Self-Punishment" and Paul Federn on a "The Inhibition Dream (as an expression of a conflict of wills in the sense of Freud)".

1912 April 24
WPV meeting: F. gives "An epilogue on the discussion on masturbation".

1912 May
F.'s mother is ill with herpes zoster.

1912 May 1
WPV meeting: critical reviews and papers published in the *Zentralblatt*.

1912 May 2
– Hans Blüher gets in touch with F. He had become aware of F.'s writings through Heinrich Körber and was particularly interested in homosexuality in light of F.'s neurosis theory.
– F. recommends to Oskar Pfister that he should not offer his manuscript "The Psychoanalytical Method" to Deuticke, as the latter always makes difficulties.

1912 May 8
WPV meeting: Eduard Hitschmann speaks about Arthur Schopenhauer.

1912 May 15
– F. receives antique glasses from Gisella Pálos, presumably from the trove of the treasure digger of Duna Pentele.
– WPV meeting: F. reads a manuscript "Über das Tabu" ("On the Taboo"). "The reading took three hours and caused several deaths" (F. to Ferenczi, 16.5.1912).

1912 May mid
F.'s daughter Sophie goes to Hamburg for almost two months and gets engaged to Max Halberstadt there.

1912 May 19
F. acquires Gustave Le Bon's book *Psychology of the Masses*.

1912 May 22
WPV meeting: reviews and clinical communications.

1912 May 24–28
Short visit in Kreuzlingen to Ludwig Binswanger
F. is in Kreuzlingen on Lake Constance with Ludwig Binswanger, but did not plan to visit Carl Gustav Jung in Zurich, but hoped that the latter would come to Kreuzlingen. Jung did not, but interpreted F.'s "Geste von Kreuzlingen" ("Gesture of Kreuzlingen") personally.

1912 May 24
Departure from Vienna in the evening.

1912 May 25
– Arrival in Kreuzlingen in the morning of May 25; F. changed trains in St. Margarethen.
– That day and the next, F. and Binswanger go for walks around Lake Constance. Binswanger reads to F. from a planned paper on "Freud's significance for psychiatry".

1912 May 26
- Car trip to the Untersee, which also includes Wolfgang Stockmayer, who had worked for Jung in Zurich as a volunteer doctor in 1908/09 and became his follower.
- In the evening, F. is invited to dinner at the estate Brunegg, above Kreuzlingen, the family estate of the Binswangers. On this occasion, he calls Adolf Friedländer a "pig".

1912 May 27
F. visits Leopold and Babette Löwenfeld in Munich late in the evening on his way back from Kreuzlingen.

1912 May 28
Arrival in Vienna.

1912 May 29
WPV session: Theodor Reik speaks on "Cynicism".

1912 May end
- F. sends Ludwig Binswanger Victor Hugo's novel *Notre-Dame de Paris*.
- The publisher Hugo Heller tells F. "that he doesn't trust himself to recommend *Imago* in his Viennese circle because he would lose customers" (F. to Ferenczi, 30.5.1912).

1912 June
F. publishes "Ratschläge für den Arzt bei der psychoanalytischen Behandlung".

1912 June 3
Emil Oberholzer begins an analysis with F. (until July).

1912 June 11
F. has the idea of comparing the Judgment of Paris with Shakespeare's *King Lear*. This idea then enters F.'s paper "The Motif of the Box Choice", published a year later.

1912 June 14
Ernest Jones and Loe Kann arrive in Vienna.

1912 June 15
F. asks Oskar Pfister by telegraph to come to Vienna as quickly as possible for a week in order to help Elfriede Hirschfeld – whose therapist he was before F. – in her attempt to "give up guarding" (F. to Pfister, 15.6.1912).

1912 June 16
- Oskar Pfister is in Vienna for a week.
- Loe Kann, Ernest Jones' mistress, begins an analysis with F. It lasts until 1914 July 10.

1912 June mid
The WPV's end-of-year party takes place on the Konstantinshügel.

Summer 1912
- Foundation of the "Secret Committee" at the suggestion of Ernest Jones. Members are: F., Sándor Ferenczi, Otto Rank, Karl Abraham, Hanns Sachs, Ernest Jones and from 1919 Max Eitingon.
- Mosche Wulff, a Russian doctor and follower of psychoanalysis from Odessa, visits F.

1912 June 23

F. believes "that the entrance scene in Lear must mean the same as the choice scene in The Merchant of Venice" (F. to Ferenczi, 23.6.1912). F. later developed this idea in his paper "Das Motiv der Kästchenwahl", which will appear in 1913.

1912 June 27

F. sends Havelock Ellis the medal with his portrait made by Karl Maria Schwerdtner in 1906, after he had received a portrait photo of Ellis some time ago and hung it up in his surgery.

1912 July beginning

F. signs the founding manifesto of the "Gesellschaft für positivistische Philosophie" ("Society for Positivist Philosophy").

1912 July 3

Hans Blüher sends F. the manuscript of his book *Die deutsche Wandervogelbewegung als erotisches* Phänomen.

1912 July 5

Sophie returns from Hamburg and tells her parents that she has become engaged to Max Halberstadt. F. invites his future son-in-law to Karlsbad, where he and Martha start a spay stay on July 14.

1912 July 14

An "Aufruf an Männer und Frauen aller Kulturländer" ("Appeal to Men and Women of All Cultural Countries") signed by F. is published in the journal *Die Neue Generation* edited by Helene Stöcker. The appeal argues "that the striving for the health of human sexual relations, the idea of the higher development of the human race must not stop at the borders of a country", and concludes with the words: "Fighting present evils, awakening the sense of responsibility of the living generation, we are in league with the future. Whoever wants to stand up with us for the realization of these high goals should be welcome!" (SFG 12, p. 499).

1912 July 14–August 14
Spa stay with Martha in Karlovy Vary

F. is with Martha at the spa in Karlsbad (Hotel Goldener Schlüssel). Breakfast is in the "Freundschaftssaal". Jan van Emden also comes back to Carlsbad to continue his analysis.

1912 July 14

Departure from Vienna in the evening.

1912 July 15

– Arrival in Karlovy Vary in the morning.
– F. and Martha meet Mary Philipp, the second wife of Martha's uncle Elias Philipp. She is in Vienna with her son Oscar, Martha's cousin.

1912 July 17

Max Halberstadt, the fiancé of F.'s daughter Sophie, comes to Karlsbad for a few days to introduce himself to him and Martha at F.'s request. He "behaved very sweetly and engagingly, even though he was still a little shy" (F. to Sophie, 20.7.1912).

1912 July 27

An advertisement of the engagement of Max Halberstadt and Sophie Freud appears in the *Hamburger Fremdenblatt*.

1912 July 28

– An advertisement of *the* engagement of his daughter Sophie to Max Halberstadt, initiated by F., appears in the *Neue Freie Presse*.
– F. and Martha meet with Max Halberstadt's aunt Cäcilie Wolff.

1912 August 2

Jung informs F. that he has asked Eugen Bleuler whether he could temporarily take over the editorship of the second half-volume of the *Yearbook of Psychoanalysis* during Jung's trip to America. He also states that he will put his presidency up for discussion at the next International Psychoanalytical Congress "so that the Association can decide whether or not to tolerate dissenting views" (Jung to F., 2.8.1912).

1912 August 10

F. meets with Ludwig Jekels, and they agree on an analysis.

1912 August 12

Jan van Emden departs from Carlsbad.

1912 August 14

In the morning, departure from Karlovy Vary, and drive via Munich to Bolzano.

1912 August 15 September 14

Summer stay in South Tyrol with wife Martha, sister-in-law Minna and Anna, Sophie and her fiancé Max Halberstadt

1912 August 15

Arrival in Bolzano and family reunion.

1912 August 16

Trip to Karersee. Alfred Winterstein is also on holiday in Karersee, and F. occasionally takes longer walks with him. Hans Lampl comes to visit, and F. gives him "lessons in sponge hunting" (F. to Jeanne Lampl de Groot, 2.6.1929).

1912 August 20

F. hopes that Jung will remain faithful to psychoanalysis.
    1912 August 22
    F. writes about the events in Zurich "most regrettable is the certainty that togetherness of Jews and anti-Semites, whom I hoped to unite on the foundation of psa., miscarried" (F. to Rank, 22.8.1912).

1912 August 25

F.'s pregnant daughter Mathilde is seriously ill.

1912 August 29

Death of Theodor Gomperz. In 1879, F. had taken over the translation of the last volume of the complete edition of John Stuart Mill's works edited by Gomperz. From the mid-1880s to the mid-1890s, Gomperz's wife Elise was in treatment with F.

1912 August 30

F. and his family move from Karersee to Bozen (Hotel Erzherzog Heinrich). There, they meet two friends of F.'s son Ernst: Felix Augenfeld and Richard Neutra. F. goes to the cinema with the three friends.

1912 August end

F. is asked by the lawyer Leopold Sternau to justify his statement about Adolf Friedländer of May 26 – F. had called Friedländer a "pig" – in favor of one of his opponents at the Honor Court. However, Friedländer was acquitted by the Court of Honor.

1912 September 1

Sándor Ferenczi arrives in Bolzano. F. picks him up at the station, and at Waltherplatz, they meet Paul Klemperer and Emmy Eisenberg, the daughter of the gynecologist James Eisenberg and niece of Ludwig Eisenberg, in whose artist's and writer's encyclopedia *Das geistige Wien* an autobiographical contribution by F. had appeared. F. welcomes Emmy, but not the Adler follower Klemperer.

1912 September 2

F. has to go to Vienna urgently, as the illness of his daughter Mathilde makes an abortion necessary. Afterward, Mathilde remains childless. Ferenczi accompanies him to Vienna. His family moves to San Cristoforo at Lago di Caldonazzo (Hotel Seehof). F.'s attention was drawn to this place by his sister Mitzi.

1912 September 8

F. arrives in San Cristoforo coming from Vienna.

1912 September 10

Emma Jung sends F. an offprint of the second part of Carl Gustav Jung's *Wandlungen und Symbole der Libido*.

1912 September 14–28
Trip to Rome with Ferenczi

F. enjoys Rome "as never before", and his retirement plan is firm: "not Cottage, but Rome" (F. to Martha, 20.9.1912). He visits Michelangelo's statue of Moses in S. Pietro in Vincoli every day, about which he "will perhaps write a few words" (F. to Martha, 25.9.1912).

1912 September 14

– Around noon, departure from San Cristoforo.
– Arrival in Florence, where F. meets Ferenczi.

1912 September 15

Travel to Rome; arrival 11.45 pm, overnight at Hotel Eden.

1912 September 16

Visit to the Palatine and the Monument to Victor Emmanuel II. Then shopping: at the hat shops Miller (Via Condotti) and Martinoli (Palazzo Fiano), and at the antique shops Adriano d'Innocenti (Via del Babuino), Benedetto di Segni (Via Condotti), Alberto Funaro (Piazza di Spagna) and Guiseppe Sangiorgi (Palazzo Borghese).

1912 September 17

Visit to the Tarpeia Rock, at the southern end of the Capitol, Monte Pincio and Villa Borghese; walk along the banks of the Tiber.

1912 September 18

– In the morning, visit of the Campo de' Fiori with the statue of Giordano Bruno and the Roman Forum.

- In the afternoon, visit of antique shops: three shops of Ettore Jandolo (Via Sistina, Via Margutta, Via del Babuino and the shop of Knill (Via del Babuino).

1912 September 19

- Another visit to Monte Pincio, then to the Mausoleum of Augustus, the Palazzo Borghese and the Lateran; he makes detailed notes on the statue of Moses, which F. visits again.
- In the evening, F. and Ferenczi go to the theater to see a "new patriotic operetta" (F. to Martha, 20.9.1912).

1912 September 20

F. buys a Gardenia, the scent of which "put him in the best of moods" (F. to Martha, 20.9.1912).

1912 September 21

F. and Ferenczi go in the afternoon to the festivities on the occasion of the capture of Rome 42 years ago at the Porta Pia. He had already briefly attended this event five years earlier.

1912 September 24

Ferenczi travels alone to Naples for four days.

1912 September 25

F. does some small shopping – presumably gifts, and acquires Guglielmo Ferrero's book *The women of the caesars*.

1912 September 27

Ferenczi returns from Naples. F. and he drive together to Udine.

1912 September 28

F. arrives back in Vienna.

1912 September end

F. receives a request from Lou Andreas-Salomé, who wants to come to Vienna for a few months, if she can attend his lectures and take part in the meetings of the WPV. The sole purpose of her stay in Vienna, she says, is to devote herself to the cause of psychoanalysis.

1912 October

In the winter semester (until March 1913), F. offers lectures once a week on "Einzelne Kapitel aus der Lehre von der Psychoanalyse" ("Individual Chapters from the Psychoanalytic Theory"), location: lecture hall of the Psychiatric Clinic, Saturday 7–21 pm, fee ten Kronen.

1912 October beginning

- Ernest Jones is in Vienna.
- F. has influenza.
- F. receives from Friedrich Kraus, Professor of Medicine and Director of the Medical Clinic at the Charité in Berlin, the request whether he would like to write the articles on hysteria and obsessive-compulsive neurosis for an encyclopedia of internal medicine.

1912 October 4

Bruno Veneziani, chemist and son of a manufacturer from Trieste, begins an analysis with F. It lasts until 1913 May 31.

1912 October 6

Wilhelm Stekel gives F. his book *Die Träume der Dichter* with *the* dedication "Seinem Führer in treuer Anhänglichkeit!"

1912 October 9
- WPV meeting: Regular General Meeting with statement of accounts and re-election of the Executive Committee.
- F. receives the anthology *Selected papers on hysteria and other psychoneuroses,* in which F.'s writings on the subject translated by Abraham Brill are published.

1912 approx. October 13
F. receives from Johann Marcinowski his book Der Mut zu sich selbst. Das Seelenleben des Nervösen und seine Heilung (The courage to face oneself: The inner life of the nervous and its healing).

1912 October 15
Ludwig Jekels begins an analysis with F. It lasts until the end of 1913 July.

1912 October 16
WPV meeting: Hanns Sachs speaks on "The Methodology of the theory of instincts".

1912 October 17
F. compares himself to Moses.

1912 October 18
F. reads an article in the *Neue Freie Presse* about the Brixen Cathedral cloister. It mentions a painter from Cologne, Andreas de Bembis de Freud, as the painter of one of the paintings on the vaults of the cross. F. and his brother Alexander then decided to go to Brixen to see if it could be an ancestor.[31]

1912 October 20
F. invited a committee of speakers (Rudolf Reitler, Eduard Hitschmann, Victor Tausk, Paul Federn and Sándor Ferenczi as an external member) who were to deliver papers for F. on what he considered to be problematic new publications. The paper on Jung's book *Wandlungen und Symbole der Libido (Transformations and Symbols of the Libido) was to be written by* Ferenczi, to whom F. wrote in this context: "So, we will open the hostilities. The best defense is a good offence" (F. to Ferenczi, 17.10.1912).

1912 October 23
WPV meeting: reviews and communications; Bernhard Dattner talks about "Marcinowski's analyses of numbers", Gaston Rosenstein makes "Critical remarks on Juliusburger's 'alcoholism'", Otto Rank talks about "Psychoanalytic from Multatuli" and Victor Tausk makes an "Analysis of a forgetting".

1912 October 25
F. acquires William Lloyd's *book The Moses of Michelangelo: A study of art, history and legend.*

1912 October 25
Lou Andreas-Salomé comes to Vienna for five months to learn more about psychoanalysis from F. She attends his lectures and takes part in the meetings of the WPV. Andreas-Salomé publishes the diary entries from this time under the title "In der Schule bei Freud" ("In School with Freud"). She also attends a college run by Hermann Swoboda.

1912 October 26
F.'s first lecture on "Individual Chapters from the Doctrine of Psychoanalysis" is attended by almost 60 listeners, including Lou Andres-Salomé.

1912 October 30
- WPV meeting: F. presents a case, "combined with some polemical observations". It is about his patient Elisabeth Mannes.
- Ernest Jones informs F. that he wants to dedicate his *Papers on psycho-analysis, which are* in preparation, to him.

1912 October end
- F. resigns as a co-editor of the Zentralblatt due to differences with Stekel, and Stekel becomes a sole editor.
- F. immediately begins to prepare the foundation of a new journal, which will appear from January mid as the *International Journal of Medical Psychoanalysis* (IZP).

1912 November beginning
- Wilhelm Stekel resigns from the WPV.
- F. receives photos of Donatello statues in Florence from Ernest Jones.

1912 November 2
F. gives a lecture in the psychiatric clinic (topic: Unconscious, complex, drive).

1912 November 6
WPV meeting: Isidor Sadger speaks on "On the sadomasochistic complex". Wilhelm Stekel's resignation from the Vienna Union is announced.

1912 November 8
F. gives "a small souper" in honor of Otto Rank's passing of his doctoral examination.

1912 November 9
F. has a lecture at the psychiatric clinic.

1912 November 11
- F. asks his followers who have submitted a manuscript for publication in the *Zentralblatt für Psychoanalyse* to withdraw their contributions and make them available to him for the new journal.
- Because of the events surrounding F.'s resignation from the editorship of the *Zentralblatt,* Jung invites the chairmen of the various European local groups to a conference in Munich on December 24.

1912 November 13
WPV meeting: Isidor Sadger continues his talks on the sadomasochistic complex.

1912 November 14
The name of the new journal has been decided: *International Journal of Medical Psychoanalysis.*

1912 November 16
F. has a lecture in the psychiatric clinic (topic: Dream symbols).

1912 November 20
- WPV meeting: reviews and clinical communications, including F. speaking on "Two women's fates", that of Charlotte, Empress of Mexico and that of Eugenie, Empress of France.
- Sándor Ferenczi is coming to Vienna for a few days.

1912 November 23–26
Conference of Chairmen in Munich Park Hotel

1912 November 23

Departure from Vienna in the evening.

1912 November 24

- In the morning, after a sleepless night, arrival in Munich.
- Decision to found the *IZP* and discussion of Wilhelm Stekel's resignation from the WPV. Present besides F.: Karl Abraham, Ernest Jones, Carl Gustav Jung, Johan van Ophuijsen, Franz Riklin and Leonhard Seif. The discussion lasted from 9.30 am to 11.30 pm. During the meeting, F. had a fainting fit, possibly triggered by a disagreement between F. and Jung about the position of Amenophis IV (Akhenaten) in relation to his father. However, the sleepless night could also be responsible.
- After the meeting, F. and Jung take a walk to talk things out; among other things, the "Kreuzlingen gesture" is discussed and largely clarified.

1912 November 25

Departure from Munich in the evening.

1912 November 26

Arrival in Vienna in the morning.

1912 November 27
WPV meeting: Viktor Tausk speaks on "Two Contributions to the Psychoanalysis of the inhibition of Artistic Productivity".

1912 November 30
F. has a lecture in the psychiatric clinic (topic: Desire Dream. Disgust and Sexuality).

1912 December 4
WPV meeting: reviews and clinical communications about cases, F. mentions Alfred Adler.

1912 December 7
F. has lecture in the psychiatric clinic (topic: Libido)

1912 December 8
Lou Andreas-Salomé visits F. in the afternoon.

1912 December 11
WPV meeting: Alfred von Winterstein makes "Psychoanalytic observations on the History of Philosophy".

1912 December 14
F. lectures at the Psychiatric Clinic (topic: Neurosis therapy, transference, intellect and affect).

1912 December 18
- Jung draws F.'s attention to the fact "that your technique of treating your pupils like your patients is a mistake" (Jung to F., 18.12.1912).
- WPV meeting: case reports and reviews; Ludwig Jekels speaks about a "case of promises", Isidor Sadger about "child slander", Eduard Hitschmann about a "case of blushing" and Victor Tausk shares an "observation of a form of obsessive neurotic fantasies".

1912 December 21–24
Karl Abraham visits F. in Vienna. F. secretly pays Abraham's hotel bill.

1912 Winter
Hans Blüher sends F. an "Open Letter", which he publishes a little later as an introduction to his writing *The Three Basic Forms of Sexual Inversion.* In this letter, he discusses certain points of F.'s view with which he did not agree.

1912 December 23
Ernest Jones sends F. from Rome two photographs of Michelangelo's Moses statue.

1912 Christmas
Loe Kann hosts a Christmas party at the Schlosshotel Cobenzl, where F. is invited along with Hanns Sachs and his wife Emmy.

1912 December 26
F. asks Jones to send him an illustration or drawing of the lower part of the tablets of the Law of Moses statue and encloses a sketch of his own for illustration.

1912 December 30
- F. attends a performance of *Don Juan* at the Court Opera, but only the third act.
- Sophie's fiancé Max Halberstadt spends a few days with the Freud family to discuss details of the upcoming wedding.

1912 December 31
F. is back at the Hofoper and attends a performance of Die *Fledermaus* by Johann Strauss.

1913

- Hans Blüher sends F. his book *Die drei Grundformen der sexuellen Inversion (Homosexualität). Eine sexuologische Studie* with the dedication "Vom Verfasser dankbarst zugeeignet. Hans Blüher".
- Havelock Ellis sends F. the second edition of the third volume of his *Studies in the psychology of sex* with the dedication "To Professor Freud with the Author's best regards".
- Eduard Hitschmann gives F. the second edition of his book *Freuds Neurosenlehre nach ihrem gegenwärtigen Stande zusammenfassend dargestellt* with the dedication "Herrn Professor Freud in Verehrung und Ergebenheit d. V".
- Hermine von Hug-Hellmuth gives F. her book *Aus dem Seelenleben des Kindes* with the dedication "Ihrem hochgeschätzten Lehrer, Herrn Professor Dr. S. Freud in dankbarer Verehrung überreicht von der Verfasserin".
- Carl Gustav Jung gives F. his paper "Versuch einer Darstellung der psychoanalytischen Theorie" with the dedication "Herrn Prof. Dr. Freud in dankbarer Hochachtung überreicht vom Verfasser".
- Otto Rank and Hanns Sachs give F. their jointly written book *Die Bedeutung der Psychoanalyse für die* Geisteswissenschaften with the dedication *"Herrn Professor Freud in Dankbarkeit und Verehrung von seinen Schülern: Dr Otto Rank Dr Hanns Sachs"*.

1913 January
- Alfhild Tamm, Swedish psychiatrist, visits F.
- David Eder, British psychiatrist, begins an analysis with F.

1913 January 3
F. decides to stop private communication with Carl Gustav Jung.

1913 January 8
WPV meeting: Paul Federn speaks about "An example of libido replacement during the course of treatment".

1913 January 10–12
Sándor Ferenczi is in Vienna. F. and Ernest Jones, who is in Vienna, visit him at the Hotel Regina late in the evening of January 10.

1913 January 11
- Leonhard Seif arrives in Vienna.
- Sándor Ferenczi is having lunch at F.
- F. has lecture in the psychiatric clinic (topic: Dream and Fairy Tale).

1913 January 12
F. spends the day together with Sándor Ferenczi, Ernest Jones, Leonhard Seif and David Eder on Cobenzl.

1913 January 14
Ball of the Lese- und Redehalle jüdischer Hochschüler ("Library and speech hall of Jewish university students") in Vienna. F. was a member of the honorary committee and may have been present.

1913 January 15
WPV meeting: F. speaks on "Animismus, Magie und Allmacht der Gedanken" ("Animism, Magic and Omnipotence of Thoughts"), the third part of *Totem and Taboo*.

1913 January 18
F. has lecture in the psychiatric clinic (topic: Two children's lies).

1913 January 22
WPV meeting: Emil Lorenz speaks on "The story of the miner of Falun".

1913 January 25
F. has a lecture in the psychiatric clinic (topic: The Neurotic. The Healthy).

1913 January 26
Wedding of F.'s daughter Sophie to Max Halberstadt at Berggasse 19. Hans Lampl, who was in love with Sophie, has to fetch her to F.'s study, where her bridegroom is waiting. This demonstrates that Lampl agrees to the wedding.

1913 January 27
The first issue of the *International Journal of Medical Psychoanalysis* appears; publisher is F., and editors are Sándor Ferenczi, Otto Rank and Ernest Jones.

1913 January 29
WPV meeting: brief communications; i.e., Fliess' theory of periodicity is discussed.

1913 February beginning
F.'s daughter Sophie and her husband Max Halberstadt move into their own flat in Hamburg; F. congratulates them and transfers the rest of the dowry of 8550 Kronen[32] to Max Halberstadt's account.

1913 February 1
− Ernest Jones leaves Vienna for Toronto.
− F. has a lecture at the psychiatric clinic.

1913 February 2
Lou Andreas-Salomé visits F. at his invitation and has a long conversation with her, and he tells her a lot about his life.

1913 February 5
WPV meeting: Isidor Sadger speaks on "Sexuality and Eroticism in Childhood". Hugo Heller is co-opted as a publisher of the two psychoanalytic journals.

1913 February 8
F. has a lecture in the psychiatric clinic (topic: Child traumas). Among the listeners are Lou Andreas-Salomé and the Austrian poet Richard Beer-Hofmann.

1913 February 9
Lou Andreas-Salomé visits F. in the afternoon.

1913 February 12
WPV meeting: reviews and clinical communications, including Hanns Sachs on the "Star as a Genital Symbol" and Eduard Hitschmann on "Paranoia and Anal Eroticism".

1913 February 13
Lou Andreas-Salomé visits F. for dinner and stays until 1.30 am. F. then takes her home.

1913 February 15
F. lectures at the Psychiatric Clinic (subject: Bisexuality, Neurosis and Sexuality, Dream Interpretation).

1913 February 19
WPV meeting: Karl Weiss speaks on "On the psychogenesis of refrain and rhyme".

1913 February 23
Lou Andreas-Salomé is visiting F.

1913 February 26
WPV meeting: Paul Federn speaks on "Disturbances in work and professional activity resulting from Neurosis".

1913 February end
Max Brod gives F. the book *Anschauung und Begriff* written by him and Felix Weltsch.

1913 March
– Loe Kann invites F., Otto Rank and Hanns Sachs to a dinner with her fiancé, the American writer Herbert Jones.
– Helene Stöcker is invited home by F. during her stay in Vienna.

1913 March beginning
Carl Gustav Jung gives F. his book *Wandlungen und Symbole der Libido* with the dedication "Dem Lehrer und Meister zu Füssen gelegt von einem ungehorsamen aber dankbaren Schüler". It contains the two parts already published in the *Yearbook*.

1913 March 1
F. has a lecture at the Psychiatric Clinic (Final College).

1913 March 1–2
Sándor Ferenczi is in Vienna.

1913 March 3
F. asks Otto Rank to see him in the late evening about an "urgent intervention" in the *IZP*.

1913 March 5
WPV meeting: Theodor Reik speaks on "Psychoanalytical remarks on Schnitzler's poetic works". In the discussion, F. makes remarks on narcissism.

1913 March 12
WPV meeting: Viktor Tausk speaks on "The Father Problem".

1913 March 14
Lou Andreas-Salomé visits F. for dinner. She stays until 2.30, and F. then takes her home.

1913 March 19
WPV meeting: clinical communications and reports; F. talks about "A dream representation that reveals a piece of the dreamer's infantile sexual behavior (penis envy) in hypocritical disguise", and Josef Friedjung shares "Observations on the source of the child's sense of shame (onanism)".

1913 March 20–26
Short trip through Upper Italy with daughter Anna
1913 March 20

F. leaves Vienna for Bolzano in the evening.

1913 March 21

– F. arrives in Bolzano at 11.45 am. There, he meets his brother Alexander and his wife Sophie, as well as Anna, who had been staying in Merano since November to recover after her Abitur.
– At 2.30 pm, continue with Anna to Verona; arrive at 5.00 pm, overnight at Hotel Londra.

1913 March 22

F. and Anna drive to Venice (overnight stay at the Hotel Britannia). It rains heavily there.

1913 March 23–24

F. and Anna now experience Venice "in the most beautiful sunshine" (F. to Sophie, 26.3.1913).

1913 March 25

Return journey via Trieste to Vienna.

1913 March 26

F. arrives back in Vienna.

1913 March end

Martha goes to Hamburg to visit daughter Sophie; the visit is possibly connected with a therapeutic abortion performed on Sophie – presumably by Rudolf Kaufmann.

1913 April 2

WPV meeting: Hanns Sachs speaks about Jonathan Swift.

1913 April 6

Lou Andreas-Salomé is on her last visit to F. before she leaves Vienna.

1913 April 9

– WPV meeting: Isidor Sadger speaks about "An Autoerotic".
– Eduard Hitschmann gives F. his book *Freud's theories of the neuroses* with the dedication "In dankbarer Verehrung Dr Hitschmann".

1913 April 12

Alfred Jekels begins an analysis with F.

1913 April 16

– WPV meeting: Eduard Hitschmann speaks on "Neurosis and celibacy".
– Maximilian Steiner gives F. his book *Die psychischen Störungen der männlichen Potenz* with the dedication "Herrn Prof. Freud in Dankbarkeit und Verehrung Dr Steiner".

1913 April 19–20

Sándor Ferenczi is in Vienna.

1913 April 23

WPV meeting: Isidor Sadger speaks on "Autoeroticism and Narcissism".

1913 April 30
WPV meeting: brief communications.

1913 May 7
WPV meeting: Karl Weiss speaks on "Education and Neurosis".

1913 May approx. 10
F. receives an unexpected visit from his brother Emanuel from Manchester.

1913 May 12
F. completes his work *Totem and Taboo*.

1913 May 14
WPV meeting: Edoardo Weiss presents "A Contribution to the mechanism of name forgetting".

1913 May 18
Ludwig Binswanger and Paul Häberlin visit F. in Vienna. F. devotes the whole Sunday to them – partly at home, partly at the Cobenzl – and the three men essentially discuss philosophical and psychoanalytical-political questions.

1913 after May 19
Ernest Jones comes to Vienna, stays until June 1 and then goes to Budapest with Ferenczi.

1913 May 21
WPV meeting: Otto Rank talks about fairy tales.

1913 May 24–25
Sándor Ferenczi comes to Vienna.

1913 May 25
– In the morning, Ferenczi visits F.
– In the afternoon, first meeting of the Secret Committee; F. gives each member a gem.

1913 May 28
WPV meeting: reviews.

1913 June
Pauline Hüft, the daughter of Theodor Herzl, had some sessions with F.

1913 June 4
WPV meeting: F. speaks about "Totem".

1913 June 21
Oskar Pfister sends F. his book *Die psychoanalytische Methode*, to which F. had written a preface with the dedication "Dem Eroberer Sigmund Freud/sein dankbarer und getreuer Etappenlieutenant".

1913 June 23
Death of Max Kassowitz. F. had worked in the second half of the 1880s at the I. Public Children's Hospital Institute in Vienna, which was directed by Kassowitz, and had also had private contact with him.

1913 June 29

The Viennese analysts give a "totem party" for F. on Constantine Hill in the Prater to mark the completion of *Totem and Taboo*. F. is presented with an Egyptian figurine by Loe Kann and sets it up in front of his plate as a totem. Ernest Jones and Sándor Ferenczi are also present.

1913 Summer

Hans Herzl, the son of Theodor Herzl, visits F. He wants to know, among other things, whether F. wants to start an analysis with his sister Pauline Hüft after the first sessions with her. He himself also has some sessions with F.

1913 July 1

F. gives Eduard Hitschmann and Hedwig Schick a carpet for their wedding.

1913 July 13–August 11
Spa stay with wife Martha, sister-in-law Minna and daughter Anna in Marienbad

F., Martha, Minna and Anna are in Marienbad (Villa Turba) for a spay stay. F.'s brother Alexander and his wife Sophie have already been in Marienbad since July 8 and are also staying in the Villa Turba. F.'s daughter Sophie comes to Marienbad with her husband Max. Anna Freud falls in love with her cousin Edward Bernays, who had come from America, and has thoughts of marriage.

1913 July 13

Departure from Vienna in the evening.

1913 July 14

Arrival in Marienbad (now Mariánské Lázně) in the morning.

1913 July 21

Max Eitingon comes to visit for a day.

1913 July 26

F.'s brother Alexander and wife Sophie leave.

1913 July 28

Trip to Karlsbad together with nephew Edward Bernays.

1913 July 29

F.'s daughter Sophie and her husband Max leave.

1913 July end

F. visits Ferenczi's mother Rosa, who is also in Marienbad for a spa stay.

1913 August beginning

F. learns that Adolf Friedländer wants to sue him because of his statements about him on 1912 May 26 in Kreuzlingen.

1913 August 3

Ferenczi's mother Rosa pays F. a return visit.

1913 August 11

Departure from Marienbad.

1913 August 13–September 5
Summer stay with family in San Martino di Castrozza

F. is with Martha and Anna in San Martino di Castrozza (Hotel des Alpes). During this holiday F. has the dream of the "*Pope was dead*".

1913 August 13

Arrival in San Martino di Castrozza

1913 August 15

Arrival of Ferenczi.

1913 September 1

Karl Abraham arrives in San Martino di Castrozza.

1913 September beginning

F. goes for a walk with the writer Walter Benjamin, who is staying in the same hotel. They are accompanied by a "silent friend", presumably Karl Abraham. The conversation revolves around the passing of beauty. Two years later, F. publishes a paper on this problem under the title "Vergänglichkeit".

1913 September 5

In the morning, F., Abraham and Ferenczi leave for Munich.

1913 September 5–9
IV. International Psychoanalytical Congress
in Munich

The Congress takes place in the Hotel Bayrischer Hof. At the Congress, there is a definitive break with Carl Gustav Jung.

1913 September 5

F., Abraham and Ferenczi arrive in Munich in the evening.

1913 September 6

F. intends to buy antiques; however, the antique dealer Sabetai Gabai at Maximiliansplatz has nothing for him, and F. buys a single piece from another dealer.

1913 September 7

F. gives a lecture "Zum Problem der Neurosenwahl" ("On the problem of neurosis choice"). This lecture appears a few months later under the title "Die Disposition zur Zwangsneurose".

1913 September 8

Rainer Maria Rilke attends the Congress and sits almost next to F. Lou Andreas-Salomé introduces him to F., and together with Sándor Ferenczi and Viktor von Gebsattel, they sit together until late at night.

1913 September 9

F. goes for a walk with Lou Andreas-Salomé in Munich's Hofgarten and has a long confidential conversation with her.

1913 September 9–30
Journey to Rome with Minna

F. travels to Rome via Bologna. There, he writes the preface for the book version of *Totem and Taboo and* an outline of the paper "Zur Einführung in den Narzissmus". He likes Rome better with each passing year.

1913 September 9

Departure to Bologna. F. meets sister-in-law Minna there.

1913 September 10

Travel from Bologna to Rome (overnight stay at Hotel Eden); arrival 11.50 pm.

1913 September 12

F. meets the antique dealer Ettore Sandolo on the street.

1913 September 13

Visit to Michelangelo's statue of Moses in San Pietro in Vincoli.

1913 September 21

Visit to the Tombe Latine, an ancient burial site on the Via Appia.

1913 September 22

Visit Tivoli and the waterfalls there, about 30km east of Rome.

1913 September 27

Jerome Alexander, a chemist from New York, asks F. for his autograph. He and his family were sitting next to F. and Minna at the hotel. F. had given Alexander's two daughters a bar of chocolate each. The younger one – six-year-old Dorothy – and F. had occasionally winked at each other, and F. had come to their table and had a short conversation.

1913 September 28

Departure from Rome at 11.50 pm.

1913 September 29

Drive via Florence, Bologna, Padua, Venice and Pontebba.

1913 September 30

Arrival in Vienna at 7.38 am.

1913 October
– In the winter semester (until March 1914), F. offers lectures once a week on "Einzelne Kapitel aus der Lehre Psychoanalyse" ("Individual Chapters from the Theory of Psychoanalysis"); location: lecture hall of the Psychiatric Clinic, Saturday 7–21 pm, fee ten Kronen.
– George Smeltz, budding analyst from Pittsburgh, is in Vienna for a few weeks, and Eduard Hitschmann takes him along to some WPV meetings as a guest.

1913 October beginning
F. is invited by Albert Moll to join the Society for Sexual Science.

1913 October 8
WPV meeting: General Meeting. The previous Executive Committee is re-elected. F. "gave a very honest account" of the IV. International Psychoanalytical Congress in Munich (F. to Abraham, 8.10.1913).

1913 October 9
Reuben Stein, grain merchant from Stockton in California, begins a nearly three-week analysis at F.

1913 October 12
F. is again considering a trip to Egypt.

1913 before October 13
Kurt Tucholsky and Kurt Szafranski ask F. – like many other prominent figures from science, literature and art – to participate in the planned journal *Orion*. F. declines for reasons of time; the journal also did not come into being because of the outbreak of war.

1913 October 15
– F.'s son Ernst goes to Munich to continue his studies.
– WPV meeting: Theodor Reik speaks on "Obsessive-Compulsive Symptoms".

1913 October 18
Martha goes to Hamburg to visit her daughter Sophie's family.

1913 October 22
WPV meeting: discussion on totemism.

1913 October 25
F.'s first lecture in the winter semester. He notices an analogy between "Breuer's first running away from the discovery of sexuality behind the neuroses and the last boys" (Freud to Abraham, 27.10.1913).

1913 October 27
Carl Gustav Jung resigns from the editorship of the *Yearbook* because he considers further collaboration with F. impossible.

1913 October 29
WPV meeting: Hermine von Hug-Hellmuth speaks on "On some papers by Stanley Hall and his school. Seen from the viewpoint of psychoanalysis".

1913 October 30
The writer Lucy Hoesch-Ernst begins an analysis with F. (until March 1914).

1913 November
The painter and graphic artist Max Pollak begins work on an etching by F. that Hugo Heller had commissioned. He comes about seven times, each time for an hour.

1913 November beginning
F.'s book *Totem und Tabu* is published.

1913 November 2
Sándor Ferenczi is in Vienna. F. had asked him to come in order to discuss further steps with him after Jung's resignation as an editor of the *Yearbook*. *At* a meeting attended by F., Ferenczi, Rank, Sachs and the publisher Hugo Heller, it is decided that Eduard Hitschmann and Karl Abraham should take over the editorship of the *Yearbook*.

1913 November 4
F. gives a lecture to B'nai B'rith on the topic "Was it Psychoanalyse?" ("What is psychoanalysis?").

1913 November 5
WPV meeting: critical reviews.

1913 November 12
WPV meeting: Herbert Silberer speaks about "Homunculus".

1913 November 19
WPV meeting: Sándor Ferenczi talks about experiments with telepathy and brings the fortune teller Alexander Roth and his wife, but they fail, and the meeting turned into a fiasco.

1913 November 23
F. holds a thought transference session in his flat with Alexander Roth and his wife – she was the medium. Present are Eduard Hitschmann, Hans Sachs and their wives, as well as Otto Rank, Alexander Freud and F.'s children. Mrs Roth was supposed to pick out a book from F.'s library that he had thought of. This did not work and the meeting "went very miserably, hardly any indication of success" (F. to Ferenczi, 23.11.1913).

1913 November 26
Session of the WPV: brief clinical communications.

1913 December 3
Session of the WPV: clinical communications and reviews.

1913 December 10
– The Austrian composer Bruno Granichstädten begins an analysis with F. (until 1914 July).
– WPV meeting: Karl Landauer speaks on "On the psychology of schizophrenia".

1913 December 14
F. finishes work on the fourth edition of The *Interpretation of Dreams.*

1913 December 17
WPV session: critical reviews.

1913 December 21
Ernest Jones comes to Vienna.

1913 December 24–29
Visit from daughter Sophie in Hamburg

F. stays at the Hotel Esplanade, but takes his meals with Sophie and Max. During their stay, John Philipp, a cousin of Martha, makes a drawing of F.

1913 December 24

Departure from Vienna in the evening.

1913 December 25

– Arrival in Berlin at Anhalter Bahnhof at 8.00 am; F. freshens up in the Hotel Excelsior, opposite the station.
– In the morning, he visits Max and Mirra Eitingon and his sister Mitzi and her family.
– From lunch onward, he spends the afternoon at the Abrahams' home with Karl Abraham.
– 8 pm departure from Berlin.

1913 December 26

Arrival in Hamburg at 7.00 am.

1913 December 28

Departure from Hamburg to Vienna.

1913 December 29

Arrival in Vienna in the morning.

1914

- The American psychiatrist and neurologist William White campaigns for F. to be awarded the Nobel Prize. [33]
- Books received:
- Ludwig Binswanger sends F. an offprint of his paper "Klinischer Beitrag zur Lehre vom Verhältnisblödsinn" published under the pseudonym Lothar Buchner with the dedication "Mit herzlichem Gruss und der Bitte einmal nur die [illegible] zu lesen!"
- Herbert Silberer gives F. his book *Probleme der Mystik und ihrer Symbolik* with the dedication "Dem verehrten Herrn Prof. Dr Freud ergebenst überreicht".
- Hans Sperber sends F. his writing *Über den Affekt als Ursache der Sprachveränderung* with the dedication "In aufrichtiger Verehrung der Verfasser".

1914 January

F.'s paper "The Moses of Michelangelo" is published. F. decided to publish it anonymously, "partly as a pleasantry, partly out of shame at the obvious amateurishness which it is hard to avoid in the Imago papers, and finally because my doubts about the findings are stronger than usual and I published it only as a result of editorial pressure" (F. to Abraham, 6.4.1914).

1914 January 7
WPV Meeting: Hanns Sachs speaks about Ferenc Molnár.

1914 January 12
F. writes "furiously" (F. to Ferenczi, 12.1.1914) on the "Geschichte der psychoanalytischen Bewegung".

1914 January 14
WPV meeting: clinical Communications.

1914 January 21
WPV meeting: reviews.

1914 January 25
Ferenczi is in Vienna.

1914 January 28
WPV meeting: Viktor Tausk speaks about "Narcissism".

1914 January 29
F. attends Frederik van Eeden s lecture on Rabindranath Tagore and is invited to the subsequent banquet, at which Hugo von Hoffmansthal is also present.

1914 February
Hans Abels, WPV member, begins an analysis with F.

1914 February
F. writes his papers "Zur Einführung in den Narzissmus" and "Zur Geschichte der psychoanalytischen Bewegung".

1914 February 1
- Magnus Hirschfeld visits F. in the morning.
- Frederik van Eeden, Hugo Heller and Otto Rank are at lunch at F.

1914 February 4
WPV meeting: reviews and clinical communications.

1914 February 10
Working dinner of the *IZP* editors at F.

1914 February 11
WPV meeting: Hermine von Hug-Hellmuth speaks about "Children's Games".

1914 February 15
F. finishes writing the "Geschichte der psychoanalytischen Bewegung".

1914 February mid
– F.'s daughter Anna is ill and has a fever.
– F. receives from Gerbrandus Jelgersma his rector's address on the 339th anniversary of Leiden University.

1914 February 18
WPV meeting: brief clinical communications.

1914 February 20
F. invites to an "official Moses evening, at which the fate of this experimental piece is supposed to be decided" (F. to Ferenczi, 15.2.1914). Hugo Heller, Otto Rank, Hans Sachs and Max Pollak, who made the drawings for the article, are present.

1914 February 25
WPV meeting: first discussion on the infantile Oedipus complex.

1914 March 4
WPV meeting: Paul Federn speaks on "On the Demarcation of the Reality and Pleasure Principle".

1914 March 7
Martha travels to Hamburg because Sophie is expecting a baby.

1914 March 11
– WPV meeting: F. speaks about "A case of foot fetishism".
– Birth of Ernst, F.'s first grandson, son of daughter Sophie. F. talks to her on the phone in the morning.

1914 March mid
F. finishes his paper *Zur Einführung in den Narzissmus.*

1914 March 17
– F. discusses an attack on Carl Gustav Jung with Otto Rank and Hanns Sachs at the suggestion of Karl Abraham.
– F. has had a picture by Karl Abraham framed and now puts it in the place of Jung's picture.

1914 March 18
WPV meeting: Second discussion on the infantile Oedipus complex and discussion on Otto Rank's "Biographical Material".

1914 March 19
- Eugénie Sokolnicka, Polish-French natural scientist, begins an analysis with F. (until June).
- F. receives two books: Lloyd Tuckey's *Treatment by Hypnotism* and Morton Prince's *Unconscious*.

1914 March 22
Sándor Ferenczi is in Vienna.

1914 April beginning
F.'s daughter Anna has whooping cough.

1914 April 1
WPV meeting: Otto Rank speaks about "The Double".

1914 April 5
F. suffers from overtiredness and tobacco intolerance.

1914 April 8
- F.'s son Oliver embarks on a trip to Egypt.
- WPV meeting: third discussion on the infantile Oedipus complex.

1914 April 9–13
Easter journey with Sándor Ferenczi and Otto Rank to the island of Brioni
For F., it is a wonderful stay, but too short a rest.

1914 April 9
Departure by night train from Vienna to Pola.

1914 April 10
In Divača, Ferenczi gets on; late morning, arrival in Pola, and at 2.30 pm, crossing to Brioni.

April 12
Departure from Brioni.

April 13
Arrival in Vienna.

1914 April mid
- F. had severe tracheitis/laryngitis.
- F. speaks to two members of the American Psychoanalytic Association. They assure him that Jung's influence on them is not significant. They were employees of the Manhattan State Hospital in Ward's Island, probably August Hoch and George Kirby.

1914 April 20
Jung submits his "resignation" as President of the IPA to the Conference of Presidents. Karl Abraham is entrusted with the provisional management of the Association's business.

1914 April 22
WPV meeting: Ludwig Jekels speaks about Napoleon.

1914 April 29
WPV meeting: reviews.

1914 May 6
WPV meeting: Karl Landauer speaks about "Psychosis".

1914 May 7
F. suffers from your bowel disorder, and Walter Zweig, a specialist in gastrointestinal diseases, performs a colonoscopy. F.'s suspicion that it could be bowel cancer is dispelled.

1914 May mid
F. would like to see Karl Abraham as the new President of the IPA.

1914 May 20
WPV meeting: fourth discussion on the infantile Oedipus complex.

1914 May 27
WPV meeting: reviews.

1914 May end
- F.'s paper Zur Einführung in den Narzissmus is published.
- Hanns Sachs tells F. about his visit to Berlin.

1914 May 31–June 1
Ride with Otto Rank to wedding of Loe Kann in Budapest

1914 May 31

F. travels from Vienna to Budapest.

1914 June 1
- Loe Kann, F.'s patient and former lover of Ernest Jones, marries Herbert Jones. F. and Rank are witnesses to the marriage.
- F. travels back to Vienna on the same day.

1914 June 3
WPV meeting: F. gives "An Introduction to Narcissism".

1914 June 22
F.'s paper "Geschichte der psychoanalytischen Bewegung" is published. F. comments on this with the words: "So the bombshell has now burst" (F. to Abraham, 25.6.1914).

1914 June 28
After the news of the assassination of the Austrian heir to the throne Archduke Franz Ferdinand in Sarajevo, F. believes that its "consequences cannot be foreseen" (F. to Ferenczi, 28.6.1914).

1914 June 29
Sergei Pankejeff (the "Wolf Man") says goodbye to F. after finishing his analysis. When the conversation turned to the assassination of the heir to the Austrian throne the previous day, F. said that in the event of Franz Ferdinand's accession to the throne, there would probably also have been a war between Austria and Russia.

1914 July
C. G. Jung resigns from the IPA.

1914 July 1
Otto Rank gives F. his book The myth of the birth of the hero with the dedication "Herrn Prof. Freud in herzlicher Dankbarkeit der Verf.".

1914 July 2
Karl Abraham sends F. the Dutch translation of his book *Traum und Mythus* with the dedication "Mit herzl. Grüssen K.A.".

1914 July 11
– Sándor Ferenczi comes to Vienna.
– Sándor Ferenczi, Otto Rank and Hanns Sachs visit F.

1914 July 12–August 5
Cure with Martha in Karlovy Vary
F. lives with his wife in the Villa Fasolt on the Schlossberg near Karlsbad. He writes "Erinnern, Wiederholen, Durcharbeiten" and "Bemerkungen über die Übertragungsliebe". He has also begun to study Shakespeare's Macbeth and is writing down some thoughts on it.

1914 July 12
In the evening, departure from Vienna by night train to Karlovy Vary.

1914 July 13
F. and Martha arrive in Karlsbad in the morning.

1914 July 21
Emmanuel Régis and Angelo Hesnard send F. their jointly written book *La psychanalyse des névroses et des psychoses* with the dedication "Hommage des auteurs et des éditeurs".

1914 July 22
The painter Hermann Struck, who is also in Carlsbad, asks F. to let him draw him. F. gives his consent on July 27.

1914 after July 25
Due to the partial mobilization on July 25, the staff in all spa facilities is reduced to half and the *Karlsbader Tagblatt* sells four extra issues daily, which "means their acquisition is a considerable increase in spa costs". (F. to Alexander Freud, 27.7.1914)

1914 July 28
Ludwig Binswanger applies for admission to the WPV.

1914 July end
Hermann Struck portrays F.

1914 August 4
Departure from Karlovy Vary by night train.

1914 August 5
Arrival in Vienna.

1914 August after 5
F. makes a kind of inventory of his antique collection and labels some pieces.

1914 August 11
F.'s son Ernst comes to Vienna for a visit.

1914 August 12
F.'s son Martin volunteers for the Austrian army.

1914 ca. August 25
Anna Freud arrives back in Vienna after a four-week stay in England. Shortly after the end of the war, she had been able to take advantage of one of the last opportunities to leave the country as an "enemy alien". She traveled back to Vienna via Gibraltar with the Austrian ambassador Albert Graf von Mensdorff-Pouilly-Dietrichstein, who had been expelled from England, and his entourage.

1914 September 6
F. visits his son Martin in Mühlau near Innsbruck.

1914 September 12–13
Sándor Ferenczi is in Vienna.

1914 September 16–27
Trip to Berlin and Hamburg
F. visits his daughter Sophie and son-in-law Max Halberstad in Hamburg. The main reason for the trip is to see his six-month-old grandson.

1914 September 14
Departure from Vienna to Hamburg.

1914 September 15
Arrival in Berlin. F. meets with Karl Abraham; presumably he also visits his sister Mitzi and meets with Max Eitingon.

1914 after September 16
Journey from Berlin to Hamburg.

1914 after September 17
F. is very happy about his grandson Ernst, who is "a charming little fellow, who manages to laugh so engagingly whenever one pays attention to him; he is a decent, civilized being, which is doubly valuable in these times of unleashed bestiality" (F. to Abraham, 22.9.1914).

1914 September 25
– Departure from Hamburg to Berlin. At the station, F. gives a stretcher full of grapes and a roll to a wounded man, which Sophie had given him as provisions for the journey. "Two other rolls were taken from me by a senior naval officer who had been travelling since Kiel and was very hungry" (F. to Sophie, 27.9.1914).
– Arrival in Berlin at 1.10 pm. Lunch at the home of Karl Abraham and his wife Hedwig. F. also spends the afternoon with the Abrahams.
– Departure by night train to Vienna at 18.00. On the train, he makes the acquaintance of Vicco von Bülow, a nephew of the former Reich Chancellor Bernhard von Bülow.

1914 September 26
Departure to Vienna in the evening.

1914 September 27
F. arrives in Vienna from Berlin. Anna and Oliver are waiting for him at the station.

1914 after September 27
Marie Thalberg, the wife of the Adler follower Friedrich Thalberg, begins an analysis with F. It lasts until the beginning of 1915. On January 10, she throws herself from the third floor of a house on Alserbachstrasse 5 and is killed immediately.

1914 September 30
- F. titles a sheet "Das Urbild der Lady Macbeth" ("The prototype/archetype of Lady Macbeth").
- Sándor Ferenczi is coming to Vienna for four weeks.

1914 October
- F. offers lectures "Einzelne Kapitel aus der Psychoanalyse" ("Individual Chapters from Psychoanalysis") in the winter semester (lecture hall of the Psychiatric Clinic, fee ten Kronen).
- F. writes on the medical history of the "Wolf Man".

1914 October 1
WPV meeting: General Meeting (first part).

1914 October 7
WPV meeting: General Meeting (second part).

1914 October 11
Martin is called up as a gunner to Marburg (today Maribor in Slovenia).

1914 October 14
F.'s Gymnasium celebrates its 50th anniversary. It is now called Erzherzog Rainer-Real-Gymnasiums and has published a commemorative volume to mark the occasion. F.'s contribution was dedicated to the "Psychologie des Gymnasiasten" and introduces the volume.

1914 October 16
F. gives lectures on "Einführung in die Psychoanalyse" ("Introduction to Psychoanalysis") in the winter semester.

1914 October 17
Death of F.'s brother Emanuel. He is killed in a railway accident. F. learns of his death on November 10.

1914 October 21
WPV meeting: brief communications.

1914 approx. October 23
F. receives Adolf Friedemann's book *Das Leben Theodor Herzl.*

1914 October 28
F.'s first meeting with Theodor Reik, who wants to start an analysis with him.

1914 October end
F. sends Hermann Struck an offprint of his paper Aufsatzes "Der Moses des Michelangelo".

1914 November 2
Hermann Struck sends F. five proofs of the lithograph and three of the etching for inspection and possible suggestions for changes. He had portrayed F. in Karlsbad at the end of July.

1914 November 4
WPV meeting: discussion on narcissism introduced by Victor Tausk and Paul Federn.

1914 November 10
F. learns of the death of his brother Emanuel, who died in a railway accident on October 17.

1914 November mid
Martha is in Hamburg visiting daughter Sophie and son-in-law Max.

1914 November 18
WPV meeting: Hanns Sachs talks about his "London impressions" after his visit to Ernest Jones.

1914 before November 24
F. informs Hermann Struck that he likes etching better than lithography.

1914 November 24
Hermann Struck asks F. to personally sign a limited number of prints of the etching and the lithograph.

1914 November 20
The Hungarian astronomer Sándor Gothard begins an analysis with F. It lasts until 1915 July.

1914 November end
F. receives the prints of Hermann Struck's lithographs and etchings from Hugo Heller for signing.

1914 December 2
WPV meeting: brief communications.

1914 December 3
Leo Kaplan sends F. his book *Grundzüge der Psychoanalyse* with the dedication "Seinem hochverehrten Lehrer Prof. S. Freud in Dankbarkeit der Autor".

1914 December 8
F. acquires René Dussaud's book *Les civilisations préhélleniques dans le bassin de la mer Egée*.

1914 December 14
Theodor Reik begins an analysis with F.

1914 December 15
Martha comes back from Hamburg.

1914 December 16
WPV meeting: Theodor Reik speaks about "Puberty Rites".

1914 December 20
Trigant Burrow visits F. and offers him his house in Baltimore as a "refuge" if F. wants to leave Europe because of the war.

1914 December 20–21
Sándor Ferenczi is in Vienna.

1914 December 30
WPV meeting: Viktor Tausk presents "Contributions to a Psychoanalytic Exposition of Melancholia".

1914 December end
Sándor Ferenczi is coming to visit Vienna for a day or two.

1915

- F. is nominated for the Nobel Prize (Medicine) for the first time. Signatories include Alfred Döblin, Knut Hamsun, Walter Hasenclever, Max Liebermann, Thomas Mann, Romain Rolland, Bertrand Russel, Jakob Wassermann, H. G. Wells, Franz Werfel, Virginia Woolf and Arnold Zweig.
- F. is portrayed by Bernard Henke. The painter gives the picture the title "A Portrait of a Gentleman" (36.2x25.5cm).
- Emanuel Loewy sends F. his work *Stein und Erz in der statuarischen Kunst* with the dedication "Mit besten Grüssen d. Vf.".

1915 January 1
Marco Levi Bianchini sends F. the Italian translation of the five lectures *Über Psychoanalyse* with the dedication "An den hochgeehrten Herrn Prof. S. Freud mit/achtungsvoller Freundschaft/M Levi Bianchini".

1915 January 13
WPV meeting: case material and reports.

1915 January 20
- F.'s son Martin is transferred to the front in Galicia. F. bids him farewell at Vienna's Nordbahnhof and thinks "in total clarity about the doubt there is whether and how we shall ever see him again" (F. to Abraham, 25.1.1915).
- Rosa and Karl Mayreder visit F. on Paul Federn's recommendation.

1915 January 20
Karl Mayreder, Austrian architect, begins an analysis with F. It lasts until the end of March.

1915 January end
Martha hangs the etching by Hermann Struck above her desk.

1915 February 3
WPV meeting: brief communications and reviews.

1915 February 7
F. begins to write down his lecture "Wir und der Tod".

1915 February 16
F. gives a lecture to B'nai B'rith on the subject of "Wir und der Tod".

1915 February 17
WPV meeting: clinical communications and reviews.

1915 March 3
WPV meeting: F. presents the medical history of Sergei Pankejeff ("Wolf Man").

1915 March 11
Friedrich (Fritz) Eckstein advises Rosa Mayreder not to leave her husband Karl in treatment with F. for longer than until Easter (April 2).

1915 March 15
F. begins writing his work "Triebe und Triebschicksale"; he finishes it on April 4.

1915 March 17
WPV meeting: discussion of the medical history of Sergei Pankejeff ("Wolf Man") presented by F. on March 3.

1915 March
F.'s paper "Wir und der Tod" is published.

1915 March 31
WPV meeting: Tausk speaks on "On the psychology of alcoholic occupational delirium".

1915 April 4
F. begins writing his work "Das Unbewußte". It is completed on April 23.

1915 April 6
F. has "fresh inflammation of the trachea" (F. to Ferenczi, 8.4.1915).

1915 April 9
Martha travels to Hamburg for an extended period to visit her daughter Sophie's family.

1915 April 14
WPV meeting: Leo Kaplan speaks about the "Genesis of traumatic primordial fantasies".

1915 April mid
– Oskar Pfister is in Vienna.
– F.'s paper "Zeitgemäßes über Krieg und Tod" is published.

1915 April 23
– F. begins writing the two works "Metapsychologische Ergänzung zur Traumlehre" and "Trauer und Melancholie" and finishes them around May 4.
– F. sends an offprint of his paper "Zeitgemäßes über Krieg und Tod" to Ludwig Binswanger.

1915 April 24
F. sends Ludwig Binswanger an offprint of his paper "Zeitgemäßes über Krieg und Tod".

1915 April 28
WPV meeting: Hanns Sachs speaks about Schiller "The Ghost-Seer".

1915 May
F.'s paper "Das Unbewußte" is published.

1915 May 12
WPV meeting: clinical communications and reviews.

1915 May 26
WPV meeting: brief communications.

1915 before June 26
Anna passes her teacher's examination.

1915 June 26–29
Search for summer quarters in the Berchtesgadener Land

1915 June 26

Drive from Vienna via Salzburg to Bad Reichenhall; meet Minna there.

1915 June 28

- F. and Minna are in Königssee.
- Departure from Königssee.

1915 June 29

Arrival in Vienna.

1915 July beginning

F.'s paper on "Triebe und Triebschicksale" is published.

1915 July 7

F.'s son Martin is slightly wounded at the front by a grazing shot.

1915 July 8–9

F. has dream of the "Death of the sons".

1915 July 14

- F.'s son Ernst comes to Vienna for a short visit.
- Otto Rank visits F.
- F. begins by "clearing away the antiquities", probably because he wants them to be better protected during his absence from Vienna and the unpredictable development of the war. "Lonely still stands the Egyptian king's son on the desk, abandoned by all the gods, only the Nubian head and the long Neit of Sais still keep company. On the whole, little is destroyed, only the contents of the small display case had to be emptied. If, contrary to expectations, the Russians should come to Vienna in the meantime, they will notice the gap immediately" (F. to Anna, 14.7.1815).

1915 July 15

Emanuel Loewy visits F.

1915 July 16

F.'s brother Alexander is a guest at F.'s for dinner.

1915 July 17–August 12
Spa stay with Martha in Karlovy Vary

F. and Martha live in the Rudolfshof.

1915 July 17

At 10.14 pm, departure from Vienna to Karlovy Vary.
1915 July 24
F. has an appointment with the spa doctor Rudolf Kolisch.

1915 July 26

- F. gives Martha a barometer for her birthday.
- F. donates 100 crowns to a charity Martha has chosen.

1915 July end

F. writes a short poem for a man who offers spa guests to be weighed in front of the dining room, replacing the "gruesome quatrain" (F. to Anna, 1.8.1915) that the man himself had written.

1915 August 12

At 11.26 am, departure. The journey continues via Eger and Munich to Berchtesgaden, where they arrive shortly after midnight and spend the night.

1915 August 13–September 13
Summer stay with Martha and Anna in

Schönau am Königssee

Accommodation at Pension Hofreit.

1915 August 13

At 6.14 am, travel from Munich via Berchtesgaden to Schönau.

1915 August 18

F. is in Bad Ischl for his mother's 80th birthday.

1915 September beginning

F.'s son Oliver gets engaged to Ella Heim, a medical student he met on a trip to Egypt two years ago.

1915 September 13

Departure of F. and Minna to Munich.

1915 September 13–15
Short trip with Minna to Weimar and Berlin

1915 September 13

Arrival in Weimar. F. shows his sister-in-law Minna the city she is in for the first time.

1915 September 14

Trip to Berlin.

1915 September 15

F. continues alone to Hamburg.

1915 September 16–26
Sophie and family visit Hamburg

1915 September 16

Arrival in Hamburg.

1915 September 17–24

During his stay in Hamburg, F. made the first observations of his grandson Ernst's "Fort-Da" ("gone") play, which he later described in his book *Jenseits des Lustprinzips (Beyond the Pleasure Principle).*

1915 September 25

– Departure to Berlin.
– Together with Jan van Emden, F. visits Abraham's wife Hedwig; Karl Abraham was stationed in Allenstein (today Olsztyn) at the time.
– Dinner with Jan van Emden at the Hotel Excelsior, then on to Dresden, where van Emden will disembark.

1915 September 26

Arrival in Vienna.

1915 October 4

Aranka Schwarcz begins an analysis with F. It lasts, with interruptions, until the beginning of 1918 March. She comes from Szolnok, about 100km east of Budapest, and occasionally brings news and food from Ferenczi.

1915 October

F. offers "Vorlesungen zur Einführung in die Psychoanalyse" once a week in the winter semester (until 1916 March).

1915 October 9–10
Visit to Sándor Ferenczi in Pápa (Hungary)

Sándor Ferenczi was stationed in Pápa with a hussar regiment.

1915 October 13

- F.'s son Martin is passing through on a visit to his parents in Vienna.
- WPV meeting: General Assembly.

1915 October 23

F. offers lectures on "Einzelne Kapitel aus der Psychoanalyse" ("Individual Chapters from Psychoanalysis") in the winter semester (lecture hall of the Psychiatric Clinic, fee ten Kronen). About 70 people attend, including F.'s daughters Mathilde and Anna, and Oliver's fiancée Ella Haim.

1915 October 31

F. considers a trip to Constantinople.

1915 November 1

Rózsi von Freund, Anton von Freund's second wife, begins an analysis with F. It lasts with interruptions until 1917 December.

1915 November

F. is writing the paper "Vergänglichkeit".

1915 November 3

WPV meeting: Eduard Hitschmann speaks on "On Gottfried Keller" (Part 1).

1915 November 13

The young poet Arthur Fischer-Colbrie begins an analysis with F. It lasts, with interruptions, until 1919 July.

1915 November 14

F.'s son Oliver is on a short visit to Vienna.

1915 November 17

WPV meeting: Eduard Hitschmann speaks on "On Gottfried Keller" (Part 2).

1915 November end

F.'s son Martin is on leave in Vienna for ten days.

1915 December
- F. donates six crowns a month to an aid campaign for refugees from Galicia and Bukovina.
- F.'s son Oliver was ordered to Mosty in the Jablunka Pass, where he was employed in tunnel work. He was therefore initially exempted from military service, as the tunnel was important for the war.

1915 December beginning
- Miklos Sisa, one of the younger followers of psychoanalysis in Budapest, attends F.'s lecture on Ferenczi's recommendation. He had published a popular article on psychoanalysis in 1914, and F. takes him under his care.
- Ferenczi sends Martha a package of flour.

1915 December 1
WPV meeting: Hanns Sachs speaks on "On Schiller's Maid of Orleans".

1915 December 15
WPV meeting: casuistic communications and papers.

1915 December mid
Anton von Freund, a rich Budapest brewery owner, visits F. His second wife Rózsi has been receiving treatment from F. since the beginning of November.

1915 December 18
F.'s son Oliver arrives in Vienna.

1915 December 19
Wedding of F.'s son Oliver to Ella Haim in Vienna. F. was best man, but hopes that the marriage will soon be divorced. Rainer Maria Rilke is also a wedding guest.

1915 December 20
Rainer Maria Rilke visits F. and is a "charming companion" (F. to Ferenczi, 24.12.1915).

1915 before December 24
- F.'s daughter Anna goes to Hamburg over Christmas to visit her sister Sophie and her nephew Ernst.
- Ferenczi sends Martha another parcel of flour.

1915 before December 31
F.'s son Martin is promoted to lieutenant, son Ernst to ensign.

1915 December end
Ferenczi is coming to Vienna over the turn of the year.

1916

- F.'s son-in-law Max Halberstadt is drafted for military service.
- F.'s son Martin meets his future wife Esti Drucker at a party.
- Richard Wagner, former WPV member, visits F. during a furlough.

1916 January 1
F.'s son Martin becomes a lieutenant, son Ernst an ensign, i.e. officer candidate.

1916 January 2
F.'s daughter Anna returns from Hamburg.

1916 January 6
Otto Rank leaves for Krakow, where he takes up the position of editor of the Krakauer Zeitung – the only German daily newspaper in Galicia – as he is unfit for field service.

1916 January
F. begins to write down the lectures he gives as *Vorlesungen zur Einführung in die Psychoanalyse*.

1916 January 5
WPV meeting: Eduard Hitschmann speaks about claustrophobia.

1916 January 12
Adolf Friedemann visited F. He had been a participant in the Zionist congresses since 1898 and had accompanied Theodor Herzl on his trip to Egypt in 1902.

1916 January 19
WPV meeting: brief communications and discussion on war psychoses. Hans Sachs speaks on "Language symbols".

1916 January 26
Leo Kaplan sends F. his book *Psychoanalytische Probleme* with the dedication "Dem verehrten/ Lehrer/Herrn Prof. Dr. Freud/der Autor".

1916 January end
F. has influenza.

1916 February beginning
F. reads four newspapers daily: The "miserable" *Neue Freie Presse,* the *Vossische Zeitung*, the *Arbeiterzeitung* and the *Krakauer Zeitung* (F. to Ferenczi, 4.2.1916).

1916 February 1
F.'s daughter Mathilde gets an injection, possibly because of a relapse after one of her many illnesses associated with complications.

1916 February 6
The Karlovy Vary doctor Ignaz Zollschan visits F. Presumably the contact was made through the painter Hermann Struck.

1916 February 9
WPV meeting: communications and presentations.

1916 February 10
F.'s son Ernst has three weeks' leave from the front and spends this time in Vienna, Hamburg and Berlin.

1916 February 12
Martha falls ill with influenza.

1916 February 14
Herbert Silberer gives F. his book *Durch Tod zum Leben* with the dedication "Herrn Prof. Dr S. Freud/ergebenst überreicht/vom Verfasser".

1916 February 15
– F. gives a lecture to B'nai B'rith on Anatole France's novel *La Révolte des Anges.*
– F.'s son Ernst leaves for Hamburg.

1916 February 17
Rainer Maria Rilke reports to F. about his poor mental condition; he had considered several times that F. might help him out of his "entombment".

1916 after February 18
F. sends Romain Rolland's novel *Jean Christophe* to his son-in-law Max Halberstadt.

1916 February 22
F.'s son Oliver comes to Vienna from Mosty. He got home leave because of influenza.

1916 February 23
– WPV meeting: Hanns Sachs talks about the detective novel *Fine Threads* by Edwin Balmer and William Mac Hary, and F. talks about the "connection between symptom and symbol".
– F.'s son-in-law Max Halberstadt, who is on the Western Front, is wounded in the head by a grazing shot. F. learns of this four days later.

1916 February 26
F.'s son Ernst returns from Hamburg.

1916 February 27
F.'s son Ernst returns from Hamburg from visiting his sister and reports on Sophie and Ernst.

1916 March 1
F.'s son Ernst back to the front.

1916 March 3
F.'s son Oliver is going to Mosty again.

1916 March 9
Martha goes to Hamburg for her grandson Ernst's second birthday. F. gives him 200 marks from the fee for the Dutch translation of the Psychopathologie *des Alltagslebens* – with the warning to the parents: "But don't invest it in papers, spend it!" (F. to Sophie, 9.3.1916).

1916 March 10
F. tries to find out more about son-in-law Max's injury from the chief physician of the sixth Army stage hospital in Valenciennes. The head of the military hospital, the Jewish chief medical officer Benno Koppenhagen, replies to F. on March 15 that the wound is healing well and Max can be discharged in about two weeks.

1916 March 15
WPV meeting: Eduard Hitschmann speaks on "Thomas Mann's 'Friedrich der Grosse'" and "Dream with following change of mind", Paul Federn on "Dream of deceased" and "Age melancholy" and F. on an "Archaeological parallel to a compulsive neurotic theme".

1916 March 20
Martha sends photos of grandson Ernst from Hamburg.

1916 March 22
F.'s son Martin comes to Vienna unexpectedly. The reason for Martin's visit was a rearmament of his battery. It was converted to heavy artillery and transferred to Salzburg on April 12.

1916 March 25–26
Max and Mirra Eitingon visit F. Max had been on leave from his post as head of the psychiatric observation department for a few weeks due to illness and on their way to a spay stay in Karlsbad they stopped off in Vienna.

1916 March 28
Oliver's wife Ella has a spontaneous abortion. F. writes on this occasion: "Ella had an abortion yesterday. The two of them are not very lucky. We attach a faint hope to the mishap, of which one must not yet speak aloud. It would really be a relief for us, because we believe Oli would not lose much if he became free again" (F. to Max Halberstadt, 29.3.1916). In fact, the couple divorced again in 1916 September.

1916 April 1–2
Sándor Ferenczi is in Vienna.

1916 April 2
Death of Betty Hammerschlag, the wife of F.'s former religion teacher Samuel Hammerschlag. F. had known her since 1873. Her daughter Anna was his patient between 1895 and 1900 and plays a central role in the dream of "Irma's Injection".

1916 April 3
F. is at Betty Hammerschlag's funeral in her flat and meets Josef Breuer there. It is the last encounter between the two men.

1916 April 5
WPV meeting: brief communications and reviews; Hermine Hug-Hellmuth speaks on "An anatomical children's fantasy about the sunset", F. on a "A case of speech disorder" and Isidor Sadger on "On the question of periodic limb paralysis".

1916 April 11
Lilly Freud, the daughter of F.'s sister Mitzi, makes her first public appearance as a reciter in Vienna. At the instigation of the Burgtheater, Hugo Heller had engaged her to perform Asian poetry. All members of the F. family living in Vienna, including grandmother Amalia, attended the performance. F. had a large bouquet of colorful flowers handed to her on the podium. He sent a telegram to his sister Mitzi and cousin Moritz: "lovely evening beautiful success congratulations = arden".

1916 April 12
Departure of F.'s son Martin with his battery to Salzburg.

1916 April 16
F. receives Edwin Holt's book *The Freudian Wish and its Place in Ethics.*

1916 April 17
Martha comes back from Hamburg.

1916 April 22–25
Visit to son Oliver at the Jablunka Pass

F.'s son Oliver is often employed as an engineer in tunnel construction during the first years of the war – including in Mosty on the Jablunka Pass.

1916 April 22

Departure from Vienna.

1916 April 23

F. looks at the tunnel on Easter Sunday and talks to Oliver about the formalities of the forthcoming divorce from Ella.

1916 April 24

F. and Oliver visit the nearby town of Teschen (today Český Těšín). From there, F. drives back to Vienna.

1916 April 25
F. arrives in Vienna in the morning.

1916 April 25
Otto Rank, who had come to Vienna from Krakow, visits F.

1916 April 26
WPV meeting: Ludwig Jekels speaks about Shakespeare's "The Merchant of Venice". F. receives a bouquet of orchids on the occasion of his upcoming 60th birthday.

1916 May 6
– Johann Marcinowski sends F. his book *Ärztliche Erziehungskunst und Charakterbildung* with the dedication "Seinem hochverehrten Lehrer/in aller Dankbarkeit/Dr Marcinowski".
– For F.'s 60th birthday, Eduard Hitschmann sent him a birthday speech, for which F. thanked him with the words: "As beautiful and as affectionate as your speech, which was not given, is otherwise only an obituary in the central cemetery" (F. to Hitschmann, 7.5.1916).
– F. receives a birthday letter from Julius Wagner-Jauregg in which he expresses his friendly sentiments.

1916 May 16
Hugo Heller visits F. and introduces him to his second wife – Hedwig Neumayr – whom he had married on May 2.

1916 June 1
Start of correspondence between F. and the young writer Arthur Fischer-Colbrie.

1916 June 7
WPV meeting: Viktor Tausk speaks on "Psychoanalytic War Experiences".

1916 June 10–15
F.'s son Oliver is in Vienna to settle the divorce formalities.

1916 June 13
Sándor Ferenczi is coming to Vienna for three weeks for his analysis.

1916 June 15
F.'s daughter Anna had developed a tonsil abscess as a result of angina, which was now opened with an incision to allow the pus to drain.

1916 Summer

Rudolf Kriser turns to F. for treatment again after five years. In July mid, he has ten sessions, then continues the analysis from 1917 January to 1918 December.

1916 June 23

F.'s son Martin is transferred from Italy to the Russian front, and visits his parents for a few hours while passing through Vienna.

1916 June 30

F.'s son-in-law Robert Hollitscher is released from military service.

1916 July 1

The French teacher Selma Leitner visits F. one day before her wedding to the publisher Heinrich Glanz because she had suddenly become afraid of getting married. F. reassured her and told her to get married. F. knew her future husband because his daughter Anna had taken religion lessons and Hebrew lessons with him in 1914 and 1915 in preparation for her teaching exam.

1916 July 8

The first part of the *lectures on the introduction to psychoanalysis is* published.

1916 July 10

Minna and F.'s daughter Anna travel to Weißenbach am Attersee. From there, they travel on to Salzburg on July 13, where they met up with F. and Martha on July 16, who are on their way to Badgastein.

1916 July 11

Emanuel Loewy visits F.

1916 July 13

The Swedish journalist and writer Eira Hellberg visits F. She belonged to the circle of friends of August Strindberg. F. considers her to be analyzed and recommends that she be treated by Ferenczi.

1916 July 16–September 15

Summer holiday with wife Martha and sister-in-law in Badgastein and Salzburg

Accommodation in the Villa Wassing (today Villa Excelsior). Visiting for several days are Brother Alexander with wife Sophie, daughter Mathilde with husband Robert, Martin, Ernst and Anna. F. meets Selma and Heinrich Glanz in Salzburg, who are on their honeymoon.

1916 July 16

Departure from Vienna.

1916 July 17

Arrival in Salzburg, where F. and Martha are expected by Minna and Anna. Continue to Badgastein.

1916 July 19

Departure from Badgastein to Salzburg. The stay was planned to be longer, but due to the difficult supply situation, the company decided to spend the rest of the holiday in Salzburg; first, they stay at Hotel Bristol, where they meet relatives of Martha (Anna Thorsch with one of her daughters); later, they move to the sanatorium in Parsch.

1916 July 21

Serena Szabó begins an analysis with F. She is a sister of Anton von Freund's second wife Rózsi and the wife of René Spitz's uncle Alexander Szabó. The analysis lasts, with interruptions, until 1917 November.

1916 after July 22

Kurt and Therese Rie visit F. with their son Robert in the Parsch sanatorium.

1916 July 29–31

F. is in bed with influenza.

1916 August beginning

Paula Haas from Mainz begins an analysis with F. It lasts until December mid. She is the owner of the painting "Der Bach im Tal" by the German painter Hans Thoma and probably also had contact with him.

1916 August 1

- F. receives from Josef Popper-Lynkeus the dissertation by Heinrich Straus *Über den Rhythmus in den Lebenserscheinungen* published in 1825.
- F.'s son Ernst is promoted to lieutenant.

1916 August 2

Visit to a concert by the Fitzner Quartet at the Mozarteum. The program includes Mozart's String Quartet in D minor, Schumann's String Quartet in A major and Brahms Quintet in B minor for clarinet and string quartet.

1916 August 4

- F.'s daughter Mathilde and son-in-law Robert come to Salzburg.
- Visit to a concert of the quartet Fitzner with the pianist and Bruckner student Ferdinand Löwe at the Mozarteum. The program includes Mozart's Divertimento for Violin, Viola and Violoncello in E-flat Major, Brahms Piano Quartet in G Minor and Beethoven String Quartet in F Minor.

1916 August 6

F.'s son Martin is on leave and comes to Salzburg.

1916 August 7

F.'s son Ernst is on leave and comes to Salzburg for a week. F. has his photo taken with the two lieutenants Martin and Ernst.

1916 August 13

F. meets Leopold Königstein, who had come to Salzburg for the funeral of the table glass manufacturer Ignaz Glaser.

1916 August 14

Anna and Ernst drive to Aussee.

1916 August 16

Hanns Sachs comes to Salzburg.

1916 August 18

F., Martha and Minna are in Aussee for the 81st birthday of F.'s mother Amalia. There, they meet Selma Glanz again.

1916 August 20

- Return to Badgastein; stay there until September 14.
- F. undergoes a spa treatment and finds Badgastein "tremendously beautiful, far more so than San Martino di Castrozza" (F. to Abraham, 27.8.1916).
- Among the spa guests is Heinrich Waldeyer. F. and Martha and Minna sit at a table with him every evening for three weeks. Waldeyer had already assumed in 1881 that the nerve cell is to be understood as the basic functional unit of the nervous system. He introduced the term "neuron" for it. F. had quoted Waldeyer extensively in his neuropathological work and had come to the same conclusion in his "Entwurf einer Psychologie".

1916 August 23–24

F. is mushroom hunting as the weather is better after a few days of rain.

1916 at August 24

There is no more white bread in Badgastein. In Ludwig Schurk's bakery, you have to pay with jewelry to get rusks, as the brown bread is hardly enjoyable. F. is of the opinion that the baker "rightly bears his name Schurk [villain]" (F. to Anna, 26.8.1916).

1916 August 25

F. buys two Chinese porcelain dogs from an antique dealer, one for Anna and one for his brother Alexander.

1916 September beginning

F. played cards with the Viennese historian Alfred Pribram – a good friend of F. – every afternoon. Pribram was also F.'s tarot partner occasionally on Saturdays in Vienna.

1916 September 2

F. goes mushroom hunting at Prossau, a hiking destination about 300 m higher up, east of Badgastein in the Kötschachtal. He suspects that after most of the spa guests have left, there are more mushrooms there than in the high season.

1916 September 13

The marriage of F.'s son Oliver to Ella Haim is divorced.

1916 September 14

Departure from Badgastein.

1916 September 15

Arrival in Vienna.

1916 after September 23

Selma Glanz begins an analysis with F. It lasts until the end of 1917 March, and F. takes no fee.

1916 September 25

Otto Rank visits F. on his way from Constantinople to Krakow.

1916 September 27

- F. sends Oskar Pfister a copy of his *Vorlesungen zur Einführung in die Psychoanalyse* with the dedication "Herrn Dr. O. Pfister/herzlich/d. Verf.".
- F. sends Abraham Brill a copy of his *Vorlesungen zur Einführung in die Psychoanalyse* with the dedication "Dr. A. A. Brill/d Verf.".

1916 September 28
Robert Bárány, who was the first Austrian to receive the Nobel Prize for Medicine in 1914 and had known F. since 1897 at the latest, intends to propose F. for the Nobel Prize for Medicine.

1916 September 29
Sándor Ferenczi is coming to Vienna for two weeks in order to continue his analysis.

1916 September 30
F. notes the end of summertime, which was first introduced in Austria-Hungary on 1916 April 30 and lasted until September 30.

1916 October
F. offers lectures on "Einführung in die Psychoanalyse" once a week during the winter semester (until 1917 March) (location: lecture hall of the Psychiatric Clinic, Saturday 7–21 pm, fee ten Kronen).

1916 October 7
F. hands Robert Bárány documents for the nomination for the Nobel Prize, presumably his curriculum vitae and a list of his publications.

1916 October 11
WPV meeting: Business discussion on the election of new officers.

1916 October 13
F. receives food from Anton von Freund.

1916 October 14
Ferenczi has his last analysis session with F., who informs him a month later that he considers the analysis "finished, – finished, not terminated […]". (F. to Ferenczi, 16.11.1916).

1916 October 16
F.'s son Martin receives the medal of honor "Signum laudis" (Sign of Praise).

1916 October 28
F.'s son-in-law Max Halberstadt, who had been classified as "unfit for field service" after being wounded on February 23, becomes an aviation photographer in Hanover.

1916 November 3
Emil Rosenthal, a brother-in-law of Max Kassowitz), begins a short analysis with F. (until the end of November).

1916 November 8
WPV meeting: Hermine von Hug-Hellmuth reports "From the lives of three 'Urninden'" (lesbians).

1916 November mid
F. meets with Hugo Ignotus.

1916 November 17
F.'s daughter Sophie comes to Vienna for six months with her son Ernst.

1916 November 18
The German writer Albrecht Schaeffer sends F. his book *Rainer Maria Rilke* with the dedication "Dem Entdecker der Kindheit dem ausserordentlichen Manne/Professor Dr. Sigm. Freud/in Ehrfurcht und Dankbarkeit zugeeignet/Schaeffer".

1916 November 20
F.'s son Oliver finishes his work at the tunnels in Mosty and comes to Vienna.

1916 November 23
F. sends to Lou Andreas-Salomé Edwin Holt's book *The Freudian Wish* and James Putnam's paper "The Work of Alfred Adler, Considered with Especial Reference to that of Freud".

1916 November 26
F.'s son Martin has a riding accident.

1916 December 1
F.'s son Oliver was called up for military service and, at his request, transferred to Krakow to join a pioneer troop. He had chosen Krakow because Otto Rank, with whom he had a very good relationship, worked there as an editor.

1916 December 2
F.'s son Oliver leaves for Krakow.

1916 December 6
WPV meeting: discussion evening.

1916 December 10
F. Martin, the son, is temporarily transferred to the Cadre in Vienna. This meant that he was not exposed to direct combat and could often visit Berggasse.

1916 December 13
– WPV meeting: brief communications; Victor Tausk speaks on "Two parapraxes. A case of concealment", Hanns Sachs on "Two cases of misreads", Eduard Hitschmann on "Bedwetting in a 52-year-old woman" and F. on "Leonardo da Vinci and a Memory of his Childhood"
– Erzsébet Révész-Radó. begins an analysis with F.

1916 December 16
The second part of F.'s *lectures on the introduction to psychoanalysis is* published.

1916 December 22
F. ordered Jean-Baptiste de Lamarck's *Zoologische Philosophie* from the university library, as he had envisaged a work on "Lamarck and Psychoanalysis" together with Ferenczi.

1916 Christmas
Hugo Heller gives F. the *Spruchwörterbuch* by Franz Lipperheide with the dedication "Frohes Weihnachten u alles Schöne f 1918 H. H.".

1916 December 28
For F., it is the first working day in years that he has not taken anything in. Shortly before, he had written to Abraham: "I have little to do, so that at Christmas, for instance, I will again have reached rock-bottom" (F. to Abraham, 18.12.1916).

1916 December 29

F.'s son Martin travels to Budapest for the coronation of Karl I. as King of Hungary, which took place on December 30. Charles had already been de facto Emperor of Austria and King of Hungary since the death of Emperor Franz Joseph on November 21. Martin "is still very delighted by his impression of the ardennal [...]" (F. to Ferenczi, 4.1.1917).

1916 December end

The director of the Budapest joint-stock company "Harmonia", Stefan Szanto, visits F. and asks him to give a lecture for an "honorary fee" of 1000 Kronen.[34] The joint-stock company runs a music publishing house, and an art and piano shop, and organizes concerts and lectures. F. intends to accept the offer for 1917 February 2, but Ferenczi strongly advises him against it for various reasons, and F. does not give the lecture.

1917

– F. is nominated for the Nobel Prize (Medicine) for the second time.

Books received:

– Georg Groddeck sends F. his book *Psychische Bedingtheit und psychoanalytische Behand-lung organischer Leiden* with the dedication "Herrn Prof. F. überreicht/vom Verfasser".
– Oskar Pfister sends F. a collection of lectures on the subject "Was bietet die Psychoanalyse dem Erzieher?" ("What does psychoanalysis offer the educator?" with the dedication "Herrn Prof. Dr F. übersendet/das jüngste Enkelchen/d. V.".
– Lou Andreas-Salomé sends F. her book *Drei Briefe an einen Knaben* with the dedication "Herrn Prof. S. Freud zum Gruß von der dankbaren Verf.".

1917 January
Sándor Ferenczi is diagnosed with pulmonary tuberculosis and Graves' disease.

1917 January 1
F. begins to read Lamarck's *Zoologische Philosophie* and sends a first draft of the "Lamarck paper" to Sándor Ferenczi. Its core idea is that the "Allmacht der Gedanken" ("omnipotence of thought") was also once a reality.

1917 January 2
Rudolf Kriser continued his analysis with F. It lasted until December 1918. He called F. a swin-dler and exploiter, among other things, but successfully completed the analysis after two years and remained attached to F. in veneration.

1917 January 10
WPV meeting: Hermann Nunberg speaks about "Observations on a case of hypochondria".

1917 January mid
– F. learns that Robert Bárány, who has nominated him for the Nobel Prize, is getting a profes-sorship in Uppsala and comments on this in a letter to Ferenczi with the words. "With that, my prospects for the prize increase from five to six percent" (F. to Ferenczi, 22.1.1917). In fact, some members of the Karolinska Institute let Bárány know that F. had little chance, as his work on psychoanalysis the results were "too hypothetical for the time being" (Ida Bárány-Kurt Eissler, 18.5.1964).
– Eira Hellberg reports back to F.

1917 January 15
Desirée (Daisy) Brody, a niece of Alexander Szabó and sister of René Spitz, begins an analysis with F. It lasts until May.

1917 January 18
The archeologist and art historian Ludwig Pollak begins an analysis with F. (until April).

1917 before January 20
F. has difficulties in obtaining the literature he wants for the Lamarck paper; among other things, he asks Karl Grobben and writes to the Court Library.

1917 January end
F. gets some books on Lamarck.

1917 February 4
Sándor Ferenczi is in Vienna for a day.

1917 February 7
WPV meeting: Lajos Lévy speaks on "The Sexual Symbolism of the Biblical Story of Paradise".

1917 February 12
F. Daughter Anna goes to the sanatorium in Sulz in the Vienna Woods.

1917 February 18
- F. visits his daughter Anna in Sulz.
- Ella Götzl begins an analysis with F. It lasts until 1920 December. Ella Götzl was the daughter of the kaiserliche Rat (Imperial Councillor) Adolf Pick, the boss of the metal cufflink factory "Pick und Fleischner". F. kept in contact and exchanged letters with her until the end of his life.

1917 February 21
F.'s daughter Anna comes back to Vienna from the Sulz.

1917 March
F. gives a lecture to B'nai B'rith on "Phantasie und Kunst" ("Imagination and Art").

1917 March 2
F.'s son Oliver is transferred from Krakow to Krems and stays two days in Vienna.

1917 March 7
WPV meeting: Ludwig Jekels presents an "Essay on Macbeth".

1917 March 15
F. notes in his calendar "Revolution in Russia". Ten days later, he writes: "Since the revolution I have seen every other interest shrivel up, and since one can't do anything in this one, one does nothing at all. The tensions are now too great. How intensely would one have experienced this splendid change if today the first consideration were not for peace" (F. to Ferenczi, 25.3.1917).

1917 March 17
Death of Franz Brentano. F. had listened to lectures by the philosopher as a student and was temporarily so strongly under his influence that he considered "to take my Ph.D. in philosophy and zoology" (F. to Silberstein, 7.3.1875).

1917 March 27
F.'s son Martin comes from Linz to visit Vienna for a fortnight.

1917 March 29
Siegfried Bernfeld begins his analysis with F. (until 1920 April).

1917 April 8
F.'s son Oliver is coming from Krems to visit Vienna over Easter.

1917 April 11
- F.'s son Martin has to return to the Cadre.
- WPV meeting: speeches and contributions.

1917 April 13
Sándor Ferenczi is in Vienna for a day.

1917 April 15
F.'s son Ernst comes to Vienna for a holiday. This time, he did not stay in Berggasse, but with his sister Mathilde in Türkenstrasse 29, about three minutes' walk away.

1917 April 18
WPV meeting: brief communications; Eduard Hitschmann speaks on "Child observation (of a three-year-old girl)", Hanns Sachs on "Ethnological parallels to infantile sexual theories", Paul Federn on "Narcissism and egoism" and F. on "A childhood memory of Goethe and an analytical observation".

1917 April 25
F. notes in his calendar: "No Nobel Prize 1917". No Nobel Prize was awarded in 1917 for physiology and medicine – the category for which F. was eligible.

1917 April 27
F.'s son Martin is passing through Linz on his way to a short military training course in Bruck an der Leitha for a short visit to Berggasse.

1917 May 3
F.'s son Ernst goes back to the front.

1917 May 4
F.'s son Martin stops in Vienna for two days on his way back from Bruck to Linz and stays until his father's birthday on May 6.

1917 May 7
F.'s son Oliver makes a half-hour visit to Berggasse on his way from Krems to a Hungarian mission.

1917 May 7–10
Sándor Ferenczi is on his way back from a spay stay at Semmering in Vienna.

1917 May 12–13
F.'s son Oliver stops for a night in the Berggasse on his way back from Hungary to Krems.

1917 May 14
– Another shipment of bread from Ferenczi arrives in Berggasse.
– F.'s daughter Sophie leaves for Hamburg again after six months in Vienna with her son Ernst; F. gives her some bread from Ferenczi.

1917 May 16
WPV meeting: Paul Federn speaks about the "early stage of dementia praecox".

1917 before May 21
An official from Anton von Freund's brewery in Budapest delivers a "monster giant bread" to Berggasse.

1917 May ca. 21
F. receives a 700-page manuscript from Meinrad Haberl entitled "Zur Metaphysik der Gefühle" ("On the Metaphysics of Feelings").

1917 before May 23
Selma Glanz gives F. an orchid plant, which she had bought specially from the Kaiser's greenhouse.

1917 May 26–27
F.'s sons Martin and Oliver are visiting Vienna over Whitsun.

1917 May 27
Beginning of the correspondence between F. and Georg Groddeck.

1917 May 29 before
Eira Hellberg demands suggestive treatment from F., which he refuses.

1917 June 6
- WPV meeting: the meeting takes place in the lecture theater of the Wagner-Jauregg's clinic. His assistant Otto Pötzl speaks on "Experimentally excited dream images as an illustration for Freudian dream analysis".
- The third part of F.'s *Vorlesungen zur Einführung in die Psychoanalyse* is published.
- F. receives "ammunition", i.e. food, from Hungary. Both Sándor Ferenczi and especially Anton von Freund regularly supply F., the latter among other things with 20 kg of lard.

1917 June 6–8
Otto Rank comes to Vienna for three days from Krakow, where he has been the *Krakauer Zeitung* since the beginning of 1916.

1917 June 13
F.'s son Ernst receives the medal of merit "Signum laudis" (sign of praise).

1917 June 15
F.'s sister-in-law Minna goes to Bad Reichenhall for a spay stay.

1917 June 17
F. visits his son Oliver in Krems.

1917 June 19
Death of F.'s nephew Hermann Graf, the son of his sister Rosa. He had been wounded on the Italian front on June 18 and had now died in a field hospital in Tossa (about 20 km south of Bolzano). F. learns of his death on June 25.

1917 June 23
F.'s son Oliver unexpectedly comes to Vienna for one night.

1917 June 24
Before his summer holiday, F. asks Selma Glanz to give the greenhouse from which the orchid vines she had given him four weeks ago "the order to collect them at our expense and to keep them in care over time. We are leaving at the end of this week and can do nothing more for them" (F. to Selma and Heinrich Glanz, 24.6.1917).

1917 June 25
F. brings the news of Hermann Graf's death to his mother, F.'s sister Rosa, who was in the process of packing a parcel for her son. According to F.'s niece Lilly, he says "Don't bother anymore, Rosa, Hermann has fallen – SHOUT!"

1917 June 30–September 1
Summer stay with wife Martha and daughter Anna in the High Tatras

F., Martha and Anna stay in Csorbató in Villa Maria Theresia for the holidays. During this time, Max Eitingon and Otto Rank visit him. F. organizes a "hunting contest" for mushrooms and offers 20 Heller as the first prize and ten Heller as the second prize.

1917 June 30

Departure from Vienna at 11.49 pm.

1917 July 1

Arrival at Oderberg (today Bohumín) at 8.51; onward journey at 10.10 to Csorbató and arrival there around 16.00.

1917 before July 13

F. Ilona Berger from the hospital kitchen of the reserve hospital in Ujpest in the north of Budapest receives a consignment of bread and cheese arranged by Ferenczi.

1917 July 15

Hanns Sachs comes to Csorbató for three weeks with his partner the actress Grete Ilm – a sister of Ernest Jones's future wife Katherine.

1917 July 19

– Ferenczi sends bread, cheese and salami to Csorbató.
– Eitingon sends a basket with eggs.

1917 July 21

Ferenczi comes to Csorbató for 14 days.

1917 July 29

F. goes mushroom picking for the first time during this holiday.

1917 August 4

Ferenczi and Sachs leave.

1917 August 6

F.'s son Ernst is transferred to a hospital in Zagreb because of a stomach ulcer.

1917 August 7

– F. and Martha drive to Lomnicz (today Tatranská Lomnica) to say goodbye to Gisella Pálos.
– Kata Lévy, the sister Anton von Freund's and her husband Lajos come from Lomnicz to Csorbató to question F. about the upbringing of their son Willy.

1917 before August 8

– F. receives consignments of chocolate, beef salami and 50 cigars from Ferenczi.
– Sándor Varyas – a high school teacher and follower of psychoanalysis – brings eggs, butter, flour and smoked sheep's cheese.
– Kata Lévy brings primsen cheese – a sheep's cheese sewn into goat skins – and butter.

1917 August mid

F.'s son Ernst is transferred to Graz for a few days.

1917 August 17

F.'s brother Alexander is awarded the Order of the Iron Crown by the Emperor for his services to the tariff system in Austria-Hungary.

1917 August 19

Anna leaves Csorbató and spends the rest of her summer holidays with Ferenczi's sister Ilona Zoltán in Kótaj near Nyíregyháza.

1917 August 20

- Move to a veranda room on the ground floor of the villa.
- F. receives from Ludwig Binswanger the manuscript of the first chapter of Part 2 of a planned book on psychoanalysis.
- F. receives a basket of eggs from Max Eitingon, who is in Miskolcz.

1917 August 21

F.'s son Martin informs his parents by telegram that he has to return to the front.

1917 August 23

F.'s son Ernst is transferred to the hospital of the Stiftskaserne in Vienna. There, he lies in the same room as F.'s cousin Simon Nathansohn.

1917 September 1

- Departure for Vienna. On the train journey, F. writes down his paper "Eine Kindheitserinnerung aus ,Dichtung und Wahrheit'".
- Arrival in Vienna; Oliver is at the station to pick up his parents.

1917 September 2

Anna returns to Vienna after a two-week stay at Ilona Zoltán's estate.

1917 September 15

F.'s son Oliver is transferred from Krems to Krakow again and is in Berggasse for a short visit.

1917 September 11

Max Brod, Franz Kafka's friend and patron, begins an analysis with F. (until 1918 June).

1917 September mid

F.'s son Ernst is on sick leave for four weeks because of gonorrhea and spends it in the Berggasse.

1917 September 18

Sascha Tschernjakow, a wood manufacturer and trader from Russia, begins an analysis with F. It lasts until 1918 February. His second wife, Beate Kolisch, was married to Oskar Taussig before him. During the analysis with F., he often exchanges ideas with Max Brod, the friend of Franz Kafka, who is being treated by F. at the same time.

1917 September 25

Leo Kaplan sends F. Book *Hypnotismus, Animismus und Psychoanalyse. Historisch-kritische Versuche* with the dedication "Dem verehrten/Lehrer/Herr Prof. F./der Autor".

1917 September 27

The opera singer Marie Gutheil-Schoder begins an analysis with F. It lasts until October.

1917 September 28

Max Eitingon is in Vienna for a few hours and has dinner with Freud.

1917 October 10

WPV meeting: General Assembly, statement of accounts. Re-election of officers. Hanns Sachs speaks on "The basic motif of Shakespeare's last creative period and its shaping in the 'Tempest'".

1917 October 28

F.'s son Oliver receives his marching orders to the Russian front and is deployed to build a bridge over the Dniester.

1917 October 25

F. sends a handwritten short autobiography to Albert van Renterghem for the use of Renterghem's preface to his Dutch translation of the *Lectures for Introduction to Psychoanalysis*.

1917 October 29

Maximilian Steiner gives F. his book *Die psychischen Störungen der männlichen Potenz* with the dedication "Herrn/Prof. Dr. Sigm. F./in heartfelt gratitude and sincere veneration/Dr Steiner".

1917 November beginning

After F.'s cigar supply was used up, he has palpitations, complains of fatigue and discovers a painful swelling of the palate. He thinks it is possibly a carcinoma. Then, he receives 50 cigars from a patient and "the gum irritation rapidly abated!" (F. to Ferenczi, 6.11.1917).

1917 November 2

Anton von Freund von begins an analysis with F. (until 1919 March).

1917 November 9

– F.'s son Martin is transferred to Palmanova, a good 20 km south of Udine. From Palmanova, Martin sends a box of coffee, canned goods, leather, soap, fabrics and shoes to Vienna. They came from an Italian depot, and F. comments on the shipment in a letter to Ferenczi with the sentence: "From Martin there came a case of booty from Palmanova" (F. to Ferenczi, 20.11.1917).

– Otto Pötzl gives F. an offprint of his paper on "Experimentell erregte Traumbilder in ihren Beziehungen zum indirekten Sehen" with the dedication "Herrn Professor Sigmund Freud arden bescheidenes Zeichen begeisterter Verehrung und Bewunderung gewidmet. Otto Pötzl".

1917 November 14

WPV meeting: communications and reviews, including Wilma Federn on Psycho-Analysis and Maids: An attempt to peace, Otto Pötzl on "déjà raconté", Leo Kaplan on the consequences of an attempt to intimidate a schizophrenic, F. on an example of dream, on symbols and on convincing in psychoanalysis, and Hermann Nunberg on "incest with daughter and its psychical consequences".

1917 November 15

F.'s son Ernst is transferred to Steinamanger (Szombathely) in western Hungary.

1917 November 20

F. receives Alfred Adler's paper *The Problem of Homosexuality*. He calls it "a very stupid and remarkably inadequate piece of writing" (F. to Ferenczi, 20.11.1917).

1917 December

F. publishes paper "Eine Kindheitserinnerung [Goethes] aus Dichtung und Wahrheit".

1917 December 6

– F.'s son Ernst is transferred from Steinamanger (Szombathely) to Vienna.

– F. follows the armistice negotiations between Germany and Russia with great interest, but without knowing that Adolf Joffe is the head of the Russian negotiating delegation. Joffe had lived as a political émigré in Vienna between 1906 and 1912. There, he had been a member of the editorial board of Pravda, published by Trotsky, and a patient of Alfred Adler. Trotsky wrote in this context: "Through Joffe, I became acquainted with the problems of psychoanalysis, which fascinated me […]" (Trotsky 1930, p. 171). During his time in Vienna, Joffe had also visited F. In 1918, he became Soviet Russia's ambassador to Germany.

1917 before December 11
- F. receives 20 kilos of the finest flour from a "Hungarian friend".
- F. meets Robert Bárány, who has been teaching at Uppsala University for over a year, and who had nominated him for the Nobel Prize in 1916.

1917 December 11
- F. receives 100 cigars and a bottle of petrol from a patient.
- A crate of apples arrives from Merano, which Martha had ordered.

1917 December 12
WPV meeting: F. speaks on "Das Tabu der Virginität".

1917 December 25
Otto Rank visits F.

1917 December 27
F. cannot bring himself to finish the Lamarck work.

1917 December 31
F. again receives a porcupine from Ferenczi in memory of their visit to America in 1909, during which they had seen a dead porcupine in the Adirondacks. Ferenczi had already given him a porcupine at the end of 1909 November.

1918

- F. is nominated for the Nobel Prize (Medicine) for the third time.
- Anton von Freund donates 1 million crowns to psychoanalysis, which are largely lost in the following years due to the devaluation of money.
- F. loses all his assets invested in Austrian government securities (150,000 crowns) and 100,000 crowns of his wife's life insurance.

Books received:

- Horace Frink sends F. his book *Morbid fears and compulsions* with the dedication "To Prof. F./with the writer's compliments/H. W. Frink".
- Alphonse Maeder sends F. his book *Heilung und Entwicklung im Seelenleben* with the dedication "Herrn Prof F./in Verehrung/A M".
- Oskar Pfister sends F. his book *Wahrheit und Schönheit in der Psychoanalyse* with the dedication "Herrn Prof. Dr F./in herzlicher Gesinnungs-/gemeinschaft/d. V ".
- Isaac Silverman sends F. his book *The psychical function of the cerebellum* with the dedication "To Professor Sigmund F./with the Author's compliments".

1918 January 1
F.'s son Oliver becomes a platoon leader.

1918 January 2
Georgina Weiss, a sister of Edoardo Weiss, begins an analysis with F. It lasts until June 26.

1918 January 3
F. s son Ernst travels to Dresden, Berlin and Schwerin for a fortnight. In Schwerin, he visited his sister Sophie, who had temporarily moved to Schwerin with her son Ernst in 1917 May, as her husband Max was active there in training for air reconnaissance by aviators.

1918 January 7
Julius Riesz, partner of the leather company H. Riesz Söhne, begins a short analysis at F. It lasts until 1919 January.

1918 January 9
WPV meeting: brief communications and reviews.

1918 January 14
The Austrian ethnologist Rudolf Trebitsch presents himself to F. for treatment, but nothing comes of it, probably because he died at the beginning of October as a result of influenza.

1918 January mid
The Madrid publisher R. Castillo asks for permission to translate *Psychopathology of Everyday Life into* Spanish.

1918 January 16
WPV meeting: Victor Tausk speaks on "The emergence of the 'influence apparatus' in schizophrenia".

1918 January 30
WPV meeting: discussion on Victor Tausk's presentation of January 16.

1918 February
Silvia Mels-Colloredo from the Waldsee-Mels line of the Colloredo noble family begins an analysis with F. It lasts at least until 1920 July.

1918 February
F. has dream of "Sohn im Sportkostüm" ("son in sports costume").

1918 February 3–4
Sándor Ferenczi is in Vienna.

1918 February 13
WPV meeting: Theodor Reik presents "Psychoanalytical Studies in Biblical Exegesis".

1918 February 15
- F. receives 10,000 crowns[35] more than requested from his patient Sascha Tschernjakow, who has been receiving treatment from him since September mid.
- Ernst Simmel sends F. his *book Kriegs-Neurosen und psychisches Trauma* with the dedication "Herrn Professor Dr. Freud in aufrichtiger Verehrung. Dr Simmel". This is also the beginning of the correspondence between F. and Ernst Simmel.

1918 February mid
Wilma Federn wanted to dedicate her drama *Die Treibjagd to* F., but he urged her "to refrain from the intended dedication [...] and not to spoil her chances by such a confession" (F. to Wilma Federn, 17.2.1918).

1918 February 17
F.'s son Martin comes from the Italian front on leave and brings coffee and rice.

1918 February 19
Lajos Lévy and Anton von Freund visit F.

1918 February 26
F.'s son Oliver gets home leave for a good two weeks, mainly because of eczema and indigestion.

1918 March
F. meets the deputy director of the library in front of the university library. By chance, Paul Federn and Siegfried Altmann, the later director of the Israelite Institute for the Blind in Vienna-Döblin, pass by and Federn introduces Altmann to F.

1918 March 1
F.'s son Martin becomes first lieutenant.

1918 March 4
István Hollós begins an analysis with F.

1918 March 13
- WPV meeting: F. speaks on slip of the tongue as a faulty act and melancholy, Helene Deutsch on an "Association attempt in melancholy" and Otto Fenichel on a "Letter of a seven years old boy: Interpretation of dreams".
- F.'s son Oliver goes back to his company.

1918 before March 15
Esti Drucker, who has been dating F.'s son Martin for two years, is invited to dinner in the Berggasse.

1918 March mid
Istváan Hollós is with F. for analysis.

1918 March 16
F.'s son Martin goes back to the Italian front.

1918 March 22
F. receives the book by the psychiatrist Paul Schilder *Wahn und Erkenntnis. A psychopathological study.*

1918 March 27
Otto Rank gives F. his book *Der Künstler. Ansätze zu einer Sexual-Psychologie* with the dedication *"Prof. F. in herzlicher Dankbarkeit/Dr Rank"*.

1918 April
F.'s daughter Anna takes her teacher's exam.

1918 April beginning
F. has "gouty pains (age arthritis)" in his right hand (F. to Ferenczi, 7.4.1918).

1918 April 3
Anton von Freund, who has been undergoing treatment with F. again since the end of February, pays 7000 crowns for this phase of the treatment.[36]

1918 April 5
F. suggests to his brother Alexander to provide Dolfi, who takes care of the mother, with enough money that the mother does not know about and thus does not learn about the actual costs of the household.

1918 April 11
F. learns that Sophie's husband Max's brother, the pediatrician Rudolf Halberstadt, was killed in action in France on April 5.

1918 April 12
– F.'s son Ernst is found unfit for service due to lung catarrh.

1918 April 15
F.'s daughter Anna passed the teaching qualification examination, having already passed her teacher's examination in 1914. From 1915 to 1918, she taught at the Cottage Lyceum, which now also offered her an employment contract.

1918 April 17
WPV meeting: Otto Fenichel speaks on "On a derivative of the incest conflict".

1918 April 19
– F.'s daughter Anna takes the religion exam.
– Walter Schmideberg visits the F.'s and gives Martha "a small package" from Max Eitingon – presumably food. Schmideberg had met Eitingon in Meran and had been made aware of F. and psychoanalysis by him. He visits F. again a few days later.

1918 May 5
F.'s Martin is awarded the Medal of Merit Signum laudis for outstanding service in the war for the second time.

1918 May 6
On his birthday, F. learns that his daughter Sophie is pregnant again.

1918 May 7
Minna goes to Bad Reichenhall for a spay stay.

1918 May 8
F.'s Ernst goes to Abbazia for six weeks to be treated for his lung catarrh.

1918 May 13
F. receives Oskar Pfister's book *A New Approach to the Old Gospel.*

1918 May 15
WPV meeting: Theodor Reik continues his lecture on "Psychoanalytical Studies on Biblical Exegesis" from February 13.

1918 after May 28
F. has his patient Rudolf Kriser paint his portrait after the analysis for a fee. F. finds the drawing "quite fine, and not very gratifying" (F. to Ferenczi, 2.6.1918), but has it reproduced.

1918 June 5
WPV meeting: Otto Pötzl speaks on "Metapsychological traces in the spatial arrangement of the visual centers of the cerebrum" (first part).

1918 June 11
F. signs the contract for the summer holiday in Csorbató.

1918 June 12
WPV meeting: Otto Pötzl continues his talk on "Metapsychological traces in the spatial arrangement of the visual centers of the cerebrum" (second part).

1918 June 17
– The People's Nutrition Office cuts bread rations by half because it is becoming increasingly difficult to import grain. This means that per capita only 630g of flour could be given per week. F. is thus even more dependent on the support of his Hungarian friends.
– F.'s son Ernst returns from Abbazia.

1918 June 27
F. again receives a generous fee from Anton von Freund, this time for the treatment period from the beginning of April to the end of June.

1918 July beginning
Martha goes to Schwerin to visit her daughter Sophie. She is accompanied to Berlin by Richard Mises, a distant relative.

1918 July 2
F.'s son Martin comes to Vienna from the Italian front.

1918 July 6
Julius Wagner-Jauregg proposes to the medical faculty that F. be awarded the title of full professor.

1918 July 8–August 1
Summer stay in Budapest

F. and his daughter Anna are invited by Anton von Freund to stay at his official residence in Budapest-Steinbruch until August 1. As a guest gift, F. brings the etching by Max Pollak. In Budapest, he begins work on the fifth edition of The *Interpretation of Dreams*. Ferenczi visits occasionally, also Lajos Lévy. F.'s son Ernst comes on leave from the front for a few days. During the stay, a carriage with two horses was provided. So F. and Anna could also visit the center of Budapest.

1918 July 8

Travel by boat from Vienna to Budapest.

1918 after July 8

Kata Lévy begins an analysis with F. He takes no fee for it, probably because her brother Anton von Freund supports psychoanalysis so generously financially.

1918 July end

F. grants Zsófia Dénes an interview. Dénes is a Hungarian journalist and niece of Ferenczi's wife Gisella. She had worked for a few years since 1912 as Paris correspondent for the Hungarian newspapers *Pesti Napló* and *Világ. The* interview then appeared in the *Világ (World)* on August 4.

1918 August 1–September 25
Summer stay in the High Tatras

F. is on holiday in the High Tatras with his wife. They stay at the Kriváň' Hotel. Sándor Ferenczi and F.'s son Ernst also come to Csorbató.

1918 August 1

Journey from Budapest to Csorbató, together with Ferenczi and seven-year-old Willy Lévy. Martha – coming from Schwerin, where she had visited daughter Sophie and family – arrives two hours before F. and waits for her husband at the station.

1918 August 4

Regine Vidor, a sister of Anton von Freund, and her husband Emil Vidor visit F. and Martha in Csorbató, presumably to discuss details of their stay in September.

1918 September

F.'s son Martin becomes engaged to Esti Drucker. The official engagement is not until 1919 September.

1918 September 4

Move from Csorbató to Lomnicz. There, they were guests of Regine Vidor, a sister of Anton von Freund and her husband Emil Vidor.

1918 before September 9

F. receives from Hermann Hesse's essay "Künstler und Psychoanalyse" (Artists and Psychoanalysis).

1918 September 14

F., Martha and Ernst make an excursion to Késmark (today Kežmarok), about 15km east of Lomnicz.

1918 September 15

Kata and Lajos Lévy come to Lomnicz for a few days and play cards with F. occasionally.

1918 September mid

Hanns Sachs comes to Lomnicz.

1918 September 25

Rail journey from Lomnicz to Budapest.

1918 September 28–30
V. International Psychoanalytical Congress in Budapest

The Fifth International Psychoanalytical Congress takes place in Budapest. It was originally planned in Breslau, but is now held in the conference hall of the Hungarian Academy of Sciences; the participants are accommodated in the Hotel Gellért fürdö. At the General Assembly, on the proposal of the previous President of the IPA Karl Abraham, Sándor Ferenczi is unanimously elected President and Anton v. Freund is elected Secretary of the Association.

1918 September 29

– F. gives a lecture on "Wege der Wege der psychoanalytischen Therapie", in which he expresses the hope that analytical therapy could be made available not only to intellectuals but also to low-income earners and children by providing free treatment in outpatient clinics.
– Sándor Ferenczi gives F. the Hungarian translation of *Totem und Tabu* with the dedication "Seinem lieben Professor F./zur Erinnerung an den Budapester Kongress/Dr Ferenczi".

1918 September 30

Rail journey from Budapest to Vienna.

1918 September 30

After returning from the Budapest Congress, F. wrote to Ferenczi: "I am swimming in satisfaction, I am lighthearted, knowing that my problem child, my life's work, is protected and preserved for the future by your participation and that of others" (F. to Ferenczi, 30.9.1918).

1918 after September 30

Anna Freud begins an analysis with her father. It lasts until 1922 autumn.

1918 October

– F. offers lectures on "Psychoanalytischen Neurosenlehre" ("Psychoanalytic Theory of Neurosis") in the winter semester (lecture hall of the Psychiatric Clinic, fee $4 or 20 Krone).
– Martha gives Mathilde Zissermann, who had moved in from Russia with her four children above the F.'s to her mother Stefanie Matthias at Berggasse 19, beds, children's furniture, clothes and toys. Later, F. occasionally invites Mathilde Zissermann to tea in his study.

1918 October 1

The two Dutch psychoanalysts Johan H. W. van Ophuijsen and Jan van Emden meet in Vienna on their way back from the Budapest congresses and stay for four days.

1918 before October 2

F. receives Eugen Bleuler's paper "The Psychological Direction in Psychiatry".

1918 October 2

– Margarethe Rie begins an analysis with F. It lasts, with interruptions, until 1938 June.
– F.'s sister-in-law Minna comes back to Vienna from Bad Reichenhall.

1918 October 3
F. learns of the death of his cousin Simon Nathansohn.

1918 October 5–6
Lajos Lévy and Kata Lévy are visiting Vienna.

1918 October 6
F. goes to Rekawinkel (today a district of Pressbaum in the Vienna Woods), presumably to the Rekawinkel Sanatorium, a private institution for "nervous and emotionally ill people", which he occasionally recommended to patients for treatment.

1918 October 7
F. Children Anna, Ernst, Mathilde and Oliver have the "Spanish flu". It has been rampant in Austria-Hungary since September mid. [37]

1918 October 16
Hanns Sachs visits F.

1918 October 27
F.'s son Martin ends up in English captivity.

1918 October 28
F.'s son Ernst goes to Munich. He had only been classified as fit for clerical service and had been granted permission to resume his architectural studies in Munich.

1918 November beginning
F.'s son Martin becomes a prisoner of war and is admitted to a convalescent hospital in Teramo in Abruzzo.

1918 November 2
F.'s son Oliver comes to Vienna. He had originally been to be transferred from Venzone to Bosnia. However, a Hungarian officer had decided on his own authority that after his country's declaration of independence, no trains with Austrian soldiers were allowed to pass through the national territory. He therefore confiscated all weapons and diverted the train toward the Austrian border.

1918 November 4
- F. enters "Nobel Prize done" in his calendar. However, no Nobel Prizes were awarded for medicine in 1918 because of the war.
- F. takes over the disposal of the foundation from Anton von Freund. In 1918, he had decided to use a foundation he had already established specifically to found and support a psychoanalytic polyclinic with a teaching institute in Budapest.

1918 November 11
Otto Rank introduces F. to his wife Beata, whom he had married two days earlier.

1918 November 12
F. enters "Panic participated" in his calendar. This refers to a demonstration in front of parliament, during which there was a shootout. The panicked crowd fled, leaving many injured and two dead.

1918 November 16
F. enters in his calendar: "Republic in Hungary".

1918 November 17
F. proposes to the "Secret Committee" to offer two prizes annually from the interest of Anton von Freund's foundation.

1918 November 19
Meeting of the WPV; Siegfried Bernfeld speaks on "Poetic writing by youth".

1918 November 21
F. learns that his son Martin has been in English captivity since October 27.

1918 November 29
Otto Pötzl gives F. an offprint of his paper "Über die räumliche Anordnung der Zentren des menschlichen Grosshirns with the dedication "Herrn Professor Sigmund Freud in unbegrenzter Verehrung und Bewunderung überreicht von Dr. Otto Pötzl".

1918 November end
The writer Ernst Lothar visits F. and has a long conversation with him about the end of the monarchy and Austria as a homeland.

1918 December 2
Helene Deutsch begins an analysis with F.

1918 December 3
F. receives the first personal message from son Martin, dated November 14.

1918 December 8
Birth of F. grandson Heinele (Heinz), son of daughter Sophie.

1918 December mid
Viktor Tausk asks F. to analyze him. Tausk refuses and sends him to Helene Deutsch, who in turn is analyzing him.

1918 December 22
WPV meeting: General Assembly.

1918 December end
F.'s paper "Aus der Geschichte einer infantilen Neurose" is published. It is the case of Sergei Pankejeff ("Wolf Man")

1919

- F. is nominated for the Nobel Prize (Medicine) for the fourth time.
- F. becomes a member of the board of trustees of the "Jewish Scientific Institute" (YIVO) founded in Vilnius. The other members are as follows: Eduard Bernstein, Simon Dubnow, Albert Einstein, Moses Gaster, Edward Sapir, David Swinsen, Bernhard Wachstein and Chaim Zhitlovsky.
- The International Psycho-Analytical Press is founded in London as a branch of Internationale Psychoanalytische Verlag. Ernest Jones becomes a director.
- Ernst Papanek introduces the nine year old Wolfgang Foges to F., whom he had identified as a problem child within the framework of the project "Playmates" which he had initiated. He meets with F. a total of three times. The contact was established through Mathilde Zissermann, who lived on the floor above F. and was involved in the same project.
- Louis Ferriére, a Swiss psychiatrist who works for the International Red Cross in Vienna, offers to bring F. vital items from Switzerland. F. asks for soap and chocolate.

Books received:

- Honorio Delgado sends F. his book *El psicoanalisis* with the dedication "Herr Prof. Dr. Freud:/ Mit der grössten Hochach-/tung und Bewunderung/des Verfassers".
- Eduard Hitschmann gives F. his book *Gottfried Keller. Psychoanalyse des Poets, seiner Gestalten und* with the dedication "Herrn Professor F./in dankbarer Verehrung/d. V".
- The American psychiatrist Isador Coriat sends F. his book *What is psychoanalysis?* With the dedication "To Dr. Sigmund Freud/with the author's/kindest regards".
- Paul Federn gives F. his book *Zur Psychologie der Revolution. Die vaterlose Gesellschaft* with the dedication "Herr Prof. Dr S. Freud/verehrungsvoll d Verf.".
- The American writer and sociologist Waldo Frank sends F. his book *Our America* with the dedication "To Dr Freud/our master without Whom/our generation could not/express itself/ Waldo Frank/New York".

1919 January mid

The Internationale Psychoanalytische Verlag is founded in Vienna from the funds of Anton von Freund's foundation. F., Sándor Ferenczi, Anton von Freund, Otto Rank (business manager) and Theodor Reik (assistant) become directors. The publishing house is located at Grünangergasse 3–5 (until 1924).

1919 January 5
WPV meeting: Theodor Reik speaks on "The Birth of Music from the Spirit of Tragedy".

1919 January 19
WPV meeting: Siegfried Bernfeld speaks on "The Poetry of Young People".

1919 January 26
Sergei Pankejeff (the "Wolf Man") visits F.

1919 January 31
F. makes a first will and stipulates that his wife Martha is to decide on the distribution of the estate. He forbids eulogies and asks for the funeral to be announced later. "If it is convenient and cheap: Cremation".

1919 February 2
WPV meeting: Victor Tausk speaks on "War Neuroses and Psychoses".

1919 February 16
Elections to the National Assembly take place in Austria. As women are entitled to vote for the first time, Martha and Anna celebrate "their entry into political life" (F. to Martin Freud, 16.2.1919).

1919 February 23
WPV meeting: Walter Fokschaner speaks on "Analysis of a case of paranoia".

1919 March
- Robert Jokl, assistant at the Burghölzli in Zurich, begins an analysis with F. It lasts until May.
- F.'s wife Martha falls ill with severe influenza and pneumonia, from which she only recovers after several months.
- Romain Rolland sends F. his book *Liluli* with the dedication "Au Destructeur d'Illusions/ Prof. Dr F./en arden de respect/et de cordiale sympathie/Romain Rolland".

1919 March 2
Sándor Ferenczi marries Gisella Pálos.

1919 March 3
Cyril Strauss from Frankfurt begins an analysis with F. It lasts until 1920 December.

1919 March 6
Margit Dubowitz, Anton von Freund's mistress, begins an analysis with F. It lasts until around 1920 December.

1919 March 9
WPV meeting: Josef Friedjung presented "Some thoughts on the problem of the will".

1919 Spring
- The publisher Urban & Schwarzenberg asked F. to write a contribution on the subject of "Psychoanalytic Neurosis Theory" for the *Special Pathology and Therapy of Internal Diseases* edited by Friedrich Kraus and Theodor Brugsch. However, F. forwarded the request to Karl Abraham after hesitating for some time.
- F. writes the draft for his writings *Jenseits des Lustprinzips* and *Massenpsychologie und Ich-Analyse.*
- F. grants Charles Rosebault an interview. It was published in the *New York Times* on August 24 under the title "Americans Who Were More German Than Germans".

1919 March 23
WPV meeting: Paul Federn speaks on "The fatherless society".

1919 March 25
Sándor Ferenczi is appointed full university professor by the Hungarian People's Commissioner for National Education Zsigmond Kunfi.

1919 March 30
Five days after the proclamation of the soviet republic in Hungary, F. published his paper "Kell-e az egyetemen a ardennalysis tanitani?" ("On teaching of psycho-analysis in Universities"), which later is published under the German title "Soll die Psychoanalyse an den Universitäten gelehrt arden?"

1919 April beginning

Sándor Ferenczi prompts F. to (re-)read **Börne** s article "The Art of Becoming an Original Writer in Three Days" ("Die Kunst, in drei Tagen ein Originalschriftsteller zu arden").

1919 April 2

WPV meeting: Alfred Winterstein speaks on "The Origin of Greek Tragedy".

1919 April 5

Theodor Reik gives F. his book *Das Werk Richard Beer-Hofmann* with the dedication "Herrn Professor S. Freud ergebenst/Th. Reik".

1919 April 9

After reading Ludwig Börne's article "Die Kunst, in drei Tagen ein Originalschriftsteller zu arden" ("The Art of Becoming an Original Writer in Three Days"), F. wrote that he was "astonished at how much some things that are in there correspond almost word for word with some things that I have always represented and thought. So he could really be the source of my originality" (F. to Ferenczi, 9.4.1919).

1919 April 11

Otto Rank returns from a stay at a spa in Switzerland and immediately visits F.

1919 April mid

– A private analytic society founded in Leipzig contacts F. He sends a complete set of *Imago* and recommends reading and discussing the articles until someone can come to Leipzig to train psychoanalysts.
– The Hungarian soviet government instructs its legation in Vienna to pay the money from Anton von Freund's Budapest fund to F. in installments.

1919 April 16

WPV meeting: Victor Tausk speaks on "Questions from the psychoanalytical technique".

1919 April 17

F. sends the medical historian Max Neuburger F. his biographical data at his request.

1919 April 21

Sergei Pankejeff (the "Wolf Man") visits F. during a stay in Vienna and receives from him the fourth volume of the *Sammlung Kleiner Schriften zur Neurosenlehre*, which also contains his case under the title "Aus der Geschichte einer infantilen Neurose. F.'s dedication reads: "Seinem lieben/Dr. Sergei Pankejeff/Freud".

1919 April 30

WPV meeting: Announcements and papers, including F. report on the founding of a psychoanalytic society in Leipzig, Otto Rank on the psychoanalytic movement in Switzerland and the rest of the world, and Eduard Hitschmann "About a case of an eating disorder".

1919 May

The first volume to be published by the newly founded Internationaler Psychoanalytischer Verlag (International Psychoanalytical Publishing House, from now on "Verlag") is the anthology edited by F. *Zur Psychologie der Kriegsneurosen (On the Psychology of War Neuroses),* which contains the contributions to the discussion on this subject from the fifth International Psychoanalytical Congress in Budapest in 1918.

1919 May 14
WPV meeting: Alfred von Winterstein speaks on "The Nausicaa Episode in the Odyssey".

1919 May mid
Martha has flu with fever and pneumonia.

1919 May 16
Hans Hattingberg brings F. a consignment of sugar, butter and flour from son Ernst in Berlin.

1919 May 18
Maximilian Steiner brings sugar and 50 cigars, presumably also from son Ernst.

1919 May 10
Martha gets influenza with pneumonia and high fever, which she suffers from for a week.

1919 May 28
WPV meeting: Hermann Nunberg speaks "On a case of catatonia".

1919 June 16
WPV meeting: F. presents a summary of *Jenseits des Lustprinzips*.

1919 June 18
- WPV meeting: Walter Fokschaner makes "remarks on a case of lunar addiction".
- F. receives 50 cigars and sugar, brokered by Maximilian Steiner.

1919 June 25
Käthe Hammerschlag, the granddaughter of F.'s religion teacher Samuel Hammerschlag and niece of his former patient Anna Hammerschlag commits suicide with cyanide. F. therefore visits her parents Albert and Leontine Hammerschlag the next day.

1919 before June 26
Eli Bernays sends 100 marks "to keep the passive members of the family on top in these hard times […]". (F. to Ernst Freud, 26.6.1919).

1919 July
Heinrich Meng begins an analysis with F. It usually takes place on weekends when Meng comes from Stuttgart to Vienna.

1919 July 2
- WPV meeting: Announcements and papers, including Hermine Hug-Hellmuth on "A Child's Analysis", Otto Rank on "A Child's Poetry", Hermann Nunberg on the "Interpretation of an Ornamental Drawing" and Paul Federn "On a Case of Obsessive Neurosis. Strange dreams".
- Viktor Tausk apologizes in writing to F. for his absence from the WPV meeting.

1919 July 3
Viktor Tausk writes a farewell letter to F.

1919 July 4
Death of Viktor Tausk; he shoots himself.

1919 July 6
Julius Wagner-Jauregg submits an expert opinion to the Ministry of Education in which he approves F.'s appointment as a full professor.

1919 July 9
Wagner-Jauregg submits his expert opinion on F. to the "Standing Commission" for the award of the venia arden.

1919 July 14
F. hands Otto Rank a large sum of money to distribute to various people.

1919 July 15–August 12
Spa stay with sister-in-law Minna in Badgastein
Accommodation is again at the Villa Wassing. Here F. reads for the first time Arthur Schopenhauer and writes *Jenseits des Lustprinzips*. – F. tells Eduard Hitschmann, who is also in Badgastein with his wife, how he discovered transference (in his patient Anna von Lieben).

1919 July 15
F., Martha and Minna leave Vienna. Martha leaves the train in Salzburg and starts a spay stay at the sanatorium Parsch (near Salzburg). At 7.45 am, F. arrives in Badgastein; at the station they are met by Guido Brecher, a relative of Martha and member of the WPV who worked as a spa doctor in Badgastein in the summer.

1919 July 16
Julius Wagner-Jauregg proposes F. for appointment as full professor. In his report of July 6, however, there is an error: Instead of Ordinarius, he writes Extra-Ordinarius, a title F. had held for a long time. The "Standing Commission for Habilitations" of the College of Professors proposes F. as full professor by 18 votes to 7. The commission's proposal is forwarded to the Ministry of Education on July 24.

1919 before July 21
F. meets Ludwig Riesz, a brother of his patient Julius Riesz.

1919 July 21
F. is not deterred by the heavy rain and fetches magnificent white orchids (Platanthera bifolia) from "a certain area […]". (F. to Anna, 21.7.1919),

1919 July 25–26
F. visits his wife Martha for her birthday in the Parsch sanatorium near Salzburg; there he meets son Ernst and they all attend a reading of verses Anton Wildgans by Hilda Wegner on the 25th. On the 26th, F. goes back to Badgastein with his son Ernst.

1919 July 27
At Max Neuburger's request, F. sends him a condensed description of psychoanalysis, consisting of only a few lines.

1919 July 28
F.'s son Ernst leaves Badgastein.

1919 July 30
F. takes a hike to Böckstein, about 4km south of Badgastein.

1919 July end

Otto Rank sends F. a Schopenhauer edition at his request.

1919 August 2

F.'s former patient Julius Riesz comes to Badgastein with his wife Mathilde and daughter Anna for a spay stay. In the evening F. plays tarot with him – and probably also Minna. The following evenings are also dedicated to playing tarot.

1919 August 6

F.'s son Martin returns to Vienna from captivity.

1919 before August 10

– Karel Wenckebach, one of the co-founders of modern arrhythmia diagnostics, who has worked at the First Medical Clinic in Vienna since 1914, visits F.
– F. has a therapeutic session with the painter Anna Wassing at her request.

1919 August 13–September 9
Summer stay with Martha and Anna at Badersee near Garmisch-Partenkirchen

F. had asked his son Ernst to rent "a balcony room for two persons and next to it a smaller one for Anna" (F. to Ernst Freud, 26.6.1919) in the Alpenhotel. F. has a view of the Zug-spitze from his desk.

1919 August 13

– F. drives with Minna from Badgastein to Salzburg. There they meet up with Martha and Anna and drive to Munich together in the afternoon.
– Visit to Harry Kahn's comedy *Der Ring* at the Munich Kammerspiele. Afterward, every-one went to dinner at the Hotel Marienbad with F.'s son-in-law Arnold Marlé, who was on stage himself that evening.
– In the evening, continue to Lake Badersee.

1919 August 18

F.'s sister Mitzi and her daughter Margarethe come to visit.

1919 before August 19

F. and Martha meet F.'s sister Rosa and her daughter Cäcilie in Munich.

1919 August 19

– F. writes about the supply situation: "Here, of course, one becomes rapidly impover-ished. Bavaria and Germany in general are actually even more expensive than German Austria. I spend fabulous sums every day […] There is no shortage of bad cigars here, somewhat cheaper than here in the sneak trade". (F. to Alexander Freud, 19.8.1919)
– The sons Martin and Ernst come to Badersee and stay for just under two weeks.

1919 before August 28

F. receives from the German-American writer and publicist George Sylvester Vierecks his book *Roosevelt. A Study in Ambivalence*, with the dedication "Prof. Dr. Sigmund Freud the Discoverer of a New World his humble Disciple the author George Sylvester Viereck".

1919 before August 31

F. receives Albert Mordell's book *The Erotic Motive in Literature* from Oskar Pfister.

1919 September 1

Max Eitingon and his wife Mirra come to Badersee for just under a week.

1919 before September 7

Son Ernst comes to Badersee.

1919 September 9

F., Martha and Ernst travel together to Munich, then on to Berlin with Eitingons.

1919 September 9–25
Visit of daughter Sophie in Hamburg with Stopover in Berlin

F. and Martha visit their daughter Sophie and her family in Hamburg. On this occasion F. has himself photographed by his son-in-law for a new official portrait. It is the famous picture with cigar and watch chain.

1919 September 10

Arrival in Berlin.

1919 September 10–12

F. visits his sons Ernst and Oliver, his sister Mitzi as well as his niece Margarethe and her husband Erwin Magnus.

1919 September 13

Journey from Berlin to Hamburg.

1919 September 21

– Journey from Hamburg to Berlin; arrival 3.40 pm at Lehrter Bahnhof. F. and Martha are received by Max Eitingon and Karl Abraham. F. is invited to Abrahams for lunch and dinner.
– Karl Abraham takes F. to the Anhalter Bahnhof; departure 9.40 pm In Leipzig, Mirra Eitingon and Eitingon's parents Chaim and Chasya arrive at the station and give F. a "basket full of gifts of love" (F. to Eitingon, 12.10.1919).

1919 September 22

Arrival in Munich in the morning. Son Ernst picks up his parents at the station.

1919 September 25

F. arrives back in Vienna.

1919 September 27

– Sándor Ferenczi comes to Vienna. F. proposes Max Eitingon for the "Secret Committee".
– Ernest Jones and Eric Hiller come to Vienna.

1919 September 28
– Julius Hering from Warsaw begins an analysis with F. It lasts until December.
– Ernest Jones invites the Freud family and Otto Rank to lunch at the Hotel Cobenzl.
– In the evening, the engagement of F.'s son Martin to Ernestine (Esti) Drucker takes place.

1919 September 29
Margarethe Csonka begins an analysis with F. It lasts until December. F. publishes her case history in 1920 under the title "Über die Psychogenese eines Falles von weiblicher Homosexualität".

1919 October
– F. becomes "Titular-Ordinarius".
– Franz Alexander visits F. for the first time.

1919 October beginning

F.'s daughter Anna joins the English department of the Internationale Psychoanalytische Verlag as an assistant.

1919 October 3

– F. issues a power of attorney for Ernest Jones for the purpose of disposing of the psychoanalytical foundation.

– F. and Martha are having coffee with Martin's parents-in-law Leopold and Ida Drucker.

1919 October 4

Ernest Jones and Eric Hiller depart from Vienna.

1919 October 6

David Forsyth, British doctor, starts an analysis at F. It lasts until November 18.

1919 October 10

Max Brod gives F. his book *Die Einsamen* with the dedication "Herrn Prof. Freud mit freundlichem Gruß/Max Brod".

1919 October 12

F. hires an English teacher, presumably because he was expecting a number of American and English education candidates for analysis in the near future.

1919 October 16

Beginning of the correspondence between F. and Heinrich Meng.

1919 October 19

Georg Groddeck sends F. the manuscript of his book *Der Seelensucher. Ein psychoanalytischer Roman.* F. "was delightfully entertained" by it (Freud to Groddeck, 8.2.1920).

1919 October 20

F. receives the official portrait photos taken during his visit to Hamburg from his son-in-law Max Halberstadt.

1919 October 25

Marco Levi Bianchini sends F. the Italian translation of the second edition of *On the Dream (Il sogno)* with the dedication Widmung "An den hochgeehrten Herrn Prof. S. Freud mit/achtungsvoller Freundschaft/M Levi Bianchini".

1919 October 29

F. attends a piano concert by the visually impaired pianist Paul Emerich with works by Johann Sebastian Bach in the small concert hall at the invitation of his dentist Sigmund Strach. Emerich had consulted him once eight years ago.

1919 October 30

F. reads an article about Emerich's piano concerto in the *Neue Freie Presse* and gives it to Sigmund Strach, who immediately forwards it to Emerich's mother Johanna.

1919 November

F. signs an "Aufruf für die Kinder der vom Hunger heimgesuchten Länder" ("Appeal for the Children of Hunger Stricken Countries") initiated by the IPA.

1919 November beginning
F. writes to Bernhard Schwarzwald, the director of the Parsch sanatorium, that he and his psychoanalytic colleagues will not send patients to his sanatorium because an advertisement placed by Schwarzwald excludes the assignment of patients to Parsch. The advertisement describes the sanatorium as a "Physikal.-diätet. Kuranstalt und Erholungsheim" which offers "fattening cures and psychotherapy (according to Dubois)".

1919 November 2
WPV meeting: Theodor Reik speaks about "Oedipus and the Sphinx". Melanie Klein is present as a guest.

1919 November 12
Oskar Pfister visits F. in the evening and brings food from Emil and Mira Oberholzer from Zurich. He had come with a children's aid train that sent children from poorly supplied post-war Austria to Switzerland. Pfister had been involved in this and similar aid campaigns.

1919 November 13
Sándor Ferenczi leaves Vienna.

1919 November mid
- Georg Sylvester Viereck sends F. his essay "The President sees snakes" and offers to send him food. F. accepts with the remark "that meat food will certainly lift my production capacity again" (F. to Eitingon, 19.11.1919).
- Honorio Delgado sends F. his paper "El psicoanalisis" with the dedication "Herr Prof. Dr. Freud: Mit der größten Hochachtung und Bewunderung des Verfassers".

1919 November 24
Anton von Freund undergoes surgery in Vienna and is diagnosed with metastases from his testicular sarcoma. Guido Holzknecht then begins radiation therapy, combined with the introduction of radium. In view of his approaching death, he decreed that his ring, which he had received from F. as a member of the "Secret Committee", should be returned to F. so that he could hand it over to Eitingon as von Freund's successor on the committee.

1919 November 30
WPV meeting: General Assembly; Siegfried Bernfeld speaks on "Psychoanalytical Problems from the History of Pedagogy".

1919 November end
- F. receives a consignment of black tea, cocoa, margarine, corned beef and biscuits from his nephew Sam in Manchester.
- A suitcase belonging to F.'s daughter Mathilde, who had checked it in for the return journey to Vienna after a visit to Berlin, arrives in Vienna a day late and "was then emptied of everything edible and smokable, everything else remaining intact, a selection that suggests a well-mannered railway gang". (F. to Eitingon, 2.12.1919).

1919 December beginning
Ernö Garami, the brother of Margit Dubowitz and Minister of Trade in Budapest before the soviet republic, visits F. and informs him about the status of Ferenczi's attempts to bring Anton von Freund's foundation to safety.

1919 December 2
F. receives notification from Max Eitingon that he has set up a deposit of 3000 Swedish kronor for him.[38]

1919 December 6
The New York dentist Louis Bieber, originally from Hungary, begins an analysis with F. It lasts, with interruptions, until 1921 January.

1919 December 7
Wedding of F.'s son Martin with Esti Drucker. In the afternoon, Esti's parents invite the wedding party home.

1919 December 18
- Ferenczi's sister-in-law Charlotte Leichtmann visits F. and gives him a letter from Ferenczi describing matters concerning Anton von Freund's Budapest Foundation.
- F.'s nephew Edward Bernays, who lives in New York, informs him about the preliminary work for the publication of the English translation of the lectures on Introduction to Psychoanalysis and the expected fee of 15% of the sales price. Furthermore, Edward had been asked by the publisher Boni & Liveright to inform F. that he was prepared to pay $10,000[39] for a lecture tour by. F., however, declined.

1919 December 21
- Oskar Pfister leaves Vienna.
- WPV meeting: General Assembly; Walter Fokschaner speaks on "On a case of paranoia".

1919 December 23
The President of the National Assembly awards F. the title "Ordentlicher Professor".

1919 Christmas
Hugo Heller gives F. the book by Austen Layard *Nineveh and its remains* with the dedication "Herrn Prof. Dr Sigm Freud/dankbarst/in Verehrung/Hugo Heller".

1919 before December 25
F. sets up a money deposit in London.

1919 December 28
- F. discusses the difficulties of importing the food into Austria with Julius Wagner-Jauregg, who together with him had been asked by the Zurich Aid Society for the Mentally Ill to take over the distribution of a large donation of food to Viennese mental patients. To Oskar Pfister he writes in this context: "What do you say to an administration that shrieks to the outside world for aid and then does not admit it when it comes?" (F. to Pfister, 27.12.1919).
- Lajos Lévy comes to Vienna to see his brother-in-law Anton von Freund once more, and delivers a letter from Ferenczi to F.

1919 December 31
The Viennese newspapers report F.'s appointment as full professor.

1920

- F. is nominated for the Nobel Prize (Medicine) for the fifth time.
- Founding of the *International Journal of Psycho-Analysis*.
- Clarisse Philipp, the wife of Martha's cousin Oscar has mild epileptic seizures and Ernest Jones, whom Oscar had consulted, suggests analytical treatment. F. writes to Oscar that he is very surprised as this is not a case for analysis, only bromine can help.
- Dora Karplus, later Heinz Hartmann's wife, begins an analysis with F.

Books received:

- Isador Coriat sends F. his books *The hysteria of Lady Macbeth* with the dedication "To Dr. Sigmund Freud with the author's kindest regards" and *Repressed emotions* with the dedication "To Prof. Dr. Sigmund Freud with the best wishes of the author".
- Smith Ely Jelliffe, American psychiatrist, sends F. his book *The technique of psychoanalysis* with the dedication "Prof. Sigmund F./Compliments of/Smith Ely Jelliffe".
- Ernest Jones sends F. his book *Treatment of the neuroses* with the dedication "Professor Freud/With the author's kindest regards".
- Hanns Sachs sends F. his book *Ars amandi psychoanalytica oder psychoanalytische Liebesregeln* with the dedication "'Wollust und Würde tun sich/im Olymp nicht weh.'"/ In dauerder Dankbarkeit u./Ergebenheit Ihr/H. S".
- Stefan Zweig sends F. his book *Drei Meister. Balzac, Dickens, Dostojewsky* with the dedication "Herrn Professor Siegmund Freud/dem grossen Wegweiser ins Unbewusste/in immer wieder erneuter Verehrung/Stefan Zweig".

1920 January beginning
F. is now asking his patients 200 Kronen[40] "more naturally more from the victors [of World War I]" (F. to Abraham. 6.1.1920).

1920 January 1
Otto Rank returns from London and brings several boxes of food bought in Holland and a pair of shoes for F.

1920 January 2
- WPV meeting: discussion on the foundation of a society for the cultivation of psychoanalysis; Siegfried Bernfeld presents the intentions and organization of the society.
- William Fairbairn, Scottish philosopher, theologian and physician, begins an analysis with F.

1920 before January 4
F.'s daughter Sophie informs her father that she is pregnant again.

1920 before January 5
Georg Sylvester Viereck announces to F. that a consignment of meat products is to arrive in Hamburg. F. asks his daughter Sophie to take care of a smooth pick-up.

1920 January 7
The Dean's Office of the Faculty of Medicine is informed by the Ministry of Education of F.'s appointment as full professor.

1920 January 8
F. receives 1200 cigars which he had ordered abroad and has to pay 1000 crowns in customs duty. He cedes 300 cigars to his brother Alexander.

1920 January 14
The Medical Doctors' College of the Faculty of Medicine is informed by the Ministry of Education of F.'s appointment as a full professor.

1920 January 15
F.'s niece Cäcilie (Mausi), the daughter of his sister Rosa, moves in with Freud for half a year. Her widowed mother lives a good 2km away.

1920 January mid
- The Freud family receives a food shipment from Alexander Szabó and his wife Serena from Switzerland.
- Elma Pálos visits F.

1920 January 17
F.'s last visit to Anton von Freund, who is in hospital.

1920 January 18
WPV meeting: continuation of the discussion on the foundation of a society for the cultivation of psychoanalysis.

1920 January 19
F. sends the Dutch physician Herman Joseph Gerard Wyers a copy of the second edition of his *Eine Kindheitserinnerung des Leonardo da Vinci* with the dedication "Herr J. G. Wyers/dVerf".

1920 January 20
- Death of Anton von Freund.
- The Education Office sends the Dean's Office of the Faculty of Medicine the decree of appointment as full professor and asks that it be handed over to F.

1920 January 22
F. attends the funeral of Anton von Freund at the Central Cemetery in Vienna.

1920 January 25
- Death of F.'s daughter Sophie in St. Georg's Hospital in Hamburg. After Sophie had become pregnant again, an abortion was performed and after three days sepsis set in, which led to her death. In the evening Hans Lampl visits F. He says to him: "One thing is so wonderful that no one knows yet that Sophie is dead. Then as it will be known, people will come. And I am so glad that I am alone" (interview with Hans Lampl by Kurt Eissler, 1953). After Sophie's death, F. wears a small medallion with Sophie's picture on his watch chain until the end of his life.
- Oskar Pfister's 20-year-old son Oskar is at F.'s for lunch.

1920 January 27
An obituary formulated by F. for his daughter Sophie is published in the *Neue Freie Presse.*

1920 January 28
Cremation of F.'s daughter Sophie in Hamburg. F.'s sons Oliver and Ernst, as well as Max Eitingon attend. F. and Martha were unable to travel because the train service with Germany had been suspended.

1920 February 1
WPV meeting: announcements and papers, including Eduard Hitschmann on "On urethral eroticism in obsessive neurosis", Hermine Hug-Hellmuth on "On hearing colours in children",

Hermann Nunberg on "On right and left in dreams" and "On the link between sadism and eating" and Walter Schmideberg on the "accuracy of the unconscious".

1920 February 3
Mr. Popper, who had attended the funeral service for F.'s daughter Sophie in Hamburg, visits Freud's and reports on the ceremony and delivers the eulogy by Felix Rosenthal the director of the Hamburg Israelite Hospital.

1920 February 5
Friedrich Tinti, Austrian landowner and future politician, begins an analysis with F. It lasts until 1920 August.

1920 February 6
Jenö Varga visits F.

1920 February 9
– Claude Daly, a major in the Indian army, starts an analysis with F. and gives him two books: Havelock Ellis' *The Philosophy of Conflict* and Wilfrid Lay's *Man's unconscious conflicts.* The analysis lasts until December.
– F. receives a food shipment from his nephew Sam in Manchester.

1920 February 14
In Berlin, the Berlin Psychoanalytic Association opens an outpatient clinic for the psychoanalytic treatment of nervous illnesses.

1920 February 15
F.'s son Oliver returns from Berlin, bringing with him food that Eitingon has procured for Freud.

1920 February mid
F. receives a detailed medical report on his deceased daughter Sophie from the Hamburg doctor Arthur Lippmann.

1920 February 20
Jozsef Eisler begins an analysis with F. It lasts until 1920 December.

1920 February 22
WPV meeting: Hermann Nunberg speaks on "On the course of the libido conflict in schizophrenia".

1920 February 23
In connection with the accusations against Julius Wagner-Jauregg, F. draws up a "Gutachten über die elektrische Behandlung von Kriegsneurotikern" ("Memorandum on the Electrical Treatment of War Neurotics").

1920 March
F. accumulates "Valuta in Amsterdam". (F. to Ernst Freud, 2.4.1920).

1920 March 2
F. receives Thomas Mann's book *Herr und Hund. Gesang von Kindchen.*

1920 March 4
Minna returns from a long spay stay in Bad Reichenhall.

1920 March 7
WPV meeting: Paul Schilder speaks on "On Identification".

1920 March mid
F. has headaches and dizziness. He thinks a nasal purge is the cause.

1920 March 21
WPV meeting: announcements and papers, including Eduard Hitschmann speaking on "A castration dream as a contribution to the genital symbolism of teeth", Hermann Nunberg on "On an apparent secretion disorder" and Theodor Reik on the "Technique of psychoanalysis applied to the humanities".

1920 Spring
– F.'s paper on his patient Margarethe Csonka is published under the title "Über die Psychogenese eines Falles von weiblicher Homosexualität".
– F.'s paper "Zur Vorgeschichte der analytischen Technik" is published. In it F. discusses the influence of Ludwig Börne's writing "Die Kunst, in drei Tagen ein Originalschriftsteller zu arden" ("The Art of Becoming an Original Writer in Three Days") on the development of the psychoanalytic method.
– Most of the food shipments to Freud's come from Loe Kann in The Hague.

1920 March 19
After consulting with Hanns Sachs, Alexander Szabó invites F. to Switzerland for the summer and assures him that he can secure enough paying patients from whose fees F., Martha and Anna can cover a stay of several months. Szabó also raises the question of moving F.'s residence to Switzerland.

1920 March end
A new food shipment arrives from F.'s nephew Sam in Manchester.

1920 April 2
– F. goes to the meeting of the committee for the foundation of a children's recreation home, of which he is a member. It was initiated by German-Americans under the chairmanship of the former American envoy in Vienna Frederic Penfield and is to receive start-up funding of 3 million crowns – 1 million of which is to come from F.'s brother-in-law Eli Bernays. Other members are the medical dean Albin Haberda, the undersecretary of the health department Julius Tandler and the pediatrician Clemens Pirquet. The meeting is held at the Vienna Mayor Jakob Reumann.
– Sándor Ferenczi comes to Vienna.

1920 April 7
WPV meeting: Ernest Jones speaks on the "Progress of Psychoanalysis in England and America" and Hanns Sachs on "The Psychoanalytic Movement in Switzerland".

1920 April 15
– John Rickman, British doctor, begins an analysis with F. It lasts, with interruptions, until 1924 February.
– F. rejects Alexander Szabó's offer to spend the summer in Switzerland.

1920 April 19
Martha goes to Hamburg to visit her widowed son-in-law Max and the two grandchildren. She stays until the beginning of June.

1920 April 21
WPV meeting: Walter Schmideberg speaks on "On psychological changes during captivity".

1920 May

Barbara Low, David Eder's sister-in-law, sends F. her book *Psychoanalysis. A brief account of the Freudian theory* with the dedication *"Professor Freud"*.

1920 May beginning

Motty Eitingon from New York, a brother-in-law and cousin of Max Eitingon, supports psychoanalysis by donating 1 million crowns.[41]

1920 May 5

WPV meeting: announcements and papers, including Hermine Hug-Hellmuth speaking on "On Children's Drawings", Karl Weiss speaking on the subject of "From the Soul Life of the Child" and Eduard Hitschmann speaking on the "Influence of the Dream by the Sleeping Companion".

1920 May 6

For his birthday, F. receives a sum of $5000 from Max Eitingon[42] for psychoanalysis.

1920 May 8

– F. attends the inauguration of the children's home "Tivoli". It has been financed by German-Americans and F.'s brother-in-law Eli Bernays has contributed 1 million Kronen. On this occasion, F. sees Richard Wagner, WPV member from 1910 **to** 1913, for the last time.
– F.'s nephew Sam sends another food parcel from Manchester, including tea, chocolate, cocoa, biscuits, sardine cheese and dried milk from Nestle.

1920 before May 13

Hector Munro, doctor from London and member of the Independent Labor Party, visits F. and brings two boxes of Havana cigars from Ernest Jones.

1920 May 17

F.'s daughter Anna travels to Berlin for the wedding of her brother Ernst and on this occasion presents the ring that F. had given Anton von Freund as a member of the Secret Committee to his successor Max Eitingon. F. had once worn the ring himself.

1920 May 18

Marriage of F.'s son Ernst to Lucie Brasch.

1920 after May 18

F.'s brother-in-law and cousin Moritz, his sister Mitzi's husband, has a heart attack. F. believes that he will not survive the next one.

1920 May 21

WPV meeting: Otto Fenichel speaks on "On Sexual Issues in the Youth Movement".

1920 May 26

F.'s daughter Anna returns from Berlin from the wedding of her brother Ernst.

1920 June

F. receives from Ludwig Jekels "delicious cherries, which have met with undivided applause from young and old" (F. to Jekels, June 1920).

1920 June 2

WPV meeting: Paul Schilder speaks about the causality problem.

1920 June 16
WPV meeting: Discussion of a work by Karl Jaspers and the problem of causality. F. ends the discussion with a "philosophical-critical lecture".

1920 June 18
F. gives Minna money for her birthday as a contribution toward a marquise ring and a silk jacket.

1920 Summer
- The American socialist and pacifist Prynce Hopkins visits F. to begin an analysis with him. But since F. had to go to the Congress in The Hague, Hopkins decides to start an analysis with Ernest Jones.
- At the request of Moshe Wulff, F. sends a box of psychoanalytical literature to Moscow with an English delegation.

1920 June 30
WPV meeting: Business.

1920 July beginning
Max Eitingon has a bust of F. made by Paul Königsberger from a photograph as a gift from the Berlin Association for F.'s 65th birthday.

1920 July 3
Hermann Struck sends the proof print of his slightly improved portrait of F.

1920 July 3
Wilhelm Stekel asks F. to resume their relationship.

1920 July 4

From now on, F. begins his letters to Eitingon with the salutation "Dear Max".

1920 approx. July 6
Paul Königsberger comes to Vienna and F. sits nine times until the end of July, almost always at lunchtime, so that the latter can improve his bust made in Berlin. F. always places a figure from his collection next to Königsberger's plate to please him. Königsberger gives F. a Chinese offering bowl for his collection.

1920 July 7
WPV meeting: Business.

1920 July mid
- The American psychologist Gordon Allport visits F. He has the impression that F. still assumes that insight into the symptomatology is therapeutically helpful.
- F. finishes his book *Jenseits des Lustprinzips.*

1920 July 20
F. receives from his nephew Edward Bernays in New York the English translation of the *lectures introducing psychoanalysis*, which had just been published by Boni & Liveright under the title *A General Introduction to Psychoanalysis.*

1920 July 25
F. goes to Tulln, presumably to visit a patient. Guiolo Bonvicini, a friend of F., had a sanatorium for the mentally ill in Tulln.

1920 July end
Sándor Ferenczi and Lajos Lévy visit F.

1920 July 30–August 28
Spa with sister-in-law Minna in Badgastein

F. is at the spa in Badgastein with Minna. They again stay in the same rooms in the Villa Wassing as the previous year. Here F. is writing his book *Massenpsychologie und Ich-Analyse*. Son Martin is also in Badgastein with his wife Esti and her parents. His brother Alexander is also there with his wife from August 20. Paul Königsberger also comes to finish his bust. F. has regular contact with his former patient Julius Riesz and his wife Mathilde. Eduard Hitschmann and his wife are also in Badgastein.

1920 July 30

Journey from Vienna to Badgastein. F. sees Friedrich (Fritz) Adler on the train, the son of Victor Adler, who had shot the Austrian Prime Minister Karl Stürgkh in 1916 and had been sentenced to death but amnestied in 1918. F. had seen him for the first time in the summer of 1886, when he had visited Friedrich Adler's father Victor with Heinrich Braun.

1920 July 31

F. welcomes Julius Tandler, who is also in Badgastein for a spay stay.

1920 August 2

F.'s nephew Edward Bernays informs his uncle of the great interest and laudatory reviews of *the General Introduction to Psychoanalysis* in America.

1920 August 7

F. is seven hours picking mushrooms, from which they make dinner.

1920 August 20

F.'s brother Alexander comes to Badgastein with his wife Sophie and son Harry.

1920 August 28

Departure from Badgastein and journey to Bad Ischl, where he meets Martha and Anna.

1920 August 30–September 6
Visit with daughter Anna from Son-in-law Max in Hamburg

It is F.'s first visit to Hamburg after the death of daughter Sophie.

1920 August 30

Departure from Bad Ischl to Munich.

1920 August 31

Journey from Munich to Berlin.

1920 September 2

Journey from Berlin to Hamburg

1920 September 3–5

F. and Anna spend two days with Max Halberstadt.

1920 September 6

Journey from Hamburg via Bremen and Osnabrück to The Hague. In Osnabrück the Berlin Congress participants board F.'s train. Karl Abraham had arranged for each of the younger analysts to have the opportunity to talk to F. alone.

1920 September 6–11
VI International Psychoanalytical Congress in The Hague

The Congress will take place in the Louis XV room of the "Pulchri Studio", a building that belonged to the Hague Society of Artists.

1920 September 6

F. and Anna arrive in The Hague; overnight stay at Hotel Paulez.

1920 September 7

- F. gives a welcoming speech in the evening.
- Death of F.'s brother-in-law and cousin Moritz Freud, husband of his sister Mitzi.

1920 September 8

Introductory speeches by Sándor Ferenczi and Ernest Jones.

1920 September 9

- F. gives a lecture under the title "Ergänzungen zur Traumlehre".
- F. and daughter Anna have lunch with Ludwig Binswanger.

1920 September 10

Official dinner.

1920 September 11

Morning business meeting; Ernest Jones replaces Sándor Ferenczi as President of the IPA; afternoon lectures.

1920 September 12–28
Journey through Holland with daughter Anna, Jan van Emden and Johan van Ophuijsen

Originally, F. had planned to travel to England with Anna, but that fell through because Anna's visa did not arrive in time.

1920 September after 11

F. and daughter Anna visit Antje van Ophuijsen (née Mastrigt), her mother Cornelia and her husband, the analyst Johan van Ophuijsen. Antje van Ophuijsen gives F. a Chinese jade dog, which F. had wanted to buy, but then renounced because of the high price.

1920 September 28–30
Visit to Berlin

1920 September 28

Journey to Berlin; Anna separates from F. in Osnabrück and continues to Hamburg to her widowed brother-in-law Max Halberstadt.

1920 September 29

- F. visits his sister Mitzi, who has just been widowed.
- F. visits the Abrahams. He gives Karl and Hedwig Abraham money so that they can buy the children Hilda and Gerd bicycles for Christmas.

1920 September 30

Travel from Berlin to Vienna; arrival in the late evening.

1920 October
- Ernest Jones visits F.
- Edward Bibring introduces himself to Freud.

- Monroe Meyer, American psychiatrist, begins an analysis with F. It lasts until 1922 March.

1920 October beginning
- Raymond de Saussure, son of the linguist Ferdinand de Saussure, begins an analysis with F.
- F. writes a letter of recommendation for Jan van Emden in Holland for Marie Paneth, the daughter-in-law of his friend Joseph Paneth, who died in 1890. She needed it for the planned emigration to the Dutch Antilles with her husband Otto Paneth.
- Martha would prefer to exchange the flat in Berggasse for a flat in Döbling or in the Cottageviertel.
- Freud has a new maid: Marianne from Aussee. She only stays for an ample year, as she was obviously overqualified for a maid.
- F. receives from Stefan Zweig his book *Drei Meister. Balzac, Dickens, Dostojewski* with the dedication "Herrn Professor Siegmund Freud/Dem großen Wegweiser ins Unbewußte/ In immer wieder neue Verehrung/Stefan Zweig/Salzburg 1920". F. reads the volume with extraordinary pleasure. As far as Dostoevsky is concerned, F. provides Zweig supplementary material.

1920 October 2
- F. proposes to his nephew Edward Bernays to write a series of popular scientific articles on psychoanalysis for an American magazine. The title of the first article should be: "One should not use psychoanalysis in polemics".
- F. and Martha are visiting daughter Mathilde and son-in-law Robert.

1920 October 3
- F. goes to Tulln, presumably again to the patient he had already visited on 25 July.
- Alix and James Strachey arrive in Vienna. Each begins an analysis with F. It lasts until 1922. James gives him John Meynard Keynes' book *The economic consequences of the peace* right at the beginning, in which the author criticized President Woodrow Wilson and predicted that the Treaty of Versailles would lead to disaster.

1920 October 4
- On his first day at work after the summer, F. takes 10,000 Kronen[43] and writes: "Since the Kronen is constantly losing value, I will soon be a millionaire". (F. to Anna, 5.10.1920).
- F. and Martha are visiting Oskar and Melanie Rie.

1920 October before 11
- F. speaks for an hour Anthony Gustav de Rothschild from London. The contact was established via Charlotte Rosenbacher, a sister of F.'s former patient Helene Schiff. Rothschild, however, decides against treatment.
- F. receives a coffee machine from Ferenczi's sister-in-law Charlotte Leichtmann from Rome.

1920 October 12
Alfred Pribram tells F. that he was expected in Cambridge on September 27 for a lecture on "Totem and Taboo". Apparently, F. had forgotten to cancel – his daughter Anna had not got her visa in time – or his message had not reached Cambridge.

1920 October 13
WPV meeting: Wilhelm Reich speaks about the "Libido Conflict in 'Peer Gynt'".

1920 October 14
- George Young, English historian, begins an analysis with F. It lasts until 1920 December.

– F. appears as an expert witness in the commission of "Erhebung militärischer Pflichtverletzungen" ("Inquiry into Military Breaches of Duty"), which meets in the parliament building. Julius Wagner-Jauregg had been accused of abusing soldiers with electric shocks. F. criticizes Wagner-Jauregg's method, but exonerates him from the accusation of having deliberately tortured patients. F.'s expert opinion is dated 1920 February 23.

1920 October 24
The commission for the "Investigation of Military Breaches of Duty" absolves Wagner-Jauregg of all guilt.

1920 October 29
WPV meeting: General Assembly. Re-election of functionaries; Aurel Kolnai speaks on the "Psychoanalysis of Anarcho-Communism".

1920 October 30
F. "got excellently over the fact that the distribution of the Nobel Prize passed me over twice" (F. to Abraham, 31.10.1920).

1920 November
– F.'s book *Jenseits des Lustprinzips* was published. Four months later he writes about the book: "I have been punished enough for 'Jenseits', it is very popular, brings me quantities of letters and praise, I must have done something very stupid there. (F. to Eitingon, 27.3.1920).
– F. analyzes four to six hours a day in English.

1920 November 5
Six parcels arrive from F.'s nephew Sam in Manchester with "lots of good and useful things" (F. to Anna, 5.11.1920).

1920 November 8
Clarence Seyler visits F. He gives him his *Vorlesungen zur Einführung in die Psychoanalyse* with the dedication "Mr. Cl. A. Seyler in friendly memory. Sigm. Freud".

1920 November 9
Minna returns from a spay stay in Merano.

1920 November 11
WPV meeting: Dorian Feigenbaum speaks on "On a special kind of ecnosia".

1920 November 25
WPV meeting: Frieda Teller speaks on "The interrelation of psychological conflict and physical suffering in Schiller".

1920 November end
F. receives from Oskar Pfister his book *Der psychologische und biologische Untergrund expressionistischer Bilder (The psychological and biological basis of expressionist paintings).*

1920 December
– The International Psycho-Analytical Press, a London branch of Internationale Psychoanalytische Verlag, moves to Vienna. Jones' assistant Eric Hiller therefore also comes to Vienna.

1920 December 7
Ernst and Lucie Freud are on their way back from a holiday in Italy to spend a week in Vienna visiting their parents.

1920 December 8
WPV meeting: Robert Jokl speaks on "On the psychogenesis of writer's cramp".

1920 December 16
WPV meeting: Jozsef Eisler speaks on "On the theory of countertransference".

1920 before December 17
F. receives a portrait photo from Honorio Delgado.

1920 December 18
The German psychiatrist Ernst Harms visits F. because he is seeking an analysis with him. As two telegrams crossed to make an appointment, F. was not prepared for the visit and he sends Harms away again after five minutes and gives him a new appointment in 1921 January.

1920 December Christmas
F. receives from Oskar Pfister his book *Die Behandlung schwer erziehbarer und abnormaler Kinder (The Treatment of difficult and abnormal Children) and the* book *Vermeintliche Nullen und angebliche Musterkinder (Alleged Zeros and Alleged Model Children)*.

1921

– Start of correspondence with Viktor Frankl.

Treatments:

– Lionel Blitzsten, American psychiatrist and neurologist, begins an analysis with F.
– Salomea Kempner, Polish doctor, starts an analysis at F.
– Albert Polon, American psychiatrist, begins an analysis with F.

Books received:

– William White sends F. his book *Foundations of psychiatry* with the dedication "Prof. Sigmund Freud/Compliments of/Dr. W. A. White".
– Abraham Brill sends F. his book *Fundamental conceptions of psychoanalysis* with the dedication "To Prof Freud With sincere and affectionate regards from A. A. Brill".
– Edward Kempf sends F. his book *Psychopathology* with the dedication "To Prof. Sigmund Freuds/with my grateful appreciation/Edward J Kempf".
– Joel Rinaldo sends F. his book *Psychoanalysis of the "reformer". A further contribution to the sexual theory* with the dedication "With Author's Compliments".
– Hermann Rorschach sends F. his book *Psychodiagnostik. Methodik und Ergebnisse eines wahrnehmungsdiagnostischen Experiments* with the dedi*cation* "Herrn Professor Freud/in Verehrung u. Dankbarkeit/zugeeignet/H. Rorschach".
– Wilfred Trotter sends F. his book *Instincts of the herd in peace and war* with the dedication "With the compliments/of the author".

1921 January
– F. works on his paper Massenpsychologie und Ich-Analyse.
– Ernst Harms begins an analysis with F., but breaks it off after nine sessions.

1921 January 5
WPV meeting: Alfred Winterstein speaks about the "collector".

1921 January 15
Siegfried Bernfeld visits F. for the first time. He wants to move from Berlin to Vienna, and F. hopes to employ him in the publishing house and provide him with analyses.

1921 January 19
WPV meeting: small communications, including Hermann Nunberg speaking on "On becoming tired and falling asleep during analysis", Helene Deutsch on "An observation from analysis", Paul Schilder on "On compulsive impulses", Robert Jokl delivers a "Contribution to the origin of the womb fantasy", Theodor Reik speaks on "A remark by Gustav Mahler", Eduard Hitschmann lectures "From Lasalle's life and writings", Karl Weiss speaks on "Goethe's correspondence with Zelter", and F. reports on an "English Promise".

1921 January 24
Max Eitingon sends F. Traugott Oesterreich's book *Occultism in the Modern World View.*

1921 February 2
WPV meeting: Paul Schilder speaks on "On Narcissism".

1921 February 4
F. asks his nephew Edward Bernays for an affidavit for Ernst Kassowitz, son of Max Kassowitz, who wants to emigrate to the USA.

1921 February 6
Elma Pálos visits F.

1921 February 9
WPV meeting: discussion on answering the questions of the central leadership.

1921 February 16
WPV meeting: small communications, including Aurel Kolnai speaking on "On Sadism and Masochism", Eduard Hitschmann on "On Sexual Neurasthenia" and Wilhelm Reich delivering a "Contribution to Anal Eroticism".

1921 February 17
Hans Lampl visits F.

1921 February 18
Beginning of the correspondence between F. and Nikolai Osipov. However, there were certainly occasional letters before that on the occasion of sending offprints or in connection with Ossipov's translations of some of F.'s writings into Russian.

1921 February 21
– F. receives photographs of Sophie's grave in Hamburg from Max Halberstadt.
– F. visits Otto Rank.

1921 March 2
WPV meeting: Theodor Reik speaks on "St Epiphanius Prescribes".

1921 March 7
F. issues William Fairbairn a certificate that he has completed 25 hours of analysis with him.

1921 March 10
Horace Frink, American psychiatrist, begins an analysis with F. It lasts until 1923 Christmas.

1921 March 13
F.'s son Oliver goes to Romania and in this context F. "quite suddenly took a step into real ageing. Since then the thought of death has not left me at all". (F. to Ferenczi, 8.5.1921).

1921 March 14
Eugen Fried, a general practitioner, files a complaint against F. and Robert Stigler (professor at the Hochschule für Bodenkultur). He claims that F. and Stigler had committed attacks on his personal honor against him as the author of the pamphlet *Der Vaginismus und die Ehen perverser Männer*. Fried applies for disciplinary proceedings to be instituted.

1921 March 16
WPV meeting: small communications, including Raymond de Saussure speaking on "On French Expressions on Anal Eroticism", Helene Deutsch on "A Pseudo-Persecutory Delusion" and Otto Rank on "On Psychic Potency".

1921 Spring
- Amalia Götzl, eldest sister of Edoardo Weiss, begins an analysis with F. Her younger sister Giorgina had already been analyzed by F. from 1917 to 1920.
- The British physiologist Ivor Tuckett begins an analysis with F.

1921 March 26
F. receives James Putnam's *Addresses on psycho-analysis.*

1921 March 27
- F. goes by car to an "asylum" on the morning of Easter Sunday to see three cases, so it is probably a consultation.
- The Viennese publicist and writer Robert Weil publishes a "Naturgeschichte der Frau" under the pseudonym "Homunculus" in the *Neue Freie Presse*, which states, among other things: "The misunderstood woman is psychoanalytically inclined. Her only joy is Freud".
- F. hears that the Austrian writer Hermann Bahr "recently stated publicly that I am the most famous Austrian" (F. to Eitingon, 27.3.1921). It is possible that this was a statement made by Bahr in the Café Grinsteidl.

1921 March 30
WPV meeting: Helene Deutsch speaks on "On Pseudology".

1921 April
- F. writes the preface to the sixth edition of the *Traumdeutung*.
- Anna Guggenbuehl, née Koellreuter, begins an analysis with F. It lasts until July.

1921 April 1
Philippe Sarasin, Swiss psychiatrist, begins an analysis with F. It lasts until the spring of 1923.

1921 April 3
Birth of F.'s grandson Anton Walter, son Martin. F. sees him when he is a few hours old in the Rudolfinum, a private hospital in Vienna.

1921 April 4
F. goes to the Rudolfinum again to see his grandson.

1921 April 10
F. is back at the Rudolfinum to see his grandson.

1921 April 13
WPV meeting: discussion on F.'s *Jenseits des Lustprinzips*.

1921 April 14
F. sends the British botanist Arthur Tansley a copy of the sixth edition of the *Traumdeutung* with the dedication "Herr Prof. Tansley/zur freundlichen Er-/innerung an den/Verf.".

1921 April mid
F. receives from Oscar Schmitz his book *Das Dionysische Geheimnis. Erlebnisse und Erkenntnisse eines Fahnenflüchtigen.*

1921 April 24
F.'s nephew Edward Bernays gives a dinner in New York on the occasion of his uncle's 80th birthday. 76 guests are invited.

1921 April 27
WPV meeting: Isidor Sadger speaks on "Neurosis and Castration Complex".

1921 May
Girindrashekhar Bose sends F. his book *The Concept of Repression* with the dedication "Presented to Prof. Sigmund Freud L.L.D. as a humble token of the author's most sincere admiration for his devotion to truth. Girindrashekhar Bose".

1921 May 6
F. receives the bust made by Paul Königsberger as a gift from the Berlin Society. It now waits "as an eerily threatening iron double for a definitive installation in some place in the flat" (F. to Ferenczi, 8.5.1921).

1921 May 11
WPV meeting: small communications, including Wilhelm Reich speaking on "Daydreams of an Obsessive-Compulsive Neurotic", Theodor Reik on "Psychoanalytic Technique" and Paul Federn on F.'s book "Jenseits des Lustprinzips".

1921 May 22
F. reads Edward Freeman's *History of Sicily under the Phoenicians, Greeks and Romans*.

1921 May 25
WPV meeting: Theodor Reik speaks on "The Gospel of Judas Iscarioth".

1921 June 8
WPV meeting: Wilhelm Reich speaks on "On Triebenergetics".

1921 June 16
Martin becomes an authorized signatory of "Treuga", a large Dutch-Austrian trading company.

1921 June 26
F. and Martha make an excursion to the Kahlenberg and meet son Martin on the way back. In the evening, they go to the Stadtpark to see the Johann Strauss monument, which was ceremoniously unveiled in the morning. F.'s comment on it: "Bronce is no material for trousers" (F. to Anna, 29.6.1921).

1921 June 29
F. receives information about the fate of his mother's relatives in Odessa: His cousin Jascha died of typhus in early 1920. The son-in-law of Jascha's sister Anna (married Deiches) – a Russian prince – is also dead, and she emigrated to Krakow with her granddaughter sometime after the October Revolution.

1921 June end
- After all the children except Anna have moved out, renovations are carried out at Berggasse 19, and some of the rooms are given new purposes.
- F. receives 200 cigars from Hans Lampl from Berlin.

1921 July
- The Austrian journalist Adolf Storfer becomes an assistant at Internationale Psychoanalytische Verlag.
- The Internationale Psychoanalytische Verlag buys all rights to F.'s books from Hugo Heller for 65,000 marks.[44]

1921 July 14

F.'s book *Massenpsychologie und Ich-Analyse* is published.

1921 July 15–August 14

Spa stay with Minna and niece Lucie in Badgastein

Accommodation is again Villa Wassing. Jan van Emden visits three times for two days, the last time with his wife. At the same time, the American economist Carl Snyder and the singer Selma Kurz, married to the Viennese gynecologist Josef Halban, are also in Badgastein. He is also in frequent contact with his niece Lucie Wiener (daughter of his sister Anna) and her children, who have been in Badgastein since the end of July. He analyzes with Lucie why she lost her beloved cigarette case.

1921 July 15

Departure to Badgastein.

1921 July 16

- F. picks white orchids in a mown meadow.
- The academic senate of the university decides that there are no grounds for initiating disciplinary proceedings against F. and Robert Stigler as demanded by Eugen Fried in March.

1921 July mid

- The American parapsychologist Hereward Carrington asks F. if he would collaborate on a new occult magazine. F. declines.
- Girindrashekhar Bose requests a photo of F.

1921 July 31

Birth of F.'s grandson Stephan Gabriel, son of Ernst.

1921 August

The "Artists' Aid for the Starving in Russia" is founded. F. becomes a member of its committee, which also includes Hermann Bahr, Felix Salten, Arthur Schnitzler and Julius Tandler. The Society of Friends is led by Fridtjof Nansen.

1921 August beginning

F. receives the French translation of the five lectures *Über Psychoanalyse*.

1921 August 2–4

F. writes down his work "Traum und Telepathie", possibly inspired by several letters from representatives of occultism.

1921 August 6

The linguist and cultural scientist Julian Obermann visits F. for dinner.

1921 August 9

Jan van Emden and wife come to Badgastein.

1921 August 12

- Smith Ely Jelliffe and his wife Belinda visit F. He receives them somewhat unfriendly, as he had seen Jelliffe in the company of Wilhelm Stekel, who is also in Badgastein for a spay stay. Twelve years later, F. apologizes for the unfriendly treatment.
- F. and Martha meet Josef Friedjung's family at Böckstein station, and they all take a long walk together.
- Beginning of the correspondence between F. and Joan Riviere.

1921 August 14

Departure from Badgastein to Innsbruck.

1921 August 14–September 14
Summer stay with family in Seefeld in Tyrol

F. spends several weeks with his family (Martha, Anna, niece Cäcilie and grandson Ernst) in Seefeld in Tyrol (Pension Kurheim). He is visited there by Jan van Emden, Sándor Ferenczi, Abraham Brill. Helene and Felix Deutsch, as well as Eduard and Hedwig Hitschmann, are also in Seefeld. The jurist Hans Kelsen, who is also on holiday in Seefeld, meets F. by chance and tells him the dream of a colleague who is a friend, which F. interprets correctly, although he did not know the dreamer.

1921 August 14

F. is expecting Martha, Anna and Ernst in Innsbruck.

1921 August 15

Drive from Innsbruck to Seefeld.

1921 August end

During walks, F. has ringing in the ears, palpitations and heart pains, which he considers to be signs of "rapid ageing of the heart and arteries" (F. to Eitingon, 29.8.1921). However, these complaints quickly pass.

1921 September 11

Start of correspondence between F. and the Dutch doctor Jeanne de Groot (later Jeanne Lampl-de Groot).

1921 September 14

Drive from Seefeld to Munich.

1921 September 14–21
Visits by the sons to Berlin and of the son-in-law in Hamburg

1921 September 14

F., Martha and grandson Ernst take the night train from Munich to Berlin at 7.15 pm.

1921 September 15

At 7.37 am, arrival at the Anhalter Bahnhof. F. is picked up by son Ernst and Max Eitingon. Miss Jacob, Max Halberstadt's housekeeper, receives grandson Ernst in the afternoon and takes him to Hamburg.

1921 September 15–16

F. visits son Oliver, his sister Maria, and meets Karl Abraham.

1921 September 17–18

F. visits his widowed son-in-law Max Halberstadt and his grandchildren in Hamburg.

1921 September 19

Drive to Lübeck.

1921 September 21

Journey from Lübeck to Hildesheim.

1921 September 21–September 29
Harz Journey of the "Secret Committee"

On this journey, F. introduces his companions (Karl Abraham, Max Eitingon, Sándor Ferenczi, Ernest Jones, Otto Rank, Hanns Sachs) to the basic ideas of the following texts: "Über einige neurotische Mechanismen bei Eifersucht, Paranoia und Homosexualität", "Bemerkungen zur Theorie und Praxis der Traumdeutung" and "Psychoanalyse und Telepathie".

1921 September 21

The members of the "Secret Committee" meet at the Hotel Kaiserhof in Hildesheim.

1921 September 22

Visit to the Egyptian Museum in the Pelizäus-Haus in Hildesheim.

1921 September 24

Stay in Goslar.

1921 September 25

Stay in Hahnenklee.

1921 September 26

- Trip to Schiercke (Hotel Stolberg); on the way, F. and Karl Abraham talk about Hanns Sachs, of whom Abraham is partly critical.
- Eitingon travels back to Berlin early, presumably because his wife is not well.

1921 September 27–28

Stay in Halberstadt and excursion to the Brocken.

1921 September 28

Journey to Leipzig. From there, at 19.00 departure by night train via Passau to Vienna.

1921 September 29

Arrival in Vienna.

1921 September 29
The American psychiatrists Abraham Kardiner and Monroe Meyer are waiting for F. at the station.

1921 October 1
- F. begins treatment of Scofield Thayer, an American poet, art collector and editor of the literary magazine *The Dial, through the* mediation of his nephew Edward Bernays. *The* treatment lasts, with interruptions, until 1926.

1921 October 2
Leonard Blumgart, Abraham Kardiner, Monroe Meyer, Clarence Oberndorf and Albert Polon meet in the afternoon at F. One of them was supposed to change to another analyst because F. could not accommodate all of them in his schedule. Anna F., however, had the idea that each of them would give up one hour per week so that they could all stay with F.

1921 after October 2
- Leonard Blumgart begins an analysis with F. It lasts until 1922 March.
- Abraham Kardiner begins an analysis with F. It lasts until 1922 April 1.

- Monore Meyer begins his analysis at F. It lasts until the summer of 1922.
- Clarence Oberndorf begins an analysis with F. It lasts until 1922 February.
- Albert Polon begins an analysis with F. It lasts until 1922 April.

1921 October 10
- F. grants the French Surrealist poet André Bretón an interview. It is published on 1922 March 1 under the title "Interview du Professeur Freud à Vienne" in the journal *Littérature.*
- F. and Otto Rank discuss with Theodor Reik the meeting on the reorganization of the "Referatenzentrale" ("center for reviews") of the psychoanalytic journals.

1921 October 12
WPV meeting: Hans Prinzhorn speaks on "On Drawings by the Mentally Ill and Primitives". As the WPV could no longer use the meeting room at Franz-Josefs-Kai 65, the meeting was held at Theodor Reik's home.

1921 after October 12
Hans Prinzhorn visits F.

1921 October 21
Internationale Psychoanalytische Verlag moves from Grünangergasse to temporarily rented premises at Fleischmarkt 1.

1921 October 26
WPV meeting: Siegfried Bernfeld speaks on "Some Remarks on Sublimation".

1921 November
Max Rosenberg, a rich American whom Horace Frink, had sent to F., and begins an analysis with F. It lasts until at least 1923.

1921 November 8
Lou Andreas-Salomé comes to Vienna for six weeks and stays with Freud's.

1921 November 9
WPV meeting: small communications, including Siegfried Bernfeld on "On the symbolism of ties", Paul Schilder on "Psychosis after cataract surgery", Eduard Hitschmann on "On questions of teaching in psychoanalysis" and Hermann Nunberg on two cases of particularly strong love relationships between fathers and daughters.

1921 November 11
Sergei Pankejeff visits F.

1921 November 13
Minna breaks her right forearm after a fall on an icy path.

1921 November 17
F. becomes honorary member of the Dutch Association of Psychiatry and Neurology.

1921 November 23
WPV meeting: Gustav Bychowski speaks on "On the psychology of schizophrenic persecutory delusions".

1921 November 30
WPV *meeting*: Hans Kelsen speaks on "The Concept of the State and Freud's Mass Psychology ".

1921 December
F. becomes an honorary member of the Dutch Society of Psychiatry.

1921 December 14
WPV meeting: small communications, including Gustav Bychowski speaking on "A Buddhist womb fantasy", Hermann Nunberg on "A case of projection", Paul Schilder "On the pathology of the ego ideal", Wilhelm Reich on "A contribution to the conversion-hysterical symptom complex" and Eduard Hitschmann on "Hirschlaff's statistics on hypnosis cures".

1921 December mid
Applications are received from Moscow and Calcutta for the formation of local groups of the IPA.

1921 December 16
Marco Levi Bianchini comes to Vienna and presents F. with the Italian translation of the *Vorlesungen zur Einführung in die Psychoanalyse (Introduzione allo studio della psicoanalisi)* to which he has written a preface with the dedication *"To his most honoured teacher/Prof. S. Freud/the most faithful Italian student/Levi Bianchini"*.

1921 December 17
Start of correspondence between F. and Ruth Blumgart (later Ruth Mack Brunswick)..

1921 December 20
Lou Andreas-Salomé leaves after spending six weeks visiting Freud's.

1921 before December 21
F. receives an article on psychoanalysis from the Colombian newspaper *La Nacion from* the Colombian doctor Rafael Gonzales Sanchez.

1921 December 21
WPV meeting: Small communications, including Helene Deutsch speaking on "Drawing from the Unconscious", Paul Federn on "A Motif of Seasickness", Siegfried Bernfeld on "A Motif for the Production of Occasional Poems", Robert Jokl on "Supra-religious Motifs in Neuroses" and Paul Schilder on "On the Fantasy of Rebirth in an Epileptic State of Drowsiness".

1921 Christmas
- Otto Rank gives F. the second edition of his book *Der Mythus von der Geburt des Helden* with the dedication "Herrn Professor Freud/in tiefster Dankbarkeit/Dr Otto Rank".
- The Belgian teacher Julian Varendonck visits F. The publication of his book *Über das vorbewusste phantasierende Denken (On Preconscious Fantasizing Thought)* in Internationale Psychoanalytische Verlag was imminent.

1921 December 26
The Spaniard Antonio Carlos Rodríguez Pastor, who teaches in London, visits F. and delivers a Christmas present from Ernest Jones.

1922

Treatments:

- The urologist Joseph Asch begins an analysis with F. He is the head of the urology clinic at Lenox Hill Hospital and co-founder of the New York Psychoanalytic Group.
- Joan Riviere begins an analysis with F. It lasts intermittently until 1926.
- Mira Oberholzer begins an analysis with F.

Received books and offprints:

- Charles Baudouin, French psychoanalyst and pacifist, sends F. his book *Études de psychanalyse* with the dedication "Prof. Sigmund Freud en profonde admiration Charles Baudouin".
- David Forsyth sends F. his book *The technique of psycho-analysis* with the dedication "Prof. Dr Freud/in grateful remembrance/from the Author".
- Horace Frink gives F. Alexander Goldenweiser's book *Early civilisation* with the dedication "Prof. Freud/With best wishes from/H. W. Frink".
- Serge Jankélévitch sends F. the French translation of the *Vorlesungen zu Einführung in die Psychoanalyse* wit the dedication "Au Dr S. Freud/hommage respectueux de son/traducteur/ Dr Jankélévitch".
- Emanuel Loewy sends F. an offprint of his paper "Neuattische Kunst" with the dedication "Sigmund Freud/für Gradiva/d. Vf".
- Arie Querido sends F. the Dutch translation of *Jenseits des Lustprinzips* (Het levensmysterie en de psycho-analyse) with the dedication "Vom Übersetzer".
- Hanns Sachs gives F. his book *Die Elemente der Psychoanalyse* with the dedication "In dauernder Dankbarkeit u. Ergebenheit/Ihr/Hanns Sachs".
- Paul Schilder gives F. his book *Über das Wesen der Hypnose* with the dedication "Herrn Prof. Freud/in Verehrung/v. Verf".
- Smith Ely Jelliffe sends F. his book *Psychoanalysis and the drama* with the dedication "Prof. Sigmund Freud:/Compliments of/Smith Ely Jelliffe".
- F. gives Horace Frink the portrait photo of him taken by Max Halberstadt.

1922 January
- F. writes in his paper "Eine Teufelsneurose aus dem 16. Jahrhundert"
- F.'s son Oliver becomes engaged to Henny Fuchs.

1922 January 3–7
Karl Abraham, Sándor Ferenczi, Hanns Sachs and Géza Róheim come to Vienna and give lectures to American and English training candidates. Ferenczi and Abraham stay with Freud's at Berggasse 19.

1922 January 4
WPV meeting: Felix Deutsch speaks on "Psychoanalysis and Organic Diseases".

1922 before January 15
F. receives from the American journalist William Bayard Hale his book *The Story of a style,* *which* examines Woodrow Wilson's literary style.

1922 January 18
WPV meeting: Hans Sperber speaks on "A Linguistic Observation on Grillparzer's Father Complex".

1922 January 22
Karl Abraham comes to Vienna to give two lectures, the first on January 22, the second on January 23.

1922 January 25
WPV meeting: small communications, including Monroe Meyer speaking on "The dream form as a content representation", Karl Abraham on "The spider as a dream symbol" and Paul Federn on "On scientific plagiarism".

1922 January 26
Foundation of the Indian Psychoanalytical Society in Calcutta. Girindrashekhar Bose invites F. to give lectures in Calcutta.

1922 January 30
Hans Sachs comes to Vienna for a fortnight.

1922 February
- F. writes the preface to Raymond des Saussures *La méthode psychanalytique*.
- After receiving F.'s tax return, the tax authority doubts that he has declared his income correctly, as everyone knows that his reputation extends far beyond the borders of Austria. F. replies that he feels very honored to receive a communication from the government. It was the first time that the government had taken notice of him. However, he had to disagree on one point: His reputation did not extend far beyond the borders of Austria, it began at the border.

1922 February 3
The Neue Freie Presse publishes an appeal by the "Artists' Aid for the Starving in Russia", also signed by F.

1922 February 5
F. orders a pair of shoes from his nephew Sam in Manchester.

1922 before February 13
F. receives an etching by Rembrandt as a gift from his son Ernst.

1922 February 15
WPV meeting: Siegfried Bernfeld speaks on "On a typical form of male puberty" and Clarence Oberndorf on "The role of an organic inferiority in a neurosis".

1922 February 20
- F. sends Girindrashekhar Bose an assessment of his book *The Concept of Repression*, which Bose needs for his agent. It says, among other things, "It was a great and pleasant surprise that the first book on a psychoanalytic subject which came to us from that part of the world (India) should display so good a knowledge of psychoanalysis so deep an insight into its difficulties and so much of deep-going original thought" (F. to Bose, 20.2.1922).
- F. receives from Wilfred Trotter the second edition of his book *Instinct of the Herd in* Peace and War with the dedication "With the compliments of the author".

1922 February 27
Joan Riviére, English translator, begins an analysis with F. It lasts until 1926 November.

1922 March
- The Internationale Psychoanalytische Verlag moves to Andreasgasse 3.

- The American publicist and journalist Walter Lippmann sends F. his book *Public Opinion* with the dedication "To Professor Doctor Sigmund Freud/Respectfully from/Walter Lippmann".

1922 March beginning
Anna travels to Hamburg to visit her brother-in-law Max Halberstadt and his children. She stays there for more than six weeks, then travels to Berlin to visit her brothers and her aunt Mitzi's family and then on to Göttingen to Lou Andreas-Salomé, only returning to Vienna at the end of April.

1922 March 1
- F. declines Girindrashekhar Bose's invitation to Calcutta on grounds of age.
- WPV meeting: small communications, including Eduard Hitschmann speaking on "Blood Glands and Psychology" and Helene Deutsch delivering a "Contribution to the Formation of the Conversion Symptom".

1922 March 2
The shoes ordered by F. from his nephew Sam arrive.

1922 March 5
- Ida Adler (née Bauer), F. Patient "Dora" from the "Bruchstück einer Hysterieanalyse" visits F. with her husband Ernst.
- F. asks Julius Figdor to bring him cigars from Holland and specifies the brands: Viktoria, Wersche Vollendamer, Soberano, Genadore. F. had met Figdor through his wife Melanie, who was a close friend of Minna. Figdor was in the jewelry business, had a courier passport and was not checked at the border.
- Otto Rank is at F. for a meeting.

1922 March 6
Rudolf Urbantschitsch visits F. The conversation is mainly about the establishment of a psychoanalytical sanatorium in Baden, which Urbantschitsch wants to finance with the proceeds from the sale of his Cottage sanatorium and shares in the Bodencreditanstalt. The project was not realized, partly because the Bodencreditanstalt went bankrupt.

1922 March 15
WPV meeting: Walter Fokschaner speaks on "On Chess".

1922 March 19
F. sees "The Marriage of Figaro" in the Redoutensaal in Vienna.

1922 March 26
F.'s daughter-in-law Esti "ran away from here in a very unmotivated fit of rage without saying goodbye" (F. to Anna, 27.3.1922). But the next day she apologizes.

1922 March 27
F. pays 1,660,000 Kronen in taxes.[45]

1922 March 29
WPV meeting: Hermine Hug-Hellmuth speaks on "On sexual education".

1922 March 31
Arthur Tansley begins an analysis with F. It lasts until the end of 1922 June and from 1923 September to December.

1922 March end
Ernst Blum, a German-Swiss psychiatrist, begins an analysis with F. It lasts until the spring of 1923.

1922 April
Herbert Graf (the "Little Hans") visits F. He had previously discovered his medical history in his father's library and wanted to talk to F. as a result.

1922 April 2
– F. is in the Purkersdorf sanatorium by car.
– F. visits Helene Schiff in the afternoon.

1922 April 3
– F. visits his grandson Anton Walter for his first birthday.
– F. receives Oskar Pfister's book *Die Liebe des Kindes und ihre Fehlentwicklung* with the dedication "Patri spirituali/fraterculus physicus".
– Arthur Tansley sends F. his *book The new psychology and its relation to life* with the dedication "Prof. Dr. Freud/from the author".

1922 April 7
WPV meeting: Siegfried Bernfeld speaks "On a motive for producing some satirical poems".

1922 April 12
– WPV meeting: F. remarks that "the number of guests is getting out of hand" (F. to Anna, 13.4.1922).
– F. receives $50[46] fee advance for the printing of an American translation of "Traum und Telepathie", which was probably never published.

1922 April 13
F. has a security lock installed for his practice rooms by the Viennese company Salvo.

1922 April 15
WPV meeting: continuation of the discussion on Hugh Hellmuth's lecture "On Sexual Education" of March 29.

1922 April mid
– Jeanne de Groot, Dutch doctor, begins an analysis with F. It lasts until 1925. After a long interruption, she has a few more sessions in 1931.
– F.'s mother has a fainting spell.

1922 April 18
A meeting of the "International Psycho-Analytical Press" takes place at F.'s house. F., Eric Hiller, Otto Rank, Joan Riviere, James Strachey and John Rickman discuss the question of whether Eric Hiller, who ran the "Press" in Vienna, could not be replaced by someone else. Jones had suggested Anna Freud. A decision is not made.

1922 before April 24
F.'s mother suffers from the consequences of a fainting spell.

1922 April 26
WPV meeting: Otto Rank makes "Remarks on Mozart's 'Don Juan'".

1922 May 3
WPV meeting: business meeting – Consultation on outpatient clinic matters.

1922 May 5
- Max Eitingon arrives in Vienna. He had traveled from Leipzig with F.'s daughter Anna, who had stayed overnight with Eitingon's parents, coming from Göttingen.
- Death of Ignaz Rosanes. He had been one of F.'s closest friends since their time together at the Gymnasium.

1922 May 10
WPV meeting: Small communications, including Eduard Hitschmann speaking on "On the Perineal Eroticism of Men".

1922 May 14
F. writes down thoughts on the theme of "The Head of Medusa".

1922 May 22
The Psychoanalytic Outpatient Clinic opens at Pelikangasse 18.

1922 May 24
WPV meeting: Theodor Reik speaks on "Oedipus and the Sphinx".

1922 May 25
Beginning of the correspondence between F. and Sándor Radó.

1922 May 31
WPV meeting: Anna Freud gives her test lecture on "Schlagephantasien und Tagträume" ("Beating Fantasies and Daydreams").

1922 June 13
WPV meeting: business meeting – Anna Freud is elected as a member.

1922 June 16
Arthur Schnitzler visits F. for dinner in the Berggasse. F. gives him a copy of the fourth edition of the *lectures introducing psychoanalysis*. He then accompanies Schnitzler home to Sternwartenstrasse 71, a journey of over an hour. On the way, they both talk about aging and dying.

1922 June 21
WPV meeting: General Assembly. August Aichhorn speaks on "Education in reformatories".

1922 June 22
Raymond de Saussure sends F. his book *La méthode psychanalytique* with the dedication "A Monsieur le Professeur S. Freud/hommage respectueux/R. de Saussure". It arrives at F.'s home on June 24.

1922 June 30–August 1
Spa stay with Minna in Badgastein
Accommodation again in the Villa Wassing. F. begins work in Badgastein on his book *Das Ich und das Es (The Ego and the Id) and* writes down the paper "Bemerkungen zur Theorie und Praxis der Traumdeutung" and "Über einige neurotische Mechanismen bei Eifersucht, Paranoia und Homosexualität". Kurt Redlich and George Morgenthau (ENT doctor from Chicago and in analysis with Paul Federn) also stay in Badgastein. In addition, F.'s niece Judith, daughter of his sister Anna, is in Badgastein with her husband Victor Heller.

1922 June 30
Departure to Badgastein in the evening.

1922 July 1

Arrival in Badgastein.

1922 July 9

F. and Minna are in the Nassfeld, a southwestern side valley of the Gasteinertal.

1922 July 10

F. meets Leopold Königstein, who is in Badgastein for a week. One evening they play tarot together.

1922 July 15

Friedrich Georg Steiner, the director of the British-Austrian Bank and F.'s advisor in financial matters, sends his secretary to Badgastein to ask F. about a treatment for Luisa Strauss, the sister-in-law of the Dutch bank director Ernst Frohnknecht, who is a friend of his. The treatment was to take place in Switzerland, but F. refused and the lady then came to Berchtesgaden two weeks later, where F. spent the rest of the summer.

1922 July mid

– The spa doctor Guido Brecher, a distant relative of Martha, asks F. to examine a lady from Merano and possibly start a treatment, which Brecher could then continue in Merano.
– F. receives from Honorio Delgado his book *Algunos aspectos de la psicologia del niño* with the dedication *"Al padre del/Psicoanálisis,/con le más/profunde admi/ración del más/humilde cultor de la disciplina H F Delgado"*.

1922 July 17

Horace Frink and his mistress Angelika Bijur come to Badgastein and F. analyzes Angelika Bijur daily.

1922 July 23

An Englishman comes to Badgastein to negotiate with him about a lecture cycle in Cambridge. But nothing comes of it.

1922 July 29

Paul Federn comes to Badgastein for a short visit.

1922 August 1

Departure from Badgastein in the morning.

1922 August 1–September 14
Summer stay with family in Berchtesgaden

F. and his family spend several weeks in the Moritz Pension on the Salzberg near Berchtesgaden. Horace Frink and his lover Angelika Bijur have also come with them from Badgastein to Berchtesgaden.

1922 August 1

Arrival in Berchtesgaden at 4.00 pm.

1922 August 5

– Luisa Strauss, sister-in-law of the Dutch bank director Ernst Frohnknecht, begins an analysis with F.
– Oliver arrives in Berchtesgaden.

1922 August 10 approx.

– F. is in Salzburg.

– F. and Anna go on a trip to Munich by car with Horace Frink and Angelika Bijur. There they dine at the posh Boettner restaurant at Theatinerstrasse 8. When Angelika Bijur suggests they go to a nightclub afterward, Anna is close to fainting, but her father is interested. When they arrive at the nightclub, however, it is closed.

1922 August mid

Arthur Schnitzler comes to Berchtesgaden and spends an afternoon alone with F. on his veranda. One of the topics of conversation is Schnitzler's marriage, which he had divorced less than a year before.

1922 August 16

Ludwig Binswanger sends F. his book *Einführung in die Probleme der allgemeinen Psychologie* with the dedication "In dankbarer Erinnerung an meine Besuche in Wien und ganz besonders an Ihren Besuch in Kreuzlingen! Ludwig Binswanger".

1922 August 18

Death of F.'s niece Cäcilie (Mausi), daughter of F.'s sister Rosa Graf. She commits suicide with Veronal. Her mother is temporarily admitted to a clinic.

1922 September 4

Max Eitingon comes to Berchtesgaden for two days with his wife Mirra.

1922 September 8

F. transfers 20,000 marks to Lou Andreas-Salomé, as she can hardly treat patients for health reasons.

1922 September 14

Departure from Berchtesgaden to Munich.

1922 September 14–21
Short visit to grandchildren and son-in-law in Hamburg

F. visits his widowed son-in-law Max Halberstad and his grandchildren Heinele and Ernst in Hamburg. F. takes Heinele – after a stopover for the Congress in Berlin – to Vienna, where he is taken in by daughter Mathilde and her husband Robert.

1922 September 14

Arrival in Munich.

1922 September 15

Departure from Munich in the evening.

1922 September 16

Arrival in Hamburg in the morning.

1922 September 21

Departure to Berlin.

1922 September 21–27
VII. International Psychoanalytical Congress in Berlin

The Congress takes place in the house of the Brüderverein in Kurfürstenstrasse. F. sets as the prize task the topic: *Relationship of analytical technique to analytical theory.* The prize money is 20,000 marks. It is the last Congress in which F. takes part.

1922 September 21

Arrival in Berlin. F., Martha, Anna and Heinele stay overnight with Eitingons at Rauchstrasse 4.

1922 September 23

Meeting of the "Secret Committee". On this occasion, a photo of all the members is taken, which Abraham's daughter Hedwig later calls "Das Fähnlein der sieben Aufrechten" (The Banner of the Upright Seven), after a novel of Gottfried Keller.

1922 September 24

Informal private meeting of the local group presidents. In the evening, they attend the operetta *Orpheus in the Underworld* by Jacques Offenbach at the Grosse Schauspielhaus.

1922 September 25

Opening of the Congress by Ernest Jones.

1922 September 26

- F. gives a lecture – with a heavy cold – on the subject of "Etwas vom Unbewußten". Among other things, F. tells us that he has adopted the concept of the "it" from Georg Groddeck, Among the audience is Olga Székely-Kovács, the then 22-year-old daughter of Vilma Kovács. She was so impressed by F.'s lecture that she made a sculpture of F. after her return to Budapest.
- Business meeting; among other things, the Indian Psychoanalytic Association is admitted to the IPA and its President Girindrashekhar Bose becomes a member of the editorial board of the *IZP.*
- F. presents a prize competition on the topic: "Relationship of analytical technique to analytical theory". The prize is endowed with 20,000 marks.

1922 September 27

The English group gives a lunch in F.'s honor. F. sits next to Barbara Low. The conversation is mainly about English writers.

1922 September 28

Departure for Vienna. F. and his grandson Heinele have Horace Frink and Angelika Bijur as travel companions.

1922 after September 28

Ruth Blumgart, Leonard Blumgart's sister-in-law, begins an analysis with F.

1922 September end

Max Eitingon gives F. Leopold Ziegler's book *Der ewige Buddho. Ein Tempelschriftwerk in vier Unterweisungen* with the dedication "Zur guten Erinnerung/an den/Berliner Kongress".

1922 September 29

Arrival in Vienna in the evening. Heinele is delivered to daughter Mathilde and her husband Robert and will live there.

1922 October beginning

Thaddeus Ames visits F. to begin an analysis with him. F. had promised him in writing, but now refuses – presumably because of Frink – and sends him to Otto Rank.

1922 October 4

F. meets with Otto Rank to follow up on the Berlin Congress.

1922 October 8

Horace Frink and Angelika Bijur invite F. and Martha to a performance of *Don Juan at the* Court Opera.

1922 October 18

WPV meeting: General Assembly.

1922 October 22

F.'s answer to a survey "Was wird mit Europa?" ("What about Europe?") by the Hungarian literary-scientific weekly *Tüz (Fire)* is published. F. writes: "Unfortunately, I don't know how to answer any of your questions about fate. My expectations for the future fluctuate with my mood. I lack all material for a judgement of interest to others. I myself would be very glad if someone would teach me about these problems" (SFG 17, pp. 165–167).

1922 October end

F. receives Stefan Zweig's book *Amok. Novellen einer Leidenschaft* with a dedication, to which F. replies: "it goes undeservedly far".

1922 October 30

– Ernst Haberl, the son of F.'s former maid Christine Haberl, shoots his father, who was about to rape Ernst's half-sister, and seriously injures him. On November 12, F. hires the lawyer Valentin Teirich to defend Ernst Haberl. Haberl was acquitted on 1923 September 19.
– F. draws up a will and authorizes son Martin and Alfred Rie to execute all the provisions contained therein.

1922 November

Clarence Seyler visits F. and receives from him a copy of the *Vorlesungen zur Einführung in die Psychoanalyse* with the dedication "Zur freundlichen Erinnerung/Sigmund Freud".

1922 before November 5

F. sends Arthur Schnitzler Georg Groddeck's novel *Der Seelensucher.*

1922 November 1

WPV meeting: Herbert Silberer speaks about "Observations on Dreams".

1922 November 6

F. receives the book by Charles Richet *Traité de Métapsychique* from Max Eitingon with the dedication "Mit herzlichen/Grüßen aus Paris/Max Eitingon".

1922 before November 13

Rudolf Payer, the director of the former Imperial entail library, brings F. the manuscript of a "bond with the devil" from the end of the 17th century. F. plans a small paper on this, which is published in the journal *Imago* at the beginning of 1923 under the title "Eine Teufelsneurose im siebzehnten Jahrhundert".

1922 November 15

WPV meeting: Wilhelm Reich speaks about "Limits of memory activity in the psychoanalytic cure".

1922 November 19
Death of Heinrich Obersteiner. F. had a three-week substitution in his private sanatorium Oberdöbling in 1885 June and had many scientific and personal points of contact with him.

1922 November 30
The municipal sanitary authority demands the discontinuation of the outpatient clinic; but three months later, it can be reopened.

1922 Autumn end
Roger Money-Kyrle, English philosopher, begins an analysis with F. It lasts until 1924 June.

1922 December 8
Birth of F.'s grandson Lucian (son of Ernst Freud).

1922 December mid
F. orders three new volumes of the *Encyclopaedia Britannica*.

1923

– F.'s contributions "Libidotheorie" and "Psychoanalyse" are published in the *Handwörter-buch der Sexualwissenschaft,* edited by Max Marcuse.

Receive books and offprints:

– Édouard Claparède sends F. his paper "Théodore Flournoy. Sa vie et son oeuvre, 1854–1920" with the dedication "à Mr. le Prof. S. Freud très cordial hommage Ed Cl".
– Israel Levine sends F. his book *The unconscious. An introduction to Freudian psychology* with the dedication "To the Master/From a very grateful pupil/I. Levine".
– Oskar Pfister sends F. his book *Der seelische Aufbau des klassischen Kapitalismus und des Geldgeistes* with the dedication "Herrn Prof. Freud/herzlich & dankbar/d. V".
– Paul Schilder gives F. his book *Das Körperschema. Ein Beitrag zur Lehre vom Bewusstsein des eigenen Körpers* with the dedication "Herrn Prof. Freud/in Verehrung/v. Verf".
– Paul Schilder gives F. his book *Seele und Leben. Grundlagen zur Psychologie der Schizo-phrenie und Paraphrenie, zur Psychoanalyse und zur Psychologie überhaupt* with the dedi-cation "Herrn Prof Freud/ergebenst überreicht/v. Verf".
– Julian Varendonck sends F. his book *Over esthetische symboliek* with the dedication "To Professor S. Freud/with deepest reverence./J. Varendonck".

1923 January 2
The expressionist painter Emil Lüthy, a cousin of Emil Oberholzer, begins an analysis with F., but F. breaks it off after a few weeks.

1923 January 3
WPV meeting: small papers and announcements; Walter Fokschaner on "Déja raconté in con-nection with an opposing memory illusion" and Paul Schilder on "The unconscious".

1923 January 12
Death of Herbert Silberer. He died by hanging.

1923 January 17
WPV meeting: small papers and announcements, including Siegfried Bernfeld speaking on the "Analysis of a Pedagogical Action", Hermann Nunberg on "An Induced Dream" and Wilhelm Reich on the "Course of Treatment of a Psychogenic Tic".

1923 January 23
Viktor Frankl, Maximilian Silbermann and Fritz Wittels found the "Akademischen Verein für medizinische Psychologie" ("Academic Association for Medical Psychology"), which aims to "smuggle in medical psychology through a back door" as a supplement to the official offer of the Medical Faculty (interview of Maximilian Silbermann by Kurt Eissler, 14.11.1956). F. welcomes the foundation and becomes a member of the scientific advisory board. Guido Holz-knecht supports the association financially.

1923 January 31
WPV meeting: Felix Deutsch speaks on "Illustrations of Psychoanalysis".

1923 February 4
F. and daughter Anna are at the wedding of his niece Beatrice Winternitz and Ernst Waldinger.

1923 February 9
F. asks the French writer Edouard Monod-Herzen to say to Romain Rolland "a word of respectful reverence for one unknown to him". (F. to Monod-Herzen, 9.2.1923).

1923 February 14
WPV meeting: Frieda Teller speaks on "Transmissions in Analysis".

1923 February 9
F. asks the French writer Edouard Monod-Herzen to say to Romain Rolland "a word of respectful reverence for one unknown to him" (F. to Monod-Herzen, 9.2.1923).

1923 February 21
Karl Abraham sends F. images of the antechamber of the tomb of Tutankhamun, which had been opened on February 16 by Howard Carter; he also encloses a newspaper article entitled "Neue Funde in Ägypten" ("New finds in Egypt").

1923 February 22
Romain Rolland thanks F. in a detailed letter for the greetings he sent him via Monod-Herzen. Rolland calls F. the Columbus of a new continent of the spirit ("Vous avez été le Christophe Colomb d'un nouveau continent de l'esprit) (Rolland to F., 22.2.1923) and sends him his fairy play *Liluli* illustrated with woodcuts by Frans Masereel with the dedication "Au Destructeur d'Illusions/Prof. Dr Freud en/hommage de respect/et de cordiale sympathie/Romain Rolland".

1923 February 28
WPV meeting: Theodor Reik speaks on "Tabnith, King of Sidon".

1923 February end
- F. discovers the first signs of his oral cavity cancer.
- Hermann Keyserling visits F.
- F. writes his paper "Die infantile Genitalorganisation".

1923 March 1
F. grants George Sylvester Viereck an interview. It is published in August in two parts under the headline "Freud's first interview on psychoanalysis" in the *New York American.*

1923 March 4
WPV meeting: small communications and papers, including Paul Federn on the "History of Melancholia" and "On a Variety of an Inhibition Dream", Anna Freud on "On a Hysterical Symptom in a Young Child", Hermann Nunberg on "On a Dream as a Neurosis Triggering Moment" and Eduard Hitschmann on the "Prehistory of a Suicide that Occurred in the Last Week".

1923 March 11
Georg Groddeck sends F. a manuscript by Eberhard von Roeder on Aristotle. F. replies very skeptically: his understanding and judgment had been paralyzed by the style.

1923 March 14
WPV meeting: Wilhelm Reich speaks on "On some relations between narcissism and guilt".

1923 March mid
Ernst Blum falls in love with F.'s daughter Anna.

1923 March 17
The International Psycho-Analytical Press is moved separately from Internationale Psychoanalytische Verlag from Vienna back to London; Eric Heller also leaves Vienna.

1923 March 20

The Argentinian psychiatrist Fernando Gorriti sends F. his work *Anamnesis general de 5000 enfermos mentales clasificados* with the dedication "Al sabio profesor de Psiquiatría de la Universidad de Zurich, Dr Freud, homenaje del autor:/Fernando Gorriti".

1923 Spring

– F. gives an interview to the French journalist Raymond Recouly. It is published in *Le Temps* on August 14 under the title "Une visite à Freud".
– F. donates to the restoration of St. Stephen's Cathedral.

1923 March end

F.'s grandson Heinele has a fever, but Oskar Rie is not worried about it.

1923 April

Johannes van der Hoop, Dutch psychiatrist, sends F. his book *Character and the unconscious. A critical exposition of the psychology of Freud and of Jung* with the dedication "Herrn Prof Freud/in dankbarer Anerkennung und/Hochachtung zugeeignet vom Verfasser".

1923 April 1

– Beata Rank sends F. the Polish translation of *Über den Traum* (O marzeniu sennem) with the dedication "Herrn Prof. Freud/in Verehrung überreicht/von/Beata Rank/Ostern 1923".
– F. attends a performance of Hugo von Hoffmansthal's *Der Unbestechliche* at the Raimundtheater with Max Pallenberg in the leading role.

1923 April 7

– Felix Deutsch visits F., and the latter asks him to look at his palate. Although Deutsch suspected cancer, he diagnosed it as "leukoplakia" in order to reassure F.
– F.'s wife Martha and son Martin go to Oliver's wedding in Berlin.

1923 April 10

Wedding of F.'s son Oliver to Henny Fuchs. Of F.'s family, only Martin came to Berlin.

1923 after April 12

F. receives from Douglas Barbour, follower of psychoanalysis from Oxford, his book *Psycho-Analysis and Everyman* with the dedication "Prof. Sigm. Freud/with the humble admiration/of the Author".

1923 April 16

Theodor Reik sends F. his book *Der eigene und der fremde Gott. Zur Psychoanalyse der religiösen Entwicklung* with the dedication *"Meinem verehrten* Lehrer/in dankbarer Ergebenheit./Th. Reik".

1923 April 18

– F.'s grandson Heinele has an operation on his tonsils.
– WPV meeting: Paul Schilder speaks on "Psychoanalysis and Encephalitis" and Paul Federn on "A case of sexual dysfunction".

1923 April 19

The educational counseling center is opened as part of the outpatient clinic. Hermine Hug-Hellmuth takes over the management.

1923 April 21

F. consults the rhinologist Markus Hajek and the dermatologist Maximilian Steiner about a tumor on the palate. He is operated on by Hajek in his clinic at the General Hospital in the presence of Felix Deutsch and Ludwig Rosenberg. The operation is poorly prepared and the excision is only performed under local anesthetic. Rosenberg is of the opinion that Hajek removed far too little of the tumor. When post-operative bleeding occurs, a dwarf waiter who had also been operated on there saves F.'s life by fetching help. The histological findings revealed a carcinoma, but the doctors did not tell the patient. F. is treated with radium: Three times a week, three hours each time at intervals of one week. F. remains in the clinic until April 23.

1923 April 27 approx.
F.'s book *Das Ich und das Es* is published.

1923 April 29
Markus Hajek demonstrates F. to his students

1923 April end
F.'s sister-in-law Minna is at the Cottage Sanatorium for heart treatment; its former owner and director was Rudolf Urbantschitsch, a member of the WPV from 1907 to 1914.

1923 May 5
Max and Mirra Eitingon come to Vienna for three days to personally check on F.'s condition.

1923 May 7
Max Eitingon, who had come for F.'s birthday, travels back to Berlin.

1923 May 8
F. is at Markus Hajek's for a follow-up examination.

1923 May 10
Ernst, who had come for F.'s birthday, travels back to Berlin.

1923 May 16
WPV meeting: Salomea Kempner speaks on "Oral Sadism".

1923 May 18
Beginning of the correspondence between F. and René Laforgue.

1923 May 26
F. has his fifth radium irradiation.

1923 May 30
– The health of F.'s grandson Heinele deteriorates rapidly, and the doctors diagnose miliary tuberculosis and abandon him.
– WPV meeting: Beata Rank speaks on "The role of the in the development of human society".

1923 June 5
Wilhelm Knöpfelmacher, the director of the Karolinen Children's Hospital in Vienna, examines Heinele and diagnoses "glandular fever".

1923 June 10
F. Son-in-law Max Halberstadt arrives in Vienna. He had been called because of the hopeless state of health of his son Heinele. In view of the imminent death of his grandson, F. writes: "I can bear this loss so badly, I don't think I have ever experienced anything more difficult […]" (F. to Lajos and Kata Lévy, 11.6.1923).

1923 June 13
WPV meeting: Paul Schilder speaks on "On Source Areas of Psychic Energy".

1923 June 18

F. sees the laryngologist Conrad Stein because of a palatal tumor, who – like Felix Deutsch – diagnoses leukoplakia.

1923 June 19

- Death of F.'s grandson Heinele, son of F.'s daughter Sophie Halberstadt. F. writes to Ferenczi: "My dear child died yesterday" (F. to Ferenczi, 20.6.1923).
- In the evening, Felix Deutsch visits F. to ask him whom he should go to in analysis against. On this occasion, F. asks Deutsch to look at his palate again. Deutsch is now sure that the tumor is cancer.

1923 June 30–July 30
Spa stay with sister-in-law Minna in Badgastein

1923 June 30

Departure to Badgastein.

1923 July 1

Arrival in Badgastein.

1923 July

Joseph Severn sends F. his book *Popular Phrenology* with the dedication "To Professor Sigmund Freud/Vienna/With the author's/good wishes".

1923 July 7

F. gives Sándor Ferenczi a copy of the *Encyclopaedia Britannica* for his 50th birthday.

1923 before July 9

F. receives from Eduard Hitschmann the book by Selma Lagerlöf for the first part of her autobiography Märbacka.

1923 July 9

Daughter Anna comes on a short visit from Annenheim, where her mother and Ernst Halberstadt – the son of F.'s deceased daughter Sophie – have already been staying since July 6.

1923 July 10

Death of F.'s nephew Theodor ("Theddi"), son of sister Mizzi. He had drowned while bathing.

1923 July mid

Ruth Blumgart is in Badgastein and goes for walks with F. several times.

1923 July 16–17

F. he goes for two days to Annenheim on Lake Ossiach, where the rest of the family spends the summer.

1923 July 19

Julius Banko, the director of the Collection of Classical Antiquities at the Kunsthistorisches Museum issues an expert opinion on the authenticity of "Oedipus Solves the Riddle of the Sphinx" of F.'s collection, probably a Greek Hydria.

1923 July 22

F. takes Ruth Blumgart on a trip to the Nassfeld, a southwestern side valley of the Gastein Valley.

1923 July 30–31

F. goes again for a short visit to Annenheim on Lake Ossiach and from there continues with his family to Lavarone.

1923 July end

F. receives Havelock Ellis' book *Dance of Life* with the dedication "To Professor Freud/ with best regards of/Havelock Ellis".

1923 August 1–31
Summer stay with family in Lavarone

In Lavarone, the family – including Ernst, the son of his deceased daughter Sophie – stays at the Hotel du Lac. Edward Kempf visits F. on the recommendation of Stanley Hall. Max Eitingon also comes to Lavarone for a visit.

1923 August 1

– F., Martha, Anna and grandson Ernst travel to Bolzano, where they meet up with Mathilde and Robert Hollitscher and travel on together to Lavarone.
– Ernest Jones comes to Lavarone.

1923 August 10

Car trip to two of the forts, "which are being allowed to develop into interesting ruins" (F. to Ernst, 14.10.1923)

1923 August 26

– The "Secret Committee" meets in Castel Toblino, then in San Cristoforo, but without F. At the last meeting of the "Committee" in San Cristoforo, the members learn of F.'s cancer; there are also disputes with Otto Rank.
– Felix Deutsch visits F. at the insistence of F.'s daughter Anna and recommends that F. no longer be treated by Markus Hajek for his palate ulcer, but by Hans Pichler. He allows F. to go to Rome with Anna.

1923 August 29

The "Secret Committee" pays a collective visit to F. in Lavarone. Abraham tries hard to clarify and mediate the differences within the committee.

1923 August 30

Max Eitingon takes F.'s grandson Ernst to Berlin.

1923 August 31

Departure from Lavarone; Martha goes to Meran to visit Minna and F. leaves for Rome with Anna.

1923 August 31–September 23
Trip to Rome with daughter Anna

Accommodation at the Hotel Eden. While in Rome, F. buys an onyx ashtray for Felix Deutsch. At the same time, his brother Alexander and his wife Sophie are in Rome. They do many things together.

1923 August 31

F. and Anna travel to Verona.

1923 September 1

Journey to Rome. On the train to Rome, F. gets a lot of bleeding in his mouth.

1923 September 1

In the afternoon, F. and Anna stroll along Via del Corso, which connects Piazza del Popolo with Piazza Venezia.

1923 September 2

Morning visit to the Forum and Capitol; afternoon visit to Pincio.

1923 September 3

Morning visit to the Palatine; afternoon Gianicolo and Vatican.

1923 September 4

Morning visit to the National Museum; afternoon visit to the Pantheon, Colosseum, Piazza Navona, Maria Sopra Minerva and Giordano Bruno Monument.

1923 September 5

In the morning visit to the Vatican Museums; in the afternoon, F. shows his daughter Michelangelo's Moses in St. Pietro in Vincoli; then visit to the Bocca della Verità, the portico of Octavia and an ancient prison.

1923 September 6

Morning visit to the Capitoline Museums; afternoon visit to Janus, Palatine and Protestant Cemetery.

1923 September 7

Morning visit to the Sistine Chapel and Raphael's Stanzas; afternoon visit to the churches of S. Sabeo, S. Sabina, Monte Aventino and the Pyramid of Cestius.

1923 September 8

In the morning, Castel Sant'Angelo; in the afternoon, tomb of Caecilia Metella, Via Appia and Columbarium of Pomponius Hylas.

1923 September 9

Morning visit to Villa Giulia; afternoon visit to the Church of Saint Paul Outside the Walls and the Church of San Paolo alle Tre Fontane.

1923 September 10

Morning visit to the Vatican, the loggias and the library; afternoon visit to the Celio district and the tombs on Via Latina.

1923 September 11

Visit to the Lateran Basilica in the morning; cinema in the evening.

1923 September 12

Morning visit to Monte Tarpeo, Church of Santa Maria in Aracoeli; afternoon visit to Fontana dell'Acqua Acetosa and Ponte Molle (Milvian Bridge).

1923 September 13

Morning excursion to Tivoli; afternoon Villa d'Este.

1923 September 14

Morning visit to the Palazzo Doria-Pamphilj.

1923 September 15

In the morning the Vatican Picture Gallery, the Church of S. Maria del Popolo; in the afternoon Santa Prassede, Maria Maggiore, Santa Croce in Gerusalemme, S. Laurentius outside the walls and the Tomb of Eurysaces.

1923 September 16

Morning visit to the Zoological Gardens and Galleria Borghese; afternoon visit to Maria sopra Minerva, Maria della Pace, Camera commerciale, Isola Tevere, Palazzo Farnese, Palazzo Spada, Palazzo della Cancelleria and Villa Massimi.

1923 September 17

Morning visit to Palazzo Corsini and Villa Farnesina; afternoon visit to Piazza Pia, the Church of Jesus and the Church of S. Clemente.

1923 September 18

Afternoon shopping, including a silver necklace.

1923 September 19

Morning visit to Campo di Fiori; afternoon visit to Via Appia, San Sebastiano and burial chamber of Marcus Clodius Hermes with the oldest wall paintings with biblical themes.

1923 September 20

Morning shopping on Via Nazionale, which connects Piazza della Repubblica and Piazza Venezia; including leather shopping; afternoon Monte Mario hill, Camilluccia; evening Fontana Trevi.

1923 September 21

Shopping in the morning; Palatine and Café Aragno in the afternoon.
– Departure from Rome in the evening.

1923 September 23

F. and daughter Anna arrive back in Vienna.

1923 Autumn
– The sculptress Catherine Barjansky finished a bust of F. She had already made one of Einstein and was also the art teacher of Elisabeth of Bavaria, Queen of Belgium since 1909.
– F. carries out control analyses on daughter Anna.

1923 September 26
– F. is examined by the laryngologist Markus Hajek and the surgeon Hans Pichler at Lichtenfelsgasse 1; they detect a recurrence of the cancer and decide on a second operation.
– Pichler makes a new prosthesis. F. demands to be treated by Pichler as a "paying patient" and not as a colleague.
– After Ernst Haberl had been acquitted on September 19, F. transferred 500,000[47] Kronen to Valentin Teirich, who had defended Haberl, and was also prepared to pay the costs of a possible further trial in the amount of 1,500,000 Kronen.

1923 September 27
Hans Pichler cleans and examines F.'s teeth.

1923 October
- F. begins writing a paper "Psychoanalysis: Exploring the Hidden Recesses of the Mind", which is published in 1924 in volume two of *These Eventful Years. The Twentieth Century in the Making, as told by Many of its Makers*, edited by Franklin Hooper and published by *Encyclopedia Britannica*.
- F. niece Hella Bernays divorces her husband Maurice Murray Cohen and lives in Vienna for the next four years. On F.'s advice, she is analyzed by Hermann Nunberg.

1923 October 4
Hans Pichler performs a submandibular and cervical gland removal and ligation of the external carotid artery on F. at the Auersperg Sanatorium (Auerspergstr. 9). Assistant is Anton Bleichsteiner. The removed material was not carcinogenic.

1923 October 8
Death of F.'s brother-in-law Eli Bernays, brother of his wife Martha.

1923 October 11
Hans Pichler performs a partial resection of the right posterior maxilla and the ascending mandibular branch under local anesthesia at the Auersperg Sanatorium. In addition, parts of the buccal and lingual mucosa are removed. The assistants are Otto Hofer and again Anton Bleichsteiner. That same evening F. smokes again, but is later forced to wear a prosthesis in his mouth, which severely hinders him in eating and speaking. However, he has to stay in the sanatorium for another two weeks. F. is unable to treat any patients until the end of the year.

1923 October 12
F. is not yet able to speak after the operation, but is already drinking and eating apple puree, for example.

1923 October 13
F. has a brief rise in temperature to 39 degrees, associated with a feeling of weakness.

1923 October mid
- Felix Deutsch and F. end their doctor-patient relationship because Deutsch had concealed his cancer diagnosis from F., although there had been a pact between them according to which Deutsch had to tell his patient the unrestricted truth. Privately, both men remained in contact.

1923 October 17
WPV meeting: General Assembly – elected to the Executive Committee were the following: F. (Chair), Otto Rank (Deputy), Paul Federn and Siegfried Bernfeld (Secretaries), Richard Nepallek (Treasurer) and Theodor Reik (Librarian). The management of the outpatient clinic was entrusted to: Eduard Hitschmann (chairman), Paul Federn and Felix Deutsch.

1923 October 19
F.'s tampon is renewed.

1923 October 22
Death of F.'s sister-in-law Maria, the wife of his brother Emanuel.

1923 October 24
F. is discharged home and visited by Pichler.

1923 October 28
F. is pain-free for the first time since the operation and has slept one night without narcotics.

1923 October 30
In view of his state of health, F. supplements the previous arrangements regarding the inheritance and entrusts son Martin – in agreement with Alfred Rie – with the execution of all provisions.

1923 October 31
WPV meeting: small communications, including Wilhelm Reich speaking on "Introspection of Schizophrenia", Siegfried Bernfeld on "The Magito Membrane" and Theodor Reik on "On Unconscious Guilt".

1923 October end
Otto and Vera Schmidt from Moscow visit F.

1923 November 5
F. has gradually increasing pain. After rejection of a necrotic clot, a fissured ulcer is visible. Some pus comes out at one point.

1923 November 9
Hans Pichler grinds F.'s prosthesis down a bit and it now fits better.

1923 November 10
F. has more severe pain again, which decreases when the prosthesis is removed.

1923 November 12
Hans Pichler, assisted by Otto Hofer and Ernst Hertzka (the husband of Oliver F.'s first wife Ella Haim), operates on F.'s tumor recurrence at the Auersperg Sanatorium and removes most of the right soft palate and the pterygoid process (bone process of the sphenoid bone).

1923 November 14
The surgical suture between the soft palate and the prosthesis has come loose and the stent clot has slipped into the mouth, where it causes F. severe discomfort. It is cut up and taken out.

1923 November 15
Visit by Hans Pichler.

1923 November 16
Visit by Hans Pichler.

1923 November 17
– On the recommendation of Paul Federn and Rudolf Urbantschitsch, F. undergoes a Steinach operation (ligature of both vas deferens) in the hope that his cancer will be positively affected. F. had taught the inventor of this surgical method, Eugen Steinach, microscopy as an assistant. However, the operation was carried out by Robert Lichtenstern (1874–1955). Since then, F. has been very interested in hormone research. Three quarters of a year later, F. thinks that the operation has not achieved any success.
– Visit by Hans Pichler

1923 November 19
F. has severe pain, but no fever.

1923 November 20
F. tells Otto Rank a "funny dream", which Rank interprets in a letter to F.

1923 November 21
F. is in the Auersperg Sanatorium for another operation and is discharged the following day.

1923 November 27
Hans Pichler tries again to fit F.'s prosthesis better.

1923 before December 8
F. receives from Joan Riviere the book by Howard Carter and Arthur Mace *Tut-ench-Amun: An Egyptian royal* tomb *discovered by Earl of Carnarvont and Howard Carter*, "which interested me more powerfully than anything since my illness" (F. to Joan Riviere, 8.12.1923).

1923 before December 9
F. receives from George Sylvester Viereck his book *Rejuvenation. How Steinach makes people young* with the dedication "For Prof. Sigmund Freud/as a token of admiration/with the good wishes of/the author/George Sylvester Viereck/(George F Viereck)".

1923 December 10
F. can swallow and speak well again.

1923 December 19
F. meets Arthur Schnitzler in the center of Vienna.

1923 December 20
F.'s prosthesis now fits better. He can now remove and reinsert it on his own. During a consultation with Guido Holzknecht, it is decided to treat F. with X-ray radiation. The first session takes place on the same day.

1923 Christmas
- F. receives from Fritz Wittels. an advance copy of his book *Sigmund Freud. Der Mann, die Lehre, die Schule* with the "In unwandelbarer Verehrung,/in Erinnerung an Zeiten, die nun schon lange vergangen sind Dr Fritz Wittels". F. encloses a list of corrections to a letter of thanks to Wittels.
- F.'s son Oliver and his wife Henny are visiting F. over Christmas.
- Hanns Sachs comes to Vienna.

1923 December 25
Oskar Pfister sends F. his book *Zur Psychologie des philosophischen Denkens* with the dedication "Seinem lieben Grosspapa Prof. S. Freud/wünscht frohen Jahreswechsel dieses/Schmöker-lein/von O. Pfister".

1923 December 31
- Sándor Ferenczi sends F. his book *Versuch einer Genitaltheorie* with the dedication "Herrn Professor Freud in Dankbarkeit/zugeeignet von/seinem ergebenen/Ferenczi".
- Jeanne de Groot visits F. at his invitation to set the next analysis hours.

1923 December end
- F.'s new prosthesis is ready.
- F. receives an invitation to Lausanne, but cancels for health reasons.

1924

- The Internationale Psychoanalytische Verlag moves to Andreasgasse 3 (until the spring of 1928).

Treatments:

- Maryse Choisy, French journalist and pilot, begins a brief analysis at F.
- Lillian (Meena) Gunn begins an analysis with F. F. asks her husband, the Egyptologist George Gunn, to look at the Egyptian pieces in F.'s collection. Gunn is convinced that most of them are fakes.

Received books and offprints:

- Louise Brink sends F. her book *Women characters in Richard Wagner. A study in "The Ring of the Niebelung"* with the dedication "Prof. Dr. Sigmund Freud, With deep respect and gratitude Louise Brink".
- Josef Friedjung gives F. an offprint of his paper "Zur Kenntnis kindlicher Milieutypen" with the dedication "Herrn Prof. Freud in dankbarer Verehrung/der Verf".
- René Laforgue sends F. his book *La psychanalyse et les névroses,* written together with René Allendy with the dedication "A mon maître Monsieur le Professeur Freud/ce téimoignage de mon admiration respectueuse/René Laforgue".
- John Landquist sends F. the French translation of *Psychopathologie des Alltagslebens* (Vardagslivets psykopatologi), which he has done together with Emmy Groddeck, with the dedication "Professor Dr Sigmund F./mit ehrfurchtsvollem Gruss/von John Landquist".
- Sante de Sanctis sends F. his book *La conversione religiosa. Studio bio-psicologico* with the dedication "Al Maestro Sigm. Freud/senza del quale questo libro/non sarebbe stato scritto/ Sante de Sanctis".
- Paul Schilder gives F. his book *Medical Psychology for Doctors and Psychologists* with the dedication "Herrn Professor/Freud in Verehrung/v. Verf".
- Georges Villey-Desméserets sends F. his book *Contribution à l'étude des doctrines en médecine mentale* with the dedication "A Monsieur le Professeur/S. Freud/très respectueux hommage/G. Villey".
- Georg Wanke, neurologist from Friedrichroda, sends F. his book *Psychoanalyse. Geschichte, Wesen, Aufgaben und ihre Wirkung* with the dedication "Meinem hochverehrten Lehrer u. Meister/Herrn Professor S. Freud, der Verf".

1924 January beginning
F. receives manuscripts of two papers from Heinrich Gomperz, one of which F. recommends to the journal *Imago* for publication. It is published in the same year with the title "Psychologische Beobachtungen an griechischen Philosophen".

1924 January 2
- Death of Leopold Königstein. F. had been friends with the ophthalmologist since their time together at the General Hospital. Königstein played a role in F.'s cocaine studies and the discussion of male hysteria.

– WPV meeting: Sándor Ferenczi speaks about the book *Developmental Goals of Psychoanalysis,* co-authored with Rank.

1924 January 4

F. goes to Guido Holzknecht for X-ray treatment in the afternoon.

1924 January 16

Death of F.'s brother Philip.

1924 January 21

F. completes the writing of his paper on "Das ökonomische Problem des Masochismus".

1924 February 4

F. tries on a new prosthesis made by Hans Pichler.

1924 February 7

F. gets the new prosthesis after final corrections by Pichler. It fits more firmly and is lighter than the first one, and can be used better, and F. finds it easier to speak with it.

1924 February 8

An article about F. by Alfred Winterstein is published in the *Neue Freie Presse.*

1924 February 11

After changes to the new prosthesis, F.'s pronunciation deteriorates again.

1924 February 14

Oskar Pfister sends F. his book *Love in children and its aberrations. A book for parents and teachers* with the dedication "Seinem geistigen Nährvater/Sigmund Freud/in Treue/O. Pfister".

1924 February 26

The modified prosthesis fits quite well. However, F.'s speech is very poor.

1924 March 2

F. begins writing his paper "Der Untergang des Ödipuskomplexes"; the article is finished on March 21.

1924 March 6

F. has pressure marks and pain from the prosthesis.

1924 March 14

Hans Pichler has a consultation with the speech specialist Hugo Stern, who finds that there is virtually no rhinolalia. F. feels a considerable improvement and facilitation of speech due to the last milling of the prosthesis. However, it is now rather difficult to insert the prosthesis so that it slips into the fold. F. should practice inserting it by biting on a piece of wood with the molars on the upper and lower right.

1924 March 19

– F. has lengthy academic discussions with Otto Rank.
– Giovanni Capone sends F. his book *La dottrina psicoanalitica di S. Freud* with the dedication "Al Chiarissimo Signor Prof. S. Freud ommagio devoto di G. Capone".

1924 March 20
F. is against the publication of the experiments on thought transference.

1924 Spring
- F.'s *Collected Writings* begin to appear, starting with volume 4, the *Psychopathology of Everyday Life.*
- F. is elected honorary member of the American Neurological Society.
- Frédéric Weil, former young supporter, visits F. He is considering having an analysis done on him.

1924 March 26
F. has a new typewriter on which his daughter Anna increasingly writes his letters.

1924 March 29–30
F. is so unwell that for the first time in his medical life he interrupts work during the weekend and goes to the "Kurhaus" on the Semmering.

1924 April 5–6
F. again spends a weekend at the "Kurhaus" on the Semmering.

1924 April 10
Hans Pichler mends the milled holes in the prosthesis, and F. gets his old prosthesis back as a modest replacement for this time.

1924 April 13
Max and Mirra Eitingon come to Vienna.

1924 April 14
F. sends a greeting address to Ernest Jones to be read at the VIII. International Psychoanalytical Congress in Salzburg with the text: "Absent for the first time, I warmly greet all participants and wish their work every success".

1924 April 15
Sándor and Gisella Ferenczi come to Vienna.

1924 April 17–24
F. spends Easter at the "Kurhaus" on the Semmering.

1924 April 20
Paul Federn and Heinrich Meng give F. the special volume of the *Ärztliche Volksbuch*, published by Meng and August Fiessler with the dedication "Herrn Professor Sigmund Freud/Ostern 1924/ verehrungsvoll überreicht. Dr Paul Federn Dr. Heinrich Meng".

1924 April 21
Hermine von Hug-Hellmuth gives F. her book *Neue Wege zum Verständnis der Jugend.* with the dedication *"Herrn Professor Freud/in Dankbarkeit überreicht von der Verfasserin",*

1924 April 21–23
The VIII. International Psychoanalytical Congress takes place; F., however, is absent because of influenza.

1924 April 24
Birth of F.'s grandson Clemens, son of son Ernst.

1924 April 24–26
Ernest Jones is in Vienna.

1924 April 25
F. receives the honorary title "Citizen of the city of Vienna". The *Neue Wiener Tagblatt* publishes the following news on April 26: "Yesterday, in a confidential meeting, the Vienna City Council appointed Dr. Sigmund Freud a citizen of the city of Vienna in recognition of his great services to medical science".

1924 May
- The British botanist Ernest Pickworth Farrow visited F. He had been inspired to take an interest in psychology by Arthur Tansley.
- Otto Rank visits F.
- F. becomes Vice-President of the World Union of Jewish Students founded by Albert Einstein.

1924 May beginning
Romain Rolland asks to visit F. via Stefan Zweig.

1924 May 5
Extraordinary meeting of the WPV.

1924 May 6
Julius Tandler and Josef Friedjung visit F. and present him with the "Citizen's diploma of the city of Vienna". On this occasion F. gives Julius Tandler the *Pychoanalytische Studien an Werken der Dichtung und Kunst* with the dedication "Herrn Prof. J. Tandler, hochachtungsvoll, d. Verf.".

1924 May 7
The *Arbeiterzeitung* celebrates F. "in a nice little article" (F. to Oliver Freud, 7.5.1924).

1924 May 12
- On the occasion of the presentation of the citizenship diploma to F., the Wiener *Morgen* publishes a caricature of F. and Robert Gersuny, who had also received the diploma.
- Rudolf Urbantschitsch visits F.

1924 May 14
Stefan Zweig and Romain Rolland visit F. in the afternoon. Rolland has been in Vienna since May 10 on the occasion of the Richard Strauss Festival Week.

1924 before May 28
Flora Kraus, the wife of the bank director Maximilian Kraus and patron of psychoanalysis, "has the firm intention to build a house for the polyclinic" (F. to Ferenczi, 28.5.1924).

1924 June 2
Oskar Pfister sends F. his book *Die psychoanalytische Methode* with the dedication *"Verjüngt und entjungt,/Entadlert und dem Adler ange-/glichen, überbringt dieses Buch/Herrn Prof. Freud herzlichen Gruss/von O. Pfister"*.

1924 June 12
Hanns Sachs sends F. his book *Gemeinsame Tagträume* with the dedication *"In dauerder Dank-barkeit/und Verehrung/Hanns Sachs"*.

1924 June mid

Freud declines an invitation from the Hearst Press to come to New York for the duration of a trial of two young men (Nathan Leopold and Richard Loeb) accused of murder, for health reasons.

1924 June end

Robert McCormick, the editor of the *Chicago Tribune*, offers F. "$25,000[48] or any sum" if he analyzes the two young men charged with murder. F. declines because he "cannot be expected to give my opinion as an expert witness solely on the basis of newspaper reports and without the possibility of a personal examination of the persons and deeds" (F. to Georg Seldes, 29.6.1924). F. had already declined the invitation of the Hearst Press to come to New York for the duration of the trial a few days earlier.

1924 June 24

F. issues a certificate for Rudolf Urbantschitsch that he "has used the last two years to create a thorough education in the theory and practice of psychoanalysis here in Vienna and in Budapest".

1924 July 4

Death of Josef Herzig. The chemist had courted F.'s sister Rosa in 1884 and played an important role in F.'s cocaine studies.

1924 Summer

The differences with Otto Rank come to a head.

1924 July 1

F. feels disturbed by a feeling of pressure and tension on the right side for which no cause can be found. Hans Pichler suspects the cause to be the sinuses, which are treated by Heinrich Neumann. He advises F. to take the prosthesis out more often.

1924 July 8–September 29
Summer stay at Semmering

F. spends the summer at the Villa Schüler on Semmering and works on his "Selbstdarstellung". Dorothy Burlingham, the daughter of the American entrepreneur, painter and glass artist Louis Comfort Tiffany, lives with her children in the house next door. From Semmering, F. travels to Vienna once a week to be examined by Hans Pichler. Edmund Jerusalem, the son of Wilhelm Jerusalem, visits F. together with his wife Anna, the daughter of Max Kassowitz.

1924 July mid

On the recommendation of Carl Gustav Jung, F. begins the treatment of William Blumenthal, a rich American diplomat with a germ phobia. It lasts until 1928 December. Blumenthal lives in the Südbahnhotel, not far from the Villa Schüler. F.'s niece Lucie is staying in the same hotel and learns from the chambermaid that he needs 25 towels a day. Blumenthal has also had his hotel room repainted.

1924 July 30

Death of F.'s former patient Emma Eckstein. She died as a result of cervical cancer and an unsuccessful operation.

1924 August beginning

F. receives a request from Albert Cohen in Geneva, who is going to publish a *Revue Juive,* to send him a contribution. F. chose "Résistances a la Psychanalyse", later also published in English under the title "The Resistances to Psycho-Analysis".

1924 August 6

Birth of Sophie, the first daughter of F.'s son Martin and thus F.'s first granddaughter.

1924 August 8

F. grants Carl Dymling an interview. It is published in *Dagens Nyheter* on September 14 under the title "Hos pejlaren av själslivets djup" ("In the depths of the soul").

1924 August 10

Karl Abraham visits F.

1924 before August 24

– F. receives an invitation from the Schopenhauer Society to give a public lecture, but cancels for health reasons.
– F. receives a small booklet of verses from Georg Sylvester Viereck, presumably the volume *Gedichte* published in 1922.

1924 August 27

F. receives the first volume of the *Ärztliches Volksbuch* written by Paul Federn and Heinrich Meng with the dedication "Das erste Exemplar des Buches überreichen wir Ihnen, Herr Professor verehrungsvoll und dankbar Dr Paul Federn Dr Heinrich Meng".

1924 August 29

Max and Mirra Eitingon visit F. and spend the night in the Villa Schüler.

1924 September

Mark Brunswick, American composer, begins an analysis with F. It lasts until the spring of 1928 and 1934 until 1938.

1924 September beginning

F. receives from Franklin Hooper the anthology *These Eventful Years. The Twentieth Century in the Making, as told by Many of its Makers*, to which F. had contributed a chapter entitled "Psychoanalysis: Exploring the Hidden Recesses of the Mind".

1924 September 3

Birth of F.'s granddaughter Eva, daughter of son Oliver. F. writes: "On the third of the month, Oli's wife gave birth to a little daughter at her father's in Berlin, the second granddaughter. There are now seven; none can make me forget the lost Heinele." (F. to Ferenczi, 6.9.1924).

1924 September mid

F.'s hearing on the right side is deteriorating badly.

1924 Autumn

Lionel Penrose, who is studying psychology for a year in Vienna, seeks out F. to find out from him how he can get psychoanalytic training.

1924 September 28

F. is elected in absentia as President of the WPV, Paul Federn as Vice-President. Until then, F. was chairman and Otto Rank deputy chairman.

1924 September 29

Departure to Vienna.

1924 September 30
The new prosthesis only brings F. relief for three days; he is now feeling worse again.

1924 September end
Arthur Schnitzler sends F. his novella *Fräulein Else* with the dedication "Hrn Prof. Sigmund Freud/in herzlicher Verehrung/Arthur Schnitzler".

1924 October
- F. has a sharp dispute with Poul Bjerre, who had published works by him in an anthology together with papers by Alfred Adler and Carl Gustav Jung without his knowledge.
- Siegfried Altmann, who had been introduced to F. by Paul Federn in 1918 and who had been director of the Israelite Institute for the Blind on the Hohe Warte in Vienna since 1922, approached F. with the question of whether he would like to become a member of the Board of Trustees of the Institute for the Blind. F. agrees. Arthur Schnitzler and Richard Beer-Hoffmann had also already given their consent.

1924 October 1
F. continues the treatment of William Blumenthal. Because of his germ phobia, Blumenthal rents three floors in a Viennese hotel, but only occupies the middle one.

1924 October 6
Hans Pichler is trying to further improve the prosthesis.

1924 October 3
Rudolf Urbantschitsch gives F. an offprint of his lecture "Psychoanalysis. Ihre Bedeutung und ihr Einfluss auf Jugenderziehung, Kinderaufklärung, Berufs- und Liebeswahl" with the dedication *"Seinem genialen Lehrer u. Meister/Prof. Dr. Sigmund Freud/in bewundernder Verehrung Dr Rudolf Urbantschitsch"*.

1924 October 7
F. consults Helene Deutsch about the current problems with Otto Rank.

1924 October 8
Heinrich Meng visits F.

1924 October 10
The Vienna Medical Association files charges against the non-medical analyst Theodor Reik with the Vienna Magistrate on the basis of the "Kurpfuschereigesetz" ("law on quackery").

1924 October 15
WPV meeting: Robert Wälder speaks on "Creative and schizophrenic thinking".

1924 October mid
- Flora Kraus, who wanted to finance the construction of a building for the Psychoanalytic Outpatient Center, has to abandon her intention because of her divorce. F. writes: "With that my last hope that something respectable would become of ΨA in Vienna goes down the drain" (F. to Ferenczi, 12.10.1924).
- Jan van Emden is in Vienna and asks F. to have a daily analysis lesson for four weeks, but F. refuses.

1924 October 26

Otto Rank has a three-hour conversation with F. in the afternoon, which, however, does not lead to a clear clarification of Rank's scientific position.

1924 October 28

– F. is pain-free for the first time since the operation.
– WPV meeting: General Assembly – F. is elected Chairman.

1924 October 31

Sándor Ferenczi and Max Eitingon come to Vienna for two days and discuss with F. and Otto Rank the tensions that have arisen between them and Rank and their consequences for the publishing house.

1924 November

Anna introduces her friend Eva Rosenfeld to her father.

1924 November 5

F. answers a request from Stefan Zweig concerning the dedication of his book *Der Kampf mit dem Dämon. Hölderlin, Kleist, Nietzsche* positively. The dedication reads: "Professor Dr. Sigmund Freud to the penetrating spirit, the inspiring designer of this triad of pictorial endeavour".

1924 November mid

The physiologist Arnold Durig asks F. to prepare an expert opinion on lay analysis. F. complies with the request and also has a verbal exchange with Durig, which resulted in far-reaching agreement between him and Durig.

1924 November 12

F. submits the housing tax return. He has to pay 261,000 Kronen per month.[49]

1924 November 16

Sándor Radó, Hungarian doctor and psychoanalyst, comes to Vienna and takes over Otto Rank's business.

1924 November 19

– Otto Rank makes his farewell visit to F.
– F.'s prosthesis does not cause him pain for the first time.

1924 November 26

WPV meeting; Helene Deutsch speaks on "The Menopause of Women".

1924 November 28

Helene Deutsch presents F. with the plan to form a new teaching committee and to organize psychoanalytic teaching in close accordance with the Berlin model.

1924 November end

– F. has a "presidential letter" from Karl Abraham read out in the WPV.
– F.'s prosthesis causes renewed pain.

1924 December

F. begins treating the writer Lilian Powers. It lasted until the end of 1925. Powers was friends with Scofield Thayer, another of F.'s patients.

1924 December 3
Anna Freud becomes a member of the "Secret Committee" in place of Otto Rank.

1924 December 4
F. discusses with the lawyer Paul Rosenfeld – a brother of Otto Rank – the transfer of Otto Rank's powers of attorney to Max Eitingon.

1924 December 8
Oskar Pfister sends F. his book *Die Liebe vor der Ehe und ihre Fehlentwicklung* with the dedication *"Herrn Prof. Dr Freud/in herzlicher Dankbarkeit/d. Verf"*.

1924 December mid
Otto Rank visits F. "in order to – confess" (F. to Ferenczi, 21.12.1924), and F. is again much more positive toward him.

1924 December 15
– Helene Deutsch proposes the foundation of a psychoanalytic teaching institute. After its opening, she herself becomes director, Siegfried Bernfeld vice-director and Anna Freud secretary.
– F. becomes an honorary member of the Greek Psychiatric Association.

1924 December 17
Erwin Magnus sends F. the book by Georg Brandes *Cajus Julius Caesar* with the dedication "Dem grossen Onkel meiner kleinen Margit in aufrichtiger Verehrung Erwin Magnus".

1924 December 18
– F. is at the farewell party for Salomon Ehrmann, who was given emeritus status on the occasion of his 70th birthday.
– Karl Abraham sends F. the second edition of his book on *Giovanni Segantini* with the dedication "Herrn Prof. Freud mit herzlichen Grüßen der Verf.".

1924 December 19–20
Max Eitingon is coming to Vienna for two days.

1924 December 23
F. has hardly any pain, but can chew and drink less easily because fluid flows out through the nose.

1924 Christmas
Arthur Tansley sends F. Alan Milne's book *When we were very young* with the dedication "Prof. Dr. Sigmund Freud/from A G T. "

1924 December 29
F. concludes that Otto Rank "has come back to us completely" and that he "account[ed] for his behavior in a way that deserves tolerance and pardon" (F. to Joan Riviere, 29.12.1924).

1924 December 30
The Viennese newspaper *Der Tag* reports under the headline "Blitzlicht" that Samuel Goldwyn, whose company "Goldwyn Pictures" had just been absorbed into Metro-Goldwyn-Mayer (MGM), wanted to recruit F. for the artistic direction of his film *Romeo and Juliet*.

1924 December end
The lawyer Robert Hermann from Brno visits F. in connection with a possible treatment of a client's wife. The contact between Robert Hermann and F. had been arranged by Salomon Ehrmann.

1925

- F. noticed small alabaster dishes from Egypt in the antique shop of Ludwig Lustig at Helferstorferstrasse 2, right next to the bookshop of his publisher Franz Deuticke. Lustig's son Robert had placed them in the shop window. Since then, F. has been a customer at Lustig's and buys something almost every week, which his son Robert then brings to Berggasse.
- Chaim Bloch, a Hasidic and Kabbalist rabbi and publicist, visits F. and shows him the manuscript of his introduction to the memoirs of the Kabbalist Chaim Vital.
- Only personal encounter between F. and Viktor Frankl.

Treatments:

- Medard Boss, Swiss psychiatrist, begins an analysis with F.
- Heinz Hartmann, Austrian psychiatrist, begins an analysis with F.

Received books and offprints:

- Ernest Pickworth Farrow sends F. his book *Plant life on East Anglian heaths. Being observational and experimental studies of the vegetation of Breckland with* the dedication "To Professor F. with the Author's Esteem".
- George Sylvester Viereck sends F. the collection *Little blue books* edited by him with the dedication "Admiringly/George Sylvester Viereck".
- F. receives from Helene Deutsch her book *Psychoanalyse der weiblichen Sexualfunktionen* with the dedication "Herrn Professor F./in dankbarer Verehrung/überreicht von/Verfasserin".
- Johannes Heinrich Schultz sends F. his book *Die Schicksalsstunde der Psychotherapie* with the dedication "Dem Schöpfer der Psychoanalyse/in aufrichtiger Verehrung/v. V".
- Leo Kaplan sends F. his book *Schopenhauer und der Animismus. Eine psychoanalytische Studie* with the dedication "Dem verehrten/Lehrer Herrn/Prof. F./der Autor".
- Margit Ornstein F. sends the book of Josef Popper-Lynkeus *Gespräche* edited by her and her brother Heinrich Löwy with the dedication "Herrn Professor Dr Sigmund Freud/in größter Verehrung und Dankbarkeit/Margit Ornstein".
- Gustav Bychowski sends F. an offprint of his paper "Zur Frage nach den Beziehungen zwischen der Psyche und dem weiblichen Genitalsystem" with the dedication "Herrn Prof. Freud in Verehrung GBychowski".
- The French psychiatrists Adrien Borel and Gilbert Robin give F. their *book Les rêveurs éveillés* with the dedication "Au Professeur S. Freud en respectueux hommage. A Borel et G Robin".
- The British nurse and psychoanalyst Mary Chadwick sends F. her book *Psychology for nurses. Introductory lectures for nurses upon psychology and psycho-analysis* with the dedication "With deepest gratitude from Mary Chadwick".

1925 January
The WPV's teaching institute opens with 15 listeners.

1925 January beginning
F. receives an invitation for the opening of the Hebrew University in Jerusalem planned for April 1, but declines for health reasons.

1925 January 5
- The French playwright Henri Lenormand visits F. to talk to him about his play "Don Juan", which has just been performed in Vienna.
- The "Wiener Psychoanalytische Lehrinstitut" ("Vienna Psychoanalytic Teaching Institute") opens.

1925 January mid
The lawyer Robert Hermann visits F. with Mrs Eisner – the wife of a client – about possible treatment. F. has three sessions with Mrs Eisner and refers her to Lou Andreas-Salomé.

1925 January 19
F. receives from the philosopher Hans Vaihinger his article on "Schopenhauer and Psychoanalysis", which had been published in the *Münchner Neueste Nachrichten on* 1925 January 4.

1925 January 23
F. grants Friedrich Porges an interview. It is published in *Die Stunde* on January 24 under the title "Professor Freud macht keinen Seelenfilm" ("Professor Freud does not make a soul film"). In the interview, F. makes it clear that he has no intention of receiving Samuel Goldwyn – who is on his way to Vienna – and accepting his offer.

1925 January 23–27
Max Eitingon is in Vienna.

1925 before January 27
F. receives a box of cigars from Ann and Louis Bieber from New York.

1925 February beginning
William Inman, ophthalmologist from Portsmouth, who studies the relationship of psychoanalysis to ophthalmology, visits F.

1925 February 2
F. writes on a sheet of paper: "My teacher Brücke used to say that nature is in no hurry and what she does costs her nothing. Sigm. Freud. 25.2.25.".

1925 before February 9
F. receives from Fritz Wittels his book *Die Vernichtung der Not. On Popper-Lynkeus and his work "Die allgemeine Nährpflicht"*.

1925 February 10
F. has complaints because his prosthesis wobbles.

1925 February beginning
- F.'s "Selbstdarstellung" is published in the fourth volume of Louis Grote's anthology *Die Medizin der Gegenwart in Selbstdarstellungen*.
- F. sends Havelock Ellis an offprint of his "Selbstdarstellung".

1925 February 12
- F. gives Abraham Brill an offprint of his "Selbstdarstellung" with the dedication "Seinem lieben Dr. A.A. Brill. Freud".
- F. gives Oskar Pfister Brill an offprint of his of his self-representation with the dedication "Seinem lieben Dr. O. Pfister, Freud".

1925 February mid
- F. is so impressed by a report by the Australian-born classical philologist Gilbert Murray on telepathic experiments before the Society for Psychical Research that he is prepared to "give up his opposition to the existence of thought transference" (F. to Secret Committee, 15.2.1925).
- F. gives Arthur Fischer-Colbrie an offprint of his of his "Selbstdarstellung" with the dedication "Auf Deinen Wunsch/l. Arthur/Freud".

1925 February 17
- F. gives Ruth Mack (divorced Blumgart) an offprint of his "Selbstdarstellung" with the dedication "Seiner lieben Ruth/ zum 17. Februar 1925/Freud".
- F. gives his nephew Sam (son of brother Emanuel) Brill an offprint of his "Selbstdarstellung".

1925 March
The municipal health department threatens to close the outpatient clinic if lay people work there.

1925 March beginning
F. conducts experiments on thought transference with Ferenczi and his daughter Anna. He also has a discussion with Otto Rank.

1925 March 3
F. sends Jeanne de Groot an offprint of his "Selbstdarstellung"-

1925 March 5
Jakov Kogan sends F. his Russian translation of *Massenpsychologie und Ich-Analyse* (*Psikhologiya mass i analiz chelovecheskogo*) with the dedication "Velichaishemu myslite/Lyu nashego vremeni/Prof. Freidu./Perevodchik./Odessa".

1925 March 8
F. turns to Arnold Durig and protests against the decision of the Vienna magistrate prohibiting Theodor Reik from practicing psychoanalysis. He asks Durig to "grant Reik an interview in his cause" (F. to Durig, 8.3.1925).

1925 March 10
Hans Pichler pulls out F.'s tooth and does a root canal filling.

1925 March 20
Oskar Pfister sends F. his book *Die Frömmigkeit des* Grafen *Ludwig von Zinzendorf* with the dedication "Herrn Prof. Freud herzlich/Pfister".

1925 Spring
- F. gives his daughter Anna a German shepherd dog, which he had acquired from a police captain, so that she can go for a walk on her own. He is given the name "Wolf".
- Henry Benjamin, a student of Eugen Steinach, visits F. Steinach had asked F. to receive him.

1925 March 27
F. sends a greeting address to the Board of Trustees of the Hebrew University in Jerusalem on the occasion of its official opening on April 1.

1925 April
- Wilhelm Reich gives F. his book *Der triebhafte Charakter. Eine psychoanalytische Studie zur Pathologie des Ich* with the dedication "Meinem verehrten Lehrer/Herrn Professor F./in Dankbarkeit/Dr Wilhelm Reich".

- Max Friedemann visits F. He is an employee at Oskar Kohnstamm's sanatorium in König-stein in Taunus and had done an analysis with Max Eitingon in the early 1920s.

1925 April 1
Anna represents her father at the official opening of the University of Jerusalem.

1925 April 6
Anna von Vest starts treatment with F. again.

1925 April 9
René Laforgue asks F. if Marie Bonaparte could make an analysis with him. Marie is a great-grandniece of Napoleon I, great-great-granddaughter of Lucien Bonaparte and daughter-in-law of King George I of Greece.

1925 April 12
Visit from F.'s Franz Alexander, Karl Landauer and Oskar Pfister.

1925 April 14
- F. meets Georg Brandes and Arthur Schnitzler at the Hotel Sacher.
- Lajos Lévy is in Vienna and examines F.; he finds "objectively everything very good".
- F. receives Stefan Zweig's book *Der Kampf mit dem Dämon. Hölderlin – Kleist – Nietzsche*. He reads through the first essay on Hölderlin "in one go" (F. to Zweig, 14.4.1925). The printed dedication read: "Professor Dr. Siegmund Freud/To the penetrating spirit, the inspiring designer/This triad of pictorial endeavour". Zweig added in handwriting: "Faithful Stefan Zweig, Easter 1925".
- F. informs René Laforgue that he can take Marie Bonaparte into analysis from October 1.

1925 April 15
F. visits Georg Brandes in his hotel and tries to clear up the latter's greatest misunderstandings about psychoanalysis. Afterward, Brandes wrote to his translator Erwin Magnus, the husband of F.'s niece Margarethe: "I have been stupid and prejudiced. Now I see Freud for the great man he is" (interview with Margarethe Magnus by Kurt Eisler, n.d., SFP). In addition, the conversation revolves around Georges Clemenceau. Arthur Schnitzler is also present.

1925 April 24
Hans Pichler fits F. with a new prosthesis, but it only caused no discomfort for one day.

1925 April 29
Erwin Hanslik sends F. his book *Wesen der Menschheit* with the dedication "Prof. Sigmund Freud/in besonderer Verehrung/Erwin Hanslik".

1925 May 6
- For F.'s 69th birthday, Sándor Ferenczi and Max Eitingon come to Vienna, and his daughter-in-law Lucie is also there. A total of over 30 guests are present.
- F.'s niece Hella and her son Peter visit F.'s mother Amalia in the Gymnasiumstrasse with the photographer Jerome Lachenbruch. A little later, F. comes to visit his mother and Lachenbruch photographs him.
- General Assembly of the Internationale Psychoanalytische Verlag.

1925 May 8
Otto Rank visits F.

1925 May 12
– F.'s daughter-in-law Lucie leaves.
– Hermann Keyserling visits F. in the evening.

1925 May mid
The Vienna Commercial Court confirms the assignment of the company shares of Internationale Psychoanalytische Verlag from Otto Rank and Sándor Ferenczi to Max Eitingon.

1925 May 28
The French journalist André Gaucher sends F. the manuscript of his planned book *L'Obsédé* with the request and his opinion on obsessive thoughts and obsessive neuroses. F. replies in two letters, which Gaucher then publishes in his book.

1925 May 29
Sante de Sanctis visits F.

1925 June 5
Hans Neumann, the director of Neumann Produktion G.m.b.H. (LLC) suggests to Karl Abraham that he should collaborate as a competent analyst on a film about psychoanalysis that he wants to make. Later, it was decided that Neumann would be the producer and the Austrian Georg Wilhelm Pabst the director. Abraham also involves Hanns Sachs and Max Eitingon.

1925 June 9
F. asks Ernest Jones to send the British politicians Arthur Balfour and Richard Haldane each an offprint of his "Selbstdarstellung".

1925 June mid
F.'s note about the "Wunderblock" is published. It is about a "novel notepad" made by the Viennese company August Stier. It is a tablet made of resin or wax mass whose "construction shows a remarkable agreement with my hypothetical structure of our perceptual apparatus" (SE 19, p. 228).

1925 June 16
Richard Coudenhove-Kalergi, the founder of the Pan-European Union, sends F. a questionnaire on the necessity and possibility of a union of Europe.

1925 June 20
Death of Josef Breuer. F. had published the *Studies on Hysteria* with him in 1895.

1925 June 29
Arthur Fischer-Colbrie visits F.

1925 June 30–September 30
Summer stay at Semmering
F., Martha, Minna, Anna and their German shepherd Wolf are again staying at the Villa Schüler. F.'s niece Lucie Bernays is also at Semmering and Karl Kraus is staying in July mid at the Südbahnhotel, to which the Villa Schüler belongs. F. writes two papers: "Die Verneinung" und "Einige Folgen des anatomischen Geschlechtsunterschieds" and his book *Hemmung, Symptom und Angst*. Once a week F. goes to Pichler by car. He is visited by Isador Coriat and his wife Etta.

1925 July beginning

F.'s condition is very changeable. The prosthesis causes him great discomfort.

1925 July

F. receives the "Heredity questionnaire" from John Kendrick, fills it out and sends it back to Chicago.

1925 July 7

F. receives a questionnaire from the Ernst Heimeran publishing house in Munich on the question "Is there a representation of your esteemed person in works of visual art?" In his answer he lists: The etching by Max Pollak, the bust by Paul Königsberger and the medal by Karl Schwerdtner.

1925 July 9

F. receives an issue of the newspaper *Le Matin,* published in Port-au-Prince (Haiti), with a lead story on psychoanalysis.

1925 July mid

F.'s obituary of Josef Breuer is published.

1925 before July 21

F.'s nephew Edward Bernays comes to the Semmering for a day with a wife Doris.

1925 July 21

F.'s son Martin comes to the Semmering.

1925 July 23

Otto Rank visits F.

1925 August

– F. formulates his own obituary, which reads, among other things: "The body was cremated on xx" and "This form of notice follows an instruction from the deceased".
– Elizabeth Severn, Ferenczi's patient, visits F. to discuss a possible analysis with him.

1925 August 1

Siegfried Bernfeld gives F. his book *Psychologie des Säuglings* with the dedication "Herrn Professor Freud in Verehrung und Dankbarkeit überreicht vom Verfasser".

1925 August 3

Sándor and Gisella Ferenczi come to visit Semmering for a day.

1925 before August 7

F. has his best week in two years.

1925 August 10

F. writes to Hanns Sachs about what he sees as the incorrect actions of the film people at Neumann Produktion.

1925 August 14

The *Neue Freie Presse* reports that UFA (Universum Film AG) will produce the film "Geheimnisse einer Seele" ("Secrets of a Soul") with the participation of Hanns Sachs and Karl Abraham.

1925 August 15

Lou Andreas-Salomé comes to Semmering for a fortnight.

1925 August 22

George Davis Bivin, who among other things deals with imaginary pregnancy, visits F. Possibly it is him, whom F. tries to offend by proposing "that the Statue of Liberty in New York harbor should be replaced by a monkey holding up a Bible" (F. to Ferenczi, 27.8.1925).

1925 August 25

The *Neue Freie Presse* publishes a letter by F. in which he declares that he is in no way involved in filmic undertakings on the subject of psychoanalysis.

1925 August 30

August Aichhorn gives F. his book *Verwahrloste Jugend* with the dedication "Herrn Professor Freud in tiefer Verehrung überreicht. Aichhorn"

1925 September 2–5

The IXth International Psychoanalytical Congress takes place in Bad Homburg. F. does not take part.

1925 September 4

– Alexander Luria, Soviet psychologist and psychoanalyst, sends F. his Russian translation of *Jenseits des Lustprinzips* (Po tu storonu printsipa udovol'stviya), made together with Lev Vygotsky, with the dedication "Herrn Professor S. Freud/hochachtungsvoll/mit herzlichsten Grüssen/von der Moskauer Vereinigung/Al. Luria/Homburg".
– Theodor Reik sends F. his book *Geständniszwang und Strafbedürfnis. Probleme der Psychoanalyse und der Kriminologie* with the dedication "Meinem verehrten und geliebten Lehrer/Th. Reik".

1925 September 9

– Hans Pichler discovers a bumpy elevation on the roof of F.'s mouth, which he believes to be a cancer recurrence.
– The *Neue Wiener Journal* prints an excerpt from F.'s paper "Die Widerstände gegen die Psychoanalyse" under the headline "Abrechnung mit meinen Gegnern" ("Reckoning with my Opponents").

1925 September 15

Carl Liebmann, son of the American brewery owner Julius Liebmann, begins an analysis with F. It lasts until 1930.

1925 September mid

– F. gives his niece Lucie (daughter of sister Anna) an offprint of his "Selbstdarstellung" with the dedication "Seiner lieben Lucie zur Erinnerung an den Sommer 1925 in Villa Schüler Onkel Sigm".
– F. receives from George Sylvester Viereck a collection of English poems edited by him under the title *Little blue books* with the dedication "Admiringly George Sylvester Viereck".

1925 September 17

F. is asked by James Garvin, the editor of the 13th edition of the *Encyclopaedia Britannica,* to write an article on psychoanalysis for the third volume of the "New Supplement Volumes". F. sent the article a week later and it was published in 1926 under the title "Psychoanalysis: Freudian School".

1925 September 30

F. returns to Vienna.

1925 September 30

– Marie Bonaparte, who arrived in Vienna the day before, visits F. in the afternoon; she stays at the Hotel Bristol and has at least one session with F. every day until December mid.
– Protest meeting of the WPV because of a commemorative publication decided in Berlin.

1925 Autumn

The Brazilian psychiatrist João Cesar de Castro sends F. his book *A concepção freudeana das psychoneuroses* with the dedication "A M. le Prof. Dr. Sigm. Freud j'ai l'honneur d'offrir cette brève notice de son oeuvre géniale repectueusement. Cesar de Castro Porto Alegre (Brésils)".

1925 October

The German psychotherapist Fritz Mohr sends F. his book *Psychophysische Behandlungs-methoden;* F. raises "energetic objections to some things" in a letter to the author (F. to Mohr, 16.10.1925).

1925 October 5

Samuel Orgel, American psychiatrist, begins an analysis with F. It lasts until at least 1930.

1925 before October 8

Mordecai Tenenblatt, Editor of the *Daily News Bulletin of* the Jewish Telegraph Agency sends F. an article from the *Bulletin* about F. He criticizes and corrects "gross inaccuracies" in the article (F. to Tenenblatt, 7.10.1925)

1925 October 15

Death of Eduard Silberstein. F. had met Silberstein at the Gymnasium in 1866 and later learned Spanish together with him, founded an "Academia Castellana" and wrote humorous texts.

1925 October 28

WPV meeting: General Assembly – F. is re-elected as Chairman.

1925 November

Beata Rank lends money to the Internationale Psychoanalytische Verlag.

1925 November 17

F. is being irradiated because of an inflammation in the mouth area.

1925 November 19

Hans Pichler pulls out F.'s tooth, which had grown together with an inflammatory bone.

1925 November 24

Georg Groddeck and wife visit F. for lunch.

1925 December

– F. revises the manuscript of his paper *Inhibition, Symptom and Anxiety.*
– Marie Bonaparte gives F. her books *Guerres militaires et guerres sociales* with the dedication "Au Professeur Freud a` la se're'nite' le faible echo des cruelles agitations des hommes Marie Bonaparte" and *Le printemps sur mon jardin* with the dedication "Au Professeur Freud, ces fleurs, ces êves, ces oiseaux, dont, plus sage encore que le Roi Salomon, il sait entendre le mystérieux langage. Marie Bonaparte".

1925 December 3
Ernst Waldinger, lyricist and husband of F.'s niece Beatrice, sends F. Thomas Mann's *Bekenntnisse des Hochstaplers Felix Krull (Confessions of Felix Krull)* with the dedication "Gern trinkt die Liebe auch aus irdnem Kruge/Gleich tapfer härte dich für Tun und Leiden!/Der Glaube ackert mit dem besten Pfluge –/Geduld und Mut – hab du nur diese beiden!/In herzlicher Freundschaft Ernst".

1925 before December 13
The writer Emil Ludwig visits F. for an evening. The conversation revolves around Goethe, Napoleon and Leonardo da Vinci.

1925 December 17
Marie Bonaparte leaves Vienna.

1925 December 22
Otto Rank visits F.

1925 Christmas
Maximilian Steiner gives F. his book *Die psychischen Störungen der männlichen Potenz* with the dedication *"Herrn/Prof. Dr Sigm. Freud/in constant loyalty and gratitude/Dr Steiner"*.

1925 December 25
- Death of F.'s student Karl Abraham in Berlin.
- The liberal *Prager Tagblatt* publishes the views of "eminent contemporaries" on the "modern dictator" Benito Mussolini. F.'s reply was the shortest: "It doesn't occur to me to comment on Mussolini!" In addition to F., Alfred Adler, Kurt Hiller, Theodor Lessing, Wilhelm Stekel and Fritz Wittels, among others, responded to the survey.

1925 December mid
F. gives Lillian Powers a copy of his paper "Aus der Geschichte einer infantilen Neurose" with the dedication "Frau Dr. Lillian Powers zur Erinnerung an ihre Analyse beim Verf.".

1925 December 26
- Stefan Zweig visits F. in the morning.
- Sándor Ferenczi visits F. in the afternoon.
- Georg Schwarz sends F. the novel *Lydia Sergiyevna* by Claude Anet, which he has translated, with the dedication "Herrn Professor Sigmund Freud verehrungsvoll überreicht vom Übersetzer Georg Schwarz".

1925 December end
F. writes an obituary for Karl Abraham, which is published in the *IZP in the* first months of 1926.

1926

– F. meets William Bullitt, American diplomat and Deputy Secretary of State under Woodrow Wilson, and his wife Louise. Both began an analysis with F. before the end of 1926.

Books received:

– René Allendy, French psychoanalyst, sends F. his book *Les rêves et leur interprétation psychanalytique* with the dedication "Au Professeur S. Freud En témoignage de respect et d'admiration je dédie modestement ce travail R Allendy".
– René Laforgue sends F. his *book Le rêve et la psychanalyse* with the dedication "Meinem hochverehrten u geliebten/Meister/Herrn Professor Freud/dieser bescheidene Beitrag seines/ Schülers/R Laforgue".
– Alfred Machard sends F. his novel *Printemps sexuels* with the dedication "Au Professeur Freud/Son admirateur/Alfr Machard".
– Oskar Pfister sends F. his book *Die Legende Sundar Singhs. Eine auf Enthüllungen protestantischer Augenzeugen in Indien gegründetdete religionspsychologische Untersuchung* mit der Widmung "Herrn Prof. Dr S. Freud/in herzlicher Dankbarkeit/d. Verf".
– Peter Schmidt sends F. his book *The Theory and Practice of the Steinach Operation* with the dedication "Siegmund Freud/in reverence/the author".
– Stefan Zweig sends F. his book *Verwirrung der Gefühle* with the dedication "Professor Siegmund Freud/In alter inniger Verehrung/Stefan Zweig"

1926 January beginning
Max Eitingon is in Vienna.

1926 January 3
Marie Bonaparte arrives in Vienna again and stays (with short interruptions) for about five months.

1926 January 6
F. gives an emotional speech at the WPV's memorial meeting for Karl Abraham, who died on Christmas Day 1925. It is the first official meeting F. has attended in three years and the only one until Hitler's invasion of Austria in 1938 spring.

1926 January mid
– F. receives Enrico Morselli's two-volume book *La psicanalisi* and comments very disparagingly on it; he asks Edoardo Weiss to write a detailed review for *IZP.*
– F. is in bed for several days with flu and fever. During this time he reads "several intimate publications about Anatole France, which indicate a not very transparent picture of his person". (F. to Ferenczi, 18.1.1926).

1926 January 24
The Neue Freie Presse publishes excerpts from a volume of *tributes* to *the sixtieth birthday of* Romain Rolland initiated by Georges *Duhamel*, Maxim Gorki and Stefan Zweig. F. participated with a letter to the birthday boy.

1926 January 25
Rudolf Urbantschitsch gives F. the offprint of his lecture "Selbsterkenntnis mit Hilfe der Psychoanalyse. An Fällen aus der psychoanalytischen Praxis gemeinverständlich dargestellt" with the dedication "In tiefer Verehrung/überreicht vom Verfasser".

1926 January 28 ago
Friedrich Thieberger, the editor of the *B'nai B'rith Monatsblätter of the Grand Lodge for the Čechoslovak State*, asks F. for a contribution for an issue on the occasion of F.'s 70th birthday.

1926 January 28
F. sends Friedrich Thieberger a sheet with a text on B'nai B'rith, but refuses to tolerate a special number for his birthday.

1926 January 29
- Hanns Sachs visits F.
- The volume initiated by Georges Duhamel, Maxim Gorki and Stefan Zweig on the occasion of Romain Rolland's 60th birthday is published in precious print in Emil Roninger s Rotapfel-Verlag. Richard Strauss had composed a song especially for it and F. had also contributed a birthday greeting.

1926 February
- F. becomes an honorary member of the British Psychological Society.
- Alyse Gregory visits F. She was in Vienna with Lillian Powers to visit their mutual friend Scofield Thayer, who was undergoing treatment at F.'s.

1926 February beginning
F. was invited by Ferdinand Schmutzer to "let him etch" (F. to Radó, 11.2.1926). F. then visits him and is photographed by Schmutzer several times. Schmutzer wanted to finish the etching by F.'s birthday and in this context visited F. on the following Sundays.

1926 February 5
- Death of Sigmund Exner. F. had attended lectures on physiology with him and was proposed by him as a member of the Society of Physicians in 1887.
- F. asks Stefan Zweig for a copy of the birthday volume for Romain Rolland published on January 29.

1926 before February 13
WPV meeting: on the question of character analysis. F. develops his idea of how, with the help of psychoanalysis, a study of personality will be possible from three different points of view: the dynamic, the historical and the static.

1926 February mid
F. succeeds in preventing the publication of a special issue of the *Vienna Medical Journal*; presumably it was to be devoted to the critique of psychoanalysis.

1926 February 17 and 19
F. has attacks of angina pectoris on the street and consults his friend, the cardiologist Ludwig Braun, about it. On Braun's advice, F. undergoes treatment at the Cottage Sanatorium in March.

1926 February end
- F.'s book *Inhibition, Symptom and Anxiety* is published.
- F. receives from Rudolph Loewenstein, French doctor and psychoanalyst, a manuscript on the subject of "transference".

1926 March beginning
John Stirling-Gilchrist, Scottish physician, begins a brief analysis of 15 sessions at F.

1926 March 2
Lajos Lévy and Ludwig Braun examine F. and insist on a longer stay in a sanatorium because of F.'s heart attacks.

1926 March 5–April 4
Stay at the Cottage Sanatorium

F. undergoes "heart therapy" there. Anna, Marthe and Minna take turns in looking after him and live in the next room. Felix Salten visits F. in the sanatorium.

1926 March 8

F. sends Arthur Schnitzler his recently published work *Inhibition, Symptom and Anxiety.*

1926 March 12

Arthur Schnitzler visits F.; his flat is only 350m from the Cottage sanatorium.

1926 March 13

F. receives reproductions by Leonardo from Marie Bonaparte.

1926 March 24

The film "Geheimnisse einer Seele. Ein psychoanalytisches Kammerspiel" premieres at Berlin's Gloria-Palast.

1926 March 26

Arthur Schnitzler visits F. They talk about the difficulties of writing and Hermann Keyserling, among other things.

1926 April 4

Return from the Cottage Sanatorium to Berggasse.

1926 April 4–5
Sándor Ferenczi visits F. in Vienna.

1926 April 12
Otto Rank comes for a last visit to F.

1926 April mid
A "real friendship" begins to develop between Anna Freud and Dorothy Burlingham, "from which we both derive much good" (Anna Freud to Eitingon, 19.4.1926).

1926 before April 21
The April issue of the *B'nai B'rith Monatsblätter der Grossloge für den Čechoslovakischen Staat* publishes contributions on F.'s 70th birthday and a text by F. on the Order of B'nai B'rith. The contributions are by Otto Sittig, Eduard Hitschmann, Salomon Ehrmann, Edmund Kohn and Friedrich Thieberger.

1926 April 30
An unsigned article illustrated by a photograph of F. is published in the *Berliner Illustrierte Zeitung* under the headline "Die Entdeckung des Unbewussten (zu Professor Freuds 70. Geburtstag)". The newspaper sends a copy of the article to F., who thanks it on May 2 with the following lines: "I thank you most sincerely for sending me the issue of your magazine which contains my photograph. The essay below obviously originates from an opponent of psychoanalysis who had to put himself under great duress in writing it" (F. to the *Berliner Illustrierte Zeitung*, 2.5.1926).

1926 May
- F. gives Paul Federn a testimonial in which he describes him, among other things, as a worthy representative of psychoanalysis in Vienna.
- Charles Baudouin visits F. in Vienna and gives him his book *Le symbole chez Verhaeren. Essai de psychanalyse de l'art* with the dedication "Au maître S. Freud en hommage et vive admiration et en profonde reconnaissance/Baudouin/Institut de Psychagogie, 3rd Taconnerie, Genêve".
- Paul Federn and Heinrich Meng give F. the second volume of the *Ärztliches Volksbuch, edited by Heinrich Meng und August Fiessler,* with the dedication "Herrn Professor Dr S. F./in grosser Verehrung/und Dankbarkeit/von Paul Federn/u Heinrich Meng".
- Otto Rank gives F. his book Technique of Psychoanalysis with the dedication "Herrn Prof. S. Freud/in alter Verehrung/überreicht/vom Verfasser".
- Fritz Wittels gives F. his book *Die Technik der Psychoanalyse* with the dedication "Für Professor Freud/Ein Schelm gibt mehr als er hat/In Verehrung/Fritz Wittels".

1926 May 4
Ernest Jones arrives in Vienna.

1926 May 5
Sándor Ferenczi arrives in Vienna.

1926 before May 6
Beginning of the correspondence between F. and Yvette Guilbert.

1926 May 6
- More than 150 well-wishers come to F.'s 70th birthday, all of whom sign a leather-bound guest book.
- F. gives $10 to each invited birthday guest over 14 and $5 to each guest under ten.
- Austrian radio broadcasts an appreciation of F.'s life and work.
- Sándor Ferenczi gives the ceremonial address on F.'s 70th birthday.
- The Social Democratic Mayor of Vienna, Karl Seitz and Julius Tandler present F. with a diploma artistically designed by Max Pollak for the honorary title of "Citizen of the city of Vienna" awarded to him two years ago.
- The *Neue Freie Presse* publishes an essay by Paul Schilder, a feature article by Stefan Zweig and a welcoming poem by Hans Vaihinger.
- In the evening, at the invitation of the "Akademischen Vereines für medizinische Psychologie" ("Academic Association for Medical Psychology"), Sándor Ferenczi and Theodor Reik speak about F.'s significance in a lecture hall at the university.
- In Berlin, a celebration of F.'s birthday takes place at the Esplanade Hotel in Berlin. Ernst Simmel introduced the celebration, lectures were given by: Director of the First Medical Clinic of the Charité Wilhelm His, the writer Alfred Döblin, Secretary of State Julius Hirsch, The painter Emil Orlik and the composer Franz Schreker. Among the participants were Albert Einstein, Georg Wilhelm Pabst and Jenö Varga. Hermann Hesse, Siegfried Jacobson, Thomas Mann, Hans Vaihinger, Jakob Wassermann and others were invited but canceled with good reason.

Gifts:

- Ferdinand Schmutzer's etching by F.
- A deluxe edition of Nietzsche's works by Otto Rank.

- A collection of 30,000 marks, which had been collected by his students. F. forwards 24,000 marks to the Internationale Psychoanalytische Verlag, the rest goes to the Ambulatorium.
- An eight-page "Bekenntnis zu Freud" ("Confession to Freud") by Lou Andreas-Salomé, later published in the *Almanach der Psychoanalyse 1927*.
- An old Persian miniature from the librarians and booksellers Gertrude Kvergic-Kraus and Ilse Moebius.
- A walking stick with ivory handle by Sándor Ferenczi.
- A precious antique bronze statue of Marie Bonaparte.
- The issues of *IZP* and *Imago* published on his 70th birthday.
- Anatole Frances *Oeuvres complètes by the* French Psychoanalytical Association.
- Nietzsche's *Collected Works* by Otto Rank.
- The first four volumes of The Cambridge ancient history by Mark Brunswick.
- An offprint *Sigmund Freud* with the dedication *"Dem hochverehrten Lehrer/zum 6. Mai 1926/vom Verfasser"* by Carl Müller-Braunschweig.
- A birthday wish in Kleinian "Stachelschrift", a Braille script readable by the sighted, from the children of the Israelite Institute for the Blind in Vienna.

1926 May 7
- F. attends a meeting of the "Secret Committee" for the last time.
- Elsa Leipen goes to F. with her sister Olga Barsis to congratulate him afterward. Both are sisters of Hanns Sachs.

1926 May 8
A festive meeting of the B'nai B'rith on the occasion of F.'s 70th birthday was held in the Festsaal of the Industriehaus. The event was opened by speeches by Felix Kohn (President of the Lodge "Vienna"), Salomon Ehrmann (Grand President of the Federation of B'nai B'rith Austria), F.'s pupil Eduard Hitschmann, his old friend Ludwig Braun and Alexander Freud. Alexander also reads F.'s speech.

1926 after May 9
Max Eastman, American writer, comes to Berggasse 19, but is turned away. as F. is banned from visiting by his doctors after three days of birthday bustle.

1926 before May 11
F. sees the etching by Ferdinand Schmutzer in the shop window of the Artaria publishing house. He thanks Schmutzer again "for the trouble you took in reproducing my nasty face". He feels "only now that it has been preserved for posterity" (F. to Schmutzer, 10.5.1926).

1926 May mid
- Arnold Ascher sends F. the issue of *B'nai B'rith Mitteilungen für Österreich* dedicated to F.'s 70th birthday – of which Ascher was editor at the time – with the dedication "Br. Sigm. Freud in Verehrung Dr Arnold Ascher".
- The American journalist Dorothy Thompson borrows $500 from F.[50] so that she can travel to Warsaw to report from there on Marshal Piłsudski s coup.

1926 before June 21
F. receives a consignment of Greek honey from Marie Bonaparte.

1926 June

F. begins work on his paper "Die Frage der Laienanalyse".

1926 June mid

Ferdinand Schmutzer sent F. a drawing by him, "which is incomparably better than the etching. (F. to Eitingon, 18.6.1926)

1926 June 16

Sergei Pankejeff (the "Wolf Man") visits F. and receives the money donation collected for him every year. Ruth Mack takes over his treatment from now on.

1926 June 17–September 29
Summer stay at Semmering

F. again lives in the Villa Schüler. Dorothy Burlingham rents the neighboring villa. F.'s niece Lilly and her husband Arnold Marlé visit F. in Semmering. His niece Hella Bernays is in Prein with her son Peter and F. visits her once. F. also occasionally goes to Vienna to see his doctors, as he suffered from Hertz complaints and the ill-fitting prosthesis during the first week of his stay.

1926 June 28–30

Max Eitingon visits F. Anna had picked up Eitingon from Vienna with a car including a chauffeur from the Südbahnhotel. On the way from the railway station in Vienna back to Semmering, the chauffeur ran over a 14-year-old girl between Vösendorf and Wiener Neudorf. He immediately took her to the Franz-Josefs-Spital; there the girl succumbed to her internal injuries a week later.

1926 June 30

Angelo Hesnard sends F. his book *La vie et la mort des instincts chez l'homme* with the dedication *"Au Professeur S. Freud/avec le souhait que cet hommage/lui apparaisse ce qu'il est rééllement/un regret de l'avoir pas su le comprendre/Dr Hesnard".*

1926 June end

F. begins work on his paper "Dostojewski und die Vatertötung".

1926 July

F. grants George Sylvester Viereck an interview. Viereck himself published the interview in several versions of varying length and with different titles. First, an abridged version appeared in the *London Weekly Dispatch* on 1927 July 28 under the title "Mean Men Explained by Freud", a somewhat longer one with the headline "Cheerful Humility Marks Freud at Seventy" appeared in the Baltimore *Sun on* August 28, and was finally followed by an extended reproduction in the October issue of the *American Monthly* entitled "Surveying Life at Seventy".

1926 July 4

Ludwig Braun visits F. and examines him.

1926 July 12

Marie Bonaparte continues her analysis with F. (until August 8). She gives F. Giorgio Vasari's book *Leonardo da Vinci* with the dedication *"Au Professeur F./en souvenir et en* reconnaissance/des heures heureuses/passées à traduire/ *"Un souvenir d'enfance de Léo-nard"/* près de Celui qui enfin le comprit./Marie Bonaparte *".*

1926 July 18

F. publishes an article in the *Neue Freie Presse* on "Dr. Reik und die Kurpfuschereifrage". He had felt compelled to also comment in the press before the publication of his book *Die Frage der Laienanalyse, which was* already in print, because "the Reik process was going through all the newspapers in a very unpleasant way" (Anna Freud to Eitingon, 15.7.1926).

1926 July 28

F. is in Vienna for one day.

1926 July 29

The British psychoanalyst Marjorie Franklin visits F.

1926 August beginning

F. reads to Marie Bonaparte his article Zur Frage der Laienanalyse".

1926 August mid

Philip Lehrmann, an American follower of F. and friend of Abraham Brill, visits F. He is willing to accept him as an analysand in one to two years.

1926 August 22

Sándor Ferenczi comes to Semmering for a week with his wife Gisella.

1926 before August 27

F. and Ferenczi meet with Frankwood Williams, the Medical Director of the National Committee for Mental Hygiene, and enlighten him about Otto Ranks, whom Williams was treating.

1926 September

Josephine Jackson, American doctor and psychoanalyst, sends F. her book *Outwitting our nerves. A primer of psychotherapy* with the dedication *"To/Sigmund Freud/Whose mes-sage it is the mission/of this book to further./Josephine A. Jackson".*

1926 September beginning

– F.'s book The *Question of Lay Analysis* is published.
– Stefan Zweig sends F. his book *Verwirrung der Gefühle* with the dedication "Professor Dr Siegmund/ in alter inniger Verehrung/Stefan Zweig".

1926 September 1

Friedrich Eckstein gives F. the book *Dostojewski am Roulette,* edited by him and René Fülöp-Miller with the dedication "Herrn Professor Dr. Sigmund Freud mit dem Ausdruck unwandelbarer Verehrung ergebenst Friedrich Eckstein".

1926 September 4

In a letter to Stefan Zweig, F. analyzes his novellas *Twenty-Four Hours from the Life of a Woman, Downfall of a Heart* and *Confusion of Emotions.*

1926 September 7

Visit from daughter Mathilde.

1926 before September 12

- Havelock Ellis sends F. the book by Isaac Goldberg *Havelock Ellis. A biographical and critical survey* with the dedication "To Professor F. with/cordial greetings from/Havelock Ellis".
- Franz Werfel visits F. and, following the meeting, he reads Werfel's drama *Paulus unter den Juden,* which the poet had given him with the dedication "Herrn Professor/Sigmund Freud/in tiefer Verehrung/Franz Werfel/Breitenstein ".

1926 September mid

Arthur Fischer-Colbrie sends F. some of his poems, presumably most of which were published a good year later under the title *Music of the Seasons.*

1926 September 15–16

Ernst Simmel visits F. on the Semmering.

1926 September 18

Paul Federn delivers the *Psychoanalytische Volksbuch* (*Psychoanalytic Chapbook)* to F., which is "very significant in terms of content" (F. to Ferenczi, 19.9.1926).

1926 September 26

- Max Eitingon visits F. on the Semmering.
- F. asks Max Marcuse to remove his name from the International Committee for the Preparation of the Congress for Sexual Research because of Albert Moll's spiteful remarks toward psychoanalysis.

1926 September 29

Move from Semmering to Berggasse 19.

1926 September 30
- F. receives from Max Eitingon Dostoevsky *Briefe (Letters)* with the dedication "Herrn Professor Freud in dankbarer Erinnerung an das Gespräch üb. D. a. Semmering Sept. 26. M. Eitingon".
- F. donates a large number of books and journals to the WPV library.
- F. receives from Georg Sylvester Viereck an article entitled "The Dance 'Mania'" published in *Vanity Fair* magazine by the New York neurologist Joseph Collins, in which F. is also mentioned.
- F. receives Honorio Delgado book *Sigmund Freud* with the dedication "Al insigne Maestro Prof. Dr. Sigm. Freud,/en testimonio de profunde admiración/y respeto./H F Delgado". Two years later, he sends Delgado some biographical corrections to it.

1926 Autumn
Dorothy Burlingham picks up F. and Anna and Wolf the sheepdog every morning for a car trip in the Ford so that the dog can run free somewhere.

1926 October
- The Brazilian psychiatrist Durval Marcondes sends F. his writing *O symbolismo esthetico na literatura. Ensaio de uma orientaçao para a critica literaria, baseada nos conhecimentos fornecidos pela psycho-analyse* with the dedication "Á sabedonia do Mestre, a admiração do/ discipulo/Durval Marcondes".
- Sergei Pankejeff (the "Wolf Man") visits F. again, as he has fallen ill again.

1926 October 1
Marie Bonaparte comes to Vienna to continue her analysis. F. gives her back an Anubis statuette that he had received from her, as Anubis plays a major role in her analysis.

1926 October 6
F. receives 10,000 Swiss francs from Emil von Freund from the Anton von Freund Fund.

1926 before October 9
At a joint meeting of the WPV Executive Committee and Teaching Institute, it is decided to hold an informal meeting once a month in future to discuss current issues. The meetings took place at 9pm in F.'s flat.

1926 October 19
F.'s niece Martha (Tom), married Seidmann, comes to Vienna for two and a half months and lives in the Bettina boarding house in Hardtgasse in the XIX district. There, she meets Ruth Lachenbruch, the wife of the photographer Jerome Lachenbruch.

1926 October 20
WPV meeting: General Assembly – F. is re-elected as chairman.

1926 October 24
Death of Salomon Ehrmann. F. had known the dermatologist since his student days. As former president of the humanitarian association "B'nai B'rith" in Vienna, he had given a speech to celebrate F.'s 70th birthday.

1926 October 25
F. visits Rabindranath Tagore in a Viennese hotel and is impressed by his appearance.

1926 November
Julio Porto-Carrero from Rio de Janeiro visits F. and gives him his *textbook on psychiatry.*

1926 November 9
Marie Bonaparte arrives back in Vienna to continue her analysis with F. and stays until December 7.

1926 November 10
Hans Pichler fits F. with his fourth prosthesis. It fits quite well, but F. can only speak indistinctly.

1926 November 12
Informal meeting of the WPV at Berggasse 19: Wilhelm Reich talks about his new technical experiments, and F. comments on them in a two-hour contribution.

1926 November 14
An appeal signed by F. for the erection of a monument to Josef Popper-Lynkeus is published in the *Neue Freie Presse.*

1926 November or December
Heinrich Meng visits F. He is "a very pleasant visitor; the man is very agreeable, a hard worker, and he achieves extraordinary things in the way of sensible propaganda by means of books for the general public, and periodicals" (F. to Ferenczi, 13.12.1926).

1926 December beginning
– F. becomes an honorary member of the Swiss Psychiatric Association.
– The Indian philosopher Surendranath Dasgupta from Kolkata visits F.

1926 before December 2
The Frankfurt psychiatrist Walter Riese asks F. to sign a public critique of contemporary psychiatry. F. refuses on the grounds that "a change can only come from the inner progress of science" (F. to Riese, 1.12.1926).

1926 December 7
Marie Bonaparte leaves Vienna.

1926 before December 20
F. receives from Ernst Pringsheim the book *Die Physiologie des Saftsteigens* by the Indian researcher Jagadish Bose, which he has translated.

1926 before Christmas
The Swiss psychoanalyst and philosopher Henri Flournoy visits F. He is the son of the psychiatrist Theodore Flournoy and brother-in-law of Raymond de Saussure.

1926 before December 25
Sándor Ferenczi visits F. in Vienna.

1926 December 25–1927 January 2
Visit to the sons Ernst and Oliver in Berlin

F. and his wife Martha live in the Hotel Esplanade. Of his colleagues, he sees only Max Eitingon and Ernst Simmel; also Karl Abraham's widow. An acquaintance shows F. a marble bust from Alexandria, which reminds him of the young Disraeli.

1926 December 25

Arrival in Berlin. Mirra Eitingon receives F. and Martha at the station.

1926 December 26

F. and Martha visit the sons Oliver and Ernst. F. writes about this: "The strongest impression of Berlin is little Evchen [Oliver's daughter], an exact repetition of Heinele, square face with coal-black eyes, the same temperament, lightness of speech, cleverness, fortunately looks stronger [...] (F. to Anna, 27.12.1926)

1926 December 27

– F. meets Arthur Schnitzler by chance in the hotel.
– In the afternoon, F. meets Max Eitingon for a longer time and discusses Anna's planned lecture tour to Berlin and the problems with Wilhelm Fliess.

1926 December 29

– F. meets Albert Einstein and his wife at the home of his son Ernst. F. writes about the meeting: "He is cheerful, confident, and kind, understands as much about psychology as I do about physics, and so we had a very good conversation" (F. to Ferenczi, 2.1.1927).
– In the evening, a visit to Oliver's new flat.

1926 December 30

F. and Martha attend a performance of the Russian theater "Die Fledermaus" ("Летучая мышь") by Nikita Balieff with Eitingons. Eitingon's wife Mirra was formerly an actress at this theater.

1927

- F. is nominated for the Nobel Prize (Medicine) for the sixth time.
- Winifred Ellerman (pseudonym "Bryher"), daughter of the shipping magnate John Reeves Ellerman, and her husband Kenneth McPherson arrive in Vienna by plane to visit F. Bryher had a letter of recommendation from Havelock Ellis.
- F. gives Julius Fürth a letter of recommendation for his immigration to Argentina.
- The Sociedade Brasileira de Psychanalyse is founded, the first psychoanalytical society in South America.

Received books and offprints:

- Mark Brunswick sends F. Volumes 5 and 6 of *The Cambridge ancient history*.
- Karl Federn sends F. the book he translated, Herman Melville's *Taïpi. Ein Südsee-Erlebnis* with the dedication "Herrn Prof. Dr S. F./in Verehrung/der Übersetzer".
- Max Fleischer sends F. his *book Der Porzellanpavillon. Nach Dichtungen chinesischer Lyrik* with the dedication "Dem Denker und Deuter/der Seele,/ihres Wesens, ihres Lebens, ihres Geheimnisses,/ihrem heilenden Helfer,/Sigmund Freud,/in Dankbarkeit für sein Werk!/Max Fleischer".
- Yvette Guilbert sends F. her memoir *La chanson de ma vie* with the dedication "Au Professeur/Sigmund Freud/avec admiration/Yvette Guilbert".
- Prynce Hopkins sends F. his book *Father or sons? A study in social psychology* with the dedication "To Prof. Dr. Sigmund Freud/with sincere regards/from/Prynce Hopkins".
- René Laforgue sends F. the book *L'évolution psychiatrique* written by him and Angelo Hesnard with the dedication "A mon cher Maître/Monsieur le Professeur Freud/ce témoignage de mon affection respectueuse/R. Laforgue".
- Ilse Ronjat sends F. an offprint of her paper "Le cas de Jeannette. Psychanalyse et guérison d'une jeune fille hystérique opérée sept fois" with the dedication "In Verehrung/I. Ronjat".
- Hans Zulliger sends F. his book *Gelöste Fesseln. Studien, Erlebnisse und Erfahrungen* with the dedication "In Verehrung überreicht/vom Verfasser".

1927 January 1
- F. goes to the Tegel Sanatorium in the morning to meet Ernst Simmel's patient Baroness von Vietinghoff and her husband at their request. He then discussed the case with Johannes Heinrich Schultz, who was also involved in the treatment.
- In the afternoon, departure of F. and Martha from Berlin.

1927 January 2
Arrival in Vienna in the morning.

1927 January 4
Arbitration meeting of the WPV because of Rudolf Urbantschitsch. Presumably it was about his article published in the *Wiener medizinische Wochenschrift* "Über die Abkürzung der Behandlungsdauer psychoanalytischer Kuren". Urbantschitsch had already been deprived of his guest privileges in the WPV in 1924 November because of "tasteless advertisement for his praxis" (F. to Abraham, 28.11.1924).

1927 January 14
Informal meeting of the WPV at Berggasse 19.

1927 before January 26
Max Eitingon is in Vienna for a few days.

1927 February 1
F. and Anna visit the German shepherd Wolf, who is in a veterinary clinic because of eczema.

1927 February 6
Marie Bonaparte arrives in Vienna to continue her analysis with F.; she stays with short interruptions until May 7.

1927 February 8
- F. and Anna visit Wolf the German shepherd again, who is in a veterinary clinic because of eczema.
- F. asks Oskar Pfister and Mira Oberholzer to send Wilhelm Reich Swiss patients or teaching analysands, as he is in Davos for six months for a spay stay and is dependent on income.
- Death of Heinrich Braun. F. had known him since their time together at the Gymnasium and they both became friends; among other things, he learned French with him. Braun was a social democrat and the brother-in-law of Victor Adler.

1927 before February mid
Johannes Ruths begins an analysis with F. which – with interruptions – lasts almost five years. Ruths was a Swedish industrialist and multimillionaire. He had developed a method of heat storage – the so-called "Ruths accumulator" – which kept water constantly boiling. He had also financially supported the anthroposophist Rudolf Steiner, which F. commented thus: "His critical abilities are obviously not on a par with his other talents, otherwise he would not have fallen for the impostor Steiner of anthroposophy so thoroughly" (F. to Eitingon, 16.2.1927).

1927 February 16
F. buys a Mycenaean ceramic vessel.

1927 February 24
Theodor Reik sends F. an offprint of his lecture *Wie man Psychologe wird* with the dedication "Meinem verehrten Lehrer in alter Anhänglichkeit und Liebe/Th. Reik".

1927 March 1
Harald Schultz-Hencke sends F. his book *Einführung in* die *Psychoanalyse* with the dedication "In Dankbarkeit und/Verehrung überreicht/vom Verfasser".

1927 Spring
- F. gets a new prosthesis, which "is a great improvement" and makes his "existence much easier" (F. to Ferenczi, 25.3.1927).
- Henri Flournoy begins an analysis with F. It lasts until the end of April.

1927 March 18
Beginning of the correspondence between F. and Arnold Zweig. Arnold Zweig asks F. to dedicate his book *Caliban oder Politik und Leidenschaft to* him. F. accepts.

1927 March 19–20
Anna goes to Berlin to give a lecture to the association there.

1927 March 24
Marjan Albinski, Polish philologist and literary scholar and major in the Polish army, sends F. his book *Wojskoszkola charakterów* [Military School of Characters] with the dedication "Hochwohlg. Geehrter Herrn Prof. Dr. Sigmund Freud/Dr. Marjan Albinski".

1927 March 25

F. grants Max Eastman an interview. It is published in 1942 under the title "The Crotchety Greatness of Sigmund Freud" in Max Eastman's book *Heroes I Have Known*.

1927 before March 28

F. issued an expert opinion for the opera singer Richard Tauber that he is undergoing psychoanalytic treatment in Berlin, cannot travel and therefore cannot fulfill his obligations at the Vienna State Opera. However, should legal obligations present themselves, Tauber can interrupt his treatment.

1927 March 30

Oskar Pfister sends F. an offprint of his contribution to *Die Pädagogik der Gegenwart in Selbstdarstellungen* with the dedication *"Patri spirituali/Sigmund Freud/auctor"*.

1927 April 7–28

F.'s daughter Anna and Dorothy Burlingham spend a holiday together in Italy.

1927 April 11

– Paul Federn visits F. at his invitation to discuss, among other things, "the necessary rescheduling of the next social evening" (F. to Federn, 4.4.1927).
– The new prosthesis begins to torment F.

1927 April 14–28

Stay at the Cottage Sanatorium. F. is back in Cottage Sanatorium because of his heart problems; Martha and Minna also move with him.

1927 April 15

Ruth Mack visits F. and brings F. a new coffee machine.

1927 April 16

F.'s weekly tarot party takes place in the sanatorium this time.

1927 April mid

The Austrian-American violinist Marion Knight, daughter of the violin virtuoso Otto Scheda, asks F. for support as she is planning a concert in Vienna. F. refuses on the grounds that he has no influence in Viennese society, knows nothing about music and is an old man.

1927 before April 17

– F. learns that William Bullitt is planning to write a play about Wilson. F. is very curious about it.
– Rudolf Kriser is again treated by F. after the death of his wife.

1927 April 17

F. reads an article in the *Neue Freie Presse* by Wilhelm Ostwald entitled "Bekenntnis zum Optimismus" ("Confession of Optimism"). In it Ostwald writes, among other things, that "Freud's psychoanalysis and psychotherapy [are] on the path of scientific influence on existence". F. perceives this as a "compliment for analysis" (F. to Anna, 20.4.1927).

1927 April 18

Fritz Wittels gives F. his book *The Liberation of the Child* with the dedication *"Herrn Professor Freud in Verehrung/Fritz Wittels"*.

1927 April 20

– Marie Bonaparte undergoes a gynecologic operation by Josef Halban in the Löw sanatorium.
– The *Arbeiter-Zeitung* publishes a manifesto signed by F. and others under the title "Eine Kundgebung des geistigen Wien" ("A manifestation of intellectual Vienna"). It was intended as a response to Ignaz Seipel's campaign against the "Marxist united front".
– Ludwig Braun visits F.
– F. goes to see Hans Pichler about his prosthesis.

1927 April 28

F. moves back to Berggasse 19.

1927 April 28

F. wants to give himself a present for his birthday and asks his son Ernst to bring him a Mycenaean bowl from the antique dealer Philipp Lederer in Berlin. As an alternative, F. has a gold ring in mind on whose red to orange-white quartz is carved a hand tugging at an ear. "This stone would have a special – analytical – interest for me because of the object" (F. to Ernst Freud, 28.4.1927).

1927 May beginning

Heinrich Gomperz draws F.'s attention to an anticipation of psychoanalytic sublimation theory by François Hemsterhuis. F. suggests to Gomperz that he write a short note on this for the *IZP*. This is published in issue 3 of the journal.

1927 before May 4

F. receives from the American neurologist Israel Wechsler his book *A text-book of clinical neurology* with the dedication "To Professor Sigmund Freud, with highest regard and sincerest wishes, from the author, I. S. Wechsler".

1927 May 6

F. Mark Brunswick receives the first volume of *The Cambridge ancient history*.

1927 May 7

Marie Bonaparte leaves Vienna.

1927 May

Carl Müller-Braunschweig, German philosopher and psychoanalyst, sends F. his paper *Das Verhältnis der Psychoanalyse zu Ethik, Religion und Seelsorge* with the dedication "Herrn Prof. Freud in Ergebenheit/d. Verf.".

1927 May 14

Oskar Pfister sends F. his book *Religionswissenschaft und Psychanalyse* with the dedication "Seinem lieben Prof. Dr Sigmund Freud/herzlich/Pfister".

1927 May mid

Edward Bernays sends F. his just published book *An outline of careers: A practical guide to achievement by thirty-eight eminent Americans*. F. immediately lends it to his son Martin, as he "will unfortunately soon have occasion to consider a new career" (F. to Edward Bernays, 20.5.1927).

1927 May end
The public prosecutor's office discontinues the criminal proceedings against Theodor Reik on the grounds of quackery. Among others, F., Julius Wagner-Jauregg and Alfred Adler had been asked to give expert opinions.

1927 June
F. works on the supplement to his work "Der Moses des Michelangelos" and writes the "Nachwort zur Frage der Laienanalyse".

1927 June beginning
The graphic artist Max Pollak asks F. for recommendations in connection with his forthcoming emigration to the USA. F. promises him, among other things, to arrange contacts with the Tiffany Company (through Dorothy Burlingham), Ruth Mack and Edward Bernays.

1927 June 2
F. receives Arnold Zweig's book *Caliban oder Politik und Leidenschaft*. The printed dedication reads "Sigmund Freud respectfully".

1927 June 7
The American writer Ludwig Lewisohn sends F. his book *The case of Mr. Crump* with the dedication "Herr Professor Dr. Sigmund Freud, dem grossen Seelenforscher in tief aufrichtiger Verehrung/Ludwig Lewisohn".

1927 before June 9
F. receives "$5,000[51] for our institutions" from the women's rights activist and psychoanalyst Grace Potter (F. to Ferenczi, 9.6.1927).

1927 June 9
F. is treated by Hermann Wolf for a periodontal abscess.

1927 June 15–September 29
Summer stay at Semmering
F. spends the summer at the Villa Schüler again, but occasionally goes to Vienna. The French psychoanalyst Georges Parcheminey is also at Semmering and visits F.

1927 June mid
– F. receives Karl Bühler's book Die Krise der Psychologie.
– F. receives from Oskar Pfister his *book Analytische Seelsorge. Einführung in die praktische Psychoanalyse für Pfarrer und Laien* with the dedication "Herrn Prof. Freud/in Liebe/O. Pfister".
– F. receives the first volume of Otto Rank's *Grundzüge einer genetischen Psychologie auf Grund der Psychoanalyse der Ich-Struktur.*

1927 June 28
Ernst and Oliver come with their families to the Semmering.

1927 June end
F. constantly switches between the fourth and third prosthesis to get used to the new one more easily.

1927 July beginning
F. suffers severely from prosthesis and therefore goes to Vienna twice.

1927 July beginning

The American politician and journalist Arthur Sweetser decides to support psychoanalysis in Vienna financially after the death of his 11-year-old son Harold, who was in analysis with Anna. He and his wife Ruth sent at least four checks for $1000 each within a few weeks.[52]

1927 July 26

Wilhelm Reich visits F.

1927 August

– Oliver, Henny, Eva and Ernst are visiting.
– Georg Groddeck seeks Nobel Prize for F.

1927 August beginning

F. is working on his paper on "Fetischismus". He asks Fritz Wittels to give him the basic idea of Wilhelm Stekel's book *Der Fetischismus dargestellt für Ärzte und Kriminologen* before sending his article to *IZP.*

1927 August 6

Marianne Rie visits F.

1927 August 8–10

F. writes his paper "Der Humor".

1927 before August 13

F. received a request from Joseph Pulitzer, a son of Joseph Pulitzer, the founder of the Pulitzer Prize, whether he would be willing to contribute to the anniversary issue of the *St. Louis Post-Dispatch.* However, the conditions formulated by F. were not accepted so that F. did not write an essay for the newspaper.

1927 September 1–3

– Innsbruck is the venue of the X. International Psychoanalytical Congress takes place. F. does not take part.
– Max Eitingon sends F. a telegram on behalf of the Congress participants with wishes for "undiminished strength and full health". F. replies, wishing "fruitful scientific work" and expressing the hope that the participants "will find the strength to agree on practical questions from the feeling of a common task".
– The "Secret Committee" becomes the board of the IPA, Eitingon becomes president, Ferenczi and Jones vice-presidents, Anna Freud secretary; Johann van Ophuijsen treasurer; Hanns Sachs leaves the committee.

1927 after September 3

– Visiting F. are: Max Eitingon, to whom he reads *The Future of an Illusion*, Sándor Ferenczi, Smith Ely Jelliffe and Honorio Delgado. From the latter, he receives an antique drinking vessel as a gift.
– Ernest Jones visits F. and gives him Bertrand Russell's book *The analysis of* matter with the dedication "Professor Sigm. Freud/from E. J.".

1927 September 5

Marie Bonaparte comes to Vienna to continue her analysis with F.; she stays until 17 December.

1927 September 16–17

Ludwig Binswanger visits F.; the conversation revolves around Elfriede Hirschfeld, among other things.

1927 September 17

F. gives a dinner attended by Dorothy Burlingham, Ludwig Binswanger and wife, Marie Bonaparte, René Laforgue and daughter Anna.

1927 September 29

F. returns to Vienna.

1927 September 30

The *Illustrierte Kronen-Zeitung* reports that F. had received an "honorary gift of 100,000 dollars" from the New York Psychoanalytical Society so that he could "continue his scientific research without economic worries". On October 2, *Illustrierte Kronen-Zeitung* publishes a letter from F. in which he denies this report.

1927 September end

David Brunswick, American psychologist and brother of Mark Brunswick, begins an analysis with F. It lasts until 1930 June.

1927 October beginning

- F. sends the ten volumes of his *Collected Writings* published to date to the Jewish National Library in Jerusalem.
- *Felix Valyi, the editor of the Review of Nations published in Geneva*, visits F. on Max Eitingon's recommendation.
- F. receives from Fritz Wittels his small book Die Psychoanalyse. Neue Wege der Seelenkunde.

1927 October 12

Theodor Reik sends F. his book *Dogma und Zwangsidee. Eine psychoanalytische Studie zur Entwicklung der Religion* with the dedication *"Meinem verehrten Lehrer/in alter Anhänglichkeit/ und Dankbarkeit/Th. Reik"*.

1927 October mid

- F.'s main work critical of religion, *Die Zukunft einer Illusion,* is published; he sends a copy to Max Eitingon with a personal dedication, one to Oskar Pfister, because of whom he had delayed the publication of the book, and one to Eva Rosenfeld with the dedication "Der tapferen Eva d. Verf." – Eva Rosenfeld had lost her 15-year-old daughter Rosemarie ('Mädie') in a mountain accident in the summer.
- F. is in severe pain again due to his prosthesis.
- F. arranges for the Internationale Psychoanalytische Verlag to send Georg Sylvester Viereck a photograph with his name on it.

1927 October 19

WPV meeting: General Assembly – F. is re-elected chairman.

1927 October 21

Martha goes to Berlin for several weeks to visit her children and their families.

1927 before October 30

- F. receives from Georg Sylvester Viereck his interview with Kaiser Wilhelm II, which had appeared on October 15 under the title "What life means to the Kaiser".
- Julie Braun-Vogelstein, the widow of F. School friend Heinrich Braun, asks F. to provide her with memories for a planned biography.

1927 October 30
Ernst Kris gives F. the book *Die Kameen im kunsthistorischen Museum* written by him and Fritz Eichler with the dedication "Herrn Prof. Freud in Dankbarkeit und Verehrung überreicht/E. Kris".

1927 November 4
F.'s fourth prosthesis causes swelling and disturbs hearing, perhaps due to closure of the tube.

1927 before November 14
F. receives Brazilian cigars from Ludwig Jekels, but only smokes one Havana a week, but has heart trouble for a day afterward.

1927 November 15
Oskar Pfister and Marco Levi Bianchini give F. the Italian translation of Pfister's book *Was bietet* die Psychoanalyse dem Erzieher *(Pedagogia e psicoanalisi)* with the dedication *"Herrn Prof. S. Freud/in Verehrung angeboten/vom Verfasser und vom/Uebersetzer/Zürich – Teramo/O. Pfister/M Levi Bianchini"*.

1927 before November 27
The Vienna City Administration informs F. via councilor Julius Tandler that they will allocate a plot of land to the WPV on which a building for the Psychoanalytic Outpatient Clinic can be erected.

1927 November end
F. tries to place the German writer and left-wing socialist revolutionary Ernst Toller – after seeing him two or three times – as a patient with Lou Andreas-Salomé, but in the end, he goes to Franz Alexander.

1927 before December 2
F. receives Arnold Zweig's book *Der Streit um den Sergeanten Grischa* with the dedication "In die Hände von Sigmund Freud/Arnold Zweig".

1927 December 11
Arthur Schnitzler sends F. his book *Sprüche und Bedenken* with the dedication "Professor Sigmund Freud/in Verehrung/mit herzlichen Grüßen/Arthur Schnitzler".

1927 December mid
Maria Montessori addresses F. with the request to sign the appeal for the foundation of the teaching and training center for Maria Montessori's pedagogy planned by Hedwig Schaxel in Vienna. F. agrees, but the plan could not be realized.

1927 December 17
Marie Bonaparte leaves Vienna.

1927 December 23
Heinz Hartmann gives F. his book *Die Grundlagen der Psychoanalyse* with the dedication *"Herrn Prof. Sigm. Freud/in Verehrung und Dankbarkeit/Hartmann"*.

1927 Christmas
– F. receives from Erwin Magnus, the husband of his niece Margarethe, the book by the Danish writer Johannes Vilhelm Jensen *Metamorphosis of the Animals*, which he has translated.

– For Christmas, Arthur Tansley sends F. a reproduction of Leonardo's Anna Selbdritt, which F. had discussed in detail in his 1910 work *Eine Kindheitserinnerung des Leonardo da Vinci*. F. hangs the picture on the door of his study so that he could see it from his desk.

1927 December end

The Brazilian psychiatrists Francisco Franco da Rocha and Durval Marcondes found the Brazilian Psychoanalytic Society in Sao Paulo and inform F. about it.

1928

- F. gives M. Platzeff a copy of his paper "Zeitgemäßes über Krieg und Tod" with the dedication "Herrn M. Plazeff/zur freundl. Erinnerung/Freud".

Books received:

- Mark Brunswick sends F. Volume 7 of *The Cambridge ancient history.*
- Isador Coriat sends F. his book *Stammering. A psychoanalytic interpretation* with the dedication "To Prof. Dr. Sigm. Freud/in deep appreciation./Isador Coriat*".
- Richard Nicolaus Coudenhove-Kalergi *sends* F. his book *Held oder Heiliger* with the dedication "Professor Sigmund Freud/in grösster Verehrung/R N Coudenhove-Kalergi".
- Ernest Jones sends F. his book *Psycho-analysis* with the dedication *"Prof.* Freud/with kindest regards from Ernest Jones*".
- Ernest Jones sends F. his book *Zur Psychoanalyse der christlichen Religion* with the dedication *"To Professor Freud/With the respects of/a fellow infidel/Ernest Jones".*
- Paul Schilder sends F. his book *Gedanken zur Naturphilosophie* with the dedication "Herrn Prof S. Freud/in Verehrung/d Verf".
- The Norwegian theologian Kristian Schjelderup sends F. his book *Die Ascese. Eine religionpsychologische Untersuchung* with the dedication "Herrn Professor Dr. Sigm. Freud/in aufrichtiger Verehrung/von/Kristian Schjelderup".
- George Sylvester Viereck and Paul Eldridge give F. their jointly written book *My first two thousand years. The autobiography of the wandering Jew* with the dedication *"To Prof. Sigmund Freud,/In Token of Our/Admiration,/George Sylvester Viereck/Paul Eldridge".*
- The British biographer and writer Lytton Strachey sends F. his book *Elizabeth and Essex. A tragic history* with the dedication "To Sigmund Freud/with profound admiration/from/Lytton Strachey".
- F. receives from Stefan Zweig his book *Drei Dichter ihres Lebens* with the dedication "Professor Siegmund Freud/In unveränderlicher Liebe/und Verehrung/Stefan Zweig/1928".

1928 January 3
Adolf Storfer visits F.

1928 January 7
István Hollós sends F. his books *Hinter der gelben Mauer* with the dedication "Herrn Professor Freud/Dr Hollós" and *Búcsum a sárga háztól* with the dedication "Budapest 1928. Januar/D Hollós István*".

1928 before January 12
F. receives from Felix Frisch his book *Das vegetative System der Epileptiker.*

1928 January 13
Informal meeting of the WPV at Berggasse 19: F. tries "with much humour and interest [...] to soften Reich's overly far-reaching genital theories" (Anna Freud to Eitingon, 18.1.1928).

1928 January 15
Géza Róheim, Hungarian ethnopsychoanalyst, visits F.

1928 January mid
F. receives from Edward Petrikowitsch, a typesetter who emigrated from Austria to the USA in 1921, an article from the *St. Louis Post-Dispatch dealing with* F.'s just published book *The Future of an Illusion* and claiming that the book has disappointed and divided his followers.

1928 January 27
Max Eitingon is coming to Vienna for four days.

1928 February mid
F. suffers from conjunctivitis, which lasts about two weeks.

1928 February beginning
Sándor Ferenczi visits F. in Vienna.

1928 February 12
John Campbell Hill sends F. his book *Dreams and education* with the dedication *"*To the Master/ Professor Sigmund Freud./J. C. Hill".

1928 February 15
Albert Einstein responds negatively to Heinrich Meng's inquiry as to whether he would support F.'s re-nomination for the Nobel Prize.

1928 February mid
Georg Sylvester Viereck again tries to persuade F. to go on a lecture tour of the USA.

1928 before February 19
F. receives from Yvette Guilbert her book *L'art de chanter une chanson* with the dedication "A Monsieur/le Professeur/S. Freud/en toute respectueuse/Amité/Yvette Guilbert".

1928 February 22
Carl Gustav Jung gives a lecture on "The Structure of the Soul" at the invitation of the Vienna Cultural Association. In an interview published the previous day in the *Neues Wiener Journal* he expresses the opinion that sexuality does not play the important role in the life of the soul that F. assigns to it. F. follows the reports on Jung's visit in the Viennese press.

1928 February 26
The French Marxist philosopher Georges Politzer sends F. his book *Critiques des fondements de la psychologie* with the dedication "À Monsieur le Professeur S. Freud, fondateur de la 'psychologie concrète' hommage respectueuse Georges Politzer".

1928 March 8
Hans Pichler tries to fit F. with the fifth prosthesis, but this is not successful because of a lock in the jaw.

1928 March 18
William Boven, a Swiss psychiatrist from Lausanne, visits F. He wants to get to know psychoanalysis through self-analysis. F. refers him to Eduard Hitschmann.

1928 March 29
– F. is the best man at the wedding of Ruth Mack and Mark Brunswick.
– Ferenczi comes to Vienna for a weekend and gives the next day a lecture on "Kriminalität im Lichte der Psychoanalyse" ("Crime in the light of psychoanalysis") at the Wiener Verein für angewandte Psychopathologie (Vienna Association for Applied Psychopathology and Psychology).

1928 March 31
Ludwig Rosenberg, one of F.'s long-time tarot partners, visits F. until late in the evening. At parting, F. says to him "So this month we have killed. It is now a struggle between us and the time. It is now a life and death struggle between us and time" (F. to Eitingon, 1.4.1928).

1928 April 1
Death of Ludwig Rosenberg. He had only complained of mild stenocardial complaints in the last two weeks.

1928 before April 2
F. receives Ludwig Binswanger's book *Wandlungen in der Auffassung und Deutung des Traumes von den Griechen bis zur Gegenwart*, and reads it "through in one go" (F. to Binswanger, 2.4.1928).

1928 April 2
F. wears his fifth prosthesis for a few hours.

1928 before April 6
The Internationale Psychoanalytische Verlag moves from Andreasgasse to the stock exchange building at Börsegasse 1 (until 1936 May).

1928 April 7
Theodor Reik sends F. his book *Das Ritual* with the dedication "Meinem verehrten Lehrer/mit den herzlichsten/Ostergrüßen und -wünschen/Theodor Reik".

1928 April 14
Sándor Ferenczi is coming to Vienna for the weekend.

1928 before April 22
F. receives a philosophical treatise from Max Eitingon Leo Schestow, presumably his booklet *Potestas Clavium oder Die Schlüsselgewalt*. F. reads it "in one go, […] without becoming clear about the personal attitude of the author himself" (F. to Eitingon, 22.4.1928).

1928 April 22
Judith Rosenberg visits F., who was a friend of her husband Ludwig, who died on April 1.

1928 April 24
It turns out that F. cannot wear the fifth prosthesis because it is too thick and too big.

1928 April 26
F. writes some positive lines in appreciation of Magnus Hirschfeld:: "I have always held the view that the life struggle of Dr Magnus Hirschfeld against the cruel and unjustified interference of legislation in human sexual life deserves universal recognition and support". It is published in May in a volume *For Magnus Hirschfeld on his 60th birthday*, edited by Richard Linsert and Kurt Hiller – both communist publicists and champions of the rights of sexual minorities.

1928 April end
F. receives as a gift from Stefan Zweig his book *Drei Dichter ihres Lebens. Casanova – Stendhal – Tolstoi* with the dedication "Professor Sigmund Freud/ In unveränderlicher Liebe/ und Verehrung/Stefan Zweig".

1928 May 1
F.'s answer to a radio question on the inheritance of mental talent is published in the journal *Volksaufartung, Erbkunde, Eheberatung*. The initiator was the Wuppertal doctor and medical councilor Leonard Leven. He wanted to find out whether the "Schopenhauerian thesis […] that the intellect of sons comes from the mother, the character from the father" could be empirically confirmed or refuted. To this end, he sent out a questionnaire in 1928 to well-known personalities, including F. Further replies were sent by Lujo Brentano, Wilhelm Dörpfeld, David Hilbert, Karl Kautsky, Heinrich Mann and Thomas Mann, among others.

1928 May 5
Max Eitingon comes to Vienna for a few days.

1928 May 5–6
F. has dream of "extended family".

1928 May 6
Ruth Mack Brunswick gives F. for his birthday the book by Thomas Looney *"Shakespeare" identified in Edward de Vere the 17th Earl of Oxford* with the dedication "Professor von Ruth. Ruth Mack Brunswick". The book makes a strong impression on him and he reads it again a year later.

1928 May 7
F. gets the modified fifth prosthesis.

1928 before May 12
F. receives the seventh volume of Havelock Ellis's *Studies in the psychology of sex* with the dedication "To Dr. S. Freud with/affectionate regards from/Havelock Ellis".

1928 May 18
For the first time, F. has the feeling of having "a tolerable prosthesis in his mouth", "with which it is possible to exist" (F. to Marie Bonaparte, 18.5.1928).

1928 before May 19
The Parisian psychiatrist Gilbert Robin visits F. and publishes an account of his encounter with F. in the *Nouvelles Littèraires on* May 19.

1928 June
The German psychiatrist Alfred Storch sends F. an offprint of his probation lecture "Die Psychopathologie in ihren Beziehungen zu den Natur- und Geisteswissenschaften" with the dedication "Im Bewußtsein des Gemeinsamen, das uns durch das Trennende einigt, und mit den besten Wünschen zum neuen Jahr von/Ihrem Alfred Storch".

1928 June 1
The mathematician Hermann Weyl sends F. his book *Der Epileptiker. Narrative* with the dedication "Herrn Professor/Sigmund Freud/in Verehrung überreicht/Dr. Hermann Weyl".

1928 June 2
The French psychiatrist and child analyst Sophie Morgenstern sends F. an offprint of her paper *Un cas de mutisme psychogène* with the dedication "Herrn Professor S. F./in tiefster Verehrung/ überreicht von/S. Morgenstern/Paris d. 2 Juni 1928".

1928 June 13
F.'s new prosthesis begins to cause him discomfort again.

1928 June 16–August 30
Summer stay at Semmering
This time, F., Martha, Minna and Anna stay at the Hotel Südbahnhof until the end of June and then at the Villa Schüler. F. meets the lawyer Julius Lederer, with whom he has been friends since their time together in the reading club of the German students of Vienna. Israel Wechsler also visits him, and F. tells him about his encounters with Dorothy Thompson – F. develops a strong interest in astronomy and gets himself a telescope.

1928 Summer

- George Young asks F. to let him talk about the English painter Richard Rees.
- Philip Lehrman, an American doctor, begins an analysis with F. It lasts about a year. During this time, Lehrman, an amateur filmmaker, makes numerous film recordings of F.

1928 before June 21

Dorothy Burlingham begins her analysis with F. and gives him a small Chow Chow bitch; F. names her Lün. Dorothy goes on afternoon excursions in her chauffeur-driven car for a week, inviting F., his daughter Anna and Antje Mastrigt.

1928 June 23–24

Franz Ernst, an employee of the director of the dental clinic of the Charité in Berlin, Hermann Schröder, comes to Vienna to prepare the production of a new prosthesis for F.

1928 June 26

F. visits Ludwig Braun because of his heart complaints.

1928 before June 27

F. receives the first issue of the *Revista Brasileira de Psychanalyse* from Durval Marcondes. F. buys a small Portuguese grammar and a German-Portuguese dictionary so that he can read the magazine himself and learn Portuguese at the same time.

1928 June end

Ernest Jones's wife Katharina (née Jokl) – a cousin of Robert Jokl – is visiting Semmering.

1928 July

F. receives from Georg Sylvester Viereck the books Days in Doorn, the *Autobiographie des ewigen J*uden and his interview with Georges Clemenceau. F. particularly liked the latter "extraordinarily" (F. to Viereck, 20.7.1928).

1928 July 7–9

- Max Eitingon comes to Semmering for a visit. He sees a color etching by Max Pollak by Tatjana Barbakoff at F.'s and decides to buy a copy for his wife Mirra. F. organizes the purchase and shipment to Berlin; Albert Einstein is also involved.
- General Assembly of the Internationale Psychoanalytische Verlag.

1928 July 14

Ernst Simmel sends F. the manuscript of his paper "Die psychoanalytische Behandlung in der Klinik" ("Psychoanalytic treatment in the clinic"), which had already been accepted for publication by the *IZP*.

1928 July mid

- Lucy von Weizsäcker, the wife of the psychologist Adolf von Weizsäcker, asks F. for permission to make a graphological analysis of his handwriting. F. answers reservedly and promises "that I will not pursue you with my resentment if you bring the misdeed to fruition after my demise" (F. to Lucy von Weizsäcker, 17.7.1928).

- Julio Porto-Carrero informs F. about the foundation of the Brazilian Psychoanalytic Association. F. replies that it is very important to him "that your society soon feels at home within the International [Association]" and asks him to submit a report on the history of the society for the *IZP* (F. to Porto-Carrero, 24.7.1928).

1928 July 16–17

Philipp Sarasin visits F. on the Semmering.

1928 July 27

F. takes the train to the Rax and picks flowers among the rocks.

1928 before July 29

F. takes the cable car up the Rax.

1928 July 29

Sándor Ferenczi and his analysand George Amsden, American doctor, visit F. at Semmering.

1928 August

F. asks daughter Mathilde to come to Semmering and wants to get her a nice room.

1928 August 30

Departure from Semmering to Vienna.

1928 August 30–November 1
Stay in Berlin-Tegel for prosthesis fitting

F., his daughter Anna and Chow Lün live on the upper floor of the doctors' villa at the Tegel sanatorium. Marie Bonaparte visits F. in Berlin and then drives back to Vienna with him. Sándor Ferenczi and Lou Andreas-Salomé also visit F. in Berlin. In addition, Johannes Heinrich Schultz visits F. for a consultation. F. is not happy with the chauffeur named Lillich, because he is unpunctual and does not have good manners. Ernst Simmel makes sure that F. gets another chauffeur for his next stay in 1929 spring.

1928 August 30

After a few hours' stay in Vienna, departure for Berlin.

1928 August 31

Arrival in Berlin.

1928 September

Johannes Ruths comes to Berlin for treatment. He is there in connection with the installation of his storage facilities and offers F. a large sum if he would move to Berlin. For a while, at least, F. probably seriously considered it.

1928 September 1

- F. has his first session with Hermann Schroeder. He thinks he has a good idea of what he has to do.
- F.'s daughter-in-law Lucie comes to visit from Hiddensee.

1928 September 2

— Oliver, Henny and Eva visit F.
— Philipp Lehrman comes to Berlin to continue his analysis.

1928 September 3

Ernst and Lucie come for dinner.

1928 September 6

— Jean Lampl-de Groot and her husband Hans visit F.
— F. is with Hermann Schroeder for 1½ hours.

1928 September 8

— F. is with Hermann Schroeder for 1½ hours in the morning.
— Jean Lampl-de Groot and her husband Hans visit F.

1928 September 9

— F.'s son-in-law Max Halberstadt visits F. with his wife Bertha, whom he had married three years after Sophie's death.
— Marie Bonaparte arrives in Berlin.

1928 September 11

Hermann Schroeder thinks that F. has the worst part of the treatment behind him.

1928 September 14

F. is back with Hermann Schroeder.

1928 September 15

F. loses one of two artificial teeth and has to go to Hermann Schroeder.

1928 September 16

— F. goes on a boat trip on Lake Tegel with Oliver and Ernst Simmel.
— In the evening, a game of tarot with Ernst.

1928 September 19

— F. is with Hermann Schroeder for an hour in the evening.
— Ernst comes to dinner.

1928 September 21

F. gets a new prosthesis. But he has to change back to the old one after two days.

1928 Autumn

F. declines to contribute to the anthology *Sex in Civilization* planned by Curt Goetz (pseudonym Victor Calverton) and Samuel Schmalhausen.

1928 September 23

F. is with Hermann Schroeder twice for two hours.

1928 September 26

F. is with Hermann Schroeder both in the morning and in the evening and wears the new prosthesis again.

1928 September 27

F. visits his sister Mitzi with daughter Anna, who is visited by his eldest sister Anna from New York. Afterward, they visit Lampls.

1928 before September 29

F. meets up with his sister Anna, who spends part of the summer in Europe.

1928 September 30

Ceremonial opening of the new premises of the Berlin Institute, which had moved from Potsdamerstrasse 29 to Wichmannstrasse 10. F. is represented by daughter Anna, but had visited the premises beforehand.

1928 October 2

F. visits son Ernst and meets his brother Alexander there.

1928 October 16

F. is without his prosthesis for a day; he only gets it back in the evening. Schroeder tells him that he will charge the work of the technician and the material, but not his own work. F. writes: "That was spoken so earnestly and sincerely that I knew nothing to answer. […] I was prepared for about M 10,000; – if he had charged me about half out of collegiality, I would have felt rich and light. As it is, I do not yet know what to do" (F. to his family, 7.10.1928).

1928 October 17

– Anna buys her father a pair of gloves.
– Oliver and Henny come for dinner.

1928 October 29

F. flies for the first time. He makes a sightseeing flight over Berlin from Tempelhof airport in a Lufthansa plane. He finds "the sensations startling and rather pleasant" (F. to Sam Freud, 6.12.1928).

1928 before October 31

F. gives Ernst Simmel a ring similar to those that the members of the "Secret Committee" had received.

1928 October 31

Departure to Vienna.

1928 November 1

Arrival in Vienna.

1928 November 4

F. visits his mother.

1928 November 5

F. sends Max Eitingon two photographs of himself for the new rooms of the polyclinic.

1928 November 10
Paul Federn and Heinrich Meng give F. their *Psychoanalytische Volksbuch* with the dedication "S. Freud/Dem verehrten und/geliebten Meister/Dr Paul Federn/Heinrich Meng".

1928 November mid
Anna F. introduces her father to the few-month-old son of the later child analyst Marie Briehl.

1928 before November 16
F. receives from the founding member of the Indian Psychoanalytic Association Sarasilal Sarkar his article "A peculiarity in the imagery in Dr. Rabindranath Tagore's poems".

1928 November 17
F. receives Volume XII of the Spanish translation of his works.

1928 November 20
Marie Bonaparte, who is back in Vienna, falls ill with cystitis and has to stay in hospital for a longer time. In the Löw sanatorium, she receives medical care from Max Schur. Through her, Schur gets to know F. and later becomes his doctor – also thanks to Marie Bonaparte's efforts.

1928 December
- Informal meeting of the WPV at Berggasse 19: Heinz Hartmann speaks on "Psychoanalysis and Weltanschauung". In the discussion, Freud remarks that he is a socialist but is against terror and bloodshed, like Schiller.

1928 before December 2
- F. receives from his nephew Edward Bernays his recently published book *Propaganda* F. picks it up "not without apprehension […] it might be […] too American", but finds it "so clear, clever and comprehensible that I can read it with pleasure" (Freud and Edward Bernays, 2.12.1928).
- Silvio Tissi asks F. if he may dedicate his book *La psicoanalisi to* him.

1928 December 5
- WPV meeting: General Assembly – F. is re-elected chairman.
- The Romanian psychiatrist and psychoanalyst Ioan Popescu sends F. his book *Doctrina lui F. (psihanaliza)* with the dedication "Veuiller bien agréer Maître, comme une/modeste expression d'une activité consacrée à/l'éxtension (consacrée) struck through de la psychanalyse dans/notre pays – cette étude, que j'ai en même temps/présentée comme ma thèse de doctorat en médecine et chirurgie à l'Université de Iassy. Avec le plus profonde respect et l'admiration le plus dévouée/Dr Popescu-Sibiu /Botoşani (Moldavie)".

1928 December 6
Ida Fliess asks F. to let her have any of her husband Wilhelm's letters that may still be available – possibly only on loan. F. replies a good week later that, according to his recollection, he "destroyed the greater part of our correspondence sometime after 1904", but does not consider it impossible "that a select number of letters were kept and can be brought to light by a careful search in the rooms I have occupied for 37 years" (F. to Ida Fliess, 17.12.1928).

1928 before December 9
F. receives from Richard Dyer-Bennet the manuscript of a planned book entitled "Gospel of Living". F. finds little to criticize in it, but believes that the ideas developed are "overly optimistic" (F. to Dyer-Bennet, 9.12.1928).

1928 December 9
- F. grants William Smyser an interview. It is published under the title "The Czar of Psychoanalysis" in the *New York Herald Tribune* on August 28.
- Informal meeting of the WPV at Berggasse 19: Theodor Reik speaks about F.'s book *Die Zukunft einer Illusion*.

1928 before December 12
F. receives from the musicologist Robert Lach his ceremonial speech, which he had given on November 19 at the University of Vienna on the occasion of the 100th anniversary of the death of Franz Schubert. It was entitled *Das Ethos in der Musik Schubert's*, and F. read the speech with great pleasure.

1928 December mid
- F. reads the book *Der Verbrecher und seine Richter* by Franz Alexander and Hugo Staub. He thinks the basic ideas are accurate and that they deserve a lot of attention.
- F. gives Marie Bonaparte Thornton Wilder's book *The Bridge of San Luis Rey* with the dedication "Prinzeß Marie aus Anlass einer Erkrankung und einer Einsicht/Freud/Dez 1928". After reading the book, F. describes it as "something quite unusually beautiful" (F. to Ernst Freud, 16.12.1928).
- Arthur Tansley visits F.

1928 December 19
The French doctor and biologist Jean Troisier visits F., and he gives him the fifth edition of the *Vorlesungen zur Einführung in die Psychoanalyse* with the dedication "Dr J. Troisier bon souvenir de Vienne/Freud".

1928 Christmas
- F. receives from Lytton Strachey his book *Elizabeth and Essex. A tragic history* with the dedication "To Sigmund Freud with profound admiration from Lytton Strachey".
- F. Son Oliver is visiting the Freud's with his family.

1928 December 30
F. informs Ida Fliess that he "is very much inclined to believe that the entire correspondence has been destroyed. But since I have not found other things that I certainly wanted to keep, such as the Charcot letters, I do not consider the matter closed" (F. to Ida Fliess, 30.12.1928).

1928 December end
- The Berlin antiques dealer Philipp Lederer is in Vienna and looks at F.'s collection and is very appreciative of it.
- The Internationale Psychoanalytische Verlag closes its balance sheet for 1928 with a deficit of $15,000[53].

1929

- F. is nominated for the Nobel Prize (Medicine) for the seventh time. Among the signatories are Alfred Döblin, Knut Hamsun, Walter Hasenclever, Max Liebermann, Thomas Mann, Romain Rolland, Bertrand Russel, Jakob Wassermann, Herbert George Wells, Franz Werfel, Virginia Wolf and Arnold Zweig.
- The caricaturist Henry Major produces a charcoal drawing of F., presumably from photographs.
- F. subscribes to *Die Antike*, a Journal for Art and Culture of Classical Antiquity.
- The French historian and sociologist Maxime Leroy asks F. to comment on some dreams of Descartes that he had just published in his book *Descartes, le philosophe au masque*. F. answers in detail.

Books received:

- Franz Alexander sends F. the book *Der Verbrecher und seine Richter*, written together with Hugo Staub, with the dedication "Mit ergebenem Gruss Dr Alexander".
- Iwan Bratt sends F. the Swedish translation of Heinrich Meng's and Paul Federn's *Psychoanalytischen Volksbuchs* (*Psykoanalysen i populär framställning*), edited by him, with the dedication "Herrn Professor Sigmund Freud/mit grösster Verehrung/von dem schwed. Herausgeber".
- Havelock Ellis sends F. his book *The art of life* with the dedication "To Professor Freud with/ the best regards of/Havelock Ellis".
- Smith Ely Jelliffe sends F. his *Técnica del psicoanálisis* with the dedication "To Prof. Sigmund Freud/With best wishes/Smith Ely Jelliffe".
- Emanuel Loewy sends F. his book *Polygnot. Ein Buch von griechischer Malerei* with the dedication "Sigmund Freud/in herzlicher Freundschaft/E. L".
- Heinrich Meng and Paul Federn give F. the first volume of the second edition of the *Ärztliches Volksbuch, edited bei Heinrich Meng und August Fiessler*, with the dedication "Herrn Professor S. Freud/in Ehrfurcht überreicht/von/Dr. Heinrich Meng manu propria/Dr Paul Federn".
- Wilhelm Reich sends F. the second edition of his book *Sexualerregung und Sexualbefriedigung* with the dedication "Herrn Prof Freud/ergebenst/Verfasser".
- Kristian Schjelderup sends F. the Danish translation of the *Vorlesungen zur Einführung in die Psychoanalyse (Forelaesninger til indførelse i psykoanalyse)* with the dedication "Herrn Professor Dr. Sigm. Freud/in aufrichtiger Verehrung/von/Kristian Schjelderup".
- Ernst Simmel gives F. Hans Prinzhorn's book *Gedanken zur Zeit. Neue Fragen der Seelenerkenntnis* with the dedication "Herrn Professor Freud/sehr ergebenst übersandt/Ernst Simmel".
- Silvo Tissi sends F. his book *La psicoanalisi. Scienza dell'io o del mistero-problema psichico con saggi di analisi psichica su drammi di Pirandello, Shakespeare, Ibsen, Tolstoi e Shaw* with the dedication "A/Sigmund Freud/creatore della 'Psicanalisi'/questo fervido omaggio/ umile e ardente offre/l'Autore/Milano/Via Gherardini,/10".

1929 January
Charles Maylan wrote an open letter to F., which he himself described as "an intellectual attack against the creator of the psychoanalytic method" (Maylan to F., January 1929). He had visited

F. earlier at a "time when I was still available to anyone who wanted something from me. He visited me then to get advice on how to get training in psychoanalysis" (F. to Else Mediner, 12.8.1930).

1929 January beginning
Max Schur becomes F.'s personal physician on Marie Bonaparte's recommendation.

1929 January 12
Marie Bonaparte leaves Vienna.

1929 January 14
- Eva Rosenfeld begins an analysis with F., for which he takes no fee. It lasts until 1932.
- Informal meeting of the WPV at Berggasse 19: Paul Federn speaks on "Characters of Analysis".

1929 January 27
Max Eitingon and Sándor Ferenczi visit F.

1929 February
Charles Baudouin sends F. his book *Psychanalyse de l'art* with the dedication "Et avec toute ma reconnaissance pour son bon accueil à Vienne en 1926 Baudouin".

1929 February beginning
Moritz *Károlyi*, a former assistant of Hermann Schroeder in Berlin, takes over the "care" of F.'s prosthesis.

1929 February 7
William Blumenthal comes back to F. and is referred by him to Ferenczi.

1929 February 8
In Vienna, there are problems with the gas and water supply, which also affects Berggasse 19. In addition, the coal deliveries do not work well and the Freuds' flat is often unheated.

1929 February 9
Johannes Ruths gives F. the bronze sculpture of an Egyptian frog god that he had bought in Aswan. An expert opinion from the Kunsthistorisches Museum four weeks later declares the sculpture to be a copy.

1929 February 12
- F. answers a questionnaire on smoking sent to him by Victor Richard Rubens (actually Richard Vasvary). Rubens had sent the questionnaire to prominent people with the intention of publishing the answers in an anthology under the title *On smoking and smokers,* but this did not happen.

1929 February 13
Start of correspondence between F. and Albert Einstein (the two men had already met at the end of 1926). Einstein asks F. to support an initiative Carl Frankenstein's to promote Jewish scientists, artists and writers.

1929 February 15
Ilse Moebius and Gertrude Kvergic-Kraus, a great-niece of Max Kassowitz, open a "Foreign Language Lending Library" in Naglergasse in Vienna. From its opening until their emigration in

1938, Minna or Martha regularly pick up English literature for F. – exclusively detective novels, up to 14 books per week.

1929 February 26
– Heinrich Meng sends F. Hans Prinzhorn's book *Gedanken zur Zeit. Neue Fragen der Seelenerkenntnis* with the dedication *"Herrn Prof F./in Verehrung/Heinrich Meng"*.
– F. asks Julius Figdor again to bring him cigars from Holland.

1929 March
Arnold Zweig sends F. his book *Pont und Anna* with the dedication "Siegmund Freud/this analytical history/in due gratitude/to Arnold Zweig".

1929 March 1
Heinrich Meng sends F. Walther Riese's book *Die Unfallneurose als Problem der Gegenwartsmedizin* with the dedication *"Herrn Prof Freud/in Verehrung/H Meng"*.

1929 March 8
– Charles Maylan sends *Freuds tragischer Komplex* with the dedication "To the creator of analytical/science and art/in reverence/and gratitude/Ch. E. Maylan".
– Oskar Pfister sends F. his book *Die Psychoanalyse im Dienst der* with the dedication "Herrn Prof. Dr Freud sendet herzlich/ein promoviertes Enkelkind/O. Pfister".

1929 March 9
An appeal, also signed by F., for the amnesty of the French journalist Henri Guilbeaux is published in the Berliner *Vorwärts*.

1929 March 10–March 23
Stay in Berlin-Tegel for prosthesis fitting
F. is again living in the Tegel sanatorium. He is again accompanied by his daughter Anna. Philip Lehrman also goes to Berlin to continue his analysis. F. gives Hermann Schröder a copy of the book *Die Urgestalt der Brüder Karamasoff* with the dedication "Seinem verehrten Helfer Prof. H. Schröder/März 1929/Sigm. Freud". Lou Andreas-Salomé visits F. twice – first personal meeting with Arnold Zweig and his wife Beatrice. Frequent meetings with Max and Mirra Eitingon – F. buys a Hellenistic sphinx and some smaller pieces from the antique dealer Philipp Lederer.

1929 March 10
Journey from Vienna via Passau to Berlin.

1929 March 11
Arrival in Berlin.

1929 March 14
– F. visits his sister Mitzi.
– Lou Andreas-Salomé comes to Berlin.
– Oliver and Henny come to dinner, later Max Eitingon too.

1929 before March 15

F. receives from Yvette Guilbert her book *La passante émerveillée* with the dedication "Au Professeur Freud/Au grand Savant/A l'homme simple/et charmant/qui aime les/ Chansons de France! He writes to her: "I admired your judgement of America in it and was pleased to find confirmation of a prejudice of mine, namely that a great man always loves the truth and also has the courage to tell the truth" (F. to Yvette Guilbert, 14.3.1929).

1929 March 15

Ernst Simmel, as director of the psychoanalytic sanatorium, sends an appeal to the Prussian Minister of Culture Carl Heinrich Becker, asking for support to set up a foundation to ensure the survival of the clinic. The letter is also signed by F.

1929 March 17

– Oliver, Henny, Eva and Max Halberstad come for lunch.
– Lou Andreas-Salomé and Max Eitingon come to dinner.

1929 before March 18

F. buys a 5000-year-old smoking bowl from Philipp Lederer as a replacement for the Egyptian frog god, exposed as an imitation, which Johannes Ruths had bought for him in Egypt and given to him at the beginning of February.

1929 March 18

– Arnold Zweig and his wife Beatrice come for coffee.
– Ernst and Lucie come for dinner.

1929 March 19

– Margarethe Nunberg comes for lunch.
– Ernst and Lucie come for dinner followed by a game of tarot.
– Anna, Lou Andreas-Salomé and Ernst Simmel go to a meeting of the Berlin Psychoanalytical Association. F. remarks: "I think the visit to the monkeys in the zoo this morning was already preparation" (F. to his family, 19.3.1929).

1929 March 21

Oliver and Henny come for dinner.

1929 March 22

Last visit to Hermann Schroeder.

1929 Spring

F. signs an "Appeal for the Creation of a Fund for the Psychoanalytic Clinic Schloss Tegel".

1929 March 23

Departure to Vienna.

1929 March 25
F. meets Adolf Storfer and hands him two checks for the Internationale Psychoanalytische Verlag, which F. had received via Abraham Brill and Ruth Mack Brunswick and a patient, respectively.

1929 April
Fritz Wittels for readmission to the WPV; he had been attending meetings as a guest again since 1926.

1929 April beginning
Robert Sommer, Chair of Psychiatry at the University of Giessen, gives F. a commemorative coin with his portrait.

1929 April 4
Theodor Reik sends F. his book *Der Schrecken und andere psychoanalytische Studien* with the dedication "Meinem verehrten Lehrer in/alter Anhänglichkeit/Reik".

1929 April 16
The Hungarian orthodontist Moriz Károlyi begins to deal with F.'s prosthesis. Through reductions, F. temporarily has fewer problems.

1929 April 27–28
Anna and Dorothy Burlingham fly to Salzburg to look for accommodation in Berchtesgaden for the summer. F. comments: "A real trip – through the air, there and back, in 1h 35 from here in Salzburg!" (F. to Ernst Freud, 12.5.1929).

1929 before April 30
Walter Kluge, the former analyst of Arnold Zweig, asks F. if he can visit him. F. replies positively.

1929 April end
Israel Wechsler asks his publisher to send F. his new book The Neuroses. He also asks F. if he would be willing to give manuscripts of his books to the Hebrew University in Jerusalem.

1929 May 3
Informal meeting of the WPV at Berggasse 19. Fritz Wittels had just returned from America and is present as a guest.

1929 May 6
- As a birthday present for F., the first issue of the journal *Die psychoanalytische Bewegung is* published.
- Among the visitors on F.'s birthday are Lou Andreas-Salomé, Ludwig Binswanger, Max Eitingon.
- As birthday presents, F. receives, among other things: an Egyptian wooden mask from son Ernst, the second volume of Arthur Evans' book The palace of Minos by Ruth Mack Brunswick.

1929 after May 6
F. receives Julio Porto-Carrero's book *Ensaios de psychanalyse* with the dedication *"In humble respect/and admiration/J. Porto-Carrero/Rio de Janeiro".*

1929 May 13
WPV meeting; Robert Wälder speaks on overdetermination. F. is reported to have said, "I understand myself better since I heard this lecture" (interview with Edward Bibring by Kurt Eissler, 31.5.1952, p. 50).

1929 May 14
Informal meeting of the WPV at Berggasse 19.

1929 May mid
F. is asked by the Paul Zsolnay Verlag to write a congratulatory letter for Felix Salten's 60th birthday coming up on September 6, which was to be published in the Zsolnay Verlag yearbook together with other wishes from well-known people.

1929 before May 29
F. receives from the Russian philosopher Leo Shestov his book *Auf Hiobs Wage. Über die Quellen der ewigen Wahrheiten.*

1929 May 31
The American psychiatrist and psychoanalyst Leon Pierce Clark visits F.

1929 June
Paula Fichtl becomes the new housekeeper for the Freud family. She had previously been employed by Dorothy Burlingham for three years.

1929 June after 2
Clinton McCord, American doctor, begins an analysis on F.; it lasts until September 4.

1929 June 18–September 14
Summer holidays near Berchtesgaden
F., Martha, Minna, Anna, grandson Ernst and the dogs Lün and Wolf spend the summer in Haus Schneewinkellehen between Berchtesgaden and Königssee. The Burlingham's live in another house on the same property. F. works here on his book *Das Unbehagen in der Kultur*, originally titled *Das Unglück in der Kultur*. – Marie Bonaparte continues her analysis.
Visitors include the following:

- F.'s brother Alexander with family.
- F.'s son Oliver with family.
- F.'s son Martin for a week.
- Georg Sylvester Viereck with wife.
- Karl Landauer with his wife and children.
- Marie Bonaparte, Paul Federn, Vladimir Gurevich, René Laforgue, Rudolph Löwenstein, Clarence Oberndorf Joan Riviere.

1929 June 18

Drive from Vienna to Berchtesgaden. Arrival in House Schneewinkellehen in the evening.

1929 June 20

Johannes Ruths comes to Berchtesgaden with his family and continues his analysis. He starts a relationship with his daughter's friend during this time.

1929 June 21

Clinton McCord continues his analysis.

1929 Summer

David Brunswick is in Berchtesgaden to continue his analysis and brings his mother Cecilie with him.

1929 June 23

Ernst Jones comes to Berchtesgaden with his wife by car for two days.

1929 June 30

Sándor Ferenczi and his wife are in Berchtesgaden for a day. In conversation, F. makes the remark that Ferenczi's "appearance was an indication of premature senility". This had made a "shocking impression" on Ferenczi (Ferenczi to F., 6.11.1929). After that, Ferenczi writes fewer letters to F. and begins to withdraw from him. However, F. cannot remember having made such a statement (F. to Ferenczi, 13.12.1929).

1929 July

F. receives a questionnaire "Über geistige Begabung mit besonderer Berücksichtigung des Geschlechts" ("About mental talent with special consideration of sex") by Leonard Leven and partially fills it out.

1929 July 11

Abraham Brill comes to Berchtesgaden for a day.

1929 July 13

Max Eitingon comes to Berchtesgaden.

1929 July 14

F. asks Romain Rolland if he may use his remark about an "oceanic feeling" for his book *Das Unbehagen in der Kultur*. Rolland immediately replies positively.

1929 July 21

F.'s son Ernst and wife Lucie come to Berchtesgaden for a few days.

1929 July 23

F. takes the whole family on a trip to St. Bartholomä.

1929 July 24

F. visits his daughter Mathilde and her husband Robert in Gmain, some 40km west of Linz, with his son Ernst and Lucie. In the evening, F. wins nine marks at tarot.

1929 July 27

F.s book *Das Unbehagen in der Kultur* is finished for the time being.

1929 July 27–31

The XI International Psychoanalytical Congress takes place in Oxford. Anna goes there, F. does not take part but sends a telegram of welcome.

1929 July end

Isaac Landman, the editor of *The American Hebrew* in New York, asks F. to contribute to the anniversary issue. F. declined on the grounds that he was "no more attached to the Jewish religion than to any other. Any allusion to it would probably make your readership uncomfortable" (F. and Landman, 1.8.1929).

1929 August beginning

F.'s nephew Edward Bernays makes F. an offer from his publisher Boni & Liveright to publish a biography of F. In his reply, F. writes: "By the way, it is a real American naivety on the part of your publisher to expect a hitherto decent man to commit such a vulgarity for $5000.[54] The temptation for me would begin at a hundred times that sum, but even then would be rebuffed after half an hour" (F. and Edward Bernays, 10.8.1929).

1929 August 2

Anna returns from Oxford from the International Psychoanalytical Congress.

1929 August 5

Jan van Emden comes to Berchtesgaden.

1929 August 7

Marie Bonaparte arrives in Berchtesgaden.

1929 August 23

F. draws the attention of the American brewery owner Julius Liebmann, the father of F.'s patient Carl Liebmann, to the precarious situation of the Tegel sanatorium and asks him to consider a business involvement. Liebmann's commitment to Tegel can indeed prevent its closure for the time being.

1929 August 25

F. has a lengthy conversation with Dorothy Burlingham's son Robert and her father-in-law Charles Culp Burlingham, who question him about Dorothy Burlingham's condition.

1929 August end

F.'s Chow Chow Lün is run over by a train in Salzburg; Eva Rosenfeld was supposed to bring him back to Vienna, but he broke loose from the leash in Salzburg and was only found four days later.

1929 September

– Joseph Ishill sends F. the anthology he edited *Havelock Ellis. In Appreciation* with the dedication "To Dr. Sigmund Freud, with the compliments of Joseph Ishill".
– F. issues an evaluation for Ruth Mack Brunswick in which he certifies that "in the five years she spent in Vienna as my personal pupil, she learned psychoanalysis both practically and theoretically, treated several patients with understanding and success, and made herself known through two valuable clinical publications" (F. to Mack Brunswick, September 1929).
– F. gets the daughter of Anna's German shepherd Wolf named Adda to replace Lün, who has been run over.

1929 September 2

The American psychiatrist Smiley Blanton begins an analysis with F. It lasts, with major interruptions, until 1938 August.

1929 September 4

F. sends a sample of his handwriting to the German physician Carl Haeberlin with the remark: "I myself am a layman and heretic with regard to graphology. But let it be admitted that I regard illegible handwriting as an expression of contempt for the recipient" (F. to Haeberlin, 5.9.1929).

1929 before September 6

F. congratulates Felix Salten on his 60th birthday and writes that Salten "belongs to those poets whom one immediately becomes personally fond of" (F. to Salten, before 6.9.1929).

1929 September 11

Ruth Mack Brunswick is in Berchtesgaden for a day.

1929 September 14

F., Anna and Smiley Blanton leave Berchtesgaden for Berlin.

1929 September 15–October 26
Stay in Berlin-Tegel for prosthesis fitting

F. is in Tegel for a consultation with Hermann Schröder; he is again accompanied by his daughter Anna, who meets Robert Fliess during the stay. Marie Bonaparte is in Tegel at the same time. Smiley Blanton has also come to Berlin with me so that he does not have to interrupt his analysis.

1929 September 15

Arrival in Berlin.

1929 September mid

F. receives as a gift from Stefan Zweig his book *Joseph Fouché. Bildnis eines politischen Menschen* with the dedication "Dem Meister der Seelenkunde/Unserm Lehrer im Wissen/ um den Menschen/Siegmund Freud/Diese Bildnis eines Politers/In Verehrung/Stefan Zweig".

1929 September 20

F. issues a certificate for Ruth Mack Brunswick that she was his pupil for five years and learned psychoanalysis theoretically and practically.

1929 September end

F. meets his niece Martha (Tom), her husband Jakob (Jankew) Seidmann and their daughter Angela.

1929 October 14

F. meets with his niece Margarethe and her husband Erwin Magnus.

1929 October 19

The husband of F.'s niece Martha (Tom), Jakob Seidmann, hangs himself.

1929 October 20

F. visits his niece Martha (Tom) in the Flatow sanatorium. Her husband Jakob Seidmann had hanged himself the day before.

1929 October 25

Departure from Berlin.

1929 October 26

F. arrives back in Vienna.

1929 after October 26

The nurse Mimi Schulhof consults F. about her feeling of inferiority and her fear of exams; F. refers her to Eduard Hitschmann.

1929 October end

When the Nobel Prizes are awarded, F. is once again passed over: The Nobel Prize for Medicine was awarded to Christiaan Eijkman and Frederick Hopkins for their work on vitamins, and the Nobel Prize for Literature went to Thomas Mann.

1929 November

- F. gives Marie Bonaparte a ring with a gem, as the members of the Secret Committee had also received.
- F. gives Smiley Blanton his *Collected Writings* with a dedication and a photograph of himself.

1929 November beginning

F. puts his paper *Das Unbehagen in der Kultur* to print.

1929 November 1

The American journalist Montgomery Belgion sends F. his book *Our present philosophy of life* with the dedication "For Sigmund Freud with the respects of the Author".

1929 November 2

- The British psychoanalyst John Rickman visited F. He had compiled the *Index Psychoanalyticus 1893–1926* published by Hogarth in 1928.
- F. plays tarot again for the first time after the summer holiday and the stay in Berlin.

1929 before November 4

The Viennese art historian Fritz Novotny informs F. about his impression of F.'s patient Carl Liebmann, who was at the Institute for Art History, where Novotny is an assistant. Novotny subsequently visits F. about six more times, each time in connection with Carl Liebmann.

1929 November 4

F. carries has an ulcerated finger and therefore seeks out his tarot partner, the surgeon Julius Schnitzler.

1929 November 6

- F. discusses mountings of pieces in his collection with the art historian and curator of the Vienna Kunsthistorisches Museum Ernst Kris.
- Henri Flournoy visits F.

1929 November 7
F. notes: "Anti-Semitic disturbances". This probably refers to the interruption of the lecture by the Jewish anatomy professor and city councilor Julius Tandler by right-wing students, who carry the riot into other parts of the building and onto the street.

1929 November 11
F. suffers from neuralgic pain.

1929 November 14
F. has a heart and intestinal attack".

1929 November 16
F. is at the Rothschild Hospital for a consultation with his friend, the heart specialist Ludwig Braun.

1929 November 17
Thomas Mann sends F. his book *Die Forderung des Tages. Reden und Aufsätze aus den Jahren 1925–1929* mit der Widmung "Sigmund Freud/in großer Verehrung/München, 17. XI. 1929/ Thomas Mann".

1929 November 20
F. attends a concert by Yvette Guilbert at the concert hall and gives her flowers.

1929 November 21
F., Martha and Anna are invited to tea at the Bristol Hotel by Yvette Guilbert.

1929 November 22
F. attends another concert by Yvette Guilbert at the Konzerthaus.

1929 November 23
- F. visits the dentist Bernhard Gottlieb, who since the end of the 1920s had been working on research into growths and tissue changes caused by excessive strain on the teeth; he lived in Vienna IX, Türkenstr. 15, quite close to F.
- F. went to Hans Pichler with the dentist Josef Weinmann, who is now treating him. He suspected a recurrence. However, Pichler found that it was a harmless spot where the nasal mucosa had spread to the remains of the palate. F. commented succinctly: "False alarm with Pichler".

1929 November 28
The Dutch psychiatrist Gerbrandus Jelgersma asks F. if the Internationale Psychoanalytische Verlag would be prepared to publish the German edition of his textbook on psychiatry. It was the only textbook for psychiatry in which psychoanalysis was appreciated.

1929 November 30
Marie Bonaparte leaves Vienna.

1929 November end
Else Hofmann, an assistant of Emanuel Loewy, who occasionally visits F. in connection with the latter's collection of antiquities, procures an antique golden laurel wreath for F. from the Greek envoy. Originally, the publisher Paul Zsolnay had sought the wreath for the poet's coronation Gerhart Hauptmanns.

1929 December

The Austrian writer Wladimir von Hartlieb sends F. his book *Das Antlitz der Provence* with the dedication "Herrn/Prof. Dr. Sigm. Freud/in Verehrung und Bewunderung/W. Hartlieb".

1929 December 4

On his daily walk, F. discovers a poster advertising Charles Maylan's book *Freud's Tragic Complex*.

1929 December 7

Charles Maylan gives a lecture directed against F. in the small concert hall in Vienna under the title: "The Mythology of the Ego: Nietzsche versus Freud".

1929 December 7–10

F. notes: "Bad heart days". He writes to Sándor Ferenczi: "A veritable mosaic of measures to force the recalcitrant organs into service. Most recently, the heart has been added to the list with extrasystoles, arrhythmias, fibrillation attacks. My wise personal physician, Prof. Braun, says that none of this is of serious significance. Is he already starting to deceive me?" (F. to Ferenczi, 13.12.1929).

1929 December 12

Informal meeting of the WPV at Berggasse 19.

1929 December 13

F. calls Sándor Ferenczi his "paladin and secret grand vizier" (F. to Ferenczi, 13.12.1929).

1929 December 17

F. buys some gems.

1929 December 21

The art historian Wolfgang Born sends F. an offprint of his paper "Der Traum in der Graphik des Odilon Redon" with the dedication "Prof. Dr. Sigmund Freud verehrungsvoll überreicht vom Verfasser".

1929 before December 24

F.'s book *Das Unbehagen in der Kultur is* published.

1929 December 24–26

Max Eitingon visits F. and receives a copy of *Das Unbehagen in der Kultur* as a Christmas present. Their conversations also include the Japanese psychologist Yaekichi Yabe, who would like to do an analysis in Europe.

1929 Christmas

The American psychiatrist Edith Jackson arrives in Vienna. She stays in the same boarding house as Margaret and Smiley Blanton, who has arranged for her to have an analysis with F.

1929 December 26

Eva Rosenfeld starts an analysis at F. It takes about two years.

1929 December 27

F. gives Martha pearls for New Year.

1929 December 29

F. agrees to join the Honorary Presidium of the Board of Trustees of the Jewish Scientific Institute (YIVO).

1929 December 30

Death of the shepherd dog Adda; F. had got her as a replacement for Lün, who had been run over.

1930

Books received:

- Ernst Aster sends F. his book *Die Psychoanalyse* with the dedication "In tiefer Verehrung überreicht vom Verf.".
- Mark Brunswick sends F. Volume 8 of *The Cambridge ancient history*.
- The American journalist Floyd Dell sends F. his book *Love in the Machine Age. A Psychological Study of the Transition from Patriarchal Society* with the dedication "To Sigmund Freud/creator of a new age of thought/a novelist turned student/offers very respectfully/his attempt at a Freudian interpretation/of current social history/Floyd Dell".
- Alexandre Hérenger, Swiss poet and writer, sends F. his writing *Exorcismes* with the dedication "À Monsieur le Professeur Sigmund F.,/au génial exorciste de la psyché humaine,/ces quelques verses, en faible témoignage de ma/respectueuse et profonde admiration./Alexandre Hérenger".
- The American political scientist Harold Lasswell sends F. his book *Psychopathology and politics* with the dedication "To Professor/Sigmund Freud,/with respect./Harold D. Lasswell".
- Karl Menninger, American psychiatrist, sends F. his book *The human mind* with the dedication "For/Professor Sigmund Freud/from a loyal disciple/of the third generation./Karl A Menninger MD".
- Roger Money-Kyrle sends F. his dissertation *The meaning of sacrifice* with the dedication "To Prof Freud/from/R E Money-Kyrle".
- Wilhelm Reich gives F. his book *Geschlechtsreife, Enthaltsamkeit, Ehemoral* with the dedication "Herrn Professor F./ergebenst gewidmet/vom/Verfasser".
- Philipp Sarasin sends F. his book *Goethe's Mignon. Eine psychoanalytische Studie* with the dedication "In tiefer Verehrung/und großer Dankbarkeit/überreicht vom Verf".
- George Sylvester Viereck and Paul Eldridge give F. their jointly written book *Salome the wandering Jewess. My first two thousand years of love* with the dedication "To Sigmund Freud,/George Sylvester Viereck/Paul Eldridge".
- Kristian Schjelderup sends F. the Danish anthology *Psykoanalysen i praksis* with F.'s writings translated by him with the dedication "Herrn Professor Sigm. Freud/in aufrichtiger Verehrung/von/Kristian Schjelderup".
- Werner Zimmermann, Swiss writer and life reformer, sends F. his book *Psycho-sexuelle Heilbehandlung* with the dedication "With the Author's compliments". He had published it under the pseudonym P. N. Teulon.
- Viktor von Weizsäcker and Karl Müller give F. Weizsäcker's book *Soziale Krankheit und soziale Gesundung* with the dedication "Herrn Prof. Sigm. Freud/mit dem Ausdruck der Verehrung/Viktor Weizsäcker/Karl Müller".

1930 beginning
Richard Beer-Hofmann visits F. Max Schur had initiated this visit.

1930 January
- Informal meeting of the WPV at Berggasse 19. Richard Sterba speaks on the "Problematic of the Doctrine of Sublimation".
- F. gives Hermann Schröder a copy of his book *Das Unbehagen in der Kultur* with the dedication "Herrn Prof. H. Schröder/mit den herzlichsten Neujahrsgrüßen/der dankbar ergeben Verf./1930".

1930 January 1
- A part of *Das Unbehagen in der Kultur* is published under the title "Die Wege zum Glück" ("The ways to happiness") in the supplement to the *Neue Freie Presse.*
- F. gives Eva Rosenfeld his book *Das Unbehagen in der Kultur* with the dedication "Seiner lieben Großen d. Verf.".

1930 January 2
Edith Jackson begins an analysis with F. It lasts until 1936 May.

1930 January 3
F. receives cigars from Karl Landauer.

1930 January 9
- Informal meeting of the WPV at Berggasse 19.
- The Austrian poet and founder of the Sesam publishing house, Helene Scheu-Riesz – a former patient of F. – asks F. if he would receive the American poet Robert Schauffler and talk about a problem in his latest book. F. declines because of an increased need for rest.

1930 January 10
F. refuses to pay the fee bill of his doctor Max Schur because of "disrespectful disregard for medical services" and demands a "more appropriate" bill (F. to Schur, 10.1.1930).

1930 January 10–11
F. buys gems again.

1930 January 15
- In response to Marie Bonaparte's inquiry about treatment options for the religious mania (e.g. regular sex with Jesus Christ) of her sister-in-law Alice Battenberg, F. proposes to achieve premature menopause or temporary suppression of the period by X-ray irradiation of the ovaries. In addition, she was to be observed analytically. At the beginning of April, Alice goes to the Tegel Sanatorium in Berlin for two months, where these recommendations are carried out under the supervision of Ernst Simmel, although he initially has reservations.
- F. receives back some clay figures that he had mounted on a base.

1930 January 16
F. receives from Romain Rolland his books *La Vie de Ramakrishna* and *La Vie de Vivekananda.*

1930 January 18
Death of Felix Wiener, the husband of his niece Lucie Bernays.

1930 January 19
The French-Thai legal philosopher René Guyon sends F. his book *La légitimité des actes sexuels. Études d'ethique sexuelle* with the dedication "Au professeur Sigmund Freud, maître de la psychanalyse, ce volume est dédié en très respectueux hommage/R. Guyon".

1930 January 21
- F. receives a visit from Charmian London, Jack London's second wife. She came from Berlin, where F.'s niece Margarethe was translating books by her husband.
- F. has a biliary colic.

1930 January 24
- F. meets with Max Schur.
- F. buys a Roman bronze statuette of an acrobat through the mediation of the Kunsthistorisches Museum.

1930 February
Arnold Zweig begins an analysis with F. It lasts until May 1933.

1930 February 3
Nerio Rojas, forensic pathologist from Buenos Aires, visits F.

1930 February 6–7
F. has a "dream of Nestroy".

1930 before February 8
Martha Oppenheimer, the wife of the Frankfurt gynecologist Hermann Oppenheimer, asks F. for a writing sample.

1930 February 8
F. learns of the death of his niece Martha (Tom), daughter of sister Mitzi. She had taken her own life after the death of her husband on February 7.

1930 February 9
- Arnold Zweig visits F.
- Ernst Kris visits F. and examines some pieces from his collection.

1930 February 10
Theodor Reik sends F. his book *Warum verliess Goethe Friederike?* with the dedication *"Meinem verehrten Lehrer/mit den herzlichsten Grüßen/Reik"*.

1930 February 13
Informal meeting of the WPV at Berggasse 19: Franz Alexander (together with Hugo Staub) presents a case entitled "Ein leidenschaftlicher Autofahrer" ("A Passionate Motorist"). He also brings F. cigars from Max Eitingon.

1930 February 14
- F. receives from Samuel Lifschitz his book *Hypnoanalysis* with the dedication *"Prof. Dr./S. Freud/in reverence/from the author/Moscow/S. Lifschitz"*.
- F. gives Smiley Blanton four volumes of his *Collected Writings*.
- F. gives daughter Anna a jade necklace.

1930 February 15
F. acquires the fragment of an Egyptian bust, possibly the upper part of a basalt bust of an Egyptian official from the Middle Kingdom, which F. from then on used as a paperweight.

1930 February 16
F. gives Ruth Mack Brunswick an opal necklace for her birthday.

1930 February 17
F. receives the book *Animism, magic and the divine king* by the Hungarian psychoanalyst Géza Róheim.

1930 before February 21

F. receives Abraham Roback's book *Jewish Influence in Modern Thought* with the dedication "To Professor Sigmund Freud/With the high esteem of/A A Roback". He thanks him and writes at the end of his letter: "I was brought up so un-Jewish that today I am not even able to read your dedication, which is obviously in Jewish script" (F. to Roback, 20.2.1930).

1930 February 23

F.'s sister Mitzi is in Vienna. Presumably the fate of her orphaned granddaughter Angela Seidmann is at stake.

1930 February 26

Gregorio Bermann from Argentina visits F. Bermann was a forensic pathologist at the University of Cordoba.

1930 February 28

– Fritz Trebitsch, an assistant to Hermann Schroeder, is in Vienna making corrections to F.'s prosthesis.
– F. notes in his "Kürzeste Chronik" ("Shortest Chronicle"): "Eisinger about Angela". Arpad Eisinger was the executor of the will of F.'s niece Martha (Tom) Seidmann. He was in possession of a letter from her which expressly forbade the adoption of Angela Seidmann by F.'s daughter Anna. Furthermore, any contact of Angela with psychoanalysis was to be prevented.

1930 March beginning

F. suffers from intestinal problems, such as irritability and spasms of the colon.

1930 before March 3

The writer Josef Perlberger asks F. if he would put up a Jewish National Fund collection box at home. F. answers positively, but fears that the box will remain empty as he no longer holds an ordination.

1930 March 4

F. acquires a jade piece for his collection.

1930 March 5

– F. receives an inquiry from the Prussian Ministry of Culture, presumably in connection with a possible teaching position for Siegfried Bernfeld at the Berlin University.
– F. is at the doctor's because of heart problems.

1930 March 8

– The art historian and writer Carl Einstein asks F. for the surrealist magazine *Documents* "to send us a few lines [without delay] in which you set down what is significant to you about Picasso" (Einstein to F., 8.3.1930).
– Abraham Roback sends F. his book *Popular Psychology with Chapters on Character Analysis and Intelligence Tests* with the dedication "Professor Sigmund Freud/With fondest regards and hopes that he will/not be too disappointed/A A Roback".

1930 March 9

F. gets a new Chow Chow bitch from Dorothy Burlingham and names her Jofi. She is a half-sister of Lün, who was run over by a train at the end of 1929 August. Jofi stays with F. for seven years.

1930 March 16–17

Yvette Guilbert gives two concerts in the middle concert hall. F. attends both, and Yvette sang primarily for him. The audience also looked at least as interested in F. as in the singer.

1930 March 20
Informal meeting of the WPV at Berggasse 19: Paul Federn lectured on *Das Unbehagen in der Kultur* and F. responded with critical remarks on his own book.

1930 Spring
Felix Augenfeld, architect and friend of F.'s son Ernst, designs a desk chair for F. at Mathilde's request, intended as a birthday present.

1930 March 24
F. receives a number of Roback's writings from Abraham Roback. In addition to offprints, these probably include the books *The Psychology of Character* and *Popular Psychology.*

1930 March 26–27
Anna goes to Budapest and gives a lecture to the Hungarian Psychoanalytic Association.

1930 March 27
Max Eitingon is visiting Vienna.

1930 March 29
Martha goes to Berlin for a fortnight, among other things to be there on her son Ernst's birthday (April 6).

1930 before March 31
- Richard Flatter, Austrian translator and poet, sends F. his translation of *King Lear* and F. takes this opportunity to read the "mighty work" once again.
- F. receives from Heinrich Löwy his biography of Josef Popper-Lynkeus published in the *Jüdische Lexikon.*
- Lajos Lévy is visiting Vienna.
- F. visits Oskar Rie, partly because of the illness of his wife Melanie.

1930 April 5–6
F. has a heart attack during the night. F.'s friend, the cardiologist Ludwig Braun, does not think any special therapy is necessary. However, he restricts his smoking to three cigars a day.

1930 April 7
Hans Zweig from Brno visits F. Zweig had published a collective report on "Psychotherapy in Czech Literature from 1920–1930" in the February issue of the *Zentralblatt für Psychotherapie.*

1930 April 9
F. receives a consignment of Berchtesgaden cigars from Max Eitingon.

1930 April 10
Stefan Zweig visits F. He had come to Vienna from Salzburg on April 7 to attend the premiere of his tragicomedy *Lamb of the Poor at* the Burgtheater on April 12.

1930 April 12–13
Sándor Ferenczi visits F. There is a brief improvement in relations between the two men.

1930 April 13
- Martha comes back from Berlin.
- Marie Bonaparte, who had arrived in Vienna the day before, visits F. in the evening.

1930 April 14
One of the springs of F.'s prosthesis is broken.

1930 April 15–17
Anna and Dorothy Burlingham are in Paris.

1930 after April 15
Ernst Kris and F. choose a stone from F.'s collection for Ernst's wife Marianne.

1930 April 18
F. receives from Hanns Sachs the manuscript of his book *Bubi. The Life Story of Caligula*. Three weeks later, Sachs asks F. to tell him his impression of the manuscript.

1930 April 21–May 3
Stay at the Cottage Sanatorium
Because of heart and intestinal problems, F.'s doctors urge him to go to the Cottage Sanatorium again for treatment. Daughter Anna accompanies him.

1930 April 21
F. moves to the sanatorium.

1930 April 25
F. gives up smoking completely (temporarily) and starts to feel better.

1930 April 29
The board of trustees for the award of the Frankfurt Goethe Prize meets in Frankfurt. Nominees include Hermann Hesse, Edmund Husserl, Fritjof Nansen, Romain Rolland, Bertrand Russel and F. Alfred Döblin makes a strong case for F., but a decision is not made.

1930 May 3
F. is released from the sanatorium.

1930 May
Hugo Sonnenschein (pseudonym "Sonka") sends F. his book *Der Bruder Sonka und die allgemeine Sache, oder, Das Wort gegen die Ordnung* with the dedication "Sigm. Freud,/dem grossen Revolutionär,/in Ehrfurcht/Sonka/Wien".

1930 shortly before May 4
F. receives from Marie Bonaparte a Roman sarcophagus lid depicting the slain Hector.

1930 May 4–July 24
Stay in Berlin-Tegel for prosthesis fitting
F. is again living in the medical center of the Tegel sanatorium; his daughter Anna accompanies him. Coming to Berlin for analysis are Smiley Blanton, Edith Jackson, Dorothy Burlingham and David Brunswick. F. consults Fritz Langstadt, a former Dresdner Bank trustee and tax advisor, about an investment he made in a Berlin property that has yielded only 4.5% instead of the promised 5%. He meets Langstadt twice at the Hotel Eden.

1930 May 4
Departure by night train to Berlin. While still at the station, Eva Rosenfeld tells him that the pediatrician Wilhelm Knöpfelmacher has declared his grandson Ernst healthy.

1930 May 5
Arrival in Berlin.

1930 May 6
- F. learns that Hermann Schröder does not want to adjust the prosthesis, but wants to make a new one.

- F. receives 74 roses from Max Eitingon for her birthday.
- Daughter Anna presents him with a poem on behalf of Jofi and gives him a live turtle.

1930 May 7

- F. visits the antique dealer Philipp Lederer. It is the first of six visits in 1930 to Lederer's shop at Kupfergraben 4. By buying antiques, F. compensated for abstinence from smoking and wrote in this context: "Only the cigar is missing, what one tries against it, drinking wine, writing letters, biting dates, is no substitute. Antiques might have been, but you can't buy that much" (F. to his family, 9.5.1930).
- F. receives a mail item from Sándor Ferenczi with an Egyptian Osiris figure.
- Yaekichi Yabe visits F. in the evening and presents him with volumes 3 and 4 of the Japanese translation of the *Gesammelte Schriften* edited by him with the following dedications: Vol. 3: "To Prof. Dr. S. Freud dedicated by Kenji Ohtski [translator]", Vol. 4: "To Prof. Freud/presented/by/Y. K. Yabe/Supervisor of the translation".

1930 May 11

F. visits the antique dealer Philipp Lederer again (second visit 1930).

1930 May mid

The Prussian Minister of Culture Carl Heinrich Becker visits F. with six of his staff.

1930 May 17

- F. visits son Ernst in Caputh.
- William Bullitt visits F. and tells him that he intends to write a book on the Treaty of Versailles, which should also include studies on Clemenceau, Lloyd George, Lenin and Wilson – all politicians whom Bullitt had met personally. F. suggests that he write the chapter on Woodrow Wilson together.

1930 May 18

F. starts smoking again after a short period of abstinence – one cigar a day.

1930 May 19

F. and William Bullitt agree to write a book together about the American President Woodrow Wilson.

1930 May 25

Max Halberstadt, F.'s widowed son-in-law, comes to Tegel for a visit.

1930 May 26

F. visits the antique dealer Philipp Lederer again (third visit 1930).

1930 May 29–31

F. visits his son Ernst with Anna, who has a house on the island of Hiddensee. Here, he meets Raymond de Saussure again for the first time.

1930 May end

F. he reads Axel Munthe's work *The Book of San Michele.*

1930 June

Emanuel Loewy sends F. an offprint of his lecture "Ursprünge der bildenden Kunst" with the dedication "Sigmund Freud/herzlich grüßend/d. Vf".

1930 before June 2

F. receives from Max Levy-Suhl his book *Die seelischen Heilmethoden des Arztes. Eine Lehre vom neurotischen Menschen.*

1930 June 4

F. visits the antique dealer Philipp Lederer again (fourth visit 1930).

1930 June 8

F. meets with Robert Fliess, the son of his former friend Wilhelm Fliess. Fliess was currently undergoing psychoanalytic training and one of the topics of the conversation was the theory of life and death instincts.

1930 June 13

– F. learns of the death of Trude Hammerschlag, the granddaughter of F.'s religion teacher Samuel Hammerschlag. She had died in a fire at her workplace in the chemistry laboratory at Vienna University on February 11. F. writes about this: " [...] the horribly clumsy end of Trude H. has also shaken me very much" (F. his to family, 14.6.1930).
– Martha rents the Villa Rebenburg in Grundlsee for her summer stay.

1930 June 14

F. visits the antique dealer Philipp Lederer again (fifth visit 1930).

1930 before June 15

Cyril Clemens, a distant relative of Mark Twain (real name: Samuel Langhorn Clemens), asks F. if he would accept the vice-presidency of the International Mark Twain Society founded in 1930. F. accepts with thanks.

1930 June 17

Franz Alexander visits F. He was visiting from the USA, where he is a visiting professor of psychoanalysis at the University of Chicago Medical School.

1930 June 18

Josef Weinmann, a specialist in diseases of the oral cavity and a student of Hermann Schröder, examines F.

1930 June 20

The lawyer Hugo Staub visited F. Staub had worked with Franz Alexander on crime and psychoanalysis.

1930 June 21

– F.'s just widowed niece Lucie Wiener (daughter of F.'s sister Anna) visits F. She had come to Europe to look for work because she did not want to stay in America.
– Around midnight, F. sees "the Zeppelin very low over our house as if it had paid us a special visit" (F. to his family, 22.6.1930). It was indeed the "Graf Zeppelin", which had landed on Staaken airfield, very close to Tegel Palace, on this day during its tour of Germany. The occasion was the second World Power Conference, which took place in Berlin from 1930 June 16 to 25.

1930 June 24
- F.'s son-in-law Max Halberstad comes to Berlin for two days.
- Dorothy Burlingham leaves.

1930 June 30
F. has an attack of cardiac neuralgia with diarrhea.

1930 July
Harry Price sends F. his book *Rudi Schneider. A Scientific Examination of his Mediumship* with the dedication "To/Professor Dr. Freud,/with kind regard,/Harry Price".

1930 July 1
- F. visits the antique dealer Philipp Lederer again (sixth and last visit 1930). Among all the purchases made at Lederer's, a small Athens figurine is the main item.
- F. divides the fee for the eighth edition of The Interpretation of Dreams between his sons Martin and Oliver.

1930 July 3

- Arnold Zweig visits F., who writes: "On Thursday evening Arnold Zweig and his wife were with us. The poor boy is half blind, he can no longer read for himself. In the mirror of such fates one is silent about his" (F. to his family, 5.7.1930).
- The board of trustees for the award of the Frankfurt Goethe Prize meets in Frankfurt. No decision is made at this meeting either, but F. learns that he has been nominated.

1930 July 5
F. receives the finished prosthesis; however, it causes such discomfort that he "actually longs for the old one that was taken off" (F. to Ruth Mack Brunswick, 8.7.1930).

1930 July 7
F. visits Hermann Schroeder, who makes corrections to the prosthesis.

1930 July 23
F. says goodbye to Hermann Schröder.

1930 July 24
Departure from Berlin.

1930 July 25
F. arrives back in Vienna.

1930 July 27–September 28
Summer stay at the Grundlsee
F., Martha, Minna and Anna – who arrives later – live in the Villa Rebenburg in Grundlsee. F. has a piano in his room removed. Visitors include Marie Bonaparte, Vladimir Gurevich, Eva Rosenfeld, Robert Wälder, son Ernst and daughter Mathilde. Wilhelm Reich also comes to Grundlsee. He as a sharp disagreement with F.

1930 July 27

Drive from Vienna to Grundlsee.

1930 July 29

F. receives the news through a letter from Alfons Paquet that the city of Frankfurt has awarded him the Goethe Prize endowed with 10,000 Reichsmark. Paquet had been secretary of the board of trustees of the Goethe Prize since 1927.

1930 August 2

Paul Federn, Heinrich Meng and István Hollós visit F. At F.'s request, Meng reads out the speech that F. had written for the awarding of the Goethe Prize and which was later read out by Anna in Frankfurt.

1930 August 6

F.'s daughter Mathilde arrives in Grundlsee and stays for three weeks.

1930 August 8

F. visits his mother in Bad Ischl. He has three cars for the 30km journey: Dorothy Burlingham's, Ruth Mack-Brunswick's and Marie Bonaparte's.

1930 after August 8

F. acquires a fragment of a Roman sarcophagus lid from the 2nd century from Ludwig Pollak through the mediation of Ernst Kris.

1930 August 16

– Felix Salten visits F.
– F.'s brother Alexander visits F. together with his wife Sophie and son Harry.

1930 August 17–18

F. is in to Bad Ischl for his mother's 95th birthday.

1930 August 21

Alfons Paquet sends F. his book *Städte, Landschaften und ewige Bewegung* with the dedication *"Herrn Professor Sigmund Freud/in Verehrung/mit herzlichen Gruß/Alfons Paquet"*.

1930 August 24

– Max Michel, Councillor of Frankfurt, comes to Grundlsee to present F. with the check for 10,000 Reichsmark for the Goethe Prize. He is accompanied by his wife Lotte and Liselotte Graf, the wife of Herbert Graf (the "little Hans"), who is now Kapellmeister in Frankfurt. F. sends the check for 10,000 Reichsmark to his son Ernst in Berlin so that he can set up an account for him there.
– F. visits his mother in Bad Ischl and writes: "It is hoped to bring her back to Vienna alive tomorrow" (F. to Ernst Freud, 24.8.1930). This is the last time F. sees his mother.
– F. formulates tqo drafts of anobituary for his mother

1930 August 25

– Paul Federn picks up F.'s mother in Bad Ischl and accompanies her to Vienna. It is clear to F. that he would probably not see her again: "Things are bad with my mother, we are glad that she got from Ischl to Vienna alive with Federn's help" (F. to Eitingon, 26.8.1930).
– Death of Melanie Rie, the wife of F.'s friend Oskar Rie.

1930 August 28

In Frankfurt, the ceremonial awarding of the Goethe Prize to F. takes place in front of a small circle of invited guests in the Goethehaus. He is represented by his daughter Anna, who also reads his speech.

1930 August 31

Ernst Simmel and René Laforgue visit F. Laforgue films scenes of the visit. Simmel stays for a good week.

1930 September 2

Hanns Sachs visits F.

1930 September 3

Siegfried Bernfeld visits F.

1930 September 3–5

Alfons Paquet visits F.

1930 September 7–8

Max Eitingon, Paul Federn, and Josef Weinmann visit F.

1930 September 8

F. increases his cigar consumption from one to two a day.

1930 September 12

Death of F.'s mother. She dies at the age of 95 after weeks of illness from gangrene of one leg. Until her death, she had been cared for by the nurse Wilhelmine Siner.

1930 September 14

– Funeral of F.'s mother. F. does not attend, but Anna goes to the funeral in Vienna.
– Fernando Gorriti sends F. his book *Psicoanálisis de los sueños en un sindrome de desposesión* with the dedication "Al sabio psiquiatra Profesor/Dr Sigm. Freud, homenage de/la mais grande admiración,/con esta tan pequeña obra de su Escuela. Fernando Gorriti Buenos Aires".

1930 September 15

Anna and Dorothy Burlingham go on holiday to Italy.

1930 September 16

Marie Bonaparte leaves Grundlsee.

1930 September 17

F.'s sister Dolfi, who had taken care of her mother all her adult life and nursed her in recent years, comes to Grundlsee to recuperate.

1930 September 18

– F.'s son Ernst goes to Vienna with Chow Chow Jofi.
– Eva Rosenfeld moves into the Villa Rebenburg.

1930 September 19

An appeal "Für das Arbeitende Palästina" ("For Working Palestine") signed by F. is published in the *Ostjüdische Zeitung*. The appeal was initiated by Histadruth, the umbrella organization of Israel's trade unions. In addition to F., signatories were as follows: Eduard

Bernstein, Léon Blum, Max Brod, Martin Buber, Simon Dubnow, Albert Einstein, Lion Feuchtwanger, Arnold Zweig.

1930 September 28

Departure from Grundlsee back to Vienna.

1930 September 29

Anna and Dorothy Burlingham return from their trip to Italy.

1930 September 30

- F. goes to the radiologist Gottwald Schwarz at the Cottage Sanatorium for X-rays of the stomach. It was found that F.'s colic has no organic cause.
- The Swiss psychoanalyst Gustav Graber sends F. his book Die *Kreuzfahrt des Lebens* with the dedication "Herrn Prof. Dr. S. Freud,/dem Gewinner des Goethe-Preis 1930/in tiefer Verehrung/der Verf./Stuttgart".

1930 September end

Anna Freud and Dorothy Burlingham buy a farmhouse in Hochrotherd, about 30km southwest of Vienna. They furnish it with the help of Anna's brother Ernst.

1930 October

- A "Manifest gegen die Wehrpflicht und die militärische Ausbildung der Jugend" ("Manifesto against compulsory military service and the military training of youth") signed by F. is published in the journal *Die neue Generation.*
- The St. Petersburg-born writer and journalist André Beucler sends F. the French translation of the book *Dostoyevsky* by Dostoyevsky's second wife Anna Dostoyevskaya that he had arranged with the dedication "À Dr. Sigmund Freud/avec l'admiration et/les remerciments du/ traducteur/André Beucler".

1930 after October 1

Ferenczi visits F.

1930 October 3

- F. had noticed that a tumor had appeared behind the prosthesis on the palate and now consulted Pichler. He wanted to observe F. for a week and then possibly operate.
- F. acquires a new display case for his archeological collection. It is placed behind F.'s desk and smaller oriental antiques are stored in it.

1930 October 8

WPV meeting: General Assembly – F. is re-elected chairman.

1930 October 9

Naum Ischlondsky sends F. his book *The Conditioned Reflex and its Significance in Biology, Medicine, Psychology and Pedagogy* with the dedication "To the great master of psychological thought with sincere admiration and deep reverence/N. Ischlondsky/Paris".

1930 October 10

Hans Pichler removes a small papillary leukoplakia.

1930 October 14

Hans Pichler, assisted by Arwed Berg and Josef Weinmann, removes a small papillary leukoplakia by excision and skin transplantation (Thierschung).

1930 October mid
F. receives Arnold Zweig's little comedy Laubheu und keine Bleibe. He reads it and finds it "not at all funny" (F. to Arnold Zweig, 22.10.1930).

1930 October 16
F. has severe pain and spoils his stomach by taking Veramon and Pantopon and vomits.

1930 October 17
- F. has a fever, probably as an after-effect of the operation. Pneumonia develops and lasts for almost two weeks. F. asks Hans Pichler to remove the prosthesis. Pichler agrees but puts it back in later.
- William Bullitt visits F. in connection with their planned joint work on Woodrow Wilson. He stays for at least two weeks.

1930 October 18
Hans Pichler sends the histological findings of a small piece of tissue to Max Schur. He finds no evidence of a malignant process in the examined sections.

1930 October 31
F. leaves the flat for a walk for the first time since his pneumonia.

1930 October end
Sándor Ferenczi visits F.

1930 November
- F. receives the Italian translation of *Totem und Tabu (Totem e tabu) from* Edoardo Weiss with the dedication *"Meinem hochverehrten Lehrer/Herrn Prof. Dr. Sigmund Freud/in Ergebenheit/ Dr Edoardo Weiss".*
- F. receives from Hanns Sachs his book *Bubi. Die Lebensgeschichte des Caligula* with the dedication "Herrn Prof. Freud/in dauernder Dankbarkeit./H. S".

1930 November 2
F. smokes a first cigar after the operation and pneumonia.

1930 November 5
F. acquires the missing fragment of the Roman sarcophagus lid, of which he had already received a fragment from Ludwig Pollak in August.

1930 November 6
F. notes: "Conclusively passed over for Nobel Prize". This probably refers to the fact that he was not nominated for the Nobel Prize in 1930. Between 1915 and 1938, F. was nominated by a total of 32 people – always for medicine, only in 1936 by Romain Rolland for literature.

1930 November 9
Sándor Ferenczi visits F.

1930 November 11
Alexandre Hérenger sends F. a manuscript in which he compares F. and Goethe. It is published six months later under the title "Goethe und Freud" in the *Psychoanalytischen Bewegung*.

1930 November 15
F. receives the volume *Ten Years of the Berlin Psychoanalytic Institute, for* which he had written a preface.

1930 November 20
F. receives the fragments of the Roman sarcophagus mounted on a wooden base were. He placed the piece on the bookshelf in the treatment room facing the window.

1930 November 25
F. attends one of Yvette Guilbert's recitals in the middle concert hall. After the concert, he sends her flowers to the hotel.

1930 November 29–30
Max Eitingon is in Vienna. The conversations with F. include Eitingon's future as president of the International Psychoanalytical Association and his relations with the members of the Berlin Psychoanalytical Society.

1930 November 30
F. visits Yvette Guilbert at her hotel.

1930 December 3
The Swiss psychologist and psychoanalyst Gustav Graber sends F. his book *Zeugung, Geburt und Tod – Werden und Vergehen im Mythus und in der Vorstellung des Kindes* with the dedication "In Verehrung und Dankbarkeit/überreicht vom/Verfasser/Stuttgart".

1930 December 4
F. carries the feeling that he is finished with his contribution to the book on Woodrow Wilson on which he is working together with William Bullitt.

1930 before December 8
F. receives from the national economist Eugen Schwiedland his paper "Zur Krise des Abendlandes".

1930 December 11
– Edoardo Weiss visits F.
– Informal meeting of the WPV at Berggasse 19.

1930 December 12
William Bullitt has a long argument with F. over a passage on the "death drive" in their joint book on Woodrow Wilson.

1930 December 13–14
Anna goes to Budapest to give a lecture to the Hungarian Psychoanalytical Association.

1930 December 14
A statement by F. on the expert opinions in the appeal proceedings against Philip Halsmann, who had been accused of killing his father, is published in the *Neue Freie Presse*. Halsmann later became famous for his photographs of Albert Einstein, Fernandel, Salvador Dali and Richard Nixon.

1930 December 17

F. visits Max Pollak, to whom he had promised that he would be allowed to draw his "last likeness, which one is wont to make of a departing man" (F. to Max Pollak, 6.9.1930).

1930 Christmas

– Richard Coudenhove-Kalergi sends F. his book *Los vom Materialismus!* with the dedication "Dr. Siegmund Freud in Verehrung herzlichst R N Coudenhove-Kalergi".
– René Laforgue sends F. his book *Devant la barrière de la névrose. Etude psychanalytique sur la névrose de Charles Baudelaire* with the dedication "Herrn Professor Freud/mit dem Ausdrucke meiner Dankbarkeit/Laforgue".

1931

F. supports the nomination of Richard Coudenhove-Kalergi for the Nobel Peace Prize in 1931.

Books received:

- René Allendy sends F. his book *La psychanalyse* with the dedication "A M. le Prof. Sigmund Freud En hommage de profonde vénération R Allendy".
- Siegfried Bernfeld gives F. his book *Trieb und Tradition im Jugendalter* with the dedication "Herrn Professor Freud in Verehrung und Dankbarkeit der Verfasser".
- Eva Clark sends F. her book *Hidden allusions in Shakespeare's plays* with the dedication "To Prof: Dr: Freud, from the Author, Eva Turner Clark". Margaret and Smiley Blanton also give F. this book with the dedication "To Professor Freud With affectionate regards Margaret & Smiley".
- Josef Friedjung gives F. his book *Die Fehlerziehung in der Pathologie des Kindes* with the dedication "Herrn Prof. Freud in Verehrung u. Dankbarkeit/der Verf".
- Ernest Jones sends F. his book *On the nightmare* with the dedication "To Professor Freud/ With the kindest regards/from/Ernest Jones".
- Arthur Ramos, Brazilian psychoanalyst, sends F. his book *Estudos de psychanalyse* with the dedication "Ao Professor S. Freud,/modestissima homenagem do/ultimo dos seus discipulos/ Arthur Ramos".
- Harald Schultz-Hencke sends F. his book *Schicksal und Neurose* with the dedication "In dankbarer Verehrung/vom Verfasser überreicht".
- Susan Isaacs, English educational psychologist and psychoanalyst, sends F. her book *Contribution à la psychologie sociale des jeunes enfants* with the dedication "With the author's gratitude".
- René Laforgue sends F. his book *L'échec de Baudelaire. Etude psychanalytique sur la névrose de Charles Baudelaire* with the dedication "A mon vénéré maître/le Dr. Freud/le témoignage de ma reconnaisance/Laforgue".

1931 beginning
F. works on his writings "Über libidinöse Typen" and "Über die weibliche Sexualität".

1931 January 8–10
Son Ernst and daughter-in-law Lucie are visiting Vienna. F. gives Lucie a necklace similar to those he had given Martha and Anna.

1931 January 10
Jofi gets a puppy, he is called Tatoun.

1931 January 12
F. is the first German-speaking scientist after Rudolf Virchow to receive an invitation from the University of London to give the Huxley Lecture. However, F. declines for health reasons.

1931 January 14–15
F. has acute periostitis with severe pain.

1931 January 17
Anna is in Prague, presumably to give a lecture to a Prague student group.

1931 January 18
Adrien Turel, Swiss writer, sends F. his book *The Conquest of the Beyond.*

1931 January 19
Marie Bonaparte meets in Vienna to continue her analysis. She stays until March mid.

1931 January 20
F. begins an X-ray treatment at Karl Presser, an associate of Guido Holzknecht, which extends over 20 sessions.

1931 at January 21
Most members of F.'s family are suffering from the effects of flu.

1931 January 22
– F. is elected Deputy Honorary President of the "International and Spanish Speaking Association of Physicians, Dentists and Pharmacists".
– F. sends a short assessment of Siegfried Bernfeld in a letter of recommendation in which he calls Bernfeld "perhaps the strongest head among my pupils and followers" (F. to Rudolf Olden, 22.1.1931).

1931 January 26
F. agrees, at the request of Siegmund Leverie, that a league of Viennese high school graduates will include his name in its honorary presidium.

1931 January 29
Theodor Reik sends F. his book *Gebetmantel und Gebetriemen der Juden. Ein psychoanalytischer Beitrag zur hebräischen Archäologie* with the dedication *"Meinem verehrten Lehrer in alter/Anhänglichkeit/Reik"*.

1931 February 3
Hans Pichler discovers a wart-like elevation at the surgical site.

1931 February 4
F. buys a Corinthian vase from Otto Fröhlich, one of the antique dealers with whom F. had been in contact since the mid-1920s. It could be the painted alabaster vessel for oil or perfume from the 6th century BC, on which a winged "ruler of the animals" is depicted.

1931 February 7
Hans Pichler removes a wart-like papilloma from F. Anton Bleichsteiner was the assistant. Max Schur and Josef Weinmann were also present. Due to edema around the wound, F. cannot open his mouth well or chew afterward.

1931 February 9
Death of Mathilde Breuer, wife of his former mentor and friend Josef Breuer.

1931 February 11
– F. suffers from a short-term lockjaw.
– F. receives Stefan Zweig's book *Die Heilung durch den Geist* from the Insel publishing house in Leipzig on his instructions.

1931 February 13
F. can hardly stand the pain caused by the prosthesis. Hans Pichler persuades him to leave the prosthesis in, because otherwise it will cause more and more discomfort, which finally succeeds.

1931 February 14
F. received a request from Werner Richter, Ministerialdirektor and head of the Higher Education Department in the Prussian Ministry for Science, Art and National Education, to comment "in detail on [Bernfeld's] scientific achievements" (F. to Bernfeld, 14.2.1931). Bernfeld had applied for a lectureship in psychology or psychoanalytical pedagogy at the University of Berlin. F. sends his expert opinion on February 20.

1931 February 16
– F. resumes work after the operation on February 7.
– Sándor Lorand, Hungarian psychoanalyst from New York, sends F. his book *The morbid personality* with the dedication *"*With respect/Sándor Lorand/New York".

1931 February 20
F. had sent an expert opinion on Siegfried Bernfeld to Oswald Richter, head of department in the Berlin Ministry for Science, Art and Education.

1931 before February 27
Rudolf Lipschitz, a doctor from Berlin, sends F. a manuscript entitled "God created man in His own image". F.'s reaction is "I lack one basic condition to go along with you. I have no faith in the authenticity of mediumistic phenomena" (F. to Lipschitz, 26.2.1931).

1931 February 27
Informal meeting of the WPV at Berggasse 19. Siegfried Bernfeld gives a lecture.

1931 February 28–29
Max Eitingon visits F.

1931 February end
F. writes down the first draft of his work "Über die weibliche Sexualität".

1931 March 20
F. becomes an honorary member of the Society of Physicians in Vienna and sends a letter of thanks.

1931 Spring
The Academic Association of Jewish Physicians decides to offer F. the honorary presidency.

1931 March 27
Informal meeting of the WPV at Berggasse 19. Sándor Radó gives a lecture.

1931 April 3
F. rents a villa in Pötzleinsdorf for the summer.

1931 April 12
F.'s grandson Ernst (son of daughter Sophie) leaves Vienna because he cannot take the Matura at the Burlingham-Rosenfeld School in Hietzing. He moves to Berlin and moves into the Scharfenberg school farm on an island in Lake Tegel.

1931 before April 14
Max Schur discovers a new lesion in F.'s oral cavity.

1931 April 14
Hans Pichler diagnoses a rapidly growing tumor and, after consultation with Guido Holzknecht, considers an operation necessary. F. is against it – he has had enough operations. But Holzknecht convinces him with the argument that he himself has already had 25 operations.

1931 April 15
Adolf Storfer visits F.

1931 April mid
Max Schur suggests asking the director of the Curie Institute in Paris Claudius Regaud to attend the consultation in Vienna. Rigaud, however, refuses and recommends against radium treatment as long as the tissue is not malignant.

1931 April 20
Guido Holzknecht is against irradiation and in favor of excision including the somewhat altered transplanted surface of the surrounding area.

22 April
Hans Pichler performs another excision and a skin transplantation.

1931 April 23–May 5
Stay at the Auersperg Sanatorium

1931 April 23

Surgical removal of the tumor tissue by Pichler. Assistants are Alexander Berg and Josef Weinmann; Max Schur and Ruth Mack Brunswick were also present. The prosthesis is refitted. F. is still somewhat dazed in the evening.

1931 April 24

The histological findings by Jakob Erdheim show that the removed tumor tissue is precancerous and that nicotine plays a major role in the etiology.

1931 April 26

F. has two severe attacks of pain; otherwise, he feels much better and no longer has a temperature.

1931 April 30

Post-operatively, a pulmonary complication is diagnosed but responds well to treatment.

1931 May 5

F. is dismissed.

1931 May
- Charles Baudouin sends F. his book *Mobilisation de l'énergie* with the dedication "Au maître Sigm. Freud ce livre qui lui doit le meilleur de sa substance avec mon souvenir respectueux et dévoué Baudouin".
- René Guyon sends F. his *Essai de psychologie matérialiste* with the dedication "Au professeur S. Freud, hommage de respect/R. Guyon".

1931 after May 5

Marianne Kris, the daughter of F.'s friend Oskar Rie, begins an analysis with F.

1931 May 6

- WPV festive session to celebrate F's 75th birthday. Paul Federn gives the welcome and introduction, and Sándor Ferenczi gives the festive lecture on "Die Kinderanalyse beim Erwachsenen" ("Child Analysis in Adults").
- F. receives a letter of congratulations from the Society of Physicians (signed by Julius von Wagner-Jauregg, among others) on his 75th birthday.
- Adolf Grimme, Carl Heinrich Becker's successor as Minister of Culture in Prussia, congratulates F. on his 75th birthday. In a letter of thanks, F. writes that he "enjoys […] the perception that my work is having an effect" (F. to Grimme, 15.5.1931).
- Ferenczi visits F. for two minutes, and F. had canceled all other visitors.

Gifts:

- A Vishnu statute, two copies of a congratulatory address printed in Sanskrit on silk, three copies of the English translation of the address and three copies of the minutes of the meeting of the Indian Psychoanalytic Association on the occasion of its meeting on F.'s 75th birthday (from the Indian Psychoanalytic Association).
- A Greek vase from the 4th century BCE with a representation of Dionysus. It is the same vase in which F.'s ashes will be interred at Golder's Green Crematorium on 1939 September 26 (by Marie Bonaparte).
- Homer's *Ilias* with the dedication "Am 75. Geburtstag/gedenkt Ihrer/in steter Verehrung!/ Schaeffer/Rimsting a. Chiemsee" (by Albrecht Schaeffer, who translated the text).
- A somewhat 100-page open letter entitled "My thanks to Freud" (by Lou Andreas-Salomé). The text is later published in the Internationale Psychoanalytische Verlag.

1931 May 11

F. resumes work after his operation, for the time being only one hour in the morning and one hour in the afternoon.

1931 May 14

F.'s son Oliver is visiting.

1931 after May 17

Arnold Groeneveld, a Dutch doctor, sends F. his lecture *Das Problem der Aggressivität* with the dedication "Hochachtungsvoll,/ergebenst vom Verfasser".

1931 May 31

- Death of Edith Rischawy, the niece of F.'s son-in-law Robert Hollitscher and friend of F.'s daughter Anna.
- Ernst Steinmann, German art historian, sends F. his book *Michelangelo im Spiegel seiner Zeit* with the dedication "Rom im Mai 1931/Sigmund Freud/dem grossen Forscher/verehrungsvoll und dankbar/zugeeignet von/Ernst Steinmann".

1931 June 1–September 26
Summer stay in Pötzleinsdorf

F. and his family spend the summer in Pötzleinsdorf. They live in a late Baroque country house at Khevenhüllerstr. 6, which originally belonged to Konrad Mautner. During the revolution of 1848, prominent political refugees hid here. The park is divided by a fence for the dogs Wolf and Jofi.

1931 June 1

Relocation from Berggasse to Pötzleinsdorf.

1931 June 2

Eduard Hitschmann gives a lecture to the B'nai B'rith on the occasion of Sigmund Freud's 75th birthday.

1931 June 3

Funeral of Edith Rischawy.

1931 June 6

Otto Fleisch, brother of F.'s friend and mentor Ernst Fleischl, visits F.

1931 June 13–15

Max Eitingon visits F.

1931 June 20–23

F.'s son Ernst comes to visit.

1931 Summer

F. is appointed to the honorary board of the League for Working Palestine in Austria, founded at the end of 1928.

1931 before June 25

F. receives from Immanuel Velikovsky his paper "Über die Energetik der Psyche und die physikalische Existenz der Gedankenwelt".

1931 June 28

– F. meets with Adolf Storfer. Presumably it was also about his position in the publishing house.
– Otto Fleischl has joined the tarot at F.

1931 before June 30

Georg Fuchs, German writer, sends F. his book *Wir Zuchthäusler. Erinnerungen des Zellengefangenen Nr 2911* and asks him to intercede for the book. F. finds the book "poignant, beautiful, clever and good", but declines to intercede because he "has a low opinion of today's cultural mankind" and believes that the poor treatment of prisoners is "entirely in keeping with our culture" (F. to Georg Fuchs, June 1931).

1931 July

– Sophie Morgenstern sends F. her book *La psychanalyse infantile et son rôle dans l'hygiène mentale* with the dedication *"Mit freundlichsten Grüssen/die Verfasserin"*.
– F. gets from Theodor Lessing his book *Der jüdische Selbsthass* with the dedication "Prof. Dr. Sigmund Freud verehrungsvoll übersendet von seinem Gegner Th. Lg.".

1931 July 14

The sculptor František Juran, who comes from F.'s birthplace, comes to Pötzleinsdorf to work on the design of a commemorative plaque for F.'s birthplace in Freiberg (Příbor), which is to be unveiled on October 25.

1931 July mid

F. sister Mitzi is visiting Vienna.
1931 July 19
Death of Johanna Rie, the sister-in-law of F.'s friend Oskar Rie.

1931 July 23

– F. is on a condolence visit to Alfred Rie, whose wife Johanna had died four days earlier.
– Johannes van der Hoop, co-founder of the Dutch Association for Psychotherapy, visits F.

1931 July 24

– The sculptor Oskar Némon begins work on three busts of F., in stone, wood and bronze. He had received the commission for this through Paul Federn, who had Elisa Gluck, an aunt of Oskar Némon, as a patient. The bust was intended as a belated gift for F.'s 75th birthday. Némon had made a bust from photographs of F. in the spring, which Federn considered unsuccessful.
– F. acquires the Egyptian mummy portrait of a young bearded man from the 4th century. It originally came from the collection of the carpet dealer Theodor Graf. F. has it hung above his armchair next to the couch.
– F.'s brother Alexander and his niece Lilly (daughter of sister Mitzi) are visiting in the evening.

1931 July 27

Death of Auguste Forel. F. had met the Swiss psychiatrist for the first time in July 1889 at his patient Fanny Moser's home in Schloss Au on Lake Zurich and had discussed his book *Der Hypnotismus* in the same year. F. learns of his death one day later.

1931 July 31

The well-known oral surgeon Varaztad Kazanjian from Harvard University comes to Vienna for a day and a half at the instigation of Ruth Mack Brunswick to try to improve F.'s prosthesis.

1931 August

An appeal signed by F. of the Bund der sozialistischen Freidenker (League of Socialist Freethinkers) for "Menschlichkeit und Frieden" ("Humanity and Peace") is published in the journal *Der sozialistische Freidenker,* the organ of the Bund der sozialistischen Freidenker founded in Leipzig in 1926.

1931 August

Marie Bonaparte comes to Vienna.

1931 August 1

Varaztad Kazanjian has finished a new prosthesis, and F. is very satisfied with it for the time being, also because it is smaller and lighter than the old one. Kazanjian leaves Vienna, convinced that he has finished his work.

1931 August 3

Irmarita Putnam, the wife of Tracey Putnam, a nephew of James Putnam, begins an analysis with F. It lasts until 1932 January.

1931 August 6

Ruth Mack Brunswick phones Kazanjian and asks him to come back to Vienna, as F. is not satisfied with the prosthesis. Kazanjian calls Hans Pichler and asks him to take over further work on the prosthesis. Marie Bonaparte then goes to Paris to bring Kazanjian back to Vienna. She offers him $6000[55] for his loss of earnings in America. In the end, however, F. pays the treatment costs.

1931 August 7

F. consults the laryngologist Conrad Stein about nosebleeds.

1931 August 10

Marie Bonaparte arrives in Vienna with Varaztad Kazanjian, his wife and daughter. Kazanjian now treats F. partly in Hans Pichler's surgery and makes in Josef Weinmann's lab two more prostheses out of materials that remain soft; with them, F. can speak better but cannot smoke and he always bites his tongue.

1931 August 25

The psychoanalytic sanatorium Tegel ceases operations for economic reasons.

1931 August 29

Varaztad Kazanjian leaves Vienna.

1931 August 31

Minna has an accident on the road.

1931 September

– Charles Baudouin sends F. his book *L'âme enfantine et la psychanalyse* with the dedication "Au Prof. Sigm. Freud, ces quelques pas nouveaux dans la route qu'il nous a ouverte, avec ma respectueuse gratitude Baudouin".
– Julia Deming, American psychoanalyst, begins an analysis with F.

1931 September 1

F.'s friend Oskar Rie suffers a heart attack.

1931 September 7

Franz Alexander visits F. He discusses with him, among other things, the possibilities of founding a psychoanalytic institute in the USA.

1931 September 8

Hans Pichler discovers a new ulcer on the right edge of the tongue, but decides against an operation as it does not seem to be growing.

1931 September 11

Max Eitingon comes to Vienna for three days. Essentially, he and F. discuss the problems of the Internationale Psychoanalytische Verlag.

1931 September 12

Marie Bonaparte leaves Vienna.

1931 September 13

Hermann Nunberg says goodbye to F. as he goes to the USA for a year to give introductory lectures on psychoanalysis at the Mental Hygiene Institute of the University of Pennsylvania.

1931 September 16

Minna goes to Merano for a month's spay stay.

1931 September 17

- Jan van Emden visits F.
- Death of F.'s friend Oskar Rie.

1931 September 18

F. is on a condolence visit to Margarethe Nunberg, the daughter of Oskar Rie.

1931 September 26

Relocation from Pötzleinsdorf back to Berggasse.

1931 September 30
John Rickman visits F.

1931 October
- F.'s son Martin starts working at Internationale Psychoanalytische Verlag.
- Pierre Jouve, French writer and literary critic, sends F. his book *Vagadu* with the dedication "pour Sigmund Freud/à qui l'intelligence et l'art doivent/une si grande reconnaissance./ Pierre Jean Jouve".

1931 October 5
Death of Tatoun, a Chow Chow born in January; he probably died of distemper.

1931 October 6
F. acquires a 19th-century guanyin for his collection. It is a jade figure sitting on a wooden base, representing a Bodhisattva, an Aspirant to future Buddhahood. He also buys a figure from the Tang dynasty, possibly the woman who now stands on F.'s desk.

1931 October 8
- Paul Federn visits F. Presumably they discuss the upcoming celebration of the unveiling of a commemorative plaque at F.'s birthplace in Freiberg, which Federn will attend.
- F. acquires a priestly figure for his collection, perhaps one of the two Buddhist Lohans from the Ming dynasty.

1931 October 12
- F. receives from the sculptor František Juran the plaster cast of the commemorative plaque Juran had made for the celebration on October 25 in Freiberg (Příbor).
- Anna presents her father with an album containing photos from the summer stay at the villa in Pötzleinsdorf. The photos are briefly annotated by Anna, partly in the form of rhymes.

1931 October 15
F. acquires an equestrian figure and a guardian figure for his collection.

1931 October 17
- F.'s son Ernst comes to Vienna, among other things to discuss renovation plans for the recently acquired house in Hochrotherd – about 40km southwest of Vienna – with Anna and Dorothy Burlingham.
- F. has pneumonia, which lasts until November 1.

1931 October 21
Death of Arthur Schnitzler. F. had been in contact with him for decades.

1931 October 22
Albrecht Schaeffer and his wife Olga visit F. He gives Schaeffer a Tanagra figure from his collection.

1931 before October 25
The portrait painter Irene Hölzer-Weinek sends F. three etchings. One of them depicts Victor Adler, and F. buys it.

1931 October 25
A commemorative plaque made by the sculptor František Juran is unveiled at F.'s birthplace in Freiberg. The street where F.'s birthplace is located is renamed "ulica Freudova". Among others, Anna and Martin Freud, Paul Federn and Max Eitingon took part in the celebrations. The local organizer was František Beneš, the director of the District Health Insurance Institute. A male choir sang a composition by Smetana. The ceremonial address was given by the radiologist František Slabihoudek from Ostrava. Afterward, the commemorative plaque was solemnly unveiled and a male choir sang the national anthems of Austria and Czechoslovakia to conclude the ceremony.

1931 October 28–31
Sándor Ferenczi visits F. They try to overcome their increasing estrangement.

1931 October 29
F. can choose one of the three busts commissioned by Paul Federn from Oskar Némon for the WPV. F. decides on the wooden one, "which promises to be a pleasant roommate with its lively and friendly expression" (F. to Paul Federn, 1.11.1931).

1931 October 31
- Death of Guido Holzknecht. He had treated F. with X-rays since the end of 1923. It died as a result of skin cancer caused by the X-rays.
- F. notes: "Nepenthe". Presumably this name for a pitcher plant refers to a bust that F. had received as a gift from the WPV at the end of October.
- Jeanne Lampl-de Groot leaves Vienna.

1931 November 5–6
F. has a severe gastrointestinal disorder, and a colonic spasm even forces him to cancel an analysis lesson.

1931 November 8
F. travels to carries Hochrotherd.

1931 November 10
F. has intestinal problems again.

1931 November 13
F. acquires for his collection an Egyptian wooden figure, which he calls a "camel driver", and a jade piece.

1931 November 19
F. buys pearls and rings, the former for Anna for her birthday.

1931 November 21
- Eugen Bleuler visits F. in the afternoon. On the 19th, he had given a lecture on "Psyche als Lebensfunktion" ("Psyche as a Life Function") at the Academic Association for Medical Psychology; in the evening after the visit to F., he spoke at the Austrian Society for Psychical Research on the "Problem of Parapsychology".
- F.'s son Martin goes to Berlin to prepare the takeover of the Internationale Psychoanalytische Verlag from Adolf Storfer with Max Eitingon.

1931 November 22
F. notes: "Oppenheimer". Possibly this entry refers to an article of Carl Oppenheimer, "Otto Warburg und die Zellatmung" ("Otto Warburg and cell respiration"), which was published on November 13. This article emphasizes the importance of Warburg's theory for understanding malignant tumors. However, the painter Max Oppenheimer could also be meant, who had made an oil painting of F. in 1909.

1931 November 29
The *Neue Freie Presse* publishes a "Vorschlag Freuds zu Winterhilfe" ("Freud's proposal on winter aid)"). The "Winterhilfe" had been founded by the Vienna city council on 1931 October 15. The chairman was Julius Tandler, professor of anatomy at the University of Vienna and head of the welfare office of the city of Vienna.

1931 November 30
F. attends a concert by Yvette Guilbert at the concert hall and sends her flowers to the Bristol Hotel afterward.

1931 December beginning
F. receives his book *Junge Frau von 1914 as* a gift from Arnold Zweig.

1931 December 1
Adolf Storfer hands F. a consignment of Berchtesgaden cigars that Max Eitingon had given him during a visit to Berlin.

1931 December 3
F. gives his daughter Anna pearls for her 36th birthday.

1931 December 4
– F. receives Lou Andreas-Salomé's *My Thanks to Freud, which* had just been published by Internationale Psychoanalytische Verlag.
– Arnold Zweig sends F. his novel *Junge Frau von 1914* with the dedication "Professor Sigmund Freud:/Froh, so weit gekommen/zu sein, grüßt Ihr/immer dankbarer/Arnold Zweig".

1931 December 9
F. receives the ivory statuette of Vishnu, which the Indian Psychoanalytical Society had given him for his 75th birthday. For various reasons, it arrived in Vienna five months late, F. put it on his desk and commented: "The sensation of these days was a delightful ivory statue about 20 cm high of the god Vishnu given by the psa group in Calcutta, which was made with great care after an old stone image from Travancore and came with a fine wooden base with Sanskrit inscription" (F. to Ernst Freud, 13.12.1931).

1931 December 15
F. learns of the death of Gustave Le Bon and suspects that Marie Bonaparte is now also expecting his death and is therefore not writing for some time. Ruth Mack Brunswick confirms F.'s assumption.

1931 December mid
Mark Brunswick hands F. two boxes of Berchtesgaden cigars that Max Eitingon had given him during a visit to Berlin.

1931 December 31
Durval Marcondes sends F. the Portuguese version of the five Lectures *Über Psychoanalyse (Cinco liçoes de psicanalise)* with the dedication "Dear Prof. Freud,/I have the honour to offer you the first copy/of the Portuguese translation of your work 'On Psychoanalysis (Five Lectures)./My pleasure is all the greater as this is the first Portuguese translation of one of your works. Durval Marcondes".

1932

- F. is nominated for the Nobel Prize (Medicine) for the eighth time.
- The Internationale Psychoanalytische Verlag is struggling because of the global economic crisis.
- Suzanne Bernfeld begins an analysis with F. (until 1934). At the very beginning, he sends her to Friedrich Eckstein for tea, who is supposed to give him information about her education and her knowledge of Greek.

Books received:

- Mark Brunswick sends F. Volume 9 of *The Cambridge ancient history*.
- Félicien Challaye, French philosopher, sends F. his book *Nietzsche* with the dedication "Au Maître Sigmund Freud, Respectueux hommage. Félicien Challaye".
- Vincenzo Girone, Italian psychiatrist, sends F. his book *Lampada spenta* with the dedication "L'autore/Dr V. Girone/Orzinuovi/(Brescia)".
- Abraham Kardiner sends F. his book *The bio-analysis of the epileptic reaction* with the dedication "To Professor Dr. Sigmund Freud/with kindest regards/A. Kardiner".
- René Laforgue sends F. his book *Misère de l'homme* with the dedication "Herr Professor S. Freud/With the expression of deep/Gratitude and veneration./His pupil/R. Laforgue".
- Emanuel Loewy sends F. his book *Zur Frage: Monogenismus oder Polygenismus?* with the dedication "Herzlichst grüßend/d. Vf".
- Hermann Nunberg gives F. his book *Allgemeine Neurosenlehre auf psychoanalytischer Grundlage*, for which Freud has written a preface, with the dedication "Herrn Prof. Freud in Dankbarkeit von/seinem treuen Schüler/Hermann Nunberg".
- Ludwig Pollak sends F. his book *Zum hundertsten Todestage Goethes* with the dedication "Herrn Professor F./in wahrer Verehrung/L. P".
- Ioan Popescu sends F. his book *Doctrina lui Freud* with the dedication "To the Master, as a token of/great esteem./Dr Popescu-Sibiu".
- Harald and Kristian Schjelderup give F. their jointly written book *Über drei Haupttypen der religiösen Erlebnisformen und ihre psychologische Grundlage* with the dedication "Herrn Professor Dr. Sigm. Freud/in aufrichtiger Verehrung/von/den Verfassern".
- Stefan Zweig sends F. his book *Marie Antoinette* with the dedication "Professor Siegmund Freud/Der uns menschliches Verstehen/Lernte in Dankbarkeit und Treue Stefan Zweig".
- Stefan Zweig, Alzir Hella and Olivier Bournac give F. Zweig's book *La guérison par l'esprit. Sigmund Freud* with the dedication "Dem grossen Manne/dies kleine Bildnis/in getreuer Verehrung/Stefan Zweig/en témoignage de/respectueuse admiration/Les Editeurs/A Hella Bournac".

1932 January
F. chooses Paul Federn and Eduard Hitschmann as editors for *IZP*, Ernst Kris and Robert Wälder for *Imago*.

1932 January 1
- F. has stomach complaints that last until January mid.
- F. has the feeling that Wilhelm Reich and Otto Fenichel are misusing the psychoanalytic journals "for Bolshevik propaganda […]" (F. to Eitingon, 9.1.1932), and wants to take action against Reich.

– Oskar Pfister sends F. the Polish translation of his book *Psychoanalyse und Pädagogik (Psychanaliza na uslugach wychowania)* with the dedication "Herrn Prof. Dr S. Freud/ein herzlicher Neujahrsgruß/von O. Pfister".

1932 January 9
F. tries a new prosthesis; however, it is very uncomfortable.

1932 January 16–17
Max Eitingon comes to Vienna. One of the issues is the transfer of the publishing business from Adolf Storfer to Martin Freud. Before that, Federn and Jekels had tried to mediate between F. and his son Martin on the one side and Storfer on the other.

1932 January 16
F.'s son Martin takes over the management of Internationale Psychoanalytische Verlag. An application for the deletion of the previous managing director Adolf Storfer and the registration of Martin Freud goes to the Vienna Commercial Court.

1932 January 20
F. and William Bullitt sign an agreement to split the royalties of their planned book on Woodrow Wilson. Bullitt pays F. $2500[56] and receives two thirds of the rights to the manuscript and F. one third. The royalties are to be divided accordingly. F. immediately forwards the $2500 to the IPA.

1932 before January 24
F. rents the villa in Pötzleinsdorf again from May mid.

1932 January 27
F. cannot stand the prosthesis for more than ten minutes.

1932 January 30
To save the IPA, Edith Jackson donates $1000.[57] Abraham Brill collected the same amount and forwarded it to Vienna.

1932 February
F. appeals to the WPV because of the publisher's situation.

1932 February beginning
F. works on the *New Series of Lectures for Introduction to Psychoanalysis*.

1932 February 5
F. acquires a figure of a Chinese polo player from the Tang dynasty for his collection.

1932 February 10
F. writes the preface to *Neue Vorlesungen zur Einführung in die Psychoanalyse,* which he plans for the Internationale Psychoanalytische Verlag.

1932 February 11
The Japanese psychiatrist and follower of psychoanalysis Heisaku Kosawa visits F. (together with Toshio Kurokawa, who translated for him) and gives him a color print of Fujiyama by Kiyoshi Yoshida. F. gives him a letter of recommendation for Paul Federn, but Kosawa eventually begins an analysis with Richard Sterba, as he cannot afford the fee with F. or Federn.

1932 February 19
F. Martin's son achieves a moratorium on Internationale Psychoanalytische Verlag's liabilities to creditors until the summer. This was his first success in restructuring the publishing house as managing director.

1932 February 22
F. and daughter Anna are suffering from an infection with a cold.

1932 March 7
Hans Pichler operates on F. and removes a leukoplakia. There are increasing difficulties in closing the surgical wounds with sutures or a plastic.

1932 March 8
- F. learns of the death of Aristide Briand; he was French Prime Minister several times and Marie Bonaparte's lover between 1913 and 1919.
- Jacob Steil from Karlsruhe sends F. an article from the *Landauer Anzeiger* with the title "Die Psychoanalyse hat abgewirtschaftet" ("Psychoanalysis has failed").

1932 March 13
F. acquires a large Greek kelebe – a vessel for storing drinks or honey – for his collection from the art dealer Otto Fröhlich.

1932 March 17
Thomas Mann visits F. It was the poet's first visit to him. F. writes: "Thomas Mann's visit was very pleasant. He behaved genuinely and at ease, one was immediately familiar with him, and what he said was understandable and sounded like background" (F. to Eitingon, 20.3.1932).

1932 March 19
Géza Róheim sends F. his book *A csurunga népe (The People of Csurunga)* with the dedication "Herr Professor/Sigmund Freud/hochachtungsvoll/gewidmet/vom/Verfasser".

1932 Spring
- Beginning of the writing of the *New Series of Lectures for Introduction to Psychoanalysis*.
- F.'s and William Bullitt's joint book on Woodrow Wilson is finished in outline.

1932 March 23–30
Marie Bonaparte is in Vienna for a week.

1932 March 27–28
F. writes a circular letter to all psychoanalytic societies and important members with the proposal that the Internationale Psychoanalytische Verlag should be formally recognized as an institution by the IPA.

1932 March 28
Franz Günther Stockert, a grandson of Theodor Meynert, visits F.

1932 April 4
Martha goes to Berlin to attend son Ernst's birthday and to see her grandchildren. She stays until April 19.

1932 April 6
Géza Róheim visits F.

1932 before April 8
Irene Hölzer-Weinek sends F. etchings again. F. buys them.

1932 April 14
Smith Ely Jelliffe sends F. his book *Psychopathology of forced movements and the oculogyric crises of lethargic encephalitis* with the dedication "Professor Sigmund Freud,/with sincere regards/Smith Ely Jelliffe".

1932 April 16
F. receives from Edoardo Weiss the *Rivista* italiana di Psicoanalisi *founded by* him and thanks Weiss: "The journal, your Rivista, makes a very respectable impression, both externally and in terms of content. The reviews in it also seem quite appropriate" (F. to Weiss, 24.4.1932).

1932 April 17
F. is in Hochrotherd.

1932 April 19
- F.'s son Martin travels to Leipzig; the Internationale Psychoanalytische Verlag's camp was located there.
- Martha comes back from Berlin.

1932 April 22
Ludwig Binswanger and his daughter Hilde visit F. The day before, Binswanger had given a lecture on "Klinik und existenziale Anthropologie" ("Clinic and Existential Anthropology") at the Academic Association for Medical Psychology.

1932 May 6
F. celebrates his birthday "as a mean weekday" (F. to Eitingon, 8.5.1932): He drives with the dogs to their second home at the Nausch shelter in Kagran, visits Hans Pichler in the afternoon, has four analytical sessions and plays cards in the evening. Among the few visitors was Arnold Marlé, the husband of F.'s niece Lilly. The play "Disraeli" by Louise Mayer and Arthur Rundt had been performed under his direction at the Burgtheater the previous evening. Arnold brought with him a small album depicting Lilly's walk through Goethe's Weimar in photographs she had taken herself. The occasion was the rumor that a bust of F. was to be erected in the Goethe House.

1932 May 8
F. is in Hochrotherd.

1932 May 11
Editorial meeting of the Internationale Psychoanalytische Verlag. F. proposed to move the editorial office of *IZP* and *Imago* to Vienna. Paul Federn and Heinz Hartmann became editors of the *IPZ* alongside Sándor Radó. Ernst Kris and Robert Wälder took over the editorship of *Imago*.

1932 May 14–September 17
Summer stay in Pötzleinsdorf
F. is back in the country house at Khevenhüllerstr. 6, where he is working on the *new series of lectures on the introduction to psychoanalysis, among other things*. Because of his prosthesis, F. goes to Josef Weinmann almost every week.

1932 May 14

Move to Pötzleinsdorf.

1932 May 19

Mary Chadwick sends F. her book *Adolescent girlhood* with the dedication "With best wishes from the Author".

1932 May 31

F. receives the first issue of the newly launched *Psychoanalytic Quarterly.* It was edited by Dorian Feigenbaum, Bertram Lewin, Frankwood Williams and Gregory Zilboorg.

1932 May end

- F.'s sister Mitzi is visiting Vienna.
- F. receives the Italian translation of Stefan Zweig's *Die Heilung durch den Gei*st, which portraits him alongside Franz Anton Mesmer and Mary Baker Eddy. F.'s comment is: "I found myself again very interesting, although not altogether similar" (F. to Ferenczi, 2.6.1932).

1932 June

F. sends the preface to the book on Woodrow Wilson planned by him and William Bullitt to the publisher.

1932 June 15

F. and William Bullitt sign the publishing contract for the book on Woodrow Wilson.

1932 June 16

Leon Steinig, the secretary of the Institut International de Coopération Intellectuelle, an institution of the League of Nations, asked F. on behalf of the League of Nations to enter into a correspondence with Einstein "on a problem from the field of psychoanalysis" (Steinig to F., 16.6.1932). The idea came from Einstein himself, who was thinking of topics such as psychoanalysis and the peace movement, the share of the unconscious in the outbreak of warlike conflicts and the instinct of aggression and war. F. answered immediately, declared his willingness and left the choice of topics to Einstein.

1932 Summer

- Friedrich Tinti offers F. the family Schallaburg near Melk as the headquarters of the psychoanalytical movement. F. refuses, among other things because psychoanalysis is tied to a large city because of the teaching.
- Jacob Bendahan sends F. the May/June issue of the journal *Les anciens* with the dedication "to the honoured Prof Dr Sigmund Freud from Jacob J. Bendahan".

1932 June 23

Hans Pichler discovers two papillomas at the lower edge of F.'s maxillary sinus.

1932 June 24

F.'s son Ernst, daughter-in-law Lucie and grandson Stephan Gabriel are visiting Vienna.

1932 after June 24

The Jungian Edward Bennett visits F and asks him, among other things, how the rifts between him, Jung, Adler and Stekel came about and why there is no longer any contact between them. F. answers briefly: Adler could not have analyzed, he personally did not get on with Stekel and Jung was a great loss.

1932 June 28

– F. notes: "Large horse bought". This probably refers to one of the two Chinese copies of figures from the Tang period.
– Edith Jackson donates again for the publishing house: this time, 2000$.[58]

1932 June 29

F. sends Marie Bonaparte the preface to her book *Edgar Poe, étude psychanalytique.*

1932 before July 10

The philosopher Siegfried Hessing asks F. if he would be willing to contribute to the commemorative publication for the 300th anniversary of the birth of Spinoza. F. declines because he "does not know anything to say that has not already been said by others" (F. to Hessing, 9.7.1932).

1932 July 11

Martha receives the volume *Jacob Bernays* edited by Michael Fraenkel. *Ein Lebensbild in Bildern* with the dedication: "Professor Martha Freud née Bernays in Dankbarkeit und Verehrung überreicht vom Verf.". The volume is dedicated to F., and the preface ends with the words: "The book is dedicated to Professor Freud in a grateful spirit. May it also be worthy to bear his name at the head!"

1932 July 13

F. learns of the death of Mathilde Halberstadt, the mother of F.'s son-in-law Max Halberstadt, who had died on July 11.

1932 July 16

F.'s Chow Chow Jofi comes back from the shelter in Kagran.

1932 July 18

F.'s speech is disturbed again. He has a feeling of swelling and tension. On Pichler's recommendation, he therefore seeks out the ENT doctor Oskar Hirsch, who can relieve him of his discomfort for a time. In gratitude, he gives Hirsch his book *Das Unbehagen in der Kultur* with the dedication "Meinem lieben Professor Dr. Hirsch in Dankbarkeit von seinem Zeitgenossen Freud".

1932 before July 20

F. granted Nicolas Neumann, a Hungarian photographer, translator and journalist living in Paris, an interview that he published on 1932 July 20 in the French magazine *VU* under the pseudonym Nicolas Bandy.

1932 July 20

Franz Alexander visits F. together with Alfred Stern, an influential politician and founder of the Chicago Institute for Psychoanalysis in Chicago, and his wife Marion.

1932 July 26

Celebration of Martha's birthday in Hochrotherd. Marie Bonaparte is among the guests.

1932 July 29

Hans Pichler performs excisions and coking of small papillomas on F.

1932 August beginning

F.'s sister Maria is visiting.

1932 August 1

Leon Steinig visits F. and delivers a letter of Einstein dated July 30, which marks the beginning of the exchange of letters on the subject of "Why War?"

1932 August 10

F. has new complaints, especially when speaking, and Hans Pichler discovers a new granulating protrusion in the size of a peppercorn.

1932 before August 11

F. receives Hermann Keyserling's *South American Mediations.*

1932 August 11

The daily newspaper *Freiheit*, organ of "Communist Party of Germany, Section of the Communist International" publishes an appeal signed by F. for the holding of an "anti-war Congress". The appeal had originally been published by Henri Barbusse and Romain Rolland in the French newspaper *L'Humanité* and sent in a slightly modified form by the Berlin doctor Felix Boenheim to colleagues all over the world. Over 200 people signed Boehnheim's appeal, including F.

1932 August 14

F. acquires a Corinthian pyx from the 5th century BC for his collection; it is a painted container for storing jewelry.

1932 August 15

Jeanne Lampl-de Groot visits F.

1932 August 16

Hans Pichler performs excisions and coking of small papillomas on F. At the outer edge of the maxillary sinus, a wart-like thickened, overhanging edge has formed again. It is destroyed with diathermy.

1932 August 17

F. receives from the American psychologist Joseph Jastrow his book *Freud: His Dream and Sex Theories.* "It is really one of the stupidest and most arrogant pieces of criticism that our Analysis has ever suffered" (F. to Jelliffe, 17.8.1932).

1932 August 21

Sándor Ferenczi, the designated next President of the IPA, decides "after a long agonizing hesitation […] to renounce the presidential candidacy" (Ferenczi to F. 21.8.1932).

1932 August 23–24

Abraham Brill visits F. One topic of conversation was certainly the newly founded psychoanalytic associations in the USA, which resisted Brill's attempts to unite them under one roof.

1932 August 27–30

F.'s son Ernst is visiting Vienna.

1932 August 28

Abraham Brill and Sándor Radó visit F. They tell him about Ferenczi's poor health.

1932 August 31

- F. completed the *New Series of Lectures for Introduction to Psychoanalysis*.
- Kata and Lajos Lévy visit F.

1932 August end

Sándor Ferenczi and Abraham Brill visit F. in Vienna.

1932 September

Edoardo Weiss sends F. his book *Elementi di psicoanalisi,* for which F. has written a preface, with the dedication *"Herrn Prof. Dr. Sigmund Freud/in Ergebenheit/Dr Edoardo Weiss"*.

1932 September 1

Anna travels to Göttingen and visits Lou Andreas-Salomé. She then travels on to the XII. International Psychoanalytical Congress in Wiesbaden.

1932 September 2

Sándor Ferenczi with wife Gisella visit F. Ferenczi reads F. a lecture in which he "made a full regression to aetiological views which I believed 35 years ago and abandoned […]". (F. to Anna, 3.9.1932).

1932 September 4–7

The XII. International Psychoanalytical Congress takes place. F. did not take part.

1932 September 6

F. finishes his reply letter to Einstein on "Why war?"

1932 September 9

F. learns of the death of Christian von Ehrenfels, who had died the previous day and whom he had known personally since 1904.

1932 September 17

Return to Berggasse 19.

1932 September 17

Roger Money-Kyrle sends F. his book *Aspasia. The future of amorality* with the dedication *"To/Prof Freud/from/R Money-Kyrle"*.

1932 September 20

F. receives Richard Flatter's translation of *Shakespeare's Sonnets*. On this occasion, F. rereads the book by the English Shakespeare scholar Gerald Rendall *Shakespeare sonnets and Edward de Vere.*

1932 September 21

The Österreichische Kampfkomitee gegen den Krieg (Austrian Combat Committee against the War), represented by Josef Riese and Sigismund Peller, invite F. to a meeting of the committee for September 23 so that he can "assist the anti-war physicians of Austria […] in organizing the fight against the war with [his] advice" (Edith Jackson to F., 21.9.1932). The invitation was extended because F. had supported the convening of the Amsterdam anti-war Congress. The next day, F. declined for health reasons.

1932 September 25
F. spends a day in Hochrotherd.

1932 September 27
- F.'s sister Anna is in Vienna and stays at the Hotel Imperial. F. visits her there.
- Franz Brücke, a great-grandson of F.'s teacher Ernst Brücke, visits F.

1932 Autumn
André Breton sends F. his book *Les Vases Communicants* with the dedication "A Sigmund Freud avec le désir de concilier son enseignement avec le seul autre qui merite d'être reçu. (Pardon de certaines impertinences qu'il s'expliquera trés facilement). Avec man admiration et man affection sans bornes. André Breton 42 rue Fontaine Paris IXe".

1932 October 2
F. goes with Ruth Mack Brunswick and her husband Mark to Hochrotherd for a day.

1932 October 4
- Hans Pichler diagnoses a somewhat larger area in F.'s oral cavity that is sensitive and has a clearly papillary structure. He considers removal to be absolutely necessary.
- Anna flies to Berlin. There, she gives a lecture at the "Congress for Infant Education" on September 5. The next day, she flies back to Vienna.

1932 October 6
Hans Pichler performs excisions and coking of small papillomas on F.

1932 October 11
Jakob Erdheim diagnoses an extensive inflammation in F., which is a consequence of tobacco abuse. It is very clear to see how the inflammation appears first and, as a consequence, the typical leukoplakia.

1932 October 12
WPV meeting: F. is re-elected chairman.

1932 October mid
- Stefan Zweig sends F. his book *Marie Antoinette* with the dedication "Professor Siegmund Freud/ Der uns menschliches Verstehen/ lernte in Dankbarkeit und Treue Stefan Zweig".
- Viktor von Weizsäcker sends F. the manuscript of "an interesting analysis of a neurosis mixed with organic disease" (F. to Eitingon, 20.10.1932), which F. finds so good that he recommends its publication in the *IZP*.

1932 October 29
Death of Alfred. Oskar Rie's brother had been hit by a lorry on the Schottenring the previous day and succumbed to his injuries that night. F. learns of his death the next day.

1932 November
Robert Neumann, Austrian writer and publicist, sends F. his book *Unter falscher Flagge. Ein Lesebuch der deutschen Sprache für Fortgeschrittene* with the dedication "Herrn Professor/ Sigmund Freud/ergebenst/Neumann".

1932 November beginning
F. has a cold with an infection of the upper airways and an inflammation of the middle ear. Max Schur examines him and F. shows him pictures of Crete and Rhodes and tells him about daydreams of the sunny Mediterranean and Greek temples in Sicily.

1932 before November 3
F. reads the book by the Viennese doctor Hans Robicsek *Language, Man and Myth. Einführung in die Differentialanalyse der Sprache* and shares his decidedly critical assessment with the author.

1932 November 3
F. seeks the ear, nose and throat specialist Erich Ruttin for his middle ear infection. Ruttin punctures it so that the accumulated fluid can drain off.

1932 before November 21
The Austrian writer and translator Marie Herzfeld sends F. her essay "Über ein Skizzenblatt Leonardos als Beitrag zur Charakterdeutung des Meisters" ("About a sketch by Leonardo as a contribution to the character interpretation of the master").

1932 November mid
F. has a very unpleasant severe flu with right-sided otitis, but strangely enough it was completely painless.

1932 November 24
Arnold Zweig sends F. his book *De Vriendt kehrt heim* with the dedication "Dieses erste gebundene Exemplar des de Vriendt in Ihre Hände, Vater Freud. Arnold Zweig".

1932 before November 27
F.'s *New Series of Lectures for Introduction to Psychoanalysis* is published. The official year of publication was 1933.

1932 November 27
– F. sends Arnold Zweig the volume edited by Michael Fraenkel, *Jacob Bernays, Ein Lebensbild in Briefen*. Jacob Bernays was an uncle of Martha.
– Heisaku Kosawa pays a farewell visit to F. Kosawa gives him a copy of the recently published *New Lectures on Introduction to Psychoanalysis* for his teacher Kiyoyasu Marui.

1932 November 30
Yvette Guilbert performs "Chansons von ehemals" ("Chansons of yesteryear") in the Vienna concert hall. Afterward, F. visits her in the hotel.

1932 December
– Pierre Jouve *sends* F. his book *Histoires sanglantes* with the dedication "Pour le Professeur Sigmund Freud ces (HISTOIRES SANGLANTES) avec l'hommage que la poésie doit à son génie. Pierre Jean Jouve".
– F. proposes Mosche Wulff for a chair of psychoanalysis to be established at the University of Jerusalem.

1932 December 8
Hans Pichler performs excisions and boils of small papillomas. Jakob Erdheim's finding is leukoplakia.

1932 December 12
– F. sends Hermann Schröder a copy of his *Neue Folge der Vorlesungen zur Einführung in die Psychoanalyse* with the dedication "Dem unvergessenen, gütigen Helfer/Prof. H. Schröder mit herzlichsten Grüßen d. Verf.".
– Kemal Cenap sends F. his writing *Terminologie internationale en turc apre`s l'adoption de l'alphabet latin* with the dedication "Herrn Prof. S. Freud mit bestem Gruß Kemal Cenap".

1932 December 12–13
William Bullitt is in Vienna for two days and works with F. on the Wilson book.

1932 December mid
F. grants the Austro-Hungarian journalist János Békessy an interview. It appeared on December 25 under the title "Berggasse 19: Professor Freud and the Afterlife" in the Budapest newspaper *Magyar Hírlap*. The interviewer signed with the pseudonym Hans Habe.

1932 December 18
F. receives Hilda Doolittle's book *Palimpsest* from an "American friend" (F. to Hilda Doolittle, 18.12.1932). Hilda Doolittle was the pseudonym of the American writer Hilda Aldington and became known by the initials "H. D.".

1932 December 19
Ernest Jones informs the IPA board – and thus also F. and Anna – of the danger that Isidor Sadger's written memoirs of F. could be published in England.

1932 December 28
F. issues a certificate for Franz Alexander.

1933

- F. is nominated for the Nobel Prize (Medicine) for the ninth time.
- F. gives Eva Rosenfeld the *Neuen Folge der Vorlesungen zur Einführung in die Psychoanalyse* with the dedication "Seiner lieben Eva d. Verf.".
- F. gives an employee of the Viennese judge Franz Ulrich a signed copy ("Sigm. Freud/1933") of each of the following books: *Zur Psychopathologie des Alltagslebens, Vorlesungen zur Einführung in* die *Psychoanalyse* and *Neue Folge der Vorlesungen zur Einführung in die Psychoanalyse.*

Received books and offprints:

- Ludwig Binswanger sends F. his book *Über Ideenflucht* with the dedication "Mit herzlichsten Grüssen v Verf.".
- Eva Clark sends F. her book *The satirical comedy* with the dedication "To Prof: Dr: Freud, from the author. Eva Turner Clark".
- Havelock Ellis sends F. his book *Psychology of sex* with the dedication "To Professor F./with affectionate/greetings from/Havelock Ellis".
- Poul Faergeman, Danish psychoanalyst, sends F. his book *Freud i moderne litteratur* with the dedication "Herrn Professor S. Freud/von P. F".
- Paul Federn gives F. an offprint of his lecture "Verhalten des Hausarztes gegenüber den Neurosen" with the dedication "Herrn Prof Dr S. Freud/in Ehrerbietung d Verf." and the offprint of his lecture "Zirkuläre Freundschaftsbeziehungen" with the dedication "Herrn Prof Dr S. F./in Ehrerbietung und Ergebenheit/d Verf".
- Yrjö Kulovesi, Finnish doctor and psychoanalyst, sends F. his book *Psykoanalyysi* with the dedication "Herrn Professor Freud/dankbar/der Verf".
- Kostis Meranaios, Greek writer, journalist and translator, sends F. his Greek translation of *Das Ich und das Es* (Τό έγώ καϊ τό έκεϊνο) with the dedication "To Dr Sigmund Freud. A humble offering of my boundless admiration".
- Julio Porto-Carrero sends F. his book *Sexo e cultura* with the dedication "A M. le professeur/ Dr. Sigmund Freud/en respectueux hommage./J. Porto-Carrero" and the book *A psicologia profunda ou psicanálise* with the dedication "A mon cher Maître/M. le prof. Sigmund Freud/ en lui priant pardon de/si peu de nouvelles./J Porto-Carrero".
- Silvio Tissi sends F. his book *Al microscopio psicanalitico. Pirandello, Ibsen, Shakespeare, Tolstoy, Shaw, Borguet, Gide* with the dedication "Omaggio al Freud".
- Rebecca West, British writer and journalist, sends F. her book *St. Augustine* with the dedication "To Professor Freud/With deep gratitude/from Rebecca West".
- Arnold Zweig sends F. his volume of stories *Mädchen und Frauen* with the dedication "Dieses ist der zweite Band/Nimm auch ihn in deine/Hand/Und verweile mit Vergnügen/in den Bildern, Worten, Lügen/A. Z".
- Stefan Zweig sends F. his book *Freud* with the dedication "Dem verehrten Meister/im Jahr der Verbrennung/sein getreuer/Stefan Zweig".

1933 January beginning
The 10,000 Reichsmark with which the Goethe Prize was endowed, which F. had received in 1930, had been used up. F. wrote: "[…] I find it saddening that the Goethe Prize did not last longer than 2½ years" (F. to Ernst Freud, 15.1.1933).

1933 January 4
The Gross-Schweinbarth doctor Richard May, who had described the case of a patient to F. at the end of 1932, visits F. Perhaps May wanted to discuss the publication of the case with F.

1933 January 6
Siegfried Bernfeld visits F.

1933 January 5
F. learns of the death of Gabriel Anton. F. had known him since his time at the General Hospital. He learns of his death two days later.

1933 January 7
Suzanne Bernfeld visits F.

1933 January 18
F. learns of the death of Louis Comfort Tiffanys, the father of Dorothy Burlingham, the partner of daughter Anna. He had died the day before.

1933 before January 21
F. receives a paper by the lawyer Hans Moser from the editor of the "Rundbriefe der deutschen Jugendbünde in Amerika" Gilbert Perleberg, in which the author assigns the problem of conscience a central position in psychoanalysis. F. rejects this as inaccurate.

1933 January 27
Max Eitingon visits, among other things to discuss with F. the political situation in Germany and the possibilities for the further work of the Berlin Psychoanalytic Institute. They also discuss the possibility of Sadger's memoirs of F. being published in England. F. wants to inform the WPV Executive Committee about this.

1933 January 31
– F. notes: "Hitler Reich Chancellor". The Viennese newspapers had reported that Hindenburg had appointed Adolf Hitler as Reich Chancellor on January 30.
– F.'s Chow Chow Jofi comes back from the shelter in Kagran.

1933 January end
William Bullitt visits F. for two days. He is "[…] the only American who understands something about Europe and wants to do something for Europe" (F. to Lampl-de Groot, 17.2.1933).

1933 February beginning
– The lawyer Rudolf Bienenfeld visits F. and presents him with his book *Die Haftungen ohne Verschulden.*
– Irene Hölzer-Weinek discusses the design of an ex-libris with Minna and would like to paint F.'s portrait, but he refuses. However, Hölzer-Weinek makes sketches of F. at home and then a portrait etching, which she sends to F. and which he likes.

1933 February 5
F. sends a first bundle of letters he had received from Karl Abraham to Max Eitingon, who had asked for them. He also agrees that Abraham's widow may allow him to see F.'s letters to Abraham.

1933 February 12
Pierce Clark, American psychiatrist and psychoanalyst, sends F. his book *Lincoln. A psychobiography* with the dedication "To Sigmund Freud, With very best wishes, L. Pierce Clark".

1933 February 15
– Fernando de Allende Navarro, Peruvian psychiatrist, sends F. his book *El valor de la psicoanálisis en policlínica. Contribución a la psicología clinica.* with the dedication "A mon Maître Monsieur le Prof. Sigmund Freud; très respectueusement. F De Allende Navarro Sgo, Chili".
– F. complains again about swelling and some pressure when inserting the prosthesis.

1933 February mid
F. reads *Southwind* by the Scottish writer Norman Douglas.

1933 February 17
F. acquires for his collection the iron bust of a Bodhisattva, a companion of Buddha.

1933 February 21
F. receives from Ladislav Kratochvíl his Czech translation of *Eine Kindheitserinnerung des Leonardo da Vinci (Vzpomínka z dĕetství Leonardo da Vinci)* with the dedication "Dem Urheber der Psychoanalyse/Lad. Kratochvíl".

1933 February 28
– After the Reichstag fire on the night of February 27–28, F. notes: "Berlin parliament on fire".
– F. feels neglected as a patient and urges Hans Pichler to treat him more often.

1933 March 1
Hilda Doolittle begins an analysis with F. It lasts until June 15 and from 1934 October until December 1.

1933 March 13
F. acquires for his collection an Egyptian fabric painting, presumably pieces of linen from Egyptian mummies from the Ptolemaic-Roman period (100 BCE–200 CE).

1933 March mid
– The WPV receives a donation from Winifred Ellerman (Bryher).
– René Spitz visits F. and reports to him on the situation of the analysts in Prague.

1933 March 17
F. acquires for his collection a glazed Chinese ceramic of a seated woman.

1933 March 21
F. explains to Max Eitingon three ways of dealing with the Berlin Institute under the conditions of National Socialism.

1933 March 22
F.'s correspondence with Albert Einstein on the question "Why war?" is published in Paris in three languages under the title *Warum Krieg? Pourquoi la guerre? Why War?* in an edition of 2000 copies per language.

1933 March 27
- Lajos Lévy reports to F. about Ferenczi's state of health.
- F.'s Chow Chow gets injured.

1933 March 29
- Mariano Barilari, Argentinian doctor from Buenos Aires, visits F. He was interested in psychosomatics and prepared a publication on the subject (*Contribucion a la medicina psiquica).*
- Ferenczi urgently advises F. to leave Austria.

1933 March 31
Winifred Ellerman (Bryher) visits F. Among other things, it is about the fee of her friend Hilda Doolittle, which Ellerman paid.

1933 April
Johannes van der Leeuw, General Secretary of the Dutch Theosophical Society and founder of the Association of Practical Idealists, begins an analysis with F. He was an enthusiastic pilot, was called "The Flying Dutchman", and F. treated him because he flew riskily and was constantly in danger of flying too high or too fast.

1933 April 2
F.'s grandson Ernst arrives in Vienna. He had just been able to leave Berlin for Austria, accompanied by Eva Rosenfeld.

1933 April 3
- F.'s Chow Chow Jofi has an offspring. The two puppies, which were born after a complicated birth, are named Fo and Tatoun.
- The Scottish writer Norman Douglas visits F. He had come to Vienna with his girlfriend Winifred Ellerman (Bryher).

1933 after April 3
F. reads Norman Douglas's travelogue *Old Calabria,* which Douglas had presumably given him on his visit.

1933 April 4
F. concludes a contract with the publisher W. W. Norton for an American edition of the *New Series of Lectures for Introduction to Psychoanalysis.*

1933 April 6
F. language is disturbed, and he is going through a worst week.

1933 April 8
F.'s son Oliver and his wife Henny come to Vienna to talk to his father about his future prospects. Oliver has been unemployed for a year and is dependent on F.'s financial support.

1933 April 10
F. receives Abraham Roback's book *Jewish Self-consciousness and its treatment* with the dedication "To Pierre Janet – Dean of psychiatrists/With the high esteem of /A A Roback". Roback had obviously sent F. a copy intended for Pierre Janet.

1933 April 12
Norman Douglas sends F. his writing *Paneros. Some words on aphrodisiacs and the like* with the dedication "To Professor Freud/from/Norman Douglas".

1933 April mid
- The Australian psychoanalyst Roy Winn suggests that F. write an intimate self-biography. F. replies that he "only [expects] the world to leave me alone and rather turn its interest to psychoanalysis" (F. to Winn, 23.4.1933).
- Georg Sylvester Viereck sends F. a published letter from the former German Crown Prince Wilhelm von Preussen, in which he assures that no one in Germany has to fear disadvantages because of their religion. Also enclosed is a letter from Viereck about German students and the burning of books to the *New York Herald Tribune* of May 28.

1933 April 17
Felix Boehm, a German doctor and psychoanalyst, visits F. to seek his advice on the situation of psychoanalysis in Germany after Hitler's rise to power. At F.'s request, Paul Federn is present at the meeting.

1933 April 22
The newspaper *Der Wiener Tag* publishes a long interview with the conductor Otto Klemperer on the occasion of his first concert with the Vienna Philharmonic Orchestra the next day. The interview is entitled "Der Katholizismus und das Absolute" ("Catholicism and the Absolute"). F. briefly and succinctly notes "Klemperer".

1933 April 23
Yvette Guilbert sends F. her book *Mes lettres d'amour* with the dedication *"Au grand Freud/ avec les sentiments/dévoués et admiratifs/d'Yvette Guilbert"*.

1933 April 26
Edoardo Weiss and the Italian writer Giovacchino Forzano visit F. Forzano was a friend of Mussolini and had written the book *Campo di Maggio* with the dictator. During the visit, he presented F. with the German translation entitled *Hundert Tage (Hundred Days)* with the dedication "A Sigmund Freud/che venderà migliore il mondo,/con ammirazione e/riconoscenza/ Benito Mussolini und G. Forzano". At Forzano's request, F. returns the gift with a copy of *Why War* and the dedication "Benito Mussolini mit dem ergebenen Gruß eines alten Mannes, der im Machthaber den Kulturheros erkennt. Freud".

1933 April end
- F. wants to give Winifred Ellerman (Bryher) a Chow Chow puppy as a thank you for her help with the Internationale Psychoanalytische Verlag. But she diplomatically refuses.
- Arnold Zweig comes to Vienna with his wife for ten days.

1933 May 4–September 30
Summer stay in Döbling

F. spends the summer in Unterdöbling, Hohe Warte 46. However, he regrets that they did not rent again in Pötzleinsdorf. F.'s niece Lucie visits him for the last time and brings him Chinese jade pieces. In addition, the photographer Hans Casparius arrives; F. takes longer walks with him, and Casparius takes pictures of him.

1933 May 4

Move to Unterdöbling.

1933 May 5

F.'s son Ernst and grandson Clemens come to Vienna for ten days.

1933 May 6

- F. has a dizzy spell on the morning of his birthday.
- Paula Fichtl dresses F.'s little Chow Chows in Styrian traditional costume. F. forbids her to do anything similar in the future – the animals would suffer.
- Arnold Zweig gives F. his play *Die Umkehr* for his birthday with the dedication "Dem Vater Freud/zum 77./in großer/Herzlichkeit/A. Z.".
- Marie Bonaparte gives F. a Chinese camel statuette for his collection.
- Ruth Mack Brunswick gives F. an Egyptian alabaster vase.

1933 May 7

Max Eitingon resigns as chairman of the Berlin Institute.

1933 May 10

F.'s books are burned in Berlin, and at the same time, the following sentence is read out by a speaker: "Against soul-grinding overestimation of the instinctual life. For the nobility of the human soul. I hand over to the flame the writings of Sigmund Freud". The next day, F. notes: "Burning in Berlin" and sarcastically says that in the Middle Ages they would have burned him themselves, but today they are content with his books.

1933 May 11

F. condoles Josef Halban, whose wife Selma, née Kurz – an important singer – had died the day before.

1933 May 15

- Hans Pichler operates F.
- Arnold Zweig visits F. He strongly advised him not to return to Germany, as he would be sent to a concentration camp. It is Zweig's last visit before his emigration to Palestine.

1933 May 16

- F. has severe pain after the operation, and Pichler treats the upper gums under anesthesia.
- Jeanne Lampl-de Groot visits the Freud family for five days.

1933 May 18

The Flaubert specialist Hélène Frejlich sends F. her book *Flaubert d'après sa correspondance* with the dedication "A Monsieur Sigmund Freud/Hommage respectueux/Hélène Frejlich".

1933 May 20

Pietro Zanfrognini, Italian writer, sends F. his book *Cristianesimo e psicanalisi* with the dedication "Al Maestro/devotamente/Pietro Zanfrognini/Staggia Modenese/(Modena)".

1933 May 21

– F. has colitis.
– Siegfried van Vriesland, Dutch consul in Palestine, visits F. He was committed to psychoanalysis in Palestine.

1933 May 22

Death of Sándor Ferenczi. F. writes an obituary for the *IZP*.

1933 May 23

F. receives the first issue of the Japanese Journal of Psychoanalysis.

1933 May 24–25

Anna and Martin are in Budapest for Ferenczi's funeral.

1933 May 25

Heinrich Meng visits F.

1933 May 26

Hans Pichler removes dead tissue from F.'s lower jaw so that the lower part of the prosthesis is relieved.

1933 May 28

– F. learns of the arrival of son Oliver's family in Paris. The family had left Berlin on May 27 and emigrated to France. After a stopover in St. Briac-sur-Mer, they moved to Rue George Sand in Paris.
– After the first Jewish colleagues of F. had left Germany, he wrote: "The persecution will help us to spread" (F. to Alfred Gross, 28.5.1933).

1933 May 29

F. receives Marie Bonaparte's three-volume work *Edgar Poe, étude psychanalytique*, to which he had written a preface, with the dedication "Au Professeur Freud, A mon maître aimé, ces pages inspirées par son oeuvre et son esprit, et où l'auteur s'est complu, pour pénétrer en l'un des psychismes les plus sinistres qui furent, à suivre longuement les voies ouvertes par celui qui, le premier, pénétra l'inconscient des hommes".

1933 May 30

F. acquires a white stone Buddha bust for his collection.

1933 June 4

F. concludes the obituary of Sándor Ferenczi.

1933 June 5

The English writer Herbert George Wells visits F. with his partner Moura Budberg.

1933 before June 6

F. receives an "interesting, perhaps too flattering essay" from the Budapest lawyer, publicist and translator Eugen Kerpel (F. to Eugen Kerpel, 5.6.1933).

1933 June mid

F. wonders "whether the events of 1683, when the wave of Turkish attacks fell on the walls of Vienna, will now be repeated in the face of the barbarians from the other direction" (F. to Marie Bonaparte, 22.6.1933).

1933 June 16–18

Max Eitingon visits F. The most important topic of the visit was the further fate of psychoanalysis in Germany.

1933 June 17

Hilda Doolittle leaves Vienna.

1933 June 18

Paul Federn and Heinrich Meng give F. the Spanish translation of the *Psychoanalytische Volksbuchs (El psicoanálisis y la vida moderna)* with the dedication "Herrn Professor Freud/in Verehrung überreicht/Paul Federn/und/Heinrich Meng".

1933 June 24

Death of Paul Hammerschlag, the son of F.'s religion teacher Samuel Hammerschlag and husband of Josef Breuer's daughter Bertha.

1933 before June 26

The Swiss doctor Jeanne Stephani-Cherbuliez asks F. to write a foreword for her book *Le sexe a ses raisons: Instruction et éducation sexuelles*. F. refuses on the grounds that he decided a few months ago not to write any more forewords and introductions for books by colleagues.

1933 June 26

Fritz Wittels visits F. and gives him his paper "Nachtrag zu meinem Buche 'Sigmund Freud' (1923)". ("Addendum to my book 'Sigmund Freud' (1923")"). In it, Wittels relativizes some of the book's statements. F. notes "Wittels' remorse".

1933 end of June/beginning of July

Hilda Doolittle and Johannes van der Leeuw visit F. Hilda, then travel to London; Van der Leeuw flies to Cape Town and sends F. a picture postcard from a stopover in Egypt.

1933 Summer

Japanese psychiatrist Kiyoyasu Marui visits F.

1933 July 4–5

F. receives two books from the British politician David Davies: Suicide or Sanity? An Examination of the Proposals before the Geneva Disarmament Conference. The Case for an International Police Force with the dedication "To Dr Freud/in appreciation of his services to the cause of Science and World Peace with the compliments of the author" and The Problem of the Twentieth Century. A Study in International Relationships with the dedication "To Dr Siegmund Freud/in appreciation of his great services to humanity with the esteem and compliments of the author". Davies was probably in Vienna and paid F. a visit. He was in correspondence with Albert Einstein and had certainly read Warum Krieg?

1933 July 8

F.'s son Martins has furunculosis, probably as a result of blood poisoning. At the end of August, he has to go to hospital.

1933 July 9

F. and his former classmates Wilhelm Knöpfmacher and Julius Wagner celebrate the 60th anniversary of the Matura together. When F. shows Knöpfmacher an antique sculpture on his desk, the latter thinks F. is collecting old sculptures to make himself feel younger.

1933 July mid

Hans Hattingberg, a non-Jew and former IPA member, is given a lectureship in psychotherapy at the Medical Faculty of the University of Berlin.

1933 July 17–24

Marie Bonaparte comes to Vienna to continue her analysis.

1933 July 23

F. congratulates his double Ludwig Horch – by now President of the Vienna Steam Saw and Planning Works and Romanian Consul General in Vienna – on his 70th birthday.

1933 July 27

F. receives from Abraham Roback, American psychologist and linguist, his book *Curiosities of Yiddish Literature* with the dedication "To Professor Sigmund Freud/With the highest regards/A A Roback".

1933 August

- F. begins to look again at the figure of Moses.
- Honorio Delgado sends F. his book *A vida e a obra de Freud* with the dedication "Al mi ilustre Maestro/el Prof. Dr. Freud,/dedico este modesto/tributo de admira-/ción/H F Delgado".
- Kiyoyasu Marui visits F. and gives him the Japanese translation of the *Gesammelte Schriften* with the dedication "To Prof. Dr./Sigmund Freud/with/heartfelt thanks and/ reverence/from the/translator/(Kiyoyasu Marui)/Sendai Japan"

1933 August 2

William Bullitt visits F.

1933 August 8

F. visits the Israelite Institute for the Blind with Ernst Kris. It was located at Hohe Warte 32, only a few meters from the summer flat. He was very interested in the blind and Braille, which Paul Emerich had explained to him in detail 20 years earlier. F.'s *lectures on the introduction to psychoanalysis were* also published in Braille by the Hohe Warte publishing house.

1933 August 10

F. visits the Israelite Institute for the Blind again because he was so moved by his first encounter with the blind children two days earlier. He asks the director Siegfried Altmann a long series of questions. At the end of the visit, F. writes in the guest book: "Professor Dr. Sigmund Freud in neighbourly admiration. 10 August 1933".

1933 August 11

Max Eitingon visits F.

1933 August 12

- F. goes to Hochrotherd for a short visit.
- Stephen Wise visits F.

1933 August 17

Marie Bonaparte visits F. and stays for a week.

1933 August 25

Ruth Mack Brunswick travels to America to talk to the members of the New York Psychoanalytical Society about some problems.

1933 August 31

Roy Grinker, an American psychiatrist, begins an analysis with F. It lasts until the summer of 1934.

1933 September 3

– René Laforgue visits F. One topic of conversation is the career prospects of F.'s son Oliver, who has just arrived in France.
– Winifred Ellerman (Bryher) uses her recently deceased father's fortune to set up a foundation to promote analytical education in Vienna.

1933 after September 5

Hans Pichler performs excisions and cochleations of small papillomas on F. F. feels unwell after the operation, and has coronary insufficiency with angina pectoris and pneumonia in the right lower lobe.

1933 September mid

F. is diagnosed with thrombosis in the leg.

1933 September 16

F.'s son Ernst visits his parents with his family. It is the last visit before emigration to England. Ernst's wife Lux leaves on September 19, the rest of the family on September 22.

1933 September 18

David Beddow, Canadian psychiatrist, begins an analysis with F. It lasts until 1934 July.

1933 September 19

Hans Pichler comes to Döbling for a consultation.

1933 September 30

Return to Berggasse 19.

1933 October beginning

F. can leave the bed again after his thrombosis.

1933 October

Wilhelm Reich gives F. his book *Massenpsychologie des Faschismus. Zur Sexualökonomie der politischen Reaktion und zur proletarischen Sexualpolitik* with the dedication *"Professor Freud/ in Verehrung überreicht/veröffentlicht als Antwort/auf die Kulturbarbarei/des Faschismus/Wilhelm Reich"*.

1933 October 4

The Austrian journalist and writer living in Switzerland Ludwig Bauer visits F. and talks to him about psychoanalysis. Bauer later uses this conversation in several newspaper articles, in a way that angered F. greatly.

1933 October 5
- F.'s son Martin passes his bar exam.
- F. sends a letter of recommendation for Max Eitingon to the King David Hotel, where the Eitingons and his wife were staying temporarily.

1933 October 6
Hans Pichler performs excisions and coking of small papillomas on F.

1933 October 9
F. leaves Berggasse 19 for the first time since returning from his summer home.

1933 before October 15
F. receives from Sigurd Naesgaard, Danish psychoanalyst, his two-volume work Psykoanalyse.

1933 October 18
WPV meeting: F. is re-elected chairman.

1933 October 19
F. Martin, the son, goes to Zurich, among other things to establish a management for the International Psychoanalytical Publishing House. He stays until November 4.

1933 October 29
Wilhelm Reich visits F.

1933 October 30
F. provides Theodor Reik with a testimonial in which he writes: "It cannot have remained unknown to any connoisseur of psychoanalytic literature that the numerous works of Dr. Theodor Reik on the application of psychoanalysis, very particularly those concerning religion and ritual, are among the best and most successful in this field […]".

1933 November
Julio Porto-Carrero sends F. his book *Psicanalise de uma civilizaçao* with the dedication *"A M. le professeur/Sigmund Freud/Mon cher Maître/J'ai essayé de tirer de/ 'Die Zukunft einer Illusion' et de/ 'Das Unbehagen der Kultur ' les/conclusions des ces quelques pages. Je me sens de plus en plus in-/te'gré dans la Psychanalyse. Ceci est presque une profession de foi scientifique. Votre humble élève J Porto-Carrero".*

1933 November 2
Leon Pierce Clark sends F. his book *The Nature and Treatment of Amentia* with the dedication "To/Professor Freud/With best regards./L. Pierce Clark".

1933 November 4
F. gives Heinz Hartman his *Collected Writings for his* birthday.

1933 November 6
F. receives a scarf made by Marie Bonaparte.

1933 November 8
F. suffers from stomatitis.

1933 November 9
Hans Pichler visits F. because he has sensitivity disorders of the oral mucosa and therefore has trouble sleeping.

1933 November 10
Erik Carstens addresses F. on behalf of the Danish Psychoanalytical Association with a request to support the Danish psychoanalysts in their struggle against the Danish authorities and the "wild" analysts.

1933 November 16
– F.'s son Ernst, who had returned to Vienna from England, leaves Germany for good.
– F. acquires Cypriot seals for his collection.

1933 November end
F. gets a carrying chair so that he can be carried down and up the stairs in the stairwell.

1933 before December 6
F. receives Xavier Boveda, Argentinian poet, whose poetry collection *Integracion del hombre: Poemas en profundidad*. Boveda had read an article by Ludwig Bauer about F. shortly before – Bauer had visited him on October 4 – and contacted F. on this occasion.

1933 December 17
F. sends Judah Leon Magnes, the Chancellor of the Hebrew University in Jerusalem, a letter of recommendation for Max Eitingon at his request.

1933 November 25–28
Max and Mirra Eitingon come to Vienna for a visit.

1933 December 3
F.'s sister Mitzi suffers a heart attack at Anna's birthday party.

1933 before December 11
F. receives a bunch of chincherinchees from Meta Harris from Cape Town, but they "suffered from the frost of the last days of their journey […]" (F. to Meta Harris, 10.12.1933). Meta Harris was born Rosenthal from Breslau.

1933 December 11
F. falls in the flat.

1933 December 12
Arnold Zweig sends F. his stories *Spielzeug der Zeit* with the dedication "Vater Freud/für ein paar/leichtere Stunden!/Arnold Zweig".

1933 December end
Marie Bonaparte visits F. and stays for a week.

1934

- Ernest Jones becomes President of the IPA.
- Margarete Bienenfeld begins an analysis with F. Her husband, the lawyer Rudolf Bienenfeld, is simultaneously being treated by Edward Bibring, and the two analysts exchange views.

Received books and offprints:

- Marie Bonaparte gives F. her book *Introduction à la théorie des instincts* with the dedication "A mon cher Maître, Ces quelques aperçus dans les profondeurs instinctuelles – avec la reconnaissance d'une élève qui osa les professer! Marie".
- Jean Bruller, French writer and caricaturist, sends F. his book *Ce que tout rêveur doit savoir de la méthode psychanalytique d'interprétation de rêves* with the dedication "Ce que tout rêveur doit savoir de la méthode psychanalytique d'interprétation de rêves; suivi d'une nouvelle cle' des songes avec vignt aquarelles de l'auteur repre'sant les rêves typiquess".
- Rudolf Brun, Swiss doctor, sends F. an offprint with book reviews with the dedication "Herrn Prof. Freud verehrungsvoll überreicht vom Verfasser".
- Mark Brunswick sends F. Volume 10 of *The Cambridge ancient history*.
- Karen Horney, German doctor and psychoanalyst, sends F. an offprint of her paper "The overvaluation of love" with the dedication "With best regards/Karen Horney".
- Humberto Salvador, Ecuadorian lawyer, sends F. his book *Esquema sexual* with the dedication "Para el ilustre maestro/S. Freud,/la más alla gloria de la ciencia/y del arte./Respetuoso homenaje de admi-/ración/Humberto Salvador".
- Franz Werfel sends F. his novel *Die vierzig Tage des Musa Dagh* with the dedication "Herrn Professor Dr/Sigmund Freud/in treuster Verehrung/Franz Werfel".
- Robert Wälder gives F. the anthology *L'esprit, l'éthique et la guerre. Lettres de Johan Bojer, Johann Huizinga, Aldous Huxley, André Maurois, Robert Waelder* with the dedication "Herrn Prof. Freud in Verehrung R Wälder".
- Viktor von Weizsäcker sends F. his book *Ärztliche Fragen. Vorlesungen über allgemeine Therapie* with the dedication "In Ehrerbietung und Dankbarkeit/vom Verfasser".

1934 January
Julio Porto-Carrero sends F. his book *Ensaios de psicanálise* with the dedication "Sincerely/J Porto-Carrero".

1934 January 5
- F.'s son Martin undergoes a kidney stone operation with Adolf Edelmann, the director of the Cunning Childs hospital.
- Departure of Marie Bonaparte.
- Martha and Minna's cousin Oscar Philipp from London visits his cousins. Martha gives Oscar three scarves for her grandchildren, who have been living in London for three months.

1934 January 12
Hans Pichler diagnoses the beginning of papillary change of the surface epithelium. He attempts a superficial cauterization, which causes F. severe pain.

1934 January 16
F. has severe pain and a feeling of pressure. Hans Pichler again treats the painful area with potash lye, which is less painful this time.

1934 January 23
F.'s pain intensifies. Consultation with the radiologist Fritz Eisler and Max Schur. A small wart is discovered on the upper lip near the corner of the mouth. The painful area is to be irradiated with low doses at F.'s home.

1934 January 24
First X-ray exposure in the Berggasse. The X-ray machine is in Minna's room.

1934 February 7
F. gives his daughter Mathilde and son-in-law Robert a radio for their silver wedding anniversary – together with Anna, Dorothy Burlingham and Ruth Mack Brunswick.

1934 February 9
After a good two weeks of X-ray irradiation, there has only been a slight improvement, so the irradiation is continued.

1934 February 10
F.'s son Martin is discharged after his kidney stone operation.

1934 February 12
A four-day civil war begins in Austria between the ruling Austrofascists and the Social Democrats. The latter call a general strike. The electricity in Berggasse is cut off for 24 hours. F. says: "It was a consolation that at least the matches still lit" (F. to Ernst Freud, 20.2.1934).

1934 February 17
Rolf Ehrenfels, the son of Christian von Ehrenfels, visits F.

1934 February 20
Martin goes to a sanatorium in Baden near Vienna to recover from a kidney stone operation.

1934 February 22
Michael Fraenkel sends F. his book *Theodor Mommsen, Jacob Bernays and Paul Heyse* with the dedication *"Herrn Professor Dr Sigmund Freud und Frau/Martha geb. Bernays/in Dankbarkeit und Verehrung überreicht von Michael Fraenkel"*.

1934 February 24
F. is irradiated by the radiologist Fritz Eisler, but the pain does not improve. On the contrary, the last reduction of the prosthesis, perhaps also wearing the prosthesis at night, has brought a clear improvement in pressure and lockjaw.

1934 before February 29
Saul Rosenzweig, American psychologist, sends F. some of his experimental work to test psychoanalytic hypotheses, which F. takes "note of with interest" (F. to Rosenzweig, 28.2.1934).

1934 before March 3
F. receives from Pierre Laroque, French civil servant in the Ministry of Labor and Social Affairs, his *Essai sur l'e'volution du "moi"*.

1934 March 7
James Bransom, British literary scholar, sends F. his book *The tragedy of King Lear* with the dedication "To Sigmund Freud, In recognition of a debt that can never be paid; from the Author, James S. H. Bransom". F. studies the book eagerly.

1934 March 8
- The American ambassador George Earle visits F.
- F. acquires an Egyptian mummy mask from the 13th century BCE for his collection.

1934 March 9
F. acquires a gilded mummy case from the 7th or 6th century BCE for his collection from the antiquities dealer Ludwig Lustig.

1934 March 12
F. has an inflammation of the mucous membranes.

1934 March 13
Death of Vinzenz Läufer. He was a "specialist in nose, throat and lung diseases". F. learns of his death one day later; presumably he was occasionally treated by him.

1934 March 19
Consultation with the radiologists Herbert Fuhs and Fritz Eisler, Max Schur is also present. It is decided to insert 50 mg of radium at the site of the papillary growth with an old duplicate prosthesis. The old prosthesis is reduced in size after a cast.

1934 March 22
Arnold Zweig sends F. part of a book that later is published under the title *Bilanz der deutschen Judenheit 1933. Ein Versuch.*

1934 March 23
The duplicate prosthesis with 50mg radium is inserted for one hour; all metal parts are covered with varnish and wax. On the advice of Herbert Fuhs, F. is now irradiated with radium about every three to four weeks. However, the treatment had to be discontinued at the end of July because F. developed migraine and severe general disorders.

1934 April beginning
F. sends Arnold Zweig the 11 volumes of his *Gesammelte Schriften* published so far.

1934 April 2
Arnold Zweig sends F. a large-format portrait photo at his request.

1934 April 5
The Freud family is visited by inspectors from the census commission who check the information in the questionnaires of the census that took place on March 22.

1934 April 13
F. is driven by car to Strassergasse 47 in Grinzing and rents the house for the summer.

1934 April 15
F. receives the German translation of Marie Bonaparte's *Edgar Poe, A Psychoanalytical Study*, published by Internationale Psychoanalytische Verlag.

1934 April 20
F.'s son Oliver is visiting from Paris and will stay until April 26.

1934 April 21
Claude Daly visits F. His wife had died, and he settled in Vienna for four years and continued his analysis with F.

1934 April 23
Second radium irradiation.

1934 April 24
F. acquires a 12-volume historical-critical complete edition of *Sämtlicher Werke* Johann Nestroys.

1934 April 25
Ludwig Jekels says goodbye to F. before moving to Stockholm at F.'s suggestion to support the newly founded Finnish-Swedish Psychoanalytic Association together with Otto Fenichel.

1934 April 26
- F. acquires volume 2 of Leonard Woolley's *The royal cemetery. A report on the predynastic and Sargonid graves excavated between 1926 and 1931*, in which Woolley describes his excavations in Ur, in present-day Iraq.
- Johannes van der Leeuw visits F. in the evening. He stays for a few days for a short analysis. On this occasion, Freud gives him an original lithograph of his portrait that Ferdinand Schmutzer had made with the dedication "Herrn Dr. Joh. van der Leeuw in freund Erinnerung/Sigm. Freud".

1934 April 28–October 13
Summer stay in Grinzing

F. spends the summer at Strassergasse 47. The study, bedroom and bathroom are on the ground floor – by now this was a condition for F. – and there is a large covered terrace.

Visitors:

- Theodor Reik visits F. with the Dutch psychoanalyst Catharina Versteeg to settle a dispute. First Reik talks to F. for an hour, then Catharina Versteeg.
- Antje van Mastrigt, who probably came to Vienna with Reik and Catharina Versteeg.
- The Swiss psychiatrist Max Müller visits F.

1934 April 28

Relocation to Strassergasse 47.

1934 May 6

Sándor Ferenczi's widow Gisella visits F. on his birthday. Actually, "all visits […] had been vigorously forbidden" (Martha to Lucie, 8.5.1834). But since F. had a very good relationship with Gisella Ferenczi, an exception was made for her.

1934 May 7

F. receives – presumably as birthday gifts for his collection – an ivory Buddha (16th or 17th century) from the border region between Burma and Thailand and a stone Chinese Fohund (guardian lion).

1934 May 8

The Italian poet Giovanni Papini visits F. He had given him a Hellenistic marble statue of Narcissus as a birthday present. In an accompanying letter, he dedicated the gift to the "discoverer of narcissism". F. then invited him to visit him at Berggasse 19. In the conversation during the visit, F. expresses his anger that he had allowed others to steal the honor and the expected profit associated with the discovery of cocaine as an anesthetic from him.

1934 after May 11

F. intends to read Erich Friedrich Podach's book *Gestalten um Nietzsche,* since Arnold Zweig had recommended it to him. In this context, F. sends Arnold Zweig a "crazy announcement by a psychotic who has probably been cured wrong and who wants to have seen through Friedrich Nietzsche's mystery" (F. to Arnold Zweig, 11.5.1934).

1934 June

Edoardo Weiss sends F. his Italian translation of the *Neue Vorlesungen zur Einführung in die Psychoanalyse (Introduzione alla psicoanalisi. Nuove lezioni)* with the dedication "Herrn Prof. Dr. Sigmund Freud/mit Ergebenheit/Dr Edoardo Weiss":

1934 June beginning

F. regularly reads English detective novels one hour before going to sleep.

1934 June 4

F. acquires for his collection a figure of Serapis (Egyptian Hellenistic god) and a "fountain bull" (possibly an Etruscan drinking vessel in the shape of a bull).

1934 June 6

F.'s sister Rosa has to go to hospital because of a gall bladder disease.

1934 June 14

– Death of Stella Zweig, the sister of Bertolt Brecht's wife Helene Weigel. She was a sole procurator at Internationale Psychoanalytische Verlag and a valued co-worker of F.'s son Martin and died of polio. On this occasion, F. asks Roy Grinker, who is a neurologist, to inform him about the latest research results on polio.
– F. learns of the death of Georg Groddeck, who died on June 14.

1934 June 15–16

On the occasion of the meeting between Hitler and Mussolini in Venice, F. suspects that Italy will not abide by the signed declaration on Austria's independence and writes: "Perhaps at this very moment the intriguer M[ussolini] in Venice is selling us to the captain of the thieves H[itler]" (F. to Jones, 16.6.1934).

1934 June 21

Third radium irradiation with a new radium prosthesis.

1934 Summer

– F. is considering writing something about important changes in certain of his views on basic questions of psychoanalysis. However, he fears that this would upset his followers and affect the psychoanalytic movement.
– Robert Fliess, son of F.'s long-time friend Wilhelm Fliess, visits F. in Grinzing. The subject of the conversation is the theory of seduction.

- Suzanne Bernfeld comes regularly for analysis and one day has a Fontane letter with her that her husband had given her. Minna reads the letter and has no intention of giving it back to Suzanne Bernfeld. F. rather stands by Minna in this situation.

1934 June 27

Fourth radium irradiation.

1934 June 30

F. learns of the S.A. revolt and the dismissal of Chief of Staff Ernst Röhm. He has "only one feeling: What? After the starter I am supposed to get up from the table! And then nothing follows! I'm still hungry!" (F. to Arnold Zweig, 15.7.1934).

1934 July

Franz Alexander visits F. Karl Menninger was also in Grinzing, but during the conversation between F. and Alexander, he was in the garden with Anna. Alexander wanted to introduce Menninger to F., but he refused.

1934 July 4–5

F. has a severe attack of ciliated scotoma-migraine, which is attributed to the radium, but wrongly so, as Hans Pichler believes.

1934 July 6

- F. has severe right-sided nosebleeds.
- The dean's office of the medical faculty informs F. that the competent federal minister may grant him an exemption to extend his authorization to teach.

1934 July 9

F. asks his nephew Harry, who is in Karlsbad, to bring him a meteorite; he would like to have a piece on his desk "that has not grown on this miserable earth". (Harry Freud, interview with Kurt Eisler, 5.9.1952, SFP). F. had seen a meteor stone at the C.W. Kessler company, which dealt in minerals, during earlier spa visits to Karlsbad, but had not purchased it for reasons of cost.

1934 July 12

- F.'s grandson Ernst takes off on a holiday tour.
- F. acquires for his collection a "lion dragon", presumably a Chinese jade lion from the Chinese Qing Dynasty, which F. later used as a paperweight.

1934 July 13

Philipp Sarasin visits F.

1934 July 17

Wulf Sachs, a Russian-born doctor and psychoanalyst from Johannesburg, visits F.

1934 July 21

F.'s son Ernst comes to visit.

1934 July 22

Marie Bonaparte visits F. and stays in Grinzing for a week.

1934 July 25

– The Austrian Federal Chancellor Engelbert Dollfuss is murdered by an SS standard. F.'s son Martin goes to the funeral.
– Michael Balint, Hungarian physician and psychoanalyst, visits F.

1934 July end

F. has pain, swelling and fatigue with every radium irradiation, also stenocardial attacks. Therefore, the irradiation is stopped.

1934 August 2

Death of Reich President Paul von Hindenburg. F. writes on this occasion: "No one can say what consequences the German development may have for our poor Austria" (F. to Jelliffe, 2.8.1934).

1934 August 9

– F. begins writing the first version of his book *The Man Moses and the Monotheistic Religion.*
– F. has migraines, heart problems, worsened speech and severe local discomfort.

1934 August 20

Hermann Nunberg comes from America to visit F.

1934 August 22

Ernest Jones visits F. and Anna. An important topic of the visit is the preparation of the XIII International Psychoanalytic Congress in Lucerne.

1934 August 24

Ernest Jones drives to Hochrotherd with Anna.

1934 August 25

– Franz Alexander visits F.
– Anna leaves for Lucerne.

1934 August 26–31

The XIII International Psychoanalytical Congress takes place in Lucerne. F. does not take part.

1934 August end

F. receives the first issue of the new magazine *Marriage Hygiene* from Bombay.

1934 September beginning

F. sends Havelock Ellis his New Series of Lectures for Introduction to Psychoanalysis.

1934 September

The radium specialist Wilhelm Schloss treats F.

1934 September 4

F. learns of the death of Johannes van der Leeuw. He had crashed in his De Havilland over Tanzania on August 29 on the return flight from a conference in South Africa. F. feels von Leeuw's death "as a personal loss" (F. to Hilda Doolittle, 24.9.1934).

1934 September 6

F. acquires an Eros statue from Myrina (2nd century BCE) for his collection. It is the largest of seven Eros figures he owns.

1934 September 14

The twelfth and last volume of F.'s *Gesammelte Schriften is* published – six years after the eleventh.

1934 September 23

F. finishes writing the first version of his book *The Man Moses and the Monotheistic Religion.*

1934 September 27

Marie Bonaparte visits F. and stays for ten days.

1934 October

Julio Porto-Carrero sends F. his book *Grandeza e miserias do sexo* with the dedication "A M. le professeur Dr Sigmund Freud/mon Maître très vénéré et dont/je sens l'image, à coté de celle/cher Maître de mon enfance – mon/Père – dans la structure de mon/Idéal du Moi – de mon Sur-Moi./J. Porto-Carrero".

1934 October 4

Arnold Zweig sends F. a manuscript of his play *Bonaparte in Jaffa.* F. reads it "with much pleasure". (F. to Arnold Zweig, 6.11.1934).

1934 October 9

– Joseph Wortis, American psychiatrist, begins an analysis with F. It lasts until 1935 January 31.
– The University of Vienna informs the Dean's Office of the Faculty of Medicine that F.'s authorization to teach expires.

1934 October 13

F. is back at Berggasse 19.

1934 October 17

WPV meeting: F. is re-elected chairman.

1934 November–December

Renewed radium treatment, which F. tolerates badly.

1934 November 3

F.'s daughter-in-law Lucie is visiting.

1934 November 8

Siegfried Altmann sends F. the book by Ludwig Münz and Viktor Löwenfeld *Plastische Arbeiten Blinder* with the dedication "Herrn Univ.-Prof. Dr Sigmund Freud/Dieses aus Arbeiten unseres/Institutes resultierende/Buch überreicht in tiefster/und herzlichster Verehrung/Dr. S. Altmann".

1934 November 12

Géza Róheim sends F. his book *The riddle of the sphinx* "To/Prof. Sigmund Freud/most respectfully/dedicated/by/the/author".

1934 November 24

Else Heilpern, German curative teacher and sister-in-law of F.'s son Oliver, visits F.

1934 November 26

- F. learns that his lectureship has expired.
- F. now receives hormone injections at regular intervals, to which he responds well.

1934 December 14

F. has arrhythmias and the doctor Alexander Fleischer is called. On January 3, F. thanks Fleischer for his intervention and asks for the fee note to be sent to him.

1934 December 16

- F. has a vagus attack.
- F. acquires the book *Norddeutsche Backsteindome* by the German photographer Albert Renger-Patzsch.

1934 Christmas

Roy Grinker visits F.

1935

- John Dorsey, an American psychiatrist, begins an analysis with F. It lasts a good two years.

Received books and offprints:

- Luís Varela Aldemira, Portuguese painter, sends F. his book *A arte e a psicánalise* with the dedication "ao Dr. Freud oferta de V. Aldemira".
- Edmund Bergler sends F. his book *Talleyrand, Napoleon, Stendhal, Grabbe. Psychoanalytisch-biographische Essays* mit dem Widmung "Herrn Prof. Freud in dankbarer Verehrung/der Verf.".
- David Forsyth sends F. his book *Psychology and religion* with the dedication "Prof. Freud/from the Author/with kindest remembrances".
- Margaret Fries, American pediatrician and psychoanalyst, sends F. an offprint of her paper "Interrelationship of physical, mental and emotional life of a child from birth to four years of age" with the dedication "With the Author's Compliments/Margaret E. Fries".
- Arnold Groeneveld sends F. offprints of his papers "La psychologie du travail" and "Le role de l'autorité dans la vie de l'enfant" with the dedication "Mit kollegialen Grüssen,/vom Verfasser".
- Bernard Jaffe, American chemist and historian of science, sends F. his book *Outposts of science. A journey to the workshops of our leading men of science* with the dedication "To/Dr. Sigmund Freud/by an admirer./Bernard Jaffe".
- Rudolph Loewenstein sends F. his French translation of the five Lectures *Über Psychoanalyse (Cinq psychanalyses)*, which he has done together with Marie Bonaparte, with the dedication "Au Professeur F./pour ses quatre vingts ans/cet 'enfant' qui en a déjà/dit/avec tout l'attachement/d'une fille spirituelle/Marie Bonaparte/Au Professeur F.,/mon maître,/en faible te'moignage de ma ve'ne'ration et de ma profonde gratitude. R. Loewenstein".
- Heinrich Meng sends F. the book by Hans Zulliger *Schwierige Schüler* with the dedication "S. Freud/In Verehrung/Meng".
- Merrill Moore, American psychiatrist and poet, sends F. an offprint of his paper "Contributors to the history of syphilis of the nervous system – Ulrich von Hutten (1488–1524)". with the dedication "With compliments to Dr. F./Dr Merrill Moore".
- Sacha Nacht, Romanian-born French psychiatrist and psychoanalyst, sends F. his book *Psychanalyse des psychonévroses et des troubles de la sexualité* with the dedication "A Monsieur le Professeur Freud,/avec l'expression de mon admiration,/ce modeste travail qui n'est/qu'un essai de diffusion de/son oeuvre géniale./S. Nacht".
- Jorge Thenon, Argentinian doctor and psychoanalyst, sends F. his book *La neurosis obsesiva* with the dedication "A l'illustre Maître Sigmund Freud/hommage de l'auteur".

1935 January 1
F. has a stomach attack with vomiting.

1935 January 7
F. commissions his son Martin to execute his "testamentary provisions".

1935 January 9
F.'s son Martin returns from Nice, where he had visited his brother Oliver.

1935 January 23
Death of F.'s former patient Anna von Vest.

1935 January 27
F. produces a postscript to his "Selbstdarstellung" of 1925.

1935 February 6
Lucien Lévy-Bruhl, the editor of the *Revue Philosophique*, visits F. and gives him his book *La mythologie primitive. Le monde mythique des Au straliens et des Papous* with the dedication "Mr le Professeur Dr. S. Freud, en souvenir de notre récent entretien L. Lévy-Bruhl". Lévy-Bruhl gave a lecture on "La mentalité des Primitifs" the same evening at the Austrian Cultural Association.

1935 February 12
The Spanish writer and diplomat Salvador de Madariaga y Rojo visits F. He was in Vienna for a lecture at the Kulturbund on "L'Espagne Contemporaine". The visit was arranged by Jolande Jacobi, a long-time colleague of C. G. Jung. G. Jung and at that time vice-president of the Austrian Cultural Association. In 1931, Madariaga had commented on the question of the importance of international intellectual cooperation in a volume published by the Institute for Intellectual Cooperation of the League of Nations. The next volume in this series was F.'s correspondence with Einstein on the subject of "Why War?"

1935 February 13
After F.'s daughter Anna gave two lectures on the "Ego and the mechanisms of defence" at the WPV (on January 23 and February 6), which were apparently very well received, F. wrote to Arnold Zweig: "I must remind myself to remember the only beautiful fact that my daughter Anna is currently making such good analytical discoveries and reporting on them in – as everyone says – masterly lectures. A reminder, then, not to believe that the world will end with my death" (F. to Arnold Zweig, 13.2.1935).

1935 February 15
Quintin Frazer, a student of Fritz Wittels in New York, sends F. an paper he has written on the Schreber case under the title "Additional remarks on a case of paranoia".

1935 February 18
The American psychiatrist Ralph Gerard visits F. on behalf of the Rockefeller Foundation. He came from Leningrad, where he had previously visited Ivan Petrovich Pavlov. He told him that he had been inspired to change an experimental arrangement by reading F.'s writings. He now expected that future research into human behavior would be determined by a synthesis of the doctrine of the conditioned reflex and psychoanalysis. When Gerard recounted this statement to Pavlov's F., the latter's shoulder-shrugging response was, "It would have really helped if he had said that a few decades earlier" (Memoirs of Ralph Gerard, 23.4.1958).

1935 February 22
Minna travels to Merano for a spay stay. She stays until April 6.

1935 February 25
Death of Otto Fleischl. F. learns of this on February 28.

1935 March 3
F. gives Friedrich Eckstein the *Almanach 1935* with the dedication "Seinem lieben Freunde Fritz Eckstein in Erwartung einer wertvolleren Gegengabe. Sigm Freud".

1935 March 16
- F. rents the house in Grinzing at Strassergasse 47 again for the summer.
- The Reich government in Germany announces the reintroduction of compulsory military service. F. makes a note of this the next day, presumably also because he had signed in 1930 a "Manifest gegen die Wehrpflicht und die militärische Ausbildung der Jugend" ("Manifesto against compulsory military service and the military training of youth").

1935 March 20
Max Schur notices the development of a suspicious lesion after a break of one and a half years. Hans Pichler wants to remove it if it does not recede.

1935 March 23
Hans Pichler performs a diathermy destruction of small papillomas. Jakob Erdheim's finding was "proliferating leukoplakia, probably still in a precancerous state".

1935 March 29
F. receives an electric clock, presumably as a gift from Jeanne Lampl-de Groot.

1935 April
- Dorian Feigenbaum sends F. an offprint of Victor Tausk's paper "On the origin of the 'influencing machine' in *schizophrenia*", translated by him, with the dedication "Herr Professor Freud,/in reverence and with the/very best regards,/the translator".
- Julio Porto-Carrero sends F. his book *Psicologia judiciaria* with the dedication "Ao Mestre Magnifico/Sr. Prof. Dr. Sigmund Freud/com muita honra oferece/o discípulo dedicado/J. Porto-Carrero".
- Adolf Storfer sends F. his book *Wörter und ihre Schicksale* with the dedication "Herrn Prof. Freud/in Verehrung/der Verfasser".

1935 April 11
F. receives the American translation of the *eue Folge der Vorlesungen zur Einführung in die Psychoanalyse.*

1935 April mid
F.'s son Martin is in Zurich, presumably in connection with the transfer of F.'s foreign assets to Switzerland.

1935 April 17
Jakob Erdheim examines a "high-grade leukoplakia"; based on his histological findings, he still considers it to be precancerous.

1935 April 18–October 18
Summer stay in Grinzing

1935 April 18

Relocation to Strassergasse 47.

1935 April 20

Theodor Reik and Karl Landauer visit F. Both were living in Holland at the time and were. The main topic of the visit was probably the conflict over training issues and lay analysis between the two divided psychoanalytic associations in Holland.

1935 April 21

Ernest Jones visits F. with wife Katherine, son Mervyn and daughter Nesta May.

1935 April 22

F. has neuralgic pain.

1935 April 23–25

Ernest Jones and Walter Schmideberg visit F. The visit was mainly about increased cooperation between the London and the WPV, but in a separate conversation with Jones also about the differences between Anna Freud and Melanie Klein.

1935 April 26

- F. receives a bowl from Clinton McCord, possibly a piece for his collection.
- F. receives Stefan Zweig's book *Maria Stuart*.
- F. acquires the counterpart of a yellow dragon for his collection. Thus, he has a pair of dragons made of jade.

1935 April 28

At the suggestion of the Fischer publishing house, F. writes "a short greeting for Thomas Mann's 60th birthday" (F. to Arnold Zweig, 2.5.1935).

1935 April 30

Hans Pichler performs electrocoagulation of precancerous tissue. After the operation, F. has severe pain and difficulty inserting the prosthesis.

1935 May

Claude Défalèze, Swiss writer, sends F. his book *Vivendo* with the dedication "A Monsieur le Professeur Sigmund Freud,/au père courageux en tenace de la/psychanalyse, en respectueux hommage/d'un suisse romano/Claude Défalèze".

1935 May 5

- William Bullitt visits F.
- F. has extraordinarily severe pain and notes: "Beginning of prosthetic misery".

1935 May 6

On his birthday, F. can hardly use the prosthesis. Hans Pichler decides to make a new prosthesis. It is finished on June 22.

1935 May 8

Enrico Carpani sends F. his writing *Nirvâna* with the dedication "A Sigmund Freud, con devozione E. G. Carpani".

1935 May 20

William Bullitt, American ambassador to Moscow since 1934 April, visited F. He had presumably come from Warsaw, where he had attended the funeral of Józef Piłsudski on May 17.

1935 May 21

F. is unanimously elected honorary member of the Royal Society of Medicine

1935 June 8–10

The four-country meeting of representatives of psychoanalysis from Italy, Austria, Czechoslovakia and Hungary takes place in Vienna. F. invites the participants home and talks to each of them.

1935 at June 9

Frances Deri (originally Franziska Herz), Austrian midwife and psychoanalyst, visits F. Together with Annie Reich and Steff Bornstein, she had founded the Prague Psychoanalytic Working Group and was its director. Deri discusses with F., among other things, an paper on sublimation that she had begun to write.

1935 June 10

– István Hollós, president of the Hungarian Psychoanalytic Association since 1933, visits F.
– Edoardo Weiss visits F.

1935 June 11

F. grants Suniti Chatterji, Indian literary scholar and educator, an interview. It is published in Bengali in Calcutta in the same year.

1935 Summer

Ernst Blum visits F.

1935 June 22–23

– Anna gives two lectures to the psychoanalytical working group in Prague.
– F. receives the new prosthesis.

1935 July 8

F. learns of the death of Albert Hammerschlag, son of F.'s religion teacher Samuel Hammerschlag. F. had been friends with him since the early 1880s. Both were colleagues at the Vienna General Hospital, and Albert had helped him with the translation of Charcot's *New Lectures on the Diseases of the Nervous System*. Albert Hammerschlag had died the previous day.

1935 July 8

F. entrusts his son Martin "with the care of the execution of my testamentary provisions" (F. to Martin Freud, 8.7.1935).

1935 July 17

F. has a heart attack and extrasystoles.

1935 July 21

F. grants Cornelius Tabori, Hungarian writer and journalist, an interview. It is not published until 1951 in Tabori's *My Occult Diary*.

1935 July 21–28

Marie Bonaparte visits for and stays a week.

1935 August 1

The Rockefeller Foundation begins funding research on "Studies of Reflex Behavior in Relation to Neuroses" with $10,400[59] The next day, F. notes the name of the foundation's chairman "Rockefeller Jr." – John D. Rockefeller. And a few days later, F. received from Howard Liddell a reprint of the article "Observations on experimental neurosis in sheep", written together with Oscar Anderson, with the dedication "To Dr. Sigmund Freud with cordial esteem H S Liddell". Liddell was the main beneficiary of the money as a professor at Cornell University Medical College.

1935 August 2

F. acquires an Egyptian metal statuette of Isis nursing the young Horus (ca. 6th century BCE) from Ludwig Lustig for his collection. It finds a place on F.'s desk.

1935 August 3

Smiley Blanton is back in Vienna and continues his analysis for a fortnight.

1935 August 6

Max Eitingon visits F.

1935 August 14

F.'s son Ernst visits his parents in Vienna with his son Lucian.

1935 August mid

The YIVO (Jewish Scientific Institute) Congress in Vilnius from 14–19 August elects F. as an honorary member of YIVO.

1935 August 17

At the end of the second phase of the analysis, F. gives Smiley Blanton the *Traumdeutung* with the dedication "Meinem lieben Dr. Smiley Blanton zur Erinnerung".

1935 August 19

Hans Pichler performs a diathermy destruction of a brown dry keratosis. Erdheim has no suspicion of malignant deep growth.

1935 August end

Howard Liddell sends F. an offprint of the article "Observations on experimental neurosis in sheep" written jointly with Oscar Anderson with the dedication "To Dr. Sigmund Freud with cordial esteem H S Liddell".

1935 September 1

Philipp Sarasin and his lover Salomea Kempner, a Polish doctor and psychoanalyst, visit F.

1935 September 3

F. writes a greeting for the 40th anniversary of the "Vienna" lodge of B'nai B'rith. The "Vienna" had been founded on 1895 October 13, and F. had been its member since 1897 September 29.

1935 September 5

F. acquires a Chinese jade bowl and a camel for his collection. The camel is a 20th-century fake in the style of the Tang dynasty.

1935 September 9

Arnold Zweig sends F. his book *Erziehung vor Verdun*.

1935 September 15

- Jan van Emden visits F.
- Stefan Zweig visits F., and he tells him in detail about his planned Moses book.
- Willy Haas visits F.

1935 September 29

James Jeans, British physicist and astronomer, visits the Austrian capital on the occasion of his wedding to Susi Hock, a Viennese. Jeans was a member of the Royal Society, of which he was elected honorary member in 1925.

1935 October 1

F. acquires a Buddha statue from the Song dynasty for his collection; however, it is probably a copy.

1935 before October 5

F. receives Franz Alexander's book *The medical value of psychoanalysis with* the dedication "Herrn Prof. Dr. Sigm. Freud mit tiefster Verehrung Dr Franz Alexander".

1935 October 10

F. writes an accompanying card to a birthday gift for Dorothy Burlingham. The gift was a cut gem, which was to be made into a ring by the watchmaker Rudolf Löwy. At one point in the sentence, he accidentally inserted the word "bis". F. immediately analyzed this blunder and wrote down his small paper "Die Feinheit einer Fehlhandlung".

1935 October 11

Hans Pichler performs diathermy destruction of a brown dry keratosis.

1935 October 13

Thornton Wilder visits F. They talk about the use of psychoanalysis for novels and about religion.

1935 October 18

Return to Berggasse 19.

1935 October 21

Death of Richard Wahle. F. had known him since their time together at the Gymnasium and was close friends with him until around 1886.

1935 October 28

F. wrote a "postscript" for the second edition of the English translation of his "Selbstdarstellung". He also made some additions to the text.

1935 November 6

Death of Victor Dirsztay, treated by F. from 1909 to 1920.

1935 November 10

Yvette Guilbert visits F. She had performed chansons in the Middle Hall of the Konzerthaus on November 9.

1935 November mid

Siegfried Fehl, the director of the Jewish Museum in Nikolsburg, visits F. He gives the museum some of his works, a picture and copies of his diplomas; also an offprint of the Russian translation of the *Drei Abhandlungen zur Sexualtheorie* with the dedication "Dem jüdischen Museum in Nikolsburg/Freud/1935".

1935 before November 22

John Dollard, American psychologist, sends F. his book *Criteria for the life history. With analysis of six notable documents.*

1935 November 23

F.'s son Oliver comes to visit for a week from Nice. Among other things, it was about F.'s financial support for the purchase of the photo shop that Oliver ran. While he was still in Vienna, the owner rejected Oliver's (and F.'s) offer of 200,000 francs[60] by telegram.

1935 December 2

Georges Parcheminey sends F. his book *Le problème de l'hystérie* with the dedication "Hommage de l'auteur/G. Parcheminey".

1935 December 3

F. acquires a Chinese rifle from the Han dynasty. It is possibly not for his collection, but a gift for Anna's birthday.

1935 December 10

F.'s grandson Ernst goes to Palestine for six months for professional orientation.

1935 December 15

Serynes Pereira Franco, Brazilian forensic pathologist, sends F. the first volume of *Biologia forense* with the dedication "Ao creador da Psychanalyse/homenagem/do/author/Victoria".

1935 December 16

The Vienna City Office issues F. a recognition card with the number 00476085.

1935 December 23

Death of Paul Hollitscher, the brother of Mathilde's husband Robert. He was institutionalized for depression and threw himself out of a window the day before his planned release.

1935 Christmas

John Dorsey sends F. his book The *Foundations of Human Nature. The Study of the Person* with the dedication "To Professor Freud/John M. Dorsey".

1935 December 27

Percy Allen, English journalist and writer, sends F. his book *The life story of Edward de Vere as "William Shakespeare"* with the dedication "To Dr. S. Freud with regard & respect from Percy Allen".

1935 December end

F. receives John Hill's book *The teacher in training from an* Irish Jungian, but immediately passes it on to Anna.

1936

F. is nominated for the Nobel Prize (Medicine) for the tenth time and for the Nobel Prize for Literature (by Romain Rolland) for the first time.

Books received:

- Smiley and Margaret Blanton give F. their jointly written book *For stutterers with* the dedication "To Professor Freud. With affectionate regards. Smiley Blanton Margaret Gray Blanton".
- Mark Brunswick sends F. Volume 11 of *The Cambridge ancient history.*
- Roland Dalbiez, French philosopher, sends F. his book *La méthode psychanalytique et la doctrine freudienne* with the dedication "A F./R Dalbiez".
- Morris Ginsberg, British sociologist, sends F. an offprint of his paper "Montagu David Eder" with the dedication "To/Professor Freud".
- Abraham Maslow, American psychologist, sends F. the third part of his book *The role of dominance in the social and sexual behavior of infra-human primates* with the title *A theory of sexual behavior of infra-human primates* and the dedication "To Dr. Sigmund Freud/With the respects of/A H Maslow/Please comment if/possible".
- Edward Glover, British doctor and psychoanalyst, sends F. his book *The dangers of being human* with the dedication "Professor Freud/with good wishes/from Edward Glover".
- Merrill Moore, American doctor and poet, sends F. his book *Six sides to a man. New Sonnets* with the dedication "Inscribed in admiration/and esteem/to Dr. Sigmund Freud /Merrill Moore /Boston".
- René Laforgue sends F. his book *Clinique psychanalytique* with the dedication "A mon maître le Professeur Freud/Hommage reconnaissant/Laforgue".
- Carlos Noriega, Peruvian doctor, sends F. his book *Historial y tratamiento de una neurosis* with the dedication "Homenage del autor al gran/maestro, Dr. Sigmund F./C. Gutierrez N".
- Wulf Sachs sends F. his book *The vegetative nervous system* with the dedication "With the/Author's/Compliments/W S".
- Hans Syz, American psychiatrist and psychoanalyst, sends F. an offprint of his paper "Post-traumatic loss of reproductive memory and its restoration through hypnosis and analysis" with the dedication "With the compliments/of the author".

1936 January
Marie Bonaparte seeks the Nobel Prize for F. during a visit to Stockholm.

1936 January 1
Heinrich Meng and Paul Federn visit F. in the Berggasse. The conversation revolves around the repeated nomination for the Nobel Prize and a request from Victor Wittkowski to F. to contribute to a commemorative volume on Romain Rolland's 70th birthday.

1936 January 2
F.'s son Ernst comes to Vienna and, among other things, inspects the WPV's new premises at Berggasse 7 with regard to the possible variations in interior design. He stays until January 13.

1936 January 14
F. finishes his contribution to a Festschrift for Romain Rolland's 70th birthday. The Festschrift did not appear, however, and F.'s "birthday present" was later printed in the *Almanac* under the title "Eine Erinnerungsstörung auf der Akropolis".

1936 January mid
Marie Bonaparte visits F. for a few days.

1936 January 16
F. is operated on again by Hans Pichler, who extensively coagulates a wart-like growth. F. suffers from the consequences of the operation for a long time.

1936 before January 29
Oskar Némon begins work on a new bust of F., which his students want to give him for his 80th birthday. Within a week, 12 sessions take place.

1936 February beginning
F. receives from the German writer and publicist Kurt Hiller his essay on Theodor Lessing "Der Denker im Spiegel". In his reply letter, F. reports on his exchange with Lessing before the First World War.

1936 February 1
F.'s son-in-law Max Halberstadt visits F. for the last time before his emigration to South Africa. He stays for four days.

1936 February 9
Death of Robert Breuer, the son of Josef Breuer.

1936 February mid
Max Schur and Hans Pichler discover a leukoplakia in F.'s mouth, which makes to them an "unpleasant impression".

1936 February 20
– F. granted Gustav Bychowski an interview. It appeared in the journal in 1936 June under the title "A Conversation with Freud". Bychowski was a Polish psychoanalyst who had met F. in 1921 during his analysis with Siegfried Bernfeld in Vienna.
– Hans Pichler cleans two encrusted areas and discovers a new leukoplakia.

1936 March 3
– Death of Friedrich Pineles. F. had known him since 1883 at the latest.
– F.'s brother Alexander gives him an Osiris group for his collection; however, it is probably a copy.

1936 March 8
F.'s daughter Anna meets Felix Boehm in Brno and talks to him about the organizational future of psychoanalysis in Germany.

1936 before March 10
Georg Hermann, German writer, gives F. his book *Der etruskische Spiegel*.

1936 March 10
Hans Pichler cauterizes the remains of two warts and boils away the new leukoplakia.
1936 March 16
John Rickman sends F. the anthology he edited *On the bringing up of children. By five psychoanalysts: Susan Isaacs, Melanie Klein, Merell P. Middlemore, Nina Searl and Ella Freeman Sharpe* with the dedication "To Prof Freud/a friendly tribute/from/John Rickman".

1936 Spring
- Therese Benedek, Hungarian psychiatrist and psychoanalyst, visits F. shortly before her emigration to America and gives him an offprint of her lecture "The Superior Idea and its Relationship to Addictive Disease", which she gave at the XIII International Psychoanalytical Congress in Lucerne on 1934 August 28, with the dedication "Mit den besten Grüssen Ihre Therese Benedek".
- Margarethe Lutz is brought to F. by her father, as her attending doctor had diagnosed a mental illness. F. sends the father into the next room, talks to Margarethe alone for an hour. After that, she is able to resist her domineering father and determine her own life.
- F. treats the opera singer Richard Tauber for impotence. After two sessions and a conversation with Tauber's future wife Diana Napier, the impotence had disappeared, but F. refers Tauber to Berlin for follow-up treatment.

1936 before March 25
Arthur Foxe, American psychiatrist, sends F. his book *Crime and sexual development* with the dedication "To Dr. S. Freud/with/Deep admiration/A. N. Foxe".

1936 March 25
- F. has a severe migraine.
- Minna undergoes surgery on both eyes for glaucoma and stays in the sanatorium for a good four weeks.
- Angela Seidmann, the orphaned granddaughter of F.'s sister Mitzi, visits F. She had been adopted by her aunt Lilly and her husband Arnold after the death of her parents and now came to Vienna from Prague.
- The stocks of the Internationale Psychoanalytische Verlag in Leipzig are confiscated. F.'s son Martin tries to stop the destruction of the books through international intervention.
- F. has severe migraine.

1936 March 30
Death of David Eder. He was with F. for analysis in 1913/14. Three weeks later, F. wrote to Eder's sister-in-law Barbara Low: "Eder belonged to the people one loves without having to trouble about them" (F. to Low, 19.4.1936).

1936 April 3
F. acquires an Egyptian ship of the dead from the antique dealer Ludwig Lustig for his collection; however, parts of it are fakes.

1936 before April 4
F. receives from Lawrence Kubie, American psychiatrist and psychoanalyst, his book *Practical aspects of psychoanalysis* with the dedication "To Prof. Sigmund Freud/with the author's/homage,/Lawrence S. Kubie".

1936 April 4
F.'s daughter-in-law Henny comes to visit from Nice with granddaughter Eva. They stay for ten days.

1936 April 12
F. acquires an Egyptian figural group depicting a field scene from the antique dealer Ludwig Lustig for his collection. The authenticity is doubtful.

1936 April 15
Minna has to go to a sanatorium for a fortnight.

1936 April 17
F. becomes an honorary member of the New York Neurological Society.

1936 April 18–October 17
Summer stay in Grinzing

1936 April 18
Relocation to Grinzing to Strassergasse 47.

1936 April 23
Abraham Brill sends $5000[61] to Vienna; possibly they are from the New York Association for the Internationale Psychoanalytische Verlag.

1936 April 25
Arnold Zweig finishes an essay around F.'s 80th birthday, which is published in the journal *Das Neue Tagebuch* under the title "Apollon bewältigt Dionysos". Zweig sends a copy of the text to F. It is not until a month later that F. replies "frightened by the threat that you want to become my biographer. You, who have so many more beautiful and important things to do, who can install kings and survey the violent folly of men from a high vantage point. No, I love you far too much to allow such a thing. Whoever becomes a biographer commits himself to lying, to concealment, hypocrisy, whitewashing, and even to concealing his lack of understanding, for biographical truth is not to be had, and if one had it, it would not be needed" (F. to Arnold Zweig, 31.5.1936).

1936 April 29
Minna returns from the sanatorium.

1936 May
- F.'s sister-in-law Minna Bernays has to undergo cataract surgery.
- Merrill Moore sends F. an offprint of his paper "A comparison of the weights of brain, heart, spleen and kidneys of epileptic and schizophrenic patients" with the dedication "Compliments – Merrill Moore M.D.".
- Edouard Pichon, French doctor and psychoanalyst, sends F. his book Le développement psychique de l'enfant et de l'*adolescent. Evolution normale-Pathologie-Traitement* with the dedication "Au Professeur S. Freud,/dont les yeux d'aigle ont percé/tant d'horizons ennuagés,/en respectueux hommage:/E Pichon".

1936 May 4
The Viennese newspaper *Der Morgen* dedicates its "Karikatur der Woche" ("Cartoon of the Week") to F.'s 80th birthday.

1936 May 6
- On the morning of F.'s 80th birthday, his Chow Chow dog Jofi comes into F.'s bedroom "to show me her tenderness in her way, which she has never done before and not since? Well, how does a little animal know when its birthday is?" (F. to Hilda Doolittle, after 6.5.1936).
- F.'s granddaughter Sophie (Martin's daughter) makes a mistake in a recited poem: Instead of saying "that God will let you live a long time", she formulates "that God will always let you live".

- F. receives a congratulatory address on his 80th birthday written by Thomas Mann, Herbert George Wells, Romain Rolland, Virginia Woolf, Jules Romain and Stefan Zweig. It is signed by a total of over 300 people.
- The Dean's Office of the Faculty of Medicine congratulates F. on his 80th birthday with a short letter.
- Thomas Mann sends a handwritten manuscript of the speech he will give in the Konzerthaus saal on May 8.
- Albert Schweitzer congratulates with a postcard from Lambarene, Albert Einstein with a letter from Princeton.
- A Freud celebration is held in Paris to mark the 80th anniversary of his birth. The neurologist Henri Claude presides, and Marie Bonaparte gives the speech. The Austrian chargé d'affaires in Paris is also present.

Guests:

- Joan Riviere.
- Elisabeth Rotten, a German reformist educator and peace activist.

Gifts:

- Daughter Anna gives F. her book *Das Ich und die Abwehrmechanismen* with the dedication "Das Bücherschreiben als/oberstes Abwehrmittel/gegen alle Gefahren von/innen und aussen./Anna".
- Son Martin gives F. a poem written by him, which ends with the lines: "Darum verkünden wir streng vertraulich: Die nächsten acht Geburtstage feiern wir gleichfalls beschaulich!" ("Therefore we announce in the strictest confidence: The next eight birthdays we will also celebrate contemplatively!").
- F.'s daughter-in-law Esti Drucker presents F. with a cake one meter in diameter, made by K.u.K. Court confectioner Demel. On the cake was a world map, among other things with an Australian aborigine, reading *Totem and Tabu*.
- F.'s niece Lilly gives F. three essays written by her: "Sigmund Freud in seinem Heim", "Meine Begegnung mit Rainer Maria Rilke" and "Mein Freund H. Ch. Andersen". It was "of all the gifts I received […] the most beautiful, because the most tender, the most artful, the richest in feeling" (F. to Lilly Freud-Marlé, 1.6.1936).
- Emanuel Loewy an engraving by Albrecht Dürer (by Emanuel Loewy)
- F. receives a menorah from Siegfried Altmann on behalf of the Institute for the Blind with a certificate confirming its authenticity and that it was excavated in Dalmatia at the beginning of the 19th century. He also gives F. a cut glass in the name of the blind children, on which the year 1856 is engraved. F. writes in his thanks that he is very touched. To Altmann, he sends Thomas Mann's book of essays *The Suffering and Greatness of the Masters as* a gift, and a check for 100 Schilling[62] "to be used directly for the children". F. had donated the same amount every year at the Hanukkah Festival for the blind children.
- F. receives a "donation" from the "Foreign Language Lending Library" in Vienna, for the library of the Institute.
- F. receives 200 tulips for his birthday from Holland, which were delivered to Vienna by air freight.

- John Murry's book *Shakespeare* with the dedication "To Professor Sigmund Freud/ with affectionate regards on his birthday/Smiley Blanton".
- Angel Garma sends F. his book *El psicoanálisis, la neurosis y la sociedad* with the dedication "Al profesor F./en su LXXX aniversario/A. Garma".
- Franz Kobler gives F. his translation of Plato's *Gastmahl* with the dedication "Herr Professor/Sigmund Freud,/dem Durchleuchter des Eros,/zum 80. Geburtstag/in tiefster Verehrung/überreicht/von/Franz Kobler".
- Nikolai Iovetz-Tereshchenko, who was also born on May 6, gives F. his book *Friendship-love in adolescence* with the dedication "To Professor Sigmund Freud on his eightieth birthday from N. M. Iovetz-Tereshchenko".
- Alexander Lipschütz gives F. an offprint of his paper "Warum treiben wir wissenschaftliche Forschung?" with the dedication "Herrn Professor S. F./mit hochachtungsvollen Grüßen und den/besten Wünschen zum 80. Geburtstag /".
- Camilla Lucerna, philologist and German teacher from Zagreb, who had lectured with F. before 1907, gives F. Ivan Meštrović's book *Meštrović* with the dedication "Dem hochverehrten Forscher/treudankbar/Camilla Lucerna".
- Joseph Michaels presents F. with the amount of 350 Schilling on behalf of a group of American students.[63]
- Moysheh Oyved (real name Edward Good) gives F. his book *The Book of Affinity* with the dedication "For Dr. Sigmund Freud/A token of esteem for his 80th birthday/Moysheh Oyved".
- Alexander Szalai sends F. his paper *Philosophische Grundprobleme der psychoanalytischen Psychologie* with the dedication "Herrn Prof Dr. Sigmund Freud/in tiefster Ehrerietung überreicht/vom Verfasser".

1936 May 6

- Opening of the new premises for the Vienna Psychoanalytic Institute, the Ambulatorium, the WPV and the Internationale Psychoanalytische Verlag by Ernest Jones at Berggasse 7. Further speeches are given by Joan Riviere and Karl Landauer.
- F. gives notice to leave the flat at Berggasse 19 at the end of 1938 August.

1936 after May 6

F. is elected honorary member of the "Kadimah", a Jewish student association in Vienna to which F.'s son Martin belonged.

1936 May 7

- In the late afternoon, Ludwig Binswanger and his wife Hertha are guests at F.'s in Grinzing.
- In the evening, festive event of the Academic Association for Medical Psychology in the Billrothhaus of the Society of Doctors in Frankgasse. Binswanger gives a lecture on "Freuds Auffassung des Menschen im Lichte der Anthropologie" ("Freud's conception of man in the light of anthropology"); Julius Wagner-Jauregg representing the Society of Physicians, Otto Marburg for the Association for Psychiatry and Neurology and Otto Pötzl representing clinical psychiatry.
- The "Legitimistischen jüdischen Frontkämpfer" ("Legitimist Jewish Front Fighters") congratulate Martin on his father's birthday.

1936 May 8
- In the evening, Thomas Mann gives a lecture on "Freud und die Zukunft" in the Konzerthaus saal. Franz Werfel is also present.
- Death of Ludwig Braun. The cardiologist had treated F. and his family members since 1919 at the latest. On the occasion of his death, F. published an obituary in the newsletter of the Association of Jewish Doctors.
- Margaret Lowenfeld sends F. her book *Play in childhood* with the dedication "Professor Sigmund Freud/In admiration/from/The Author".

1936 May 9
Quintiliano Saldaña sends F. his book *Nueva criminología* with the dedication "A l'éminent Maître/Dr. Sigmund Freud/dans son LXXX Anniversaire/Hommage très respectueux de/l'Auteur".

1936 May 10
Olga Sachs, the sister of Hanns Sachs, brings F. a bouquet of orchids to Grinzing on behalf of her brother.

1936 May mid
Marie Bonaparte visits F. for a few days and gives F. an Eros statuette.

1936 before May 22
The painter Wilhelm Krauss asks F. to paint him. His stepson Walter Schick had inspired him to do so. F. agrees, but is not enthusiastic.

1936 June
- F. granted Odette Pannetier an interview. It appeared on July 23 under the title "Je me fais psychanalyser" in the magazine *Candide*. Pannetier was a French journalist who worked for the French weekly *Candide* and became known for her – often cunningly arranged – interviews with famous personalities. In F.'s case, she succeeds in doing this about Paul Federn and Anna Freud, to whom she had feigned a dog phobia.

1936 June 5
- F. visits the new rooms for the Internationale Psychoanalytische Verlag set up at Berggasse 7 by son Ernst. They are also to be used by the outpatient clinic, as a library and as a meeting room for the WPV.
- F. becomes an honorary member of the London "Societas pro Scientia Naturali".

1936 June 9
Arnold Zweig refrains from writing a biography of Freud. He would not take up the project again until 1944.

1936 June 14
- Siegfried Altmann visits F.
- Thomas Mann personally repeats for F. his lecture on "Freud und die Zukunft", which he had given on May 8 on the occasion of his 80th birthday in the Konzerthaus saal. The

conversation afterward revolved, among other things, around the question of whether F. still felt safe in Austria. Berman Fischer and his wife Brigitte are also present.

1936 Summer

- René de Monchy, Dutch psychoanalyst, visited F. He asked for his opinion on his approach to overcoming the split among Dutch psychoanalysts.
- Sacha Nacht, a French psychiatrist, begins an analysis with F. It only lasts a few weeks.

1936 June 29

- Ella Braun, the widow of F.'s deceased friend Ludwig Braun, visits F.
- Wilhelm Krauss begins work on a portrait of F. in Grinzing. He completes it in six sittings. F.'s brother Alexander acquires the painting, and Krauss completes one copy each for himself and his stepson Walter Schick.

1936 June 30

F. becomes a corresponding member of the Royal Society and considers it "an immense honor" (interview with Stephen Foulkes by Kurt Eissler, 7.9.1969). Alongside the diploma, he receives a volume with the corresponding members of the Royal Society and their portraits.

1936 July

- Hanns Sachs visits F. and gives him a Mayan house god from Guatemala carved out of black stone.
- Max Huhner, American urologist and Shakespearian scholar, sends F. an offprint of his essay *Shakespeare's conception of the clergy* with the dedication "Prof. Sigmund Freud/with the Compliments of/Dr. Max Huhner".

1936 July 8

The Internationale Psychoanalytische Verlag books confiscated in Leipzig at the end of March are released and taken away from Germany.

1936 July 13

Hans Pichler and Max Schur discover an ulcer near the surgical site of March 10.

1936 July 14

Hans Pichler and Jakob Erdheim operate on the ulcer.

1936 July 16

Jakob Erdheim informs Hans Pichler that this time he has found a clearly malignant change.

1936 July 17

Hans Pichler and Jakob Erdheim look at the incisions of the carcinoma operated on July 14 in the Jubilee Hospital.

1936 July 18

Hans Pichler operates on F. in the Auersperg Sanatorium. As the anesthesia is not successful, the operation has to be interrupted because of F.'s severe pain and Pichler replaces the local anesthesia with a general anesthesia. Some bone is removed, and a thorough coagulation is carried out.

1936 July 19

F. is back from the sanatorium. He has to wear an eye bandage because he sees double images after the operation. F. has to stay in bed for two more days

1936 July 22

Marie Bonaparte visits F. and stays in Grinzing for nine days.

1936 July 23

F. is better again.

1936 July 27

F. complains to Hans Pichler, who visits him, about difficulties in smoking and speaking.

1936 July 31

Anna goes to the XIV International Psychoanalytical Congress in Marienbad.

1936 August 2

The American psychoanalyst Robert Knight visits F. in Grinzing. He asks F. to sign three photographs he had bought the day before at Berggasse 7. He also talks to him about Odette Pannetier, who had visited him in June under false pretenses and subsequently reported on it in a Paris newspaper.

1936 August 2–7

The XIV International Psychoanalytical Congress takes place in Marienbad.

1936 August 12

– The London analyst Stephen Foulkes visits F. in Grinzing.
– The French analyst Rudolph Loewenstein visits F. The conversation revolves around masochism and the death instinct, among other things.

1936 August 14

Arnold Zweig and Hermann Struck come from Palestine to Vienna and visit F.

1936 August Middle

Ernest Jones visits F.

1936 August 18

F. reads Arnold Zweig from the manuscript of his work on Moses and the monotheistic religion.

1936 after August 18

Richard Rosenbacher, the brother-in-law of F.'s former patient Helene Schiff visits F. He wants F. to tell him something about Bertha Pappenheim.

1936 August 20

F. receives a plaquette made by sculptor Willy Lévy. Lévy was the son of Lajos and Katá Lévy and later became known as Peter Lambda, among other things as a screenwriter for the BBC.

1936 August 25

Death of Julius Tandler. F. had known him personally since 1920 at the latest.

1936 August 28

- Ernst Jones visits with his family F.
- F.'s grandson Ernst travels to Russia for a week. Like his trip to Palestine, this trip was dedicated to his professional orientation.

1936 September

- Richard Beer-Hofmann sends F. his *Vorspiel auf dem Theater zu König David* with the dedication "Sigmund Freud, mit vielem Dank für die so freundlichen Worte, in herzlicher Verehrung Richard Beer-Hofmann".
- David Forsyth sends F. his book *Psychology and religion. A study by a medical psychologist* with the dedication "To Prof. Freud/from the Author,/with kindest regards".
- Edwin Hirsch, American doctor, sends F. his book *The Power to Love. A Psychic and Psychologic Study of Regeneration* with the dedication "To Professor Sigmund Freud, the genius who helped liberate mankind. With kindest regards/Edwin W. Hirsch M.D.".
- Edoardo Weiss sends F. the third edition of his book *Elementi di psicoanalisi* with the dedication "Meinem hochverehrten/Lehrer, Herrn Prof. Sigmund/F., ehrerbietig/ Edoardo Weiss".

1936 September 6

A delegation of the "Kadimah" presents F. with a red-purple-gold sash.

1936 September 12

- F.'s son Ernst and his wife Lucie visit their parents on the occasion of their upcoming golden wedding anniversary.
- F. sees Anna's German shepherd Wolf for the last time before he was put to sleep.

1936 September 14

F. and Martha celebrate their golden wedding anniversary. To mark the occasion, F. gives everyone a 25-Schilling gold coin. The celebration took place in the garden of Strassergasse 47 and is partly filmed by Ruth Mack Brunswick.

1936 before September 21

F. receives from John Meier the novel by David Lawrence *Lady Chatterly's lover.* F. had read the book before.

1936 October beginning

F. receives from Ludwig Binswanger the manuscript of his commemorative lecture on the occasion of F.'s 80th birthday.

1936 October 17

Return to Berggasse 19.

1936 October 18

Richard Beer-Hofmann visits F.

1936 October 19
F. receives from Abraham Roback his book *I. L. Peretz. Psychologist of Literature* with the dedication "To Professor Freud The ever youthful investigator of the mind With the kind sentiment of A A Roback".

1936 October 24
Max and Mirra Eitingon visit F.

1936 October 26–31
Marie Bonaparte is in Vienna, among other things, to continue her analysis.

1936 October 27
F. has such a severe nosebleed that the nose has to be bandaged for 24 hours.

1936 October 30
F. acquires a horse figurine for his collection. It is presumably a more recent copy of a Chinese figure.

1936 November
- Adolf Edelmann sends F. an offprint of his paper "Über ein bisher nicht beachtetes pankreo-hepatisches Syndrom, bedingt durch Übertritt des Pankreassaftes in die Blutbahn" with the dedication "Herrn Prof. Freud in tiefster/Verehrung/vom Verf. überreicht Dr Edelmann".
- Merrill Moore sends F. an offprint of his essay "Syphilis and sassafras" with the dedication "Compliments – Merrill Moore M.D.".
- Moritz Sachs, Viennese doctor, sends F. an offprint of his lecture "Ueber die Beziehungen gewisser Funktionen zum bilateral-symmetrischen Bau des Körpers" with the dedication *"Mit dem/Ausdruck besonderer/Verehrung/M S"*.
- Rudolf Bienenfeld hands F. his book *Deutsche und Juden,* which he had just published under the pseudonym Anton van Miller.

1936 November 1
Felix Boehm comes to Vienna to inform F. about the situation in Germany. At the WPV Executive Committee meeting in the afternoon, F. urges him not to make any concessions.

1936 November 14
F. receives Max Eastman's book *Enjoyment of Laughter*.

1936 November 15
Hans Demel, the director of the Egyptian-Oriental Department of the Museum of Art History, visits F.

1936 November 21
F.'s son Oliver comes to Vienna for five days.

1936 November 20
Death of Etka Herzig, the widow of F.'s college and university friend Josef Herzig. F. learns of her death two days later.

1936 November 25
F. is with Hans Pichler.

1936 December
Ida Fliess sells F.'s letters to her husband Wilhelm to the bookseller Reinhold Stahl, from whom she acquires Marie Bonaparte at the end of the year.

1936 before December 1
F. receives from Ludwig Hopf, German mathematician and physicist, his book *Materie und Strahlung.*

1936 December 11
A change in F.'s oral cavity noticed by Anna turns out to be a cancerous ulcer.

1936 December 12
Hans Pichler coagulates the ulcer. F. writes about the consequences a few days later: "At first stabbing pains, in the following days severe swelling in the mouth, so much so that I cannot eat anything, that I have great difficulty drinking and that I sacrifice my hours by helping myself to renew hot water bottles every half hour. Relief comes only from short-wave radiation, which works wonders but does not last long enough. According to the prognosis, I will have to resign myself to this form of existence for another week" (F. to Marie Bonaparte, 17.12.1936).

1936 December mid
Hans Pichler's assistant Alexander Berg examines F.

1936 December 18
F. feels strongly bothered by the lockjaw and suffers from dysphagia. He can only really take liquids. The pain and discomfort are considerably improved by short-wave irradiation, which had already been done several times at F.'s home.

1936 before December 21
Rudolf Kallir, a third cousin of Martha, approaches F. and informs him that he has been researching the family history of the Nathansohn/Kallir family and has compiled a family tree. F. asks him to send him this family tree. He receives it on 1937 January 10.

1936 December 20
Otto Loewi, German-Austrian pharmacologist, visits F. He had supported F.'s nominations for the Nobel Prize and received it himself in 1936. During this visit, he told F. about the award in Stockholm.

1936 December 30
The Berlin art dealer Reinhold Stahl visits Marie Bonaparte in Paris and offers to buy 250 letters from F. to Wilhelm Fliess for 12,000 or Francs 1200 Reichsmark. The condition, however, is that the letters are not sold either directly or indirectly to the Freud family, because Stahl fears that they would then be destroyed. F. learns of this offer on 1937 January 2.

1936 December end
– Ernst Darmstaedter, German chemical historian, sends F. an offprint of his paper "Ein Überblick über Begründung und Ausbau der Cocain-Lokalanästhesie" with the dedication *"Ergebenst von E D".*
– René Laforgue and his wife Paulette visit F.

1937

- F. is nominated for the Nobel Prize (Medicine) for the eleventh time.
- F. becomes a control analyst for the Dutch industrialist Kees van der Leeuw, a brother of F.'s former patient Johannes van der Leeuw. Kees van der Leeuw had studied medicine in Vienna from 1931 and was in analysis with Ruth Mack Brunswick.
- F. starts treating Herman Claus, a rich Dutchman. It lasts until July 1939, and it is his last big and also very problematic case.
- F. gives Friedrich Eckstein the *Almanac 1937* with the dedication "Seinem lieben Fritz Eckstein 1937 Freud".

Received books and offprints:

- Marie Bonaparte gives F. her book Topsy. *Chow chow au poil d'or with* the dedication "Au Professeur Freud qui comprend les Hommes et aime les Bêtes en souvenir ému de Jofi et avec tous mes voeux pour Lun Marie Bonaparte".
- Medard Boss sends F. an offprint of his paper "Die Grundprinzipien der Schizophrenietherapie im historischen Rückblick" with the dedication "In Verehrung der Verf.".
- Paul Federn gives F. an offprint of his paper "Die leitungslose Funktion im Zentralnervensystem" with the dedication "Herrn Prof. Dr Sigmund Freud/in Ehrerbietung und Dankbarkeit/Dr Federn".
- Josef Friedjung sends F. an offprint of his paper "Die asthmatische Reaktion" with the dedication "Herrn Prof. Dr Freud in tiefster Dankbarkeit/der Verf".
- Alexandre Hérenger sends F. an offprint of his paper "Antijudaïsme et antichristianisme" with the dedication "A Monsieur le Professeur Sigmund F.,/en hommage et profonde et respectueuse admiration./Alexandre Hérenger".
- Eduard Hitschmann gives F. an offprint of his paper "Todesangst durch Tötungsdrang" with the dedication "Herrn Professor F./in dankbarer Verehrung".
- Johannes van der Hoop sends F. offprints of his papers "De theorie en therapie van de neurosen volgens Freud" with the dedication "Herrn Prof. Freud in besonderer/Verehrung gewidmet" and "Intuition in medical psychology" with the dedication "Prof Freud in Verehrung/vom Verfasser".
- Smith Ely Jelliffe sends F. an offprint of his paper "Sigmund Freud as a neurologist" with the dedication "Prof. Sigm. Freud. With regards of/Smith Ely Jelliffe".
- Melanie Klein and Joan Riviere give F. their jointly written paper *Love, hate and reparation* with the dedication "To Professor Freud/With our gratitude/Melanie Klein/& Joan Riviere".
- René Laforgue sends F. his paper "Relativité de la réalité. Réflexions sur les limites de la pensée et la génèse du besoin de causalité" with the dedication "A mon maître le Professeur F./Hommage reconnaissant/Laforgue".
- Karl Landauer sends F. an offprint of his lecture "Freuds Lehre vom Traum" with the dedication "Mit ergebenen Grüßen L".
- Bertram Lewin, American psychiatrist, sends F. an offprint of his paper "A type of neurotic hypomanic reaction" with the dedication "To Prof F. with/the writer's compliments".
- Heinrich Meng sends F. an offprint of his paper "Über Wesen und Aufgabe der seelischen Hygiene" with the dedication "Herrn Prof Dr Freud/in Verehrung/v. Verf".
- Joseph Michaels sends F. an offprint of his paper "Psychiatric implications of the neurological examination" with the dedication "With Best Wishes".

– Sophie Morgenstern sends F. an offprint of her paper "Contribution au problème de l'hystérie chez l'enfant" with the dedication "In tiefster Verehrung gewidmet/ihrem grossen 'maître' von/Sophie Morgenstern".

– Sacha Nacht sends F. his book *Pathologie de la vie amoureuse* with the dedication "Pour Monsieur le Professeur/S. Freud en hommage/de mes sentiments profondement/respectueux/S. Nacht".

– Gerardo Nebel, Uruguayan psychiatrist, sends F. his book *La conciencia y la sombra* with the dedication "A Segismundo Freud genial investigador del inconsciente, creador de una ciencia immortal. Con la más alta admiración. Gerardo Nebel, Las Piedras, Departamento de Canalones, Uruguay".

– John Rickman sends F. the anthology he edited *A general selection from the works of Sigmund Freud* with the dedication "To Prof. Sigm. Freud a tribute of affection and gratitude from a pupil J. R.". On the back of the title page, Rickman has written the remark: "One of a specially printed issue of twelve for private distribution. J. R.".

– Hans Syz sends F. an offprint of his paper "Recovery from loss of mnemic retention after head trauma" with the dedication "With best compliments/H. S".

1937 January 2
F. learns from Marie Bonaparte that she has bought his letters to Fliess.

1937 January 3
F. asks Marie Bonaparte not to let any of his letters to Wilhelm Fliess "come to the knowledge of so-called posterity" (F. to Marie Bonaparte, 3.1.1937). Marie later deposited them in a safe at the Rothschild Bank in Vienna and only retrieved them after the Nazi invasion in 1938 March.

1937 January 4
Hans Pichler examines F. and finds that F.'s condition has improved.

1937 January 7
Reinhold Stahl visits Marie Bonaparte in Vienna and gives her F.'s manuscripts, which belong to his correspondence with Wilhelm Fliess. She receives the letters themselves a few weeks later.

1937 January 9
F. is on the birthday of his "savior and executioner" Hans Pichler (F. to Marie Bonaparte, 10.1.1937).

1937 January 11
F.'s Chow Chow Jofi is operated on for two ovarian cysts.

1937 January 14
Death of Jofi. F. writes about it: "… one does not easily get over 7 years of intimacy" (F. to Arnold Zweig, 10.2.1937). She is buried in the garden of the Nausch animal shelter next to Anna's shepherd dog Wolf.

1937 January 15
– Thomas Mann visits F. He had read from the third volume of his Joseph trilogy the previous evening in the concert hall.

– F. took over the Chow Chow bitch Lün from Dorothy Burlingham as Jofi's successor. She bore the same name as F.'s Lün, who had been run over in 1929, and he had already had her in the house for a short time in 1933, but had to give her away because she did not get along with Jofi.

1937 January 18
F. has heart problems.

1937 January 22
F. sends two samples of his handwriting to Marie Rolland, the second wife of Romain Rolland, which she wants to sell at an auction – probably for charity.

1937 after February 3
F. presents his Moses manuscript at an unofficial meeting of the WPV in his study. One of the participants points out to F. that Goethe has also commented on Moses, and Edward Bibring shows F. Goethe's essay "Israel in der Wüste" ("Israel in the desert") in his *Sophien-Ausgabe* of Goethe's writings.

1937 February 11
F. learns of the death of Lou Andreas-Salomé. She had died on February 5. F. writes an obituary for the *IZP.*

1937 February 12
F. has a heart attack.

1937 before February 20
F. receives Johannes van der Hoop's book *Consciousness Types and their Relationship to Psychopathology.*

1937 before February 27
F. reads Euripides's *Ion* in the English translation by Hilda Doolittle.

1937 February 28
Wulf Sachs visits F. He had supported F.'s son-in-law Max Halberstad in his emigration to South Africa and urged that grandson Ernst also join him, as entry to South Africa was becoming increasingly difficult.

1937 March 1
F. asks Marie Bonaparte to make recommendations to Mirjam Czuczka, the daughter of Richard Beer-Hoffmann, as she volunteers to maintain youth hostels in Palestine.

1937 March 7
– F. compares the political situation in Vienna before a probable Nazi invasion with the siege by the Turks in 1683 – except that no relief army was ready.
– F. congratulates Julius Wagner-Jauregg on his 80th birthday.

1937 March mid
Marie Bonaparte visits F. on his way to Greece and discusses with F., among other things, the question of how to deal with the Fliess letters.

1937 March 20
F. issues an expert opinion for the expressionist painter Arthur Segal. Segal had left Berlin in 1933 and now wanted to found a painting school in London, using painting as a kind of psychotherapeutic method. For this, he needed financial and professional support. Presumably, F.'s son Ernst had lobbied his father for Segal.

1937 Spring
- F.'s paper "Moses ein Ägypter" is published. F. gives offprints of the paper to, among others, the poet Richard Beer-Hofmann with the dedication "Herrn Dr. R. Beer-Hofmann herzlich Verf." and to Thomas Mann. After its publication, F. finds a passage in Houston Chamberlain's *Grundlagen des neunzehnten Jahrhunderts (The Foundations of the Nineteenth Century)* in which Chamberlain suggests that Moses could have been an Egyptian.
- Margaret Stonborough-Wittgenstein, the sister of the philosopher Ludwig Wittgenstein, begins an analysis with F. that lasts about a year. She had already presented her pubescent son Thomas to F. about his stuttering some 15 years earlier. However, the treatment was not successful.

1937 March 22
Robert Lion, French doctor, sends F. an offprint of his paper "L'auto-coït buccal. A propos d'une perversion sexuelle peu commune" with the dedication "à Monsieur le Professeur Freud,/à qui je dois tant,/bien modeste témoignage de ma profonde admiration/et de mon respectueux dévoument/Robert Lion".

1937 March 29
F. receives a Japanese medal with his portrait, awarded as the Freud Prize of the Tokyo Institute of Psychoanalysis.

1937 April
- Josephine Jackson sends F. the second edition of her book *Outwitting our nerves* with the dedication "To/Sigmund Freud/and with a query:/does Chap. XIV. pass muster?/Josephine A. Jackson" and her book *Guiding your life with psychology as a key* with the *dedication* "To/Sigmund Freud/In this I have tried to demonstrate/the simplicity of truth./Josephine A. Jackson".
- Rudolf Urbantschitsch, who is visiting Europe, visits F.

1937 April 4
Richard Beer-Hoffman visits F.

1937 April mid
Max Schur noticed a soft, almost pedunculated, outgrown mobile wart in the place of the old hole from the last operation. However, the histological findings were negative.

1937 April 21
Arthur Kielholz, Swiss psychiatrist, visits F. and gives him an offprint of his lecture "Eine Spielmünze aus dem Militärspital von Vindonissa" with the dedication "In dankbarer Erinnerung/an den Besuch vom/21.IV.37 überreicht vom Verfasser".

1937 April 22-24
F. goes to the Auersperg Sanatorium where the wart discovered a week ago is to be operated on. F. writes: "If I come out this time too, I will go straight to Grinzing" (F. to Margaret Stonborough-Wittgenstein, 21.4.1937). The operation is performed under general anesthetic, and F. has to stay in the sanatorium for two more days.

1937 April 24–October 16
Summer stay in Grinzing

1937 April 24
Relocation to Strassergasse 47.

1937 April 29

John Dollard sends F. his book *Caste and Class in a Southern Town* with the dedication "To Professor Sigmund Freud/with the author's greetings".

1937 May

Adolf Storfer sends F. his book *Im Dickicht der Sprache* with the dedication "Herrn Professor Freud/ergebenst überreicht/vom Verf.".

1937 May beginning

Pierre Janet is in Vienna for several lectures at the invitation of the Viennese Cultural Association and would like to visit F. F. had heard about this beforehand from Marie Bonaparte and informed her that he did not want to see Janet. The visit did not take place either.

1937 May 6

István Hollós and Géza Dukes give F. their Hungarian translation of *Das Ich und das Es (Az ösvalami és az én)* with the dedication "Unserem Meister/Herrn Professor Dr Sigm. Freud/in Dankbarkeit gewidmet/von den Übersetzern:/Dr Dukes Géza Dr Hollós István".

1937 May 12

F.'s son Ernst, who had come for his birthday, leaves for London again.

1937 May 13

F. receives two Greek vases and an archaic bust from Marie Bonaparte as a belated birthday present, which she had acquired on her trip to Greece in April.

1937 May mid

Anna is in Budapest for the second four-country meeting of the representatives of psychoanalysis from Italy, Austria, Czechoslovakia and Hungary.

1937 May 18

– F. receives the certificate of honorary membership in the "Royal Medico-Psychological Association".
– Władysław Matecki, Polish psychiatrist, sends F. reprints of his papers "O popędach destrukcyjnych" ("On Destructive Drives") and "Zygmunt Freud. Lekarz-myśliciel" ("Sigmund Freud. Arzt-Denker", each with the dedication "Herrn Prof. Dr S. Freud/in tiefster Verehrung/vom Verfasser").

1937 May 24

F. begins writing his paper "Wenn Moses ein Ägypter war".

1937 May 25

Leopold Szondi, Hungarian psychiatrist and endocrinologist, sends F. his work *Analysis of marriages* with the dedication "Herrn Prof. Sigm. Freud/with respect/Your devoted L. Szondi".

1937 May 28

Death of Alfred Adler in Aberdeen. He had died during a lecture tour in Aberdeen. F. comments on his death thus: "For a Jewish boy from a Viennese suburb, a death in Aberdeen, Scotland, is an unheard-of career [...]". (F. to Arnold Zweig, 22.6.1937).

1937 June

F. signs an appeal for "The Thomas Mann Fund", an organization of emigrated German writers under the patronage of Thomas Mann. He addressed the public with a request for financial support.

1937 June 5

Emil Oberholzer and Frédéric Weil visit F.

1937 June 11

– F.'s daughter Anna has a small accident.
– F. has otitis.

1937 Summer

Edith Jackson is in Vienna.

1937 June 17

F. gives Ernst Hoffmann, a member of the WPV since 1926, a testimonial listing his activities within the framework of the WPV and the Psychoanalytic Ambulatorium.

1937 June 18

F. gives Minna money for a purse and a bag for her birthday.

1937 June 20

Hugo Knöpfmacher, the son of F.'s school friend Wilhelm Knöpfmacher, visits F. and brings him greetings from his father, who was paralyzed after a stroke.

1937 June 26

– Clinton McCord, a former patient, gives F. a cast of a bronze bust created by the American sculptor Marian Marvin.
– Johanna Wertheimstein, a granddaughter of Paul and Rosa Schiff, visits F.

1937 June 30

Heinrich Zimmer, German Indologist, sends F. an offprint of his paper "Die vorarisch-altindische Himmelsfrau" with the dedication *"Professor Dr. Sigmund F.,/(der uns als Erster Symbole/wieder lesen lehrte)/verehrungsvoll dargebracht/H. Zimmer"*.

1937 July

– Freud is appointed honorary member of the Israel Medical Association.
– Sophie Morgenstern sends F. her book *Psychanalyse infantile. Symbolisme et valeur clinique des créations imaginatives chez l'enfant* with the dedication "Herrn Professeur Freud in tiefster/Verehrung und Hochachtung/Sophie Morgenstern".

1937 July 21

Marie Bonaparte visits F. and stays until July 28.

1937 before July 23

Stephan Lackner, German writer and art collector, sends F. an offprint of his article "Thomas Mann, Freud and the 'Depth'", in which he particularly addressed F.'s paper "Moses ein Ägypter". However, F. as a subscriber to the *Neues Tage-Buch* had already read it.

1937 July 28

Max Eitingon, Arnold Zweig and his son Adam visit F. Adam receives an antique vase as a gift from F. Marie Bonaparte is filming.

1937 July 31

Smiley Blanton is back in Vienna and works for a fortnight with F. Blanton and his wife Margaret give F. Eva Clark's book *Hidden allusions in Shakespeare's plays* and her book *The man who was Shakespeare,* both with the dedication "To Professor Freud With affectionate regards Margaret & Smiley".

1937 August

The Australian Hessel Duncan Hall from the League of Nations visits F. and talks to him about the danger of an imminent war.

1937 August 10

Margaret Blanton visits F.

1937 August 11

F. ends his paper "Wenn Moses ein Ägypter war …"

1937 August 13

End of the third phase of Smiley Blanton's analysis.

1937 August mid

F. suffers from hematuria for three days as a symptom of his prostate disease.

1937 August 16

Death of Edmund Kallich. He was a pupil at the Leopoldstädter Gymnasium at the same time as F. F. learns of his death on August 24.

1937 August 20

The American psychoanalyst Martin Peck and his wife Abigail visit F. Among other things, they discuss the rigid position of the Americans with regard to lay analysis.

1937 September 1

F.'s long-time friend Emanuel Loewy turns 80.

1937 September 10

F. writes to the British physicist and biochemist Ralph Worrall, who – inspired by F.'s *Neue Folge der Vorlesungen zur Einführung in die Psychoanalyse – had* sent him reflections on the subject of psychoanalysis and Marxism, that he had learned to his satisfaction that Marx and Engels "did not at all deny the influence of ideas and superego factors. This removes the main piece of the opposition between Marxism and psychoanalysis in which I believed" (F. to Worrall, 10.8.1937).

1937 September 20

Sophie Ritholz, American child psychologist, begins an analysis with F. It lasts until 1939 August.

1937 Autumn

F. sends an offprint of his recently published paper "Wenn Moses ein Ägypter war …" to Richard Beer-Hofmann with the remark "Perhaps also only a fiction".

1937 October beginning

– Marie Bonaparte comes to Vienna for a long time with her daughter Eugénie. Eugénie begins an analysis with F.
– The American diplomat John Wiley is appointed Consul General at the American Embassy in Vienna at the instigation of William Bullitt. Among other things, he had the task of looking after F. and his family and keeping his protective hand over them. Margaret Stonborough-Wittgenstein also frequently intervened with Wiley on F.'s behalf and kept her friend Marie Bonaparte informed of his efforts.

1937 approx. October 8

F. receives from the psychoanalyst who has emigrated to Turkey Edith Weigert-Vowinckel the manuscript of a paper on "Psychoanalytische Gedanken zum Kultus und Mythos der Magna Mater" in the hope that it could be published in *Imago*. F. expresses his reluctance.

1937 October 15

– F. gets a gold crown and a bridge for the incisors.
– Stefan Zweig sends F. his book *Magellan. The Man and His Deed*. F. reads it straight away and enjoys it.

1937 October 16

F. is back at Berggasse 19, just in time for his daughter Mathilde's 50th birthday.

1937 October 19

Queen Elisabeth of Belgium visits F. She is accompanied by Marie Bonaparte, with whom she is friends and who had established the contact.

1937 October 21

Death of Wilhelm Knöpfmacher, with whom F. had been friends since his school days.

1937 October 22

Max Eitingon visits F.

1937 before October 25

– Girindrashekhar Bose sends F. the paper "Contributions of Abnormal Psychology to Normal Psychology" by Shib Mitra with the request to comment on it before the Indian Scientific Congress in Calcutta, 1938 January. F. does so in a few sentences.
– Victor Wittkowski sends F. a volume of his poems. F., however, "has not been able to enjoy poetry for many years" (F. to Wittkowski, 25.10.1937).

1937 November

Ella Sharpe, British literary scholar and psychoanalyst, sends F. her book *Dream analysis* with the dedication "To/Sigmund Freud,/from/Ella Freeman Sharpe".

1937 November 4
Death of Gustav Gärtner. F. had worked with him in Salomon Stricker's laboratory in the summer of 1878 on the nerves of the salivary gland and salivary secretion in dogs.

1937 November 5
F. is in bed with bronchitis.

1937 November 11
F.'s son Oliver comes from Nice to visit his parents.

1937 November 14
– Marie Bonaparte shows the film footage she shot in Grinzing at the end of July.
– René Laforgue, who had come to Vienna with Marie Bonaparte, tried to persuade F. to emigrate. But F. refused on the grounds that it was not the Nazis but the Roman Catholic Church that was his real enemy.

1937 November mid
F. receives as a gift from Stefan Zweig his book *Magellan. The Man and His Deed*.

1937 November 23
Rudolf Bienenfeld repeats for F. and his close students a lecture he had given on November 10 to the Society for Sociology and Anthropology of the Jews of Vienna on the subject of "Die Religion der religionslosen Juden" ("The Religion of the religionless Jews").

1937 November 28
Stefan Zweig visits F.

1937 November 30
F. drops his prosthesis, and it breaks.

1937 December beginning
André Breton asks F. to contribute an original article to his dream collection. F. refuses because for him "the wording of the dreams […] has no interest […]. […] A collection of dreams without attached associations, without knowledge of the circumstances under which they were dreamed, says nothing to me, and I can hardly imagine what it can say to others" (F. to Breton, 8.12.1937).

1937 before December 15
F. receives Hans Ehrenwald's book Über den sogenannten jüdischen Geist as a gift.

1937 December mid
– Yvette Guilbert hints in a letter to F. that she is considering moving to London. In this context, F. writes to Marie Bonapartes asking whether her connections could be helpful for Yvette.
– F. receives new chapters of his novel *The Installation of the King from* Arnold Zweig. In it, F. considers the political to have been neglected.

1937 December 18
Marie Bonaparte asks the former Prime Minister of France, Léon Blum, to intercede for the naturalization of F.'s son Oliver, which succeeds a year later.

1937 Christmas

F. begins work on the paper "Die Ichspaltung im Abwehrvorgang".

1937 after Christmas

Henry Murray, American psychologist from Boston and his wife visit F. One of the topics discussed is the importance of giving the patient a goal for life after therapy. Murray also explains why Jung, not F., was invited to the 300th anniversary celebration of Harvard University. Murray explains that this decision was made because it was clear that F. would not be able to accept the invitation.

1938

- F. is nominated for the Nobel Prize (Medicine) for the twelfth time.
- After the publication of the book La Psychanalyse du Feu by the French philosopher Gaston Bachelard, F. writes an eight-page large-format manuscript on the "Prometheus complex". Bachelard had coined this term in his book. F.'s text was never published, however, but was sold at auction in New York in 1939 February.
- Mathilde Zissermann gives F. two Chinese figures.
- Rudolf Leitner, the husband of Ida Fliess's sister Marie Bondy, begins an analysis with F.
- Received books and offprints:
- Leo Bartemeier, American doctor, educator and psychoanalyst, sends F. an offprint of his paper "The mental hygiene clinic and the school" with the dedication "With best wishes from Leo Bartemeier".
- Smiley Blanton sends F. Clara Longworth de Chambrun's book *Shakespeare rediscovered* with the dedication "To Professor Freud: From Smiley to offset Margaret's bad influence with affectionate regards".
- William Fairbairn sends F. an offprint of his paper "Prolegomena to a psychology of art" with the dedication "To Professor Sigmund Freud,/With Compliments, and as a Token/of Respect./W R D Fairbairn".
- Eduard Hitschmann gives F. an offprint of his paper "Psychogene Spermatorrhoea" with the dedication "Herrn Professor Freud in dankbarer/Verehrung/d. V".
- Ernest Jones sends F. his book *Papers on psycho-analysis* with the dedication "To Professor Freud/With kindest regards/Ernest Jones" and an offprint of his paper "The unconscious mind and medical practice" with the dedication "With kindest regards/to/Prof. Freud/from/ Ernest Jones".
- Sacha Nacht and Rudolph Löwenstein give F. their jointly written text *Le masochisme* with the dedication "À M. le Professeur S. F./ses disciples fidèles/qui rendent hommage à l'ésprit/ qui l'a toujours guidé en op-/posant à une partie de sa pensée/a peut de leur expérience …/ divergent de la science/S. Nacht/R. Loewenstein".
- Adriaan Willemse sends F. his book *Paul Verlaine. Vu par un médecin* with the dedication "Dem Grossmeister/Sigmund Freud/Der Verfasser/Dr A Willemse".

1938 January

- Felix Boehm comes to Vienna and explains the situation in Berlin in a three-and-a-half-hour lecture. Among those present are F., Anna Freud, Paul Federn, Jeanne Lampl-de-Groot, Martin Freud and Richard Sterba. Boehm offers to admit Sterba as a non-Jew to the Berlin Association. F. warns Boehm that he may make sacrifices in Germany, but not compromises.
- Karl Menninger sends F. his book *Man against himself* with the dedication "To/Sigmund Freud/with affection/and with the earnest/hope that this exposition/of his theories will/meet with his approval./Karl A Menninger MD".

1938 January beginning
Samuel Stendig, the chairman of the Psychological Society in Krakow and editor of the Encyclopaedia of Polish Jewry, invites F. to visit him. F. declines for health reasons.

1938 January 7
F. receives Abraham Roback's book *Behaviorism at Twenty-Five* with the dedication "Professor Sigmund Freud/With the greetings of the season/and heartiest/wishes for another active year/A A Roback".

1938 January 8
Death of Anna Lichtheim, née Hammerschlag: She was the daughter of F.'s religious teacher Samuel Hammerschlag and was treated by F. from 1895 to 1900. She is part of the mixed figure from the "Dream of Irma's Injection", the "specimen dream" of psychoanalysis.

1938 January mid
F. receives a Persian glass plate for his collection from son Ernst.

1938 January 22
Hans Pichler operates on F. in the Auersperg Sanatorium. Under general anesthesia, he performs an excision of an ulcerated area and coagulation of the focus. The histological findings are positive. At the same time, F. has a sebaceous cyst on his chin removed.

1938 February
Aaron Rosanoff, American psychiatrist, sends F. his book *Manual of Psychiatry and Mental Hygiene* with the dedication "To Dr Sigmund Freud, gratefully yours, Aaron J. Rosanoff./Los Angeles, Calif.".

1938 February 6
F. reads an article by the journalist and writer Richard Bermann, which appeared under the pseudonym Arnold Höllriegel in the Viennese newspaper *Der Tag* under the headline "Traum vom Wettbewerb" ("Dream of Competition"). Bermann had this dream shortly before and thought it might interest psychologists or doctors who deal with dreams. F. writes to Bermann and interprets the head waiter in the dream as Mussolini and the dream as a dream of fear of European politics.

1938 February 11
Death of Emanuel Loewy. F. had known him since his student days and was a lifelong friend of the archeologist.

1938 February 17
For F., in the case of a necessary emigration, "the temptation would be great to seek this asylum on a beautiful spot on the Mediterranean coast" (F. to Martin Freud, 17.2.1938).

1938 February 19
Hans Pichler performs an excision of a suspicious wart in the area. The histological findings are negative.

1938 February 24
- F. is in increasing pain and has to stop working for 12 days.
- In the evening, F. hears the speech of Federal Chancellor Kurt Schuschnigg on the radio, in which he announces that Austria will remain free and independent despite pressure from Hitler.

1938 March
Theodor Reik visits F. for the last time. Reik finds F. much changed and emaciated physically, but as mentally fresh as ever.

1938 March beginning
Martha's cousin Oscar Philip visits Freud's.

1938 March 2
Minna undergoes cataract surgery. A second, equally successful operation follows on March 11.

1938 March 3
Theodor Loewenstein, Romanian educator, sends F. his work *Elemente de pedagogie sexuală. Psihologia şi pedagogia adolescenţei* with the dedication "Herrn Prof. S. Freud/in Verehrung zugeeignet/Dr. Th. Loewenstein".

1938 March 10
The American Consul General in Vienna John Wiley visits F. Immediately after the visit, he reports to William Bullitt, by now American Ambassador in Paris, and five days later, he sends a telegram to Bullitt describing the dramatic nature of F's situation.

1938 March 11
Abdication of Federal Chancellor Kurt Schuschnigg. F. hears the speech live on the radio at 20.00 in the evening.

1938 March 12
- German troops march into Austria. F. notes: "Finis Austriae".
- Kurt Hiller sends F. his book *Profile. Prose from a Decade.* But it gets lost and he has it sent again in August mid directly from the Paris publisher.

1938 March 13
- John Wiley's wife Monique visits F. and offers her help whenever necessary.
- In F.'s waiting room, a meeting of the WPV Executive Committee is held, which decides that "everyone who is able should flee the country and the headquarters of the Vereinigung should be moved to where F. will settle" (Jones, 1960–1962, vol. 3, p. 262). F. does not attend, but greets everyone with a handshake.
- In the evening, F. hears the news on the radio about the "reunification of Austria with Germany" – the so-called "Anschluss".

1938 March 14
- Adolf Hitler arrives in Vienna and receives an enthusiastic welcome.
- William Bullitt calls the American Consul General in Vienna John Wiley and asks him to intercede on F.'s behalf. That same evening, Wiley visits F. again.
- Giovacchino Forzano writes to Benito Mussolini and indirectly asks for intervention in F.'s favor.

1938 March 15
- Four S.A. men search the rooms at Berggasse 19. They find 6000 Schilling in a cash box[64], which Martha hands over to them. F. comments on this with the remark that he had received significantly less for his first house visit. They also confiscate the passports of the family members. Paula Fichtl does not want to let the men in at first and was very afraid that they might kill F. F. then smiles and asks one of the S.A. men to calm Paula down. Hans Lampl is also present.
- The American General Consul John Wiley, charged with F.'s protection, telegraphs to William Bullitt: "Fear Freud, despite age and illness, in danger". The Viennese police chief promises Wiley to keep an eye on Freud.

- A raid takes place at the Internationale Psychoanalytische Verlag in Berggasse 7, during which a list of F.'s foreign bank deposits is discovered in Martin's desk. Martin is briefly arrested because the S.A. finds F.'s will in the Internationale Psychoanalytische Verlag office, which showed that he has money abroad.
- Edward Bibring alerts the S.A. men to the fact that Matthias Heinrich Göring, the director of the "Instituts für psychologische Forschung und Psychotherapie" ("Institute for Psychological Research and Psychotherapy") in Berlin, is a cousin of Hermann Göring. During the raid, Ernest Jones also arrives, to represent the international rights to the publisher and the Institute.
- Albert Hirst wants permission from F. to take his letters to Emma Eckstein out of the country. But he can only speak to Martha and Anna.

1938 March mid

F. works mainly on the translation of Marie Bonaparte's book *Topsy, Chow Chow au pail d'or.*

1938 March 16

Foreign radio stations falsely report F.'s arrest.

1938 March 17

Marie Bonaparte arrives in Vienna from Paris. She stays at the Greek Embassy and dines with Freud's. She stays in Vienna until April 10.

1938 March 18

F.'s son Martin telegraphs to Carl Müller-Braunschweig with a request to come to Vienna to save the publisher's holdings.

1938 March 19

John Wiley informs William Bullitt that F. wishes to leave with a total of 16 people – his family, a maid and his doctor and his doctor's family. The costs of the trip are shared by Marie Bonaparte, the American Embassy in Vienna and the American State Department.

1938 March 20

- WPV meeting: chaired by Anton Sauerwald, the provisional administrator of the Viennese psychoanalytic institutions appointed by the Gestapo, the WPV, under pressure from the NSDAP (Nationalsozialistische Deutsche Arbeiterpartei = National Socialist German Workers' Party) decides to propose to F. that the WPV be taken over by the German Psychoanalytic Society as trustee. Present are Ernest Jones as President of the IPA, Marie Bonaparte and Anna Freud as Vice-Presidents, Carl Müller-Braunschweig as Secretary of the German Psychoanalytical Society, from the WPV Paul Federn, Edward Bibring, Heinz Hartmann, Ernst Kris, Robert Wälder, Wilhelm Hoffer, from the Internationale Psychoanalytische Verlag Martin Freud and Berta Steiner and finally August Beranek from Berlin.
- Departure of Ernest Jones.

1938 Spring

- Martin has to undergo another kidney operation. This time, it is performed by Alfred Zinner.
- F. reads Dorothy Thompson's book *Refugees: Organization or Anarchy?*
- Elma Pálos visits F.

1938 March 22
- A group of armed men (possibly Gestapo) search F.'s flat. After the intervention of Otto Pötzl and Hans Pichler, they leave again.
- F.'s daughter Anna is interrogated for several hours by the Gestapo at Berggasse 7; she has Veronal in her handbag. After the intervention of the American Consul General John Wiley, she is released after about 12 hours.
- F. hands his son Martin "the expression of [his] last will [...]" and asks him "to take over the execution of this will (F. to Martin F., 22.3.1938). Money, securities and all belongings in the flat go to Martha. Books and collections are intended for Anna.

1938 after March 22
Ilse Moebius brings the American reporter Ferdinand Jahn to Berggasse 19. He was to find out for his newspaper whether the rumors that F. had died after being interrogated by the Gestapo were true. Martha opens the bedroom door a crack and shows the sleeping F. to the reporter.

1938 March 28
Ernest Jones reports from London that his intervention on F.'s behalf with the British Home Secretary Samuel Hoare was successful, after an application had been made to the British Consulate in Vienna for entry for F. and the following persons of the "household Prof. Dr. Freud": Martha Freud, Minna Bernays, Anna Freud, Martin Freud, Esti Freud, Anton Walter Freud, Sophie Freud, Ernst Halberstadt, Mathilde Hollitscher, Robert Hollitscher, Max Schur with his wife and two children, Paula Fichtl. F. then notes: "Acception by England assured – emigration appears possible".

1938 March end
Franz Riklin jun travels to Vienna on behalf of C. G. Jung and his father Franz to bring F. \$10,000[65] to enable him to emigrate to Switzerland. F. refuses.

1938 April
Pierre Jouve sends F. his book *Kyrie* with the dedication "Pour Sigmund Freud avec l'hommage aussi éclatant et profond che possible à un Homme Juste dans les ténèbres. Pierre Jean Jouve".

1938 April beginning
- The lawyer Alfred Indra visits F. on the recommendation of his friend Rudolf Bienenfeld. He takes over F.'s legal representation. He then receives a visit from two SS men who inform him that Hermann Göring attaches importance to F. being treated gently. Marie Bonaparte manages to get it through the Greek legation that Indra is responsible for the legal preparations for F.'s departure.
- F. hands Marie Bonaparte a list of persons for whom F. would like to obtain a visa to emigrate. In addition to F. himself, the list contains the following names: Martha Freud, Minna Bernays, Anna Freud, Martin Freud, Esti Freud, Anton Walter Freud, Sophie Freud, Ernst Halberstadt, Mathilde Hollitscher, Robert Hollitscher, Max Schur, Helene Schur, Peter Schur, Eva Schur, Paula Fichtl.

1938 April 5
- F. asks his sister Anna in New York to help his long-time Viennese ear doctor Josef Schnierer find work.
- F. issues a certificate for Gertrude Kvergic-Kraus for immigration to England, confirming that her bookshop in Vienna has been supplying him with English literature for ten years.

1938 April 8

F. tells Marie Bonaparte memories from Paris of Jean-Martin Charcot and Louise Ricchetti, as well as some details about his ancestors and his analytical couch. Marie notes down the most important points.

1938 April 9

F. and Anna finish the German translation of Marie Bonaparte's book *Topsy, Chow Chow au pail d'or (Topsy. The golden-haired Chow)*.

1938 April 11

Carl Müller-Braunschweig hands over trusteeship of the WPV to Oskar Kauffmann, Landesärzteführer (Leader of the physicians of the Nation) of Deutsch-Österreich.

1938 April 12

Minna returns from a stay in a sanatorium.

1938 April mid

Friedrich Eckstein visits F. and finds him "in good health".

1938 April 18

Marie Bonaparte's daughter Eugénie and her groom Dominik Radziwil visit F.

1938 April 19

– F. gives his brother Alexander his cigar stash for his 72nd birthday, as he hardly smokes any more himself.
– Departure of Marie Bonaparte.

1938 April 24

Heinrich Meng sends F. an offprint of his paper "Zur Sozialpsychologie der Körperbeschädigten" with the dedication "S. Freud/in Verehrung/M.".

1938 April 26

F. has an attack of deafness.

1938 April 29

Marie Bonaparte returns to Vienna and stays until May 4.

1938 April end

– F. has all the important documents for leaving the country handed over to John Wiley. He wants to pass them on to the Gestapo and obtain permission for F. and his entourage to leave the country.
– Marie Bonaparte and Anna Freud burn piles of letters and writings in Berggasse 19.
– F. sifts through his library and selects about 800 books which he does not take with him into emigration. The bookseller Heinrich Hinterberger takes them over and later sells them via the librarian Jacob Schatzky to the New York Psychiatric Institute.

1938 April 30–May 1

Max Eitingon is in Vienna.

1938 May 1

Richard Beer-Hofmann visits F. together with Marie Bonaparte.

1938 May 5
- Minna leaves Vienna for Switzerland with Dorothy Burlingham. On May 28, they both travel on to London.
- F.'s daughter Anna begins negotiations with Anton Sauerwald about the conditions of emigration. Sauerwald also invites Ernest Jones, Marie Bonaparte and Carl Müller-Braunschweig to Berggasse 7.

1938 May 6
In view of the tense situation, F. had "decided to disregard this birthday and to postpone it to 6 June, July, August, etc., in short, to a date after our liberation […]" (F. to Jones, 13.5.1938).

1938 May 7
F.'s son Martin gives notice on behalf of his father to vacate flats 5 and 6 in Berggasse 19 as of August 1.

1938 May 10
F. hopes to be able to leave within 14 days.

1938 May 12
F. and his family receive German passports for their emigration.

1938 May 14
F.'s son Martin leaves Austria with his family.

1938 May mid
- F. undertakes two carriage rides in the immediate vicinity "to say goodbye to Vienna" (F. to Minna, 20.5.1938).
- On the initiative of Anton Sauerwald, the books of the publishing house are transported to the Austrian National Library in a night and fog operation with the help of Marie Bonaparte and thus saved from destruction. Its director Paul Heigl had given his consent.
- F.'s son Ernst rents a furnished house in London at 39 Elsworthy Road.

1938 May 17
F.'s brother Alexander leaves Austria with his family.

1938 May 21
Hans Demel, Director of the Egyptian-Oriental Department of the Museum of Art History, estimates F.'s antiquities collection at 30,000 Reichsmark. This put F. far below the tax evasion limit, and the collection was released without confiscation for a levy of 400 Reichsmark.

1938 May 23
F.'s antiquities collection is released by the Nazis for emigration.

1938 May 24
- F.'s daughter Mathilde and her husband Robert leave Austria.
- The photographer Edmund Engelmann starts taking pictures of F.'s flat at Berggasse 19. He also takes pictures of F. The work takes several days.
- F. asks Abraham Brill and an affidavit for Marie and Robert Kann. Marie is a granddaughter of Josef Breuer.
- The antique dealer Robert Wadler helps F. and Anna to organize and catalog his collection. He gives Wadler almost 30 antiques as a thank you.

1938 May 25
- F., Hans Königstein and August Aichhorn play tarot in the evening.
- F.'s total assets are estimated by the office for the "Reichsfluchtsteuer" at 125,318 Reichsmark.[66] The taxable share was 31,329 Reichsmark and was due on June 1.

1938 May 26
F.'s lawyer Alfred Indra and his wife are visiting for dinner. F. gives his wife two small jade vases and an antique glass bead necklace.

1938 May 27
William Bullitt telegraphs John Wiley with urgent advice to arrange F.'s departure as soon as possible.

1938 May 28
Death of Emilie Kassowitz, the widow of Max Kassowitz. F. learns of her death two days later.

1938 June
- F. is working on the third part of his Moses book.
- Isaac Meshulam Sclare, Scottish psychiatrist, sends F. his book *Mental nursing in observation wards* with the dedication "With humble acknowledgements to the Father of Modern Psychiatry./Isaac M. Sclare June 1938".
- Victor des Hêtres sends F. a reprint of his paper "La doctrine catholique est-elle opposée à l'égalité des sexes et à l'émancipation des femmes?" with the dedication "A Monsieur le Professeur Freud/Persécuté par l'Ignorant-Roi Hommage/très/respectueux/de/V d H".

1938 June beginning
The orthodontist Moritz Tischler visits F. and discusses with him the modalities in case it would be necessary in London to adjust the upper jaw prosthesis he had made. On this occasion, F. assures him that he would try to expedite the granting of an entry visa for Tischler. F. does so, and successfully. Tischler visits him regularly in London.

1938 June 2
- F. takes a trip to the Türkenschanzpark.
- F. asks Alfred Zinner, who had operated on Martin Freud's kidney a few weeks earlier, to come to Berggasse. F. thanks him for saving Martin's kidney.
- F. receives the "tax clearance certificate", which was necessary for leaving the affiliated Austria.
- Hans Pichler examines F. for the last time before he leaves for England. A keratosis in the form of a recurring brown crust is found on one spot. In several places, there are slight, but according to previous experience, unsuspicious papillary areas.

1938 June 4
- F. signs a declaration demanded by the Gestapo and formulated by Alfred Indra that F. has been treated well, with the following wording: "I gladly confirm that up to today, 4 June 1938, no harassment of my person or my housemates has occurred./Authorities and functionaries of the Party have always treated me and my housemates correctly and considerately" (ÖNB). F. suggests – rather jokingly – the addition: "I can recommend the Gestapo to all my friends and acquaintances".
- F. issues a testimonial for his chauffeur Josef Malina.

1938 June 4–6
Emigration to London

1938 June 4

- At 2 pm F. and his companions (Martha and Anna, housekeeper Paula Fichtl, the doctor Josefine Stross and Chow Chow Lün) drive to the Westbahnhof with a lot of luggage. They are accompanied by Alfred Indra. Of the relatives, only Beatrice and Ernst Waldinger had come to the station with them. Otto Marburg, who had given one of the speeches for F.'s 80th birthday, travels in the next compartment.
- At 3.25 am, the Orient Express leaves Vienna. Lieutenant Paul Weaver, an employee of the American Embassy, is on the train. During the journey, he makes sure that F. is not bothered at the border.

1938 June 5

- At 3.45 am, F. and his companion reach the German-French border at the bridge of Kehl. F. writes about this: "We were spared the annoying revision in Kehl by a miracle. After the Rhine bridge we were free!" (F. to Eitingon, 6.6.1938).
- At 6.00 am, short stay in Nancy, where F. had stayed from July 20 to 1889 August 3 to observe Hippolyte Bernheim and Ambroise Liébeault.
- Arrival at Gare de l'Est in Paris at 10.12 am. The company is received by Marie Bonaparte (with Bentley and Rolls Royce), the American Ambassador to France William Bullitt, son Ernst and nephew Harry.
- Arrival at 11.00 am at Marie Bonaparte's house on Rue Adolphe-Yvon in the posh Paris suburb of Saint-Cloud.
- At 9.00 pm, departure to the Gare du Nord. Marie Bonaparte gives F. some new Greek terracottas. She also gives him the Greek Athena figure she had already taken to Paris for me. F. puts everything on his desk in Elsworthy Road.
- At 9.50 pm, the "Night Ferry", which has been running since 1936, leaves the station. It was the first train to connect London with Paris without changing trains.

1938 June 6

- Arrival in Dunkerque (Dunkirk) at 1.30 am. The wagons are pushed directly onto the ferry.
- Arrival in Dover at 6.15 am. The wagons are pulled off the ferry by a locomotive.
- At 6.40 am, departure for London.
- Arrival at Victoria Station around 9.00 am, but not on the usual platform, but on another one, in order to avoid the cameramen and the large crowd of onlookers. F. and his companions were received by the board of the Southern Railway and the director of Victoria Station. F.'s children Mathilde and Martin were also at the station. Ernest Jones had arrived by car and drove F. past Buckingham Palace and Piccadilly Circus through Regent Street to the family's first accommodation at 39 Elsworthy Road, right on the edge of Primrose Hill.

1938 June 6

The house in Elsworthy Road had been rented by F.'s son Ernst for three months until a property of his own is found. F.'s bedroom is on the first floor, and he has to be carried down the stairs in the morning and up in the evening. Minna has already arrived, but is in bed with a coronary thrombosis, and F. cannot see her. The house was full of flowers and welcome gifts, including antiques. F. enjoys the reception in London: "So we have really arrived in England now, it is very nice and the public, friends and strangers alike, gave us a warm welcome" (F. to Lampl-de Groot, 13.6.1938).

1938 after June 6

F. is visited by: Edith Eder (wife of David Eder), David Forsyth, Edward Glover with wife Sarah, Yvette Guilbert, Loe Jones, Hubertus Loewenstein, Barbara Low, Clarisse Philipp, Walter Schmideberg, Walter Sprott (translator of the *New Series of Lectures for Introduction to Psychoanalysis*).

1938 June 8

The Danish painter Ivan Opffer, who lived in London and had already painted portraits of Albert Einstein, Thomas Mann, James Joyce, Bertrand Russel and George Bernhard Shaw, asks F. for 25 minutes so that he can draw him. Nothing seems to have come of it.

1938 before June 9

Martha's cousin Oscar Philipp, who lives nearby, sends F. cigars. He thanks him with the remark: "You are obviously not a smoker, otherwise you would not have sent me cigars that are much too good for me" (F. to Oscar Philipp, 8.6.1938).

1938 June 9

– F.'s nephew Sam arrives from Manchester for a welcome visit.
– Ernst Simmel asks F. to correct six of his lectures on psychoanalysis. F. is reluctant, but starts correcting them two weeks later.

1938 June 10

F., accompanied by Ernest Jones and Paula Fichtl, visits his Chow Chow bitch Lün, who had to stay in a quarantine station in South Kensington for six months after arriving in England. A Pekinese named Jumbo is purchased to replace Lün.

1938 June 11

Abraham Yahuda, professor of Jewish history, who also lives in Elsworthy Road, visits F. and urges him not to publish his Moses book. Yahuda also lives in Elsworthy Road diagonally opposite, and F. visits frequently over the next few weeks.

1938 before June 14

The doctor János Plesch, who had already emigrated to London in 1933, invites F. to his home. F. replies with a return invitation, as he cannot leave the house for health reasons.

1938 June 14

Tulo Nussenblatt sends F. the *Theodor Herzl Yearbook* he edited with the dedication "Dem verehrten Meister/Prof. Freud/ergebenst überreicht/T Nussenblatt". However, they never met in person, as F. and Nussenblatt had to leave Austria after the Anschluss.

1938 June mid

– F. receives a request from the Reichsbank Head Office in Vienna to update the "Form B (Claims against patients abroad)" and submit it to counter 44. F. writes to his lawyer that he can reply "that I would hurry to appear at counter 44 if I had not promised in writing not to set foot on German soil again" (F. to Alfred Indra, 13.6.1938).

- F. receives visits from Nandor Fodor (lawyer and parapsychologist), Thomas Looney (Shakespeare scholar), Hubertus Löwenstein (journalist and writer) and Stefan Zweig.
- F. has bladder problems due to a swelling of the prostate, which prevents him from leaving the house. Max Schur treats F. with hormone injections.

1938 June 15
Max Schur arrives in London.

1938 after June 17
Chaim Weizmann, the President of the World Zionist Organization, visits F.

1938 June 18
- F. thanks William Bullitt and John Wiley for their support during the emigration.
- F. sees sister-in-law Minna for her birthday for the first time since his arrival in London.

1938 June 19
Herbert George Wells visits F.

1938 after June 19
The English painter Hilda Davis wants to give F. one of her paintings, which is currently being shown at an exhibition in London. F. accepts the gift, and Hilda brings it to him in Maresfield Gardens after the end of the exhibition.

1938 June 21
F. resumes work on the third treatise of his work on Moses.

1938 before June 22
János Plesch offers F. his support for the period of acclimatization in London. F. then sends him his telephone number and invites him to visit.

1938 June 22
- Marie Bonaparte comes to London for three days and gives F. a Cyprian head for his collection.
- F. supports a positive assessment of the eagle pendant Leonhard Deutsch by Joseph Wilder.

1938 June 23
- F. is visited by three secretaries of the Royal Society (Sir Albert Seward, Archibald Vivia Hill, Griffith Davies). They bring the Society's register of honor with them so that F. can sign it. As a gift, he receives *The signatures in the first journal-book and the charter-book of the Royal Society* with the inscription "Presented to Freud at his signing, June 23, 1938". In it are the signatures of Issac Newton and Charles Darwin, among others. Marie Bonaparte films the visit. F. concludes his speech of thanks with the words: "When I consider that this great honour has been bestowed upon me, I am ready for the first time in my life to say; Heil Hitler" (interview by Kurt Eissler with Alfred Indra, 1954 August 4).
- Cecil Roth sends F. his book *The Jewish contribution to civilization* with the dedication "For Sigmund Freud,/who adorns civilization and/honours Jewry, in profound/admiration/Cecil Roth".

1938 after June 24
Hermann and Margarethe Nunberg visit F. Nunberg gives him an offprint of his paper "Psychological interrelations between physician and patient" with the dedication "Herrn Prof. Freud in Verehrung./H. Nunberg".

1938 June 25

The English psychoanalyst Meena Gunn – married to the Egyptologist George Gunn – visits and gives him an Egyptian antique for his collection.

1938 June 26

The English writer Charles Hopper sends F. a manuscript entitled "Shakespeare as a peacemaker".

1938 before June 28

– Richard Bermann sends F. his book published under the pseudonym Arnold Hoellriegel, *Zarzura, die Oase der kleinen Vögel. Die Geschichte einer Expedition in die libysche Wüste* with the dedication "Für Sigmund Freud/in grosser Verehrung/Richard A. Bermann/(Arnold Hoellriegel)".
– F. receives visits from Hubertus Löwenstein, Bronislaw Malinowski.

1938 June end

A reception is held at Elsworthy Road to mark F.'s entry in the Royal Society's register of honor. F. only appears briefly, however, as he is working intensively on the manuscript of his Moses book.

1938 July

F. welcomes, among others, Melanie Klein, Blanche Knopf, Joan Riviére, Wulf Sachs, Margarethe Stonbourough-Wittgenstein.

1938 July 1

Chaim Raphael asks F. on behalf of the Friends of the Hebrew University to sign a letter in support of the University Hospital of the Hebrew University in Jerusalem. A few days later, Raphael brings the letter to Maresfield Gardens for signing.

1938 July 3

F. writes an evaluation for Theodor Reik, who had just emigrated to America.

1938 July 8

F. is sent Reuben Osborn's book *Freud and Marx.*

1938 July 11

After initial hesitation, F. reacts positively to an idea by Hanns Sachs to revive the magazine *Imago in* America. He suggests the name *American Imago.*

1938 July 13

– Samuel Stendig visits F.
– Wulf Sachs visits F.

1938 July 15

The oral surgeon and radiologist Georg Exner, a former student of Hans Pichler, now living in London, visits F.

1938 July mid

– F. gives his nephew Harry a confirmation for the Home Office that he is his nephew and has a decent character.
– Johann Alemann's son Ernesto, the editor of the *Argentinisches Tageblatt,* approaches F. with the request to send a letter of congratulations for the Pestalozzi School in Buenos Aires. F. refuses on the grounds that he is "still negotiating questions of the return of my household effects and my books that remained in Vienna, and I am defending myself against continued

attempts at extortion after they have taken everything that was accessible to them. Given the vigilance of the gang, I can safely assume that such a public statement by me would give them the most welcome pretext for confiscating the rest of my belongings. I do not want to do them that favor" (F. to Ernesto Alemann, 19.7.1938).

– Wilhelm Hoffer takes some photos of Freud, including one showing Freud looking through the manuscript of his Moses book.

1938 July 16
– F. inspected a house in Finchley Road, which was not bought after all.
– Walter Hasenclever visits F. in the afternoon and gives him his drama *Der Sohn* with the dedication "Dem größten lebenden Dichter". Both men also talk about the subject of "Totem and Taboo".

1938 July 17
– F. makes a final will (F. had already made first wills in 1919 and 1923).
– F. finishes work on the third part of his Moses book, which he had written "with pleasure" (F. to Arnold Zweig, 28.6.1938).

1938 July 18
F. is requested by the Vienna Foreign Exchange Office to hand over 12,000 Dutch Gulden from an illegal bank account in Switzerland to them. F. refuses, as this money came from Marie Bonaparte and was intended to pay the taxes due for leaving the annexed Austria.

1938 July 19
– Stefan Zweig visits F. and brings Salvador Dali and his wife Gala with him. Dali had tried unsuccessfully to contact Freud earlier. They are accompanied by Edward James, who owns Salvador's latest painting "The Metamorphosis of Narcissus" and had brought it with him to show F. Stefan Zweig forgets his gloves as he leaves, which F. interprets as a promise to come back.
– F. has problems with hearing.

1938 July 20
– Hubertus Löwenstein sends F. the statutes of the German Academy in Exile, which had been founded for him and Volkmar von Zühlsdorff. Löwenstein asks F. to assume the presidency of the Academy's scientific department at Thomas Mann's suggestion (Thomas Mann becomes president of the artistic department). F. should also propose who should be appointed as a full member. After some hesitation, F. agrees.
– Willy Lévy begins work on a bust of F. He gives Willy a gem with Pallas Athene.

1938 July 22
F. begins writing the *outline of psychoanalysis.*

1938 July 23
Jacques Schnier, American sculptor, writer, educator and engineer, sends F. a small bronze weight that was used to weigh rice and grain at the market in Mandalay (now Myanmar). It is given a place as a paperweight on F.'s desk.

1938 July 25
Norman Sweet sends F. his book *Personality chart: Professional psychoanalysis of personality.*

1938 July 28
- F. signs his will made on July 17.
- F. buys the house at 20 Maresfield Gardens.

1938 July 29
- Anna goes to the XV International Psychoanalytical Congress in Paris. She returns on August 5.
- Ruth Mack Brunswick arrives in London. She has some analysis sessions with F. and sees Sergei Pankejeff, whose treatment she had taken over in 1926. She stays until August 24.
- Carl Gustav Jung sends a welcome telegram on behalf of the International General Medical Society for Psychotherapy, which is holding its Congress in Oxford, to F. He thanks him with a text that Edward Bennett had previously agreed with F.'s son Ernst.
- Abraham Kanter, American doctor, sends F. his book *And the stutterer talked,* written with Abe Kohn, with the dedication "With best wishes to/Prof. Dr. S. Freud/A H Kanter MD".

1938 July 30
- William Bullitt visits F.
- Radiologist John Braine examines F.

1938 August 1
F.'s patient Herman Claus "has become ill under the pressure of analysis" (F. to Anna, 1.8.1938). After a long break, the therapy is continued by Grete Bibring, who is already treating Claus' wife Marie.

1938 August
F. receives the following visitors, among others: Isaiah Berlin, Maria Bonaparte, William and Louise Bullitt, Max Eitingon, Ruth Mack Brunswick, Willy Lévy, Munro Meyer, Hermann Nunberg, Pauline Hartwig.

1938 August beginning
The Imago Publishing Company is founded by the writer and translator John Rodker. F. immediately receives brochures from the new publishing house, which publishes *American Imago* and F.'s *Gesammelte Werke,* among others.

1938 August 4
Radiologist John Braine is back at F.

1938 August 5
F. receives the news from the Viennese company E. Bäuml, which specializes in art transports that his antique collection and household objects have been loaded into three wagons and are on their way to London.

1938 August 6
Marie Bonaparte comes to London for two days.

1938 August 8
- F.'s removal goods arrive in London. He writes in this connection: "All the Egyptians, Chinese and Greeks have arrived, survived the transport with little damage and look more imposing here than in Berggasse" (F. to Lampl-de Groot, 8.10.1938).
- Juan Marin, Chilean doctor, sends F. his book *Ensayos freudianos. De la medicina, de la historia y del arte* with the dedication *"Al ilustre Prof. Sigmund Freud,/gloria de la humanidad/ contemporánea./Con admiracion y adhesion/Dr. Juan Marin".*

– Alvan Barach, American lung specialist, sends F. his book *The Spectacle of a Man,* which he published under the pseudonym John Coignard.

1938 August 10
Theodore Faithfull, veterinarian and psychoanalyst, sends F. his book The *mystery of the androgyne: Three papers on the theory and practice of* psycho-analysis.

1938 August 13
F. inspects his just purchased house in Maresfield Gardens 20.

1938 before August 15
F. has short-lasting cases of ear infection, successfully treated.

1938 August mid
– Claudius Regaud of the Institut Curie in Paris recommends electrocoagulation at the slightest suspicious pathological change.
– Arnold Zweig sends F. his essay *Baruch Spinoza. Portrait of a Free Spirit 1632–1677.*

1938 August 19
F. gets a visit from journalists.

1938 before August 21
F. receives the manuscript of her essay "Time and the Unconscious" from Marie Bonaparte.

1938 August 21
At the request of Stefan Zweig, the photographer Marcel Sternberger takes portraits of F. Sternberger had already photographed Bernhard Shaw and Herbert George Wells.

1938 August 23
– Jan van Emden visits F.
– Lili Frohlich-Bume, the widow of F.'s art dealer Otto Fröhlich visits F.

1938 August 25
– F. receives the book *Dental surgery for medical practitioners* by the London dentist Barnett Kopkin.
– Karl Fleischmann visits F.
– Martha Hoffmann visits F.
– Julius Philipp, Martha's cousin, visits Freud's.

1938 August 26
F. receives the book *Chemistry of the Brain* by the American physiologist Irvin Page. It probably influenced the end of Chapter 6 of *Abriss der Psychoanalyse.*

1938 August 28
Olga Schnitzler visits F.

1938 August 29
– Minna is placed in a care home during the move to Maresfield Gardens.
– Maria Thalberg, the daughter of F.'s former patient Oskar Thalberg, visits F.

1938 August 30
F. receives a visit from representatives of the Hebrew University in Jerusalem.

1938 August 31
Smiley Blanton is in London working with F for a week.

1938 August end
Sergei Pankejeff, the patient known as the "Wolf Man", visits F.

1938 September 3
F. moves with Martha to the Esplanades Hotel (2 Warrington Crescent, now the Colonnades Hotel). This had become necessary because the lease in Elsworthy Road had expired before the permanent home in Maresfield Gardens was ready for occupation. Minna is accommodated in a nursing home and Robert and Mathilde in a boarding house.

1938 September 4
F.'s brother Alexander arrives in London with his wife Sophie and son Harry; later, they traveled on to Canada.

1938 September 7
– Smiley Blanton finishes his analysis at F.
– Arnold Zweig visits F.

1938 September 7–27
Stay at the London Clinic

1938 September 7
Hans Pichler arrives in London, and F. is admitted to the London Clinic, as Pichler is planning a major operation.

1938 September 8
Hans Pichler removes a large cheek tumor and another area of altered tissue. The cheek tumor is histologically negative, and the other pieces were initially mistakenly not examined. F. described this operation as the "most difficult since 1923" (F. to Marie Bonaparte, 4.10.1938).

1938 September 9
Hans Pichler is satisfied with the operation and flies back to Vienna. F.'s upper lip, however, remains paralyzed for weeks. In addition, a painful bone necrosis has formed.

1938 September 13
Louis Golding, English writer, sends F. his book *In the steps of Moses the conqueror* with the dedication "Professor Freud".

1938 September 14
Smiley Blanton delivers a book on the Earl of Oxford for F. at the London Clinic.

1938 September 16
F.'s wife Martha and housekeeper Paula Fichtl move into 20 Maresfield Gardens.

1938 September 22
F. hands over his "last will and testament" to his son Martin, namely that all "money and securities", as well as "all possessions in our house", are to become the property of his

wife Martha – with the exception of the books and collections, whose "arbitrary distribution" is to be taken care of by daughter Anna. F. asks Martin to supervise all this.

1938 September 27

F. is released from the sanatorium and moves into 20 Maresfield Gardens.

1938 September 28

F. uses for Ernst Czuczka, son-in-law Richard Beer-Hofmann in his search for employment.

1938 September 30

On the day of the signing of the Munich Agreement, F. notes "Peace" in large letters.

1938 October

Josef Breuer's daughter Marie Kann visits F.

1938 October 2

– Minna moves into 20 Maresfield Gardens.
– Martin has to go to hospital for a week because of colitis.

1938 October 10

F. recommends Ernst Waldinger, the husband of his niece Beatrice, to the German Academy in Exile for support and assistance. Waldinger had emigrated to New York with his wife and two children. He also asks Thornton Wilder, whom he knew from his visit to Vienna, for support for Ernst Waldinger.

1938 October 11

Anton Sauerwald comes to London, presumably also to discuss the forthcoming liquidation of the Internationale Psychoanalytische Verlag.

1938 October 12

Arnold Zweig, who had been in London since the beginning of September, comes with his son for a farewell visit. F. gives Adam an Egyptian Ptah.

1938 October mid

– Marie Bonaparte visits F. for four days. She is accompanied by her daughter Eugenie and her husband Dominik.
– The historian of science Charles Singer addresses an urgent warning to F. via one of his sons not to publish his book on Moses and the monotheistic religion. The English churches might take it as an attack on religion, but it was important as a bulwark against anti-Semitism. He also sends him his pamphlet *The Christian Approach to Jews*.

1938 October 20

F. begins writing a treatise with the English title "Some Elementary Lessons in Psychoanalysis".

1938 October 22

Willy Lévy visits F. at his request to show Marie Bonaparte F.'s finished bust.

1938 before October 24

Guido von Fuchs invites F. to a meeting of the "Austrian Circle for Arts and Science", which F. declines for health reasons. However, F. complies with the request to be allowed to use his name for the circle. Fuchs had emigrated to England in 1935; in Austria, he was a civil servant at the Lower Austrian Financial Directorate, but also worked as a theater and arts editor for the *Reichspost*; he is also a musician and composer.

1938 October 25

Ole Øye, Norwegian psychologist, sends F. his book *Psykologiske studier av aktuelle Samfundsspørsmål* with the dedication "Til prof. Sigm. Freud, fra forfatteren. Farbödighet og takknemlighet".

1938 October 26

The philosopher David Baumgardt and his wife Carola, who used to work with F.'s son Ernst, visit F.

1938 October 29

– Marie Bonaparte, her daughter Eugenie and son-in-law Dominik Radziwil, visit F. As a guest gift, they bring a bronze Venus with a mirror in its hand for F's collection. They leave again on November 2.
– Arthur Koestler visits F. and asks him to write an essay on the subject of anti-Semitism for the German-French exile magazine *Die Zukunft, which* he edits.
– Otto Loewy visits F.

1938 October 31

F. writes the contribution requested by Arthur Koestler.

1938 November beginning

F. receives contradictory information about the housing situation of his sisters remaining in Vienna from Alfred Indra and Anton Sauerwald. F. and his brother Alexander had left them 160,000 schillings[67]; however, most of the amount had probably been confiscated. F. thought about taking them to the French Riviera, near Nice, but was skeptical whether this was possible.

1938 November 3

– F. receives from David Baumgardt his book *Der Kampf um den Lebenssinn unter den Vorläufern der modernen Ethik* with the dedication "Professor Sigmund Freud in Verehrung und Dankbarkeit".
– F. receives Henry Murray's book *Explorations in Personality.*

1938 November 5

Abraham Roback sends F. the book by Morton Prince *Clinical and experimental studies in personality* with the dedication "To Sigmund Freud/with the highest regard and most fervent wishes of/A. A. Roback (editor)".

1938 November 7

F. has a conversation with representatives of the Jewish Scientific Institute YIVO (Jacob Maitlis, Josef Leftwitch and Isaac Nachman Steinberg). The latter was Minister of Justice in Lenin's government from 1917 December to 1918 March. The conversation is about F.'s Moses book, among other things. Steinberg is of the opinion that no one has the right to ask F. not to publish it.

1938 before November 10

René Fülöp-Miller sends F. his book *Triumph over Pain* with the dedication "Herrn Prof. Dr. Siegmund Freud, in tiefer Verehrung/René Fülöp-Müller".

1938 November 10
– The day after the Reich Pogrom Night, F. notes in English: "Pogroms in Germany".
– F. learns of the ban on his writings in Spain.

1938 November 12
– F. feels an urgent desire to tell the cartoonist David Low "how much [I] admire your glorious art and your inexorable, unfailing criticism" (F. to Low, 12.11.1938). After his arrival in England, F. had repeatedly come across cartoons by David Low, an influential British political cartoonist who at that time mainly published in the *Evening Standard.*
– The German-born psychologist Siglinde Ann Coles visits F.

1938 November 13
David Alexander Edward Lindsay, 27th Earl of Crawford, visits F.

1938 November mid
F.'s son Ernst has a lift installed in Maresfield Gardens so that F. and Minna, neither of whom can climb stairs, are more mobile in the house.

1938 November 15
– F. sends Marie Bonaparte the names and dates of birth of his four sisters remaining in Vienna, since Marie had suggested that he should work for their emigration to France.
– F. receives a request from Margaret Mackworth, second Viscountess Rhondda, if F. would make a "statement" for a special issue of *Time and Tide, the* magazine she founded, on anti-Semitism.

1938 November 16
– The BBC asked Anna if F. would give a statement "for the benefit of posterity". After consultation with her father, Anna gave the BBC a positive answer.
– F. writes a statement for Paul Federn, who had emigrated to America in September, calling it an absurdity that Federn should take an examination in general medicine so that he could practice psychoanalysis in teaching and practice.

1938 before November 17
– F. receives Dorothy Thompson's book Refugees: *A World Problem.*

1938 November 17
– F. sends the requested statement on anti-Semitism to *Time and Tide*.
– Charles Singer visits F.

1938 November 19
F. has a meeting with the American publisher Blanche Knopf about the publication of his Moses book in America.

1938 November 20
Psychoanalyst, translator and editor Douglas Bryan visits F.

1938 November 21
– F.'s nephew Morris (son of his brother Philipp) is killed in a car accident in South Africa. F. learns of his death through his niece Pauline (daughter of brother Emanuel) on November 27.
– Elizabeth Rotten, Swiss educator, visits F.

1938 November 25
– The German-French exile magazine *Die Zukunft* publishes F.'s essay "Ein Wort zum Anti-semitismus" in a special issue.
– F. receives the book *Psychological methods of healing. An introduction to psychotherapy* by the British psychiatrist and psychologist William Brown.

1938 November 28
– F. sends to Yisrael Doryon the introduction to his book *Lynceus' New State, which* Doryon had asked him to write. Originally, Doryon wanted to dedicate his book to F. However, he refused, since he "had no right to it" (F. to Doryon, 28.11.1938). Albert Einstein wrote a second introduction.
– F. receives a bouquet of gardenias, his favorite flowers, from Hilda Doolittle.
– A first piece of bone is rejected from the necrotic area that had formed after the last operation.

1938 November 29
Herbert George Wells visits F. It was his last visit to F.

1938 December
Ernest François Eugène Douwes Dekker – a distant relative of Multatuli, whom F. revered – sends F. his *writing God's geboorte* with the dedication "In admiring/devotion/Dr. Douwes Dekker/Bandoeng, Java".

1938 December beginning
Max Schur discovers a sensitive swelling in F.'s mouth with a foul-smelling secretion. F. is in severe pain.

1938 December 2
– F. writes a letter in German and English for his niece Lilly, which Lilly wants to publish in an advertising brochure for her performances.
– Rudolf Olden, German journalist and lawyer, visits F.
– Elizabeth Severn visits F.

1938 December 4
– Marie Bonaparte visits F. and stays four days.
– Representatives of the European Commission for Lay Analysis visit F.

1938 December 6
– F. recommends to the German Academy in Exile to take care of the poet Max Fleischer who is in a very distressed situation in Vienna (XIX, Gymnasiumstr. 62).
– Anna picked up Lün from the North Kensington quarantine station where she has been housed since arriving in England.
– At Anna's invitation, the Icelandic folk singer Engel Lund visits the Freuds in London and sings Icelandic and English songs. Marie Bonaparte and Dorothy Burlingham are also present.

1938 December 7
F. grants an interview to the radio journalist Howard Lynton Fletcher from the BBC at 11.00 in Maresfield Gardens.

1938 December 8
- The British psychologist William Brown visits F.
- The British psychiatrist Allan Worsley visits F.

1938 December 12
Rudolf Bienenfeld visits F. and presents him with his book *Deutsche und Juden*.

1938 December mid
- F.'s son Oliver and his family receive French citizenship. In the end, Marie Bonaparte's intercession with Finance Minister Paul Reynaud was successful. F. thanks Reynaud in writing.

1938 December 16
Reverend Cornelius Greenway of the "All Souls Universalist Church" in Brooklyn (New York), asks F. for a signed portrait photo.

1938 December 18
Omri Marlé, the son of F.'s niece Lilly, had emigrated to London and brings F. as a gift from Lilly Dante's *Divine Comedy* with the dedication "Maurice Freud's Werk – für Onkel Sigmund Freud – Lilly 1938".

1938 December 22
F. receives the portrait photos from Marcel Sternberger, which he had taken on August 21. F. thinks they are very successful.

1938 before December 23
The League of American Writers asks F. for a manuscript for an auction to benefit "anti-Nazi writers". F. complies with the request and sends the first draft of his statement on anti-Semitism, which he had formulated for the weekly magazine *Time and Tide* on November 16.

1938 Christmas
- Max Schur removes a bone quester.
- Rudolf Bienenfeld sends F. an offprint of his lecture "Die Religion der religionslosen Juden" ("The Religion of the Religionless Jews") with the dedication "Zur Erinnerung an Wien in dauernder Verehrung Herrn Professor Sigm. Freud Rudolf Bienenfeld".
- Prynce Hopkins sends F. his book *The psychology of social movements* with the dedication "To Prof. Freud/in appreciation of what/his researches have contributed to my own happiness/and with best Christmas/wishes, from/Prynce Hopkins".

1938 December 26
F. finishes the proofs of his book *The Man Moses and the Monotheistic Religion*.

1938 before December 27
F. receives as a gift from Rachel Berdach her book *Der Kaiser, die Weisen und der Tod* (published under the pseudonym R. Bardi).

1938 December 27
The BBC broadcasts the interview with F. recorded on December 7 in the series "Celebrities on Radio".

1938 December 28
Max Schur removes a bone splinter that had come loose as a result of the last operation.

1939

F. buys volume 12 of *The Cambridge ancient history*.

Books received:

- Heinz Hartmann sends F. an offprint of his paper "Ich-Psychologie und Anpassungsprobleme" with the dedication "Herrn Prof. Sigm. Freud/mit den herzlichsten Grüßen/und Wünschen/von seinem dankbar ergebenen/Heinz Hartmann".
- Smith Ely Jelliffe sends F. an offprint of his paper Sigmund Freud and psychiatry with the dedication "For Prof. F. Uncorrected".
- Merrill Moore sends F. his book *One thousand autobiographical sonnets* with the dedication "For Dr. Sigmund Freud/with admiration and esteem/Sincerely/Merrill Moore".
- Raymond de Saussure sends F. his book *Le miracle grec. Etude psychanalytique sur la civilisation héllénique* with the dedication "A Monsieur le Professeur Freud/hommage respectueux/Dr R de Saussure".
- Arthur Segal sends F. his book *Art as a test of normality and its application for therapeutic purposes.*
- Norman Symons, Canadian psychologist, sends F. an offprint of his paper "On the conception of a dread of the strength of the instincts" with the dedication "With the compliments/of the author".
- The "League of intellectual Austria" elects F. as honorary president and asks him whether he accepts the election.
- Gustave Tuck, President of the Jewish Historical Society, sends F. an offprint of Philip Guedalla's lecture "The Jewish past" with the dedication "With/Gustave Tuck's/Compliments".

1939 January
F. has lumbago and also severe bone pain as a result of the last operation.

1939 January beginning
- The All Souls Unitarian Church from Tulsa in Oklahoma asks F. for a portrait photo to hang in the church. F. politely declines.
- Samuel Lipton, American physician, begins an analysis with F.

1939 January 4
Hubertus Löwenstein asks F. for a manuscript for an auction to benefit the German Academy in Exile. F. sends him some letters, which fetch high prices at an auction in February mid.

1939 January 6
- F.'s daughter Mathilde opens the fashion shop "Robell" in Baker Street.
- Samuel Stendig sends a newspaper article written by him about his visit to F. on 1938 July 13. He also asks him for a short article on the subject of psychoanalysis in Poland, a photograph with his own signature and an offprint of his last Moses article. F. refuses all requests and adds that if Stendig nevertheless continues to represent his "theories in Poland, I will have to give you credit for it" (F. to Stendig, 21.1.1939).

1939 before January 9
Ernst Simmel asks F. if he can name the clinic he is planning in Los Angeles after him. F.'s answer is: "Your institute is not yet finished. If I am no longer alive at the time of its opening, you can do what you like anyway. If, contrary to expectations, I am still here, a cable from you will make a quick decision possible" (F. to Simmel, 9.1.1939).

1939 January 9
- F. sends Abraham Brill a paper by Robert Kann, from which the latter's interest in psychoanalysis and its applications becomes clear.
- Selma and Heinrich Glanz visit F. Glanz wants to talk to him about Moses, but F. asks him to write it down. Glanz then sends F. a manuscript on the Moses question, with which he tried to convince F. that Moses was a Jew. F. invites him a little later, but tells him he has to wait with an answer until his Moses book has appeared.

1939 January 10
- F. rejects the annual account for 1938 issued by Max Schur, because "if I present it to the Medical Association, you will probably be called to account for disrespecting medical services contrary to your profession" (F. to Schur, 10.1.1939) and demands a new account.
- Hugo Ignotus visits F.

1939 January mid
Max Schur discovers new swellings in F.'s mouth, which he believes to be epithelial cancer.

1939 before January 20
Vilém Freud from Prague asks F. for help, possibly in connection with a planned emigration to England. F. cannot promise any support. Vilém Freud and his wife Berta do not succeed in emigrating; they are deported and murdered in the Bełzec extermination camp in 1942 March.

1939 January 25
- The writer Rachel Berdach visits F. at his invitation.
- André Repond, Swiss psychoanalyst, visits F.

1939 January 28
Leonard and Virginia Woolf are invited to tea at F.'s.

1939 January 29
Wilfred Trotter visits F.

1939 January 31
F. finished a recommendation for Maximilian Steiner, who had fled Vienna for London at the end of 1938.

1939 February
- F. approaches various people in order to obtain an entry permit and employment for his niece Lilly and her husband Arnold for England.
- F. promises the Maccabi World Union that they can use his name for their "Patronage Council". The secretary of Maccabi was Valentin Rosenfeld, whom F. had known for over 30 years.

1939 February 1
Karl Federn, brother of Paul Federn, visits F.

1939 February 2
F. grants permission for the printing of his Moses book, which is published by Allert de Lange in Amsterdam.

1939 February 4 or 6
Thomas Ankles sends F. his book *A study of jealousy as differentiated from envy* with the dedication "To Prof. Sigmund Freud With kind regards T. M. Ankles".

1939 February 5
Maria Bonaparte and Ernest Jones visit F.

1939 February 10
Wilfred Trotter, brother-in-law of Ernest Jones, examines F. He only recommends continuing to observe the swellings in F.'s mouth that Schur had discovered in January mid.

1939 February 11
Max Schur diagnoses a lump and an ulcer, which he believes to be a carcinoma. As the patient is not expected to undergo an operation, radium is to be given.

1939 February 14
F. sends Arnold Marlé a letter of recommendation for him and his wife – F.'s niece Lilly – as they intend to emigrate from Prague.

1939 February 17
The translator William Robson-Scott visits F.

1939 February 19
At the auction of the League of American Writers, F.'s draft of the statement on anti-Semitism and three letters by him will be auctioned. In addition, Abraham Brill had contributed F.'s manuscript on the Prometheus complex.

1939 February 20
Wilfred Trotter examines F. again, and refuses a new surgical intervention.

1939 February 24
– David Oppenheim visits F.
– Wilfred Trotter examines F. again.

1939 February 26
Marie Bonaparte visits F. with Alexander Lacassagne, Claudius Regaud's successor as director of the Institut Curie in Paris. Lacassagne examines F. together with Wilfred Trotter. Lacassagne later sends F. an invoice for 5000 francs.[68]

1939 February 27
Arnold Zweig sends F. the draft of a planned Salomon novel.

1939 February 28
F. is X-rayed, and a tissue sample is taken. The histological findings are positive, but the doctors do not consider further surgery to be indicated.

1939 March
– Mario Degani sends F. his book *La musica nella preistoria e nelle antiche civiltà* with the dedication "To Dr. Sigmund Freud/as a sign of respectful/and devoted admiration./Mario Degani".

1939 March 2
John Rickman sends F. his English translation of three of F.'s papers under the title *Civilization, war and death* with the dedication "To Prof Sigm. Freud/in gratitude for many things/freely given./J. R.".

1939 March 3
Lacassagne, who has returned to Paris in the meantime, suggests X-ray irradiation, as radium treatment would have been more likely to damage the healthy tissue.

1939 March 4
Heinrich Meng sends F. Adrien Turel's book *Bachofen – Freud. Zur Emanzipation des Mannes vom Reich der Mütter* with the dedication "Herrn Prof Dr S. Freud/in Dankbarkeit und/ Verehrung/H. Meng". F. reads the book immediately.

1939 March 5
– Fritz Paneth, son of F.'s friend Joseph Paneth, and his wife Else visit F.

1939 March 6
– The radiologist Neville Finzi examines F. in the presence of Wilfred Trotter. Both consider another operation to be hopeless. However, after the radiologist William Harmer has also examined F., a new radium treatment with a low-dose and subsequent X-ray radiation is decided upon to alleviate the pain.
– F. receives Nandor Fodor's book *On the Nature of Cultural Transformations since the End of the Middle Ages*.

1939 March 8
Anna and Martin go to the celebration of the 21st founding anniversary of the British Psycho-analytic Society. Among the guests are Julian Huxley, Henry Moore, Herbert George Wells, Rebecca West, Virginia Woolf.

1939 before March 9
Examinations in F.'s mouth area lead to the conclusion that F. has a cancer recurrence.

1939 March 9
Beginning X-ray treatment at Neville Finzi's practice in Harley Street. As a result, exhaustion, slight dizziness and headache set in. And finally, F. begins to lose his beard and bleeds from the mouth.

1939 March 12
The journalist and historian Walter Steinthal approaches F. and tells him that his research on Moses supports F.'s theses.

1939 March 13
– Marie Bonaparte arrives in London with Alexander Lacassagne. She stays until March 19.
– F. receives two advance copies of his book The Man Moses and the Monotheistic Religion. He gives one of them to Marie Bonaparte.

1939 after March
- F.'s book *The Man Moses and the Monotheistic Religion is* published.
- Hedwig Abraham, the widow of Karl Abraham, visits F. and he gives her a copy of his Moses book with the dedication "Frau Hedwig Abraham in alter Freundschaft Verf.".
- F. gives Ernst and Lucie his book *The Man Moses and the Monotheistic Religion* is published.

1939 March 15
F. receives the first radium irradiation. Neville Finzi inserts the radiation prosthesis, Alexander Lacassagne assists; Max Schur and William Harmer are also present.

1939 March 16
F. becomes Honorary President of the Austrian Center in London. The Austrian Center had achieved, among other things, that Austrians did not have to present identity papers from the Austrian legation to the British authorities, as Germany had declared Austrian passports invalid.

1939 March 19
Heinz Hartmann visits F.

1939 March 20
William Harmer visits F. and notes a positive influence of the X-ray treatment on the diseased areas.

1939 March 22
F. accepts the honorary presidency of the Jewish Health Research and Planning Institute to be founded. The foundation had been decided by the Society for the Protection of Jewish Health (OSE) in 1939 spring.

1939 March 24
F. asks the Amsterdam publisher Allert de Lange to send one copy each of his just published book *Der Mann Moses und die monotheistische Religion* at his expense to: Thomas Mann, Albert Einstein, Abraham Brill, Ruth Mack Brunswick and Max Eitingon.

1939 Spring
- Elizabeth Severn visits F.
- Anton Sauerwald visits F., and the latter asks him to convince Hans Pichler to come to London.
- After returning to Vienna, Sauerwald drives Hans Pichler by car to London (by ferry to Dover).
- Martha's cousin Oscar Philipp visits F. with Isaiah Berlin, and introduces him. During the conversation, F.'s grandson Lucian appears and when F. asks him where he has been, he answers: "At a performance of Romeo and Juliet". To which, F. replies: "That wouldn't have been necessary, you are a Romeo".
- F. gives Edward Bibring a copy of his book *Der Mann Moses und die monotheistische Religion* with the dedication "Herrn Dr. Eduard Bibring, Redakteur im Exil".
- F. sends Havelock Ellis a copy of his book *The Man Moses and the Monotheistic Religion*.

1939 March 31
Marie Bonaparte visits F.

1939 April 2
The German doctor Adolf Sindler from Dusseldorf visits F. He was engaged in the "re-education" of Prisoners of War.

1939 April 6
The psychiatrist and psychoanalyst Charles Berg from the Tavistock Clinic sends F. a series of offprints of his publications.

1939 April 9
Jeanne Lampl-de Groot and her husband Hans Lampl visit F.

1939 April 16
F. notes the changeover to summer time.

1939 before April 18
Félicien Challaye sends F. her book *Nietzsche* with the dedication "Au Maître Sigmund Freud, Respectueux hommage. Félicien Challaye".

1939 April 21
Max Schur takes his family to New York. He returns on July 8. During his absence, he is represented by Bernard Samet – a former colleague of F.'s friend and cardiologist Ludwig Braun – and Vladimir Gurevich.

1939 April 24
– Arnold Marlé visits F.
– Charles Singer and his wife Dorothea visit F.

1939 May
Alfred Indra, the lawyer who had helped to arrange F.'s emigration, visits F. on his return journey from America together with his friend Rudolf Bienenfeld, who is already living in London.

1939 May 4
F. receives Hans Carossa's work *Wirkungen Goethes in der Gegenwart* with the dedication "Dem Goethepreis-Träger Sigmund Freud mit den herzlichsten Glückwunsch zum 6. Mai 1939 in großer Verehrung seines Werkes und seines Menschentums Hans Carossa".

1939 May 6
Marie Bonaparte comes to London for three days for F.'s birthday, as does Yvette Guilbert, who gives F. her photograph with a dedication. Marie Bonaparte's daughter Eugénie films the birthday party in the garden.

1939 May 12
Marie Bonapartes' book about her Chow Chow Topsy, translated by F. and Anna, is published.

1939 May 13
– Eva Isaacs, the chairperson of the British section of the World Jewish Congress, asks F. to support the Jewish youth organization Maccabi. However, F. had already promised the Maccabi World Union in February that they could use his name for their "Patronage Council".
– Moritz Tischler discovers a walnut-sized neoplasm between the upper lip and a bridge and immediately suspects malignancy.

1939 May 15
Georg Exner confirms the cancer recurrence, but no longer considers an operation to be indicated. Radium was given for two hours a day with the help of a prosthesis, along with deep X-ray radiation. The tumor has receded, but metastases have appeared.

1939 May mid

F.'s sister Rosa receives information from the French consulate in Vienna that now would be the right time to intervene in Paris in favor of the four Freud sisters. F. immediately forwards this information to Marie Bonaparte, but fails to get the sisters to France. They all perish in concentration camps.

1939 May 16

F. concludes a contract with the Imago Publishing Company for the publication of his writings.

1939 May 19

F.'s Moses book is published in English under the title Moses and monotheism by the New York publisher Alfred A. Knopf.

1939 May 20

Anna goes to Amsterdam to visit her friend Jeanne Lampl-de Groot.

1939 after May 26

In response to his book *Der Mann Moses und die monotheistische Religion,* published in March, F. receives an unsigned letter from a Jew in Boston: "I read in the local press your statement that Moses was not a Jew. It is to be regretted that you could not go to your grave without disgracing yourself, you old nitwit. We have had renegades like you by the thousands, we are glad we are rid of them and we hope soon to be rid of you. It is to be regretted that the Gangsters in Germany did not put you into a concentration camp, that's where you belong".

1939 May end

Edmund and Anna Jerusalem visit F.

1939 June

- David Forsyth sends F. his book *How life began. A speculative study in modern biology* with the dedication "Professor Freud/from the Author/with affectionate regards".
- F. invites Paula Fichtl into his study on the occasion of her tenth anniversary of service and thanks her for the wonderful time with her and for sharing joys and sorrows with him.

1939 June 2

Marie Bonaparte arrives in London for "a few days". She gives F. her book *Cinq cahiers écrits par une petite fille entre sept ans et demi et dix ans et leurs commentaires* with the dedication "Au Professeur Freud, en souvenir et en reconnaissance de tant d'heures d'intimite' psychanalytiques et en amitie' profonde. Marie Bonaparte".

1939 June 13

- F. asks Blanche Knopf to send one copy each of his just published book *Moses and Monotheism* to: Abraham Roback, Smith Ely Jelliffe and Herman Nunberg.
- F. grants the Austrian writer Julius Epstein permission to invoke his name with the American Guild for German Cultural Freedom.
- Robert Neumann, the president of the Austrian PEN group in London, asks F. to make him an honorary member of the PEN group. F. accepts with thanks.

1939 June 14

Heinrich Meng sends F. the third edition of the *Psychoanalytischen Volksbuch* written by him and Paul Federn with the dedication "Herrn Prof. S. Freud/in Dankbarkeit und/Verehrung überreicht/von Verleger u Herausgeber/Heinrich Meng*". F. thinks that "this work will remain the best introduction to psychoanalysis for a long time" (F. to Meng, 16.6.1939).

1939 June mid
- F. gives Wilfred Trotter a copy of his book *Moses and Monotheism* with the dedication "Wilfred Trotter mit Gruß u. Dank Sigm. Freud 1939".
- F. gives his niece Pauline Hartwig (daughter of Philipp Freud) his *Moses and Monotheism* with the dedication "To dear Poppy from Uncle Sigm".
- 1800 copies of F.'s book *Der Mann Moses und die monotheistische Religion* have already been sold.

1939 June 28
The BBC asks F. if they can send to him Anthony Weymouth in preparation for a program on "Moses and Monotheism". Behind the pseudonym "Anthony Weymouth" was Ivo Geikie Cobb, a doctor practicing in Harley Street, who also worked as an author and journalist.

1939 June 30
Abraham Roback sends F. a copy of a letter by Carl Gustav Jung in which Jung describes Hitler as a danger; at the same time, Jung reports about Hitler-friendly dreams of some of his Jewish patients. Roback asks F. to destroy the copy of the letter.

1939 Summer
The surgeon Dorian Eisenklamm visits F. at the request of Josephine Stross. The visit is about controlling pain. F. believes that pain can best be controlled by willpower.

1939 July
Hanns Sachs comes from America and visits F. daily.

1939 July beginning
F. refuses to take painkillers – except aspirin.

1939 July 2
Marie Bonaparte is in London for a few days and celebrates her 57th birthday with daughter Eugenie at F.

1939 July 3
Heinrich Meng sends F. his book *Seelischer Gesundheitsschutz* with the dedication *"Herrn Prof S. F./in Verehrung/Heinrich Meng"*.

1939 July 8
Max Schur returns from America.

1939 July 10
F. learns of the death of Havelock Ellis. Ellis had died on July 8.

1939 July 15
Death of Eugen Bleuler.

1939 July 20
Once again, representatives of a commission on lay analysis issues visit F.

1939 July 24
- F.'s granddaughter Eva is visiting London from Nice. She stays until August 25.
- Herbert George Wells, who had made advances in England to obtain F.'s British citizenship, visits F. in this matter and gives him his book The fate of homo sapiens with the dedication "To Sigmund Freud/Cher Maître/from H. G. Wells".

1939 July 29
Walter Schmideberg visits F.

1939 July end
F. has a nocturnal attack of left ventricular failure with cardiac asthma and is now also on heart medication.

1939 July 31
Marie Bonaparte comes to F for a last visit with her husband Prince George of Greece and Denmark. They stay until August 6.

1939 August
- F. signs an "Aufruf an die Oesterreicher in aller Welt" ("Appeal to Austrians all over the World"), written by the Central Association of Austrian Emigrants, calling for "the homeless Austrians to be rescued into new life opportunities".
- F. develops skin necrosis with discoloration of the cheek. Eventually, a hole develops in the cheek and the smell became so strong that it attracted flies and a mosquito net had to be stretched.
- Martha buys extra gas masks at Harrod's.
- Israel Wechsler visits F.

1939 August 1
- F. discontinues his practice. At that time, he still had four patients and two training analysands.
- Marie Bonaparte visits F. with the Parisian antique dealer Emmanuel Ségrédakis, from whom she regularly shopped.
- Hanns Sachs, who had come from America, visits F.

1939 August 12
F.'s nephew Harry sees his uncle for the last time.

1939 August 15
Abraham Roback gives F. his book *The psychology of common sense* with the dedication "Professor Sigmund Freud/With the kindest regards of/A. A. Roback".

1939 August 23
F. says goodbye to Ruth Mack Brunswick, who went back to America.

1939 August 25
- F.'s granddaughter Eva returns to Nice.
- Dorothy Burlingham travels to New York to be present at the birth of her granddaughter.

1939 September beginning

F. begins to reread Balzac's book *La peau de chagrin, which* he had already acquired in the early 1920s. It was his last reading. The hero of the novel is a man determined to commit suicide who makes a pact with a magical shagreen that promises him the fulfillment of his desires but shortens his life in return.

1939 September 1

Max Schur moves into 20 Maresfield Gardens.

1939 September mid

After the first air raid alarms, F.'s bed is moved to a safe part of the house. He still followed "with some interest" the attempts to protect his art collection from bomb damage.

1939 September 19

Ernest Jones visits F.

1939 September 21

In the morning, F. reminds his doctor Max Schur of their contract of 1929 January and asks him to put an end to his suffering: "Dear Schur, you remember our first talk. You promised me then you would help me when I could no longer carry on. It is only torture now and it has no longer any sense" (Jones 1956–1958, p. 262).

1939 September 22

After consulting Anna, Schur gives F. an injection of two centigrams of morphine, a normal dose for pain patients. F. falls into a deep comatose sleep.

1939 September 23

– As Max Schur has urgent matters to settle in connection with his family's move to America, Anna asks her friend Josefine Stross, who had already accompanied F. on the journey to emigration, to come to Maresfield Gardens.
– After F. becomes restless in the afternoon, Anna tells her friend Josefine about the contract between her father and Schur, and Josefine Stross administers another morphine injection to F., this time, with a lethal dose of 30 centigrams. F. falls into a coma and dies shortly before midnight.

1939 September 26

F.'s cremation at Golder's Green Crematorium. Ernest Jones gives the eulogy and Stefan Zweig the funeral oration.

Notes

1 Cf. these lines from the poem "Der Ichthyosaurus" by Victor von Scheffel: *Der Iguanodon, der Lümmel,/wird frecher zu jeglicher Frist,/schon hat er am hellen Tage/die Ichthyosaura geküsst. (The iguanodon, the lout,/becomes bolder at all times,/he has already kissed/the Ichthyosaura in broad daylight.)*

2 The prerequisite for applying as a one-year volunteer was passing the Matura. After one year of military service, one could be appointed reserve lieutenant.

3 Corresponds to a purchasing power of about 1300 € in 2022.

4 Corresponds to a purchasing power of about €1000 in 2022.

5 Corresponds to a purchasing power of about € 1300 in 2022.

6 This corresponds to a purchasing power of just under € 400 in 2022.

7 From 1891 September, F. lives at the same address, but in a newly constructed building.

8 Founded around 1870 by Salomon Stricker to give young doctors the opportunity to experience scientific research in statu nascendi.

9 These boards hung on the door, and you could leave messages on them.

10 100 Gulden correspond to a purchasing power of about 1400 € in 2022.

11 Actually „Verein für Psychiatrie und Forensische Psychologie".

12 Corresponds to a purchasing power of about € 21,000 in 2022.

13 Corresponds to a purchasing power of about € 14,000 in 2022.

14 Corresponds to a purchasing power of about € 1700 in 2022.

15 7000 marks correspond to a purchasing power of about 50,000 € in 2022.

16 Corresponds to a purchasing power of about € 8800 in 2022.

17 Corresponds to a purchasing power of about € 1200 in 2022.

18 Corresponds to a purchasing power of about € 25,000 in 2022.

19 Corresponds to a purchasing power of about € 63,000 in 2022.

20 Corresponds to a purchasing power of about € 7500 in 2022.

21 Corresponds to a purchasing power of plenty of €7500 in 2022.

22 Corresponds to a purchasing power of just under €700 in 2022.

23 Corresponds to a purchasing power of about € 1500 in 2022.

24 However, on 1977 May 5, a memorial stone with this very test was unveiled on the Bellevue meadow, near the spot where the Bellevue had stood.

25 From Goethe's *Faust,* II. T., V. Akt.

26 In literature, the group has become known as the "Psychological Wednesday Society". Therefore, it will also be referred to as such hereafter.

27 "Early, before the day dawns/ In the morning when the earth thaws/ Must bakers watch/ Making bread *and* rolls/ This would be a beautiful art/ If they had the flour/ for free".

28 Corresponds to the purchasing power of about € 1400 in 2022.

29 Corresponds to a purchasing power of about € 1200 in 2022.

30 Today, it is only attributed to the Titian school.

31 In reality, the painter's name is Andreas Bembis de Frend and it is a painting from 1429 above the tombstone of the Cologne city priest Johann von Cerwit (Resch, 1765, S. 22). Obviously, the correspondent of the *Neue Freie Presse* has lumped several people together in his report.

32 Corresponds to a purchasing power of about € 50,000 in 2022.

33 Between 1914 and 1938, Freud was nominated 12 times for the Nobel Prize and proposed for the Nobel Prize by 32 persons or institutions, but never received it.

34 Corresponds to a purchasing power of about 900 € in 2022.

35 This corresponds to a purchasing power of about € 5500 in 2021.

36 This corresponds to a purchasing power of just under € 4000 in 2022.

37 It was the A/H1N1 virus, a variant of what is now colloquially known as "swine flu" - but which originated from parts of an "avian flu" virus. Approximately 50 million people fell victim to it.

38 Corresponds to a purchasing power of about € 12,000 in 2022.

39 This corresponds to a purchasing power of about € 240,000 in 2022.

40 Corresponds to a purchasing power of about 20 € in 2022.

41 Corresponds to a purchasing power of about € 110,000 in 2022.

42 Corresponds to a purchasing power of about € 120,000 in 2022.
43 Corresponds to a purchasing power of about €1000 in 2022.
44 This corresponds to a purchasing power of about 20,000€ in 2022.
45 Corresponds to a purchasing power of about € 2000 in 2022.
46 Corresponds to a purchasing power of about € 1200 in 2022.
47 Corresponds to a purchasing power of about 250€ in 2021.
48 Corresponds to a purchasing power of about € 600,000 in 2022.
49 This corresponds to a purchasing power of about €110 in 2022.
50 Corresponds to a purchasing power of plenty of € 10,000 in 2022.
51 Corresponds to a purchasing power of about € 120,000 in 2022.
52 This corresponds to the purchasing power of about €110,000 in 2022.
53 Corresponds to a purchasing power of about € 300,000 in 2022.
54 Corresponds to a purchasing power of about € 120,000 in 2022.
55 Corresponds to a purchasing power of about € 130,000 in 2022.
56 This corresponds to the purchasing power of a good €60,000 in 2022.
57 Corresponds to a purchasing power of about € 25,000 in 2022.
58 Corresponds to a purchasing power of just under € 50,000 in 2022.
59 Corresponds to a purchasing power of ample€ 600,000 in 2022.
60 Corresponds to a purchasing power of about € 289,000 in 2022.
61 Corresponds to a purchasing power of about € 120,000 in 2022.
62 Corresponds to a purchasing power of 400€ in 2022.
63 Corresponds to a purchasing power of about 1500€ in 2022.
64 Corresponds to a purchasing power of about € 2000 in 2022.
65 Corresponds to a purchasing power of about € 120,000 in 2022.
66 This corresponded to €178,000 in 2020.
67 Corresponds to a purchasing power of almost 1 million euros in 2021.
68 This corresponds to a purchasing power of about 100 € in 2022.

Appendices

Abbreviations

FML	= Freud Museum London
IPA	= International Psycho-Analytical Association
IPV	= Internationaler Psychoanalytischer Verlag
IZP	= Internationale (ärztliche) Zeitschrift für Psychoanalyse
LoC	= Library of Congress
MPF	= Freud Bibliography by Ingeborg Meyer-Palmedo and Gerhard Fichtner
ÖNB	= Manuscript Department of the Austrian National Library
SE	= The Standard Edition of the Complete Psychological Works of Sigmund Freud
SFG	= Sigmund-Freud-Gesamtausgabe[1]
SFM	= Sigmund Freud Museum Vienna
SFP	= Sigmund Freud Papers in the Manuscript Division of the Library of Congress
WPV	= Wiener Psychoanalytische Vereinigung (Vienna Psycho-Analytical Society)

Note

1 Sigmund-Freud-Gesamtausgabe. 23 vols. Ed. by Christfried Toegel. Giessen: Psychosozial-Verlag 2015–2023.

English translations of Freud's writings and translations into German

Freud's writings

German title	English title
Abriss der Psychoanalyse	An Outline of Psycho-Analysis
Akute multiple Neuritis der spinalen und Hirnnerven	Acute multiple neuritis of the spinal and cranial nerves
Allgemeines über den hysterischen Anfall	Some General Remarks on Hysterical Attacks
Analyse der Phobie eines fünfjährigen Knaben	Analysis of a Phobia in a Five-Year-Old Boy
Antwort auf eine Rundfrage "Vom Lesen und von guten Büchern"	Contribution to a Questionnaire on Reading
Askese	Asceticism
Aus der Geschichte einer infantilen Neurose	From the History of an Infantile Neurosis
Beispiele des Verrats pathogener Phantasien bei Neurotikern	Two Instances of Pathogenic Phantasies Revealed by the Patients Themselves
Beitrag zur Kenntniss der Cocawirkung	Contribution to the Knowledge of the Effect of Cocaine
Beiträge zur Onanie-Diskussion	Contributions to a Discussion on Masturbation
Bemerkungen über Cocaïnsucht und Cocaïnfurcht	Craving for and Fear of Cocaine
Bemerkungen über die Übertragungsliebe (Weitere Ratschläge zur Technik der Psychoanalyse)	Observations on Transference-Love (Further Recommendations on the Technique of Psycho-Analysis)
Bemerkungen über einen Fall von Zwangsneurose	Notes upon a Case of Obsessional Neurosis
Bemerkungen zur Theorie und Praxis der Traumdeutung	Remarks on the Theory and Practice of Dream-Interpretation
Beobachtung einer hochgradigen Hemianästhesie bei einem hysterichen Manne	Observation of a Severe Case of Hemi-Anaesthesia in a Hysterical Male

Beobachtungen über Gestaltung und feineren Bau der als Hoden beschriebenen Lappenorgane des Aals	Observations on the configuration and finer structure of the lobed organs in eels described as testes
Bruchstück einer Hysterie-Analyse	Fragment of an Analysis of a Case of Hysteria
Cerebrale Kinderlähmung	Infantile cerebral paralysis
Charakter und Analerotik	Character and Anal Erotism
Darstellung der "grossen Leistung" im Traum	The Representation in a Dream of a "Great Achievement"
Das Ich und das Es	*The Ego and the Id*
Das Interesse an der Psychoanalyse	The Claims of Psycho-Analysis to Scientific Interest
Das Medusenhaupt	Medusa's Head
Das Motiv der Kästchenwahl	The Theme of the Three Caskets1
Das Nervensystem	The nervous system
Das ökonomische Problem des Masochismus	The Economic Problem of Masochism
Das Seelenleben des Kindes Vortrag	The Psychic Life of Child
Das Tabu der Virginität	The Taboo of Virginity
Das Unbehagen in der Kultur	*Civilization and its Discontents*
Das Unbewusste	The Unconscious
Das Unheimliche	The Uncanny
Der Dichter und das Phantasieren	Creative Writers and Day-Dreaming
Der Familienroman der Neurotiker	Family Romances
Der Humor	Humour
Der Moses des Michelangelo	The Moses of Michelangelo
Der Realitätsverlust bei Neurose und Psychose	The Loss of Reality in Neurosis and Psychosis
Der Untergang des Ödipuskomplexes	The Dissolution of the Oedipus Complex
Der Wahn und die Träume in W. Jensens Gradiva	*Delusions and Dreams in Jensen's Gradiva*
Der Witz und seine Beziehung zum Unbewussten	*Jokes and their Relation to the Unconscious*
Die "kulturelle" Sexualmoral und die moderne Nervosität	»Civilized« Sexual Morality and Modern Nervous Illness
Die Abwehr-Neuropsychosen	The Neuro-Psychoses of Defence
Die Bedeutung der Vokalfolge	The Significance of Vowel Sequences
Die Disposition zur Zwangsneurose	The Disposition to Obsessional Neurosis
Die endliche und die unendliche Analyse	Analysis Terminable and Interminable
Die Feinheit einer Fehlhandlung	The Subtleties of a Faulty Action

Die Frage der Laienanalyse	*The Question of Lay Analysis*
Die Freudsche psychoanalytische Methode	Freud's Psycho-Analytic Procedure
Die Handhabung der Traumdeutung in der Psychoanalyse	The Handling of Dream-Interpretation in Psycho-Analysis
Die Ichspaltung im Abwehrvorgang	Splitting of the Ego in the Process of Defence
Die infantile Cerebrallähmung	*Infantile cerebral paralysis*
Die infantile Genitalorganisation	The Infantile Genital Organization
Die psychogene Sehstörung in psychoanalytischer Auffassung	The Psycho-Analytic View of Psychogenic Disturbance of Vision
Die Sexualität in der Ätiologie der Neurosen	Sexuality in the Aetiology of the Neuroses
Die Structur der Elemente des Nervensystems	The structure of the elements of the nervous system
Die Traumdeutung	*The Interpretation of Dreams*
Die Verdrängung	Repression
Die Verneinung	Negation
Die Widerstände gegen die Psychoanalyse	The Resistances to Psycho-Analysis
Die Zukunft einer Illusion	*The Future of an Illusion*
Die zukünftigen Chancen der psychoanalytischen Therapie	The Future Prospects of Psycho-Analytic Therapy
Dostojewski und die Vatertötung	Dostoevsky and Parricide
Dr. Reik und die Kurpfuschereifrage	Dr. Reik and the Problem of Quackery
Drei Abhandlungen zur Sexualtheorie	*Three Essays on the Theory of Sexuality*
E. T. A. Hoffmann über die Bewusstseinsfunktion	E. T. A. Hoffmann on the Function of Consciousness
Ein Fall von Hirnblutung mit indirekten basalen Herdsymptomen bei Scorbut	A case of cerebral hemorrhage with indirect basal focal symptoms in scurvy
Ein Fall von hypnotischer Heilung nebst Bemerkungen über die Entstehung hysterischer Symptome durch den "Gegenwillen"	A Case of Successful Treatment by Hypnotism
Ein Fall von Muskelatrophie mit ausgebreiteten Sensibilitätsstörungen (Syringomyelie)	A case of muscular atrophy with extensive disturbances of sensitivity (syringomyelia)
Ein Kind wird geschlagen	A Child is Being Beaten
Ein religiöses Erlebnis	A Religious Experience
Ein Traum als Beweismittel	An Evidential Dream
Ein Wort zum Antisemitismus	A Comment on Anti-Semitism
Eine Beziehung zwischen einem Symbol und einem Symptom	A Connection between a Symbol and a Symptom
Eine erfüllte Traumahnung	A Premonitory Dream Fulfilled

Eine Kindheitserinnerung aus "Dichtung und Wahrheit"

A Childhood Recollection from Dichtung und Wahrheit

Eine Kindheitserinnerung des Leonardo da Vinci

Leonardo da Vinci and a Memory of his Childhood

Eine neue Methode zum Studium des Faserverlaufs im Centralnervensystem

A new method for the study of the course of nerve fibers in the central nervous system

Eine neue Methode zum Studium des Faserverlaufs im Centralnervensystem

A new method for the study of the course of nerve fibers in the central nervous system

Eine Schwierigkeit der Psychoanalyse

A Difficulty in the Path of Psycho-Analysis

Eine Teufelsneurose im siebzehnten Jahrhundert

A Seventeenth-Century Demonological Neurosis

Einige Bemerkungen über den Begriff des Unbewussten in der Psychoanalyse

A Note on the Unconscious in Psycho-Analysis

Einige Charaktertypen aus der psychoanalytischen Arbeit

Some Character-Types Met with in Psycho-Analytic Work

Einige psychische Folgen des anatomischen Geschlechtsunterschieds

Some Psychical Consequences of the Anatomical Distinction between the Sexes

Émile Zola, Vortrag, gehalten in der Vereinigung B'nai Brith in Wien zwischen 11.3. und 30.12. 1902

Émile Zola (lecture)

Entwurf einer Psychologie

Project for a scientific psychology

Ergänzungen zur Traumlehre

Supplements to the Theory of Dreams

Erinnern, Wiederholen und Durcharbeiten (Weitere Ratschläge zur Technik der Psychoanalyse II)

Remembering, Repeating and Working-Through (Further Recommendations on the Technique of Psycho-Analysis, II)

Etwas vom Unbewussten

Some Remarks on the Unconsciousness

Fécondité von Émile Zola

Fécondité by Émile Zola

Fetischismus

Fetishism

Formulierungen über die zwei Prinzipien des psychischen Geschehens

Formulations on the Two Principles of Mental Functioning

Gedankenassoziation eines vierjährigen Kindes

Associations of a Four-Year-Old Child

Gross ist die *Diana* der Epheser

»Great is Diana of the Ephesians«

Gründungsmanifest der "Gesellschaft für positivistische Philosophie"

Manifesto of the "Society for Positivistic Philosophy"

Gutachten über das Parke Cocaïn

Opinion on Parke's Cocaine

Hemmung, Symptom und Angst

Inhibitions, Symptoms and Anxiety

Hysterische Phantasien und ihre Beziehung zur Bisexualität

Hysterical Phantasies and their Relation to Bisexuality

Inhaltsangaben der wissenschaftlichen Arbeiten des Privatdocenten Dr. Sigm. Freud (1877–1897)

Abstracts of the Scientific Writings of Dr. Sigm. Freud (1877–1897)

German	English
Jenseits des Lustprinzips	*Beyond the Pleasure Principle*
Josef Popper-Lynkeus und die Theorie des Traumes	Josef Popper-Lynkeus and the Theory of Dreams
Kenntniss der cerebralen Diplegien des Kindesalters (im Anschluss an die Little'sche Krankheit)	Contribution to the knowledge of cerebral diplegias in childhood, in connection with Little's disease
Kindheitsträume mit spezieller Bedeutung	Childhood Dreams with a Particular Meaning
Klinische Studie über die halbseitige Cerebrallähmung der Kinder	*Clinical study of hemilateral paralysis in children*
Konstruktionen in der Analyse	Constructions in Analysis
Kurzer Abriss der Psychoanalyse	A Short Account of Psycho-Analysis (Kurzer Abriss der Psychoanalyse)
Les diplégies cérébrales infantiles	Cerebral diplegias in childhood
L'hérédité et l'étiologie des névroses	Heredity and the Aetiology of the Neuroses
Märchenstoffe in Träumen	The Occurrence in Dreams of Material from Fairy Tales
Massenpsychologie und Ich-Analyse	*Group Psychology and the Analysis of the Ego*
Mehr Kinder	More Children
Meine Ansichten über die Rolle der Sexualität in der Ätiologie der Neurosen	My Views on the Part played by Sexuality in the Aetiology of the Neuroses
Metapsychologische Ergänzung zur Traumlehre	A Metapsychological Supplement to the Theory of Dreams
Mitteilung eines der psychoanalytischen Theorie widersprechenden Falles von Paranoia	A Case of Paranoia Running Counter to the Psycho-Analytic Theory of the Disease
Mythologische Parallele zu einer plastischen Zwangsvorstellung	A Mythological Parallel to a Visual Obsession
Nachfrage des Herausgebers über Kindheitsträume	Request for Examples of Childhood Dreams
Nachschrift zur Analyse des kleinen Hans	Postscript to the »Analysis of a Phobia in a Five-Year-Old Boy«
Nachtrag zu dem autobiographisch beschriebenen Fall von Paranoia	Postscript to the Case of Paranoia
Nachtrag zur Arbeit über den "Moses des Michelangelo"	Supplement to »The Moses of Michelangelo«
Nachträge zur Traumdeutung	Additions to the Interpretation of Dreams
Nachwort zur "Frage der Laienanalyse"	Postscript to the Question of Lay Analysis
Neue Folge der Vorlesungen zur Einführung in die Psychoanalyse	*New Introductory Lectures on Psycho-Analysis*
Neurose und Psychose	Neurosis and Psychosis
Notiz über den "Wunderblock"	A Note upon the »Mystic Writing-Pad«

Notiz über eine Methode zur anatomischen Präparation des Nervensystems	Note on a method for anatomical preparation of the nervous system
Psychische Behandlung (Seelenbehandlung)	Psychical (or Mental) Treatment
Psychoanalyse und Telepathie	Psycho-Analysis and Telepathy
Psychoanalytische Bemerkungen über einen autobiographisch beschriebenen Fall von Paranoia (Dementia paranoides)	Psycho-Analytic Notes on an Autobiographical Account of a Case of Paranoia (Dementia Paranoides)
Psychopathische Personen auf der Bühne	Psychopathic Characters on the Stage
Quelques considérations pour une étude comparative des paralysies motrices organiques et hystériques	Some Points for a Comparative Study of Organic and Hysterical Motor Paralyses
Ratschläge für den Arzt bei der psychoanalytischen Behandlung	Recommendations to Physicians Practising Psycho-Analysis
Selbstdarstellung	An Autobiographical Study
Studien über Hysterie	*Studies on Hysteria*
Tatbestandsdiagnostik und Psychoanalyse	Psycho-Analysis and the Establishment of the Facts in Legal Proceedings
Totem und Tabu	*Totem and Taboo*
Trauer und Melancholie	Mourning and Melancholia
Traum und Telepathie	Dreams and Telepathy
Triebe und Triebschicksale	Instincts and their Vicissitudes
Typisches Beispiel eines verkappten Ödipustraumes	A Typical Example of a Disguised Oedipus Dream
Über »wilde« Psychoanalyse	»Wild« Psycho-Analysis
Über Coca	On Coca
Über Deckerinnerungen	Screen Memories
Über den Bau der Nervenfasern und Nervenzellen beim Flusskrebs	On the structure of the nerve fibers and nerve cells of the river crayfish
Über den Gegensinn der Urworte	»The Antithetical Meaning of Primal Words«
Über den Mechanismus der Zwangsvorstellungen und Phobien	On the mechanism of obsessions and phobias
Über den physiologischen Schwachsinn des Weibes (Dr. Möbius)	The Physiological Feeble-Mindedness of the Woman by Dr. Möbius (lecture)
Über den psychischen Mechanismus hysterischer Phänomene	On the Psychical Mechanism of Hysterical Phenomena
Über den psychischen Mechanismus hysterischer Phänomene. Vorläufige Mitteilung	On the Psychical Mechanism of Hysterical Phenomena: Preliminary Communication
Über den Traum	*On Dreams*

Über den Ursprung der hinteren Nervenwurzeln im Rückenmarke von Ammocoetes (Petromyzon Planeri)	On the origin of the posterior nerve-roots in the spinal cord of the ammocoetes
Über den Ursprung des N[ervus] acusticus	On the origin of the acoustic nerve
Über den Witz	On jokes
Über die allgemeinste Erniedrigung des Liebeslebens	On the Universal Tendency to Debasement in the Sphere of Love
Über die Allgemeinwirkung des Cocaïns	On the General Effect of Cocaine
Über die Berechtigung, von der Neurasthenie einen bestimmten Symptomenkomplex als »Angst-Neurose« abzutrennen	On the Grounds for Detaching a Particular Syndrome from Neurasthenia under the Description »Anxiety Neurosis«
Über die Bernhardt'sche Sensibilitätsstörung am Oberschenkel	On Bernhardt's disturbance of sensibility in the thigh
Über die Beziehung des Strickkörpers zum Hinterstrang und Hinterstrangskern, nebst Bemerkungen über zwei Felder der Oblongata	On the relation of the restiform body to the posterior column and its nucleus with some remarks on two fields of the medulla oblongata
Über die Psychogenese eines Falles von weiblicher Homosexualität	The Psychogenesis of a Case of Female Homosexuality
Über die weibliche Sexualität	Female Sexuality
Über ein Symptom, das häufig die Enuresis nocturna der Kinder begleitet	On a symptom frequently accompanying nocturnal enuresis in children
Über einen besonderen Typus der Objektwahl beim Manne	A Special Type of Choice of Object made by Men
Über einige neurotische Mechanismen bei Eifersucht, Paranoia und Homosexualität	Some Neurotic Mechanisms in Jealousy, Paranoia and Homosexuality
Über einige Übereinstimmungen im Seelenleben der Wilden und der Neurotiker	Some Points of Agreement between the Mental Lives of Savages and Neurotics
Über familiäre Formen von cerebralen Diplegien	On familiar forms of cerebral diplegias
Über fausse reconnaissance (»déjà raconté«) während der psychoanalytischen Arbeit	Fausse reconnaissance (»déjà raconté«) in Psycho-Analytic Treatment
Über Hemianopsie im frühesten Kindesalter	On hemianopsia in early childhood
Über Hypnose und Suggestion	On Hypnosis and Suggestion
Über Hysterie	On hysteria
Über hysterische Lähmungen	On hysterical paralysis
Über infantile Sexualtheorien	On the Sexual Theories of Children
Über libidinöse Typen	Libidinal Types
Über männliche Hysterie	On Male Hysteria

Über neurotische Erkrankungstypen	Types of Onset of Neurosis
Über Psychoanalyse. Fünf Vorlesungen	*Five Lectures on Psycho-Analysis*
Über Psychotherapie	On Psychotherapy
Über Spinalganglien und Rückenmark des Petromyzon	On the spinal ganglia and spinal cord of the Petromyzon
Über Träume	On Dreams
Über Triebumsetzungen, insbesondere der Analerotik	On Transformations of Instinct as Exemplified in Anal Erotism
Vergänglichkeit	On Transience
Vorlesungen zur Einführung in die Psychoanalyse	Introductory Lectures on Psycho-Analysis
Warum Krieg	*Why War?*
Was ist Psychoanalyse?	On Psychoanalysis
Wege der psychoanalytischen Therapie	Lines of Advance in Psycho-Analytic Therapy
Weitere Bemerkungen über die Abwehr-Neuropsychosen	Further Remarks on the Neuro-Psychoses of Defence
Wenn Moses ein Ägypter war ...	If Moses was an Egyptian
Wir und der Tod	Death and Us
Zeitgemässes über Krieg und Tod	Thoughts for the Times on War and Death
Zerstreute Gedanken	Scattered thoughts
Zufall und Aberglaube	Chance and Superstition
Zum psychischen Mechanismus der Vergesslichkeit	The Psychical Mechanism of Forgetfulness
Zur Ätiologie der Hysterie	The Aetiology of Hysteria
Zur Auffassung der Aphasien. Eine kritische Studie	*On the interpretation of the aphasias, a critical study*
Zur Dynamik der Übertragung	The Dynamics of Transference
Zur Einführung des Narzissmus	On Narcissism: An Introduction
Zur Einleitung der Behandlung (Weitere Ratschläge zur Technik der Psychoanalyse)	On Beginning the Treatment (Further Recommendations on the Technique of Psycho-Analysis)
Zur Geschichte der psychoanalytischen Bewegung	On the History of the Psycho-Analytic Movement
Zur Kenntniss der Olivenzwischenschicht	Concerning the knowledge of the intermediary layer of the olive
Zur Kritik der »Angstneurose«	A Reply to Criticisms of my Paper on Anxiety Neurosis
Zur Psychologie des Gymnasiasten	Some Reflections on Schoolboy Psychology
Zur Psychologie des Vergessens	The Psychology of Forgetting

Zur Psychopathologie des Alltagslebens	*The Psychopathology of Everyday Life*
Zur sexuellen Aufklärung der Kinder	The Sexual Enlightenment of Children
Zur Theorie des hysterischen Anfalls	On the Theory of Hysterical Attacks
Zur Vorgeschichte der analytischen Technik	A Note on the Prehistory of the Technique of Analysis
Zwangshandlungen und Religionsübungen	Obsessive Actions and Religious Practices
Zwei Kinderlügen	Two Lies Told by Children

Translations by Freud

[Translation of Hippolyte Bernheim]: Hypnotismus und Suggestion	Hypnotism and suggestion
[Translation of J. St. Mill]:	
– Über Frauenemanzipation	Enfranchisement of Women
– Plato	Review of Grote's Plato
– Die Arbeiterfrage	Thornton on Labour and its Claims
– Der Sozialismus	Chapters on Socialism
[Translation of Jean-Martin Charcot]: Neue Vorlesungen über die Krankheiten des Nervensystems insbesondere über Hysterie	Charcot, Jean-Martin Lectures on the Diseases of the Nervous System
[Translation of Jean-Martin Charcot]: Poliklinische Vorträge	Tuesday Lectures

Most important associations, societies and committees mentioned

B'nai B'rith

B'nai B'rith was founded in New York in 1843. The organization aimed to educate the outside world about Judaism and to conduct educational work within Judaism.

In 1889, an "Austrian-Israelite Humanitarian Association B'nai B'rith" was founded in Vienna. In 1895, the local association "Vienna" was founded, of which Freud had been a member since the fall of 1897. The headquarter of the Austrian B'nai B'rith were at Universitätsstrasse 4, where Freud also gave his lectures.

Wiener Psychoanalytische Vereinigung (Vienna Psychoanalytic Association)

The *Die Wiener Psychoanalytische Vereinigung (WPV)* emerged in 1908 from the so-called "Psychological Wednesday Society" founded in 1902 by Sigmund Freud, Wilhelm Stekel, Alfred Adler, Rudolf Reitler and Max Kahane.

The first chairman of the WPV was Alfred Adler. In 1911, Freud became chairman and remained so until 1938, when the WPV was taken over by a provisional administrator appointed by the NSDAP.

Meetings were held in Freud's apartment until 1910, after which members met in various locales: Rotenturmstrasse 19 (1910–1911), Franz-Josefs-Kai 65 (1911–1921), Pelikangasse 19 (1922–1936) and Berggasse 7 (1936–1938).

Physiologische Klub (The Physiological Club)

The *Physiologische Klub* had been founded by Salomon Stricker around 1870, "and old masters met with younger workers for joint demonstrations and discussions. Anatomical, physiological, pathological, chemical topics were discussed. Young physicians employed at the clinics had found the opportunity to see scientific research in statu nascendi" (Albert, 1898, p. 7). In the early 1870s, the "younger workers" included, among others, Sigmund Exner and Ernst Fleischl (1846–1891), which Freud admired. The "masters" were Carl Rokitansky and Ernst Brücke, "who carried more weight with me than anyone lese in my whole life" (SE, 20, p. 253; Klein, 1898, p. 25).

After Stricker's death, the Physiologische Klub, under the chairmanship of Sigmund Exner, became in 1900 the Morphologisch-Physiologische Gesellschaft Wien, which published the *Zentralblatt für Physiologie* jointly with the Physiologische Gesellschaft Berlin.

At the time of Freud's lectures, the Physiological Club met in the apartment of Ernst Fleischl at Schwarzspanierstrasse 7.

Psychiatrische Verein (Psychiatric Association)

The *Psychiatrische Verein* had been founded in 1867 by Theodor Meynert, Joseph Gottfried Riedl and Max Leidesdorf as the "Association for Psychiatry and Forensic Psychology" and renamed the "Association for Psychiatry and Neurology" in 1894 (Gabriel, 2001). It published the *Jahrbücher für Psychiatrie (Yearbooks of Psychiatry)*, in which Freud had published his paper "Die Structur der Elemente des Nervensystems".

The meetings of the *Verein* were usually held in the Lower Austrian State Mental Hospital at Lazarettgasse 14 or in the General Hospital at Alserstr. 4.

Wiener medizinische Klub (Vienna Medical Klub)

The *Wiener medizinische Klub* had been founded in 1892 by the internists Hermann Schlesinger and Max Herz. Both were in their mid-20s and understood the club as a kind of protest movement against the established Viennese medical profession (Kronfeld, 1926, p. 8). Max Herz and Freud had similar ideas about the etiology of neuroses (Andersson, 1962, p. 196; Herz, 1894; Herz, 1909).

The meetings took place in the "Alte Gewehrfabrik" ("Old Rifle Factory"), which housed the Physiological Institute where Freud had worked for almost six years (Tögel, 2015, p. 19).

Gesellschaft der Ärzte (Society of Physicians)

The *Gesellschaft der* Ärzte was founded in 1836. At the time of Freud, it was primarily concerned with anatomy, medicinal chemistry and clinical medicine. Carl von Rokitansky, who was president of the society from 1850 to 1878, had some influence on Freud. When he died in 1878, his funeral was one of the few Freud ever attended.

As early as 1884, Theodor Meynert and Hermann Nothnagel had advised Freud to lecture in the *Gesellschaft der* Ärzte (Freud & Bernays, 2015, pp. 109, 373). Freud had been a member since 1887, and in 1931, he became an honorary member.

Until 1893, the meetings of the Society of Physicians were held in the Old University on today's Dr.-Ignaz-Seipel-Platz and, thereafter, in a newly built "Haus der *Gesellschaft der* Ärzte" (from 1919 Billroth House) at Frankgasse 8.

Doktorenkollegium and Professorenkollegium (Vienna Medical Faculty)

In 1849, the faculty of the Faculty of Medicine was separated into a College of Professors and a College of Doctors. The official name since then was "Doktorenkollegium der medizinischen Fakultät".

The *Doktorenkollegium* met in its meeting room at Rotenturmstrasse 19, a space also later used by the *Wiener Psychoanalytische Vereinigung* for its meetings between 1910 and 1911.

The *Professorenkollegium* not only consisted of all full professors and at least some of the associate professors, but also included two "Privatdozenten" ("private lecturers").

Family trees[2]

Ancestors of Sigmund Freud

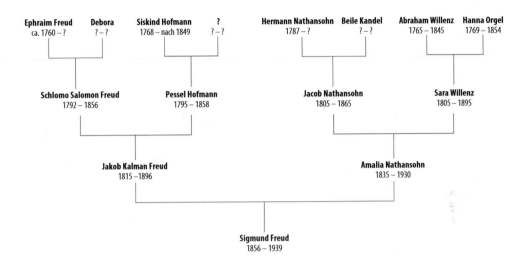

Ancestors of Martha Bernays

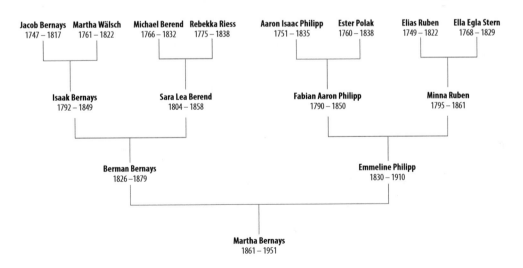

Descendants of Sigmund and Martha

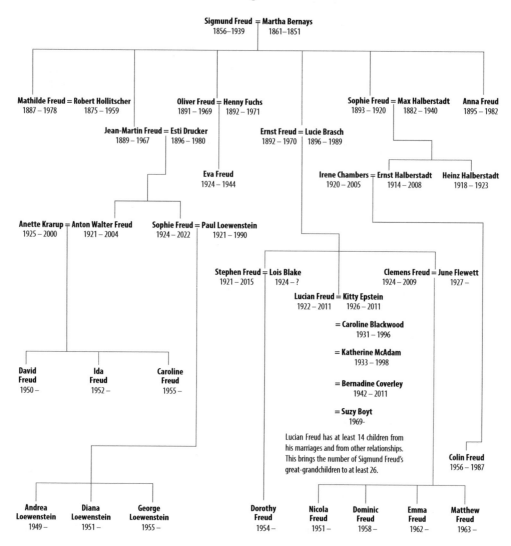

Note

2 Starting from the family trees for the Freud and Bernays families, which Hanns-Walter Lange presented in 1988 after truly pioneering work, I began in the mid-1990s to compile an integrated family tree of both families and to expand it continuously. At present, it contains more than 1400 persons. This family tree cannot be put into print, and therefore, only the most important members of both families are presented in excerpts on the following pages.

Sources used

In addition to Freud's published works and letters, the following sources have been used:

- Unpublished letters from and to Freud and documents on Freud's life, mainly in:
  - Library of Congress
    - Sigmund Freud Papers
    - Anna Freud Papers
    - Harry Freud Papers
    - Edward Bernays Papers
    - Siegfried Bernfeld Papers
    - Abraham Brill Papers
    - Paul Federn Papers
  - Freud Museum London
  - Freud Museum Vienna
  - Sigmund Freud Copyrights
  - Israelitische Kultusgemeinde Wien
  - Archive of the British Psychoanalytical Society
  - Archive of the Imperial Academy of Sciences
  - Leo Baeck Archive New York
  - Stadtarchiv Leipzig
  - Austrian War Archives
  - Wiener Stadt- und Landesarchiv (Wienbibliothek im Rathaus)

- Recollections and Interviews (SFP, Library of Congress)
- Freud's Library at the Freud Museum London
- Hotel guest books
- Passenger Lists and Passenger Records of Ellis Island
- Address books and registration slips
- Family trees, genealogical databases
- Diaries
- Course catalogs
- Personal communications from
  - Rémy Amouroux
  - Ernst Falzeder
  - Ernst Federn

- Anton Walter Freud
- Ernst Halberstadt-Freud
- Albrecht Hirschmüller
- Michael Molnar
- Paul Roazen
- Peter Swales
- Roger Willoughby

Printed matter

- Contemporary newspapers and journals (including the Korrespondenzblatt der *Internationalen Zeitschrift für Psychoanalyse*)
- Kurlisten (Spa and visitor lists), e.g. Aussee, Baden, Karlsbad, Pörtschach, Reichenau)
- Contemporary timetables and guides

Secondary literature used

Abraham, H. (1976). Karl Abraham. *Sein Leben für die Psychoanalyse*. München: Kindler.

Alexander, F. & Grotjahn, M. (Hg.). (1966). *Psychoanalytic Pioneers*. New York & London: Basic Books, Inc.

Altenkirch, R. (2002). Zwei bedeutende Persönlichkeiten der Görlitzer Medizingeschichte. II. Dr. Karl Ludwig Kahlbaum (1828–1899). *Berichte der Naturforschenden Gesellschaft der Oberlausitz*, 10, 99–104.

Amouroux, R. & Stouten, H. (2014). Als Marie Bonaparte sich taub stellte ... *Luzifer-Amor*, 27(53), 122–140.

Andersson, O. (1962). *Studies in the Prehistory of Psychoanalysis. The Aetiology of Psychoneuroses and Some Related Themes in Sigmund Freud's Scientific Writings and Letters 1886–1896*. Stockholm: Svenska Bokförlaget.

Andreas-Salomé, L. (1958). *In der Schule bei Freud: Tagebuch eines Jahres, 1912/1913*. Hg. Von E. Pfeiffer. Zürich: Niehans.

Andreas-Salomé, L. (1974). *Lebensrückblick: Grundriss einiger Lebenserinnerungen*. (5. Aufl.). Hg. von E. Pfeiffer. Frankfurt a.M.: Insel Verl.

Anzieu, D. (1990). *Freuds Selbstanalyse und die Entdeckung der Psychoanalyse*. 2 Bände. München/Wien: Verlag Internationale Psychoanalyse.

Appignanesi, L. & Forrester, J. (1992). *Freud's Women*. London: Weidenfeld & Nicolson.

Augusta, G. (2015). "Dann kamen die langen, harten Jahre". Zur Situation der Familie Freud nach ihrer Ankunft in Wien im Jahr 1859. *Luzifer-Amor*, 28(56), 108–129.

Augusta, G. (2020). *Unter uns hiess er der Rattenmann. Die Lebensgeschichte des Sigmund-Freud-Patienten Ernst Lanzer*. Wien: Mandelbaum Verlag.

Bakan, D. (1960). On the Horizon: Freud and the Zohar. *Commentary Magazine*, January.

Bauer, H. (1989). Überblick über *die Geschichte der Schule*. 125 Jahre BG/BRG Wien II (Wohlmutstrasse). Wien: Bernays & Fraenkel.

Behling, K. (2002). *Martha Freud. Die Frau des Genies*. Berlin: Aufbau Taschenbuch Verlag.

Benthien, C., Böhme, H., & Stephan, I. (Hg.). (2011). *Freud und die Antike*. Göttingen: Wallstein.

Bergstein, M. (2010). *Mirrors of Memory. Freud, Photography, and the History of Art*. Ithaca, NY & London: Cornell University Press.

Bernays, J. & Fraenkel, M. (1932). *Jacob Bernays: ein Lebensbild in Briefen*. Breslau: Marcus.

Bernays, E. (1940). *Speak Up for Democracy: What You Can Do; a Practical Plan of Action for Every American Citizen*. New York: Viking Press.

Bernfeld, S. (2018). Werke. Band 12. *Studien zu Leben und Werk von Sigmund*. Hg. Von C. Tögel. Giessen: Psychosozial-Verlag.

Berthelsen, D. (1989). *Alltag bei Familie Freud. Die Erinnerungen der Paula Fichtl*. München: dtv.

Bertin, C. (1989). *Die letzte Bonaparte. Freuds Prinzessin. Ein Leben*. Freiburg: Köre.

Billig, M. (2000). Freud's Different Versions of Forgetting 'Signorelli': Rhetoric and Repression. *International Journal of Psycho-Analysis*, 81(2000): S. 483–498.

Blanton, S. (1971). *Diary of My Analysis with Sigmund Freud*. New York: Hawthorn Books.

Boehm, F. (1978). *Schriften zur Psychoanalyse*. München: Ölschläger.

Borch-Jacobsen, M. (2021). *Freud's Patients: A Book of Lives* London: Reaktion Books

Brandenburg, D. (1974). *Berlins alte Krankenhäuser: Ihre Entstehung und Entwicklung*. Berlin: Haude & Spener.

Braun-Vogelstein, J. (1967). *Heinrich Braun. Eine Leben für den Sozialismus*. Stuttgart: Deutsche Verlags-Anstalt.

Brecht, K. et al. (Hg). (1985). *"Hier geht das Leben auf eine sehr merkwürdige Weise weiter ...". Zur Geschichte der Psychoanalyse in Deutschland*. Hamburg: M. Kellner.

Brome, V. (1968). *Freud and His Early Circle*. New York: William Morrow.

Brückner, P. (1962). Sigmund Freuds Privatlektüre. *Psyche*, 16(4), 721–743.

Burke, J. (2006). *The Gods of Freud: Sigmund Freud's Art Collection*. Sydney: Knopf.

Burlingham, M. J. (1989). *The Last Tiffany*. New York: Atheneum.

Chemouni, J. (1987). Freud et les associations juives. Contribution à l'étude de sa judéïté. *Revue française de psychanalyse*, 51, 1207–1243.

Chertok, L. (1973). Freud in Paris (1885–86). Eine psychobiographische Studie. *Psyche*, 27(5), 431–448.

Chertok, L. & Saussure, R. d. (1973). *Naissance du psychanalyste: de Mesmer à Freud*. Paris: Payot.

Choisy, M. (1974). *Sigmund Freud: A New Appraisal*. Westport, CT: Greenwood Press.

Clark, R. (1980). *The Man and the Cause*. New York: Random House.

Cohen, D. (2009). *The Escape of Sigmund Freud*. London: JR Books.

Czeike, F. (1992–1997). *Historisches Lexikon Wien* Bd. 1–5. Wien: Kremayr & Scheriau.

D'Angelo, M. (2020). *"So will ich mir entfliehen". Sigmund Freuds Italienreisen*. Giessen: Psychosozial-Verlag.

Danto, E. A. & Steiner, A. (2017). *Freud/Tiffany: Anna Freud, Dorothy Tiffany Burlingham and the 'Best Possible School'*. London: Freud Museum.

Davenport, J. C. (1992). The Prosthetic Care of Sigmund Freud. *British Dental Journal*, 7, 205–207.

Davies, K. & Fichtner, G. (2006). *Freud's Library. A Comprehensive Catalogue*. Tübingen: edition diskord.

Decker, H. (1977). *Freud in Germany. Revolution and Reaction in Science, 1893–1907*. New York: International University Press.

Decker, H. (1991). *Freud, Dora and Vienna 1900*. New York: The Free Press.

Deutsch, H. & Stein, B. (1973). *Selbstkonfrontation: die Autobiographie der grossen Psychoanalytikerin*. München: Kindler.

Doolittle, H. (1956). *Tribute to Freud*. New York: Pantheon

Drucker, Esti. (1978). *Vignettes of My Life*. Archives of Leo Baeck Institute.

Dubrovic, M. (1987). *Veruntreute Geschichte: die Wiener Salons und Literatencafés*. Frankfurt am Main: Fischer Taschenbuch Verlag.

Dufresne, T. (2006). *Killing Freud: Twentieth-Century Culture and the Death of Psychoanalysis*. London & New York: Continuum.

Ehrenburg, I. (1978). *Menschen, Jahre, Leben: Memoiren*. Berlin: Verl. Volk und Welt.

Ehrmann, S. (1926). Meine persönlichen Beziehungen zu Sigmund Freud. *B'nai B'rith Mitteilungen für Österreich*, 26(5), 132–134.

Eisenberg, L. (1889). *Das geistige Wien: Künstler- und Schriftsteller-Lexikon*. Mittheilungen über Wiener Architekten, Bildhauer, Bühnenkünstler, Graphiker, Journalisten, Maler, Musiker und Schriftsteller. Wien: Daberkow

Eissler, K. (1974). *Aus Freuds Sprachwelt und andere Beiträge*. Bern/Stuttgart/Wien: Hans Huber Verlag.

Eissler, K. (1979). *Freud und Wagner-Jauregg vor der Kommission zur Erhebung militärischer Pflichtverletzung*. Wien: Löcker Verlag.

Ellenberger, H. (1970). *The Discovery of the Unconscious*. London: Allen Lane.

Engelmann, B. (1993). *Wir Untertanen: ein deutsches Geschichtsbuch*. Göttingen: Steidl.

Engelman, E. & Scholz-Strasser, I. (1993). *Sigmund Freud: Wien IX. Berggasse 19*. Katalog. Wien: C. Brandstätter.

Engelman, E. & Scholz-Strasser, I. (1995). *Sigmund Freud: Wien IX. Berggasse 19*. Wien: C. Brandstätter.

Etkind, A. (1997). *Eros of the Impossible. The History of Psychoanalysis in Russia.* Boulder, CO: West-view Press.

Fallend, K. (1995). *Sonderlinge, Träumer, Sensitive. Psychoanalyse auf dem Weg zur Institution und Profession. Protokolle der WPV und biographische Studien.* Wien: Verlag Jugend & Volk.

Falzeder, E. (1995). Meine Grosspatientin, meine Hauptplage: ein bisher unbeachteter Fall Freuds und die Folgen. *Jahrbuch der Psychoanalyse*, 34, 67–100.

Falzeder, E. (2015). *Psychoanalytic Filiations. Mapping the Psychoanalytic Movement.* London: Karnac.

Federn, E. & Wittenberger, G. (1992). *Aus dem Kreis um Sigmund Freud. Zu den Protokollen der Wiener Psychoanalytischen Vereinigung.* Frankfurt am Main: Fischer Taschenbuch Verlag.

Ferenczi, S. (1982). *Schriften zur Psychoanalyse.* Ausw. in 2 Bd. Hrsg. von Michael Balint. Einl. von Judith Dupont. Frankfurt am Main: Fischer Taschenbuch-Verl.

Ferenczi, S. & Groddeck, G. (1985). *Briefwechsel 1921–1933.* Frankfurt am Main: Fischer Taschenbuch Verlag.

Fichtner, G. (2006). "Gegeben in unserer derzeitigen Residenz zu Lübeck". Ein Brief des frischvermählten Ehepaars Freud an Emmeline und Minna Bernays aus dem Jahre 1886. *Jahrbuch der Psychoanalyse*, 52, 193–199.

Fichtner, G. (2008). Freud und Familie Hammerschlag – eine prägende Begegnung. *Luzifer-Amor*, 21(41), 63–79.

Fichtner, G. & Hirschmüller, A. (1985). Freuds "Katharina" - Hintergrund, Entstehungsgeschichte und Bedeutung einer frühen psychoanalytischen Krankengeschichte. *Psyche*, 39, 220–240.

Fichtner, G. & Hirschmüller, A. (1988). Sigmund Freud, Heinrich Obersteiner und die Diskussion über Hypnose und Kokain. *Jahrbuch für Psychoanalyse*, 21, 105–137.

Forel, A. (1968). *Briefe - Correspondance. 1864–1927.* Hg. von Hans Walser. Bern/Stuttgart: Huber.

Fraenkel, M. (1932). *Jacob Bernays – Ein Lebensbild in Briefen.* Breslau: Marcus.

Franceschini, R. (1901). *Woher und Wohin?* Dresden/Leipzig: Carl Reissner.

Freud, E., Freud, L., Grubrich-Simitis, I. & Eissler, K. (1976). *Sigmund Freud – Sein Leben in Bildern und Texten.* Frankfurt am Main: Suhrkamp.

Freud, M. (1957). *Glory Reflected. Sigmund Freud - Man and Father.* London/Sydney/Melbourne/Wellington: Angus & Robertston.

Freud, S. (1996). *Tagebuch 1929–1939.* Kürzeste Chronik. Hg. und eingeleitet von Michael Molnar. Übersetzt von Christfried Tögel. Frankfurt am Main: Stroemfeld.

Freud, S. (2006). *Im Schatten der Familie Freud.* Berlin: Ullstein.

Freud, S. & Bullitt, W. (2007). *Thomas Woodrow Wilson. Der 28. Präsident der Vereinigten Staaten von Amerika. Eine psychoanalytische Studie.* Hg. von Hans-Jürgen Wirth. Giessen Psychosozial.

Freud-Bernays, A. (1989). Mein Bruder Sigmund Freud (1940). *Luzifer-Amor*, 2(3), 139–145.

Freud-Bernays, A. (2004). *Eine Wienerin in New York. Die Schwester Sigmund Freuds erinnert sich.* Hg. von Christfried Tögel. Berlin: Aufbau-Verlag.

Freud-Marlé, L. (2006). *Mein Onkel Sigmund Freud. Erinnerungen an eine grosse Familie.* Hrsg. von Christfried Tögel. Berlin: Aufbau-Verlag.

Fuks, E., Kohlbauer-Fritz, G., & Arnbom, M.-T. (Hg.). (2005). *Die Liebens. 150 Jahre Geschichte einer Wiener Familie.* Wien: Böhlau Verlag.

Gamwell, L. & Wells, R. (1989). *Sigmund Freud and Art: His Personal Collection of Antiquities.* Binghamton/London: State University of New York/Freud Museum.

Gamwell, L. & Solms, M. (2006). *From Neurology to Psychoanalysis: Sigmund Freud's Neurological Drawings and Diagrams of the Mind.* Binghamton: State University of New York Press.

Gardiner, M. (Hg.). (1971). *The Wolf-Man.* New York: Basic Books.

Gay, P. (1988). *Freud. A Life for Our Time.* New York: Norton.

Gelfand, T. (1987). "Mon cher docteur Freud": Charcot's Unpublished Correspondence to Freud, 1888–1893. *Bulletin of the History of Medicine*, 62(4), 563–588.

Gertz, E. (1978). *Odyssey of a Barbarian: The Biography of George Sylvester Viereck.* New York: Prometheus Books.

Gicklhorn, J. (1957). Julius Wagner-Jaureggs Gutachten über Sigmund Freud und seine Studien zur Psychoanalyse. Eine wissenschaftsgeschichtliche Notiz. *Wiener klinische Wochenschrift*, 69, 533–537.

Gicklhorn, J. & Gicklhorn, R. (1960). *Sigmund Freuds akademische Laufbahn im Lichte der Dokumente.* Wien & Innsbruck: Urban & Schwarzenberg.

Gicklhorn, R. (1965). Eine Episode aus Freuds Mittelschulzeit. *Unsere Heimat,* 36, 18–24.

Gicklhorn, R. (1969). The Freiberg Period of the Freud Family. *Journal of the History of Medicine and Allied Sciences*, 24(1), 37–43.

Gicklhorn, R. (1976). *Sigmund Freud und der Onkeltraum – Dichtung und Wahrheit.* Horn: Eigenverlag.

Giefer, M. & Tögel, C. (Hg.). (2016). *Sigmund Freud: Die Kalendereinträge von 1916–1918.* Frankfurt am Main und Basel: Stroemfeld.

Gilman, S. L. (1995). *Reading Freud's Reading.* New York: NYU Press.

Gödde, G. (2003). *Mathilde Freud. Die* älteste *Tochter Sigmund Freuds in Briefen und Selbstzeugnissen.* Giessen: Psychosozial-Verlag.

Goetz, B. (1969). *Das ist alles, was ich* über *Freud zu erzählen habe. Erinnerungen an Sigmund Freud.* Berlin: Friedenauer Presse.

Goldmann, S. (1985). Eine Kur aus der Frühzeit der Psychoanalyse. Kommentar zu Freuds Briefen an Anna v. Vest. *Jahrbuch der Psychoanalyse*, 17, 296–337.

Goldmann, S. (2003). *Via regia zum Unbewussten Freud und die Traumforschung im 19. Jahrhundert.* Giessen: Psychosozial-Verlag.

Graf, M. (1942). Reminiscences of Professor Sigmund Freud. *Psychoanalytic Quarterly*, 11, 465–476.

Graf-Nold, A. (1987). *Der Fall Hermine Hug-Hellmuth. Eine Geschichte der frühen Kinder-Psychoanalyse.* München: Verlag Internationale Psychoanalyse.

Garvy, G. (1978). Carl Snyder, Pioneer Economic Statistician and Monetarist. *History of Political Economy*, 10(3), 454–490.

Grinker, R. R. (1973). *Psychosomatic Concepts* (Rev. ed). New York: Aronson.

Grinstein, A. (1961). Freud's Dream of the Botanical Monograph. *Journal of the American Psychoanalytic Association*, 9(3), 480–503.

Grinstein, A. (1968). *On Sigmund Freud's Dreams.* Detroit: Wayne State University Press.

Grosskurth, P. (1980). *Havelock Ellis. A Biography.* New York: Alfred Knopf.

Grubel, F. (1979). Zeitgenosse Sigmund Freud. Bericht über drei Freud-Korrespondenzen im Archiv des Leo Baeck Instituts, New York. *Jahrbuch der Psychoanalyse*, 11, 73–80.

Grubrich-Simitis, I. (1993). *Zurück zu Freuds Texten. Stumme Dokumente sprechen machen.* Frankfurt am Main: S. Fischer.

Handlbauer, B. (1990). *Die Adler-Freud-Kontroverse.* Frankfurt am Main: Fischer Taschenbuch.

Harmat, P. (1988). *Freud, Ferenczi und die ungarische Psychoanalyse.* Tübingen: edition diskord.

Harris, J. & Harris, J. (1984). *The One-Eyed Doctor, Sigismund Freud: Psychological Origins of Freud's Works.* New York/London: Jason Aronson.

Heller, P. (Hg.). (1994). *Anna Freud: Briefe an Eva Rosenfeld.* Frankfurt am Main: Stroemfeld.

Hemecker, W. (1991). *Philosophiegeschichtliche Voraussetzungen der Psychoanalyse Sigmund Freuds.* München: Philosophia.

Herzogenrath, Wulf & Liška, Pavel (Hg.) (1987). *Arthur Segal 1875–1944.* Köln: Kölnischer Kunstverein.

Hirschmüller, A. (1978a). Eine bisher unbekannte Krankengeschichte Sigmund Freuds und Josef Breuers aus der Entstehungszeit der *Studien* über *Hysterie. Jahrbuch der Psychoanalyse*, 10, 136–168.

Hirschmüller, A. (1978b). *Physiologie und Psychoanalyse im Leben und Werk Josef Breuers.* Bern: Huber.

Hirschmüller, A. (1989). Freuds "Mathilde": Ein weiterer Tagesrest zum Irma Traum. *Jahrbuch der Psychoanalyse*, 24, 128–159.

Hirschmüller, A. (1991). *Freuds Begegnung mit der Psychiatrie. Von der Hirnmythologie zur Neurosenlehre.* Tübingen: edition diskord.

Hirschmüller, A. (Ed.) (1996). S*igmund Freud. Schriften* über *Kokain.* Frankfurt am Main: Fischer Taschenbuch Verlag.

Hirschmüller, A. (2021). "Die Kur ist mir sehr schwer gefallen, nach und nach gewöhnte ich mich an die Methode, besonders, da mir Dr. Freud durchaus sympathisch ist". Maggie Haller – eine Patientin Freuds. *Luzifer-Amor*, 34, 88–125.

Hook, D. (1991). *The Haskell F. Norman Library of Science and Medicine*. San Francisco, CA: J. Norman.

Israëls, H. (1989). *Schreber: Vater und Sohn: eine Biographie*. München: Verlag Internationale Psychoanalyse.

Israëls, H. (1999). *Der Fall Freud. die Geburt der Psychoanalyse aus der Lüge*. Hamburg: Rotbuch Verlag.

Janisch, H. (2007). Die Bildhauerin Margarethe Lutz. "Freud hat mich gerettet!" http://oe1.orf.at/artikel/211895, 30.12.2007.

Johnson, N. M. (1972). *George Sylvester Viereck, German-American Propagandist*. Urbana: University of Illinois Press.

Johnston, W. M. (1974). Österreichische *Kultur- und Geistesgeschichte: Gesellschaft und Ideen im Donauraum, 1848 bis 1938*. Wien: Böhlau.

Jones, E. (1927). [Besprechung von] Freud, S.: Die Frage der Laienanalyse. *Internationale Zeitschrift für Psychoanalyse*, 13, 101–107.

Jones, E. (1956–1957). *Sigmund Freud. Life and Wok*. 3 vols. London: Hogarth Press.

Jung, C. G. (1971). *Erinnerungen, Träume, Gedanken*. Olten: Walter-Verlag.

Kähler, H. (1988). Der Dichter und der Psychologe. *Sinn und Form*, 39, 1147–1164.

Kardiner, A. (1977). *My Analysis with Freud: Reminiscences*. New York: Norton.

Kempner, S. (1925). Beitrag zur Oralerotik. *Internationale Zeitschrift für Psychoanalyse*, 11, 69–77.

Kiell, N. (1988). *Freud without hindsight, reviews of his work (1893–1939)*. Madison, CT: International Universities Press.

Klein, D. (1981). *Jewish Origins of the Psychoanalytic Movement*. New York: Praeger.

Kloocke, R. (2002). *Mosche Wulff. Zur Geschichte der Psychoanalyse in Russland und Israel*. Tübingen: edition diskord.

Knoepfmacher, H. (1979). Zwei Beiträge zur Biographie Sigmund Freuds. *Jahrbuch der Psychoanalyse*, 11, 51–72.

Knöpfmacher, W. (1935). *Entstehungsgeschichte und Chronik der Vereinigung "Wien" B'nai B'rith in Wien, 1895–1935*. Wien: Verband der Israelitischen Humanitätsvereine "B'nai B'rith".

Kobler, F. (1962). Die Mutter Sigmund Freuds. *Bulletin des Leo Baeck Instituts*, 5, 149–171.

Koller, K. (1884). Über die Verwendung des Cocains zur Anästhesierung am Auge. *Wiener medizinische Wochenschrift*, 34, 1276–1278, 1309–1311.

Korotin, I. (Hg.). (2016). *biografiA. Lexikon* österreichischer *Frauen*: 4 Bände. Wien: Böhlau.

Kreuter, A. (1996). *Deutschsprachige Neurologen und Psychiater: Ein biographisch-bibliographisches Lexikon von den Vorläufern bis zur Mitte des 20. Jahrhunderts*. München: Saur.

Kuhn, P. (1999). A Professor Through the Looking-Glass: Contending Narratives of Freud's Relationships with the Sisters Bernays. *International Journal of Psychoanalysis*, 80(5), 943–959.

Kuhn, P. (2000a). The Cultivated Italian (or) Who Reminded Freud How to Remember Signorelli? *Psychoanalysis and History*, 2(1), 119–122.

Kuhn, P. (2000b). A Scandal in Salzburg: Or Freud's Surreptitious Role in the 1908 Abraham–Jung Dispute. *International Journal of Psychoanalysis*, 81(4), 705–731.

Krüll, M. (1992). *Freud und sein Vater. Die Entstehung der Psychoanalyse und Freuds ungelöste Vaterbindung*. Frankfurt am Main: Fischer Taschenbuch Verlag.

Laible, E. (1989). Über Freuds Gymnasialzeit. In Bauer, H. (1989). Überblick über die Geschichte der Schule. 125 Jahre BG/BRG Wien II (Wohlmutstrasse). Wien: Bernays & Fraenkel. S. 19–29.

Laible, E. (1992). "Durch Entbehrung zum Wissen". Unbekannte Dokumente aus Freuds Universitäts-Jahren. *Jahrbuch der Psychoanalyse*, 29, 239–264.

Lehmann, H. (1983). Freud's Dream of February 1918. *International Review of Psycho-Analysis*, 10, 87–93.

Leitner, Marina. (2001). *Ein gut gehütetes Geheimnis. Die Geschichte der psychoanalytischen Behandlungs-Technik von den Anfängen in Wien bis zur Gründung der Berliner Poliklinik im Jahr 1920*. Giessen: Psychosozial-Verlag.

Lochner, L. (1950). *Fritz Kreisler*. New York: Macmillan.

Lockot, R. (1985). *Erinnern und Durcharbeiten. Zur Geschichte der Psychoanalyse und Psychotherapie im Nationalsozialismus*. Frankfurt am Main: Fischer Taschenbuchverlag.

Loewenberg, P. (2004). Lucian and Sigmund Freud. *American Imago*, 61(1), 89–99.

Lothane, H., Zvi (2018). Freud Bashers: Facts, Fictions, and Fallacies: Freud: The Making of an Illusion. By Frederick Crews. New York: Henry Holt, 2017. *Journal of the American Psychoanalytic Association*, 66(5), 953–969.

Lück, H. & Mühlleitner, E. (1993). *Psychoanalytiker in der Karikatur*. München: Quintessenz Verlag.

Ludwig, E. (1946). *Der entzauberte Freud*. Zürich: Carl Posen.

Ludwig, E. (1973). *Doctor Freud*. New York: Manor Books.

Lynn, D. (1997). Sigmund Freud's Psychoanalysis of Albert Hirst. *Bulletin of the History of Medicine*, 71, 69–93.

Maciejewski, F. (2008). *Freud in Maloja. Die Engadiner Reise mit Minna Bernays*. Berlin: Osburg.

Mahony, P. (1986). *Freud and the Rat Man*. New Haven, CT: Yale University Press.

Marinelli, L. (Hg.). (1998). *"Meine alten dreckigen Götter". Aus Sigmund Freuds Sammlung*. Frankfurt a. M.: Stroemfeld Verlag.

Marinelli, L. (Hg.). (2003). *Freuds verschwundene Nachbarn*. Wien: Turia & Kant.

Markus, G. (2015). *Sigmund Freud und das Geheimnis der Seele: die Biographie*. München: Langen Mueller.

Masson, J. (1984). *The Assault on Truth. Freud's Suppression of the Seduction Theory*. New York: Farrar, Straus & Giroux.

Maurer, D. (1988). *Eleonora Duse*. Reinbek bei Hamburg: Rowohlt.

May, R. (1933). Brief eines Landarztes. *Psychoanalytische Bewegung*, 5, 83–84.

Maylan, C. (1929). *Freuds tragischer Komplex: eine Analyse der Psychoanalyse*. München: Reinhardt.

Mayreder, R. (1988a). *Mein Pantheon: Lebenserinnerungen*. Dornach: Philosophisch-Anthroposophischer Verlag.

Mayreder, R. (1988b). *Tagebücher 1873–1937*. Frankfurt am Main: Insel Verlag.

McGrath, W. (1986). *Freud's Discovery of Psychoanalysis. The Politics of Hysteria*. Ithaca, NY/London: Cornell University Press.

Meerloo, J. (1953). Three Artists. An Essay on Creative Urge and Artistic Perturbation. *American Imago*, 10, 247–263.

Meng, H. (1956). Freud und der Bildhauer. *Schweizerische Zeitschrift für Psychologie und ihre Anwendungen*, 15, 149–151.

Meng, H. (1973). *Psychoanalytische Pädagogik des Schulkindes*. München: Reinhardt.

Menninger, A. (2011). *Sigmund Freud als Autor in Villarets Handwörterbuch der Gesamten Medizin von 1888–1891*. Hamburg: Verlag Dr. Kovač.

Molnar, M. (1999). 20 Maresfield Gardens: A Guide to the Freud Museum, London. *Psychoanalysis and History*, 1(1), 118–120.

Molnar, M. (2014). *Looking Through Freud's Photos*. London: Karnac Books.

Monson, K. (1990). *Alma Mahler-Werfel: die unbezähmbare Muse* (Dt. Erstausg., 4. Aufl. ed.). München: Heyne.

Moser, M. (1986). *Ich habe gelebt*. Zürich: Limmat Verlag.

Mosse, W. et al. (Hg.). (1981). *Revolution and Evolution 1848 in German-Jewish History*. Tübingen: J. C. B. Mohr.

Mühlleitner, E. (1992). *Biographisches Lexikon der Psychoanalyse*. Tübingen: edition diskord.

Munk, F. & Munk, K. (1979). *Das medizinische Berlin um die Jahrhundertwende*. (2., durchges. Aufl.) München: Urban & Schwarzenberg.

Murken, B. (1981). Tom Seidmann-Freud. Leben und Werk. *Die Schiefertafel*, 4, 163–201.

Murken, B. (2004). "… die Welt ist so uneben…". Tom Seidmann-Freud (1892–1930): Leben und Werk einer grossen Bilderbuch-Künstlerin. *Luzifer-Amor*, 17(33), 73–103.

Nitzschke, B. (1996). *Wir und der Tod: Essays* über *Sigmund Freuds Leben und Werk*. Vandenhoeck & Ruprecht.

Nobus, D. (2020). The Madness of Princess Alice: Sigmund Freud, Ernst Simmel and Alice of Battenberg at Kurhaus Schloss Tegel. *History of Psychiatry*, 31(2), 147–162.

Nobus, D. (2023). *Freud in the Margins: Rethinking the History of Psychoanalysis*. New York: Columbia University Press.

Norman, H. (1991). *An Exhibition of Original Editions, Autographe Letters, and Portraits from the Library of Haskell F. Norman*. Stanford, CA: Stanford University Library.

Nunberg, H. & Federn, E. (Hg.). (1962–71). *Minutes of the Vienna Psychoanalytic Society*. 4 vols. New York: International Universities Press.

o.A. (1998). *The Haskell F. Norman Library of Science and Medicine. Part III: Modern Age*. New York: Christie's.

Oberlerchner, H. & Tögel, C. (2015). Freud in Kärnten - eine Recherche. *Luzifer-Amor*, 28, 158–168.

O'Donoghue, D. (2018). *On Dangerous Ground: Freud's Visual Cultures of the Unconscious*. New York: Bloomsbury Publishing.

Pagel, J. (1901). *Biographisches Lexikon hervorragender Ärzte des neunzehnten Jahrhunderts*. Berlin & Wien: Urban & Schwarzenberg.

Paneth, J. (2007). *Vita Nuova. Ein Gelehrtenleben zwischen Nietsche und Freud*. Hg. v. Wilhelm W. Hemecker. Graz: Leykam Buchverlag.

Pankejeff, S., Gardiner, M., Freud, S., & Brunswick, R. M. (1972). *The Wolf-Man and Sigmund Freud*. London: Hogarth Press and the Institute of Psycho-analysis.

Pessler, M. & Finzi, D. (Hg.). (2020). *Freud, Berggasse 19. Ursprungsort der Psychoanalyse*. Wien: Hatje Cantz.

Peters, U. H. (1979). *Anna Freud. Ein Leben für das Kind*. München: Kindler.

Pichler, G. (2010). Bertold Löffler's Bookplate for Sigmund Freud. *Psychoanalysis and History*, 12(1), 7–14.

Plänkers, T. (1993). "Vom Himmel durch die Welt zur Hölle". Zur Goethe-Preisverleihung an Sigmund Freud im Jahre 1930. *Jahrbuch der Psychoanalyse*, 30, 167–181.

Pohlen, M. (2006). *Freuds Analyse*. Reinbek bei Hamburg: rowohlt.

Pokorny, A. (Hg.). (1871). *Siebenter Jahresbericht des Leopoldstädter Communal-Real und Obergymnasiums in Wien*. Wien: Verlag des Leopoldstädter Communal-Real und Obergymnasiums.

Prochnik, G. (2006). *Putnam Camp: Sigmund Freud, James Jackson Putnam and the Purpose of Psychology*. New York: Other Press.

Prokop, U. (2003). *Margaret Stonborough-Wittgenstein: Bauherrin, Intellektuelle, Mäzenin*. Wien: Böhlau Verlag Wien.

Reicheneder, J. G. (1983). Sigmund Freud und die kathartische Methode Josef Breuers. *Jahrbuch der Psychoanalyse*, 15, 229–250.

Reicheneder, J. G. (1990). *Zum Konstitutionsprozess der Psychoanalyse*. Stuttgart-Bad Cannstatt: frommann-holzboog.

Reicheneder, J. G. (1994). Freud in Berlin 1886. *Luzifer-Amor*, 7, 7–16.

Reichmayr, J. (1990). *Spurensuche in der Geschichte der Psychoanalyse*. Frankfurt am Main: Nexus.

Reik, T. (1976). *Dreissig Jahre mit Sigmund Freud*. München: Kindler.

Rice, E. (1994). The Jewish Heritage of Sigmund Freud. *Psychoanalytic Review*, 81(2), 237–258.

Richebächer, S. (2005). *Sabine Spielrein. "Eine fast grausame Liebe zur Wissenschaft"*. Zürich: Dörlemann.

Rieder, I. & Voigt, D. (2000). *Heimliches Begehren. Eine verbotene Liebe in Wien*. Wien: Franz Deuticke.

Ries, P. (1995). Popularise and/or be Damned: Psychoanalysis and Film at the Crossroads in 1925. *The International Journal of Psycho-analysis*, 76(4), 759–791.

Ritvo, L. (1990). *Darwin's Influence on Freud: A Tale of Two Sciences*. New Haven, CT: Yale University Press.

Roazen, P. (1969). *Brother Animal: The Story of Freud and Tausk*. New York: Knopf.

Roazen, P. (1975). *Freud and His Followers*. New York: Knopf.

Roazen, P. (1985). *Helene Deutsch: A Psychoanalyst's Life*. Garden City, NY: Anchor Books.

Roazen, P. (1993). *Meeting Freud's Family*. Boston: University of Massachusetts Press.

Roazen, P. (1995). *How Freud Worked: First-Hand Accounts of Patients*. London: Jason Aronson.

Roazen, P. (2007). *Sigmund Freud und William C. Bullitt. Die ungewöhnliche Zusammenarbeit zwischen dem Analytiker und dem Diplomaten.* Giessen: Psychosozial-Verlag.

Robert, M. (1975). *Sigmund Freud – zwischen Moses und* Ödipus. *Die jüdischen Wurzeln der Psychoanalyse.* München: List Verlag.

Rogow, A. (1978). A Further Footnote to Freud's "Fragment of an Analysis of a Case of Hysteria". *Journal of the American Psychoanalytic Association,* 26, 331–356.

Romm, S. (1983a). *The Unwelcome Intruder. Freud's Struggle with Cancer.* New York: Praeger.

Romm, S. (1983b). Sigmund Freud and Salvador Dalí: Personal Moments. *American Imago,* 40, 337–347.

Rosenzweig, S. (1992). *Freud, Jung, and Hall the Kingmaker. The historic expedidition to America (1909).* Seattle/Toronto/Bern/Göttingen: Hogrefe & Huber.

Roudinesco, É. (2016). *Freud in His Time and Ours.* Cambridge, MA: Harvard University Press.

Roudinesco, É. & Plon, M. (2004). *Wörterbuch der Psychoanalyse. Namen, Länder, Werke, Begriffe.* Wien & New York: Springer.

Ruitenbeek, H. (Ed.) (1973). *Freud as We Knew Him.* Detroit: Wayne State University Press.

Sablik, K. (1968). Sigmund Freud und die Gesellschaft der Ärzte in Wien. *Wiener klinische Wochenschrift,* 80, 107–110.

Sachs, H. (1945). *Freud. Master and Friend.* London: Imago.

Sadger, I. (2006). *Sigmund Freud: persönliche Erinnerungen.* Hg. von A. Huppke und M. Schröter. Tübingen: Edition Diskord.

Sajner, J. (1968). Sigmund Freuds Beziehungen zu seinem Geburtsort Freiberg (Příbor) und zu Mähren. *Clio Medica,* 3, 167–180.

Sajner, J. (1981). Drei dokumentarische Beiträge zur Sigmund Freud-Biographik aus Böhmen und Mähren. *Jahrbuch der Psychoanalyse,* 13, 143–152.

Sajner, J. (1989). Die Beziehungen Sigmund Freuds und seiner Familie zu dem mährischen Kurort Rožnau. *Jahrbuch der Psychoanalyse,* 24, 73–96.

Scheidt, C. E. (1986). *Die Rezeption der Psychoanalyse in der deutschsprachigen Philosophie vor 1940.* Frankfurt am Main: Suhrkamp.

Schnack, I. (1990). *Rainer Maria Rilke, Chronik seines Lebens und seines Werkes.* Frankfurt am Main: Insel Verlag.

Schneider, S. & Berke, J. (2008). Sigmund Freud and the Lubavitcher Rebbe. *Psychoanalytic Review,* 87, 39–59.

Schnitzler, A. (1981). *Jugend in Wien.* Frankfurt am Main: Fischer Taschenbuch Verlag.

Schröter, M. (1988). Freud und Fliess im wissenschaftlichen Gespräch. Das Neurasthenieprojekt von 1893. *Jahrbuch der Psychoanalyse,* 22, 141–183.

Schröter, M. (2002). Fliess vs. Weininger, Swoboda und Freud: Der Plagiatsstreit von 1906 im Licht der Dokumente *Psyche,* 56, 338–368.

Schultz, U. & Hermanns, L. (1987). Das Sanatorium Schloss Tegel Ernst Simmels – Zur Geschichte und Konzeption der ersten Psychoanalytischen Klinik. *Psychotherapie, Psychosomatik, Medizinische Psychologie,* 37, 37–67.

Schur, M. (1982). *Sigmund Freud. Leben und Sterben.* Frankfurt am Main: Suhrkamp.

Skues, R. (2001). On the Dating of Freud's ALIQUIS Slip. *International Journal of Psychoanlysis,* 82, 1185–1204.

Skues, R. (2017). Who Was the 'Heroine' of Freud's First Case History? Problems and Issues in the Identification of Freud's patients. *Psychoanalysis and History,* 19(1), 7–54.

Spielrein, S. (2003). *Tagebuch und Briefe. Die Frau zwischen Jung und Freud.* Giessen: Psychosozial-Verlag.

Spitzy, K. (Hg.). (1987). *Gesellschaft der* Ärzte *in Wien. 1837–1987.* Wien/München: Christian Brandstätter.

Stadler, F. (1995). *Vertreibung der Vernunft: The Cultural Exodus from Austria.* Wien: Springer-Verlag.

Stekel, W. (1950). *The Autobiography of Wilhelm Stekel: The Life Story of a Pioneer Psychoanalyst.* Ed. E. Gutheil. New York: Liveright.

Sterba, R. (1985). *Erinnerungen eines Wiener Psychoanalytikers.* Frankfurt am Main: Fischer Taschenbuch.

Stone, I. (1971). *The Passions of the Mind. A Novel of Sigmund Freud.* Garden City, NY: Doubleday.

Stroeken, H. (2007). *Freud und seine Patienten*. Magdeburg: Dietmar Klotz.

Sulloway, F. (1979). *Freud. Biologist of the Mind*. New York: Basic Books.

Swales, P. (1982). Freud, Minna Bernays, and the Conquest of Rome. *The New American Review*, 1, 1–23.

Swales, P. (1986). Freud, His Teacher, and the Birth of Psychoanalysis. In P. Stepansky (Ed.), *Freud. Appraisals and Reappraisals. Contributions to Freud Studies*, Bd. 1: 3–82. Hillsdale, NJ: The Analytic Press.

Swales, P. (1988). Freud, Katharina, and the First 'Wild Analysis'. In P. Stepansky (Ed.), *Freud. Appraisals and Reappraisals. Contributions to Freud Studies*, Bd. 3: 81–164. Hillsdale, NJ: The Analytic Press.

Swales, P. (1989). Freud, Fliess, and Fratricide: The Role of Fliess in Freud's Conception of Paranoia. In L. Spurling (Ed.), *Sigmund Freud. Critical Assessments*, Bd. 1: Freud and the Origins of Psychoanalysis: 302–330. London/New York: Routledge.

Swales, P. (1997). Freud, Filthy Lucre and Undue Influence. *Review of Existential Psychology and Psychiatry*, 23, 115–141.

Swales, P. J. (2003). Freud, Death and Sexual Pleasures: On the Psychical Mechanism of Dr. Sigm. Freud. *Arc de cercle*, 1(1), 5–74.

Tabori, C. (1951). *My Occult Diary*. London: Rider & Co.

Tanner, T. (2003). Sigmund Freud and the *Zeitschrift für Hypnotismus*. *Arc de Cercle*, 1, 75–142.

Tichy, M. & Zwettler-Otte, S. (1999). *Freud in der Presse. Rezeption Sigmund Freuds und der Psychoanalyse in Österreich 1895–1938*. Wien: Sonderzahl.

Timms, E. (1992a). *Psychoanalysis in its Cultural Context*. Edinburgh: Edinburgh University Press.

Timms, E. (1992b). Zauberer und Lehrlinge: Die Begegnung Karl Kraus' mit Sigmund Freud. *Psyche*, 46, 309–335.

Timms, E. (Hg.). (1995). *Freud and the Child Woman. The Memoirs of Fritz Wittels*. New Haven/London: Yale University Press.

Timms, E. & Segal, N. (1988). *Freud in Exile. Psychoanalysis and Its Vicissitudes*. New Haven, CT: Yale University Press.

Tögel, C. (1989). *Berggasse – Pompeji und zurück. Sigmund Freuds Reisen in die Vergangenheit*. Tübingen: edition diskord.

Tögel, C. (1990). Bahnstation Treblinka. Zum Schicksal von Sigmund Freuds Schwester Rosa Graf. *Psyche*, 44, 1019–1024.

Tögel, C. (2001). Jenö Varga, the Hungarian Soviet Republic and the Development of Psychoanalysis in the Soviet Union. *Psychoanalysis and History*, 3, 193–203.

Tögel, C. (2004). Freuds Berliner Schwester Maria (Mitzi) und ihre Familie. *Luzifer-Amor*, 33, 33–50.

Tögel, C. (2006). *Freud und Berlin*. Berlin: Aufbau-Verlag.

Tögel, C. (2009). Freud, Einstein und das Institut für geistige Zusammenarbeit in Paris. Kommentierte Briefe zur Vorgeschichte des Briefwechsels "Warum Krieg?" *Jahrbuch für Psychoanalyse*, 58, 81–110.

Tögel, C. (2013). *Die Rätsel Sigmund Freuds: Von den Geschlechtsorganen des Aals zur Traumdeutung*. Giessen: Psychosozial-Verlag.

Tögel, C. (2015). *Freuds Wien. Eine biografische Skizze nach Schauplätzen*. Giessen: Psychosozial-Verlag.

Tögel, C. (2017a). Freud, die Couch und Familie Benvenisti. *Luzifer-Amor*, 30(59), 158–168.

Tögel, C. (2017b). "Elisabeth von R." – Geburtshelferin der Freien Assoziation. Neues zu Familie und Leben von Helene Weiss, verh. Gross. *Luzifer-Amor*, 30(60), 175–181.

Tögel, C. & Schröter, M. (2002). Sigmund Freud und Hermann Swoboda: Ihr Briefwechsel (1901–1906). *Psyche*, 56(4), 313–337.

Tögel, C. & Schröter, M. (2004). Jakob Freud mit Familie in Leipzig (1859). Erzählung und Dokumente. *Luzifer-Amor*, 23, 8–32.

Vickers, H. (2000). *Alice. Princess Andrew of Greece*. London: Hamish Hamilton.

Waldinger, E. (1956). Aus Freuds letzten Lebensjahren. *Aufbau*, 22, 16, 22.

Walzer, T. & Templ, S. (2001). *Unser Wien: "Arisierung" auf österreichisch*. Berlin: Aufbau-Verlag.

Weinhandl, F. & Ehrenfels, C. v. (1978). *Gestalthaftes Sehen: Ergebnisse und Aufgaben der Morphologie. Zum hundertjährigen Geburtstag von Christian von Ehrenfels* (4., unveränd. Aufl.). Darmstadt: Wissenschaftliche Buchgesesellschaft.

Weiss, H. & Weiss, C. (1984). Eine Welt wie im Traum – Sigmund Freud als Sammler antiker Kunstgegen-stände. *Jahrbuch der Psychoanalyse*, 16, 189–217.

Wells, H. G. (1939). *The Fate of Homo Sapiens. An Unemotional Statement of the Things that Are Happening to him Now, and of the Immediate Possibilities Confronting Him*. London: Secker and Warburg.

Welsch, U. & Wiesner, M. (1988). *Lou Andreas-Salomé: vom" Lebensurgrund" zur Psychoanalyse*. München: Verlag Internationale Psychoanalyse.

Welter, V. M. (2004). Ernst L. Freud (1892–1970), architect in Berlin and London. *The International Journal of Psychoanalysis*, 85, 530.

Willoughby, R. (2022). *Freud's Britain: Family, Followers and the Dissimination of Ideas before and after the Great War*. Oxford: University of Oxford.

Winter, J. (1927). *Fünfzig Jahre eines Wiener Hauses*. Wien/Leipzig: Wilhelm Braumüller.

Wittels, F. (1924). *Sigmund Freud. Der Mann, die Lehre, die Schule*. Leipzig/Wien/Zürich: E. P. Tal & Co.

Wittenberger, G. (1995). *Das "Geheime Komitee" Sigmund Freuds: Institutionalisierungsprozesse in der "Psychoanalytischen Bewegung" zwischen 1912 und 1927*. Tübingen: edition diskord.

Wolf, E. S. & Trosman, H. (1974). Freud and Popper-Lynkeus. *Journal of the American Psychoanalytic Association*, 22, 123–141.

Worbs, M. (1983). *Nervenkunst. Literatur und Psychoanalyse im Wien der Jahrhundertwende*. Frankfurt am Main: Europäische Verlagsanstalt.

Wortis, J. (1963). *Fragments of an Analysis with Freud*. Indianapolis: Charter Books.

Wyklicky, H. (1985b). Zur Geschichte des Instituts für allgemeine und experimentelle Pathologie der Universität Wien. *Wiener klinische Wochenschrift*, 97, 346–349.

Wyklicky, H. & Skopec, M. (1984). Carl Koller (1857–1944) and His Time in Vienna. In D. B. Scott (Ed.), *Regional Anaesthesia 1884–1984*. Centennial Meeting of Regional Anaesthesia, September 12–15, 1984, 12–16. Vienna.

Young-Bruehl, E. (1988). *Anna Freud. A Biography*. New York/London: Summit Books.

Zweig, A. (1996). *Freundschaft mit Freud*. Berlin: Aufbau-Verlag.

Zweig, H. (1932). Die Psychotherapie in der tschechischen Literatur von 1920–1930. *Zentralblatt für Psychotherapie*, 5, 111–119.

Zweig, S. (1932). *Mental Healers. Franz Anton Mesmer, Mary Baker Eddy, Sigmund Freud*. New York: Viking Press.

Zuckerkandl, B. (1988). Österreich *intim: Erinnerungen 1892 bis 1942*. Frankfurt am Main/Berlin: Ullstein.

Bibliography

Albert, E. (1898). Die Stellung der Pathologie, *30 Jahre experimentelle Pathologie. Festschrift für S. Stricker* Leipzig und Wien: Franz Deuticke, S. 1–12.

Andersson, O. (1962). *Studies in the Prehistory of Psychoanalysis. The Etiology of Psychoneuroses and Some Related Themes in Sigmund Freud's Scientific Writings and Letters 1886–1896.* Stockholm: Svenska Bokförlaget.

Freud, S. (1996). *Tagebuch 1929–1939. Kürzeste Chronik.* Hg. und eingeleitet von Michael Molnar. Übersetzt von Christfried Tögel. Frankfurt am Main: Stroemfeld.

Freud, S. (2002). *Unser Herz zeigt nach dem Süden: Reisebriefe 1895–1923.* Herausgegeben von Christfried Tögel unter Mitarbeit von Michael Molnar. Berlin: Aufbau-Verlag.

Freud, S. & Bernays, M. (2011). *Die Brautbriefe. 1882–1886.* Band 1. Sei mein wie ich mir's denke. Juni 1882–Juli 1886. Hg. von Gerhard Fichtner, Ilse Grubrich-Simitis und Albrecht Hirschmüller. Frankfurt am Main: S. Fischer.

Freud, S. & Bernays, M. (2015). *Die Brautbriefe. 1882–1886.* Band 3. Warten in Ruhe und Ergebung, warten in Kampf und Erregung. Januar 1884–September 1884. Hg. von Gerhard Fichtner, Ilse Grubrich-Simitis und Albrecht Hirschmüller. Frankfurt am Main: S. Fischer.

Gabriel, E. (2001). Zur Geschichte der Psychiatrie in Österreich, Gründungsmatinee Zum Welttag der mentalen Gesundheit, 3 April 2001. Wien: Naturhistorisches Museum.

Giefer, M. & Tögel, C. (Hg.). 2016. *Sigmund Freud: Die Kalendereinträge von 1916–1918.* Frankfurt am Main und Basel: Stroemfeld.

Grubrich-Simitis, I. (1993). *Zurück zu Freuds Texten. Stumme Dokumente sprechen machen.* Frankfurt am Main: S. Fischer.

Herz, M. (1894). Ueber einige vernachlässigte Hilfswissenschaften der Medizin. *Wiener medizinische Wochenschrift*, 44(16/17), 714–715, 761–763

Herz, M. (1909). *Die sexuelle psychogene Herzneurose (Phrenokardie).* Wien: Braumüller.

Hirschmüller, A. & Tögel, C. (Hg.). (2021). *Sigmund Freud: Notizbücher 1901–1936.* http://www.freud-biographik.de/freuds-notizbuecher-1901–1936/.

Jones, E. (1928). *Glossary for the Use of Translators of Psycho-analytical Works.* London: Balliere, Tindale & Cox (*International Journal of Psycho-Analysis*. Suppl. no. 1).

Jones, E. (1956–1958). *Sigmund Freud. Life and Work.* 3 vols. London: The Hogarth Press.

Klein, E. (1898). Die ersten Jahre des Institutes für experimentelle Pathologie. In *30 Jahre experimentelle Pathologie. Festschrift für S. Stricker.* 23–27. Leipzig & Wien: Franz Deuticke.

Kronfeld, A. (1926). Hofrat Professor Dr. Hermann Schlesinger. Ein Porträt. *Neues Wiener Journal*, 2(6): S. 7–8.

Resch, J. (1765). *Monumenta veteris ecclesiae Brixinensis.* Brixen: Typis Joannis Caffiani Krapf.

Steiger, R. & Reimann, A. (1982–1996). *Goethes Leben von Tag zu Tag. Eine dokumentarische Chronik. 8 Bände.* Zürich: Artemis.

Tögel, C. (2006). Sigmund Freuds Praxis. Visiten und Ordination – Psychoanalysen – Einnahmen. *Psyche*, 60(9/10), 860–880.

Tögel, C. (2015). *Freuds Wien. Eine biografische Skizze nach Schauplätzen.* Giessen: Psychosozial-Verlag.

Trotsky, L. (1930). *My Life.* New York: Charles Schribner's Sons.

Index